Readings in Criminal Justice

GLENCOE PRESS CRIMINAL JUSTICE SERIES

General Editor:

G. DOUGLAS GOURLEY

Inspector (Ret.), LA Police Department
Chairman, Department of Criminal Justice
California State University at Los Angeles
Los Angeles, California

Readings in Criminal Justice

Edward Eldefonso

Supervisor, Santa Clara County Juvenile Probation Department
Lecturer, Sociology and Criminal Justice, DeAnza College

GLENCOE PRESS
A division of Benziger Bruce & Glencoe, Inc.
New York • Beverly Hills
Collier-Macmillan Publishers
London

Glencoe Press
A division of Benziger Bruce & Glencoe, Inc.
8701 Wilshire Boulevard
Beverly Hills, California 90211
Collier Macmillan Canada, Ltd., Toronto, Canada

Library of Congress Catalog Card Number: 72-85758

First printing, 1973

Contents

v

Preface

Most teachers of law enforcement find it difficult to provide beginning students with satisfying and stimulating instruction. People entering the field have different requirements: some need a general introduction to police work, some an understanding of a particular area, and others a basis for advanced training in law enforcement. Teachers are overburdened with the effort to meet these various needs in one course, so most departments of law enforcement concentrate on the last kind of student.

Furthermore, teachers are constantly aware that, by its very nature, law enforcement covers the subject areas of many other disciplines (law, corrections, sociology, and psychology, for example). How can a teacher develop and maintain interest in a discipline that is so voluminous? Introductory courses are necessarily limited by the amount of subject matter that can be covered in the allotted time. As yet, materials have not been developed which aid the teacher in this dilemma. For courses in introductory criminal justice, there is at present no textbook that gives a comprehensive presentation of principles.

Readings in Criminal Justice attempts to present the main trends in the field of criminal justice. Along with supporting lectures and materials, it can be used as the *basic* text for a quarter or single-semester undergraduate course. It can also be used as a *supplementary* text offering rich material for discussion. Finally, the book can be rewarding for every person who wants to find out about the significant problems that face law enforcement today.

It is the editor's firm contention that students' interests are best served by presenting divergent sources and ideas in the field of law enforcement. These pages provide such repressentation from some of the most contemporary literature in the field written by distinguished authors, scholars, and practitioners in the criminal justice field. The task of including or excluding articles was formidable and required a great deal of compromise in arriving at final selections. Of course, all the subjects of interest, or ones that educators consider germane to law enforcement, could not be included. Although some excellent material was excluded, the ultimate selection was guided by a resolve to choose only articles representing important research contributions or valuable theoretical discussion or distinctive descriptive material. The descriptive selections are included for two reasons: First, in certain areas of police work, few research studies exist. Second, many areas of inquiry (i.e., police surveillance, patrol procedure, working delinquent gangs, etc.) are so far removed from the experiences of both students and instructors that the initial phase of comprehension and insight must occur through accurate description.

Brief comments open each part. These remarks are intended to tie the various selections together; they are not meant to impose a particular philosophy or point of view on the student. Critiques of the selections are not included because the presentation of divergent views is considered to be of primary importance. Each part concludes with a list of correlated selected references, annotated to generate motivation in those students who want further research in a particular area. Instructors will find these references helpful in assigning supplementary reading in specific areas of police work.

Most college libraries, faced with cuts in the budget and increases in students, simply have not been able to provide the books needed for a course in criminal justice. Because of this lack of financial resources, articles in this book have been reprinted in their entirety—with the exception of John McNamara's study of recruits' backgrounds in Part Two; because of the organization of this article, the reprinted section stands by itself.

Acknowledgments

Many obligations have been incurred during the preparation of *Readings in Criminal Justice,* some of them as hard to identify as they are to repay.

However, a special thanks must be expressed to my wife, Mildred Ann Eldefonso, *a partner in all matters,* but specifically in this project; she assisted in compiling and editing the credits for each author in this volume. I wish to further express special gratitude for the thoughtful criticism and encouragement of B. Earl Lewis, Director of the Department of Law Enforcement Education, DeAnza College, and to the staff of the Santa Clara County Juvenile Probation Department, San Jose, California, who extended their cooperation whenever possible.

Finally, and more importantly, I would like to acknowledge the cooperation and kindness of the individual authors, editors, and publishers who graciously permitted the use of their material in this volume; specific acknowledgements are noted at the bottom of the first page of each chapter.

Readings in
Criminal Justice

Part I

Understanding Crime, the Measurement of Crime, the Role of the Police

Part One introduces the student to the goals of American law enforcement, which include the protection of life and property, the preservation of peace, and the prevention of crime. In order to best meet these objectives, it is necessary that law enforcers continue in their efforts to understand crime and their role in its control.

Chapter 1 explores the question, "What Is Crime?" The answer seems self-evident, but the article shows that it is not. The definition of crime varies surprisingly according to the individual vantage point—social, moral, or legal.

Equally difficult to ascertain is the impact of crime on the society. The fear, the pain, or the loss suffered by the victim, even the economic impact, can be estimated only roughly.

Chapter 2 explores the difficulties encountered in the statistical analysis of crime, and puts forth suggestions for the improvement of crime measurement.

1

Chapters 4, 5, and 6 are devoted to the discussion of the law enforcers themselves. After presenting a historical overview of the police role, the authors go on to discuss the sociological and psychological aspects of that role. How does a policeman view himself? Is he a saint in a hostile world? Is he a disciplinarian of the enemy public? Or is he a social worker in the community? Certainly he is confronted with a multitude of problems that demand that he be a decision maker. Through Chapter 6, the student may share vicariously in the experiences of two policemen during an average day.

Finally, Chapter 7 recounts the principles of law enforcement as formulated by Sir Robert Peel, English statesman and the father of the English Police Force. These basic tenets of law enforcement are shown to be just as viable today as when set down more than a century ago.

CHAPTER 1

Criminology and the Problem of Crime

Elmer H. Johnson

Elmer H. Johnson is Professor of Sociology, Center for the
Study of Crime, Delinquency, and Corrections, Southern Illinois
University, Carbondale, Illinois. Dr. Johnson is a prolific writer and
has contributed greatly to the literature of the police science field.

From time immemorial reactions to "the criminal" have been colored
by extremes of emotion. He may be described as a monster or he may be
pictured as a hunted animal or as the helpless victim of brutality. These
wide swings of emotion are reflected in crime fiction. One story describes
the resourcefulness of the clever criminal in outwitting the police and the
courts. Another tale presents the heroic figure of the fearless policeman
risking his life and using his wits to overcome the vicious criminal. Often
the story ends with the clang of prison gates. News stories about crime
usually end at this point because this is where the public interest stops.

Curiosity as a Stimulus for Study

The drama and riddle of crime stimulate curiosity in several forms.
There is the idle curiosity which seeks entertainment and thrills and in
which the desire to learn is of minor importance. Visits to courtrooms and
prisons resemble trips to the zoo to see strange and frightening creatures.

Another form of curiosity, the prying type, is meddlesome and offi-
cious and too often is motivated by a quest for power through habitual and
impertinent inquisitiveness. The gossip gains information through a pre-
tended interest in the welfare of the offender. The interviewer presses
beyond his duties to obtain information to be used as a weapon against the
interviewee. Still another form of curiosity is the casual type in which
"something" more significant is sensed beneath the superficial aspects of

Chapter 1 from Elmer H. Johnson, *Crime, Correction and Society,* Copyright 1968. Reprinted
with the permission of the Dorsey Press, Homewood, Illinois.

3

behavior, but in which there is no follow-through. After momentary interest the observer moves on to other matters for lack of will to undertake the investigation necessary to develop and test initial impressions.

There may also exist a "practical" curiosity found among personnel with long and frequent experience in dealing with offenders. These officials ask themselves questions such as the following: "Why does this intelligent fellow repeat his crimes?" "Why do some persons remain honest under circumstances others use as excuses for crime?" "Why are there more assaults in the summer?" Frequently, this form of curiosity brings insightful answers, but usually it is sporadic and unorganized, resulting in unreliable speculation. This book assumes a more profound and enduring curiosity.

Scientific curiosity initiates the research process. At the moment it is sufficient to say that it is the most disciplined of the various types. It requires the questioner to gather and test facts systematically. In the long run it is the most useful form of curiosity because it encourages progressive accumulation of tested knowledge. It is expressed within an intellectual framework of organizing questions and for the gaining of validity and reliability in answers. It stimulates a quest for answers which can be fitted together to build general theories.

Why Study Crime?

Criminology merits this profound and enduring curiosity. Since anything affecting human behavior is pertinent to criminology, it may be said that criminology is useful as a survey of the knowledge of mankind. Efforts to explain and treat criminality have drawn on all the behavioral sciences and have made use of the concepts and principles of the physical and biological sciences.

Because criminal law reflects the fundamental values of society, it is one of the most faithful mirrors of a given civilization. In studying the operation of criminal law and the techniques of handling convicted offenders, criminology affords an opportunity to probe the nature of the institutions organizing human activities. This approach focuses attention on the reaction of society to the criminals, rather than concentrating solely on the criminals. This point of view causes the observer to examine more carefully the function and meaning of traditions he has taken for granted. New depth and freshness is given to the study of human behavior and customs.

The extent of crime demonstrates the importance of criminology as a study for the future leaders of society who will be called on to cope with the major issues of their day. Crime merits inclusion among the major social problems for reasons cited by the President's Crime Commission.[1]

---

[1]President's Commission on Law Enforcement and Administration of Justice, *The Challenge of Crime in a Free Society* (Washington, D.C.: U.S. Government Printing Office, February, 1967), p. 1.

Every citizen is, in a sense, a victim of crime. Violence and theft have not only injured, often irreparably, hundreds of thousands of citizens, but have directly affected everyone. Some have been afraid to use public streets and parks. Some have come to doubt the worth of a society in which so many people behave badly. Some have become distrustful of the government's ability, or even desire, to protect them. Some have lapsed into the attitude that criminal behavior is normal human behavior and consequently have become indifferent to it, or have adopted it as a good way to get ahead in life. Some have become suspicious of those they conceive to be responsible for crime: adolescents or Negroes or drug addicts or college students or demonstrators; policemen who fail to solve crimes; judges who pass lenient sentences or write decisions restricting the activities of the police; parole boards that release prisoners who resume their criminal activities.

Estimates of the economic impact of crime run into scores of billions of dollars. The President's Crime Commission estimated $21 billion (see Table 1-1) to indicate a rough order of magnitude, but the figures are probably conservative. The elusiveness of the factors contributing to such estimates require caution in using them. For example, four factors affect the size of the crime bill:[2]

1. *The loss of productive labor which is diverted to meeting the challenge of crime.* This would include law enforcement and criminal court personnel, insurance men, burglary alarm makers, and so on. The potentially useful labor of criminals also is lost. Estimation of such loss encounters some troublesome questions: How well are the criminals qualified by their physical and mental abilities and by their skills and motivations to assume legitimate employment? Is the economy prepared to offer productive employment for court and police personnel no longer involved in crime control?

2. *Economic waste caused by crime.* Property is destroyed or its value diminished because of crime. The cost includes a hidden charge for insurance, plant protection, allowances for expected theft, and for the portion of the tax bill which goes to pay for governmental programs directed against crime. On the other hand, there are crimes which reduce waste. For example, businessmen on occasion have invited racketeering as a means of reducing unrestrained competition. Furthermore, the costs of crimes do not fall with equal impact on all citizens. Some unknown portion of the costs of robberies, burglaries, and hijacking are absorbed by the manufacturers and distributors to keep their prices competitive.

3. *Transfer of money and property from victim to criminal.* Analysis of this effect is complicated by its relationship to the redistribution of

---

[2]E. R. Hawkins and Willard Waller, "Critical Notes on the Cost of Crime," *Journal of Criminal Law and Criminology,* Vol. 46 (January-February, 1956), pp. 657-72.

Table 1-1.—Estimated Economic Impact of Crime and Related Expenditures (In Millions of Dollars)

Crimes against Persons		$ 815
Homicide	$ 750	
Assault and other	65	
Crimes against Property		3,932
Unreported commercial theft	1,400	
Robbery, burglary, larceny $50 and over, auto theft	600	
Embezzlement	200	
Fraud	1,350	
Forgery and other	82	
Property destroyed by arson and vandalism	300	
Other Crimes		2,036
Driving under influence	1,816	
Tax fraud	100	
Abortion	120	
Illegal Goods and Services		8,035
Narcotics	350	
Loansharking	350	
Prostitution	225	
Alcohol	150	
Gambling	7,000	
Public Law Enforcement and Criminal Justice		4,212
Police	2,792	
Corrections	1,034	
Prosecution and defense	125	
Courts	261	
Private Costs Related to Crime		1,910
Prevention service	1,350	
Prevention equipment	200	
Insurance	300	
Private counsel, bail, witness expenses	60	
Total		$20,940

Source: President's Commission on Law Enforcement and Administration of Justice, *The Challenge of Crime in a Free Society* (Washington, D.C.:   U.S. Government Printing Office, February, 1967), p. 33.

national income. The loss to the victim is obvious, but what is the effect on society as a whole? It may be that the total immediate consumption of income is increased by crime through the transfer of wealth from those who would withhold it from the market to those who immediately purchase goods and services.

4. *Expenditures for crime control and care of offenders and their dependents.* These include the costs of administering the systems of law enforcement, justice, and correction. Some of the costs of caring for the indigent would be charged to this item. However, some of the services would be required even if crime could be abolished: traffic control, tracing of lost persons, and handling of crowds, for example. Prisoner labor reduces the burden of prison operations to the taxpayer. Probation and parole programs contribute indirectly to community and family integration and to the alleviation of personal problems. These services would be shifted to other welfare programs.

Although the size of the total crime bill is uncertain, the financial burden obviously is high. The social and psychological consequences of crime are further justification for concern: the fear of potential and actual victims, the effects of suspicion and hostility on relationships between citizens, the weakening of some individual's faith in moral values, and the economic insecurity created for families of victims and of imprisoned offenders.

Table 1-1 challenges several popular assumptions. Police statistics suggest that robbery, burglary, larceny, and automobile theft comprise the major share of property crimes, but other property crimes impose a much heavier burden. Employee theft, embezzlement, and other business crimes are at such volume as to raise questions concerning the sharp differentiation of adjudicated offenders from the so-called noncriminals. Although homicide makes up only a small fraction of arrest statistics, its economic impact is greater than commonly supposed. Nevertheless, driving under the influence of alcohol, an offense generally given inadequate attention, exacts a greater economic burden. The toll of syndicated crime is dominant, especially for gambling, another crime drawing an ambivalent public reaction. The Commission reports that police and, especially, corrections costs are rising rapidly, but the bulk of the costs go into personnel and nontreatment purposes such as traffic control and maintenance of prisoners.

What Is Criminology?

Criminology is the scientific study and practical application of findings in the areas of: (*a*) crime causation and criminal behavior and etiology, (*b*) the nature of the societal reaction as a symptom of the characteristics of the society, and (*c*) the prevention of crime.

Branches of Criminology

Criminology has two interdependent branches: science and practice. The criminological sciences are manned by academic and research criminologists seeking to develop a body of general principles through use of the scientific method. There is considerable debate whether their efforts are tending toward a real science of criminology, or whether they will continue to be specialists in a variety of disciplines who happen to share an interest in the scientific study of crime.

Criminological sciences appears to be a more fitting term than "criminology" when the first branch is considered. In a London symposium organized by the International Society of Criminology, the majority of participants envisaged criminology as an autonomous science.[3] But they recognized that when persons lack the clinical and experimental methods necessary for serious research, it may be necessary for criminology to resign itself to being a collection of different sciences bearing some relationship to criminal phenomena.

Internationally, the teaching of criminology is found within a multiplicity of academic structures and is subject to conflicting efforts of law, sociology, psychology, biology, and penology, respectively, to claim it as its own. Similar heterogeneity is found in United States, but with sociology more dominant.

Applied criminology, the other branch, is a loose confederation of practitioners of criminology in law enforcement agencies, criminal courts, probation and parole programs, prisons, juvenile training schools, private and public welfare agencies, and various crime prevention programs.

The teaching of criminology passes on to the practitioners the fruits of the criminological sciences, supplemented by the contributions of forensic medicine, police science, and judicial psychology. The latter three fields are more concerned with the presentation of specialized facts than with the scientific study of criminal phenomena. In addition to the regular curricula, institutes in law enforcement or correction are offered by a few universities and colleges in the form of seminars and training courses. Some law enforcement, probation, parole, and prison systems offer in-service training of various intensities and qualities. In general, the training of practitioners is far short of minimum standards, with occasional but commendable exceptions.

Difficulties of the Fields

The heterogeneity of the fields of criminology creates difficulties. First, scientific objectivity conflicts with reformist ideology accepted by

[3]Denis Carroll and Jean Pinatel, "Report on Teaching of Criminology," in *The University Teaching of Social Sciences: Criminology* (Paris: UNESCO, 1957), p. 15.

many in applied criminology. Social concern has been the mainspring of criminology from the beginning.[4] Humanitarianism and a strong sense of civic duty have been major forces motivating some individuals to devote their careers to the study and/or treatment of criminals. Even as an administrative program rationally created and deliberately implemented, applied criminology seeks to effect changes in the offender and in society itself to alleviate the crime problem. Subjectivity is even more obvious in tendencies to confuse immorality and sin with criminal behavior. Although social concern has served the purpose of giving a sense of mission to criminologists, the scientist must guard against the danger that his personal ethics or the current moral code pervert his pursuit of truth.

The nonethical quality of criminological research helps to explain the suspicion and aloofness with which many applied criminologists regard theoretical criminologists. Law enforcement officers, prison officials, and similar practitioners consider such objectivity to be inconsistent with their defense of values safeguarded by the criminal law. They regard the search for abstract truth to be unsatisfactory when they ask guidance in meeting the pressing immediate problems. On the other hand, theoretical criminologists are tempted to ignore the realities in the environment within which the practitioner must operate.

Functions of University

If a unified professional community of criminologists is to emerge, the university has key roles to play. Only the university has the resources of theoretical concepts and highly trained personnel to introduce the broad-ranging process of cultural change necessary. The intellectual storehouse of the university holds many "skeleton keys" to unlock answers to persistent difficulties. The university has the institutionalized function of providing competent and constructive criticism of traditional practice. Through teaching, students are prepared for criminological careers, and competence of practitioners is upgraded through short-term institutes. Academic training is of four types:[5] (1) Schools of social work envisage correctional work as essentially clinical and nonauthoritarian in nature. (2) Sequence of courses within departments of sociology attempt to educate future law enforcement and correctional practitioners in a program usually designed primarily to prepare students for careers in sociology per se. (3) Programs also are found within schools of public administration, social welfare, public

---

[4]Howard S. Jones, *Crime and the Penal System* (London: University Tutorial Press, 1956), p. 1.

[5]Julian Roebuck and Paul Zelhart, "The Problem of Educating the Correctional Practitioner," *Journal of Criminal Law, Criminology and Police Science,* Vol. 56 (March, 1965), pp. 45-53; Peter Lejins, "Aspects of Correctional Personnel Training as Viewed by a College Professor," *Proceedings, 85th Annual Congress of Corrections, American Prison Association,* 1955.

safety, police science, psychology, and political science. Usually, these involve a "core curriculum" without integration of criminological knowledge and experience within the theoretical studies. (4) Independent specialized programs are advocated under the beliefs that criminology does not mesh with any single behavioral science and that the generic approach of traditional departments does not provide training in the settings wherein theoretical principles are to be applied.[6]

Programs based on a single discipline assume that criminology is not a primary and self-contained discipline because its subject matter involves the full range of the social and behavioral sciences. Through intensive study within a particular discipline, the student is supposed to gain the theoretical knowledge which is a major quality of the genuine professional. However, this form of curriculum organization undermines the integration and coordination of the total body of criminological theory because members of each discipline regard crime and criminals as solely a specialized issue within their particular generic approach. Consequently, the various theoreticians are isolated from one another to the detriment of the development of the interdisciplinary approach essential to criminology.[7]

What Is Crime?

The present ferment in criminology is suggested by the very fact that such a fundamental question as "What is crime?" should be debated. From the great variety of nonconformists in a society, the criminal groups are selected according to certain criteria.

The violators of traditions and of group norms include the unorthodox participants in science, the arts, and sports. There are graduations of deviant behaviors in regard to sex, ranging from common-law marriage and serial monogamy through "free love" and other forms of sexual experimentation, to commercialized prostitution and rape by assault. Business practices range from high-pressure salesmanship and sharp business practices to fraud, swindles, and syndicated crime. Where should the line be drawn along such continuums to distinguish criminals from other unconventional persons?

---

[6]Walter C. Reckless, "Training the Correctional Worker," in Paul W. Tappan (ed.), *Contemporary Correction* (New York: McGraw-Hill Book Co., 1951), p. 40; Alfred C. Schnur, "Pre-Service Training," *Journal of Criminal Law, Criminology, and Police Science,* Vol. 50 (May-June, 1959), p. 30; J. S. Lobenthal, "Proposals for Correctional Education and Training," *Prison Journal,* Vol. 40 (April, 1960), pp. 3-12.

[7]F. Ferracuti and M. W. Wolfgang, "Clinical vs. Sociological Criminology: Separation or Integration?" *Excerpta Criminologica,* Vol. 4 (July-August, 1964), pp. 407-10; Gordon Trasler, "Strategic Problems in the Study of Criminal Behavior," *British Journal of Criminology,* Vol. 4 (July, 1964), pp. 422-42.

Morals and Criminology

Probably since the time man first developed a sense of morals, there has been a belief that crime is in violation of some universal and permanently valid moral law of which criminal law is but an imperfect and vacillating reflection. Frequently, dissatisfaction is expressed with the way criminal law functions. Somehow the "true criminal" is not affected in the way some persons think he should be. Probing the reasons for this dissatisfaction reveals this conception of crime to be colored with ideas of sin and immorality.

Acts of religious sacrilege, indecency, and vice have been and are subjected to criminal law. But can all such acts be treated as crimes without engulfing ourselves in an anarchy of personal moralities or without imposing the morality of a politically powerful minority on all members of a society?

When the criminal law becomes the means of expressing moral condemnation, serious difficulties result in a diverse culture such as ours. In the absence of universal condemnation of the "immoralities," great disparities occur in the application of criminal laws. Enforcement exaggerates differences in behavior and motivations of those persons subject to legal penalties and those not subject. Alcohol is consumed under some social circumstances which are consistent with approved values. Abortion may be stimulated by economic inability to provide adequately for additional children as well as by fear of the consequences of extramarital sex activity. Repressive laws erode the distinction between morally disapproved conduct and conduct imperiling the public order. Consequently, the drug user is less likely to receive the medical and psychological rehabilitation he requires when the law defines him as a criminal along with the antisocial persons who traffic in dangerous drugs. Legal prohibitions, in the face of a desperate demand for the forbidden services, create circumstances favorable to the development of illicit enterprises.[8]

The wide variation in penal codes of different times and governments reflect the changes in "human nature" and the relativity of its expressions through social institutions. Therefore, the criminologist turns to one of two alternatives: the legal or the social definition of crime.

Legal Definition

Crime is an intentional act or omission in violation of criminal law,

[8]Edwin M. Schur, *Crime Without Victims* (Englewood Cliffs, N.J.: Prentice-Hall, Inc., 1965); Joseph Fletcher, "Sex Offenses: An Ethical View," *Law and Contemporary Problems,* Vol. 25 (Spring, 1960), pp. 244-57; Ganville Williams, *The Sancity of Life and the Criminal Law* (New York: Alfred A. Knopf, Inc., 1957).

committed without defense or justification, and sanctioned by the law as a felony or misdemeanor.[9]

This definition assumes:

1. Crime is viewed as a legal concept: that behavior becomes criminal when it violates criminal law. Jeffery asks: "Where does crime exist, if not in the legal codes? Is crime a characteristic of criminals, or of social systems?"[10] Crime is defined by the state in the course of its efforts to protect important interests and values. When it is necessary to resort to legal coercion to protect crucial values, the selective use of criminal law reflects both the relative priority placed on certain values and the points of strain within the social structure. Hence, crime becomes an index of the patterns of interaction of members of the society, i.e., of the social system. Therefore, the crime is seen as the crucial topic, and the criminal becomes but a reflection of the workings of criminal law as a form of social control.

2. The offender cannot be assumed to be criminal until he has been found guilty through court procedure.[11] This requirement is presumed to give the legal definition its special asset in precisely differentiating with competence between the criminal and the noncriminal. Such precision, furthermore, is seen in the care with which the alleged crime is evaluated. The act, including the failure to act under certain circumstances, must be accompanied by the specific intent to do what the law prohibits. Furthermore, certain characteristics of the offender or of the situation are grounds for withholding the legal sanctions. Examples are insanity, extreme youth, and self-defense.

3. It is contended that criminal law is a particularly stable and responsible means of adjusting social control to changing social conditions. The legal definition has been criticized for its variability from time to time and from place to place. Tappan retorts by noting that all norms are relative, impermanent, and variable.[12] Since laws are products of sociocultural forces, they vary with changing conditions, but their careful consideration and consensus in development ensure some regularity of conduct while resolving the conflicting interests and values that accompany social dynamism.

Social Definition

Crime is an act which the group regards as sufficiently menacing to

---

[9]Paul W. Tappan, *Crime, Justice and Correction* (New York: McGraw-Hill Book Co., 1960), p. 10.

[10]Clarence R. Jeffery, "The Structure of American Criminological Thinking," *Journal of Criminal Law and Criminology,* Vol. 46 (January-February, 1956), p. 670.

[11]Paul W. Tappan, "Who Is the Criminal?" *American Sociological Review,* Vol. 12 (February, 1947), p. 100.

[12]*Ibid.,* p. 97.

its fundamental interests to justify formal reaction to restrain the violator. This definition assumes:

1. Criminal laws are seen as part of a larger body of norms. The criminal laws are shaped by the character and interests of those groups of the population which influence legislation. Therefore, the choice of subjects for legal sanctions and the nature of the sanctions applied against the violator reflect the same social processes whereby the group attitudes are crystallized into rules of behavior and into group resistance to the violator.

2. Crime is defined more broadly than under the legal concept. It is viewed as antisocial behavior that is injurious to those social interests which rules of behavior (including legal codes) are designed to support.[13] This means crime is defined to include a larger variety and quantity of behavior than that which the criminal law is intended to penalize.

3. The intrinsic qualities of behavior are considered to be a major focus of study, rather than only the violation of criminal law. If the characteristics of the criminal personalities and their social situations are to be studied effectively, the scientist must be free to select and classify the data appropriate to his specific research. As Sellin states, the categories set up by the criminal law are "of a fortuitous nature" and do not "arise intrinsically from the nature of the subject matter" the scientist attempts to analyze.[14]

Tests of Scientific Adequacy

To consider the relative value of the two definitions, one may subject them to three tests of scientific adequacy.

Precise Differentiation

If the definition of the criminal varies with the subjective evaluation of the person making the classification, it has less usefulness in producing reliable and valid conclusions.

Its proponents see precision as a major advantage of the legal definition, contending that conviction of the offender in court removes doubts concerning his criminality. It is argued that criminal law provides precise criteria that are lacking in the "vague, omnibus concepts" of the social definition which "allow judge, administrator, or—conceivably—sociologist, in an undirected, freely operating discretion, to attribute the status 'criminal' to any individual or class which he conceives nefarious."[15]

---

[13]George W. Wilber, "The Scientific Adequacy of Criminological Concepts," *Social Forces*, Vol. 28 (December, 1949), p. 170.

[14]Thorsten Sellin, *Culture Conflict and Crime* (New York: Social Science Research Council, 1938), p. 21.

[15]Tappan, "Who Is the Criminal?" *Contemporary Correction*, p. 99.

Critics of the legal definition deny that such precision exists, citing the large number of cases lost between crimes known to the police and conviction, the variation between jurisdictions in the efficiency of law enforcement, the fluctuations in arrest policies for minor crimes, the possibility of false conviction, the presumed failure to convict all the guilty, and the probable existence of crimes unreported to the police. It is contended that there are major tendencies among victims to ignore crimes for the sake of their own self-interest.

Universal Application

Ideally, the definition of crime should apply equally well to every time and place and to every social group. All norms are relative and impermanent because they depend on culture and the form of social organization, both of which vary with time and place. Crime is a universal phenomenon if conceptualized as nonobservance of cultural norms. But this level of abstraction is too high to have meaning for criminological analysis. Infanticide, cannibalism, homosexuality, polygamy, and similar crimes by our standards are not so considered universally. Definitions of crime have changed within our culture with the passage of time. With changes in socioeconomic arrangements and technologies, the norms are modified. For example, as the factory technology supplanted the domestic system, new organizational forms for economic production and distribution created new needs for enacted controls. Definitions of crime vary among contemporary jurisdictions. Comparison of the laws of the states of the United States demonstrates the wide variety in the specifics of legal definitions at a given time. Bensing finds confusion and lack of uniformity in the laws regulating sexual activity.[16] Eighteen states provide the death penalty for rape, but it is possible to receive only a monetary fine in three states.

Attempts to generate comparable crime rates for several jurisdictions reveal the weakness of the legal definition of crime.

In applying the social definition, the research would attempt to determine the normative patterns established by those groups dominating the society. There would be practical problems in obtaining objective and reliable information as the basis for identifying the universal normative patterns and for comparison of the relative conformity to these patterns.

Theoretical Usefulness

Scientific inquiry moves through a sequence of stages: (a) Statement of a hunch or imaginative idea as a tentative hypothesis which expresses a question occurring to the investigator in the course of his observation and

---

[16]Robert C. Bensing, "A Comparative Study of American Sex Statutes," *Journal of Criminal Law and Criminology*, Vol. 42 (May-June, 1957), pp. 57-72.

thought. (*b*) The observation and recording of data pertinent to his hypothesis in a form permitting a test of its validity. (*c*) The classification and recording of these data in a way most appropriate to his research purpose and most likely to bring reliable, valid, and significant answers. (*d*) The formulation of generalizations on the basis of his research results reflecting the patterns he has discovered in his data. Through this process of inquiry, the scientist seeks to reduce the confusion of isolated facts by discovering relationships between them and by measuring the relative significance of one fact in relation to other facts. Then he seeks to relate these generalizations to one another to create an integrated theory and, thereby, contribute to the development of science.

The generalizations and theories of science have their basis in the facts of everyday life. The problems of defining fundamental concepts reflect the difficulty of patterning the events encountered day in and day out by the policeman, judge, and prison warden. Policy is supposed to give long-term meaning to individual actions in specific events by explaining the "why," "what," and "how" of daily behavior. Why is one offender sent to prison and another only fined? What is probation supposed to accomplish? Should the homosexual be handled the same way as the habitual pickpocket? At a higher level of abstraction, science gives a similar sense of significance to each policy within a framework of policies formulated to systematize society's total reaction to crime.

Criticisms of Two Definitions

Wilber criticizes the legal definition of crime for its limitation of research to only those persons who have been convicted of violating the law when other types of nonconformists not so included may have similar characteristics.[17] He asks whether the legal definition does not sacrifice the significance of research findings for the sake of precision.

The usual manner of resolving the dispute between the competing definitions is to accept the legal definition, while acknowledging its defects. Wilber sums up: The real question is not whether the legal conception is good, but whether it is good enough.[18] Jeffery supports the legal definition on three grounds: First, criticism of the concept confuses the criminal act with the label of criminality, in that the explanation of behavior and the explanation of how certain behavior comes to be called criminal are two different matters. Second, all standards of conduct are relative and impermanent; therefore, the criticism of the relativity of the legal concept can be made of the social concept as well. Third, laws are codes of conduct and, therefore, can be subjected to analysis as norms.

---

[17]Wilber, "Criminological Concepts," p. 173.
[18]*Ibid.*, p. 168.

Wilber suggests that the existing legal framework be the starting point for the development of more adequate concepts. Short and Nye, in a similar vein, suggest development of alternative sources of data when official records are not appropriate for testing hypotheses.[19]

Immediate practical considerations compel most contemporary students of crime to depend heavily on the legal concept. The only alternative would be to amass data at expense and time beyond the resources available to most students of the subject. Since police, court, and prison statistics are based on the legal concept, this definition will continue to be in general use.

Place of Theoretical Analysis

Among the characteristics of a science are an objective attitude, a set of methods for obtaining and analyzing facts, and a goal of seeking generalized conclusions about cause and effect. However, the difficulties in defining crime as a concept illustrate how hard it is to apply the methods of science to crime. Yet the criminologist as a scientist must frame his questions with the precision of meaning essential to significant and verifiable observation of events and to the systematic integration of these observations into a theoretical framework.

For example, arrest statistics include vagrancy as a category. Vagrancy is supposed to include such offenses as vagabondage, begging, and loitering. Actually, this is a "grab bag" category which also includes a variety of other police actions. Prostitutes and criminal suspects may be arrested on this charge to hold them until an investigation can be made. But, for our immediate purpose, we will consider the first three offenses sufficient. We note at once that those offenses are too diffuse to give precise meaning to these arrests when scientific research is being conducted. Were the arrested persons idlers who refused to work? Were they happy-go-lucky wanderers who did not let poverty deny them the adventure of travel? Were they jobless husbands and fathers in search of employment? Were they professional exploiters of tenderhearted passersby?

In a research project, Foote[20] used the characteristics of a science to reach some meaningful conclusions concerning vagrancy from the hodge-podge of persons and events he observed in magistrates' courts. By framing precise questions concerning the purposes for the city of the court proceedings, he uncovered a deeper significance in them. He found the law being used to rid the city of "undesirable" persons and to control suspicious

---

[19]James F. Short, Jr., and F. Ivan Nye, "Reported Behavior as a Criterion of Deviant Behavior," *Social Problems,* Vol. 5 (Winter, 1957), p. 213.

[20]Caleb Foote, "Vagrancy Type Law and Its Administration," *NPPA Journal,* Vol. 3 (July, 1957), pp. 230-41.

persons in ways similar to those employed in 14th-century England to handle wandering beggars.

Importance of Theoretical Bases

Theory affords a means of assessing and classifying informational bits into a system which gives meaning to data collection, transformation of data into tables, analysis, and presentation of conclusions. By using a theoretical framework, the researcher is able to communicate his findings to other persons with special interest in his subject. The theoretical framework is a tool for accumulating information and discoveries for progressive penetration into the unknown. If each research study builds on the findings of another, the scientist is able to narrow his focus of attention to a particular area of facts when he begins a new study. When early studies have gathered facts within a framework of concepts appropriate to the particular subject matter, the later researcher does not have to duplicate the gathering of facts concerning matters already established. Instead he can choose a particular aspect of the area already delineated by previous studies. He has a "road map" describing the general nature of the partially explored "wilderness" of unknowns. He can use the findings of previous studies to penetrate deeper into the problem under study, rather than wasting time by making discoveries all over again. Because each theory is based on generalization of individual events into a larger pattern, discoveries are more likely to have usefulness in a large number of situations. Empirical observation tends to emphasize the uniqueness of the immediate event, rather than concentrating on similarities among events divorced in time and space.

While the causes of crime have been the subject of much speculation since ancient times, systematic study appeared only recently. Surveys of the professional journals and textbooks demonstrate the rarity of systematic studies 30 and more years ago. This is not because present-day criminologists have a monopoly on brains. Rather they have benefited from the struggles of the pioneers to develop valid, complete, and reliable information and to develop concepts and research techniques.

A survey of research in American correctional institutions and research institutes finds a large and increasing volume of research in progress.[21] However, with a few exceptions, the research in correctional systems is found to be fortuitous and haphazard.

Criminological research has been handicapped by limitations in scope, by methodological weaknesses, and by restrictions in orientation. Many studies have been concerned with minor and fragmentary aspects of problems. Often only one factor among the many associated with crime is

---

[21]Arthur L. Beeley, "The Prison as a Laboratory for the Study of the Offender," *American Journal of Correction,* Vol. 22 (July-August, 1960), p. 22.

selected for attention, without identifying the web of interactions among complex causes. Consequently, a large number of undigested and uninte-grated facts is accumulated. Multiplicity of concepts and use of jargon complicate the accumulation of established facts into a conceptual whole. Communication among various disciplines is made more difficult. Often research design and interpretations are naïve. Methodological weaknesses include inadequate or no sampling, absence of controls over complicating variables, collection of ambiguous data, and faulty statistical analyses. Much time, money, and effort are wasted in establishing what is already known or is trivial. Sometimes projects are nothing more than unguided "fishing expeditions" for information without regard for its usefulness.

There are difficulties in employing scientific methods in criminology. To study crime and the reactions to crime is to probe the fundamental values of a society—the sort of investigation unlikely to give peace to the self-righteous and the complacent. The very definition of the criminal and the forms of societal response to his conduct are founded on values which have been given deep-seated significance within the framework of emotions and beliefs acquired during the subtle processes of personality development. Emotion-charged conceptions contribute to the inconsistency and ambiva-lence which mark the evaluation of the criminal and his conduct. Tradition-ally, public interest in the criminal is sporadic and superficial, demonstrating reluctance to invest much time and treasure in restoring him to the ranks of the law-abiding population. Problems of crime causation and criminal rehabilitation are oversimplified grossly.

Applications of Statistics and Research

One of the favorable signs for the development of sound criminologi-cal research is the increased interest in collection of reliable and valid statistics. This is not to suggest that statistical information, in and of itself, is the equivalent of fundamental research; but it is a prerequisite. Data can suggest areas for fruitful study. Revealing a remarkably high number of prosecutions for a given crime may lead to an investigation into police and court practices or the socioeconomic conditions which brought about this condition. Additional prerequisites for effective research are development of research tools, acquisition of skilled personnel, and creation of a favor-able research climate.

Kinds of Research

For our purposes, there are three general patterns in the applications of criminal statistics. *Theoretical research* employs data to test hypotheses as a means of extending fundamental knowledge. *Routine administrative statistics* provide information for intelligent decision making and effective management of daily activities within an ongoing organization. *Administrative research* employs routine statistics and special studies for scientific analysis of specific problems influencing the achievement of organizational goals.

The distinctive characteristics of *theoretical research* are those which distinguish "basic research" from development in the physical sciences. Theoretical research offers less probability of short-run usefulness. It places more emphasis on discovery of general principles than on answering immediate and concrete questions. The framing of the hypotheses emerges from prolonged study of the manifold aspects of the problem. The "payoff" does not have to be immediate, tangible, specific, and practical. Theoretical research is conducted largely by university personnel, but the journals of the last decade offer evidence of increased contributions by practitioners.

Routine administrative statistics are the most common form among action agencies. Their annual reports reflect a wide range in intensity, accuracy, and sophistication of the statistical systems they use. Too many reports reveal lack of planning in data collection. They show collection of numbers in a blind and expedient manner without due examination of the significance of the numbers. They indicate lack of awareness of the relationship between the manner of counting and later use of the data in answering fundamental questions.

Routine administrative statistics provide facts essential to intelligent administration in daily operations, to justifying budgetary requests, and to answering queries from other agencies and the public. The increased size and complexity of operations have caused some agencies to develop the rationality and formality of bureaucratic organizations. Managerial control requires speedy and accurate communication of information and instructions between the groups making up the organization. In the complex organization, administrative statistics are an important means for serving the informational and control functions. When face-to-face relationships no longer suffice for serving these functions, documents of a wide variety and standard operating procedures are vital tools for coordinating diverse, and perhaps potentially conflicting, activities. Statistical collection and analysis are useful for developing and employing these tools.

Three versions of *administrative research* are operations research, correlational analysis, and experimental research.[22] *Operations research* is the employment of a scientific method of providing executive departments with quantitative basis for decisions regarding operations under their control.[23] The methods may be those of theoretical research, but the research

---

[22]James A. McCafferty, "Latent Research Findings in Corrections," paper at 61st Annual Conference of Missouri Association of Social Welfare, Kansas City, October 20, 1961.

[23]Elmer H. Johnson, "Latent Functions of an Administrative Statistical System in Correction," *Proceedings, American Correctional Association,* 1960, pp. 291-96.

aim generally is limited to a concrete problem of immediate concern. The effectiveness of a one-man patrol car is compared with that of a two-man team. Several prisoner vocational training courses are compared in terms of size of paychecks earned after release from prison.

Correlational research also employs scientific methods to guide managerial decision making, but the emphasis is on measurement over a period of time. Large populations are studied objectively to determine long-term trends. Answers are sought to such questions as: What are the characteristics of prisoners coming to our institutions today compared to ten years ago?

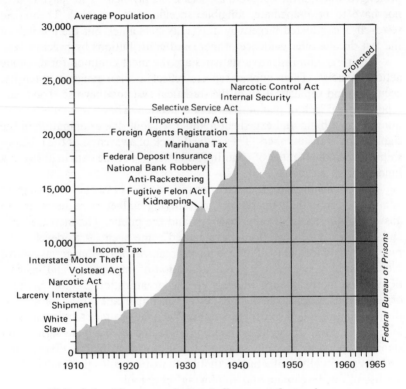

FIG. 1-1.—The cumulative influence of new laws on Bureau of Prisons population.

An example of correlational research is this analysis of the relationship between the growth of the population of federal prisons and the appearance of new federal statutes. Apart from numerical growth, the federal prisons received a different quality of offenders after World War II with a proportional decline of relatively stable liquor law violators and greater proportion of automobile thieves, narcotics violators, military offenders, forgers, and bank robbers.

Are the prisoners older? Are they more sophisticated as criminals? Are they serving shorter periods of time behind bars?[24]

Experimental research is the most sophisticated and thorough application of scientific methods within an action program. It is theoretical research in terms of study design and long-term significance of its findings to criminology as a social science. However, when such research is carried on by employees of penal institutions as part of an action program, it also is directed by practical purposes.

Administrative research has the primary advantage of providing reliable answers to fundamental questions. However, research within an action agency can have important beneficial side effects. It requires that clear questions be asked. In formulating these questions, administrators may be surprised to find themselves probing the meaning of ideas which have been taken for granted and the significance of the goals of the agency itself. Research offers a platform for discussing basic disagreements in a manner which may dissipate latent hostilities and open the way to resolution of conflict. As a source of facts, the research office draws requests from other agencies, creating opportunities for growth of understanding between allied agencies.

Problems in Use of Statistics

In spite of the usefulness of statistics and research, collection of statistics in the action agencies is a hodgepodge of poor, good, and excellent quality. Administrators usually have been slow to recognize the full value of statistical data. Researchers are unlikely to be admitted to policy-making deliberations at a time and in a role appropriate for the production and analysis of pertinent facts. However, there are more fundamental limitations.

Nomenclature

If statistical data are to be useful in measurement or in testing of hypotheses, the basic unit employed must have the same meaning to all concerned. Criminal statistics generally lack such homogeneity. First, there is wide variation in the legal labels given a particular type of crime. Burglary in one judicial system may in another be a form of larceny or theft. Second, there is a lack of uniformity in the unit of count. Assume three men are tried on an indictment charging five gasoline station holdups. The unit of count might be the trial, the number of defendants, the number of holdups, or the total number of offenses. Depending on the unit employed, the statistics could report either 1, 3, 5, or 15 crimes. Third, there is the possibility of

---

[24]McCafferty, "Latent Research Findings," p. 9.

a single offense being included several times in a statistical report when it is prosecuted more than once. The decentralization of administration of courts and law enforcement complicates any effort to develop standardized nomenclature.

Accommodations in Administration

Statistics should reflect uniform and automatic enforcement of the law. Unfortunately, through accommodations to the problems of everyday administration, agencies modify the impact of the law on some of the offenders. The system of justice operates in a way different from what "the book" says. Consequently, statistics describe the results of administration more accurately than they describe the nature of criminal conduct. These accommodations have four implications.

Discretion affects the decision-making process. Either formally or through custom, discretion is a part of the administrative system. Police agencies lack resources for complete enforcement. Full, formal adjudication of all serious criminal cases would require greatly increased court staffs and other facilities. Through encouragement of a large number of guilty pleas, the courts are able to operate a relatively expedient and economic system of administration. This is possible because the agencies of criminal justice are willing to make concessions in sentencing and to make reductions in charges. The complex pattern of decision making operates selectively to reduce the accuracy of the records of police and court business as indices of criminal conduct. For example, assault may be reduced to disturbing the peace, with the result that the actual incidence of assault is understated.

A relatively inflexible set of administrative procedures does not fit a diversity of behavioral problems. Each criminal or delinquency case includes a host of situational and personality characteristics. When the work load is heavy and when speedy processing of cases is demanded, administrators have little opportunity to recognize the full uniqueness of each case. Offense categories are used in a catchall fashion and lose their value as accurate descriptions of the events or persons included in them. Because of the variety of behaviors included under an administrative label, government reports are of sharply limited value for probing the patterns of offender behavior.

Offenses differ in their likelihood of coming to official attention. Because they reflect only those offenses which come to official notice, statistics are a distorted sample of total criminality. The possibility of a crime being included in this sample varies with the nature of the crime.[25] The crime may be of a private nature unlikely to come to official attention. The victim

---

[25]Thorsten Sellin, *Research Memorandum on Crime in the Depression* (New York: Social Science Research Council, 1937), pp. 69-70.

may not wish that the crime be known. The victim may wish to avoid the inconveniences attendant to his reporting of the crime. The public may regard the offense as trivial.

There are wide variations in the probable treatment of the same type of offender according to the characteristics of the court, the prosecutor, and the community. Griswold[26] cites a study in one state which compared the disposition of defendants detained in the jail of a metropolitan county with the disposition of defendants detained in the jail of a rural county. In the agricultural county, the similar offender is more likely to be convicted, more likely to be treated as a felon rather than a misdemeanant, and more likely to be sent to prison rather than given probation.

Organizational loyalty may subvert objective reporting. Since statistics frequently are employed as indices of organizational efficiency, administrative interest in "the facts" may be colored by desires to achieve certain results rather than to reveal the objective and ultimate truth. One's organization can be judged by statistics such as number of crimes solved, number of "successful" parole or probation cases, or number of prisoners "rehabilitated." Organizational pride and executive self-interest may motivate manipulation of statistics, destroying the usefulness of data as crime indices or as measures of organizational effectiveness.

Incomplete Control Over Extraneous Variables

If crime rates are to be valid, the influence of complicating and extraneous factors must be held constant or must be minimized. Thermometer readings do not measure room temperature in a useful way if ice is attached to the bulb at one time and a heating coil at another. Statistics are subjected to many influences extraneous to the desired purpose. Changes in police policies or an improvement in personnel and equipment can increase arrests without an upsurge in criminality. An atrocious crime may inflame public fear and anger, stimulating special legislation and sterner law enforcement and court action.

Many forms of social deviation are handled without referral to the police. Parents, school officials, and welfare agencies will deal informally with personality problems on some occasions. At other times, similar behavior results in formal criminal charges. The social class status of the offender and the reputation of his family are among the factors influencing the choice between these alternatives. The choices may vary from time to time, and place to place, and with the previous experience of the officials with the individual.

---

[26]Manzer J. Griswold, "A New Look at Offense Classifications," *Proceedings, American Correctional Association,* 1958, pp. 206-14.

Fragmentation of Data

A wide variety of agencies are interested in delinquency and crime. Some agencies gather information; some do not. There is little system in the methods employed and the types of data gathered. A complete and consistent statistical description of crime is lacking.

McCafferty classifies criminal statistical operations as being "concentric" or "fragmented" or a compromise between the two.[27] In the "concentric" form, a central agency is responsible for the collection and presentation of criminal and correctional statistics. In the "fragmented" form, each operating criminal or correctional agency collects data relevant to its activities. Police, courts, probation agencies, jails, prisons, juvenile training schools, and parole boards all collect bodies of statistics. Lack of coordination among these statistical systems prevents comparison in an effective way of crime rates at the several stages of the peno-correctional process. The problem of different units of count is aggravated. Fragmented operations increase the possibility of organizational loyalties interfering with objectivity in reporting and analysis. However, the major difficulty is the inability to maintain a continuous follow-up record on individuals who have violated the law. Ideally, a concentric statistical system for the entire nation would enable us to trace accurately the various contacts of an individual with the entire system of justice, permitting accurate count of criminals and meaningful analysis of the various patterns of criminality and of societal response to crime.

Although this system would have obvious benefits for research, enthusiasm should be tempered by consideration of the implications of the concentric system to our form of justice. Fragmented operations are symptoms of the general factors giving rise to organizational problems of American police. These factors include the emphasis on local autonomy and fear of perversion of centralized police power to serve political oppression. At the same time, local units of government have difficulty in performing the services the people ask of their government. One of the major dilemmas of our times is raised by the demands for the services of centralized government, on one hand, and demands that local self-determination and the sense of local responsibility be maintained, on the other. Advocates of local determinism are not likely to be impressed by the paramount advantages of the concentric statistical system for research when centralized control of administration is the price to be paid.

Relative Lack of Long-Term Purpose in Gathering Data

The housewife baking bread cannot transform it into cake after it is in the oven. Similarly, once the data are collected, it is difficult to utilize

---

[27]James A. McCafferty, "Prisoner Statistics—National and State," *Proceedings, Social Statistics Section, American Statistical Association,* 1960, pp. 25-33.

them efficiently for purposes other than those envisaged originally. Bodies of data are gathered routinely on the basis of a general faith that collecting such data is a good idea, rather than on the basis of careful assessment of the purposes of the data. When this general faith is the motivation, the facts collected are likewise rather general and are useless. For example, a law enforcement agency would be interested in counting "arrests." With careful planning, it would be possible to count arrests in a manner which would provide information on the age and occupation of the offender and the specifics of his offense. Because of unexpected circumstances, the police chief might want to know whether there has been a recent change in the average age of drug addicts. Care in collecting data would permit the analysis needed to provide this information.

Paucity of Information on Behavior

Labeling of the individual as a criminal is an administrative action which, of course, is a response to the behavior of the offender. However, this label is not necessarily descriptive of the etiology and motivation behind his behavior. Usually, statistical data tell us something about administrative action (such as an arrest or granting parole) and the ranking of the offender within a continuum of some general population attribute (such as age). But rarely do criminal statistics, as routinely gathered, tell us why the offense was committed or give information on the subtleties of the etiological background of the crime.

CHAPTER 2

The Measurement of Crime in the United States

Harry Manuel Shulman

Harry Manuel Shulman is Professor Emeritus of Sociology at the City College of the City University of New York. This article is based on a paper he presented at the International Congress of Criminology in Montreal, Canada, on September 3, 1965.

Crime is by its very nature not easily measureable, being subject to concealment and nonreporting—concealment by victims and nonreporting by authorities—and, as a result, the reported statistics of crime are ordinarily far short of the full volume and range of offenses. This situation holds true for the United States, in which there is as yet no comprehensive, co-ordinated body of national crime statistics, and whose reported crime statistics, compiled by a variety of agencies, fail to provide an accurate statistical base for the analysis of the volume, categories, and trends of crime in the nation.

The primary reporting of crimes in the United States lies in the hands of local police departments, who submit statistics of complaints and arrests to the Federal Bureau of Investigation of the United States Department of Justice. There are many inadequacies in this reporting process, some of which will be described later, but the underlying defect of police reporting as a measure of the volume of crime is that the police have only a very limited function in crime control, and the crimes reported by the police are only a fraction of those that occur. Important segments of crime are dealt with, not by criminal justice agencies under the auspices of criminal law but by regulatory agencies under the auspices of administrative and civil law, whose findings are hidden in the obscure and diverse reports of fifty sovereign States and the Federal government. Finally, many aspects of crime

From Harry M. Shulman, "The Measurement of Crime in the United States." Reprinted by special permission of the *Journal of Criminal Law, Criminology and Police Science* (Northwestern University School of Law), copyright © 1966, December issue, volume 57, number 4.

result in no official complaint to any form of sanctioning authority—criminal, administrative or civil—but only come to light through the operations of public departments and private agencies concerned with education, health, welfare and safety, and of private agencies and associations that serve the economic interests of many different occupations and industries.

As the result of the lack of a national policy for the comprehensive co-ordinated reporting of crime in the United States, governmental commissions and agencies assigned to the study of law enforcement and crime prevention labor under the handicap of a lack of the fundamental scientific data necessary for the study of the relationships between social policy and crime control as well as the study of the efficacy of agencies for the administration of justice. At the same time, social scientists lack the data necessary for sound national epidemiological and etiological studies of crime.

The Concealment and Non-reporting of Crime

Wide areas of criminal behavior fail to be included in crime statistics because of ambivalences and social resistances toward their reporting to sanctioning agencies, and because of opportunities for their concealment.

In sex and family relationships there is a myriad of unreported cases in which the criminal law is often in conflict with social norms and private human emotions, viz.: in homosexual relations, seduction and statutory rape, fornication and adultery, illegal abortion, bastardy (illegitimacy), miscegenation, and desertion and non-support.

Among the independent professions there are large numbers of unreported violations of law both among clients and practitioners. In the medical profession alone there are unreported illegal abortions, illegal prescriptions of narcotic drugs and illegal child adoption practices, to say nothing regarding unethical if not downright illegal practices of fee-splitting and unnecessary medical care. In the practice of law there are falsifications of claims, perjury and subornation of perjury, mingling of client's funds with those of the practitioner, and conflicts of interest.

Among the independent professions, in retail trade, and in fact wherever there is the opportunity for cash transactions, there are concealments of income for the purposes of income and excise tax evasions. Despite their undoubted frequency, very few criminal tax evasions actually become known as crimes.

Among employees there are frequent embezzlements and thefts of goods and materials commonly dealt with not by arrest and prosecution but by dismissal and sometimes by restitution. Embezzlements go unreported because supervisors are themselves guilty of related or comparable offenses. Many times, employee thefts, resulting in inventory shrinkages, are written off as customer dishonesty.

Dishonesty among customers, such as the common offenses of shoplifting and petty check forgery are ordinarily not dealt with by criminal complaint and prosecution. Shoplifting, a common and widespread customer offense, committed by housewives and 'teen-agers who are not necessarily poverty-stricken, as well as by indigents and experienced thieves, is often dealt with by department and specialty stores in the form of confiscation of the stolen goods, warnings, and sometimes by the requirement of signed confessions that are filed for the purpose of prosecution in the case of repetition of the offense on the same premises. The issuance of forged and fraudulent checks for small amounts by customers against local merchants is usually charged to profit and loss for fear of harm to community good-will arising from the prosecution of local residents.

The laws on public policy in the field of gambling are violated with impunity by millions of the general public in urban society, who in this fashion often unwittingly support criminal syndicates who monopolistically control dangerous subsidiary rackets in prostitution, narcotics, bootlegging, and usury, offenses that have their own non-reporting clientele and victims.

Among public officials and employees there are many criminal acts of omission and commission, the most common being the acceptance of bribes to grant favors in violation of law and to overlook violations. In municipal government, licensing authorities, housing inspectors, and inspectors of health hazards and dishonest weights and measures, engage often in practices of corruption without too great a danger of being caught.

Together, the crimes and offenses committed in the areas of sex and family relationship, and by professionals, business men, landlords, taxpayers, employees, customers and the general public probably number in the tens of millions of cases and must far outweigh in volume and monetary loss the offenses that are the subject of police action. Whereas there is little evidence of these offenses in the known criminal statistics, there is a large number of subsidiary sources of information from which estimates of volume and trend could be derived. There is evidence from the medical profession, the clergy, departments of education, health and welfare, and from private social agencies regarding the extent of unreported offenses in the areas of sex and family relationship, even though the identity of specific offenders may be shielded by the confidential status of the information and of the records in which they are located.

Investigative reports by legislative and other governmental commissions, in the fields of industrial medicine and insurance fraud, not to mention a variety of other violations in the fields of food and drugs, employer-employee relationships, union management, etc., are data sources. Reports of insurance underwriters and fire marshals give evidence of arson. The files of the Internal Revenue Service hold evidences of tax dishonesty, but they are not open to outside study; and relatively few have been prosecuted as crimes. Reports from trade associations throw light upon dishonest practices by employees and customers and give evidence of the extent of certain rackets, such as the bootleg manufacture, distribution, and sale of untaxed liquor.

The records of agencies of municipal government, such as those of health, housing and fire, could throw a flood of light upon violations of municipal codes on licensing and occupancy reported by inspectors but neither made the subject of sanctions nor reported in public statistics. Consumer complaints of dishonesties in retail advertising and of frauds in installment selling, reported to Better Business Bureaus, are a data source. At the present time hardly any of these sources, with the exception of legislative inquiries into organized crime, are tapped for national estimates of the amount of unreported, unrecorded, and unpunished crimes and offenses.

Reported Crimes and Offenses Dealt With under Administrative and Civil Law

There are many specialized forms of reported crimes and offenses whose punitive sanctions lie not in the criminal law but in the realm of administrative and civil law. Among these are offenses in commerce and industry, management-labor relations, union management, income tax reporting, and social security and public assistance. Some of these offenses are dealt with by regulatory agencies of the states, but the majority are dealt with by the federal government under its interstate commerce powers. These include the Internal Revenue division of the Department of the Treasury, the National Labor Relations Board, the Federal Trade Commission, the Securities and Exchange Commission, etc. Some of these offenses are dealt with under anti-monopoly laws, such as the Sherman Act, which specifically defines violations as misdemeanors and permits criminal sanctions against corporation officers, but many others are dealt with under other administrative laws whose sanctions are directed only against the corporations themselves, through stipulations and cease and desist orders, fines, and confiscations of goods deemed unfit for public sale or consumption. Still others are dealt with under civil laws that permit punitive damages to injured parties.

Among reported offenses in commerce and industry—in the fields of finance, securities, manufacturing, communications, real estate, etc.—are restraints of free competition through illegal mergers, collusive price-fixing and bidding, market control through cartels, discriminatory rebates to favored customers, fraudulent advertising claims, and violations of a wide range of legislation regulatory of real estate—including rent controls, nondiscrimination in rentals, and the maintenance of commercial and dwelling structures—so as to assure the health, welfare and safety of tenants.

In management-labor relations offenses include collusive practices between management and racket-controlled unions that result in contracts below current wage scales in industries and geographic areas; management violations of the National Labor Relations Act, such as labor spying, improper pressures upon workers in connection with union representation elections, and the discharge of workers for labor unionization activities; and in labor union management, the uses of force and illegality in the election of officers of locals and national unions, and corrupt practices in the administration of vast union pension and welfare funds.

In industry-consumer relations there are such offenses as false labelling, misrepresentation of products, false weights and measures, adulteration of products, manufacture under unhygienic conditions, etc.

In the area of taxation, aside from such violations as the evasions of payment of excise taxes (on liquor, cigarettes, tobacco, etc.) which carry criminal law penalties, there are many other offenses, particularly in the area of taxes on income, in which, despite the generally high level of tax collection at source, or of withholding at source, there is extensive misrepresentation of income and dishonesty in declaration of deductions. The majority of the latter offenses are dealt with as civil offenses and punished by fines, with no statistical reporting of their number.

In the areas of social legislation—unemployment and industrial compensation insurance, social security and public assistance—under whose umbrella tens of millions of citizens and residents have coverage, there are many violations which are rarely discovered; and when discovered they are rarely dealt with by criminal prosecution. In the area of public assistance alone, for example, aid to the indigent, handicapped, children, and elderly indigent, which covers some five millions of persons, the files of public agencies would disclose many forms of illegality dealt with by other than criminal prosecution.

As indicated earlier, the statistics of law violation in most of these categories of criminal offense lie buried in agency files, and sometimes they are to be found in the annual reports of public agencies, but so scattered are these information sources that they are not easily available to scientific investigators, much less the press. Moreover, much of this information has remained in bureaucratic concealment under the pleas of confidentiality or national security and it will be released only when "right to know" legislation makes them available to the public. In the rare instances in which violations of court orders have resulted in punishments for contempt, or where prosecutions under federal criminal law has resulted in conviction, the statistics of conviction are to be found in the annual reports of the administrative office of the federal court system, but even here the statistics are so garbled that specific offenses, small in number but qualitatively significant, are concealed through inclusion in broader categories. What the total of this range of offenses may be, in commerce and industry, taxation and social legislation, is open to conjecture. Their gross volume must run into the millions of cases, of which only a relatively few are reported and dealt with under administrative and civil law, so that even a well-organized access to the statistics of reported cases would afford but a slight glimpse of their volume and characteristics.

Crimes Known to the Police

Only one body of crimes and offenses that occur in the United States is systematically reported on a national scale. These are the crimes known to the police and reported by them to the Federal Bureau of Investigation for publication in *Uniform Crime Reports.* Included among them are the major so-called *common crimes* of homicide, assault, robbery, burglary, and theft. These statistics have been given national prominence through regular distribution for the past thirty-five or more years in quarterly and annual reports and through regular conspicuous publication in the national press. As a result of this focus upon common crimes, as well as the constant cultural reference to and repetitious use of common crime themes in newspaper articles, radio, television, novels, detective stories, etc., the term *crime* has come to have an application almost entirely restricted to common crimes, and so respected has police crime reporting become that until recently mass communication agencies have given to their readers the impression that the statistics of common crimes are a scientific measure of the American crime volume.

From our previous discussion it should already be clear that this is not the case, and that crimes known to the police are a highly unrepresentative sample of American criminal offenses. The nature of this sample, evidences of its nonrepresentativeness even of common crime, and the legal, administrative and sociological circumstances that limit the function of the police in dealing with crime, and hence limit their role in crime reporting, call for some further discussion.

The police reporting of common crime consists of two markedly different sets of data, one of citizen *complaints,* i.e., "crimes known to the police", and the other of *arrests.* One refers to offenses and the other to persons, and there is no necessary statistical relationship between them since in some crimes a number of individuals may be involved and for others a single individual may have committed more than one offense.

There is markedly incomplete police reporting of offenses. Only seven *serious* forms of crime are regularly reported in Uniform Crime Reports: murder and non-negligent manslaughter, forcible rape, robbery, aggravated assault, burglary, larceny of $50 and over, and auto theft.[1] The remaining citizen complaints to the police are, with one exception (larceny of $50 and under), not reported in Uniform Crime Reports, and are not comparable for either volume or trend, although the basic data exist in the files of individual police departments.

The police rationalization of this selective reporting of citizen complaints is that minor offenses tend not to be reported to the police and that only complaints of serious crimes, which are said to be more commonly reported, can serve as an *Index of Crime.* However, since the crime index concept is itself a dubious one, in the light of evidence that police records as a whole are a highly selective measure of crime, its use to explain the non-reporting of the majority of complaints in the 29-category schedule of crimes used in Uniform Crime Reports is itself highly dubious. This point will be elaborated.

The selective reporting of crime complaints leaves only one category of police crime data free from criticism on this score, i.e., that of arrest. By arrest is meant persons taken into custody and charged with a criminal offense, as differentiated from those merely questioned and released. In 1964, in a registration area comprising some 132 million persons, some 4,582,000 persons were arrested, of which close to 2,000,000 arrests were either for drunkenness (1,458,000 cases) or disorderly conduct (475,000 cases). An additional 378,000 cases involved other aspects of drinking, viz.: driving under the influence (225,000 cases), and liquor law violations (153,-000 cases).[2] Thus, of 4,582,000 arrests, some 2,311,000, or more than 50 percent, involved either drunkenness or disorderliness, or both. It would thus be fair to state that the job of the police, as judged by these statistics, is largely to cope with drunken and disorderly persons, a task of some importance in the maintenance of public order and safety, but not one bulking large in criminal threat to the security of the society.

The next largest category of arrests is for larceny-theft (some 358,000 cases) of which the bulk were probably for thefts under $50, and since arrests for larceny-theft bear a ratio of one arrest to every five complaints, or 20 percent, it can properly be stated that for this category arrests are a disproportionately low measure of predatory crime.

However, it is in the category of public policy arrests—for gambling, prostitution, and narcotics (offenses almost lacking in citizen complaint)— that police arrest statistics can be most highly criticized as a measure of societal midconduct. In 1964, in an urban registration area of some 3,000

---

[1]The word *serious* as used in Uniform Crime Reports is somewhat of a value judgment, since it includes such offenses as the theft of automobiles for pleasure use, and petty thefts.

[2]*Uniform Crime Reports,* Federal Bureau of Investigation, United States Department of Justice, 1964 Washington, D.C., 1965, p. 106.

cities, these offenses resulted in some 160,000 arrests (98,000 of gambling; 27,000 of prostitution; and 35,000 of narcotics), a somewhat impressive total until subjected to closer analysis. First of all, public policy arrests represented less than 4 percent (3.9 percent) of all arrests. The relative unimpressiveness of the statistics on public policy arrests becomes more apparent when their average distribution by cities is analyzed.[3]

Some 98,000 gambling arrests, distributed among some 3,000 cities, averaged out to 32 arrests per city per year, a figure that would include syndicate and independent operators, bookmakers, policy runners and collectors, customers, and repeated arrests of all these. Some 27,000 prostitution and commercialized vice arrests in the same number of cities averaged out to 9 arrests per city per year, a figure that would include overlords, madams, pimps, establishment prostitutes and streetwalkers, and repeated arrests for all these, as well as (in some jurisdictions) patrons. Some 36,000 narcotic drug arrests in the same number of cities averaged out to some 12 arrests per city per year, for syndicate and independent operators, distributors, addict-sellers and addicts, plus repeated arrests.

The small number of arrests for public policy offenses in a field of criminal operation reputed to derive huge revenues (estimated from seven to twenty-two billions of dollars per year for gambling alone) for syndicated operators known as "families" would suggest that these low arrest figures are not to be taken as a serious measure of the volume of public policy offenses in the United States. When compared to the high volume of arrests in connection with drinking, the small proportion of arrests on public policy charges in a crime area that operates as a cancer in the American society, is suggestive of selective arrest patterns among the police of the United States.

Even these statistics, however, do not tell the entire story of selective public policy offense arrest patterns. Negroes, with some eleven percent of the national population, experience some 72 percent of all urban arrests for gambling, 53 percent of all urban arrests for prostitution and 40 percent of all urban arrests for possession of narcotics.

The evidence thus far is that many areas of crime are infrequently reported to the police, that in exercising their primary assignment of law enforcement the police make arrests primarily for drunkenness and disorderly conduct, and that they make relatively few arrests for larceny-theft and very few public policy arrests. Thus, neither citizen complaints nor arrests would appear to be sound measures of the volume of common crime in the United States. At best, perhaps, police statistics are a sound measure of only a handful of serious common crimes (homicide, rape, robbery,

---

[3]Inasmuch as arrest figures for individual cities were not reported, only averages can be calculated.

aggravated assault) in which there is both a high level of complaint as well as of arrest. Such conclusions raise questions as to the reasons for the selective nature of police crime statistics.

Limitations of the Police as a Crime-reporting Agency

The police, although they are in theory assigned wide powers of law enforcement, yet limited by the laws of arrest and other civil liberties and constitutional rights of the citizenry, exercise in practice a very restricted law enforcement role. They are primarily a peace preservation body whose major functions are the protection of life, limb, and property on the streets and highways, in places of public assemblage and in commercial and private properties entered illegally from public ways. As we have seen, they exercise little or no enforcement functions in crimes of sex and the family, in commerce and industry, in tax evasion, in crimes by employees and customers, and in public policy crimes by the general public and the syndicates they support. For all of these other areas there exist alternate agencies of complaint and law enforcement, some within criminal law enforcement power, such as prosecutors and attorneys-general of the states and of the federal government, or within administrative law such as state and federal regulative agencies. Indeed, even in those areas of crime in which the police function most competently, those of common crime, the crime prevention function of the police is restricted to general patrol, and their detective function occurs after the crime has occurred in their absence. The only offenses in which they exercise both a preventive and a criminal justice function are those offenses which occur in their presence and those to which they are summoned while the offenses are in process.

The circumstances in American culture and social organization that assign to the police such a circumscribed function in law enforcement, and that permits a vast range of offenses to go unreported or to be dealt with by other investigative bodies, are numerous and, in a paper concerned primarily with the measurement of crime, can be mentioned only summarily. A wide operational range of powers for police is inconsistent with American ideological beliefs and principles of limited sovereignty. Our ideological attachment to civil liberties prevents assignment to the police of roving powers of investigation such as through the unregulated tapping of the mails and other instruments of communication. The police are restricted to the exercise of the police powers of the municipality or some other governmental body of which they are agents, and they have no national police powers such as are exercised by some European police. As a result, offenders whose operations extend beyond municipal, county, and State boundaries are not subject to arrest outside of the limited jurisdiction in which their primary offense occurred, except for purposes of extradition.

At the same time, the local police are subject to the rivalry of other separate and equal branches of government. Their authority is kept in close check by the legislative branch, which has invented alternate regulatory mechanisms via the administrative law for the control of a vast network of economic forces; they are in rivalry with prosecutor's offices in the handling of criminal complaints; and they are checked by the courts in their exercise of practices that interfere with civil liberties.

Local police departments in the United States function in communities sharply divided in social values on many issues of civil rights and personal morals. Not themselves ordinarily a cross-section of the racial and ethnic composition of the local population, they are called upon to adjudicate conflicts involving breaches of the peace that have overtones on the one hand of racial and ethnic antagonisms and, on the other, of violations of civil rights. In communities in which public policy crimes are not only the subject of culture conflict, but of political protection by corrupt political machines that have venal ties with fabulously wealthy criminal syndicates, the police are subject to many malignant controls and temptations.

Finally, the recruitment and training of the police as a highly technical career body of superior men and women is a policy that has had much lip service in American politics and little implementation. Ill-trained as most of them are, lacking in standards of high general education, and rarely selected for outstanding general intelligence, they have never had the undivided admiration and loyalty of the American public or even of the press. Because of these circumstances, together with the aforesaid legal restrictions upon their functions, they are rarely called upon to handle investigations that call for technical skill, rare judgment, tact, and administrative knowledge. Under these circumstances it is not surprising that the measure of their efficiency, as determined by the relationship of citizen complaints to arrests, and by their selective patterns of law enforcement through on-sight arrest, is low.

Gaps, Discontinuities and Limitations in the Reporting of Crime

We may now pull together some of the gaps, discontinuities and limitations in the reporting of American crime. As has been indicated, vast numbers of offenses in many areas of misconduct are not included in any systematic totals of American crime volume. Nor are there adequate bodies of criminal statistics even among those arising among criminal justice agencies, i.e., the police, prosecutors and courts. The most extensive reporting system, that of Uniform Crime Reports, is deficient in many ways. Citizen complaints are reported for only eight of twenty-nine categories of offense.[4]

---

[4]Since the present paper was originally delivered some few changes have taken place in the composition of the 29 categories, but the number remains the same.

That series of categories, while appearing offhand to be sufficient for crime reporting, is actually very insufficient and conceals important categories of crime, which, because they are lumped with others, are in effect not reported at all. Thus, shoplifting, commercial crimes generally, and offenses involving landlords and tenants, are in this manner not reported. The latter category, which includes landlord complaints of vandalism and tenant complaints of persistent failure to provide basic services in housing tenancy, have a close involvement with other aspects of social disorganization and intergroup conflict in our rapidly urbanizing society and their reporting would serve a useful purpose in the study of conflicted human relationships in slum areas.

Other important offenses are not reported at all; for example, the only traffic offense reported is that of drunken driving. It is understandable that minor offenses involving stationary vehicles—parking ordinance violations, etc.,—can be safely ignored in national crime totals, but offenses involving moving vehicles such as speeding, passing on curves, driving by unauthorized persons or in unsafe vehicles, demand national reporting by reason of the large number of deaths from vehicular "accidents," some 50,000 annually, not to mention the hundreds of thousands of injuries and the monetary losses in property destruction and damage, hospital and medical bills and the loss of income and earning ability.

The use of complaints on only seven offenses in the Uniform Crime Reports as an *index of crime* is unwarranted in the light of our knowledge of the limited law enforcement functions of the police, and of the highly selective reporting by police of even those offenses over which they have primary jurisdiction. Under pressure, the Uniform Crime Reports has modified its claims to define these complaints as an index of common crime, and it is hypothesized that all other common crimes reported in police statistics vary in level as these seven do. Unfortunately, however, this hypothesis is not verifiable, because in order to use a sample as an index we must know the size and composition of the universe from which the sample was drawn and we must have assurances that the sample was a representative one. From our preceding discussion we know that the universe of crime in our society is largely unknown, both as a whole and in its particulars, and that the police sample is likely to be unrepresentative, not only in its concentration upon certain categories of crime, but owing to the fact that those categories are unduly drawn from the offenses of certain racial and ethnic minorities and social classes.

Actually, the so-called "index to crime" projects predictively only a part of even that portion of crime with which the police come into contact and serves no other predictive function than to suggest what the future of those seven offenses may be. Its claimed use as a general crime predictive instrument has never been verified, is not verifiable and should not be used by the federal government in any manner, since its use tends to conceal the fact that in truth we do not now know either the whole volume or trends of crime in the United States, in part because it is not knowable, and in part because that portion which is known has never been properly organized for analysis.

As has been indicated, many complaints by-pass the police and are reported directly to prosecutors and attorneys-general of the states and federal government, and these often comprise offenses of far greater importance to the public than those reported to the police. Thus, the range of victims may be greater. They include, for example, complaints against conspiracies such as syndicated operations in public policy crime, in labor union management, in labor-management relations, in manager-consumer relationships, within industries, and conspiracies in the operation of criminal justice itself. Complaints to prosecutors and attorneys-general, however, tend not to be systematically reported, being usually anecdotal and focussed upon dramatic cases, rather than statistical and analytical.

The judicial statistics of those cases that come to trial in the courts could throw a great deal of light upon the criminal justice process, but in most of the states these are not reported on a state-wide basis and are, as a result, not accessible for reporting and analysis.

The listing of three levels of criminal statistics, those of the police, prosecutors, and courts, defines the structure of criminal statistics necessary for the reporting of criminal complaints in any geographical and political jurisdiction and for an analysis of the criminal justice process in that jurisdiction. The flat statement can be made that in most jurisdictions this structure of criminal statistics is not available in a form convenient for criminological purposes, and is therefore not used for analytical studies. This situation is almost as true for the federal government as it is for the states.

At the federal justice level there exist administrative data at each stratum of operation, but these are neither systematically reported as criminal statistics nor made available to any central collecting agency for reporting and analysis. A handful of federal offenses are dealt with by federal marshals, who function as police and have jurisdiction over federal lands and properties. They issue no systematic reports of complaints or arrests. The major body of important federal criminal law offenses is dealt with by federal prosecutors, who issue no systematic reports of criminal complaints and their dispositions, either individually or as a whole. Another significant body of criminal complaints and dispositions arises among the armed forces, consisting of violations of civil and military law among a large group of young men of high actuarial crime risk. However, the statistics of their offenses, as handled within the military chain of command, are not available for public use, being issued only for intramural information by the Department of Defense. And, as has been indicated, a wide range of offenses against administrative and civil law carrying punitive sanctions, and handled by administrative and regulatory agencies of the Federal government, are not available as collected statistics. Only the Administrative Office of the United States courts issues valuable annual statistics of those criminal complaints that are tried in the United States District Courts, but in the absence of complaint totals and their dispositions from all federal prosecutors, these tell little regarding the volume of federal criminal law complaints and their processing. As a result of this failure to collect under one roof all statistics of federal offenses, even the United States government has no systematic information on its own system of criminal and administrative law procedures.

Steps Toward the Improved Collection and Analysis of American Criminal Statistics

If American criminal statistics are to become available for (a) epidemiological studies of volume, distribution, and trends within functional settings of the cultural, economic and political organizations of the society; (b) administrative studies of the investigative and judicial process in this volume of cases; and (c) studies of the relationship of law enforcement policies and practices to crime prevention and control, it is apparent that significant changes in their collection, reporting and analysis will have to be made, involving at the very least the following procedures:

(1) Synthesis of the presently available statistics of sanctionable violations of criminal, administrative and civil law, now scattered in the many reports of Federal, State and local policing and regulatory agencies;

(2) The collection and synthesis from the files of many agencies of unreported data indicative of the volume of sanctionable law violations, not now the subject of complaint; and

(3) Raising the technical standards of the procedures for the measurement of American crime by placing its collection, analysis and reporting in the hands of criminologically trained research personnel qualified in the methods of social science research and statistical analysis.

The first step (1) requires the designation of a federal department or agency as the center of analysis and reporting of all available American criminal statistics. The second step (2) calls for such policies by that agency that the data indicative of unreported violations would be made available for study by other public and private agencies. The third step (3) the assignment of criminal statistics collection analysis and reporting to highly qualified social science analysts, calls for some discussion.

The sociological study of criminal statistics has by now reached a relatively high level of sophistication, both theoretically and methodologically.[5] But so far there has been little utilization of this available skill in the field of criminal justice. Not since the 1930's, when federal and state commissions for the study of justice and law enforcement made systematic studies of criminal statistics has there been a proper emphasis upon the public utilization of sound social science methods and of a qualified professional personnel in their collection and analysis.[6] Currently, at every level in the criminal justice process—in the police, prosecutor's offices, courts, correctional agencies, and rehabilitative agencies such as probation and parole departments—the task of criminal statistics has been largely in the hands of persons lacking the training for that exacting specialization.

It is conceivable that the steps here proposed may be initiated in the near future, but it is necessary that there be an awareness of the resistances in our society against systematic scientific reporting of crime. Some of these resistances originate in the opposition of strong vested interests, and others have their roots in our historical traditions. There are resistances, for example, among some criminal justice agencies who object to scientific measures of their efficiency. Thus, the honesty of police reporting of complaints has been from time to time called into question by the Federal Bureau of Investigation, which has had to reject the statistics of police departments which have sought to increase the measure of their own efficiency through under-reporting of citizen complaints as compared to arrests. Other resistances are latent in the industries subject to regulation by governmental bodies. Still other resistances exist in the administration of criminal justice, which is increasingly under criticism for its very high proportion of convictions without formal trial, on a plea of guilt to lesser offenses. Supportive of these resistances is a public opinion on the subject of law enforcement having its origin in the crime definitions of an earlier simpler society.

Historical Backgrounds of Our Patterns of Crime Reporting

The American bias in favor of the reporting of "crime in the streets" as the single important category of crime has its historical antecedents. Nineteenth century American criminal law and criminal justice procedures were based upon the precedents of eighteenth century American colonial criminal law and institutions, which were in turn based upon earlier English models in common and statute law, made known to us through the writings of such commentators as Blackstone. The English society from which we derived our models of criminal law was a monarchical aristocratic society, rural and agrarian in its major economic base, founded on the rights and

---

[5]Sellen & Wolfgang, *The Measurement of Delinquency* (1964).
[6]*Report on Criminal Statistics,* National Commission on Law Observance and Enforcement, Washington, D. C., 1931.

privileges of a landed aristocracy and devoted in its commercial operations to the principles of mercantilism and monopoly.

In such a society, as it moved into a rapid industrialization and urbanization, under the influences of a growing population and a revolution in agriculture, together with the rise in inventions, the ensuing social disorders of poverty-stricken masses newly torn from the controls and protections of a rural agricultural economy were the focus of law enforcement efforts. Such a society found it natural to define crime principally in terms of the felonies and misdemeanors of the lowest, i.e., the poorest classes, and to view criminal justice as the protection of the sound and substantial elements of society against its enemies.

At the same time, as a nation with long historical traditions of civil liberties and an elective upper and middle class Parliament, the English were opposed to the exercise of broad police powers by its central government and even the powers of the small civilian police force concerned with common crimes remained sharply curtailed.

All of these principles and practices in criminal law and criminal justice administration were taken over in American criminal justice by a young nation that had suffered from arbitrary colonial government but which was itself ambivalent upon issues of republicanism and democracy. However, the latter half of the Nineteenth and the first half of the Twentieth century saw many economic and social changes in American society. From having been largely an agrarian homestead society of independent farmers and pioneers, the United States after the Civil War shifted rapidly to the industrial form of urban economy, corporate enterprise, joint stock ownership, technical management and unionized labor force. In such a society a criminal law based upon the control of highwaymen and felons was insufficient for social control and was augmented by much new legislation in other areas of social protection.

During the latter decades of the Nineteenth and early decades of the Twentieth century protections were written into law against the dangers of the unregulated factory system, for women and children, and for all labor through safety regulations, hour and wage regulations, and finally, through union recognition and the government supervised process of collective bargaining. At the same time a mass of new regulatory laws was enacted for the control of monopolistic practices in commerce and industry and frauds in the sales of corporate securities; and the federal government took giant steps toward the control of interstate commerce through the establishment of regulatory agencies for the control of aviation, communications, transportation, banks and trust companies, food and drugs industries, utilities, extractive industries, etc.

All of these innovations were consummated under the aegis not of criminal law but of administrative law, a hybrid partaking of some of the characteristics of civil law, by which agencies of government defined positively the procedures that regulate lawful commerce and industry, and some of the characteristics of criminal law, that define the punishments for the violation of administrative regulations. By the removal of commerce and industry controls from criminal law, corporations and their management were freed from the harsh criminal law mechanisms of the police, grand juries, prosecutors, courts and prisons, and, save in extreme instances, they were dealt with by the polite mechanisms of cease and desist orders, stipulations and consent decrees, supplemented by contempt of court proceedings for failure to comply with agency requests and orders.

Removal of the controls over commerce and industry from criminal law to administrative law jurisdictions resulted in ameliorations other than the substitution of fines and confiscations of contaminated goods when agency orders were disobeyed or ignored. The transfer of hearings from open courts to private agency offices screened corporations from the public ventilation of their misconduct, initially by removal from the observation of the public as observers, later by removal from the statistics of criminal justice agencies, and, most importantly, from the constant scrutiny of the press and other communication agencies.

The Twentieth century fractional reporting of crime in terms of the "man in the street" crimes of the lowest classes does violence to the full facts of criminal behavior in our society and substitutes a "cops and robbers" image of the offender as a professional criminal or social deviate, whereas in truth the majority of offenders are drawn from all social classes and all occupations. The effects of such a skewed statistical reporting of crime are many and significant. First and foremost, it reenforces the belief in a punitive approach to the control of crime by emphasizing the crimes of those who are not easily amenable to other forms of control. It shifts attention from crime as a product of the social order to concepts of its origin in constitutional defects and handicaps, poverty, and the anomic behavior of the lower classes frustrated in their drive for economic success. It permits straining after false panaceas in terms of partial solutions. It diverts solutions into areas of emotional catharsis based upon sentimentally conceived aids to the impoverished and the handicapped in a society whose technological complexities call for the highest level of rational analysis and planning. It impoverishes criminology as a field struggling to become a behavioral science by diverting its major theories from the rigorous analysis of the forces in the social and economic order that interfere with co-operative solutions of our exploitative behavior.

True enough, honest crime reporting will not go very far in substituting co-operative for exploitative approaches in American cultural behavior, but it should be one useful step in assisting the American public to rational thinking in the field of social policy on crime control.

CHAPTER 3

History and Profile of the Police

On July 23, 1965, President Lyndon Baines Johnson established the Commission on Law Enforcement and Administration of Justice. Its General Report, *The Challenge of Crime in a Free Society,* published in 1967, was a condensation of the major findings after the commission had scrutinized every facet of crime and law enforcement in America. This publication served as a forerunner for subsequent, detailed volumes reflecting the exhaustive research and analysis underlying the original report. These volumes, all published in 1967, as noted in the Foreword to the initial report, were "the result of a joint undertaking, involving the collaboration of federal, state, local, and private agencies and groups, hundreds of expert consultants and advisors, and the commission's own staff." *The Challenge of Crime in a Free Society* includes task force reports on: the police; the courts; corrections; juvenile delinquency and youth crime; organized crime; science and technology; assessment of crime; narcotics and drugs; and drunkenness.

The police—some 420,000 people working for approximately 40,000 separate agencies that spend more than $2½ billion a year—are the part of the criminal justice system that is in direct daily contact both with crime and with the public. The entire system—courts and corrections as well as the police—is charged with enforcing the law and maintaining order. What is distinctive about the responsibility of the police is that they are charged with performing these functions where all eyes are upon them and where the going is roughest, on the street. Since this is a time of increasing crime, increasing social unrest and increasing public sensitivity to both, it is a time when police work is peculiarly important, complicated, conspicuous, and delicate.

Because the police have the responsibility for dealing with crime hour by hour, where, when and as it occurs, there is a tendency on the part of

From The President's Commission on Law Reforcement and Administration of Justice, "Introduction" (retitled, for purposes of this book of readings, "History and Profile of the Police)," *Task Force Report: The Police,* 1967. Reprinted through the courtesy of the Superintendent of Documents, U.S. Printing Office, Washington, D.C.

the public, and often of the police themselves, to think of crime control almost exclusively in terms of police work. One response to the recent increases in the volume of crime has been the charge that the police lack the competence or the will to keep crime within bounds. A far more common one has been the assertion that the police could keep crime within bounds if only the appellate courts, or civilian review boards, or corrupt politicians, or an uncooperative public allowed them to. "Take the handcuffs off our police" is a cry familiar to everyone.

The fact is, of course, that even under the most favorable circumstances the ability of the police to act against crime is limited. The police did not create and cannot resolve the social conditions that stimulate crime. They did not start and cannot stop the convulsive social changes that are taking place in America. They do not enact the laws that they are required to enforce, nor do they dispose of the criminals they arrest. The police are only one part of the criminal justice system; the criminal justice system is only one part of the government; and the government is only one part of society. Insofar as crime is a social phenomenon, crime prevention is the responsibility of every part of society. The criminal process is limited to case by case operations, one criminal or one crime at a time. Some "handcuffs" on the police are irremovable. It is with that plain fact in mind that this volume, whose purpose is to propose ways in which the police can increase their effectiveness, must be read.

The volume also should be read with an understanding of what the police actually do to combat crime. This is a subject that is often neglected, with the result that public expectations of the police and prescriptions for improving police work are unrealistic. The heart of the police effort against crime is patrol—moving on foot or by vehicle around an assigned area, stopping to check buildings, to survey possible incidents, to question suspicious persons, or simply to converse with residents who may provide intelligence as to occurrences in the neighborhood.

The object of patrol is to disperse policemen in a way that will eliminate or reduce the opportunity for misconduct and to increase the likelihood that a criminal will be apprehended while he is committing a crime or immediately thereafter. The strong likelihood of apprehension will presumably have a strong deterrent effect on potential criminals. The fact of apprehension can lead to the rehabilitation of a criminal, or at least to his removal for a time from the opportunity to break the law.

When patrol fails to prevent a crime or apprehend a criminal, the police must resort to investigation. Some investigation is carried out by patrolmen, but the principal responsibility rests with detectives. Investigation aims at identifying offenders through questioning victims, suspects, witnesses and others, through confronting arrested suspects with victims or witnesses, through photographs or, less frequently, through fingerprints or other laboratory analysis of evidence found at crime scenes.

When the number of square blocks—or in some cases square miles— of city each policeman must patrol is considered in conjunction with the many ways, times and places that crimes occur, the severe limitations upon the effectiveness of patrol and investigation are placed in dramatic focus. Such consideration will also suggest why crime rates often appear to fluctuate with relatively little correlation to what the police do.

The rate of apprehension of offenders in property crimes is extremely low—approximately 22 percent of those reported. The police have greater success with violent crimes—approximately 59 percent of those reported. In large part this is because more victims of violent crimes know or can identify their assailants. The ability of a victim or witness to identify the criminal is the factor responsible for solving a large percentage of the crimes that are solved.

To say that the police have a limited ability to prevent crime is not to criticize the police. The police, more than anybody, are frustrated by the wide gap between the task they are expected to perform and the methods at their disposal to perform it.

Seen from the perspective of history, the anomalies of regarding the police as solely responsible for crime control become evident. In the preindustrial age, village societies were closely integrated. Everyone knew everyone else's affairs and character; the laws and rules of society were generally familiar and were identical with the moral and ethical precepts taught by parents, schoolmasters, and the church. If not by the clergy and the village elders, the peace was kept, more or less informally, by law magistrates (usually local squires) and constables. These in the beginning were merely the magistrates' agents, literally "citizens on duty"—the ablebodied men of the community serving in turn.[1] Not until the 19th century did policing even have a distinct name.[2] Until then it would have been largely impossible to distinguish between informal peacekeeping and the formal system of law enforcement and criminal justice. The real outlaws—murderers, highwaymen and their ilk—were handled mostly by the military when normal procedures for crime control were unsuccessful.

The greatly increased complexities of society and its laws today only make more important the kind of unofficial peacekeeping that Jane Jacobs has called the "intricate, almost unconscious, network of voluntary controls and standards among the people themselves."[3] In communities and neigh-

---

[1]Michael Banton, *The Police in the Community* (London: Tavistock Publications, 1964), p. 5.

[2]Charles Reith, *The Blind Eye of History* (London: Faber and Faber Limited, 1952), p. 9.

[3]Jane Jacobs, *The Death and Life of Great American Cities* (New York: Random House, 1961), p. 32.

borhoods where the other instrumentalities of society whose success bears directly on controlling crime have failed—families, schools, job markets, and welfare agencies—the police must handle an enormously increased volume of offenses, both serious and petty.

It is when it attempts to solve problems that arise from the community's social and economic failures that policing is least effective and most frustrating. For, while charged with deterrence, the police can do little to prevent crime in the broader sense of removing its causes. On the whole, they must accept society as it is—a society in which parents fail to raise their children as law-abiding citizens, in which schools fail to educate them to assume adult roles, and in which the economy is not geared to provide them with jobs. The most eminent of modern police administrators, August Vollmer, once said: "I have spent my life enforcing the laws. It is a stupid procedure and has not, nor will it ever solve the problem unless it is supplemented by preventive measures."[4]

The difficulties and inherent limitations of law enforcement are seldom appreciated by the public when it considers what the police can do, and reacts to what they do. Americans are a people used to entrusting the solution of their social ills to specialists, and to expecting results from the institutions those specialists devise. They have entrusted the problems of crime to the police, forgetting that they still operate with many of the limitations of constables of years past, even though today's citizens are no longer villagers.

The adjustment of conceptions of what can be expected of the police is particularly difficult for people who are themselves law-abiding and who live in a law-abiding community. For them the phenomenon of crime seems far simpler than in fact it is. The voluntary controls of society work well for them and, since they have no desire to violate the criminal law, their supposition is that crime must be a choice between right and wrong for all men, and that more effective policing alone can determine this choice. Thus public concern about crime is typically translated into demands for more law enforcement, and often into making the police scapegoats for a crime problem they did not create and do not have the resources to solve.

No one, of course, is more sensitive to demands for more law enforcement than the police themselves. They see the menace of crime most directly, and their lives are dominated by their professional task. In addition, they have encouraged and share the idea that they are inherently more capable of controlling crime then analysis has thus far shown them to be. In part, this conception derives from the efforts of modern police leaders

---

[4]August Vollmer, "Community Coordination," March-April, 1939, as quoted in V. A. Leonard, *Police Organization and Management,* 2d ed. (Brooklyn: The Foundation Press, Inc., 1964), p. 246.

to secure support and respect as professionals with a specialized ability capable of effective exercise apart from political control. And naturally enough the police, like men in all occupations, tend to view problems in terms of their own function and to have particular faith in their own skills to resolve them.

The police are fully aware of many of the restrictions that are placed upon them, and protest some of them. Their reaction is intensified by a general and often justified feeling that the very public that is responsible for these limits on effectiveness at the same time demands greater success in law enforcement. A leading police training text, for example, states:[5]

> Many police executives are frustrated today, because of the heavy pressures brought to bear upon them and their agencies to eliminate crime and delinquency hazards and to successfully solve cases. . . . Instead of pressuring legislative representatives for changes in the law, many citizens pressure their chief of police. And much such pressure is without knowledge of the law and its limitations, its restrictive interpretations by the courts, and its scope.

In its more extreme forms this reaction has had serious consequences. It has intensified police sensitivity to criticism and to contacts or controls that imply criticism. It has evoked frequent suspicion and bitterness toward those sections of the public seen as responsible for police limitations: politicians, courts, civil libertarians. In combination this sensitivity, suspicion, and bitterness has become in itself a significant limitation on police effectiveness.

In a sense, this entire volume is a discussion of how the police can either overcome or more effectively work within the limitations upon them. Many of those limitations are functions of the way the police are organized and managed; they, probably, are the easiest to surmount. . . .

History of the Police

The face of America has changed since colonial days from a collection of predominantly rural and independent jurisdictions to an industrialized urban nation. Yet in several respects law enforcement has not kept pace with this change. As America has grown and policing has become correspondingly complex, the existing law enforcement system has not always been altered to meet the needs of a mechanized and metropolitan society.

Over the years, the proliferation of independent and, for the most part, local policing units has led to an overlapping of responsibilities and a duplication of effort, causing problems in police administration and in the

---

[5]A. C. Germann, Frank D. Day, and Robert R. J. Gallati, *Introduction to Law Enforcement* (Springfield: Charles C. Thomas, 1966), p. 32.

coordination of efforts to apprehend criminals. America is a nation of small, decentralized police forces.

Other problems have plagued the police over the years. Forces have lacked an adequate number of sufficiently qualified personnel. Unattractive salaries and working conditions, and a general lack of public support have hindered police development. And the need for harmonious police-community relations has been a persistent problem, one which, unfortunately, has not been widely recognized until recently. Community relations problems are nothing new; they have existed since American cities were divided into subsocieties by virtue of different ensuing waves of immigrants from western, and later eastern, Europe, who started settling in urban centers before the turn of this century.

To understand better the prevailing problems that police agencies face today, it is helpful to examine their development in England as well as in the United States; for there are many weaknesses in the existing system that stem from practices developed in the rural colonies and from the colonial philosophy of law enforcement.

Early History of English Law Enforcement

France and other continental countries maintained professional police forces of a sort as early as the 17th century. But England, fearing the oppression these forces had brought about in many of the continental countries, did not begin to create police organizations until the 19th century. Moreover, England, in its early history, did not maintain a permanent army of paid soldiers that could enforce criminal laws when not engaged in guarding the country's borders against invaders. The cost of developing a force specifically for peace-keeping duties was believed to be too high for the royal purse. Private citizens could do the job cheaper, if given a few shillings reward for arrests. This simple law enforcement expedient, which had begun with Alfred the Great (870–901) can be recognized as the forerunner of American police agencies.

Primarily, the system encouraged mutual responsibility among local citizen's associations, which were pledged to maintain law and order;[6] it was called the "mutual pledge" system. Every man was responsible not only for his own actions but also for those of his neighbors. It was each citizen's duty to raise the "hue and cry" when a crime was committed, to collect his neighbors and to pursue a criminal who fled from the district. If such a group failed to apprehend a lawbreaker, all were fined by the Crown.

The Crown placed this mutual responsibility for group police action upon 10-family groups. Each of these was known as a "tithing." From the tithing, there subsequently developed the "hundred" comprised of 10 tith-

---

[6]Daniel Devlin. *Police Procedure, Administration and Organization* (London: Butterworth & Co., 1966), p. 3.

ings. From this developed the first real police officer—the constable.[7] He was appointed by a local nobleman and placed in charge of the weapons and equipment of each hundred.

Soon, the "hundreds" were grouped to form a "shire," a geographical area equivalent to a county.[8] A "shire-reeve"—lineal antecedent of tens of thousands of sheriffs to come—thus came into being, appointed by the Crown to supervise each county. The constable's breadth of authority remained limited to his original "hundred." The shire-reeve was responsible to the local nobleman in ensuring that the citizens enforced the law effectively. From his original supervisory post, the sheriff soon branched out to take part in the pursuit and apprehension of lawbreakers.

It was during the reign of Edward I (1272–1307) that the first official police forces were created in the large towns of England. These were called the "watch and ward," and were responsible for protecting property against fire, guarding the gates, and arresting those who committed offenses between sunset and daybreak. At the same time the constable became the primary law enforcement officer in all towns throughout England.

In 1326, to supplement the "shire-reeve" mutual pledge system, Edward II created the office of justice of the peace. The justices, originally noblemen, were appointed by the Crown to assist the sheriff in policing the county. This led in time to their taking on local judicial functions, in line with the primary duty of keeping the peace in their separate jurisdictions.

The constable, who retained the responsibility of serving as a major official within the pledge system, meanwhile gained in importance. He became an assistant to the justice, responsible for supervising the night watchmen, inquiring into offenses, serving summonses, executing warrants, and taking charge of prisoners.[9] It was here that the formal separation between judge and police officer developed.

As law enforcement increasingly became the responsibility of the central government in 14th century England, the justice, as the appointee of the King, exercised a greater degree of control over the locally appointed constables. By the end of the century the constable no longer functioned independently as an official of the pledge system. Rather, he was obliged to serve the justice. This essentially set the justice-constable patterns for the next 500 years. The "justice [remained] the superior, the constable the inferior, conservator of the peace"[10] until the second quarter of the 19th century.

---

[7]Germann, Day, and Gallati, *Law Enforcement,* p. 49.
[8]Ibid.
[9]Devlin, *Police Procedure,* p. 6.
[10]Royal Commission on the Police, "Royal Commission on the Police 1962, Final Report" (London: Her Majesty's Stationery Office), p. 12.

Meanwhile, over these years, the local pledge system continued to decline. Community support languished. And with considerable reason.[11]

What was everybody's business became nobody's duty and the citizens who were bound by law to take their turn at police work gradually evaded personal police service by paying others to do the work for them. In theory constables were appointed annually, but in fact their work was done by deputies or substitutes who so acted year after year, being paid to do so by the constables. These early paid police officers did not rank high in popular estimation as indicated in contemporary references. They were usually ill-paid and ignorant men, often too old to be in any sense efficient.

But as the local pledge system was declining, innovations in policing were cropping up in the emerging cities of the 17th and 18th centuries. Those first law enforcement officers were increasingly assisted by a paid nightwatch force. Although these nominally were responsible for guarding the cities against thieves and vandals, apparently they were not effective. Reportedly they did little more than roam the streets at night, periodically calling out the condition of the weather, the hour, and the fact that "all was well."

Industrialization in England

While England remained essentially a rural country, the dominance of the justice of the peace in law enforcement machinery aroused little formal opposition. But with the advent of the Industrial Revolution at the end of the 1700's, families by the thousands began traveling to factory towns to find work. Inevitably, as the cities grew, established patterns of life changed and unprecedented social disorder resulted. Law enforcement became a much more complex enterprise.

Government and citizens alike responded to this need for better law enforcement. A number of fragmented civic associations, such as the Bow Street Horse and Foot Patrol, were formed to police the streets and highways leading out of London and the Government passed statutes creating public offices, later to be known as police offices. Each of these housed three paid justices of the peace, who were authorized to employ six paid constables. These new posts thus helped to centralize law enforcement operations within a small area.

By the beginning of the 19th century nine police offices had been established within the metropolitan area of London, but there was little apparent effort to coordinate their independent law enforcement activities. This was reportedly due to the fact that each office refused to communicate with another for fear that the other might take credit for detecting and apprehending an offender.

---

[11]Devlin, *Police Procedure,* p. 7.

In London especially, these weaknesses combined to make the police forces seemingly powerless to combat crime. Highwaymen on the road, thieves lurking in the cities, daily bank robberies, juvenile delinquency—all presented major law enforcement problems.[12] However, out of this difficult situation emerged a unique remedy to discourage thieves from attacking citizens; in the early 1800's gaslights were introduced on the streets of London.

Many of the experiments in law enforcement before 1820 failed "because no scheme could reconcile the freedom of action of individuals with the security of person and property."[13] In 1822, Sir Robert Peel, England's new Home Secretary, contended that, while better policing could not eliminate crime, the poor quality of police contributed to social disorder. Seven years later he introduced and guided through Parliament an "Act for Improving the Police In and Near the Metropolis." This led to the first organized British metropolitan police force. Structured along the lines of a military unit, the force of 1,000 was the first one to wear a definite uniform. The men were commanded by two magistrates, later called commissioners, who were given administrative but not judicial duties. Ultimately, the responsibility for equipping, paying, maintaining, and to a certain degree supervising the "bobbies," as they later became known, was vested in the Home Secretary. Because he was made accountable to the Parliament "for the exercise of his authority over the Metropolitan police, it could [thus] be said that the new force was under the ultimate control of a democratically elected Parliament."[14]

Availability of competent manpower, then as today, became an immediate problem. It was difficult to recruit suitable men to serve in the "new police," for the salaries were poor and the commissioners selective. And there were other harassments. Parliament objected to appropriating Government funds to maintain a police force. The radicals were afraid of tyranny. The aristocracy, though willing to accept the protection of such a force, was disgruntled because the commissioners refused to abide by the traditional rules of patronage in making appointments.

Nevertheless, the London metropolitan police proved so effective in suppressing crime and apprehending criminals that within 5 years the provinces, which were experiencing increasing crime problems and violent riots, asked London for policing help.[15] Shortly after, Parliament enacted a series of police reform bills. Among them, one empowered justices of the peace

---

[12]Germann, Day, and Gallati, *Law Enforcement*, p. 59.

[13]Devlin, *Police Procedure*, p. 10.

[14]*Ibid.*, p. 16.

[15]Christopher Hibbert, *The Roots of Evil* (London: Weidenfield and Nicolson, 1963), pp. 125-128.

in 1839 to establish police forces in the counties; and in 1856 another required every borough and county to have a police force.

As regular police forces developed, the justices of the peace voluntarily relinquished their law enforcement duties and confined themselves to deciding questions of law. Before this change occurred, the police had served as the agents of the powerful justices and had consequently used the justices' authority to carry on investigation of those in custody. When the justices relinquished their law enforcement powers, the legislature gave no consideration as to what, if any, investigative responsibilities should be transferred to the police. As a result, the statutes for law enforcement officers that remain on the books today contain little recognition of the broad discretion that police continue to exercise.[16]

Law Enforcement in the American Colonies

American colonists in the 17th and 18th centuries naturally brought to America the law enforcement structure with which they were familiar in England. The transfer of the offices of constable and sheriff to rural American areas—which included most colonial territory—was accomplished with little change in structure of the offices. Drawing upon the pattern of the mutual pledge system, the constable was made responsible for law enforcement in towns, while the sheriff took charge of policing the counties. The Crown-appointed Governors bestowed these offices on large landowners who were loyal to the King. After the revolution, sheriffs and constables tended to be selected by popular elections, patronage then being on the wane.

In many colonial cities the colonists adopted the British constabulary-nightwatch system. As early as 1636 Boston had nightwatchmen, in addition to a military guard. New York and Philadelphia soon developed a similar nightwatch system. The New York nightwatchmen were known as the "Rattlewatch," because they carried rattles on their rounds to remind those who needed reminding of their watchful presence.

Urbanization in the United States

As American towns grew in size and population during the first half of the 19th century, the constable was unable to cope with the increasing disorder. As in England years before, lawlessness became more prevalent:[17]

---

[16]Edward J. Barrett, Jr., "Police Practices and the Law—From Arrest to Release or Charge," *California Law Review,* March 1962, 50: 17-18.

[17]Arthur Charles Cole, "The Irrepressible Conflict, 1859–1865," *A History of American Life in 12 Volumes,* vol. VIII, Arthur M. Schlesinger, Sr., and Dixon Ryan Fox, editors (New York: The Macmillan Co., 1934), pp. 154-155.

New York City was alleged to be the most crime-ridden city in the world, with Philadelphia, Baltimore and Cincinnati not far behind. . . . Gangs of youthful rowdies in the larger cities . . . threatened to destroy the American reputation for respect for law. . . . Before their boisterous demonstrations the crude police forces of the day were often helpless.

Again, as in England, many American cities began to develop organized metropolitan police forces of their own. Philadelphia was one of the first. In 1883, a wealthy philanthropist left a will that provided for the financing of a competent police force in Philadelphia. Stimulated by this contribution, the city government passed an ordinance providing for a 24-man police force to work by day and 120 nightwatchmen. The force was unfortunately shortlived, for the ordinance was repealed less than 2 years later.

In 1838, Boston created a day police force to supplement the nightwatch, and other cities soon followed its lead. Crime, cities were finding, was no respecter of daylight. There were certain inherent difficulties, however, in these early two-shift police systems. Keen rivalries existed between the day and night shifts, and separate administrations supervised each shift. Recognizing the evils of separate police forces, the New York Legislature passed a law in 1844 that authorized creating the first unified day and night police, thus abolishing its nightwatch system. Ten years later Boston consolidated its nightwatch with the day police.

Following the New York model, other cities developed their own unified police forces during the next decade. By the 1870's the Nation's largest cities had full-time police forces. And by early 1900's there were few cities of consequence without such unified forces. These forces gradually came under the control of a chief or commissioner, often appointed by the mayor, sometimes with the consent of the city council and sometimes elected by the people.

These first formal police forces in American cities were faced with many of the problems that police continue to confront today. Police officers became the objects of disrespect. The need for larger staffs required the police to compromise personnel standards in order to fill the ranks. And police salaries were among the lowest in local government service, a factor which precluded attracting sufficient numbers of high standard candidates. It is small wonder that the police were not respected, were not notably successful, and were not known for their vitality and progressiveness. Moreover, the police mission in the mid-1800's precluded any brilliance:[18]

---

[18]Arthur M. Schlesinger, Sr., "The Rise of the City, 1878–1898," *A History of American Life in 12 Volumes,* vol. X, Arthur M. Schlesinger, Sr., and Dixon Ryan Fox, editors (New York: The Macmillan Co., 1934), p. 115.

The aim of the police departments was merely to keep a city superficially clean and to keep everything quiet that [was] likely to arouse public [ire].

Many of the problems that troubled these first organized metropolitan police forces can perhaps be traced to a single root—political control. As one authority has explained:[19]

> Rotation in office enjoyed so much popular favor that police posts of both high and low degree were constantly changing hands, with political fixers determining the price and conditions of each change . . . The whole police question simply churned about in the public mind and eventually became identified with the corruption and degradation of the city politics and local governments of the period.

In an attempt to alleviate these problems, responsible leaders created police administrative boards to replace the control exercised over police affairs by mayors or city councils. These boards were given the responsibility of appointing police administrators and managing police affairs. Unfortunately, this attempt to cure political meddling was unsuccessful, perhaps because the judges, lawyers, and local businessmen who comprised the administrative boards were inexpert in dealing with the broad problems of the police.

Another attempt was made at police reform during the close of the 19th century. Noting that poor policing tended to occur mainly in urban areas, the State legislatures, which were dominated by rural legislators, required that police administrators be appointed by authority of the State. Thus State control became an alternative to local control of law enforcement. This move brought little success, for many problems had not been anticipated:[20]

> For one thing, the theory of state control . . . was not uniformly applied. It was primarily directed at the larger cities, by legislatures seeking to [perpetuate] rural domination in public affairs.

In spite of increased state control, the large city continued to pay for its police service, and police costs rose. One reason was that police boards were not even indirectly responsible to the local taxpaying public which they served. In cases where the State and city governments were not allied politically, friction increased. It increased further when the State-appointed administrator instituted policy out of harmony with the views of the major-

---

[19]Bruce Smith, Sr., *Police Systems in the United States* (2nd rev. ed., New York: Harper and Bros., 1960), pp. 105-106.

[20]*Ibid.,* p. 186.

ity of the city population. It was not until the first decades of the 20th century that cities regained control of police forces in all but a few cases.[21]

After these sincere attempts at reform during the last half of the 19th century, police forces grew in size and expanded in function. However, there was very little analysis of the changes in society that made expansion necessary nor of the effect such changes would work upon the role of the police. Civil service proved helpful, spreading to local police agencies and alleviating some of the more serious problems of political interference. The concept of merit employment, which some reformers had been proposing, was embraced by some forces.

One of the most notable police advancements of the 1900's was the advent of police training schools, even though on a somewhat modest basis. In the early 1900's, the new policeman learned chiefly in the school of experience:[22]

> . . . Thus, for the most part the average American city depends almost entirely for the training of its police recruits upon such casual instruction as older officials may be able and willing to give.

In numerous areas, however, it was not until the 1940's and notably in the 1950's that police departments established and, in many cases, greatly expanded their recruit training programs.

State and Federal Law Enforcement Agencies

Although a State police force, known as the "Texas Rangers," was organized in 1835 to supplement Texas' military forces, modern State police organizations did not emerge until the turn of the century. In 1905, the Governor of Pennsylvania, in the absence of an effective sheriff-constable system, created the first State force. Its initial purpose was to cope with a public dispute between labor and management. Soon such continuing factors as the inadequacy of local policing by constables and sheriffs and the inability or unwillingness of city police forces to pursue lawbreakers beyond their jurisdictional limits convinced State legislatures of the need for State-wide police forces.[23]

The majority of State departments were established shortly after World War I to deal with the increasing problem of auto traffic and the accompanying wave of car thefts. Today all States except Hawaii have some form of State law enforcement body. While some State agencies are re-

---

[21] *Ibid.,* pp. 186-187. State control of urban police continues to exist in certain cities in Missouri, Maryland, Massachusetts, Maine, and New Hampshire.

[22] Elmer D. Graper, *American Police Administration* (New York: The Macmillan Co., 1921), pp. 109-110.

[23] Smith, *Police Systems,* pp. 147-150.

stricted to the functions of enforcing traffic laws and protecting life and property on the highways, others have been given general policing authority in criminal matters throughout the State.

The role of the Federal Government in law enforcement has developed in a sporadic and highly specialized manner. Federal law enforcement actually started in 1789, when the Revenue Cutter Service was established to help prevent smuggling. In 1836, Congress authorized the Postmaster General to pay salaries to agents who would investigate infringements involving postal matters. Among the more important law enforcement responsibilities later recognized by Congress were internal revenue investigation and narcotics control. Congress authorized a force of 25 detectives in 1868 and increased the number in 1915. In 1924, J. Edgar Hoover organized the Federal Bureau of Investigation in the Justice Department.[24]

With the expansion of interstate movement of people and goods, and Federal involvement in all aspects of life, the responsibilities of Federal agencies have increased significantly within the last few years. These Federal agencies are responsible to departments of the National Government. The Treasury Department's Secret Service is, for example, charged with the protection of the President and with investigating counterfeiting and forgery of Federal documents. Civilian departmental agencies, with the sole exception of the FBI, function under civil service regulations.[25]

The manpower and jurisdiction of the FBI have increased greatly since its establishment. Some of the statutes that have been responsible for this expansion are the National Stolen Property Act, the Federal Kidnapping Act, the Hobbs Act (extortion), the Fugitive Felon Act, the White Slave Act, the National Bank Robbery Act, Federal interstate gambling laws, and the Dyer Act. The last brings within the FBI's jurisdiction automobiles stolen and taken across the border of a State. Recent passage of strong Federal legislation has enhanced the FBI's role in the enforcement of civil rights.

Modernization

Serious study of police reform in America began in 1919. The problems exposed then and those faced by police agencies today are similar in many respects. For example, in 1931 the Wickersham Commission noted that the average police chief's term of office was too short, and that his responsibility to political officials made his position insecure. The Commission also felt that there was a lack of competent, efficient, and honest patrolmen. It said that no intensive effort was being made to educate, train, and discipline prospective officers, or to eliminate those shown to be incompetent. The Wickersham Commission found that with perhaps 2 exceptions,

---

[24]Germann, Day, and Gallati, *Law Enforcement,* pp. 67-68.
[25]John Coatman, *Police* (London: The Oxford University Press, 1959), p. 50.

Table 1.—A Profile of Federal, State, and Local Law Enforcement Agencies

	Agencies	Full-time personnel				Dollars spent					
	Number in 1965	Number in 1955	Number in 1965	Percent of total in 1965	Percent average annual increase, 1955-65	Total in millions, 1955	Total in millions, 1965	Per capita expenditure, 1955	Per capita expenditure, 1965	Percent of dollars 1965	Percent average annual increase, 1955-65
Federal	50	22,000	23,000	6.2	0.5	129	220	$0.78	$1.26	8.5	7.7
State	200	22,000	40,000	10.8	8.2	139	315	.84	1.79	12.2	12.7
Local	39,750	229,000	308,000	83.0	3.4	1,001	2,051	6.60	11.35	79.3	8.8
Total	40,000	273,000	371,000	100.0	3.6	1,359	2,586	8.22	14.20	100.0	9.0
Percent increase			35.9				90.3		72.7		

Source: Memorandum from Michael S. March, Assistant Chief of Education, Manpower and Science Division, U.S. Bureau of the Budget, May 11, 1966.

police forces in cities above 300,000 population had neither an adequate communications system nor the equipment necessary to enforce the law effectively. It said that the police task was made much more difficult by the excessively rapid growth of our cities in the past half century, and by the tendency of different ethnic groups to retain their language and customs in large cities. Finally, the Commission said, there were too many duties cast upon each officer and patrolman.[26] The Missouri Crime Commission reported that in a typical American city the police were expected to be familiar with and enforce 30,000 Federal, State, or local enactments![27]

Despite the complexity of these problems, many hopeful improvements have occurred in the past few decades. Some cities, counties, and States have taken great strides in streamlining their operations through reorganization and increased use of technology and the use of modern techniques to detect and apprehend criminal offenders. Others are on the threshold of modernization. But many departments remain static. And it is these that obviously constitute a burden on the machinery of justice, and are detrimental to the process of achieving a truly professional police service.

Profile of the Police

To understand many of the analyses and recommendations in this volume, it is helpful to have as background information a profile of law enforcement organization, manpower, and expenditures in the United States today. The statistical data, which are summarized in Table 1, are explained in this section. Much of the same information will be expanded in later chapters as different aspects of policing are discussed in greater depth.

Number of Police Agencies, Distribution, and Lines of Responsibility

There are today in the United States 40,000 separate agencies responsible for enforcing laws on the Federal, State, and local levels of government. But law enforcement agencies are not evenly distributed among these three levels, for the function is primarily a concern of local government. There are only 50 law enforcement agencies on the Federal level of government and 200 departments on the State level. The remaining 39,750 agencies are dispersed throughout the many counties, cities, towns, and villages that form our local governments.[28]

---

[26]National Commission on Law Observance and Enforcement, *Report on the Police,* (Washington: U.S. Government Printing Office, 1931), pp. 5-7.

[27]Preston William Slossom, "The Great Crusade and After, 1914–1929, *A History of American Life in 12 Volumes,* vol. XII. Arthur M. Schlesinger, Sr., and Dixon Ryan Fox, editors (New York: The Macmillan Co., 1934), p. 102.

[28]Germann, Day, and Gallati, *Law Enforcement,* p. 153.

If we look at a breakdown of the numbers of local agencies, it is again apparent that distribution tends toward the local unit, for only 3,050 agencies are located in counties and 3,700 in cities. The great majority of police forces—33,000—are distributed throughout boroughs, towns, and villages.

Because the concept of local autonomy in enforcing laws has prevailed throughout our history and because the many local policing agencies have held firmly to their traditional jurisdictional authority, responsibility for maintaining public order is today extremely decentralized. This decentralization is further accentuated by the fact that a police officer's responsibility for enforcing law is usually confined to a single jurisdiction.

The problems caused by decentralization are many, particularly where a number of police agencies exist within a radius of a few miles. Jurisdictional barriers are often erected between these agencies; maintaining adequate communication is difficult, and obtaining assistance from several adjacent agencies when needed becomes a complex operation.

The problems of decentralization have been overcome in part either by creating county, State, and Federal agencies or by increasing the responsibility of existing ones. These agencies have tended in many areas of the country to supplement and coordinate the work of local police agencies.

The 50 Federal law enforcement agencies have directed their efforts mainly to enforcing national laws dealing with interstate violations or with such specific Federal violations as theft of Federal property, postal violations, and counterfeiting U.S. currency, or with enforcing such Federal statutes as those that control the import and sale of narcotics. The duties and activities of these agencies have been defined by Congress through a series of statutes passed over a number of years. It is because of America's strong tradition of local autonomy that the Federal Government has not become extensively involved in local law enforcement.

The States have the primary constitutional responsibility for maintaining order within their boundaries, and all of the States have exercised this authority by enacting broad criminal codes. But because local police departments have traditionally maintained law and order within their jurisdictions and because thousands of violations occur daily in all parts of States, the responsibility for preventing crime has been delegated by States to the local governments in which the violations occur.

Through legislation each State has defined the scope of police responsibility among its many agencies—the State police; county sheriffs; and city, township, borough, and village police. The States have not only divided the responsibility for enforcing law among these various agencies, but they have also determined the extent to which each agency may exercise its power. In addition, State legislatures have passed statutes setting the bounds of civil and criminal liability for police officers who overstep their authority.

On the State level of government the State police are the major law enforcement agents. Their primary responsibility is to enforce some State laws, to patrol highways, and to regulate traffic. They also provide services as needed to local police such as maintaining a State system of criminal identification, conducting police training programs or providing a State communications system. Some States, in addition, have created specialized agencies to enforce particular regulations, such as conservation or alcoholic beverage control laws.

At the county level of government, the sheriff is the primary law enforcement officer. He is an elected official, whose term usually spans from 2 to 4 years and whose jurisdictional responsibility primarily covers unincorporated portions of each county. His functions include keeping the peace, executing civil and criminal process, patrolling the area, maintaining the county jail, preserving order in county courts, and enforcing court orders. The sheriff as a rule performs only restricted law enforcement functions in incorporated areas within a county, and then usually only when the city requests his participation in such activities as patrol or investigation.

In suburban townships and municipalities, police officers are vested with broad law enforcement authority and perform functions similar to those of city police. In rural areas, where most of the 18,000 townships of America are located, police officers usually confine their activities to a limited range of ministerial and traffic duties. In the absence of a local police agency, the local unit of government relies upon the services of the sheriff or State police for law enforcement assistance. These duties may include patrol, investigation, or enforcement of traffic regulations.

Two additional types of police agencies operate on the local level of government. One is the police special service district, created to protect residents or industry in unincorporated portions of urban areas. But few of the Nation's 19,000 special service districts actually provide police service. Most have been created to provide fire protection, street lighting, drainage, and sewage treatment.[29] The second type is the force whose mission is highly specialized. Such forces may be established to protect parks, housing developments, ports, toll roads, and subways. But neither these forces nor police in special service districts have had significant impact on American police administration.

Personnel

There were 420,000 full and part-time law enforcement officers and civilians employed by police agencies in 1966. The majority of these persons

---

[29]Committee for Economic Development, *Modernizing Local Government* (New York: Committee for Economic Development, July 1966), p. 32.

Table 2.—Full-Time Local Police Manpower Per 1,000 Population

	Police officers and civilians	Police officers only	Range in different geographical divisions
Cities over 250,000	2.6	2.3	1.5 to 4.1
Cities of—			
100,000 to 250,000	1.7	1.5	1.3 to 2.5
50,000 to 100,000	1.5	1.4	1.2 to 1.9
25,000 to 50,000	1.5	1.3	1.1 to 1.7
10,000 to 25,000	1.4	1.3	1.2 to 1.7
Cities under 10,000	1.4	1.3	1.2 to 1.9
Total	1.9	1.7	1.1 to 4.1

Source: Federal Bureau of Investigation, U.S. Department of Justice, "Uniform Crime Reports, 1965" (Washington: U.S. Government Printing Office, 1966), p. 148-51. These data include civilian employees.

Table 3.—Full-Time Local Police Manpower by Character of Jurisdiction

	Population served	Number of agencies reporting	Number of police employees	Average number of employees per 1,000 population
City police	109,633,000	3,613	212,888	1.9
Suburban police[1]	40,251,000	1,770	55,040	1.4
County sheriffs	32,357,000	1,154	32,159	1.0

[1]Agencies and population represented in suburban area are also included in other city groups.

Source: Federal Bureau of Investigation, U.S. Department of Justice, "Uniform Crime Reports, 1965" (Washington: U.S. Government Printing Office, 1966), p. 149.

—371,000—were full-time employees, and 11 percent, or approximately 46,000, were civilians. In 1965 there was an overall ratio of 1.7 police officers to every 1,000 persons.[30] (Tables 2 and 3 show police manpower and population ratios.) The total number of police employees at the local level of government has been increasing at an average annual rate of 3.5 percent over the past 8 years.[31]

Twenty-three thousand of the full-time officers serve at the Federal level of government, and 40,000 at the State level. The remaining 308,000 officers—or 83 percent of the total—are divided among the many county and local police agencies.

Of the 308,000 police officers serving on the county and local level of government, about 197,500 enforcement officers are distributed among the 39,695 agencies with jurisdictions in county or local areas. These include:
3,645 cities of under 250,000 population,
3,050 counties, and
33,000 townships, boroughs, villages, and special districts.
The remaining 110,500 police personnel are divided among the 55 agencies enforcing law in the 55 cities of the United States of a population over 250,000.[32]

The number of personnel in local police agencies also varies to a considerable degree among locales. On the county level of government the 3,050 sheriffs' offices range from a one-man force in Putnam County, Ga., to a 5,515-man force in Los Angeles County, Calif. The average number of police officers serving on the county level is small; only about 200 counties of the 3,050 in the United States have a sheriff's staff of more than 50 officers.[33]

In the local police forces below the county level of government the size of a force may vary from the 1 to 5-man force in the many boroughs and towns of the United States to the mammoth 28,671-member New York City police force.

Even within the radius of a major city, police forces have extraordinary range in size. Chicago, for example, has a total force of 11,745 civilians and officers. Within Cook and DuPage Counties, which encompass much of metropolitan Chicago, there are only 2,187 full-time officers enforcing the law among the 119 municipalities (other than Chicago) located there. One

---

[30]Federal Bureau of Investigation, U.S. Department of Justice, *Uniform Crime Reports, 1965* (Washington: U.S. Government Printing Office, 1966), p. 32.
[31]Memorandum from Michael S. March, Assistant Chief of Education, Manpower and Science Division, U.S. Bureau of the Budget, May 11, 1966, table 4.
[32]International City Managers' Association, *The Municipal Year Book 1966* (Chicago: International City Managers' Association), pp. 444-445.
[33]Conversation with Ferris E. Lucas, Executive Director, National Sheriffs' Association, Washington, D.C., Oct. 31, 1966.

community in Cook County controls crime with only 1 full-time officer, assisted by a part-time complement of 26 people.[34]

Availability of Manpower

Due to the great difficulties of attracting capable personnel, almost all large police departments in the United States are substantially below their authorized strength. In 1965 a survey of about 300 police departments—including nearly all of the large city departments—showed that 65.5 percent of the forces polled were below authorized strength. The average force was 5 percent below its quota; the average large-city force was 10 percent below standard capacity.[35]

The difficulties in filling quotas are increased by a low rate of eligibility among police applicants. In 1961 a survey indicated that the acceptance rate dropped from 29.9 percent in 1956 to 22.3 percent in 1961. (See Table 4.)

Table 4.—Applicant Success Rates—Regional Replies—1956-61

Region	1956			1961		
	Appli-cants	Eligible	A.S.R., percent	Appli-cants	Eligible	A.S.R., percent
New England	2,934	992	33.8	2,107	700	33.2
Middle Atlantic	22,094	7,707	34.8	19,967	5,863	29.4
East North Central	7,111	1,211	17.0	5,939	878	14.8
West North Central	1,538	522	33.9	2,041	577	21.8
South Atlantic	5,518	1,580	28.6	4,851	1,125	23.2
East South Central	973	427	43.9	1,014	480	47.3
West South Central	1,881	689	36.6	3,066	754	24.9
Mountain	1,077	344	31.9	3,016	622	20.5
Pacific	7,887	1,795	22.8	13,018	1,420	10.9
Total	51,013	15,267	29.9	55,619	12,430	22.3

Source: George W. O'Conner, "Survey of Selection Methods" (Washington: International Association of Chiefs of Police, 1962), table 33.

An even further rate reduction is suggested by recent experiences in two large metropolitan areas. In 1965, Washington, D.C. was able to hire less

---

[34]Information received from the Illinois Police Association, Elmwood Park, Ill.
[35]Raymond L. Bancroft, "Municipal Law Enforcement, 1966," (*Nation's Cities:* Washington, Feb. 1966), p. 16.

than 10 percent of people applying.[36] Los Angeles reported that only 2.8 percent of police applicants were accepted, and 4.9 percent of applicants for the county sheriff's police were hired.[37]

Manpower problems are also caused by turnover in personnel. Each year an average of 5 percent of a police department's force leaves the police service. In the next 10 years, as the mass of police officers recruited just after World War II reaches retirement age, many departments will face severe recruiting needs. For example, 41 percent of the existing Los Angeles Police Department[38] and 10 percent of the 83-man force in Joliet, Ill., will be eligible to retire in 1967.[39]

The present need for manpower and the anticipated rate of turnover both indicate that over 50,000 new police officers will be required in 1967 alone.

Characteristics of Personnel

In 1960 the census showed that the median age of male local law enforcement personnel was as follows:[40]

	Years of Age
Police and detectives	37.6
Marshals and constables	50.5
Sheriffs and bailiffs	45.4

A cross section of the age distribution of male and female police officers and detectives is seen in Table 5.

The median educational level of police officers has risen slightly in this decade. Figures released by the U.S. Department of Health, Education, and Welfare set the median at 12.4 years of education in 1966, a slight rise from the 12.2 level reported by the Bureau of the Census in 1960. A recent

---

[36]The President's Commission on Crime in the District of Columbia, *A Report on the President's Commission on Crime in the District of Columbia* (Washington: U.S. Government Printing Office, 1966), p. 17.

[37]American Trial Lawyers Association, *Crime and Its Causes in Los Angeles* (Lancaster, Pa., Golden West Publishing Co., 1966), pp. 7-8.

[38]*Wall Street Journal,* Apr. 5, 1966, p. 1, col. 5.

[39]*Herald News,* Joliet, Ill., July 15, 1966, sec. 1, p. 1, cols. 5-7.

[40]U.S. Department of Commerce, Bureau of the Census, "U.S. Census of Population: 1960. Subject Reports. Occupational Characteristics," Final Report PC(2)-7A (Washington: U.S. Government Printing Office, 1963), table 6, p. 79.

Table 5.—Employed Public Police and Detective Personnel, by Age and Sex, 1960

Age range	15-17	18-19	20-24	25-29	30-34	35-44	45-54	55-59	60-64	65-69	70-74	75+	Total
Number of employees:													
Male	41	163	12,381	36,733	46,117	71,389	38,633	10,518	6,805	2,840	1,130	728	227,478
Female	0	40	364	695	881	2,077	1,179	221	60	19	20	0	5,556
Total	41	203	12,745	37,428	46,998	73,466	39,812	10,739	6,865	2,859	1,150	728	233,034

Source: U.S. Department of Commerce, Bureau of the Census, "U.S. Census of Population: 1960. Subject Reports. Occupational Characteristics," Final Report PC(2)-7A (Washington: U.S. Government Printing Office, 1963), table 6, pp. 79, 89.

national survey of 6,300 police officers indicated that approximately 24 percent of patrolmen and 31 percent of top-level department administrators had attended college.[41]

Police personnel are predominately Caucasian. The 1960 census showed that only 3.5 percent of law enforcement employees throughout the Nation were non-Caucasian. A study by the Civil Rights Commission in 1962 revealed that only one-fifth of 1 percent of State police officers were Negro. Of the 36 Negroes serving as State police officers in the Nation, 24 were employed in Illinois.[42] The same Civil Rights Commission survey polled 271 sheriffs' offices and found that in 1962 there was a Negro-white employment ratio of 1 to 20 on the county level of government.

Some cities have recently recruited a substantial number of Negro officers. In Washington, D.C., for example, Negro employment in the past few years has increased from 14 to 19 percent of the police force, and in Chicago it has increased from 9 to 20 percent of the force.[43] And a notable event occurred in the South in January 1967 when Lucius D. Amerson was sworn in as sheriff of Macon County, Ala. Amerson became the first Negro sheriff in a Southern jurisdiction since Reconstruction.

Employment Requirements

More than 70 percent of the Nation's police departments have set the high school diploma level as an educational requirement for employment. About one-fourth of the agencies require no more than some degree of elementary education.[44] Most large cities and counties maintain a high school education or its equivalent as a minimum standard, and at least 22 departments have raised their standard to require college credit. But 21 of these are located in California.

Physical requirements for police employment are rigid. The minimum standards usually require that a recruit be between the ages of 21 and 35, have nearly perfect vision, weigh between 150 and 250 pounds, and be at least 5 feet 8 or 9 inches tall. Many departments only recruit people who have lived within the police jurisdiction for a given period of time before employment. The requirement for preservice residency may vary from 6 months to 5 years. In 1965, more than two-thirds of local law enforcement officers throughout the United States were born in the State in which they were employed.

---

[41]Institute for Community Development and Services, Michigan State University, "Police Training in the Detroit Metropolitan Region: Recommendations for a Regional Approach" (draft submitted to the Metropolitan Fund, Inc., of Detroit, 1966), table 25, p. 70.

[42]U.S. Commission on Civil Rights, "Administration of Justice, 1963" (Staff report, draft submitted 1963), pp. 13-16.

[43]Ibid.

[44]George W. O'Connor, "Survey of Selection Methods" (Washington: International Association of Chiefs of Police, 1962), table 15.

Almost all local police departments require that an applicant take written intelligence tests. But these tests are in no way standard, and many are ineffective for purposes of measuring educational achievement or personal capability for service. In 1961, a survey showed that only about 15 percent of the local agencies screened their candidates for emotional fitness as a routine procedure.[45] The National League of Cities, which sampled police departments in 1965, indicated that only 27 percent of the agencies responding conducted some kind of psychiatric evaluation of applicants.

Police Compensation

In the past 30 years, police salaries have risen, and the number of hours worked in a week have been reduced. The 40-hour week is now standard in the majority of agencies. In small communities median salaries for patrolmen have risen from a figure of approximately $1,600 in 1937 to $4,600 in 1966. Maximum salaries rose from a 1938 figure of $1,800 to a 1966 figure of $5,500. In larger cities during these same years median beginning salaries for patrolmen, which had been $1,900, rose to $5,300. At the same time median maximum salaries rose from $2,400 to about $6,600. Compensation for chief administrators on a nationwide scale in 1938 ranged from $1,980 to $12,500 per annum.[46] In 1965, it had risen to a range of $3,600 to $35,000.[47]

The above compensation figures do not include retirement, health, and other benefits accrued by public police employees.

Police Training

Classroom training for recruits is a relatively new concept in American policing. During the early years of this century, experience on the job was the most prevalent method for learning police skills.[48] In the last few years, however, there has been a marked trend toward formal training programs for recruits. Of the 1,352 cities responding to a 1965 survey, 84 percent of city police forces reported formal, in-service training for police officers.[49]

In 1965, a survey of law enforcement agencies showed that 4,000 agencies had appointed over 16,000 new police officers between July 1964 and June 1965.[50] The extent of the recruit training programs provided by

[45] *Ibid.,* table 19.

[46] International City Managers Association, *The Municipal Year Book 1939* (Chicago: International City Managers' Association), p. 424.

[47] International City Managers' Association, *Municipal Year Book 1966,* p. 434.

[48] Graper, *American Police Administration,* p. 110.

[49] International City Managers' Association, *Municipal Year Book 1966,* p. 437.

[50] International Association of Chiefs of Police, "Police Training," report submitted to the President's Commission on Law Enforcement and Administration of Justice, Washington, D.C., 1966.

these agencies is reflected in Table 6. A 1966 survey indicated that 97 percent of the 269 agencies responding had formal training programs that ranged from 1 to 12 weeks.[51]

While almost 100 percent of the police departments in cities over 250,000 in population conduct their own recruit training programs, many of the smaller departments either have limited training programs or none at all. Some departments, which do not have their own training programs, use the training facilities of other local, State, and Federal agencies.[52]

Expenditures for Law Enforcement

As Table 1 shows, law enforcement services cost the Nation slightly in excess of $2.5 billion in 1965. Approximately $2 billion of this sum was allocated to local law enforcement agencies. The remainder was divided between State agencies, which received $315 million, and Federal agencies, which obtained $220 million.

The bulk of money for law enforcement is spent on salaries. At the local level a police department may spend between 85 and 90 percent of its budget for this purpose.[53]

Like other services, the cost of policing has increased in the past few years. For example, since 1955, numbers of police personnel have increased about 36 percent and expenditures have soared 90 percent. The cost increase is primarily linked to the expense of salaries and equipment. If the present average increase in expenditures of almost 10 percent per year continues, law enforcement costs will total almost $5.5 billion by 1975— more than double the 1965 figure.

Clearly, law enforcement is competing for tax dollars with a large number of other social services provided by all levels of government, for police agencies over the past 65 years have received a declining percentage of increasing total government expenditures. In 1902, for example, police agencies were allotted 4.9 percent of total governmental fiscal outlay. In 1962, this figure had declined to 3.5 percent.[54] The percentage of governmental allotments to law enforcement continues to decline even though the cost of enforcing the law has risen from $8.22 per capita in 1955 to $13.52 per capita in 1964.[55]

The costs of policing are highest in large urban areas. As depicted in Table 7, the per capita policing costs in a city of over 1 million people are

[51]Bancroft, "Municipal Law Enforcement," p. 20.

[52]International Association Chiefs of Police, "Police Training"

[53]Slossom, "The Great Crusade," p. 443.

[54]U.S. Department of Commerce. Bureau of the Census of Governments; 1962. vol. VI, no. 4, "Historical Statistics on Government Finances and Employment" (Washington: U.S. Government Printing Office, 1964) table 1.

[55]March, Memorandum, table 2.

Table 6.—Percent of Departments Providing Recruit Training by Program Length, 1965

Population group	Weeks of training									
	Less than 1	1	2	3	4	5	6	7	8	More than 8
Over 1,000,000	100.0	100.0	100.0	100.0	100.0	100.0	100.0	100.0	80.0	60.0
500,000 to 1,000,000	100.0	100.0	80.0	80.0	80.0	80.0	70.0	70.0	70.0	60.0
250,000 to 500,000	100.0	88.0	84.0	84.0	84.0	80.0	68.0	52.0	52.0	40.0
100,000 to 250,000	100.9	97.7	85.3	77.5	67.4	58.4	46.0	34.8	24.7	14.6
50,000 to 100,000	100.0	91.0	76.1	64.0	53.4	48.9	29.2	12.6	10.5	4.7
25,000 to 50,000	100.0	81.6	69.5	53.5	42.9	34.1	23.8	9.7	6.2	4.5
10,000 to 25,000	100.0	74.2	61.5	48.3	38.6	29.3	21.0	7.6	6.0	2.9
5,000 to 10,000	100.0	63.3	49.4	33.9	26.1	21.3	15.3	5.7	3.8	1.6
Under 5,000	100.0	48.6	39.0	25.3	18.0	14.7	9.6	2.3	1.5	1.0
Percent of agencies	100.0	68.3	56.0	42.0	33.4	27.7	19.0	8.1	6.0	3.5
Percent of total officers	100.0	87.6	76.6	69.0	63.1	57.9	49.5	41.0	34.7	25.9
Number of total officers	16,169	14,178	12,399	11,162	10,203	9,362	3,011	6,632	5,619	4,199

Source: International Association of Chiefs of Police, "Police Training," report submitted to the President's Commission on Law Enforcement and Administration of Justice, Washington, D.C., 1966.

Table 7.—General Services and Police Expenditures Per Capita by City Population, 1963-64[1]

City population

	50,000 and less	50,000 to 100,000	100,000 to 200,000	200,000 to 300,000	300,000 to 400,000	500,000 to 1,000,000	1,000,000 and over
City per capita expenditure on:							
General services	73.23	119.11	137.93	135.12	133.97	178.74	248.12
Police	8.74	12.19	12.78	13.92	14.82	19.21	27.31

[1]Source: U.S. Department of Commerce, Bureau of the Census, Government Finances in 1963-64, Table 4, p. 22.

69

almost twice the cost of police activity in cities of between 200,000 and 300,000 population. Furthermore, the relative cost rate in the largest cities is more than triple that of cities having fewer than a 50,000 resident population.

The trend toward greater per capita expenditure in large urban areas is not a phenomenon unique to law enforcement. It demonstrates that the complex way of life found in large, populated cities today costs more than the relatively simple life of small towns. As expenditures for education, public welfare, and public housing increase, so do police budgets. A comparison between governmental expenditures in urban and nonurban areas is presented in Table 8.

Table 8.—Per Capita Local Government Expenditure Patterns Within and Outside Metropolitan Areas in the United States, 1962

	Within SMSA's[1]	Outside SMSA's	United States
Total	267.05	199.68	242.96
Education	97.29	95.29	96.57
Highways	18.46	22.85	20.03
Public welfare	16.13	9.78	13.86
Police protection	12.59	5.28	9.98
Fire protection	7.79	2.91	6.05
Sewerage	8.44	3.98	6.85
Housing and urban renewal	8.69	1.61	6.16
Parks and recreation	6.43	1.77	4.77

[1]Standard Metropolitan Statistical Areas.

Source: Advisory Commission on Intergovernmental Relations, "Metropolitan Social and Economic Disparities: Implications for Intergovernmental Relations in Central Cities and Suburbs," "Report" A-25, Jan. 1965, p. 51.

Special Urban Problems

The relative urban-rural crime rate has been the subject of much statistical study in recent years. As crime rates have increased throughout the United States, the rate in cities has continued to be substantially higher than in less populous areas. For example, the FBI's "Uniform Crime Reports, 1965" indicates that the rate for robbery in urban areas was 88.6 per hundred thousand population, as compared to a rate of 9.9 in rural areas.[56]

The urban rate of aggravated assault was 127.7 per hundred thousand population as compared to a rural rate of 58.3—more than double. Similarly, the urban rate for burglary was 732.7 per hundred thousand population as compared to a rural rate of 308.4. And the urban rate for larceny of $50 and over was 492.0 per hundred thousand population, while the rural rate was 176.2.[57]

In addition to the greater incidence of serious crime, urban police face rising rates for other types of crimes. The increase of petty crimes, for example, is much more severe in cities than in nonurban areas. The problem of drunkenness has caused a major drain on police time in large cities, while in the small town the problem is likely to be handled quickly and informally in the relatively few cases where it comes to police attention. Major metropolitan areas also face increasing incidents of juvenile delinquency, fed by social conditions in the city. Finally, the complex city problem of daily traffic snarls requires police regulation and control different in degree from that required in small towns.

The changing makeup of urban population is another factor in explaining the increasing cost of police services today. Table 9 shows the per capita expenditures for policing in different types of urban areas.

Table 9.—Mean Per Capita Expenditure of Cities on Police Services, 1951

City type	Number of cities	Mean per capita expenditure
Major resort city	5	$11.39
Core city of major metropolitan area	77	7.33
Industrial suburb	68	7.17
High-income residential suburb	34	6.39
Low-income residential suburb	68	6.72
Core city of minor metropolitan area	106	5.56
Independent city	137	4.96
Mean for 462 cities		6.04

Source: Ruth L. Mace, "Municipal Cost-Revenue Research in the United States," Institute of Government, University of North Carolina, 1961, p. 164, computed from data in U.S. Department of Commerce, Washington Bureau of the Census, "Compendium of City Government Finances in 1951," pp. 44-61.

---

[56]FBI, *Uniform Crime Reports 1965*, pp. 94-95.
[57]Ibid.

Each large urban sprawl has one major section that serves as the commercial hub. Generally, the number of residents in this hub is relatively few in comparison to the surrounding area. During the day the middle and upper classes travel to the central area for business purposes, sometimes increasing the population enormously. Although Detroit's resident population, for example, had decreased 9.7 percent between 1950 and 1960, its weekday population had approximately doubled. The Detroit police force was, therefore, required to add 133 personnel, an increase of 2.8 percent, to serve a city whose population was decreasing.[58] Similar considerations apply to resort cities whose populations increase several-fold during the seasonal influx of tourists.

---

[58]Samuel G. Chapman, *Police Manpower and Population Changes in Michigan Communities of 10,000 or More Population, 1950–60"* (East Lansing, Mich.: Institute for Community Development and Services, Michigan State University, 1961), pp. 8-9.

CHAPTER 4

The Police Role: A Case of Diversity

Richard H. Ward

Richard H. Ward is Instructor at the John Jay College of Criminal Justice, City University of New York. In preparing this article for publication, he received assistance from Dr. Nathan Adler, School of Criminology, Berkeley, and Dr. Kermit Gruberg, Consulting Psychiatrist to the Berkeley Police Department.

The policeman's role has come under considerable scrutiny in the past few years. Unfortunately, much of the writing that deals with the subject is woefully inadequate with regard to a true understanding of the police role in contemporary society. A major failing has been the lack of an adequate definition, and this has led to much confusion. The state that now exists, then, is often one in which the policeman is seen as an individual who carries a gun, wears a badge, and is sworn to "enforce" the law. All too often he is seen, and studied in atmosphere which gives rise to the belief that police attitudes, methods and character are more than similar and do not vary much with respect to geographical location.

Thus, while many of the aims of individual police departments may be the same, there is good reason to believe that the actual roles adopted are markedly different. Germann, Day and Gallati point out that police goals refer to two major objectives:

1. The prevention of crime and disorder and the preservation of peace (for community security).

2. The protection of life and property and personal liberty (for individual security).[1]

From Richard H. Ward, "The Police Role: A Case of Diversity." Reprinted by special permission of the *Journal of Criminal Law, Criminology and Police Science,* (Northwestern School of Law) copyright © 1970. December issue, volume 61, number 4.
[1]J. Gallati, *Introduction to Law Enforcement* (Springfield: Charles C. Thomas, 1962), p. 25.

Undoubtedly, most contemporary police agencies subscribe to such goals. However, the ways in which these goals are achieved vary according to any number of criteria. The following paper attempts to shed some light on the diverse nature of the police role today.

J. Milton Yinger defines the role as a unit of culture referring to the rights and duties, or normatively approved patterns of behavior for the occupants of a given position.[2] Looking at the police role in this light, it would be difficult to argue that the role of a policeman in a small town is the same as that of one in a large metropolitan city. Recognizing this factor, it would be more apropos to classify the term policeman as a position—referring to a unit of structure.

Another important consideration is the policeman's location within a particular milieu. The tendency to stereotype police is not uncommon. In recent years he has been described as authoritarian, brutal, uneducated, ultra-right in his politics, bigoted, cynical, and a criminal in blue.[3] No doubt, some of the labels are applicable, but the evidence to back them up on a broad scale is more than insufficient. Furthermore, there is good reason to believe that much police behavior is concomitant with the overall environment in which he works.

Studies of police within the sociological framework of society have been, with the exception of a few recent works, relatively rare. Indeed, "in the twenty-five year period from 1940 to 1965 only six articles remotely concerned with the police were published in the *American Journal of Sociology* and the *American Sociological Review,* the two major sociological journals.[4] The lack of data, combined with recent public interest in the police, has led a number of sociologists, social scientists, and psychologists to take a closer look at police in the United States. To date, their efforts have offered little in the way of a complete understanding of the police field. The primary reason, it seems, is the lack of a clear understanding as to what the police role is in a given community. Needless to say, the problem of role definition is not unique to the police field; Bruce Biddle and Edwin Thomas have written:

> Perhaps the most common definition is that role is the set of prescriptions defining what the behavior of a position member should be. But this much agreement is at best but an oasis in a desert of diverging opinion. A careful review of the definitions reveals, however, that there is one nearly universal

---

[2]J. Melton Yinger, *Toward a Field Theory of Behavior* (New York: McGraw-Hill Book Co., 1965), p. 99.

[3]See, for instance, Niederhoffer on cynicism; Reiss on brutality; and Smith, Locke and Walker on authoritarianism. Norman Mailer has described police as natural criminals who happen to turn to law enforcement instead of crime.

[4]Arthur Niederhoffer, *Behind the Shield* (New York: Doubleday and Company, Inc., 1967), p. 4.

common denominator, namely that the concept pertains to the behavior of particular persons.[5]

Because of its complex nature, though, the police role has become an almost indefinable concept. In fact, in a recent survey conducted by the author, better than 85% of the officers responding agreed with the statement: "It is difficult to define the role of the policeman in today's society." This lack of consensus, or understanding, leads to innumerable problems; both for the policeman trying to carry out his role, and the sociologist trying to study it. Perhaps Niederhoffer best exemplifies the problem of understanding police when he writes:

> The policeman is a "Rorschach" in uniform as he patrols his beat. His occupational accoutrements—shield, nightstick, gun and summons book—clothe him in a mantle of symbolism that stimulates fantasy and projection.[6]

Thus, the policeman represents many things to many people. Beyond listing a number of functions and duties it becomes increasingly difficult to set down a useful definition of the police role. Bruce Smith, author of *Police Systems in the United States,* says of the policeman:

> The policeman's art consists of applying and enforcing a multitude of laws and ordinances in such degree or proportion that the greatest degree of protection will be secured. The degree of enforcement and the method of application will vary with each neighborhood and community. There are no set rules, nor even general guides, to the policy to be applied. Each patrolman must, in a sense, determine the standard to set in the area for which he is responsible . . . Thus he is a policy-forming police administrator in miniature.[7]

A number of sociologists disagree with this view, however. Jerome Skolnick, for instance, maintains that the rule of law is far from important in the police role:

> Five features of the policeman's occupational environment weaken the conception of the rule of law as a primary objective of police conduct. One is the social psychology of the police work, that is, the relationship between occupational environment, working personality, and the rule of law. Second is the policeman's stake in maintaining his position of authority, especially his interest in bolstering accepted patterns of enforcement. Third is police socialization, especially as it influences the policeman's administrative bias. A

[5]Bruce J. Biddle and Edwin J. Thomas, *Role Theory: Concepts and Research* (New York: John Wiley and Sons, Inc., 1966), p. 29.

[6]Niederhoffer, *Behind the Shield,* p. 1.

[7]Bruce Smith, *Police Systems in the United States,* rev. ed. (New York: Harper and Row, 1960), p. 18.

related factor is the pressure put upon individual policemen to "produce"—
to be efficient rather than legal when the two norms are in conflict. Finally,
there is the policeman's opportunity to behave inconsistently with the rule of
law as a result of low visibility to much of his conduct.[8]

Skolnick further contends that the police "are increasingly articulating a
conception of professionalism based on narrow views of managerial efficiency and organizational interests."[9] Ed Cray, on the other hand, postu-
lates the theory that the police field is deteriorating:

> For 100 years, police officers have been recruited from the lowest social classes
> because the job has little to offer people capable of other work. The pay is
> poor; the hours are long; the work is hazardous. As a result the cause and
> effect have been spiral. The job has low status in the community; consequently
> it attracts only the poorest candidates. In turn, these men go out into the
> community and by their actions reinforce the poor image commonly held of
> the cop, flatfoot, or fuzz.[10]

These are but a few of the views put forth by those concerned with the police
field, but they are representative of the diversity of opinion. Perhaps, the
best definition of the police role as an aggregate is set down by James Q.
Wilson:

> In sum, the order maintenance function of the patrolman defines his role and
> that role, which is unlike that of any other occupation, can be described as
> one in which sub-professionals, working alone, exercise wide discretion in
> matters of utmost importance (life and death, honor and dishonor) in an
> environment that is apprehensive and perhaps hostile.[11]

Nevertheless, the disparity between individual policemen, individual police
departments and individual geographic locations makes this definition, at
best, a guideline with which to better understand the police role.

Role Expectation and Police Conflict

A primary consideration which, heretofore, has been grossly overlooked in police research is the relationship between police service and the
total community.[12] The tendency to study police in a microscopic, rather

---

[8]Jerome H. Skolnick, *Justice Without Trial: Law Enforcement in Democratic Society* (New
York: John Wiley and Sons, Inc., 1966), p. 231.

[9]Ibid., p. 238.

[10]Ed Cray, *The Big Blue Line* (New York: Coward McCann, 1967), p. 196.

[11]James Q. Wilson, *Varieties of Police Behavior* (Cambridge, Mass.: Harvard University Press,
1968), p. 30.

[12]Skolnick, and especially Wilson, are two exceptions.

than macroscopic, light is prevalent, thus creating a vacuum-like setting in which outside stimuli are overlooked or ignored. Furthermore, there is a proclivity toward generalization of findings to the whole police sphere. Thus, if a study shows policemen in New York to be "authoritarian" it is often assumed that all policemen are authoritarian.

The fallacy in this approach is twofold; first of all, police work does vary quite considerably from area to area and, especially and most important, the role expectation, or culture, within communities varies markedly. Role expectation is best described as the way an individual, or community, believes an individual will or ought to act in a given situation. Culture, as defined by Yinger, can be thought of as the system of *norms shared* by the members of a society, the prescriptions and proscriptions indicating how things should be done or should be appraised.[13] The difference between role expectation and culture can best be thought of in terms of individuals and individual groups—with their own expectations—in contrast to the larger society which establishes the community norms. For example, a group of drug addicts might have different expectations than the local Chamber of Commerce with regard to the way policemen institute searches; and the culture, in effect, establishes the norms in which the policeman is expected to conform.[14]

The policeman, then, in any given situation, is expected to react in a certain way by a number of persons; i.e. the supervisor, the public, the adversary, etc. Often these expectations lead to a situation in which the officer must choose between one or more alternatives at variance with the expectations of those concerned. Should he make an illegal search? Should he follow the letter of the law? Should he make an arrest to satisfy a businessman, although he knows the sergeant will be angry? Should he slug a prisoner who is "asking for it"? Such problems lead to role conflict. Yinger defines four types of role conflict:

1. Internal role conflict occurs when an individual has internalized a role that includes contradictory expectations or when he occupies two or more positions that carry incompatible role expectations.

2. External role conflict occurs when an individual is confronted with incompatible expectations from two or more persons in his position network or networks.

3. Intrarole conflict occurs when an individual perceives that others hold different expectations for him as the incumbent of a single position.

---

[13]Yinger, *Field Theory of Behavior*, p. 74.

[14]As Yinger notes, these norms may be covert and poorly verbalized, but not lacking in power to influence behavior. Thus, while Supreme Court decisions prohibit illegal searches, there may be local norms which permit them.

    4. Interrole conflict occurs when an individual perceives that others hold different expectations of him as the incumbent of two or more positions. (In any of these conflict situations they may or may not be perceived or recognized by the individual.)[15]

The various categories of role conflict are not necessarily separate entities, and the expectations that lead to role conflict may be legitimate or illegitimate. Thus, on the basis of these four variables there are sixteen types of role conflict that can possibly be designated.

One other designation is deemed noteworthy, and it is what Yinger defines as internalized role[16]—which refers to that part of the self which represents a given individual's tendencies to perform a role in a given way. This designation differs from role in that it is more closely connected to the individual's predisposition to carry out his role in a certain way.

Turning now to a discussion of these factors and their influence on the police, it becomes necessary to qualify them as being general observations which could have varying degrees of validity with respect to individual police departments. No doubt, all policemen are, as are all people, faced with role expectation and role conflict. It would appear, however, that multitudinous expectations placed on police have contributed, in no small part, to the confusion that now exists in literature about them.

A great deal has been written and said about the reaction of police at the 1968 Democratic convention in Chicago. Out of the maelstrom has emerged the term "police riot," and it has now become a common phrase in many newspapers across the nation. The result of this publicity has been to link other police departments with Chicago and make comparisons therefrom.[17] Furthermore, many of the critics who have deplored the Chicago violence fail to consider the overall implications and interrelated network surrounding the action taken by police. For instance, there is some reason to believe that the police, for the most part, were living up to role expectations in taking a firm stand against demonstrators; not only by the citizenry and the city government, but by the demonstrators as well.[18] Also, according to a Gallup poll taken right after the incident, 56% of the nation's adults approved of the way Chicago police dealt with protesters.[19] True, there may be a different public attitude now, but there is some reason to believe that,

---

[15]Yinger, *Field Theory of Behavior,* pp. 115-117.

[16]*Ibid.,* p. 99.

[17]Police work is one of the few occupations in which a "share" of the guilt for something must not only be borne by those involved, but often by others who have no connection other than the occupational title policeman.

[18]See, for example, The Walker Report, *Rights in Conflict* (New York: Signet Books, 1968), especially pp. 17, 38, 72.

[19]George Gallup, "A Well Done for Chicago Police," *San Francisco Examiner,* September 18, 1968, p. 5.

perhaps, the Chicago police were reacting to something entirely different than prejudice against demonstrators, notably role expectation.

It is to this premise that many observers of the police fail to look. There is, within a system, a given culture which defines, for the most part, the manner in which police operate.[20] These are not necessarily written rules (laws, ordinances, procedure, etc.) but, rather, "unwritten" expectations for a particular action. Often they are in conflict with other rules or laws. Thus, we may find that such things as free meals, gratuities, and overlooking certain violations, while against formal rules, are within the confines or norms of a particular system. Indeed, a policeman is often *expected* to abide by them, and may be considered "deviant" if he does not. The use of firearms is another interesting case. A great deal has been written and said about indiscriminate shooting by police, yet, for the most part,[21] a policeman generally fires his weapon in a situation that is within certain limits. For example, while it may be permissible for a police officer, legally, to fire at a stolen auto, where it is a felony offense, most police officers would not do so because there is the recognition that usually a youth is involved, and shooting a youngster is generally outside expected behavior. The same situation exists on college campuses; where police are faced with situations in which they might otherwise shoot, they are *expected* not to shoot. However, they may be expected to react in other ways, such as with clubs or chemical agents.

There is, however, another side to the coin. Albeit, police are expected to act in a certain way by a number of individuals, usually those with the most say or political power. In virtually every instance there are those who expect the police to act in another way. Thus, the campus dissident may expect the police to rough him up; the newly elected candidate may expect the police to be thoroughly honest; and the local citizens group may expect the policeman to take a strong stand when handling minority groups. These factors contribute to role conflict. There is also the policeman's inner feelings about his role. He may not feel that it is professional to accept free meals; he may not want to make a certain arrest; or he may not feel that it is proper to shoot looters in a riot situation. With regard to the rule of law, Edwin Lemert notes:

> . . . It can also be held that professionalized police today generally play regulatory roles which are more directly pointed to the end of maximum protection for the community than they are to enforcement of the criminal law. This is due in no small part to *value dilemmas the policeman experiences,*

---

[20]This is prescribed by the community, the department, and an individual's peers.

[21]This would exclude those officers who do get involved in shooting incidents which are not "acceptable"—such as getting drunk and shooting someone. It is the author's opinion that these incidents are, on the whole, rare.

coupled with the limited time and energy he has available for the task. (emphasis added).[22]

The concepts of intrarole and interrole conflict add another dimension. In intrarole conflict the officer may, or may not, perceive that others hold different expectations of him as a policeman. His supervisor, his family, the businessman, the kids on the corner, and the person he is arresting may all have different expectations of him. Given a hypothetical situation, let us assume that a police officer is told by his superior to clear a certain corner of youths, who have caused the local businessman to make a complaint. The police officer is expected to obey the order but realizes that the youths have no place to go. He must satisfy the businessman, who expects the policeman to make an arrest; he must handle the youths, who expect him to be tough; and if he does make an arrest the suspect may expect him to lie in court.

Also, interrole conflict may be apparent, or nonapparent to the individual. The policeman may be a father, a member of the youth council, and a college graduate; and in the above situation all these factors may have some bearing. As a father he may identify the youth's actions with those of his own family; he may feel that the court will only hurt the youth; and he may be expected to have a better understanding of the situation because of his education.[23]

Finally, as noted, the various conflicts are not separate entities but, rather, react in a conglomerate way to produce role conflict. As Yinger notes, "Distinguishing clearly between role, internalized role, and role behavior entails difficulties,"[24] and the same is true with regard to role conflict. Nevertheless, too much of the literature that deals with the police fails to recognize the variable influences that create role behavior and, instead, focus upon a reification of such terms as "authoritarian," "prejudice," "cynical," etc. to explain police behavior.[25]

The Need for a New Approach

What is needed, then, is a methodological model designed to study the police as a part of the total system.

To understand the influence of a position or behavior, we need to relate it not only to the personalities of the occupants and to the network of reciprocal

---

[22]Edwin M. Lemert, *Human Deviance, Social Problems, and Social Control* (Englewood Cliffs, N.J.: Prentice-Hall, Inc., 1967), p. 23.

[23]An example being the New York City Police Department, which recently required a college background for those assigned to the Youth Aid Bureau.

[24]Yinger, *Field Theory of Behavior*, p. 100.

[25]Which is not to say that they have no value as variables in a system network. But to say that police may be prejudiced, without studying the system, offers little useful information.

positions with which it is connected, but also to the larger community and society structures within which it operates.[26]

The task is by no means simple, but is primary to a full understanding of police behavior. The terms "field theory" or "systems analysis" relate to such an approach and, while a number of theoretical problems continue to exist in these theories, they are becoming more widely accepted by sociologists, social scientists, and psychologists.

As Herbert Blumer has pointed out, a major problem of the variable analysis technique is the lack of rules, guides, limitations, and prohibitions with regard to selecting variables. He also cites the absence of generic variables (variables that stand for abstract categories) and a "here and now" relationship (which would include a picture or understanding of the total context).[27] Nevertheless, as Yinger notes:

> When human behavior in a natural situation is under analysis, studies concerned with the interplay of several variables are particularly valuable as complements to more abstract research procedures.[28]

The problems of choosing variables, and assigning weight to them, are manifold, and beyond the scope of this paper; however, Table 1 indicates a theoretical approach to a study of the police. It should be noted that this is a theoretical model and open to question.

In any study of this nature care must be taken so as not to lose focus on the system under study. A recent newspaper article headlines, "Science Now Screens Out Men Who Will Be 'Bad Cops'." The article claims that scientists working with the Chicago Police Department have perfected tests to screen out bad cops.[29] The findings, according to the project director, could be used to predict which patrolmen would lose control in a riot or in the face of obscene taunts or other provocation. The report "rejected a widely held theory that an aggressive patrolman who makes many arrests is a good patrolman"; that "a man who needs a 'badge' and a 'gun' as a symbol of authority and prestige is a bad policeman"; and concluded that the " 'essential attributes' for a patrolman were found to be stability and cooperation."

Nowhere in the article is the term "bad policeman" defined, and the newspaper account fails to take cognizance of the fact that Chicago police may be quite different from New York or California police; indeed, such

[26]Yinger, *Field Theory of Behavior,* p. 128.

[27]Herbert Blumer, "Sociological Analysis and the Variable," *American Sociological Review,* December, 1956, pp. 683-4.

[28]*Ibid.,* p. 130.

[29]"Science Now Screens Out Men Who Will Be 'Bad Cops'," *San Francisco Sunday Examiner and Chronicle,* Feb. 9, 1969, p. 9.

Table 1.—Theoretical Model of a Police Research Design

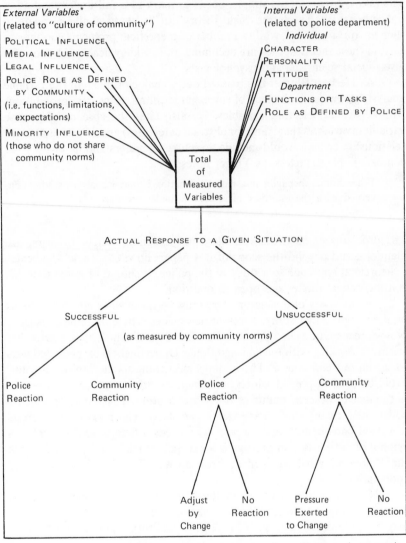

A variable measure would be used at each level and an effort made to estab-lish criteria for successful police operations, with a view toward modifying the police role where necessary.

*This is an incomplete list of variables, and merely highlights the approach.

a warning is made in the report. Furthermore, there is a question as to the usefulness of the report in the totality of the system. If a policeman should not be aggressive and make many arrests, who will make them? Will the public stand still if crime rates rise because of a lack of "aggressiveness" in a police force? What kind of a job do those men who do not "blow up" do? These are, of course, rhetorical questions, but point up the problems of limiting research to a group. Theoretically, if one wished to reduce police harassment of homosexuals he might hire them. It might reduce harassment, but would it cure the overall problem or be accepted by the public.

Police operate within the framework of a system and their actions are, generally, the result of community norms, or at least peer group norms.

> As human beings we act singly, collectively, and societally on the basis of the meanings which things have for us. Our world consists of innumerable objects —home, church, job, college education, a political election, a friend, an enemy nation, a tooth brush, or what not—each of which has a meaning on the basis of which we act toward it. In our activities we wend our way by recognizing an object to be such and such, by defining the situations with which we are presented, by attaching a meaning to this or that event, and where need be, by devising a new meaning to cover something new or different. This is done by the individual in his personal actions, it is done by a group of individuals acting together in concert, it is done in each of the manifold activities which together constitute an institution in operation, and it is done in each of the diversified acts which fit into and make up the patterned activity of a social structure or society.[30]

The police system is no different. Michael Blanton, writing on police discretion, notes that, "The police officer's judgement is usually based more on the popular morality than on the law; he sees his office as having moral authority as well as legal, which often leads to emotional involvement in the case.[31] What Blanton, and a good number of other police critics, fail to recognize is that the policeman is not an automaton capable of being completely unemotional or impartial. His particular occupational role often prescribes certain actions which, as Yinger notes, ". . . often involve privileges or *licenses* to perform acts which are deviant and forbidden outside these roles." (emphasis author's.)

Within a societal myriad the policeman functions, his role ill-defined and open to broad speculation. In order to establish an adequate field construct one must be aware of functional equivalents (the relationship between roles) and specify conditions under which various individual responses are made. Further, noting the ways in which individual responses lead back into the social system should lead to an exploration of the range

---

[30]Blumer, *Sociological Analysis,* p. 686.
[31]Michael Blanton, "Police Discretion," *New Society,* Vol. 2, No. 48, 1963, p. 6.

of these effects in a given setting. Thus, "positions and roles can be compared and contracted along a number of dimensions that are related to the direction and strength of the position and role influence."

The need for such an approach in studying the police cannot be overstated. If police service is to be improved, and the ambiguity of the police role clarified, we must begin to look at it in its perspective to society.

CHAPTER 5

Psychological Consequences of the Police Role

Hans H. Toch

Dr. Hans J. Toch is Professor of Psychology, School of Criminal Justice, State University of New York at Albany. He is the author of *Legal and Criminal Psychology* and *The Social Psychology of Social Movements.* This article is based on a text prepared for symposium presentation at the annual meeting of the American Psychological Association, September, 1963.

Gilbert and Sullivan were probably joking when they proclaimed that "a policeman's lot is not a happy one," but law enforcement officers tend to view this hypothesis as an established fact. In professional publications and in conferences concerned with police problems, the theme of the "unhappy lot" emerges with increasing frequency. The composite picture is that of dedicated missionaries hemmed in by political interference, blocked by deluded judges, cramped by tightfisted legislators, and misrepresented by a bad press. Worst of all, police spokesmen contend, the man in the street seems inclined to bite the hand that protects him. He blames the police for inevitable failures, and reacts to successful enforcement as if it represented a personal threat.

These things are perceived by some police officials in an age when police strive for the respectability of a profession. Professionalization, in turn, may be wishfully equated with currently scarce benefits, such as higher pay scales, greater job security, improved selection procedures, more sophisticated training programs, foolproof scientific methods and appropriate public esteem.

It is probably obvious that the policeman's portrait of the "policeman's lot" is only partially correct. If the situation were exactly as charac-

From Hans H. Toch, "Psychological Consequences of the Police Role, " *Police,* September-October 1965, volume 10, number 1. Reprinted through the courtesy of Charles C. Thomas, Publisher, Springfield, Illinois.

terized, only saints or madmen would be tempted to enter the police profession, whereas experience tells us that most law enforcers cannot be classified under either of these headings. However, many police *do* view themselves as playing a saintly role in a hostile world, and *this is a fact.* Their puzzlement and annoyance is also a fact, as is the hostility or indifference to police on the part of various publics, including other persons involved in the administration of justice.

What accounts for these ill feelings and resentments? How can the police be aided to find contentment and acceptance? I shall briefly comment on these two questions. As a working premise, I should like to propose that *the police role itself, as defined and practiced today, is conducive to social tensions and therefore self-defeating.* This assumption implies that greater police efficiency requires not only increased sophistication, but also *a redefinition of the role.*

What are some of the psychological and social consequences of the police role? The most obvious one, of course, is the impact of *power.* The law enforcement officer embodies the law so visibly and directly, that neither he nor the public find it easy to differentiate law and enforcement. Police speak of "contempt for the law," for instance, when they refer to persons who don't like the police. This equating of "law" and "police" is not merely semantic juggling designed to sanctify the police function but also a recognition of the broad and confused nature of the police concept in the public mind. As Bruce Smith pointed out,

> Relatively few citizens can recall ever having seen a judge; fewer still, a prosecutor, coroner, sheriff, probation officer or prison warden. The patrolman is thoroughly familiar to all. His uniform picks him out from the crowd so distinctly that he becomes the living symbol of the law—not always of its majesty, but certainly of its power. Whether the police like it or not, they are forever marked men.[1]

A police officer is partly a *symbol,* and police work consists to some extent in the creation of illusions based on symbolic attributes. It is in this fashion that an empty police car can slow down turnpike traffic, and that the presence of half a dozen officers can control a large crowd.

The police uniform is viewed as a symbolic license to judge and to punish. It does so, not only by representing the right to arrest, but also by connoting the punishing role in general. It is for this reason, for instance, that children may be threatened by means of pointed references to policemen. The punishing role does not lend itself to the promotion of a lovable

---

[1]B. Smith, "Municipal police administration." *Annals Amer. Acad. Pol. Soc. Science,* 146:1-27. p.22.

public image. It is true that law enforcement officers could echo the words
of Colonel Calverly,

> "It's one in a million
> That any civilian
> My figure and form will surpass,"

but this statement hardly takes into account the feelings of civilians.

"Policemanship," in one sense, is an easy game to play because members of the police are "one down" to begin with. They meet police officers on an unequal basis, with helplessness implicit in every encounter. The application of a sanction, such as a traffic ticket, places adults in a position equivalent to childhood experiences involving the use of sanctions, and this induces appropriate feelings of childish impotence and sheepishness. These feelings may present problems for persons who like to view themselves as autonomous, responsible adults. Strong anti-police sentiments on such occasions may therefore constitute defensive reactions against regression to the role of a child. In other words, it is the broader connotations of police actions, rather than their direct impact, which may produce most public resentment. These connotations can probably be ameliorated, but hardly completely eradicated, by police courtesy and sensitivity. Ultimately, the typical contact between police and public remains one in which there is essentially one-way communication against a backdrop of latent power.

This type of contact is not only detrimental to police-public relations, but also psychologically harmful to the police. The police officer loses his feeling of communality with the public. He exaggerates the prevalence of apathy, and sees hostility even where there is none. He interprets public resentment as an indication of his inevitable separation from the social order. According to William Wartley, who has studied police attitudes and values, the typical police officer

> regards the public as his enemy, feels his occupation to be in conflict with the community, and regards himself to be a pariah. The experience and the feeling give rise to a collective emphasis on secrecy, an attempt to coerce respect from the public, and a belief that almost any means are legitimate in completing an important arrest. These are for the policeman basic occupational values. They arise from his experience, take precedence over his legal responsibilities, are central to an understanding of his conduct, and form the occupational contexts within which violence gains its meaning.[2]

The police officer also becomes conscious of the fact that he does represent a source of power. This awareness of power can often lead to its

---

[2] W. A. Westley, "Violence and the police," *Amer. J. Sociol.,* 59:34-44, p. 35.

self-justified use. Law enforcement personnel can come to take pride in their power potential, and to view the display of power ("firmness," "authority," etc.) as an end in itself. It is in this spirit that a police official in Alabama encouraged spectators to abuses of police power with the words, "I want 'em to see the dogs work. Look at the niggers run."

The following item makes the premise even more explicit:

> In Salt Lake City, after Mrs. Agnes Haynes complained that cops surrounded her car on a downtown street, searched her as an armed-robbery suspect and left without apology while a crowd looked on, Police Chief W. C. Skousen issued a proclamation telling all citizens that if they should find themselves in a similar situation, they should 'accept the inconvenience as an exceptional opportunity to observe how police function when apprehending a criminal.'[3]

A related consequence of the police role is the fact that the use of and encounter with violence in police work create a tendency to perceive violence with comparative ease. Richard Schulte and I were able to show, for instance, that one product of an excellent police training program was an increased facility to see pictures of violent actions. We discussed this finding as follows:

> Unusual experiences, after all, become 'familiar' in the course of *any* specialization. The funeral director or the medical intern, for instance, may learn to accept corpses as part and parcel of everyday experience. The dedicated nudist may acquire a special conception of familiar attire. The pilot may come to find nothing unusual about glancing down out of a window at a bank of clouds.
>
> In the same fashion, law enforcement training can produce a revision of unconscious expectations of violence and crime. This does not mean that the law enforcer necessarily comes to exaggerate the prevalence of violence. It means that the law enforcer may come to accept crime as a familiar personal experience, one which he himself is not surprised to encounter. The acceptance of crime as a familiar personal experience in turn increases the *ability or readiness to perceive violence where clues to it are potentially available.*[4]

In similar fashion, the fact that police work entails disproportionately many contacts with socially underprivileged and emotionally disturbed persons who do not display typical middle class conduct, can shape police perception of human nature and of appropriate social behavior. Don Kooken,

---

[3] *Time,* January 19, 1959.

[4] H. Toch and R. Schulte, "Readiness to perceive violence as a result of police training," *Brit. J. Psychol.,* 52:389-393, p. 392.

formerly Captain in the Indiana State Police, points out in his volume on *Ethics in Police Service,* that

> Numerous contacts with antisocial persons are likely to cause police-men to assume a veneer of hardness. They often entertain the erroneous belief that courteous treatment of law violators by a policeman is an indication of weakness, of cringing or of servility. They will say that criminals are not entitled to the treatment accorded to gentlemen.[5]

Westley reports that "the police believe that certain groups of persons will respond only to fear and rough treatment. In the city studied, they defined both Negroes and slum dwellers in this category."[6] By thus unfavorably categorizing one segment of the community, the police involved create a double standard in human relations. Placement in the "outgroup" deprives a person of his right to customary courtesies, to friendly consideration and to frank communication. It becomes, at the very least, possible to express your contempt for him, and to deceive him and misrepresent your intentions when expedient. At worst, overt violence may be psychologically justified. Thus a former police chief in South Dakota who had subjected Indians to a variety of inhuman treatments, insisted to *The New York Times* that

> it was always necessary to handle Indians 'firmly.' The Indian is not a law-abiding person,' he said. 'As near as I can figure out, it's about like the Negroes down South: You can't let them get the upper hand.[7]

To the extent to which such compartments in the mind accommodating "gentlemen" and "criminals" or "law abiding" and "non-law abiding" citizens break down (as perforce they must to some extent sooner or later) the police officer also runs the risk of becoming a boor in relation to his friends and neighbors. He can develop a somewhat paranoid outlook in his social perceptions, with a tendency to assign evil intentions to others. *Society can come to be viewed as a vicious "dog eat dog" jungle, in which only force can insure peace and harmony.* It is consequently not surprising to find professional law enforcement groups lobbying for the death penalty, for long-term imprisonment of drug addicts, and for other legislation which reflects punitive thinking about social ills.

Chief Hoover of the FBI illustrates the prevalence of this outlook among even relatively sophisticated enforcement personnel. Bloch and Geiss succinctly summarize one of Mr. Hoover's comments about current trends in corrections. They point out that in the course of a short statement

---

[5]D. L. Kooken, *Ethics in Police Service* (Springfield: Charles C. Thomas, 1959), p. 22.
[6]Westley: "Violence," p. 40.
[7]*The New York Times,* June 13, 1962.

Mr. Hoover describes criminologists as "sentimental yammerheads" and "moronic adults" who show "asinine behavior" and "maudlin sentiment" and "inherent criminal worship." Hoover would prefer to ignore the "moo-cow sentimentality" of "hoity-toity professors."[8] Police work would appear to lead to a stress on crime as a *social problem* rather than as a *social product.*

Another aspect of the police role which reinforces this development of the law enforcer's jaundiced eye is the premium which is placed on the assignment of blame, and on securing formal convictions. Since the police officer obtains his rewards and satisfactions from the successful identification of persons responsible for misconduct, and since such success is "confirmed" through prosecution, conviction and sentencing, any interference with this sequence may be experienced as terribly frustrating. In instances where the law itself blocks the road from suspicion to disposition, the law becomes an enemy of its ostensible servants. This is almost invariably the case with laws, court decisions and administrative regulations which set limits to methods which may be used in obtaining evidence or in processing suspected offenders. Police can no more be expected to subscribe to the premise that persons whom they perceive as violators must be protected, than dedicated hunters are likely to grant the immunity of deer.

When law is seen as conflicting with enforcement or when it presents enforcement difficulties, the police sometimes operate extra-legally. They may harass prostitutes or homosexuals, for instance, when there is no recourse to prosecution. They may stage raids or "tip-overs" against gambling establishments when there are insufficient grounds for a search warrant. They may routinely frisk or search people in dark streets without reasonable grounds.[9]

When the law *does* set limits, the police frequently test them. An example is the practice of holding arrested persons in police stations for the maximum amounts of time tolerated by the courts, as documented in a study of detentions by the Chicago police between 1956 and 1958.[10]

In summary, the label "law *enforcer*" is somewhat deceptive. Police, in the words of Bruce Smith, "have made furtive, and occasionally open efforts to circumvent the law under which they operate. Laws and ordinances which were unpopular have been ignored, and others which were persistently violated have only occasionally been enforced."[11]

---

[8]H. A. Bloch and G. Geiss, *Man, Crime and Society* (New York: Random House, 1962).

[9]Material to support these generalizations is provided in an unpublished pilot project report "The Administration of Criminal Justice in the United States" circulated by the American Bar Foundation (1959).

[10]American Civil Liberties Union, *Secret Detention by the Chicago Police* (Glencoe: The Free Press, 1959.)

[11]Smith, "Municipal Police Administration," p. 1.

This situation is not in and of itself alarming or surprising. Full law enforcement is impossible. Many laws, such as those governing private sexual behavior, or those prohibiting any and all forms of gambling, are not passed with the intention of being enforced. Many laws are out of date, unrealistic, unenforceable or blantantly magical. The police are keenly aware of this fact, and have their own views about the relative merits of particular acts of legislation. Moreover, they are forced to allocate meager resources, to evaluate the circumstances surrounding each offense and to adjust to a variety of social pressures. Police discretion is thus an inescapable fact.[12]

What poses problems is not police discretion, but the frame of reference which governs the way it is exercised. An essentially punitive and negative view of the world leads to decisions in which conflicts with the community are created and reinforced. If the aim is to maximize enforcement at the expense of other values, the resulting atmosphere makes it more difficult to achieve effective enforcement. Police officers of the last generation were unable to appreciate this paradox, and even sophisticated police administrators today tend to attribute public resentment against the police to ignorance or to educational deficiencies resulting in a lack of respect for duly constituted authority.

Pioneer efforts to change the orientation behind police discretion have mainly centered on problems of race relations. After the war, a number of large municipal police departments established "human relations" training programs, and several texts and manuals for this purpose appeared. By 1950, this type of course was offered in over thirty cities. Workshops, seminars and institutes dealing with ethnic tensions and other community relations problems today awaken considerable police interest.[13] Many departments have created permanent community relations units that meet and work with civilians of all kinds. This type of development is one which suggests that the traditional police role is in fact expanding.

Other trends toward change are apparent in police work with juveniles. Units within police departments have begun to deal with youngsters from a therapeutic vantage point. Police athletic leagues and similar community programs illustrate efforts to enter into the delinquency prevention area. Attempts to improve public relations have ranged from sponsored tours of police stations to the creation of consultant or advisory boards.

Such developments are to date scattered and sometimes represent superficial gestures because many law enforcement officers view various

[12]H. Goldstein, "Full enforcement vs. police discretion not to invoke criminal process." *National Institute on Police and Community Relations,* 9th Meeting, May 22, 1963, East Lansing, Michigan.

[13]L. A. Radelet, "Police-community relations." *Social Order,* 1960, 219-225.

innovations as unpolicelike and threatening. Their view is not without a basis in fact. Police agencies which begin to render community services, to struggle with problems of crime causation, to engage in prevention programs and to assume other positive stances, are bound to start functioning differently, even in their traditional roles. Over three decades ago, Vollmer discussed the "socializing influence" of policewomen trained in psychiatric social work on their male colleagues in the Berkeley Police Department.[14] Such influence can be very real, provided institutional resistance does not block it. The infiltration of police departments by platoons of social workers in uniform would threaten two powerful institutions, both of which could be expected to react. The police, viewing their new colleagues as a malignant tumor in their collective anatomy, would at best treat them with the tolerance accorded to visiting aliens. The therapeutic professions, intent on maintaining their presumed monopoly on human relations, would distinguish between academically trained police officers carrying the sacred *imprimatur,* and the rest, whose duty it would be to conform to the traditional police stereotype. Obviously, these two types of institutional pressure can reinforce each other. Together, they can insure the segregation of therapeutic personnel in police settings.

To circumvent the push toward the treatment oriented ghetto, the arbitrary boundaries between professional human relations and professional law enforcement must be gradually *erased.* On the police side, a possible first step is the introduction of new content into police curricula. This might include sensitivity training and elements of therapeutic technique, intensive acquaintance with contemporary social problems such as urbanization, discrimination, poverty, unemployment and their social psychological consequences, a course concretizing the implications of the Bill of Rights, and seminars in which aspects of the police role and their subjective correlates are honestly examined. Police candidates can thus come to view themselves as playing a crucial role in producing the type of social order in which crime and other symptoms of interpersonal conflict are reduced. Such a view can be fully justified. Unlike many of us, law enforcement officers are not encumbered with archaic quasi-medical or quasi-educational models of social change. The police thus may be in a unique position to lead the way toward the redefinition of professional roles which the pressures of our day demand.

This, however, is probably the Utopian view. A conservative prediction would be that the police role will increasingly emphasize human relations and social involvement. As a result, the New Police Officer will come to occupy a happier and more secure place in his community. The Old Police Officer, and most of the rest of us, will be fighting this promising trend every inch of the way.

---

[14]A. Vollmer, "Meet the lady cops," *Survey,* 63:702-704.

CHAPTER 6

Law Enforcement Policy: The Police Role

The President's Commission on Law Enforcement and Administration of Justice

Law enforcement has always been a difficult task. It is especially difficult in a society such as ours that has so heterogeneous and mobile a population; that has so prosperous an economy; that has so high a degree of urbanization, with its accompanying congestion and anonymity; and that places so high a value on individual freedom, upon equality under the law, and upon local control over the police power.

The current widespread concern with crime and violence, particularly in large cities, commands a rethinking of the function of the police in American society. It calls for a reassessment of the kinds of resources and support that the police need to respond more adequately to the demands that we make upon them.

In this effort to look at the police function, the term "police" is used to refer to all persons having law enforcement responsibility, but major emphasis is upon the departments and the police officers, particularly patrolmen, who have responsibility in the large urban areas for dealing with the wide range of social and behavioral problems that are of primary concern today.

The Range of Problems
Confronting the Police

While each person has a somewhat different impression of the nature of the police function, based primarily upon his personal experiences and contacts with police officers, there is a widespread popular conception of the

From the President's Commission on Law Enforcement and Administration of Justice, "Law Enforcement Policy: The Police Role," *Task Force Report: The Police,* 1967. This report, "Law Enforcement Policy: The Police Role," was prepared by Professors Frank Remington and Herman Goldstein of the University of Wisconsin, College of Law, located at Madison. Reprinted through the courtesy of the Superintendent of Documents, U.S. Government Printing Office, Washington, D.C.

police, supported by news and entertainment media. Through these, the police have come to be viewed as a body of men continually engaged in the exciting, dangerous, and competitive enterprise of apprehending and prosecuting criminals. Emphasis upon this one aspect of police functioning has led to a tendency on the part of both the public and the police to underestimate the range and complexity of the total police task.

A police officer assigned to patrol duties in a large city is typically confronted with at most a few serious crimes in the course of a single tour of duty. He tends to view such involvement, particularly if there is some degree of danger, as constituting real police work. But it is apparent that he spends considerably more time keeping order, settling disputes, finding missing children, and helping drunks than he does in responding to criminal conduct which is serious enough to call for arrest, prosecution, and conviction. This does not mean that serious crime is unimportant to the policeman. Quite the contrary is true. But it does mean that he performs a wide range of other functions which are of a highly complex nature and which often involve difficult social, behavioral and political problems.

Individual misbehavior with which the police must deal, for example, ranges from that of the highly dangerous, assaultive sex offender to that of the petty thief or common drunk. Organized criminal activity varies from that affecting a large segment of a community, such as the "policy" or "numbers" rackets, to the two-party agreement between a burglar and the person buying his stolen property. The peace-keeping function of the police requires that they deal with human conflicts ranging from large-scale rioting to disputes between husbands and their wives. Laws enacted to preserve order within a community require the police to perform a variety of tasks, from enforcing traffic regulations to assuring that dogs, peddlers, and various businesses have their proper licenses. And, in addition, the police are called upon to provide certain emergency services which their availability and skills qualify them to fulfill—services largely unrelated to crime or potential crime situations.

It is generally assumed that police have a preventive and protective role as well. Thus, for example, the police endeavor, through such activities as patrol, to lessen opportunities for the commission of crimes; they initiate programs to reduce the racial tensions that exist in the ghettos of large cities; they conduct educational programs to promote safe driving and prevent accidents. Police are expected to afford protection to individuals who are likely to be victimized or are in some other way prey to harm—the down-and-out drunk, the mentally ill, or the naive patrons of vice activity who may be subjecting themselves to the risk of robbery or worse. Moreover, they are expected to preserve the right of free speech—even when that speech is intensely antagonistic and likely to incite opposition.

To fulfill their obligations, the police are given formal authority to invoke the criminal process—to arrest, to prosecute, and to seek a conviction. But making use of this traditional process is much more complex than is commonly assumed, due to the infinite complications that distinguish separate incidents. The police must make important judgments about what conduct is in fact criminal; about the allocation of scarce resources; and about the gravity of each individual incident and the proper steps that should be taken.

When the police are dealing with highly dangerous conduct, for example, they are expected to arrest the offender, and participate in his prosecution in order to insure correctional treatment. But when the conduct is not considered particularly dangerous as, for example, in the case of the common drunk, police may conclude—given the volume of cases—that it is not worth the effort to invoke the full criminal process. Often the police will simply pick up the drunk, detain him overnight, and release him when sober.

Domestic disputes account for a high percentage of the total number of incidents to which the police are summoned. They generally occur late at night and result in a call for the police because an assault has taken place, because there is the potential for violence, because the neighbors are disturbed, or simply because a low income couple has no other source of help in arbitrating marital conflicts. Given the nature of such disputes, the formal system of arrest, prosecution, and conviction is rarely an appropriate means for dealing with them. In the absence of likely alternatives to police involvement, police officers are left with the responsibility for dealing with such situations without being adequately equipped to do so.

When criminal activity involves a "willing buyer" and a "willing seller," a somewhat different pattern of problems is present. Widespread community support for some forms of gambling activity or an ambivalent community attitude toward some forms of sexual conduct require that a police agency decide what constitutes an appropriate level of enforcement. In the absence of a complainant, police must determine the amount of resources and the investigative procedures that they should employ to discover criminal offenses.

Because a high percentage of crimes is committed by juveniles, police are frequently called upon to deal with the youthful offender. In spite of this, there remains uncertainty as to the proper role of the police in the juvenile process. In practice most incidents involving juveniles are disposed of by the police without referral to a social worker or a judge, and consequently what police do is of great significance.

Finally, police must respond to the conflicts that arise out of what has been termed the "social revolution." It is difficult, in policing such situations, to distinguish between legitimate and illegitimate group behavior and to balance the value of free expression against the risk of public disorder. The lines which must be drawn are difficult to determine and call for policy decisions quite different from those made in traditional crimes like burglary.

It has been argued that many of the complex problems of the criminal process could be solved by more narrowly defining the police function. If drunkenness were dealt with by medically qualified people, for example, police would not have to contend with the habitual drunk. If family problems were handled by social work agencies, police would not have to deal with the many domestic and juvenile matters which now confront them. If the substantive criminal law were revised, police would not be confronted with the difficult decisions resulting from broad prohibitions against narcotics, gambling, prostitution, and homosexual activity. And if increased efforts were made to solve some of the social ills that give rise to criminality, the police could be relieved of many of their crime prevention functions.

But little effective action has been taken to develop the kind of resources required by the adoption of any of these alternatives. Some courts have recently held that it is unconstitutional to treat habitual drunkenness as a criminal offense. Presumably, this means that the police should no longer be concerned with public drunkenness, although it is possible that the police might be involved through a process which is medically rather than criminally oriented. But the test of such decisions is in whether they result in a more adequate and humane method of dealing with drunks rather than in their conformity with principle. Because few efforts have been made to develop alternatives to police involvement, the consequence of police not taking action is that drunks would be left to lie where they fall.

Proposals to relieve the police of what are essentially social services have also been lacking in their consideration of the relationship of such services to the incidence of more serious crimes. Domestic disturbances, for example, often culminate in a serious assault or a homicide. The down-and-out drunk is almost a certain victim of a theft if he is left to lie on the street and has any article of value on him. The streetwalking prostitute may, in one sense, be primarily a social problem, but many streetwalkers engage regularly in arranging the robbery of their patrons as a supplement to their incomes.

It might be desirable for agencies other than the police to provide community services that bear no relationship to crime or potential crime situations. But the failure of such agencies to develop and the relationship between the social problems in question and the incidence of crime suggest that the police are likely to remain, for some time, as the only 24-hour-a-day, 7-day-a-week agency that is spread over an entire city in a way which makes it possible for them to respond quickly to incidents of this kind.

If, as seems apparent, continued reliance is to be placed upon law enforcement agencies for meeting the wide range of functions that now comprise their task, it is important that attention be turned to the manner in which they perform those functions.

The Police Response

To urge recognition of the fact that the police task covers a wide range of activities and that it is highly complex is not to maintain that the police adequately fulfill all of their functions. It is obviously difficult and often impossible for police officers to respond in an appropriate manner to the numerous incidents called to their attention. They are under constant pressure, especially in highly congested areas, to handle a volume of cases that is beyond their capacity—forcing them to develop "shortcut" responses to run-of-the-mill situations. They lack adequate training with respect to some of the more complex social problems. And there has been little effort to provide individual officers with the guidelines which they require if they are expected to make more effective and judicious decisions in disposing of the incidents which come to their attention. In the absence of adequate resources, training, and guidance, the tendency is for individual police officers to attempt to meet largely by improvisation the varied demands made upon them.

Some indication of the manner in which this is achieved can be gathered from the following account of an observer who accompanied two police officers functioning in a congested urban area during a tour of duty that began in the early evening hours:

> After receiving routine instructions at the roll call held at the precinct station, Officers Jones and Smith located the car to which they were assigned and started out for the area in which they would spend their tour of duty. While enroute, the officers received instructions from the dispatcher to handle a fight in an alley. Upon arrival, they found a group of young men surrounded by their parents, wives, and children.
>
> One of the young men, A, had a couple of knives in his hand. While the knives were within legal limits, Officer Smith took them (and later disposed of them in a refuse container). Another of the young men, B, stood by his mother. The third, C, stood by A, from whom the knives had been taken.
>
> The mother of B was the complainant. She claimed that C had attacked her son with a knife and she demanded that C be arrested and jailed. C readily admitted he had been fighting with B, but he claimed that he had just tried to protect A. C had been drinking and was very belligerent. He indicated a readiness to take on anyone and everyone, including the police. He kept shouting and was obviously antagonizing the officers.
>
> A attempted to explain the situation. He stated that he had been the one originally fighting B and that C had merely come to his aid. B concurred in this account of what had taken place, though he did not reflect very much concern as the supposed victim of the attack.

A's mother-in-law interrupted at this time to claim that A was innocent; that the fight was B's fault. B's mother did not stand for this accusation and entered the fray.

The confusion spread. Other police officers, in the meantime, had arrived at the scene and the number of observers had grown. Officers Jones and Smith decided to take the participants to the precinct station where conditions would make it possible to make a more orderly inquiry.

At the station, the families and participants were separated and talked with individually. The mother of B insisted on signing a complaint against C and A, but finally relented as to A when he promised not to allow C to come to his apartment.

C was then formally arrested and charged with disorderly conduct. A and B were sent home with their wives and mothers. By charging C with disorderly conduct rather than a more serious crime, the officers observed that they were saving themselves some paperwork. They felt that their action in letting the mother sign a complaint against the "loudmouthed" C had served to pacify her.

After filling out the arrest reports on C, Officers Jones and Smith notified the dispatcher that they were available and resumed patrolling. But in several minutes they were dispatched to another beat to handle a domestic situation.

A young Indian girl met them at the door. There obviously had been a fight; the place was a shambles. Furniture was broken, food was on the floor, and beer cans were scattered everywhere. The girl gave an explanation to which the police officers were very much accustomed—her husband had gotten drunk, had become angry, and had gone on the "warpath." When she told the officers that her husband had been behaving in this manner for 5 years, any sympathy which they had for the girl disappeared. They explained that they were not in a position to do anything for her since her husband was not there. They advised her to go to court to obtain either a warrant for his arrest or to arrange for the issuance of a peace bond.

Upon reporting back in service with the dispatcher, Smith and Jones were assigned a domestic problem involving a couple who had been married for 27 years. The couple had only recently begun to have trouble getting along. But when the difficulty started, it was serious. The wife had been attacked by the husband a week previously and had suffered a concussion. She was now back from the hospital and wanted her husband locked up. The woman led the officers to the apartment, but the husband had, in the interval, left. They then went through the ritual of telling the wife the procedure by which she could obtain a warrant or a peace bond. They also told her to call back if she had any more trouble.

After this call, there was a short lull in activity, during which the officers patrolled the southeast corner of their assigned area. They were then told to see a complainant at a designated address.

The complainant, it turned out, was a landlord. One of his tenants had a child who had been bothering other tenants. The mother had been told to quiet the child down, but she apparently had not done so. In addition, the mother was behind in the rent. The landlord had attempted to serve her with an eviction notice but had not been able to find her at home.

The mother was at work at a lounge and the landlord asked the officers to serve the eviction notice on her there. The officers explained that they would not be able to do so since the lounge was outside the district to which they were assigned. The landlord countered this by contending that he had been a friend of the police and that he had helped them in the past. He also stressed that he was a taxpayer. Officer Jones reacted by requesting the dispatcher to assign a police officer to meet the landlord at the lounge and help him in serving the notice. The officers, in this manner, disposed of the incident.

Smith and Jones were next dispatched to investigate a noisy party. When they arrived at the scene, they found the party was going "full blast." They knocked and, when the door was answered, Officer Smith asked for the host. He told the person who then came to the door that someone had complained and that they would have to "hold the noise down." The host and others who were listening in readily agreed. When Officer Jones notified the dispatcher that the first party had been quieted, the men were dispatched to another.

The officers could not find the second party and could hear no loud noise at the address which had been given. Officer Jones requested the apartment number from the dispatcher. Both officers then went to the apartment. When the hostess came to the door, Officer Smith told her that someone had complained about a loud party. He told her that while the party seemed quiet enough at the moment, she should be careful because she evidently had some touchy neighbors.

Smith and Jones stopped for a coke before placing themselves back in service. While they were parked, Officer Jones spotted a "downer" in the doorway of the office occupied by the city council member representing the area. They called for a patrol wagon. They then went over to the drunk, awakened him, and asked him some questions. He had been sleeping and eating wherever he could, having slept the previous night in a "flophouse" downtown. When the wagon arrived, the "downer" was placed in it and taken to jail.

When the officers reported back in service, they were immediately assigned to a juvenile disturbance at a hotdog stand. They did not rush to the scene, since they had been there numerous times in the past.

The owner of the hotdog stand would not force the youths to leave, letting them stand about until the whole parking area was congested. He would then call the police. Smith and Jones dispersed the crowd. One youth started to resist but moved on when Officer Jones threatened him with jail.

The officers informed the dispatcher that they had handled the problem at the hotdog stand and then resumed patrol. They had traveled several blocks from the hotdog stand when they observed a driver run a red light. The officers gave chase and pulled the vehicle over to the side of the street. The motorist, it was revealed, had just returned from Vietnam and Officer Smith felt that he deserved a break. He released him with a suggestion that he be more careful. While Officer Smith was talking to the veteran, Officer Jones spotted a fight between two youths. He ran over, broke it up, and talked to the combatants. He sent them on their way with a warning.

The officers requested permission from the dispatcher to take time out to eat, but he responded by sending them back to the first party that they had quieted.

A great deal of damage had been done by the time they arrived. The youths had gotten drunk and loud. They had created a disturbance when the party broke up and the manager of the building had called the police. The officers advised the manager to exercise more care in deciding upon the people to whom she rented her apartments. Since the persons causing the disturbance had already gone, there was nothing else that the officers could do; they departed.

They again asked permission to take time for food, but were instead dispatched to the scene of a stabbing. They hurried to the location, which turned out to be a new portable public swimming pool.

There were three persons present—two lifeguards and a watchman. One of the lifeguards had been knifed. He was placed in the police car and officers started off for the nearest hospital. Enroute, the victim told the officers that a man had tried to go swimming in the pool after it had been closed for the night. When the lifeguard attempted to stop the intruder, he was stabbed during the scuffle. The other lifeguard called the police. At the hospital, the officers made out their reports while the victim received medical care. They later returned to the scene but found no additional information or people who would assist in the identification of the assailant. The reports were turned in for attention by the detectives.

The officers then, without asking, took their meal break, after which they reported that they had completed their work on the stabbing. They were dispatched to a party disturbance. Upon arriving at the scene, they encountered a young fellow walking out of the building carrying a can of beer.

He was stopped and questioned about the party. Officer Smith told him that "this is not Kentucky" and drinking on the street is not allowed. The fellow agreed to take the officer up to the party. When he turned to lead the way, Officer Jones observed a knife in the youth's back pocket. He took the knife away. There was not much going on at the party. Those present were admonished to keep it quiet.

Back on patrol, the officers cruised for a short period. It was soon quitting time, so they headed in the direction of the precinct station. As they turned a corner, Officer Smith saw a couple of fellows drinking on the street, but rather than get involved at this time, nothing was done.

This day in the life of Officers Jones and Smith reflects the broad and varied demands for police service, the pressures under which it is provided, and the informal and improvised responses which tend to develop. While neither articulated nor officially recognized, common responses obviously tend to develop in frequently recurring situations.

A new police officer quickly learns these responses through his associations with more seasoned officers. The fact that a response is routine does not mean that it is satisfactory. To the contrary, many routine responses are applied on the basis of indefensible and improper criteria. But once developed, the routine response is generally immune to critical reevaluation unless a crisis situation should arise. Because of their informal character, such responses tend not to be influenced by developments in police training. And, because they consist of the accumulated experiences of frontline officers, they tend to take on a vitality which continues even without the active support of the higher echelon of police administration.

Unique situations do arise, usually where the frequency of a given kind of incident is small, for which there is no routine response. Unless time permits him to confer with his sergeant, the individual officer is left to respond without any form of guidance. Under such circumstances, the decision of the individual officer will reflect his own personal values and opinions about people and about group behavior.

Improvement in the capacity of law enforcement agencies to perform the essential and highly sensitive functions that comprise the total police task requires a willingness on the part of the public and the police to take several bold steps.

There must, in the first place, be a more widespread recognition on the part of the citizenry and the police of both the range and the complexity of the problems which the police confront. Secondly, there must be a willingness on the part of the police to respond to these problems by the careful development and articulation of policies and practices which are subject to continuing reevaluation in the light of changing social conditions.

Police Attitude Toward Their Role in the Development of Law Enforcement Policies

The absence of carefully developed policies to guide police officers in handling the wide variety of situations which they confront is in sharp contrast to the efforts taken to provide detailed guidance for other aspects of police operations.

Like all military and semimilitary organizations, a police agency is governed in its internal management by a large number of standard operating procedures. Elaborate regulations exist dealing with such varied phases of an agency's internal operations as the receipt of complaints from citizens, the keeping of records, and the transportation of nonpolice personnel in police vehicles. Established procedures govern such matters as the replacement of vehicles, uniforms, and ammunition. Police agencies also have established policies with respect to certain public service functions, but these usually do not involve important criminal law issues. There are policies, for example, which provide guidance in determining whether to transport a person requiring emergency medical assistance, in deciding whether to take a stray dog into custody, and relating to the inspection of the premises of a vacationing resident.

Progressive police agencies have developed sophisticated methods for establishing procedures in these areas, methods which call for analyzing the basic problems, weighing the desirability of various alternative solutions, and then developing and adopting criteria to serve as a basis for the decisions of operating personnel.

In contrast, there have been only occasional efforts to make use of a deliberative planning process to develop policies to guide and control police officers in dealing with the wide variety of situations that require the exercise of some form of police authority.

One of the most adequate statements of enforcement policy was produced in New York State in conjunction with the enactment in 1964 of the new "stop and frisk" law. Police and prosecuting officials recognized that this newly legislated authority to stop and question persons short of arrest and to subject them to a frisk was vulnerable to attack on constitutional grounds, and they were aware that opposition to its passage would result in its implementation being closely watched.

It was for these reasons that the New York City Police Department and the District Attorney's Office joined with other law enforcement agencies throughout the state to publish a set of guidelines for operating personnel prior to the date on which the new law became effective.[1] Five pages of specific requirements, limitations, prohibitions, and examples were used to elaborate upon the legislation which itself is contained in two relatively brief paragraphs. Emphasis was not placed upon defining the law so much as it was upon urging the police to exercise restraint and to act well within the outer limits of their prescribed authority.

In the area of traffic enforcement, a number of jurisdictions have developed "tolerance policies" which establish the point above the speed limit at which officers are to warn a motorist or issue a summons to him, and also provide criteria for making similar decisions with regard to other types of motor vehicle violations. Such policies are most frequently found in State police organizations, reflecting a need for providing guidelines for

---

[1]See Attachment A, a Policy Statement on the New York "Stop-and-Frisk" and "Knock, Knock" Laws Prepared by New York State Combined Council of Law Enforcement Officials, June 1, 1964, appearing at the end of this chapter.

the isolated officer who cannot frequently consult with his supervisor or with fellow officers. They also reflect an organizational response to the demands for fairness and uniformity voiced by the cross-section of citizens who commit traffic violations—a group with the capability of insisting upon consistency in law enforcement.

There also have been some efforts on the part of police agencies to formulate policies relating to the disposition of juvenile offenders. This has, for the most part, consisted of an attempt to develop criteria to serve as a basis for deciding whether to release a juvenile offender to his parents, refer him to a social agency, or process him through the juvenile court.

Significant as these efforts are, they deal with but a small portion of the total police responsibility.

There are a number of factors which account for the general failure of police to develop policies for dealing with crime and potential crime situations, in contrast to their willingness to do so for issues of internal management of the department.

In the first place, devising procedures for handling routine matters of internal management can be done with relative certainty and assurance that the decision will not be a subject of major debate in the community. Few people are concerned about these issues. To the extent that there is public interest, police seem confident of the propriety of their making policy decisions and of their ability to defend decisions that are made. In contrast, procedures for frisking suspects in high crime areas, for dispersing crowds which gather, and for deciding who is to be arrested inevitably involve difficult and sensitive questions of public policy.

Many police administrators are caught in a conflict between their desire for effective, aggressive police action and the requirements of law and propriety. Direct confrontation of policy issues would inevitably require the police administrator to face the fact that some police practices, although considered effective, do not conform to constitutional, legislative, or judicial standards. By adopting a "let sleeping dogs lie" approach, the administrator avoids a direct confrontation and thus is able to support "effective" practices without having to decide whether they meet the requirements of law.

The police administrator has greater control over management questions than he does over the criminal justice process, responsibility for which he shares with the legislature, the courts, the prosecutor, and other agencies. The fact that the courts in particular have assumed increasing responsibility for control in this area has resulted in a prevalent attitude by police administrators that criminal justice policy decisions are not their concern. As a consequence, neither police training nor research has been directed toward these basic policy questions.

The reluctance of the police administrator to deal explicitly with important enforcement policies is reflected in a common administrative attitude toward "tolerance limits" developed in the traffic field which are usually maintained with a high degree of official secrecy. The reluctance to publicize "tolerance limits" reflects several factors: (1) a concern that the administrative action which they reflect would be criticized as a perversion of legislative intent—a concern which gives rise to the basic issue of the propriety of police policymaking; (2) a fear that publication would lead to a public debate as to what constitutes an appropriate tolerance and would lead to arguments between the officer and the offender in a given case—a concern which relates to the willingness of police to be held publicly accountable for the policy decisions which they make; (3) a concern that the existence of such a document might be used as a basis for litigation in those situations in which an officer chooses to enforce the be free to deviate from their own policy in an individual case without having to justify such deviation; and (4) a fear that widespread awareness of the existence of such tolerances would result in drivers adjusting their behavior, utilizing the established tolerances rather than the posted and published laws as their guides.

In contrast, police agencies that have formulated policies relating to juvenile offenders have generally made their policies public. The frankness with which discretion is acknowledged in the handling of juveniles is apparently attributable to (1) general recognition that it is both necessary and desirable for police to handle a large number of juvenile cases at the police level without referring them to the courts, an assumption less common with respect to adults; (2) a feeling that the juvenile process is in the "best interests" of the child while the adult process is punitively oriented—thus the sort of flexibility considered appropriate in dealing with the juvenile may be thought of as a denial of equal protection as it pertains to the adult offender; and (3) the usual existence of a specially trained group of juvenile police officers to whom the decisionmaking function is delegated.

The various factors that have been cited, taken together, account for the absence of a tradition for policy making in most aspects of police functioning that relate to crime and potential crime situations. As a result, individual officers continue to depend primarily upon routine responses and upon their individual judgment when functioning in these areas. And critical problems which the police confront do not receive the kind of attention which they require.

The Need to Recognize the Police as an Administrative Agency with Important Policymaking Responsibility

There are two alternative ways in which police can respond to the difficult problems currently confronting them:

(1) The first is to continue, as has been true in the past, with police making important decisions, but doing so by a process which can fairly be described as "unarticulated improvisation." This is a comfortable approach, requiring neither the police nor the community to face squarely the difficult social issues which are involved, at least until a crisis—like the current "social revolution"—necessitates drastic change.

(2) The second alternative is to recognize the importance of the administrative policymaking function of police and to take appropriate steps to make this a process which is systematic, intelligent, articulate, and responsive to external controls appropriate in a democratic society; a process which anticipates social problems and adapts to meet them before a crisis situation arises.

Of the two, the latter is not only preferable; it is essential if major progress in policing is to be made, particularly in the large, congested urban areas.

To assert the importance of the police playing an important role in the development of law enforcement policies in no way detracts from the importance of the legislature, the appellate and trial judiciary, or the prosecutor.

There is undoubted need for greater legislative attention to the important issues of the criminal law. Major improvement can be made by thorough revision and codification of the substantive law, following the lead of some of the States and the American Law Institute's Model Penal Code. There is need and opportunity to go further and to deal with some of the borderline types of criminal conduct which have either been ignored or dealt with inadequately in the revisions which have taken place. Major improvement can also be made by careful legislative attention to some of the basic and important questions involved in criminal procedure and administration. However, the opportunity for careful legislative attention to this field is complicated by appellate judicial opinions announcing increasingly specific rules of constitutional, procedural due process.

However great the legislative contribution may be, experience demonstrates that legislatures can never deal specifically with the wide variety of social and behavioral problems which confront police. Legislation was inadequate to deal in detail with regulation of the economy during the depression of the 1930's. As a consequence, there was a great increase in the number of economic regulatory agencies and in the importance of the administrative process. The administrative agency has survived as an essential vehicle for the introduction of needed flexibility and expertise in the economic regulatory process.

Certainly there is no reason to expect that legislatures can be more effective with respect to the work of police than they were with respect to the task of the economic regulatory agency. The "administrative process" and administrative flexibility, expertise, and, most important, administrative responsibility are as necessary and as appropriate with respect to the regulation of deviant social behavior as they are with respect to other governmental regulatory activity. This seems perfectly obvious. Yet the common assumption has been that the police task is ministerial, this perhaps reflecting an assumption that administrative flexibility and "the rule of law" are inconsistent. This assumption seems invalid. The exercise of administrative discretion with appropriate legislative guidance and subject to appropriate review and control is likely to be more protective of basic rights than the routine, uncritical application by police of rules of law which are often necessarily vague or overgeneralized in their language.

The judiciary has played and will undoubtedly continue to play an important role in the determination of what are proper law enforcement practices. It is a proper and traditional function of courts to listen to complaints from citizens alleging abuse of power by governmental agencies. And, through their interpretation of the Constitution, courts have defined the limitations upon the proper exercise of governmental power.

How specifically courts become involved with detailed law enforcement practices in the future may well depend upon how willing legislatures and police are themselves to assume the responsibility for defining appropriate practices and insuring conformity with them. However, no matter how specifically judicial review may deal with enforcement practices, it cannot be an adequate substitute for responsible police administrative policymaking. Judicial review is limited, for the most part, to cases which "go to court," and many important and sensitive police practices used in maintaining public order and settling minor disputes are seldom reflected in court proceedings. In addition, judicial review is most effective if it relates to carefully developed administrative policies rather than to the sporadic actions of individual police officers.

The prosecutor has an important responsibility in the development of appropriate law enforcement policies. But there are practical reasons why his involvement cannot adequately substitute for a commitment by police to the importance of their participating, in a major way, in the policymaking process. Usually the prosecutor, particularly in the large urban areas, confines his principal attention to cases in which there is a desire to prosecute or to issues which are important to the political life of the community. He seldom, for example, becomes involved in the development of a policy for settling domestic disturbances or dealing with the down-and-out drunk or streetwalking prostitute.

The problems which confront law enforcement today are sufficiently important and sufficiently complex to require the participation of the prosecutor, the legislature, and trial and appellate courts. But it is essential to realize that they require as well the mature participation of police, as a responsible administrative agency, in the development and implementation of enforcement policies. Some of the advantages to be gained by such participation are worth describing in some detail.

The Maintenance of Administrative Flexibility

The problems confronting police are such that it seems both necessary and desirable that police be given some flexibility to adapt law enforcement practices to changing social conditions. Giving police flexibility is not new. Police have had a great deal of flexibility in the past, but this has been as a result primarily of legislative default rather than deliberate, overt legislative choice. A traditional legislative response to difficult issues has been either to deal with them by an overly generalized statute as is the case with respect to gambling, or not to deal with the issue at all which has been the case, until recently at least, with respect to stopping and questioning suspects.

The practical consequence has been to leave police with broad flexibility, but the delegation of responsibility has been at best implicit and police have not taken it as a mandate to develop and articulate proper enforcement policies. Partly as a consequence of this, the trend has recently been pretty clearly in the direction of increasingly specific rules to govern police conduct. This is certainly the effect, for example, of the *Miranda* case. This trend is inspired in large part by a prevalent assumption that police are unwilling or unable to develop proper policies and to conform their practices to those policies.

In some situations, control by specific judicial or legislative rule may be workable. Where this is the case there is opportunity for major legislative contribution through carefully drafted code provisions which clearly and adequately prescribe proper police practice. In other situations, however, highly specific rules may result in an inflexibility which makes the system unable to react adequately to complex and changing conditions. For example, police have had broad flexibility in dealing with the domestic disturbance—the fight between husband and wife—which, in the large city, often results in a call to police. These disturbances occur in such widely varied circumstances and there are such varied ways of dealing with them, that it would be both difficult and unwise to try to specify the police response by categorical legislative treatment. Under present conditions, there seems obvious merit in allowing police flexibility in dealing with the domestic disturbance provided that this flexibility is not abused. The development by police of proper policies for dealing with the domestic disturbance and a demonstrated willingness to adhere to those policies would aid greatly in maintaining the desired flexibility.

A Sound Basis for the Exercise of Discretion

The results of efforts on the part of individual police officers, under current practice, to improvise their response to many of the situations they confront are often surprisingly good considering the absence of systematic planning: disputes are resolved; persons are disarmed; people not in control of their capacities are protected; and many are spared what, under some circumstances, would appear to be the undue harshness of the criminal process. But there are numerous situations in which mere volume and the lack of guidance result in an officer disposing of incidents less satisfactorily because of the ease with which the matter can be disposed of, the officer's personal attitudes toward the victim or the complainant, or his guess as to what form of disposition will most please his immediate supervisor. Similarly, command officers and entire departments will often respond to situations in a manner primarily dictated by the pressures exerted by the community, rather than by careful assessment of the competing values involved.

Proper and consistent exercise of discretion in a large organization, like a police department, will not result from the individual judgment of individual police officers in individual cases. Whatever the need for the exercise of judgment by an individual officer may be, certainly the development of overall law enforcement policies must be made at the departmental level and communicated to individual officers. This is necessary if the issues are to be adequately defined and adequately researched and if discretion is to be exercised consistently throughout the department.

Acknowledgment of the "Risk Factor"
Involved in Policing

Numerous factors contribute to the defensive posture commonly assumed by the police. Among them is an awareness on their part that members of the public will often question their exercise of discretion in a case in which subsequent developments focus attention upon an officer's decision. A police officer may, for example, locate one underage youth in a group of young people engaged in a drinking party. The fact that he is only under age by one month may influence the officer to release him with a warning. However, if subsequently the released youth becomes involved in a serious accident, the fact that he was released earlier in the evening will often result in the officer being castigated by his superior because he has no publicly acknowledged right to exercise discretion, although all agree that it is both necessary and desirable that he do so.

Given the range of responsibilities which the police have, they cannot be held to a system of decisionmaking which involves no risk-taking—any more than can psychiatrists in deciding whether to release a person who has attempted suicide or parole board members in voting upon the release of an inmate. The formulation of policy and its articulation to the public would, over a period of time, begin to educate the public into recognizing that the police must not only exercise discretion, but must assume a risk in doing so. Prior statements which "put the community on notice" with regard to police functioning in various areas would afford some relief from the current dilemma in which, in the absence of such policy formulations, the police are both subject to ridicule for not exercising discretion and subject to condemnation for making such judgments when they do not work out.

A Means for Utilizing Police Expertise

Many actions which the police officer takes are based upon the knowledge and experience which he has accumulated in his years of service. For example, an officer may, in deciding whether a situation is a suspicious one, reach a judgment quite different from that which would be reached by an inexperienced layman or even an experienced trial judge. An officer may have the ability to recognize the smell of narcotics or the sound of a press used in printing illegal numbers or policy tickets. Yet there has been little effort made to capitalize upon police experience or to attempt to assess its reliability: to distinguish accurate inferences from inaccurate ones; or to systematize experience so that it can be effectively communicated through police training to new police officers and to others, like judges, when the propriety of police action is challenged.

More Effective Administrative Control
Over Police Behavior

Lacking a formulated policy and thus a preannounced basis for internal disciplinary action, the police administrator is hesitant to impose sanctions upon the individual police officer who acts improperly but whose conduct does not violate the law or departmental regulations.

The police administrator finds himself caught in a conflict between his desire to be responsive to a citizen who has reason to complain about a policeman's behavior and his fear of the reaction of his force to seemingly arbitrary discipline where there is no clear breach of a preannounced standard of proper conduct.

This reluctance to characterize an officer's conduct as unwise is increased when the administrator feels that to do so will result in either the officer or the municipality being sued for damages. The administrator, therefore, may be placed in the position of defending a given action as legal, and thus seemingly "proper," even though it reflected poor judgment on the part of an officer. To minimize the chance of similar situations in the future, the administrator may urge his subordinates to use "common sense," but this is not very effective unless he is able to indicate more clearly what "common sense" is in the wide variety of situations confronted by the police officer.

Formulated administrative policies to which police officers are required to adhere would provide a basis for disciplining those who violate them and would serve also in a positive way to inform members of a force what is expected of them. Progress in elevating the quality of law enforcement is much more likely to come about as a result of trying to induce conformity to standards prescribed by department policy than by relying solely upon those minimal "legal" standards which must be adhered to to avoid civil liability or to avoid having important evidence suppressed in a criminal prosecution.

The Improvement of Recruit and Inservice Training Programs

Recruit training in police agencies is most often inadequate because the instruction bears little relationship to what is expected of the officer when he goes to work in the field. In the absence of recorded and analyzed formulations of police experience, the instructor usually is left only with the formal definition of police authority, and this is often communicated to the trainee by reading statutory definitions to him. Procedures for dealing with crime and potential crime situations are thus typically taught in doctrinaire fashion. Laws are read on the assumption that they are to be fully enforced. With this kind of formal training, the new officer finds that he has to acquire a knowledge of all the patterns of accommodations and modifications from the more experienced officers with whom he is initially assigned. As he becomes aware of the impracticality and lack of realism in much of what he learned, he may begin to question the validity of all aspects of his formal training.

The obvious need is for training related to the important problems which the officer will face in the field, training which will not only inform him of the limits of his formal authority but will also inform him of the department's judgment as to what is the most desirable administrative practice to follow in the implementation of his formal authority.

This kind of training has an additional advantage. If adequately done it ought also to serve as one important way of raising the basic enforcement issues requiring attention. Thus training can serve to improve the process by which administrative policies are developed and the adequately developed policies will, in turn, make training more effective.

A Basis for the Professionalization of the Police

It is now commonplace to refer to practically any effort that is aimed at improving law enforcement as contributing toward the professionalization of the police. Thus, improved training, the application of the computer to police work, the adoption of a code of ethics, and increased salaries have all, at one time or another, been cited as contributing toward police professionalization.

Certainly, there is much that police do today that would not, under any definition, be viewed as constituting professional work. Directing traffic at a street intersection or enforcing parking restrictions requires stamina, but little knowledge of the social structure of the community. In sharp contrast, however, the beat patrolman assigned to police a congested, high crime area is called upon to make highly sophisticated judgments having a major impact upon the lives of the individuals involved. Such judgments are not mechanical in nature. They are every bit as complicated as the decisions made by any of the behavioral scientists and in many instances are more difficult because they must be made under the pressure of the immediate circumstances.

Adequate development of administrative policies for dealing with complex social and behavioral problems will require the maximum use of police experience, research, and experimentation. The effort to systematize experience and to test its validity by research is one important mark of a profession. Another, also implicit in the development of proper administrative policy, is adherence to values more basic than those required in the interest of efficiency. These relate to the place of police and law enforcement in a democratic society.

The utilization of experience, research, experimentation, and the effort to define the proper role of police in our society would constitute a more adequate basis for the development of a true profession.

Involving the Police in the Improvement
of the System of Law Enforcement

Decisions relating to the enforcement function have traditionally been made for the police by others. The police have typically not been consulted when changes were contemplated in the substantive or procedural criminal law, despite the fact they clearly have more experience in dealing with some of the basic issues than anyone else. The reason that they have not been consulted is probably because they have not been considered qualified to deal with the complicated questions involved. But it probably is also true that police lack this skill precisely because they have not been involved in the making of important decisions in the past.

Today there is a strong commitment to the involvement of minority groups, young people and the poor in decisions about their future in the view they will respond most affirmatively if they have a feeling of participation in the initial decision. The same need is apparent in relation to police. They too are more likely to want to conform and have an ability to conform if they are part of the process for making important decisions affecting criminal justice administration.

CHAPTER 7

Professional Police Principles

By Edward M. Davis

Edward M. Davis is the Chief of Police of the city of Los Angeles. He is a member of the executive committee of the California State Peace Officers' Association; Sixth Vice-President of the International Association of Chiefs of Police; and Chairman of the Police Task Force of the National Advisory Commission on Criminal Justice Standards and Goals of the Law Enforcement Assistance Administration.

Anyone going into a business is well advised to understand the philosophy of that business. Each business has general principles and philosophies that are essential to a successful enterprise. This observation leads to asking questions of our own law enforcement business. What are the objectives of the police? What are the major functions of law enforcement? The President's Crime Commission stated that the country spends $4 billion a year on policing. For what is the money spent? Why?

Most of the answers can be found in nine principles of law enforcement first enunciated about 1822 by Sir Robert Peel, founder of the British Police system. They are ancient, but principles do not change and all the solutions to crime are here and all the solutions to community relations can be found here.

I have gone through each of these nine principles and have amplified on some of them, but I believe the essence of successful law enforcement can be drawn from these fundamental observations from a century long past.

From Edward M. Davis, "Professional Police Principles," *Federal Probation,* volume 35, number 1, March 1971. Reprinted through the courtesy of *Federal Probation,* Washington, D.C.

Prevention of Crime Is the Basic Mission of the Police

Principle Number 1.—The basic mission for which the police exist is to prevent crime and disorder as an alternative to the repression of crime and disorder by military force and severity of legal punishment.*

The goal of the police establishment still remains the absence of crime and disorder. That is the desired end product. Police engage in three major functions to achieve this primary goal. The function of first priority is prevention. When the police fail in this first function, the second function is activated—that of deterrence, or what the textbooks call repression. The third function is the apprehension of offenders and the gathering of evidence for prosecution.

Now, the police themselves cannot prevent crime. True prevention of crime is to generate in society a desire to do the right thing, to live by ethical standards of conduct. The police cannot take over the parents' job, the minister's job, and the school's job in this respect. However, the police play a major role as the catalytic agent in society to assist the process of "feeding back" to the rest of society information on what is happening in terms of crime and disorder. No one else can perform this function but the police. No one else is in contact with crime and disorder in its totality. No one else has the machinery or perception or access to the basic facts as do the police.

The police cannot prevent the development of criminality in any individual. However, through a feedback process, information on crime can be passed to social institutions which may hopefully generate programs to prevent criminality of individuals in the future.

When there is a failure to prevent crime, the police perform the next function of deterrence—attempting to be as obvious as possible and creating the impression of omnipresence. This is the reason police drive black-and-white cars; this is why police wear distinctive uniforms; this is why police attempt to be overt rather than covert in as many operations as possible.

The police helicopter is predicated largely on this second function of deterrence. Deterrence plucks the conscience strings of the guilt-ridden. The criminal who wants to do something but chickens out because of the omnipresent "chopper" is a good example of this deterrence function.

That is deterrence. That's why police don't wear green blazers with an emblem on the pocket to look like a sport. Police should look like police or they violate the very principle of deterrence.

Now, when police *fail* to deter, then they must invoke the third function, that of apprehension and gathering of evidence. The police serve as the first entryway into the criminal justice system, followed by the prosecutor, the courts, appellate courts, then institutional commitment,

---

*The nine principles presented are a paraphrase of those which have evolved since the time of Sir Robert Peel, originator of the English police system.

probation, or parole. We know from the rate of recidivism that the effectiveness of rehabilitation in this system is minimal. However, the system has value because it tends to reinforce the societal prohibitions against doing certain things and thus serves to deter prospective offenders. But police activities directed toward apprehension and gathering of evidence are of minimal value in preventing crime—the primary police goal.

The losing game of apprehension absorbs a major share of police resources. The resultant return in preventing crime and disorder is relatively small considering the vast investment. The function of deterrence absorbs a very small share of police resources, yet the return in crime prevention is better, dollar for dollar, than for apprehension. The function of prevention—the function best directed toward achieving the primary police objective—receives even less in the way of resources.

The information now gathered by police is directed wholly toward prosecution of a suspect or future apprehension of that same suspect. Police gather virtually no information for relaying to society, saying, "This is what is happening, and it is happening under these circumstances." This unarticulated but necessary mission for developing better methods of interfacing with society's institutions must be fulfilled. We must provide them with relevant, demographic data on crime that will spur them to actions which will result in an achievement of the primary goal of preventing crime and disorder.

Police Must Have the Full Respect of the Citizenry

Principle Number 2.—The ability of the police to perform their duties is dependent upon public approval of police existence, actions, behavior, and the ability of the police to secure and maintain public respect.

Arthur Niederhoffer, a 20-year New York police lieutenant, wrote a book entitled *Behind the Shield.* In it he makes observations which are not very comforting to policemen. He believes that the American police tend to hide behind a self-pity syndrome; they tend to become paranoid and withdrawn. If his thesis is correct, if policemen believe that people don't support them, that they operate in a wholly hostile environment, then there would be little hope.

The police must not allow themselves to be caught up in this "Niederhoffer syndrome." There are only two policemen for every 1,000 people in Los Angeles and five for every 1,000 in New York. The police could not even exist in a totally hostile community.

One of the important roles of police-community relations is to establish and maintain ties with all segments of the community so that the police can develop broad-based support. Associations with such groups will help individual policemen recognize the very real public support for the police which exists in every community regardless of its ethnic makeup.

A Citizen's Respect for Law Develops His Respect for the Police

Principle Number 3.—The police must secure the willing cooperation of the public in voluntary observance of the law to be able to secure and maintain the respect and approval of the public.

One hundred and thirty years ago Abraham Lincoln, then a young legislator, made the following statement:

> I hope I am over-wary; but if I am not, there is now an ill omen amongst us. I mean the increasing disrespect for law which pervades the country. Accounts of outrages committed by mobs from the every day news of the times.
>
> The question recurs, "How shall we fortify against it?" The answer is simple.
>
> Let every American, every lover of liberty, swear never to violate in the least particular, the laws of the country and never to tolerate their violation by others. Let every man remember that to violate the law is to tear the character of his own and his children's liberty. Let reverence for the laws be breathed by every American mother to the baby ... on her lap. Let it be taught in schools, and in colleges. Let it be written in primers and spelling books. Let it be preached from the pulpit, proclaimed in legislative halls and enforced in courts of justice. And in short let reverence for the law become the political religion of the nation.

This truth has not changed over the intervening years.

It is the job of every policeman to seek the willing cooperation of individuals on his beat in helping to attain the police objectives of the absence of crime and disorder. In the same tradition, it is the responsibility of every police officer to seek the voluntary observance of laws in his community. His mission is to "turn on" that community, regardless of ethnic makeup, to get the police job done.

There is a principle of "leverage" in economics. By this principle a small amount of money is manipulated to do the work of a much larger amount. Police must operate by this principle. Through the cooperation of the community, one policeman can be as many in achieving the police mission. If any policeman comes from the Academy thinking that he is going to save the world, he is going to be a total failure. We need a vision of the old-time cop-on-the-beat who never seemed to work hard. But, he had people in the community telling him things about crime and questionable activities. He had the help of his community and he got the job done. That is the only way to get the police mission accomplished.

Cooperation of the Public Decreases as the Use of Force Increases

Principle Number 4.—The degree of cooperation of the public that can be secured diminishes proportionately the necessity for the use of physical force and compulsion in achieving police objectives.

The professional, competent, emotionally secure police officer does not approach situations with a "bristle." He actively solicits the cooperation of the individual or group where the public peace is endangered. An officer with the ability to firmly but pleasantly solicit the cooperation of individuals or groups can frequently accomplish, through their cooperation, what it might take scores of officers to accomplish through the use of a "hard" approach to the situation.

In areas where there has been a pattern of using strong physical force to achieve police objectives, a concurrent pattern of resistance develops within the individual or group. The result is resistance and lack of cooperation on the part of the law violator and the subsequent necessity for resorting to force on the part of the police. The use of force is thus self-perpetuating.

Less than a year ago the British, with all their majesty, used their vast military forces to reconquer a tiny island protectorate of Anguilla. They were wise enough to take some "bobbies" along when reinstalling their administrators. During the skirmishing, two bobbies were injured. The citizens dressed their wounds and apologized to them. The reputation of the bobbies had preceded them. The British police have done a pretty good job of recognizing that when cooperation can be secured, the necessity of physical force is proportionately decreased.

Police Must Render Impartial Enforcement of the Law

Principle Number 5.—The police seek and preserve public favor, not by catering to public opinion, but by constantly demonstrating absolutely impartial service to the law, in complete independence of policy, and without regard to the justice or injustice of the substance of individual laws; by ready offering of individual service and friendship to all members of society without regard to their race or social standing; by ready exercise of courtesy and friendly good humor; and by ready offering of individual sacrifice in protecting and preserving life.

The policeman's boss is not his sergeant or the chief. The policeman does not work for the white people or the black people; he doesn't represent the "establishment." The policeman is a servant of the law.

Ten years ago Thurgood Marshall, then chief counsel for the NAACP and now an Associate Justice of the Supreme Court of the United States, made the following statement during a speech to police officers at Michigan

State University: "If there is a bad law on the books that says that a Negro cannot . . . eat at the same store counter you can, you go ahead and enforce that law. If it is a bad law, we will take care of the law; but if you enforce any of your personal prejudices, we will take care of you."

It is not the job of a policeman to determine what the legislators should say constitutes a crime. It is not the mission of the police to judge whether any law is good, bad, too harsh, or too lenient. Laws are made by legislators and are an imperfect reflection of society's mores. Laws are subject to change. However, when the law is established it is the job of the policeman to enforce that law impartially.

In California marihuana is illegal. Whether it is good or bad is a problem for the sociologists and physicians. However, as long as the law stands on the books, police should put people in jail for violating that law. Law enforcement does not have to apologize for enforcing the law, because we do not make the laws. There is an established democratic process for enacting and altering the law, but it is essential that police construe the law as it is.

The fifth principle further states: Public favor is sought by individual service, friendship to all members of society, the ready exercise of courtesy and friendly good humor, and by individual sacrifice. There are many examples of police officers sacrificing even their lives in the line of duty. If a robbery-in-progress call comes through, it may be a crummy liquor store and the police officer who responds to the call may not even like the owner. But, he would go in and give up his life in a gun battle to protect that merchant. Any officer driving down the street at 4 A.M. in the middle of a ghetto area would not hesitate to dash into a burning building to rescue the occupants. Every year the Police Department gives out medals for this type of valor. Yet the same police officer might not be friendly to the citizen he would risk his life for, because that citizen is different in some way.

The police must develop this thing called friendship for all members of society. If you were to call the Department, the man who answered might respond, "Robbery, Smith." You might receive the same stereotyped, staccato response at the "desk." The result is a reputation of cold efficiency. Members of minority groups will believe police personnel are cold to them because of prejudice; others would call it plain discourtesy. It is vitally important to police-community relations that each officer take it upon himself to maintain friendly, good-humored relations with each citizen.

A British bobby was watching the burning of the Union Jack at an English university. It is not a crime over there to burn the flag. Instead of responding with anger, he said, "Blimey, can you imagine it takes a college education to do that?" He approached that situation with friendly good humor. A prime element of any community relations program is friendliness of each officer to each member of society.

Physical Force Is Used Only as a Last Resort

Principle Number 6.—The police should use physical force to the extent necessary to secure observance of the law or to restore order only when the exercise of persuasion, advice, and warning is found to be insufficient to achieve police objectives; and police should use only the minimum degree of physical force which is necessary on any particular occasion for achieving a police objective.

The police in some areas of the country have been under fire recently because of purported cases of excessive use of force in quelling demonstrations. When this happens, the police end up being the central figure in the disturbance. Above all else, the police must remain neutral in any confrontation. The police represent only the law.

Very recently, there was a demonstration on the campus of Valley State College. During the course of the demonstration, certain laws were violated and it was, therefore, necessary to place about 200 people under arrest. The police officers were trained in weaponless defense. The 200 arrests were made in front of television cameras, and not one flailing baton appeared. The police did their job and there were no resulting charges of overreaction. The police did not become the central figure.

With calm leadership the police can talk their way around many incidents through advice, warning, persuasion. If police have to use force, that is their job, but only after the alternatives have been tried.

The Police Are the Public and the Public Are the Police

Principle Number 7.—The police at all times should maintain a relationship with the public that gives reality to the historic tradition that the police are the public and that the public are the police; the police are the only members of the public who are paid to give full-time attention to duties which are incumbent on every citizen in the interest of community welfare.

Charles Reith, in his book, *The Blind Eye of History,* delineated his belief that any civilization that depends on using its own military forces to control its people is doomed to failure. History bears out this theory. Britain was in the position of needing some force to repress disorder in the early 1800's. Finally, in 1829, Parliament passed an act establishing the British police system, the first full-time professional police department. However, Parliament was fearful of a police organization because of possible infringement on individual rights. Out of this fear the idea was spawned that it was every citizen's obligation to help police his society, but certain citizens would be set aside to do this work on a full-time basis. They would help all citizens do their job.

In England, if you smack a bobby in the eye trying to make an escape, you might get 10 years. After all, the bobby is helping every citizen do his job. England has given reality to the historic concept of the citizen being the police and vice versa. Here in America, because of a lack of philosophical leadership or because of the prohibition era, or because of the "Niederhoffer complex," the police are separate from the citizenry in many ways. The most technologically advanced, best financed, best staffed police department in the world is never going to solve the problems of crime and disorder. That is because our police have not given reality to the truth that the public are the police. Our police must communicate to the citizens that solving these problems is their job, their obligation. As police, we are merely helping them. Regardless of ethnic or economic background, the estrangement between public and police must be eliminated in favor of a coordinated effort to achieve police objectives.

A police reserve corps is one method of creating closer ties between the public and the police. It is one way of fulfilling the historic tradition that the public are the police. In having a reserve corps we open the Department to any citizen who qualifies. We have nothing to hide. We train the reserves as assistants in doing the police job.

I recently had a man tell me how much better his police organization was than the Los Angeles Police Department in every respect. I was sure he was some ranking officer. He turned out to be a reserve officer who worked as a policeman one day a week. He was a 40-hour-a-week salesman of some kind. He was also a salesman for his police organization, and for police ideals.

A trained corps of reserve officers gives tremendous flexibility to administrators in the event of any unusual occurrence. More than that, they are the public serving as the police. They will help sell the police mission to their friends, neighbors, and co-workers.

Police Represent the Law

Principle Number 8.—The police should always direct their actions strictly toward their functions and never appear to usurp the powers of the judiciary by avenging individuals or the state, or authoritatively judging guilt or punishing the guilty.

Police officers do not judge guilt; they do not punish; they do not act as executioners. Policemen represent the law. If the law says a man should go to jail for a certain act, the police arrest the man, gather the evidence, and do not take upon themselves any adjudication or correction.

I have known officers who were mad at every suspect they ever arrested. These officers were actually angry because of what the suspect had done, said, or looked like. This unprofessional, judgmental attitude breeds resistance and hostility, making the police job more difficult, if not impossible.

I have also known detectives who never seem to lose their cool. They know their job in its true light. I can think of one in particular. He always smiled. He offered the suspects a cigarette or a cup of coffee. He talked to them in friendly tones, and he made good arrests. He did not make his job any more difficult than it already was. He kept his cool. He was the epitome of a professional policeman.

The quality we look for here is equanimity. The professional policeman does not demonstrate emotional involvement in his work to the public. He does not demonstrate anger to the offender; he does not go into a rage when verbally abused. He keeps his cool.

The Absence of Crime and Disorder Is the Test of Police Efficiency

Principle Number 9.—The test of police efficiency is the absence of crime and disorder, not the visible evidence of police action in dealing with them.

If you approach the typical police officer in a radio car and ask him what he has to do to keep his job, he might tell you: "I should write 'X' number of citations every week; I have to turn in 'X' number of field interview cards; I should make 'X' number of arrests each month." On the other hand, imagine you are the chief of police and are called to City Hall and told you are going to be fired unless you could prove you are doing a good job. Are you going to tell City Hall how many traffic citations have been written and how many arrests have been made during your tenure? No, you are going to tell them that during your tenure, crime was reduced by X-percent and the number of traffic accidents has been reduced.

The higher echelon of police administration know their job is to stop crime; but there is a real danger that the officer on the street may think of his job as a "numbers game," to provide a quantity of tickets or arrests. There is a failure here. The failure is not with the policeman. He is really responding to the kind of pressures that are put on him by police management. It is easier to judge men by the quantity of tickets they write than it is to judge them on their effect on traffic flow. It is easier to judge a man by the number of arrests he makes than it is to judge him on the quality of his work stopping crime. Because the "numbers game" is easier, there is a real temptation to resort to it.

The challenge of police management is to communicate the true nature of the police mission to the man in the radio car on the street. Management has to sell the policeman a piece of geography and say, "This is your district. Your job is to stop crime and disorder here. We don't want burglaries or stickups or street-fights. If you have to arrest someone for violating any law, do it. You have been trained to stop crime. Do it in your area, and get the community to help you."

We in the police field spent a lot of time talking about "numbers" in the crime field. We spend even more time talking about mechanical gadgets and developing programs of one kind or another. I believe one of our major failings is that we have not spent enough time talking about principles.

I believe that if we can agree on the nine principles set forth by Sir Robert Peel, we can all do a better and more professional job in achieving our goal.

Part I   Selected Correlated References

Barnes, H. E., and N. K. Teeters. *New Horizons in Criminology.* 3rd ed. Englewood Cliffs, N.J.: Prentice-Hall Inc., 1959. Chapter 15 affords a particularly good commentary on police history and Chapter 18 gives a generally good background for discussing law enforcement.

Chapman, S. G., and T. E. St. Johnston. *The Police Heritage in England and America.* East Lansing: Michigan State University Press, 1962. This booklet presents a timely collection of factors in British police background.

Cressey, D. R. "The State of Criminal Statistics." *NPPA Journal* Vol. 3, No. 3 (July 1957). Concerns the positive and negative aspects of statistical information relating to crime.

Cumming, E., I. M. Cumming, and L. Edell. "Policeman as Philosopher, Guide and Friend." *Social Problems* Vol. 12, No. 3 (Winter 1965). Excellent coverage on responsibilities and role of police.

Day, F. D. "Criminal Law Enforcement and a Free Society." *Journal of Criminal Law, Criminology and Police Science* Vol. 54, No. 3 (September 1963). Scope of problems confronting law enforcement in a democratic society.

Derbyshire, R. L. "The Social Control Role of the Police in Changing Urban Communities." *Excerpta Criminologica* Vol. 6, No. 3 (May-June 1966). Explores police power and definition of role.

Devlin, P. A. "The Police in a Changing Society." *Journal of Criminal Law, Criminology and Police Science* Vol. 57, No. 2 (June 1966). An excellent discussion of impact of social change on traditional law-enforcement roles.

Griffin, J. I. *Statistics Essential for Police Efficiency.* Springfield, Ill.: Charles C. Thomas, 1958. An excellent presentation of departmental essentials in police statistical data.

Hart, H. "The Aims of the Criminal Law." *Law and Contemporary Problems* Vol. 23 (Summer 1958) 401-42. A good discussion of societal restrictions on behavior.

Ibele, O. H. "Law Enforcement and the Permissive Society." *Police* (September-October 1965). A discussion of enforcing law in cultural environments of seeming indifference.

Kooken, D. L. *Ethics in Police Service.* Springfield, Ill.: Charles C. Thomas, 1957. A discussion of nonregulated but expected police conduct.

Sowle, C. R., ed. *Police Power and Individual Freedom.* Springfield, Ill.: Charles C. Thomas, 1962. A discussion of the title subject with emphasis on potential impact of authority.

Sutherland, E. H., and D. R. Cressey. *Principles of Criminology.* 5th ed. Philadelphia: J. B. Lippincott, 1955. Penetrating analysis of the elementary principles of criminology. Excellent introductory material for students.

Tappan, P. W. *Crime, Justice and Correction.* New York: McGraw-Hill Book Co., 1960. Chapter 11 elaborates the traditional police role in detecting violations of law.

The Challenge of Crime in a Free Society, a report by the President's Commission on Law Enforcement and Administration of Justice, Washington, D.C.: U.S. Government Printing Office, 1967. An excellent overview of the dimensions of human dynamics in police problems.

Westley, C. "Violence and the Police." *American Journal of Sociology* Vol. 59, No. 34 (1953). A good discussion of the title subject from a perspective of causal relationships.

Yablonski, Lewis. *The Violent Gang.* New York: The Macmillan Co., 1962. A definitive explanation of one type of adolescent gang—the violent gang. The author discusses the violent gang as found in chaotic, urban slums. His explanation of such groups is extremely informative.

Part II

Keys to Police Effectiveness: Organization, Administration, and Personnel Selection

Recently, police departments have come to realize that the way in which they are organized is probably the key to their effectiveness. Rapid strides have been made in reorganizing police departments, particularly in the areas of operating procedures and personnel management. Chapters 8 and 9 deal with these changes, and contrast poorly organized and well-organized municipal departments.

In evaluating police effectiveness, it is vital to realize that the way in which an individual policeman performs depends in part upon how his duties are defined. As R. E. Mitchell stresses in Chapter 9, to understand these definitions and to understand the pressures under which policemen work, it is necessary to see the police in relation to the legal and illegal systems which operate in our society. In short, it is necessary to adopt a total view; Chapter 9 examines criminal organizations, legal organizations, and the way in which police departments react to both systems.

125

Chapters 10 and 11 take a long look at the way in which policemen are selected. John H. McNamara's classic article, "Uncertainties in Police Work: The Relevance of Recruits' Backgrounds and Training," examines the problems that police departments face in this regard and shows directions in which changes must take place. John Guidici describes one of the most important parts of the selection process, the oral examination, and makes pertinent suggestions about its use and changes that can make it more informative.

CHAPTER 8

Police Organization, Management, and Operations

The President's Commission on Law Enforcement and Administration of Justice

Introduction

Significant strides have been made during recent years in the organization of police departments, the management of personnel, and operational procedures. Excellent municipal police departments have been created in many urban centers. Each year, more forces abandon antiquated methods, reorganize internally, and initiate new techniques for general supervision and improved day-to-day operations. Progress has not been limited to urban forces. Several sheriffs' departments have succeeded in modernizing their departments, and now provide better protection in urban fringe areas and the nearby inhabited countryside.

Among the recommendations of the Wickersham Commission 36 years ago was one that State police forces be established to provide protection for rural areas. In 1931 there were but 21 such forces.[1] Today, 49 of the 50 States have organized State police or highway patrols, Hawaii being the exception.

In 1931, Wickersham noted that the fractionalization of law enforcement agencies and their lack of coordination were seriously affecting the fight against crime:[2]

> The multitude of police forces in any State and the varying standards of organization and service have contributed immeasurably to the general low grade of police performance in this country. The independence which police forces display toward each other and the absence of any central force which requires either a uniform or a minimum standard of service leave the way open for the profitable operation of criminals in an area where protection is

---

From the President's Commission on Law Enforcement and Administration of Justice, "Police Organization, Management, and Operations," *Task Force Report: The Police,* 1967. Reprinted through the courtesy of the Superintendent of Documents, U.S. Government Printing Office, Washington, D.C.

[1]National Commission on Law Observance and Enforcement, *Report on the Police* (Washington: U.S. Government Printing Office, 1931), p. 125.

[2]Ibid., at p. 124.

often ineffectual at the best, generally only partial, and too frequently wholly absent.

As described in detail in chapter 4, some jurisdictions have recognized these deficiencies and are taking steps to counter them by consolidating police forces or pooling common resources. For example, in Nashville, Davidson County, Tenn., the police service previously provided by numerous departments has been consolidated into one central law enforcement agency.

In Salt Lake County, Utah, and Pierce County, Wash., city and county police departments are housed in one facility, and pool several common resources. Other jurisdictions, such as Suffolk and Nassau Counties, N.Y.; Marion County, Oreg.; St. Louis County, Mo.; and Dekalb County, Ga., are devising practical plans designed to result in partial consolidation.

Some smaller communities, noting the limitations of maintaining their own police forces, have contracted with larger agencies to have them assume their policing needs. These include 62 California municipalities that have contracted for policing with 21 separate county sheriff departments; 46 Connecticut towns that by contract have a resident State police trooper; 7 cities and villages policed by the St. Louis County, Mo., police; and the unincorporated portions of Fulton County, Ga., which are policed by the Atlanta Police Department.

States are playing an increasing role in improving local police service. For example, State-level agencies in Illinois, California, and Kansas upon request provide local law enforcement forces with crime scene and laboratory analyses. The New York State intelligence and identification system spans that State, and the California Department of Justice operates the bureau of criminal identification and investigation which houses criminal records and modus operandi data on a statewide basis. Several States, including Connecticut, Rhode Island, Oregon, and Illinois provide police training for the personnel of small departments. Further, many States are now playing an active role in upgrading the preparedness of law enforcement personnel within their boundaries. To date, 23 States have programs to improve the quality of police training.

At the national level, the Federal Bureau of Investigation has since 1924 assisted local law enforcement in such important areas as fingerprint identification and training, and since 1935 in laboratory analysis of physical evidence. This assistance has had significant impact on local response to crime. Further, representatives of other Federal agencies such as the various investigative agencies within the Treasury Department and the Post Office Department work closely with State and local officials in facing common problems which have assumed area, regional, or interstate scope.

Improvement has been far from universal, however. America is still unrivaled in the number and range of quality of its police agencies; advances in technology have not as yet been widely adapted for police use, and many police departments are still plagued by poor organizational structures:[3]

> [Considering the 40,000 separate departments in this Nation] . . . the vast majority of American police agencies continue to function according to patterns laid down several generations ago.

Since traditional police practices have at best been only modestly successful in deterring criminal behavior and in apprehending offenders, it is obvious that blind adherence to tradition will not do. Also, traditional organizational structures and operational procedures have detracted from the attractiveness of police work. This is one reason for the rising resignation rates in our Nation's police departments, and for the increasing difficulty many departments have had in recruiting adequate numbers of personnel. Other than such factors as low pay and financial insecurity, these problems are caused by procedures which stifle initiative, and, in some departments, by poor direction and control, by confused responsibility, and by improper grouping of duties. Even though these conditions are apparent, there is only slight evidence that the departments most in need of reorganization are taking steps in that direction.

Existing Organizational and Operational Patterns

To assist in evaluating the present state of American police organization, management, and operations, the Commission staff:

- Conferred with expert advisory panels;
- Sought guidance from 250 police leaders and representatives from professional bodies;
- Reviewed police literature and textbooks;
- Reviewed police consultant surveys of 75 police departments;
- Reviewed a comprehensive study of police organization and management which was prepared by California State College at Los Angeles for the U.S. Department of Justice; and
- Reviewed responses to a letter sent to 2,100 police agencies by the Attorney General requesting information on effective procedures.

Findings and Recommendations

The Commission's studies enabled it to identify a number of generally prevalent deficiencies in police organization, management and operations,

---

[3]Bruce Smith, *Police Systems in the United States* (2nd ed., rev., New York: Harper & Bros., 1960), p. 209.

and suggested to it the means for correcting those deficiencies. This chapter will discuss these findings and recommendations in some detail. First, however, it is important to point out that putting the recommendations into effect will not be easy. It will require a fundamental change in attitude on the part of many police administrators and local officials. It will require spending considerable sums of money. In the police world, as anywhere, significant reform requires imagination, labor and sacrifice.

In summary, the Commission has found:

- Many departments lack qualified leadership. Police chiefs and personnel in middle management ranks should be required to have sufficient education and training to enable them to administer the complex affairs of a police force, and should receive salaries sufficient to attract and retain top administrators.

- Many departments are not organized in accordance with well-established principles of modern business management. They should be reorganized in accordance with such of those principles as best apply to the police, and those principles themselves should be periodically reexamined in the light of the changing nature of the police role.

- Many departments resist change, fail to determine shortcomings of existing practice and procedures through research and analysis, and are reluctant to experiment with alternative methods of solving problems. The police service must encourage, indeed put a premium on, innovation, research and analysis, self-criticism and experimentation.

- Many departments lack trained personnel in such fields as research and planning, law, business administration and computer analysis. Specialist units, staffed by sufficient personnel trained in a variety of disciplines, should be utilized to plan and project programs, evaluate and streamline procedures, improve management and administration, engage in special operations and establish methods for maximizing the use of personnel. In-house legal advice must be made available to medium-sized and large police forces on a full-time basis.

- Many departments fail to deploy and utilize personnel efficiently. Police administrators should study such matters as (a) the basis for deploying uniformed personnel; (b) the use of one- or two-man motor patrol; (c) whether or not, and for what purposes, men should be assigned to foot patrol, and whether men so assigned should serve alone or in pairs; (d) the feasibility of "team policing"; (e) the extent to which civilians can be used in staff and clerical work; and (f) the extent to which such police activities as jailing, communications, records, and laboratories can be "pooled" with other departments or assumed by other governmental units.

- Many departments have not adequately applied technological advances that would be beneficial to law enforcement. Regional information storage and retrieval systems, communications and command-control systems, and radio-frequency-channel sharing concepts must be adapted to the police service.

- Finally, States through their commissions on police standards or other appropriate agencies, should provide financial and technical assistance to departments to conduct surveys and make recommendations to improve police organization, management, and operations.

Developing Police Leadership

As long ago as 1921, there was recognition that the uneven development of American police organization appeared to be caused, more than by any other factor, by the lack of trained and intelligent leadership.[4] Ten years later the Wickersham Commission concurred, noting that uninformed and unimaginative leadership was a major contributing cause to existing weaknesses in police organization and management. The Wickersham Commission report said:[5]

> Not infrequently the chief is wholly incompetent to discharge the onerous duties of his position. He may lack experience, executive ability, character, integrity, or the confidence of his force, or all of them put together.

In the years following the Wickersham report, some progress has been made in upgrading the level of police leadership. Even so, the overall need for infusing police departments throughout the nation with well-trained, educated, and able administrators is still clear. For example, a 1964 study disclosed that only 33.6 percent of America's police administrators had attended college, and of these only 9.2 percent possessed one or more college degrees.[6] Unfortunately, as a rule, procedures for selecting police administrators have changed little during the past 25 years. One police executive in 1966 describes the traditional road to the top:[7]

> The time-honored, uninspired path of promotion sees an administrator fish-laddering his way up through the ranks without being prepared in any-

---

[4]Raymond B. Fosdick, *American Police Systems* (New York: The Century Co., 1921), p. 215.

[5]President's Commission, "Report on the Police," at p. 3.

[6]George W. O'Connor and Nelson A. Watson, *Juvenile Delinquency and Youth Crime: The Police Role* (Washington: International Association of Chiefs of Police, 1964), p. 79.

[7]Samuel G. Chapman, "Developing Personnel Leadership." *The Police Chief,* March 1966, 33:24.

thing more than a "by chance" manner for the new and difficult responsibilities of successive commands. The consequence is that many of today's police commanding officers are simply promoted policemen, not professional administrators carefully prepared for demanding roles in the complex enterprise that is the hallmark of contemporary police work.

The reason this condition is so prevalent is not hard to find. With few exceptions, police departments have not set minimum standards of education and achievement for administrators and middle managers, and do not offer training in administration, management and supervision to candidates for, or appointees to, such jobs. The Committee for Economic Development has pointed out:[8]

> ... young employees contemplating careers as professional administrators should receive additional training in basic administrative techniques such as those used in budget preparation and administration, organizational techniques, space and manpower studies, and procedural analysis. Local units without enough recruits each year to conduct their own on-the-job programs should use contract systems with universities, professional associations, or other governments.
>
> Beyond training for new employees, there is pressing need for continuous development of persons in responsible positions. A program of continuing education and midcareer development—with universities and professional associations—is crucial to effective administration in all local governments. Universities should accept responsibility for provision of such programs, and federal grants-in-aid for them would yield large returns at small cost compared with potential benefits. Universities should also develop or strengthen schools of public administration to play positive roles in training students for technical and managerial responsibility in governments.

The subject of standards and training is discussed in further detail ... [elsewhere]. Lateral mobility among police forces, without loss of such fringe benefits as retirement credits, is another means for increasing the numbers of qualified police middle and executive managers as well as permitting competent civilians a career opportunity in police staff work. And there will never be more than token lateral police mobility without a system of transferable retirement credits. . . . The issue of lateral mobility was posed by prominent police authority Frank Kreml at the 1965 International Association of Chiefs of Police meeting:[9]

> Why should a department be denied access to fresh outside executive talent of proven ability? What is there about the management of police

---

[8]Committee for Economic Development, *Modernizing Local Government* (New York: Committee for Economic Development, July 1966), p. 52.

[9]Franklin M. Kreml, "The Role of Colleges and Universities in Police Management," *The Police Yearbook, 1966* (Washington, D.C.: International Association of Chiefs of Police, 1966), p. 36.

resources that causes it to be different, in this respect, from all other professions? Why, only in the police field, are the managerial skills not regarded as transferable?

Other means of developing personnel, once they achieve mid-management and executive levels, is to rotate them among the various command positions within a force or temporarily exchange key personnel with other law enforcement agencies or even with nonpolice governmental agencies. Command-level personnel should be exposed to new, diverse experiences as a practical means of instilling broader executive vision, and removing narrow, parochial thinking.

Exchange and rotation programs are not without precedent in the police world. A few forces have as matter of practice rotated their command level personnel internally for several years. And one department, the Multnomah County Police, exchanged a police lieutenant for a Lancashire, England, Constabulary police inspector (a rank equivalent with lieutenant) for a 6-month period in 1966.[10] And in the summer, 1966, a police science college professor served the sheriff as visiting chief-in-residence. Programs such as these should be experimented with by other law enforcement agencies.

Finally, to insure that individual departments establish appropriate qualifications for executive positions, each State should assume responsibility for establishing minimum educational and training standards for such positions. . . .

Improving Organization

Although some forces have long been recognized as being well organized and progressively managed, far too many of America's city and county forces have serious organizational deficiencies. In fact, many police forces appear to have evolved over the years without conscious plan. These forces are characterized by diffusion of authority, confused responsibility, lack of strong lines of direction and control, and improper grouping of functions. An example of one such department is seen in Figure 1. This force of over 300 men was reported by a consultant as having:

> . . . serious deficiencies of internal communications, coordination, supervision, and direction of effort and control.
>
> This general dissipation of personnel resources—the scattering of specialized work units about the Department without the essential bond of control and direction to hold each such unit to the main objectives of the

---

[10]For a detailed description of the exchange program see: John P. deB. Kennard, *An Account of an Exchange Visit to the United States and Canada* (Lancashire, England: The Lancashire County Police, December 1966), 27 pp.

organization—has reduced the ability of the Department to function as an organized group. The ultimate result is a reduction in the efficiency of the total effort.

With virtually no exception, other consultant reports found serious weaknesses in forces that were surveyed. For example, one consultant noted the following organizational and management defects in a force having more than 450 personnel:

> Sound management practices apparently are not understood nor used by administrative and command personnel . . . Planning and research are not utilized . . . to resolve present problems of organization, personnel deployment, performance inadequacies . . . nor to prepare programs, procedures, and policies for strengthening the [department]. Career development programs have not been formulated. Staff inspection as a control device is not known . . . and therefore not used.

Another consultant body reported these findings in a force of about 3,000 persons:

> The Department suffers from a deficient organizational structure which contributes to poor management. These weaknesses make it difficult for the Department leadership to exercise full control over the entire police operation; the chain of command is confused and supervision is erratic. The excessive decentralization of the Department's operations into 14 precincts adds to these problems. One of the important consequences of poor organization and management is the diversion of police personnel to specialized or administrative assignments, thus unduly curtailing the number of men available for the street operations of the Patrol Division.

That the Nation's small police forces are also not free of organizational and management problems is confirmed in a consultant report which noted the following conditions in a 10-man force:

> It may be said unequivocally that the department has no organization pattern . . . The chief . . . has had [no] training in police administration, command, or supervision . . . [T]he chief's desk duties have created an unfavorable situation in which proper administrative and command precepts are not followed and in which field supervision and training is nonexistent.

There is little justification for American police forces not to be well organized. Available for the asking since the turn of the century has been a large and authoritative general body of guidance in public administration. And for some 30 years there have been adaptations of this to police management prepared by such knowledgeable police authorities as O. W. Wilson and V. A. Leonard, and the International City Managers' Association.[11]

The crux of the problem seems to be that relatively few police forces have taken advantage of this valuable compilation of organization and management principles. This is the more regrettable in view of successes achieved by the departments that have utilized them.

Almost all highly regarded police practitioners, public officials, management consultants and university faculty members agree that an essential need in police organization and management is for all police departments, preferably with the assistance of recognized consultants, to examine their internal organizations in order to determine whether:

- The force's work is apportioned among the various individuals and units according to a logical plan.
- Lines of authority and responsibility are made as definite and direct as possible.
- The number of subordinates who can be effectively supervised by one officer is not exceeded.
- There is "unity of command" throughout the organization.
- Responsibility, once placed, is accompanied by commensurate authority, and that once delegated, the user is held to account for the use he makes of it.
- The efforts of the organizational units and of their component members are coordinated so that all will be directed harmoniously toward the accomplishment of the police purpose. The components thus coordinated will enable the organization to function as a well-integrated unit.[12]

Police department objectives can be achieved more easily, efficiently, and satisfactorily when these principles have been applied. Figure 2 shows one form of a well organized police force. Its structure coincides with the requirements noted above.

---

[11]See O. W. Wilson, *Police Administration,* 2nd ed., (New York: McGraw-Hill, 1963), 528 pp.; V. A. Leonard, *Police Organization and Management,* 2nd ed., (Brooklyn: The Foundation Press, Inc., 1964), 459 pp.; *Municipal Police Administration,* 5th ed., (Chicago: International City Managers Association, 1951), 545 pp.; and R. Dean Smith, "Organization," *The Police Chief,* June 1962, 29: 10-34, 44, Forerunners to the above include: Leonhard Felix Fuld, *Police Administration: A Critical Study of Police Organizations in the United States and Abroad* (New York: G. P. Putnam & Son, 1909), 551 pp.; Elmer D. Graper, *American Police Administration* (New York: The Macmillian Co., 1921), 357 pp.; Raymond B. Fosdick, *American Police Systems* (New York: The Century Co., 1921), 408 pp.; and *Municipal Police Administration,* 1st ed., (Chicago: International City Managers' Association, 1938), 441 pp.

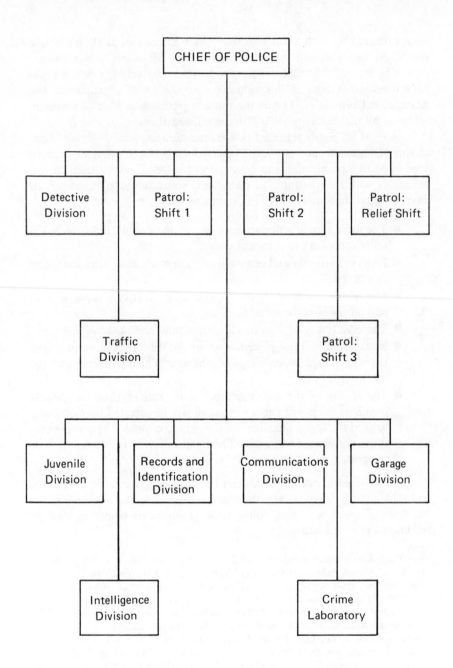

**Figure 1.—An Example of a Poorly Organized
Municipal Police Department**

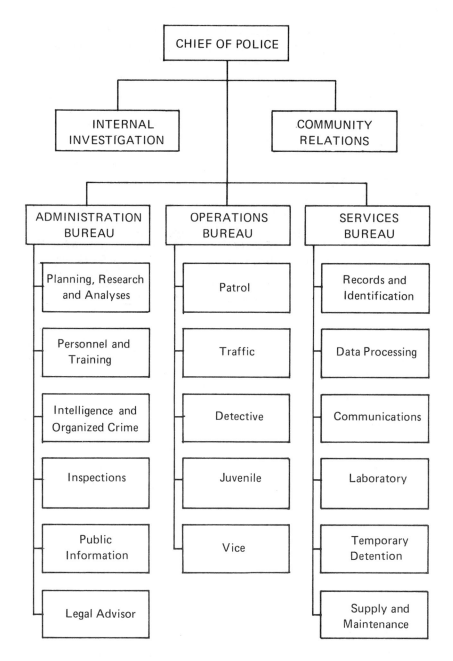

Figure 2.—One Form of a Well-Organized Municipal Police Department

Even though there is considerable knowledge about police organization, insufficient experimentation and reassessment of traditional principles is taking place in the police service today. In general, too many police departments appear unwilling to abandon outmoded concepts, to work in close collaboration with community agencies (especially social service agencies), or to encourage personnel to show initiative or offer suggestions. This prevailing attitude must change if the police are to meet the changing conditions of police service:[13]

> Every activity of police administration will require new ideas effectively put into practice to meet new conditions. This is particularly true within the area of police management.

Unfortunately, the police and academic worlds have not yet collaborated to induce necessary change. There seems to be a schism between the two, which includes mutual suspicion and lack of confidence:[14]

> Large police departments . . . are for the most part secretive about the internal life of the force. Almost anyone who undertakes research on police administration in a big city quickly discovers the extent to which he is held in suspicion and treated circumspectly . . . But the commitment to secrecy far exceeds what normal prudence would seem to dictate. Secrecy in fact is . . . one of the most important ways by which policemen defend themselves against the presumed hostility of civilians. An outsider is considered . . . to be antipolice until he is proved otherwise.

Many police departments do not have the expertise to recognize their shortcomings or to correct them when they are recognized. Most do not have the financial resources to pay the costs of organization surveys, and some cities are not interested in reform even when it is desperately needed. These are some of the reasons for the wide disparity in the effectiveness and efficiency of law enforcement agencies. Citizens within the same State, or even within the same county, do not always receive the same quality of police service because of differences in agency management and in operational policies.

---

[12]For a more comprehensive treatment of these six principles see: O. W. Wilson, *Police Administration,* 2nd ed., (New York: McGraw-Hill Co., 1963), pp. 34-36; and the International City Managers' Association, *Municipal Police Administration,* 5th ed., (Chicago: International City Managers' Association, 1961), pp. 44-45. Sixth ed., in preparation for publication by 1968.

[13]International City Managers' Association, *Municipal Police Administration,* 5th ed., (Chicago: International City Managers' Association, 1961), p. 515.

[14]James Q. Wilson, "The Police and Their Problems: A Theory," *Public Policy,* 12 (1963): 207-8.

Some departments and local governments have recognized their own limitations in assessing their police service, and have engaged outside consultant assistance to perform this task. But the costs of surveys by qualified consultants are often considered by public officials to be simply another financial burden on already over-extended city budgets. Such an attitude seems shortsighted since a comprehensive survey, if implemented, is likely to lead to a wiser allocation of funds and personnel. As Mayor John Lindsay's New York Police Task Force stated in its report:[15]

> ... Police departments must be subjected to an unrestricted and unstinting review of long-standing traditions, attitudes, and practices ... the experience of revitalized police departments in other cities as well as of other governmental and private organizations will be highly instructive to this inquiry. An effective means of tapping this expertise is through the temporary employment of individuals from outside the department. These outside experts could provide the commissioner with fresh insights and also act as a training mechanism for those in the department.

To encourage research, development, and experimentation, it seems timely for Federal and State funds to be made available to stimulate such activity, and partially offset the costs which must otherwise be borne by law enforcement agencies, universities, and private research organizations. For example, certain agencies external to the police may help improve organization, management and operations through research and analyses in collaboration with the police. These include colleges and universities, research institutes, privately funded foundations, and research arms of State criminal justice agencies and the Federal Government.

Administrative and Staff Support Personnel and Units

In addition to improving the competence of top and middle management and applying known principles of organization, police departments must establish special units whose function is the continual planning, administration and assessment of police practices and procedures. A chief of police, particularly as his force grows larger, cannot alone effectively administer a department, devise policy, or evaluate performance. He needs supporting staff, administrative personnel and management specialists who can supervise and train personnel, assist in policymaking, fulfill administrative functions, and assess the soundness of existing practices and procedures.

These personnel must be sufficient in numbers and they need not all be sworn members. For example, before a police budget can be utilized as

---

[15]Law Enforcement Task Force, *Report to Mayor-Elect John V. Lindsay* (New York: 1965), pp. 3-4.

a management device, personnel skilled in fiscal matters must be assigned
to budgetary responsibility. In medium- and large-sized police forces, lawyers should be available to provide legal advice to the chief and his staff.
Training should be handled by persons who have backgrounds and skills
in education. Planning and research should be conducted by men or women
trained in social science and research methodology.

In many forces today these functions either are not performed at all
or are performed by persons who do not possess the necessary qualifications
to perform them well. Support services historically have been weak primarily because many police chiefs feel compelled to give greater priority to
staffing operational rather than specialized service and administrative positions.

Often, city managers or city councils discourage increasing staff support by asserting that crime is fought in the streets, not in the office, and
therefore, staff support units should be cut to a minimum. For example, in
1964 the 283-man Fresno, Calif., police force had to discontinue its personnel, planning, and training division because of a major budget cutback.[16]
The 250-man Multnomah County, Oreg., police department has but 1 man
each assigned to such key special units as training, staff inspections, and
planning and research. This circumstance has existed since the units were
created in 1963 despite annual requests for additional qualified staff to make
the units truly productive.[17]

Planning, Research and Analysis

A police force cannot be effective if it is administered on a day-to-day
or crisis-to-crisis basis. It needs plans: contingency plans about, for example, how to handle a visit by the President or how to capture an armed
desperado holed up in an apartment; operational plans about how to deploy
men in various neighborhoods at various times of day or how to deal with
the problem of apartment burglaries; long-range plans about improving the
quality of personnel, installing new equipment or controlling widespread
vice activities; budgetary plans, community-relations plans, technological
plans, plans of many other kinds. It needs not only to develop new plans
but to review continually the operation of plans already in effect and to
amend them or discard them when necessary. To do this kind of planning
to best advantage, a department must first engage in research and analysis.
Crime trends, long range and short range, must be studied, as well as the
social conditions associated with them. Experimental projects must be de-
vised to test novel police techniques on a limited scale and under controlled

---

[16]International Association of Chiefs of Police, *A Survey of the Police Department of Fresno,
California* (Washington: International Association of Chiefs of Police, May 1965), p. 71.
[17]Interview with Donald E. Clark, sheriff of Multnomah County, Portland, Oreg., Dec. 21,
1966.

conditions. Such departments as Chicago, St. Louis, and Los Angeles already have good-sized, expertly staffed research, analysis and planning units, but even in those places, it can be said, the enormous possibilities of this kind of police staff work are still largely unexplored.

A department's planning and research unit should:

- Review and analyze periodically all department plans and suggest, either directly to the heads of operating divisions or to the police chief, the modernization and improvement of their plans.
- Develop plans having departmentwide application.
- Analyze the operations of plans to ascertain their suitability; when a new plan is placed in operation, discuss its weaknesses with operating and clerical personnel to effect needed improvements in it.
- Prepare statistical and other reports of police department activities, needs, and objectives.
- Prepare the annual budget and extend project fiscal and manpower requirements for up to 5 years.
- Engage in crime and traffic analyses and supply data and patterns to operating divisions.

Staff Inspection

Only a few American police forces use staff inspection as a management control process. Yet staff inspection is an essential component of modern police organization and management.

Staff inspection is a process outside the normal lines of authority and responsibility. It is detailed observation and analysis of a line or service unit designed to inform the chief of police of the performance of the unit. Staff inspection is a standard military practice and is used in one way or another by several Federal agencies. It is also a cornerstone of good police practice in many progressive police forces.

Consultants recognize the concept as important to the police. For example, in its comprehensive survey of the Baltimore police in 1965, the International Association of Chiefs of Police said:[18]

> In all organizations there is need for a system of quality control. This is usually accomplished by line supervisors, by direct observation and supervison, and by report-review. When the organization is large and decentralized there is a need for a further examination of procedures to insure that the policies of the top administrator are being followed with precision and uniformity. This can most effectively be accomplished by the creation of a staff inspection unit.

---

[18]International Association of Chiefs of Police, *A Survey of the Police Department of Baltimore, Maryland* (Washington: International Association of Chiefs of Police, 1965), p. 52.

It must be clearly understood that the staff inspection concept differs substantially from the casual daily examination of process and personnel reasonably expected of all supervisors. The staff inspection unit should look at a broader picture and seek to insure, among other things:

- That accurate records are maintained without inefficient and unnecessary duplication.
- That sworn personnel are properly deployed and not wasted on menial, clerical tasks.
- That manpower is deployed on the basis of analysis of need.
- That supervisory and command personnel operate within the framework of announced policy declarations, and adhere to objectives.
- That line and service units are coordinated.
- That policies, procedures, and regulations are carried out in the spirit for which they were designed.
- That policies, procedures, and regulations are adequate to attain the desired results.
- That resources at the force's disposal, both personnel and material, are utilized to the fullest extent and that resources are adequate to carry out the mission of the department.

Findings and recommendations should be forwarded through channels to the chief. After staff discussion, they may be sent to the planning and research unit for further study and the preparation of appropriate policy or procedures; forwarded to the internal investigations unit for action; or assigned to the training unit for additional in-service and recruit instruction. In any event, staff inspection should have a salutary effect on personnel since it seeks to counteract the inherent weaknesses of a self-inspection process.

Internal Investigation

All large police departments should maintain an internal investigation unit whose purpose is to investigate all alleged breaches of police integrity and complaints, official or anonymous, made against members of a department.[19] The function of an internal investigation unit has been described by the International Association of Chiefs of Police as follows:[20]

> ... all complaints and breaches of discipline must be thoroughly investigated and reported to administrators through channels. Responsibility and authority for investigations is placed with the internal investigation divi-

---

[19]This unit's importance in assuring that police field practices are executed in line with policy and in countering police corruption is described ... [elsewhere].

[20]*Baltimore Police Dept.*, at p. 136.

sion. Other subunits of the department are required to cooperate with these investigations. The order insures that penalties imposed for breaches of discipline are fair and equitable.

Over and above its role in the investigation of complaints and the supervision of discipline by line units, the internal investigation division should constantly and critically examine all areas of police action which represent hazards to the integrity of the department. Misconduct must be discovered at its earliest stages and prompt action taken to correct unsatisfactory conditons.

The key to an effective internal investigation unit is an impartial and fairminded staff. Properly staffed and supervised, an internal investigation unit affords protection both to the public and to the department. By exposing complaints made maliciously, it can in appropriate cases vindicate an unjustly accused officer. By investigating all complaints fully and objectively, it will serve to assure the public that harassment, undue use of force, or other police misconduct will not be tolerated.

Most of the existing internal investigation units operate by the case method—tracking down and bringing to book individual officers who misbehave. However, they should also serve in a deterrent or preventive capacity. This means identifying the problems that cause police misconduct and the neighborhoods or situations in which such misconduct is most likely to occur; devising procedures that will help solve the problems; patrolling and scrutinizing the neighborhoods; and keeping track of situations. Ways must be found to rid police mores of the pervasive feeling that an allegation of misconduct against one officer is an attack upon the entire police force, and that to report a corrupt fellow officer is a detriment, rather than a benefit, to the department. Finally, an internal investigation unit should be responsible to a department's chief and to him alone. By these means it should be possible to bring police misconduct to a minimum. . . .

The Police Legal Advisor

An addition to the police management team that seems well suited to forces of about 250 men or more is the police legal advisor. He should be a part of the department's administrative bureau staff so that he will be near the chief as well as near those engaged in training, discipline, internal investigation, crime analyses, and similar activites.

The need for continuing legal advice within a department has long been recognized by authorities on police operations, and should now be evident to everyone in view of the great interest in police practices the courts are now evincing. For example, even though Superintendent O. W. Wilson of Chicago wrote in 1962 of a need for a "legal unit" to furnish "advice to

staff and field personnel" and to survey "departmental orders and practices
in the light of actual or proposed changes" in the law, a 1965 nationwide
survey of police departments conducted by the National League of Cities
revealed that only 14 of the 276 departments responding employed lawyers,
and of these, 6 were only part-time advisors.[21]

Many municipal governments do not appear to realize the importance
of legally trained personnel in law enforcement. Given the wide range of
duties to which a legal advisor can apply his special training, this omission
is a serious one. A legal advisor could perform many services with his
special skills. He could help with training and continuing education, police
planning, community relations, legislative drafting and lobbying and departmental legal problems, and could advise on problems arising out of
specific cases. And legal skills are especially relevant to police policy planning and liaison with prosecutors.

The legal advisor's role in policy planning is linked to the fact that
total enforcement of the law is neither practical nor desirable; discretion in
the enforcement of the law must be exercised. Generally, the police have
been hesitant to articulate or record for either internal use or public information the criteria upon which enforcement decisions are made. The difficulty is that although wide areas of flexibility are now left to police agencies
without general legislative or judicial policy guidance, police have not
assumed it to be their responsibility to develop and articulate their own
policies. As a result, important policy decisions affecting such problem areas
as undercover investigations, informants, and drunkenness offenders are
seldom brought to light. It is here, in the development of policies—particularly those arising from the necessity for selective enforcement—that the
legal adviser can provide substantial assistance to troubled police executives.

Very few prosecutor's offices endeavor systematically to provide legal
counsel to the police.[22] Save for those few departments which employ legal
advisors, most police forces receive only sporadic counsel from the prosecutor's office or from individual prosecutors who have developed a special
relationship with certain squads or officers. As the American Bar Foundation researchers noted:[23]

---

[21]O. W. Wilson, *Police Planning,* 2nd ed., (Springfield, Ill.: Charles C. Thomas, 1962). p. 11;
O. W. Wilson. *Police Administration,* 2nd ed., (New York: McGraw-Hill, 1963), p. 60; and
Raymond L. Bancroft, "Municipal Law Enforcement, 1966," *Nation's Cities.* 4 (Feb. 1966):
24.

[22]Conversation with California Attorney General Thomas C. Lynch and Chief of Police
Thomas J. Cahill, Jan. 11, 1966, in Washington. These men note a few model cities, such
as San Francisco, where each of the police department's specialized investigative squads has
an assigned prosecutor, and where the police also have two lawyers on the force.

[23]Wayne R. LaFaye, *Arrest: The Decision to Take a Suspect Into Custody* (New York: Little,
Brown & Co., 1965), p. 516.

. . . While private counsel representing a business client would believe it to be of the utmost importance to consult fully with his client, prosecutors commonly proceed on the assumption that the police need not be consulted. A prosecutor who understood the problems of the police . . . could better decide what issues are in greatest need of clarification . . . . [Commonly] communications between the prosecutor and the police chief [are virtually] nonexistent.

A legal advisor could be a civilian employee, or a policeman, or a prosecutor. If he is a member of the city attorney's or district attorney's staff, he could be assigned to the force either on a rotating or permanent basis. It does seem, however, that a civilian advisor (rather than a police officer-lawyer) would be preferable in most cases; a civilian is likely to be more sensitive to the nuances and needs of other agencies, particularly governmental agencies such as welfare, education, and housing, which should coordinate their efforts more closely with law enforcement. The legal adviser would also be essential to review pending legislative proposals for the force as well as proposals drafted by nonpolice agencies whose provisions, if passed, would bear on the police.

It is impossible to calculate the number of legal advisors now needed by police agencies. An estimate of manpower needs will depend upon the duties the legal advisor will perform, which will of course, vary from department to department. For the very large departments, a legal advisory unit consisting of from 5 to 10 lawyers may be needed to meet minimum needs. For other departments one individual may be able to service the entire agency. In smaller communities, particularly suburban ones whose police force is far below 250 personnel, it may be necessary to obtain a part-time lawyer, or to share the services of one lawyer among several departments. Viewing the needs of departments for police legal advisors nationwide, approximately 250-400 attorneys knowledgeable in criminal law, administrative law, and police science seem needed on a full-time basis to meet minimum requirements.

The law schools of Northwestern University and the University of Wisconsin now have programs to train people in law enforcement legal processes. These programs alone cannot train enough people, but they do provide models for other schools to study and emulate. Private foundation and government grants to support programs for providing departments with police legal advisors would be an important step toward more just and more effective law enforcement. . . .

Searching the Crime Scene

The comments of Justice Goldberg, speaking for the majority of the Supreme Court in *Escobedo v. Illinois,* should have alerted public officials and the police throughout the country to the necessity of more adequate police crime scene searching and painstaking laboratory review:[24]

> We have learned the lesson of history, ancient and modern, that a system of criminal law enforcement which comes to depend on the "confession" will, in the long run, be less reliable than a system which depends on extrinsic evidence independently secured through skillful investigation.

More and more, the solution of major crimes will hinge upon the discovery at crime scenes and subsequent scientific laboratory analysis of latent fingerprints, weapons, footprints, hairs, fibers, blood, and similar traces. As a result, departments must train and devote greater numbers of men to searching crime scenes for physical evidence.

While forces are aware of the need to search crime scenes for physical evidence, few seem prepared to do so on a broad scale for want of adequate manpower. For example, the following summary shows by shift the small number of personnel assigned as evidence technicians in 1965 in four cities:[25]

City	Number of sworn members	Evidence technicians by shift			Total serious crimes, 1965
		Day	Evening	Night	
Buffalo	1,349	2	1	1	9,833
Cleveland	2,014	2	2	2	16,697
Omaha	403	1	1	1	5,752
Honolulu	818	1	2	0	9,281

In addition to limited manpower, forces lack equipment and training for evidence technicians. Every force, regardless of size, should devise an adequate system suited to local needs so that crime scenes are fully searched. Furthermore, the staff and facilities of the crime laboratory should be bolstered to accommodate what may be a dramatic increase in workload. This is so whether the laboratory is State, regionally, or locally administered.

---

[24]*Escobedo v. Illinois.* 378 U.S. 478, 488 (1964).

[25]Police Department of Kansas City, Mo., *1966 Survey of Municipal Police Departments (Cities of 300,000 to 1,000,000 Population, 1960 Census)* (Kansas City, Mo., Police Department, 1966), p. 22. Data on serious crime is sourced in U.S. Department of Justice, Federal Bureau of Investigation, *Uniform Crime Reports, 1965* (Washington: U.S. Government Printing Office, 1966), p. 176.

Each department should keep a statistical check on the assignments of evidence technicians so that an index of need for their services may be established. With such an index, a force may be able to distribute them better according to the demonstrated demand for their services both by location and hours of the day.

Utilizing Field Personnel More Effectively

Many American police forces do not utilize their available field personnel effectively. The most significant weakness appears to be the failure of departments to distribute patrol officers in accordance with the actual need for their presence. Other weaknesses, present to varying degrees in various forces, include too great reliance on foot patrol without providing officers with either modern communications or mobility; the extensive use of two-man motor patrol; detectives deployed in pairs; loose and insufficient patrol and detective supervision, and a lack of unity at the field level among investigators; outmoded report preparation systems; and the assignment of too many diverse tasks to police field officers. These weaknesses are outward signs of the failure of many police departments to develop field assignments on the basis of systematic evaluation of street needs.

At least seven steps must be taken to assure that police departments derive maximum utilization from field personnel:

- Distributing available field officers according to need for their services.
- Improving supervision of the field force.
- Improving coordination of effort among field personnel.
- Improving patrol techniques by critically analyzing the need for foot patrol and two-man motor patrols. Unless there is found extraordinary personnel hazards of more than an occasional nature, uniformed personnel should be deployed singly.
- Deploying investigators singly unless there is an unusual series of cases which demands that two or more men be assigned jointly.
- Modernizing report preparation and duplicating techniques.
- Relieving police officers of certain routine menial tasks.

Proportional Distribution of Patrols and Saturation Techniques

Efforts must be made to schedule police patrol at the times when, and places where, crimes are most likely to occur. This concept is known as proportional distribution of the patrol force. It involves measuring the relative need for police patrol services, and distributing personnel to beats on the basis of a crime variation index derived from data collected over an extended period.

Proportional distribution was conceived as early as 1909, when Chief August Vollmer assigned the Berkeley, Calif., patrol force (which then was bicycle-mounted and in 1911 became autoborne) to two 12-hour shifts and to beats which were laid out in accordance with the number of calls antici-pated in each part of the city. Some men worked very large beats and some patrolled areas far smaller, where "action" was more localized. Following Vollmer's move, Elmer Graper and Raymond Fosdick elaborated on the distribution concept. This in turn led to further sophistications of it by Bruce Smith and O. W. Wilson, and to its implementation by several police forces. Today in dozens of cities patrols are distributed according to the best available need-for-patrol formulas.[26] The success inherent in distributing uniformed personnel in accordance with the need for their services was noted in the "Missouri Crime Survey" in 1926 in language that seems valid today although infrequently heeded:[27]

> . . . several forces are faced with the fact that under their present scheme of distribution, uniformed patrols are inadequate in number. Rising police costs render personnel increases both inexpedient and undesirable. But this survey shows that the effect of a substantial increase can be secured if outworn schemes of distribution are abandoned, and the patrol force distrib-uted and administered not according to conditions which existed a generation ago, but in line with conditions existing today.

The concept of proportional distribution of manpower is essentially sound although not necessarily fully developed, and every force of more than a few men could advantageously be allocated on a need-for-service basis.

Several departments with computer capacity have commenced a con-tinuous statistical assessment of patrol workloads and deployment. The St. Louis police are actively engaged in implementing a program that not only will predict the police field problems for the forthcoming tour of duty but will also monitor the crime picture as it emerges, and adjust the predictions as changes develop. Although this is a highly sophisticated application and is practical for only a few departments, any agency can engage in continuing manual reassessment of patrol areas through record analysis.

Saturation is another method which makes fullest use of available operational personnel. This is accomplished by assigning additional men to

---

[26]A comprehensive discussion of distribution of police strength, applicable to the interests of both small and large forces, may be found in Samuel G. Chapman. *Police Patrol Readings* (Springfield, Ill.: Charles C. Thomas, 1964), pp. 171-233. Pages 234-276 describe the team policing concept which has had some limited application in Great Britain.

[27]*The Missouri Crime Survey* (New York: The Macmillan Co., 1926), pp. 46-47.

patrol areas that, according to available statistics, require greater-than-usual patrol coverage. Given the manpower, a chief may assign some men to a fourth shift, which overlaps two of the present shifts (i.e., serves from 7 P.M. to 3 A.M. as has been done in Toledo, Phoenix, San Diego, and Birmingham); form a tactical patrol unit as Savannah, Ga., and Berkeley have done; or pay off-duty personnel overtime to work a regular day off as is done in Washington, D.C. The purpose of each of these operations is to saturate high crime areas with officers when there is need for greater coverage and when the use of more men would not aggravate, but would help resolve, the conditions.[28]

Improving Supervision

The fact that uniformed personnel operate throughout a city at all hours of the day and night sometimes prevents the desired level of supervisory control. Accordingly, opportunities for personnel to engage in minor delinquencies, and to bestow or receive special favors, are always present. The whole scheme of patrol is such that supervisors are challenged to stimulate initiative and individual judgment. The relationship between organization, management and full utilization of personnel and supervision is well stated in the District of Columbia Crime Commission's report to the President:[29]

> Closely related to organizational and management deficiencies is the poor quality of supervision which is pervasive through the Department. The inadequacies in supervision can be attributed to the following factors: Too few supervisors at some levels, a failure to use a supervisory probation period, a lack of in-service supervisory training, inadequate transportation available to supervisors, unclear Department policies and procedures, and a failure to define supervisory responsibilities or to perform adequate line inspection. As a consequence, there is "excessive familiarity with subordinates and lack of bearing" and a "frequent loss of respect for the supervisor and administrator." These conclusions have been confirmed by the comments of many police officers to Commission representatives. Officers have repeatedly complained of the inadequacy of supervision and the lack of encouragement and support by high-ranking officers. Such attitudes reflect a low state of morale which cannot help detracting from police efficiency.

Viewed from any aspect, supervising a widely dispersed field team constitutes a difficult problem. In Denver, newspaperman Mort Stern viv-

---

[28]See *Task Force Report: The Police,* ch. 6, for a discussion of the kinds of problems in which the use of saturation patrol may be subject to question.

[29]The President's Commission on Crime in the District of Columbia, *A Report on the President's Commission on Crime in the District of Columbia* (Washington: U.S. Government Printing Office, 1966), p. 9.

idly described the events that led to the burglary indictments in 1960. He showed that when field personnel are free-lance operators and lack sufficient supervision, they are susceptible to special temptations:[30]

> The rule book forbids [delinquent acts]. But it isn't enforced. It's winked at, at all levels.

A force must provide a sufficient number of supervisors at the first command level—that of sergeant—to control adequately and direct all police activities and assure the maximum utilization of personnel. These supervisors should spend most of their time in the field, providing personnel supervision, leadership, training, and incentives, and checking on conditions throughout the city to insure that proper and immediate police action is taken. Supervisors should be charged with inducing men to apply themselves, and should also be notified of and dispatched to all incidents that might reflect discredit on the police department or on an individual officer. The additional supervisory role of police agents will be described in the next section of this chapter.

Improving Patrol-Detective Division Coordination

In almost all large police departments there is a considerable amount of organizational fragmentation. Traditionally and almost universally, patrol and investigative forces have separate lines of command and tend to be isolated from one another; often they keep separate sets of records; frequently they work different shifts or are based in different places so that there is a minimum of contact between patrolmen and detectives. In addition, investigators are more often than not divided at both headquarters and precinct levels into squads—vice, robbery, burglary, fraud, homicide, and so forth—that may themselves keep separate records, use separate informants and remain more or less isolated from each other in other ways.

At both the staff and the field levels, this overseparation of functions, or overspecialization, can have undesirable results. When intelligence is not centralized and coordinated, staff planning for the purpose of either apprehending specific criminals, or solving crime problems such as, for example, an outbreak of burglaries in some neighborhood, is almost impossible. When lines of command are kept rigidly separate, it is difficult to bring the full resources of a department to bear on crime solution. Also considerable conflict exists in many forces between uniformed branch officers and the detective division. An early report of the problem is found in the 1926 "Missouri Crime Survey":[31]

---

[30] *Denver Post,* Oct. 8, 1961, as reprinted in Samuel G. Chapman, *Police Patrol Readings* (Springfield, Ill.: Charles C. Thomas, 1964), p. 49.

[31] *Missouri Crime Survey,* at p. 49.

The ancient rivalry between the uniformed and plainclothes forces has a substantial basis. It arises from the fact that in a given case the patrolman is often the first to risk life and limb. With the arrival of detectives, however, he is automatically displaced. The plainclothes operative takes command of the situation, and the patrolman returns to his beat. This condition inspires a natural resentment, which sometimes leads to a series of retaliatory acts by the two branches. In the maneuvers which follow, the public functions of these officers are lost sight of. Their energies are directed at causing each other confusion, discomfort, and discouragement.

A 1962 consultant report shows that this issue is still current:[32]

The lack of coordination between detective and uniformed divisions leads to duplication of effort, unarticulated field work, and the loss of some cases, and the missing of arrests which might otherwise be made.

The most promising means of overcoming this problem is to combine the patrol and detective field forces under a common supervisor.

The agent-officer-community service officer recommendation made in chapter 4 of the "General Report" . . . has not only the improvement of the quality of police personnel as its objective, but also a change in the way the police work in the field. The concept, which might be called "team policing," is that police work, including patrol and criminal investigation, in a given number of city blocks should be under unified command. A "field supervisor" would have under his command a team of agents, officers, and community service officers. The team would meet at the beginning of a tour of duty and receive a briefing on the current situation in the neighborhood —what crimes were unsolved, what suspects were wanted for questioning, what kinds of stolen goods to look out for, what situations were potentially troublesome and so forth. On this basis the members would be assigned to specific areas or duties. If conditions warranted it, agents might be assigned to patrol, and wear uniforms or plainclothes. Officers might be assigned to investigation. Community service officers might be delegated to help either. In specific investigations or incidents, agents would be given authority over the actions of CSO's and officers. If the conditions in the area changed during the tour, if a major crime was committed or a major disorder erupted, the assignments would be promptly changed by the field supervisor.

Obviously, this proposal does not envision the abandonment of special duties or special squads. An agent serving as a narcotics, juvenile, or community-relations specialist, for example, would almost always cover a territory policed by several teams, and would be moved into other work only

[32]Public Administration Service of Chicago, *Police and Fire Services in Meriden, Connecticut* (Chicago: Public Administration Service, 1962), p. 36.

in emergencies. There would still be a need for squads of officers with special knowledge of certain kinds of crime.

Improving Patrol Techniques

Patrol may be executed in a host of ways. The time-honored fashion is on foot, but the mass-produced motor vehicle has brought auto and motorcycle patrol into prominence. More recently, some forces, including the Michigan State Police, Los Angeles County Sheriff's Police, and the California Highway Patrol, have integrated fixed wing aircraft and helicopters into their field forces. Of course, where large bodies of water or rivers must be patrolled, appropriate marine equipment must be used. Other forces, including many park police agencies, continue to use horses, solo motorcycles, four-wheel-drive vehicles, and bicycles for patrol as needs dictate.

Selecting the patrol method best suited to protect a city and derive at the same time maximum usefulness from personnel challenges administrators. There has been little research in this area, consequently hard facts are lacking about the practices that really are most effective. Decisions governing a force's patrol methods are, unfortunately, usually linked solely to tradition.

Foot Patrol

Many of the Nation's forces have some uniformed personnel assigned to patrol on foot. Without question, there are certain areas in some cities that require the kind of intimate, personal, police-citizen contact and police presence which only patrol on foot affords. However, in many cities, especially small ones, there is less and less justification for full-time foot patrolmen.

That there is no "standard" for foot patrol duty is clear when one studies the 1966 foot patrol deployment pattern in 37 American cities of between 300,000 and 1 million population. Of these, all but Forth Worth, Memphis, St. Paul, and San Diego had some personnel assigned to walking beats. But among cities having foot patrol beats, the total beats on each shift varied greatly, ranging from 2 in Birmingham and Phoenix, and 3 in Dallas, Kansas City, Oklahoma City, and Omaha, to 185 in Boston, 212 in Pittsburgh, and 434 in Baltimore.[33]

A decision to use foot patrols should be made only after careful analysis, since it is a highly expensive form of coverage, geographically restrictive in nature, and can be wasteful of manpower. Without transportation at hand, it provides extremely inflexible and rigid close patrol for specifically limited geographical areas and does not permit the ready reas-

---

[33] *1966 Kansas City Survey,* col. 61, table 5, p. 22.

signment of the personnel to surrounding locations when and where police services may be specifically requested.[34] Moreover, close supervision of foot patrolmen has proven very difficult.

The essence of the problem was well stated in the District of Columbia Crime Commission report:[35]

> The Department's continued reliance on foot patrol is an inefficient and outdated utilization of manpower resources . . . Leading police authorities are in general agreement that, with few exceptions, foot patrol is not the most efficient method of patrol . . . Of course, officers should be assigned walking beats in particular commercial and high-crime areas where the need can be demonstrated. As long as the Department uses foot patrol as the primary method of patrol, however, available economies will not be realized and the city will not be provided the best possible police service.

Putting the Officer "Back on the Beat"

The most significant weakness in American motor patrol operations today is the general lack of contact with citizens except when an officer has responded to a call. Forced to stay near the car's radio, waiting an assignment, most patrol officers have few opportunities to develop closer relationships with persons living in the district.

There is considerable merit in "getting the policeman back on the beat" in high crime rate areas. But this can be accomplished without depriving an officer of the many advantages of radio-equipped vehicles. For example, motor patrol officers should be equipped with very small transistorized portable police radio transmitting-receiving equipment. Small, compact portable radio devices would greatly expand the operational radii of motorized personnel by permitting them to engage in extensive foot patrol and to range well away from their vehicles at any hour of the day or night without sacrificing contact with headquarters. Police forces serving Oakland; Berkeley; Meriden, Conn.; and Kalamazoo, Mich., reported they had patrolmen so equipped. As discussed below, chapter 11 of Commission's General Report recommends Federal support to develop such equipment to be available at reasonable prices.

Chiefs may also wish to equip their footmen with motor scooters, which can be parked unobtrusively and with ease almost anywhere. New York City; Washington, D.C.; New Rochelle; North Bergen, N.J.; and Newport, R.I., have so equipped some of their footmen and report the system to be working satisfactorily. Smaller forces, which feel they must assign some men to foot patrol, should carefully consider the motor scooter-

---

[34]Police chiefs will find a Chicago Police Department staff report on foot patrol utilization very helpful in assessments of their cities' needs for footmen. This appears in Samuel G. Chapman, *Police Patrol Readings* (Springfield, Ill.: Charles C. Thomas, 1964), pp. 105-110.
[35]*Crime in District of Columbia,* at p. 53.

radio equipment concept to insure full availability of these men and their mobility.

Whether equipped with portable radios, motor scooters or standard police vehicles, patrolmen should be considered as foot officers who possess vehicles available nearby for quick, nonfatiguing transportation from one point to another. It is while out of their cars on foot that motorized patrol officers can serve very effectively as the "eyes and ears" of the police department and yet be subject to immediate recall and assignment. Consequently, by distributing the patrol force on a basis of need, and providing close supervision to its operation, the Nation's policemen will, in fact, be "on the beat" providing protection and accessibility for America's citizens.

One- and Two-Man Motor Patrol

There has been a discernible pattern away from the exclusive use of two-man cars in American cities, and a distinct movement toward the far greater use of one-man patrols as is shown in Table 1. This trend lends support to those police authorities who believe that local police problems can be most immediately met by covering a city with motorized one-man patrol units, rather than by a system of less intensive patrolling caused by an exclusive pattern of two-man units. The District of Columbia Crime Commission presents this concept in its report:[36]

> Conspicuous patrol, conveying a sense of police omnipresence, is best effected by a highly mobilized force, with considerable emphasis on one-man cars. The Commission endorses the Department's recent experimental efforts in this direction and recommends an accelerated program to increase the number of one-man cars.

Another consultant supports the view that one-man units should be the rule wherever possible:[37]

> The more men and more cars that are visible on the streets, the greater is the potential for preventing crime. A heavy blanket of conspicuous patrol at all times and in all parts of the city tends to suppress violations of the law. The most economical manner of providing this heavy blanket of patrol is by using one-man cars when and where they are feasible.

Almost all cities have long forsaken the practice of having two patrolmen walk a beat together. For the same reasons it seems generally undesirable and unnecessary to have two men in a car. One-man operations permit

[36]Ibid.
[37]International Association of Chiefs of Police, *A Survey of the Police Department of Youngstown, Ohio* (Washington, D.C.: International Association of Chiefs of Police, June 1964), p. 89.

Table 1.—Manning of Police Patrol Cars in Cities over 10,000 Population

Population group	Number cities reporting motorized patrol			Cities using 2-man patrol cars only					
				1946		1954		1964	
	1946	1954	1964	Number	Percent	Number	Percent	Number	Percent
Over 500,000	13	18	20	8	61.5	9	50.0	4	20.0
250,000-500,000	21	21	31	10	47.6	5	23.8	2	6.0
100,000-250,000	52	63	75	30	57.7	24	38.1	3	4.0
50,000-100,000	90	120	160	48	53.3	43	35.8	14	9.0
25,000-50,000	171	260	320	69	40.4	63	24.2	13	4.0
10,000-25,000	493	518	728	140	28.4	89	17.2	32	4.0
All over 10,000	840	1,000	1,334	305	36.3	233	23.3	68	4.0

Population group	Cities using 1- and 2-man patrol cars						Cities using 1-man patrol cars only					
	1946		1954		1964		1946		1954		1964	
	Number	Percent	Number	Percent	Number	Percent	Number	Percent	Number	Percent	Number	Percent
Over 500,000	5	38.5	9	50.0	15	75.0	0	0	0	0	1	5.0
250,000-500,000	10	47.6	14	66.7	25	81.0	1	4.8	2	9.5	4	13.0
100,000-250,000	19	36.5	33	52.4	59	79.0	3	5.8	6	9.5	13	17.0
50,000-100,000	35	38.9	66	55.0	102	64.0	7	7.8	11	9.2	44	27.0
25,000-50,000	77	45.0	147	56.5	171	53.0	25	14.6	50	19.3	136	43.0
10,000-25,000	238	48.3	300	57.9	342	47.0	115	23.3	129	24.9	354	49.0
All over 10,000	384	45.7	569	56.9	714	54.0	151	18.0	198	19.8	552	41.0

Source: "The Municipal Yearbook, 1947," p. 385; 1955, p. 411; and 1965, p. 426 (Chicago: International City Managers' Association).

more intensive patrol of a city with a like number of officers, prevent partners from spending much of their time aimlessly conversing with each other, and contribute to the safety of the individual officers by compelling each officer to give his undivided attention to his duties. One-man cars allow rapid assignment of more vehicles from more directions as another means of combatting crime.

Conditions which justify the use of two-man patrol cars are similar to those which dictate the assignment of two-man teams to patrol duty on foot. Such conditions include those of too many incidents for one man to handle in a physically limited, densely populated area; a high frequency of circumstances in which officers are likely to be assaulted; and the high prospect of raucous misbehavior that can only be prevented by the concerted action of two or more officers. Such decisions must be made locally and, whatever the deployment practice, forces should periodically reevaluate their one- and two-man districts to be sure of the wisdom of their decisions. For example, in its 1965 survey of the Baltimore police, the International Association of Chiefs of Police recommended a broad pattern of one-man motor patrol with some two-man units. In additon, the consultant very properly urged:[38]

> After some experience (6 months to a year) with the new distribution, workload and the incidents that seem to justify two-man cars may be reevaluated with changes made in staffing as appropriate. Workload varies in many ways, and annual study is needed. Of course, a particular event such as an assault against an officer cannot be predicted to the day, hour, and location, but the likelihood of such events can be predicted reasonably well, provided the data base is current and is a valid sample, if not the total, of all events.

Improving Investigator Deployment

The same deployment principles should apply to headquarters-based plainclothes investigative personnel. Several cities, both large and small, routinely deploy detectives in twos and sometimes threes! Since the bulk of a department's investigative work is routine, the widespread use of investigative teams is an unnecessary waste of manpower. In many departments today, including such Federal agencies as the FBI and Secret Service, investigative personnel primarily work alone. This should be the practice in all departments. A basic pattern of one-man plainclothes investigations, with exceptions as conditions indicate, would have the effect of increasing the effective manpower of those detective divisions in which two-man teams are presently the rule.

Some American forces have a formally established detective rank whose incumbents have tenure and, other than for gross misconduct, cannot

---

[38] *Baltimore Police Dept.,* at p. 93.

be removed from plainclothes status. Such a practice is basically unsound and overprotective. Plainclothes investigative positions should be filled by appointments of worthy police officers who would serve for indefinite duration. Such appointment latitude is significant for several reasons, the most important being the urgency of maintaining the vitality of a force by having some especially challenging assignments open to men who seem ready to assume greater responsibility.

Chiefs of police should take full advantage of their power to make occasional changes of personnel assignments at the patrol and investigative levels of execution. In some cities, the chief is free to do so, uninhibited by civil service restriction as to classification of detectives in a special rank complete with special pay and tenure. But where civil service precludes the chief from assigning men to plainclothes status at his discretion, he is unduly hindered and the system should be changed. The lateral transfer of men from any unit of a department to another should be the sole prerogative of the chief.

Report Preparation and Duplication

There are two other means by which the police may maximize the field time of personnel. One is to give uniformed police officers the means to prepare reports while in the field so that they need not go to headquarters or to the precinct for this purpose.

The extent of street contact hours lost to report writing at headquarters in some forces is notable. For example, in one large city, departmental procedure requires a police car team to return to the district station and prepare a report after handling almost any type of incident. Then the team returns to its prescribed patrol area. In another large city an average of 14 percent of a police officer's time is spent writing reports.

If patrol officers, investigators, and other field personnel are to be fully utilized, a force should consider implementing a system whereby reports may be dictated without requiring personnel to leave their patrol area. The same is necessary to free detectives from countless hours they are required to spend at their typewriters. One way to accomplish this is to install dictation equipment either in each vehicle or at headquarters so that an officer or detective may "call" his report onto a tape. Clerical employees could then transcribe reports and the officer could quickly resume his field duties. Many forces, including Wichita Falls, Tex.; Tulsa, Okla.; Stockton, Calif.; New Bedford, Mass.; and the Adams County, Colo., Sheriff's Police are so equipped.

Some forces report that they require their uniformed personnel to handwrite reports in the field on pre-prepared master forms suitable for subsequent offset duplication at headquarters. These include Los Angeles, Oakland, Chattanooga, and Moline, Ill.

Whether officers dictate reports while in the field or handwrite them, the means by which adequate copies of such reports are prepared and distributed at headquarters affects the optimum utilization of clerical personnel. Many small forces still find that typewritten carbon copies satisfy their distribution requirements. Larger forces, however, often require more copies than can be prepared on a typewriter, and hence have integrated various dry copy processes into their records procedures.

Routine Tasks

Another means for making better use of police officers is to relieve them of many less important tasks so that they may attend to matters criminal and preventive in nature. The real issue here centers around the role of the police and the problem of overextending available personnel. August Vollmer noted the problem in 1929:[39]

> ... Protecting lives and property and preserving the peace of a community is a huge task. Apparently it is believed to be an unimportant and small responsibility, and the legislative bodies continue to heap innumerable duties upon the police, until they are loaded to the breaking point.

The problem was noted long before Chief Vollmer's lament. For example, in 1866, the president of the Board of Commissioners of the Detroit Police Department reported to the Common Council:[40]

> ... for the last year the force has been compelled to perform an excessive amount of service, the present police establishment is not deemed sufficiently large. The force should be large enough, without being overworked, to afford protection to life and property equally throughout the city.

Related problems arise when towns and cities grow in population; the police are assigned to a broader range of tasks, and become especially involved in a host of non-criminal functions.

The police workload increases each year. Discussions with police officials and a review of several forces' annual reports over the 11-year span of 1955-65 confirm the trend. The gross workload for three cities reflected in Table 2 provides an example of this trend:[41]

Increasing caseloads compel that sworn officers be relieved of responsibility for minor tasks. ...

---

[39]August Vollmer, "The Police in Chicago" as published in the "Illinois Crime Survey" (Chicago: Association of Criminal Justice, 1929), p. 366.

[40]"First Annual Report to the Board of Commissioners of Metropolitan Police of the City of Detroit" (Detroit: Daily Post Printing House, April 1866), p.6.

[41]Telephone conversations with Superintendent Beerman, Services Division, Atlanta Police Department; Captain Smith, Records, Identification, and Communications, Denver Police Department; and Lieutenant Powers, Director of Research and Planning, Philadelphia Police Department, Dec. 5-16, 1966.

Table 2.—Number of Cases

City	1955	1960	1965	Percent increase 1965 over 1955
Atlanta	383,171	514,599	778,353	103.1
Denver	332,352	381,797	466,581	40.4
Philadelphia	1,123,477	1,319,611	1,567,088	39.5

Applying Technology to Police Service

Only token progress has been made in introducing technology into the police world. Some police departments, mainly the largest ones, have taken solid steps alone or in collaboration with nearby forces toward applying advances in science and technology to law enforcement. They have done so in spite of the costliness of equipment. Laudably, those large forces that have installed information storage and retrieval and communications systems have invited smaller forces to draw on the larger departments' facilities once the systems become operative.

Nevertheless, a majority of our Nation's police departments are constrained by limited funds and a few by lack of appreciation of the role of technology in law enforcement. Los Angeles Police Chief Thomas Reddin reported at the National Symposium on Science and Criminal Justice that:[42]

> Research should be a program of discovery and design, not merely patching the dike. . . . This nation's "knowledge explosion" has so far left law enforcement untouched. . . .

The Commission's Science and Technology Task Force has completed preliminary investigations of four specific areas in which there is promise of a major scientific contribution to law enforcement.

First, the task force determined that modern information systems can greatly assist the police in identifying persons as currently wanted; provide the basis of studies whose goal is to better deploy police personnel and analyze community crime patterns; and provide the basis for both short and long range research. This includes the outline of a national information system, but not the detailed design of the system.

---

[42]Thomas Reddin, "Police Weapons for the Space Age," *The Police Chief,* 33 (November 1966): 10-17. Chief Reddin's article suggests several police enterprises which may be broadly influenced through science, technology, and research.

Second, the task force has outlined a new command and control system with which to improve a police agency's field operations by enabling men to be more quickly dispatched to those calls which by their nature may escalate into grave disorder or where suspects are still on the crime scene or in the vicinity. The system is based on the premise that too much time elapses between the time a call for service comes in from the public and the moment cars are dispatched under present dispatching-command control techniques. Valuable minutes can be saved.

Third, the task force has attacked the problems of police radio-frequency usage and has shown how a dramatic reduction in radio frequency congestion may be made.

Fourth, the task force has proposed a research and development program for law enforcement.

The Need for Information

It is readily evident that many criminal justice problems result from the lack of complete and timely information. For example, a police officer does not know whether an arrested suspect is wanted for a more serious crime elsewhere. There are other such information problems, characterized by the inaccessibility of stored information. Government and industry have made extensive use of computer technology to solve related problems in such diverse fields as continental air defense, production scheduling, airline reservations, and corporate management. Some police agencies already use or have ordered computers.

The technical development potentially most profoundly affecting criminal justice operations is the advent of computer-based information systems. Some pioneering installations have been or in the immediate future will be established at the city, county, State, and National levels. These include the St. Louis, Chicago, and New York Police Departments, the inter-county "Police Information Network" (PIN) of Alameda County (Calif.), the State police systems of California, Pennsylvania, and New York and statewide criminal justice information systems of California and New York. The FBI is now operating a National Crime Information Center (NCIC) providing 15 police terminals around the Nation with on-line computer-based information on wanted persons, stolen vehicles, and stolen property.

A greatly expanded development of computer-based information systems is one concrete step that would make a dramatic impact on the police service. Such systems can aid the police in the following functions:

- *Police patrol.*—Enabling a police officer to check the identification of people and property against a central "wanted" file in a few minutes.

- *Crime investigation.*—Providing a police officer or investigative agent with supporting information files such as crime patterns, modus operandi, criminal associates and personal appearance and, hopefully in the future, matching latent fingerprints from a crime scene against a central fingerprint file. The latter process, when it is developed, would constitute a major breakthrough in the war on crime.
- *Manpower deployment.*—Altering police deployment in response to changing patterns of crime on an hourly or daily basis.
- *Individual protection.*—Completing arrest records to include court disposition, presenting a fairer picture to the police and judges.
- *Federal, State, and local budgeting.*—Collecting uniform statistics on agency operations and workloads, providing a basis for estimating personnel needs and for optimum allocation of men and dollars.

The Science and Technology Task Force volume contains a full discussion of the need for integrated information systems to which all criminal justice agencies can contribute.

Communications, Command, and Control

The scientific community has more to offer the modern police organization than the prospect of information storage and retrieval networks and data for research. It holds promise for improving a department's ability to operate more efficiently in the field as well by modernizing the traditional radio dispatching system in large departments. The main purpose of modernizing the dispatching function is to reduce the total time it takes an officer to reach an incident from the time a call for assistance is received.

The question of what deters people from criminal acts is very complex, and one about which little is known. Basic to deterrence is the assumption that to increase the threat of apprehension raises the risk in committing the crime, and so reduces the likelihood of the crime being committed. Projecting that threat of apprehension is a primary objective of police field operations. Improving the apprehension capability itself is one approach to raising the threat thereof.

The apprehension process can be viewed as a sequence of actions taken in response to the commission of crime. These are shown schematically in Figure 3 and listed below:

- The crime is detected—
    - (*a*) By police on patrol.
    - (*b*) By an alarm device.
    - (*c*) By a victim or another citizen.

- In the latter two cases, information about the crime is communicated to the police, usually by telephone.
- An appropriate police response (e.g., choosing a patrol car to send to the scene) is selected; this is part of the "command and control" function.
- The assignment, or "dispatch order," is communicated to the patrol force, usually by voice radio.
- The appropriate patrol cars travel to the crime scene.
- A search is conducted for the perpetrator of the crime:
    (*a*) A "hot" search at the crime scene.
    (*b*) A "warm" search in the general vicinity of the crime.
    (*c*) A "cold" investigative search by officers or plainclothes investigators.
- Throughout the search, suspects appear and have to be checked out.
- If the search is successful, a suspect is captured and evidence to support a charge is assembled.

Throughout this process, there are many opportunities for technological contributions: Better alarms, more accessible telephones to help the public reach the police, up-to-date police personnel status boards, more reliable radios, faster vehicles, nonlethal weapons, and modern crime laboratories.

Selecting the best of these technological aids from among the many possibilities requires information on the conditions that make apprehension likely.

To examine the question of what factors give rise to apprehension, Commission consultants conducted a preliminary survey of over 4,700 calls for service to a very large city police department. Over the period of the survey for 2 police divisions, all calls to the police communications center, all actions reported by the police patrol, all crimes reported, and all eventual arrests were studied. In the survey, there were 1,905 crimes examined, of which 482 (25 percent) resulted in arrests or other clearances. Of these, 70 percent involved arrests, 90 percent of which were made by the patrol force. More than half the arrests were made within eight hours of the crime, many at or near the crime scene, and almost two-thirds of the arrests were made within the first week after the crime. If a suspect is neither known to the victim nor arrested at the scene of the crime, the chances of ever arresting him are very slim. Of the 482 cleared cases, 63 percent involved "named suspects." In the 1,556 cases without named suspects, only 181 (or 12 percent) were solved later by arrest.[43]

---

[43]For a detailed description of this study see chapter 2 and Appendix B of the Science and Technology Task Force volume.

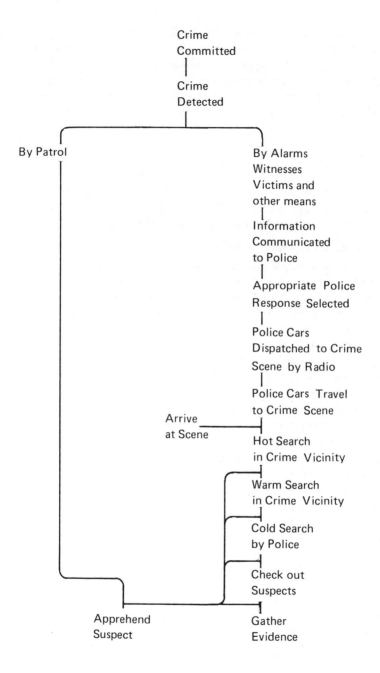

Figure 3.—Apprehension Process

Common sense suggests, and the data from the survey seem to confirm, that response time—the speed with which police can arrive at a crime scene—is important to apprehension. But to establish firmly the relationship between response time and apprehension rate, further studies are necessary. The limited research already conducted, however, supports the conclusion that a greater expenditure of funds is warranted to mount a concerted effort to reduce the total response time in the apprehension process.

The technology of communications and police command and control have developed markedly in recent years, and they can help provide better information faster both to reduce the field response time and to improve the quality of the response. The vital links in the apprehension process are the information-transfer functions indicated in Figure 3.

The Police Communications Center

The police communications center is the link that connects the citizen in trouble to the police officers who will respond. Its role has increased as the telephone has become the more common access means to police, and as more and more police officers are equipped with radios.

Considering that the communications center is the nerve center controlling the minute-by-minute deployment of the police force, it has received surprisingly little attention. It is often squeezed into a spare corner of police headquarters, frequently under the command of a sergeant or a patrolman, and usually operated with obsolete and poorly designed equipment, and in accordance with procedures that have tended to evolve by chance rather than through careful design.

An important question is what constitutes the optimum division of functions within a communications center. Few, if any, communications centers are organized in the same fashion. In some, mostly those of small forces, the same person serves as the complaint clerk and dispatcher; as forces become larger, the functions are separated. Some centers in turn have a dispatcher handling only part of a city. Other centers have a more desirable arrangement wherein dispatchers handle calls for the whole city.

The advantages and disadvantages of the various possible patterns should be experimentally assessed, both by measurements in operating centers and under laboratory control in a simulation laboratory. In this manner, standard and emergency plans and procedures can be tested, doctrine and decision rules evaluated, and training and experience can be provided police personnel under simulated extreme conditions.

Computer-Assisted Command and Control

The above modifications could surely lead to some immediate improvement. However, needed even more urgently than short-range improvements is a basic reexamination of the entire police command and control function taking full account of the promising new technological opportunities offered by computers and communications links. The review should not begin with the new technology, however. It should begin by considering questions of when, where, and how to use the police patrol force, and how to respond to various types of routine and emergency situations. It should examine on paper and by experiment the extent to which preventive patrol really deters crime, the manner in which forces should be allocated by time and by geography, optimum patrol tactics, appropriate conditions for conspicuousness and for covertness, how to respond to riots, and many other related questions. The patrol operation will then be able to benefit markedly from computer assistance—much more than if the current procedures were merely automated.

It is possible at this stage to describe only the general outlines of a computer-assisted command and control system. In such a system, a properly applied computer could reduce control-center response time significantly—from about 90 seconds under optimum conditions to about 30 seconds. For example, in a computer-aided command and control system, telephone calls to the police would still be answered by a complaint clerk, or "controller." He would enter the type of incident, the address, and a priority code into a keyboard connected to a computer. The controller can specify any additional requirements, whether a one- or two-man car should be sent, whether two, three, or more vehicles should respond, or any other requirement posed by the situation. The rest is then automatic.

The computer maintains records of street-address locations and the location and availability of each patrol car. From these it finds the closest car to respond to the call. It prepares a dispatching order which is automatically sent to the selected car as a computer-generated voice message, or by a digital data link such as teletype. If the patrol officer does not acknowledge the message within, say, 10 seconds, a second car can be sent on the call. The control orders the status of the patrol cars, events in progress, and other basic control information can also be generated by the computer and displayed to dispatching command officers who can always countermand the computer-originated orders if required. Having "override" capability, they can concentrate on the unusual while the computer deals with the routine.

Since the field response time depends strongly on the car's distance from the call, automatic electronic car location devices could be tied directly to the computer so that it could dispatch the closest car. Analysis shows that extreme precision is not essential, and that knowing position within a radius of about one-quarter mile would ordinarily be adequate.

With such a computer-assisted command and control system, many new possibilities are presented for the deployment of the patrol force. As the crime pattern in the city changes hour-by-hour, the patrol force could be redeployed to respond to it. As parts of the city are stripped of patrolmen by called-for-services, other units could be assigned as back-up. Under a riot or other emergency situation, contingency plans could be programmed so that the appropriate units are deployed to the emergency, and adequate backup maintained.

An advantage of the modern command-control system is its option that all the information stored in the computer on the locations of various kinds of calls is available when needed for complete analysis of the operations of the department. This study could be conducted daily or every few hours.

Mobile Radio Equipment

Communications must be maintained with police officers, even when they leave their cars, as well as with foot patrolmen. It is noted above that police officials are interested in securing small portable radios so that patrolmen can call for assistance in any emergency and so that more effective use can be made of the entire police force.

Miniaturized transceivers for the officer away from his car and for the foot patrolman would have similar features. Both will require base stations —the car for one and probably the precinct structure or other public buildings such as a firehouse for the other. Large-scale production economies can produce a miniaturized unit at a low cost (perhaps under $150). To assure a market warranting such production, the Commission has recommended in chapter 11 of its General Report that the Federal Government should assume leadership in initiating these two programs and should assume responsibility for guaranteeing the sale of the first production lot of perhaps 20,000 units.

A modest standardization program of car radios is possible and would add flexibility to a police department's choice of radio suppliers. Gross standardization of size, mounting brackets, receptacles and control heads can be accomplished immediately, and should go far toward making it possible to use the products of different manufacturers interchangeably. More detailed standardization of electronic equipment is less obviously useful for it may serve to inhibit the manufacturers from improving their product. Certain obvious electronic features which involve system compatibility—such as selective codes—should be standardized as early as practicable.

Digital data links to and from the police car can remove a large part of the normal voice traffic and also provide a paper copy of the message to the car. The link can be a minimal system for routine messages or a more complete teletype system. While digital links may save band-width, the need for redundant transmissions to eliminate teletype errors may substantially reduce much of that saving. Further investigation of the error characteristics of mobile digital links in a city environment is required.

Standardized Computer Code and Formats

Finally, it is essential to develop a standardized computer code and formats, fingerprint classifications, and other such uniform systems and "language" to assure national consistency of procedure when mutual support is required. Once developed, these uniform systems must be implemented, and media for dissemination must be developed. Without a standard computer code and formats, computers and systems will be unable to "talk" with each other and systems will be correspondingly weakened for lack of direct, immediate communication ability.

Overcoming Radio Spectrum Limitations

Radio-spectrum congestion and frequency compatibility seriously hamper police radio communications. For example, although 50 police cars are considered normal radio-channel capacity, New York City until recently had to control over 100 cars with 1 radio channel, and relied on the telephone to relieve its radio congestion. In the Chicago area, 38 separate cities with 350 patrol cars must all share one frequency. This congestion results in excessive delays and underutilization of the police force while patrol officers or dispatchers try to gain the air. In emergency situations, such as riots, storms, major conflagrations, aircraft disasters, and so forth where mutual support is required, neighboring police departments are unable to maintain communications because their radios operate on different frequencies.

To overcome the problems of radio-spectrum congestion and frequency incompatibility, the implementation of frequency-sharing concepts through the development of larger, more efficient police mobile radio networks should be encouraged. The larger number of small, independent, overlapping, and inefficient systems should be reduced through voluntary sharing. In this way, each user, when its demand peaks, can utilize the others' slack capacity, a basic concept common in telephone and electric-power networks. For instance, if two police departments each use their private channels 50 percent of the time, then each finds a busy signal half the time. If they were to share their channels, a user would find both channels busy about 35 percent of the time. If four such users were to group together, then all channels would be busy less than 20 percent of the time. Any peak-sharing advantages are in addition to these.

Two distinct trends must be set in motion to encourage such sharing. First, the relationship between the Federal Communications Commission and the police and other public safety band users must be restructured so that the Federal Communications Commission no longer receives piecemeal individual requests from the ultimate public safety user. Rather, coordinated requests must come through governmental entities which represent reasonably large areas and populations.

The core cities themselves are large enough to be able to develop efficient mobile radio networks for their own use, sharing their own public safety frequencies to balance the peak loads as school buses, highway maintenance, police, etc., peak at different times. With the gradual creation of coordinated networks, the Federal Communications Commission will be in a position to require projection of future needs so that radio spectrum can be allocated more rationally.

The second trend to be set in motion for more efficient use of the mobile radio spectrum requires greater use of switchable radio channels and of multichannel trunks. Generally, addressing will have to be accomplished by selective address coding rather than, as at present, by frequency. Selective coding minimizes the present system's inflexible dependence on frequency, but enables the individual user agency to retain its independence while using the system. It is evident that usage of these techniques will increase the cost of the mobile radio network. Basically, the networks will be less wasteful of radio spectrum, more flexible in use, but more costly to implement than the many small individual networks now existing. Federal Government encouragement in the form of financial support appears essential.

Finally, frequency space is available within the VHF-TV band between TV stations and within the underloaded UHF-TV band. One TV channel can provide over 100 radio channels. The Federal Communications Commission should consider allocating portions of the TV spectrum to land-mobile use from which the police should receive a significant share. This would represent a small loss (2 percent for 1 channel in UHF) to the TV community.

Operations Research

It might seem that the most important contribution that science and technology could make to public safety would be to develop equipment for law enforcement with the same degree of ingenuity that it has demonstrated in a great variety of human needs. But advanced "hardware" is only one aspect of the promise that science and technology hold for the police. One of the most promising contributions, yet one most obscure by present standards of adoption, is that which involves operations research.

As an important mechanism for innovation within police agencies, it is urged that police departments of 1,000 or more employees establish an operations research group comprising professionally trained scientists, mathematicians and engineers, including at least one person with a broad statistics background, and at least one with electronics competence. There are today about 37 State, county, and local forces of 1,000 or more personnel.

An operations research group once formed would study the organization of the department, provide technical guidance to the department management, analyze operations, and assess the effects of all experimentation within the department. Such groups, which have proven extremely effective in industry, the Federal Government, and the military, should prove to be a significant force for experimentation and innovation. The group need not be large; depending upon the size of the force, it may include up to about seven professionals. The dollar investment for thus significantly improving the effectiveness of over 1,000 men is small compared to that of most other operations of this sort and size.

State Role in Providing Consultant Assistance

Legislative bodies, city managers, mayors, and chiefs should seek consultant assistance in reviewing the organization of forces. This will lead toward police force modernization across the nation. Individual States have a key role to play in inducing improvements. Most of the organization, management, and operational suggestions presented in this chapter could be implemented locally if States were to create commissions on police standards to upgrade county and local police effectiveness through surveys and inspections. In order to overcome management and operational weaknesses, these commissions should be given certain powers and responsibilities:

- Authority to increase police effectiveness through surveys and inspections;
- Authority to see that physical resources common to a given area are jointly pooled;
- Authority to provide financial assistance to jurisdictions which comply with established standards;
- Responsibility for encouraging research in police organization, management, and operations and the publication and dissemination of such research.

The formation of commissions with power to survey the organization and management practices of police agencies, which is more fully described in chapter 8 of this volume, focuses attention on the State government as the catalyst for improving local law enforcement. Periodic surveys of the organization, management, personnel standards, and operations of all law enforcement agencies by recognized consulting experts are of such importance that each department should be so surveyed at least once every 5 years. Moreover, other State funds should not be made available to local departments unless they show good faith in their intent to implement survey recommendations which are clearly necessary and feasible.

Conclusion

Law enforcement cannot remain static and still serve the public adequately. Progress will require change in many of the time-honored ways in which numerous police officials have habitually functioned. Progress will also require an infusion of more promising police recruits, an openmindedness and daring previously unknown on the part of many police administrators, and financial and public support of higher order than that heretofore afforded the police. And progress will require time and personal commitment by public and police officials alike. The present state of police organization in the United States remains essentially similar to the way it was when summarized in 1962:[44]

> . . . about 40,000 police jurisdictions and approximately 300,000 police officers conform to no fixed or definable standard of organization, structure, public responsibility, or general efficiency. Among them are some of the best law enforcement agencies that have been developed anywhere in the world, at any level of government. Others are in the process of changing over from antiquated methods and are now embracing new techniques for popular control, general supervision, and improved day-to-day functioning. Included also are a considerable number of agencies that have failed to show any sign of renaissance and seem bypassed by constructive impulses that have brought development and progress to the first two groups. These last police forces constitute a burden on the entire machinery of justice and are detrimental to the process of achieving a professional police service held in esteem by the citizens of the nation.

The task of police executives is becoming more difficult each year, particularly as forces become numerically larger. For example, police management in the 28,671-man New York City Police Department is as demanding as supervising a vast industrial or manufacturing corporation, managing an airline or railroad, or commanding a military division. In fact, it seems that police administration is essentially similar in principle to managing any complex nonpolice enterprise. One writer asserted:[45]

---

[44]Samuel G. Chapman, *The Police Heritage in England and America: A Developmental Survey* (East Lansing, Mich.: Michigan State University Institute for Community Development and Services, 1962), p. 30.

[45]Donal E. J. MacNamara, "American Police Administration at Mid-Century," *Public Administration Review,* summer 1950, p. 188.

Study of scores of police reorganization surveys makes abundantly clear that there are few if any principles of police administration which are not at the same time principles of business, military, and general public administration.

Inducing America's police chiefs to implement proven organizational principles intended to streamline their forces and accommodate innovations is an important step forward in the war on crime. Without internal reorganization, police forces can only become larger, more inefficient likenesses of their present structure, and offer scant hope of furnishing better police service. All that such forces can promise is a steady commitment to mediocrity, drastically rising expenses over an indefinite period of time, and growing frustration among personnel. Excepting some departments from his statement, one writer thus capsulized the state of police organization and the feeling within the ranks in 1960:[46]

Typical police organization in 1960 cannot or will not utilize top brain power. Young policemen who are "too intelligent" do not remain with the police force. If they do, they all too frequently get into trouble. They become frustrated sowers of seeds of discontent. These men obviously do not fit into the general pattern of police organization in 1960.

Legislative and nonpolice administrative officials including mayors and city managers must take at least some responsibility for the current organizational condition of many police forces. These officials may induce change and modernization by demanding it, supporting modernization programs fiscally, and defending change designed to result in streamlining government citywide.

And the public must shoulder some responsibility, too. They can cause elected officials to initiate police as well as citywide governmental reforms.

Any city may have an outstanding police department—but only if it really wants one and is willing to pay for it. The public, through sustained demand for improved law enforcement, may also influence the quantitative and qualitative levels of police service. The late Chief William H. Parker wrote:[47]

Despite the most aggressive and enlightened leadership, law enforcement cannot rise above the level set by the electorate. *A condition precedent to the establishment of efficient, professional law enforcement in a community is a desire and a demand on the part of the residents for that type of service.*

---

[46]Richard A. Myren, "A Crisis in Police Management," *The Journal of Criminal Law, Criminology and Police Science,* March-April 1960, p. 600.

[47]William H. Parker, "The Police Challenge in Our Great Cities," *The Annals,* January 1954, p. 6.

CHAPTER 9

Organization as a Key to Police Effectiveness

Robert Edward Mitchell

Robert Edward Mitchell is Professor, Department of Urban
and Regional Planning, at the Institute for Social Research at
Florida State University, Tallahassee Florida.

Several competing theories of crime control have been given increasing public and legislative attention in the past few years. Many citizens who cry out against "crime in the streets" advocate solving the problem by increasing the number and power of police and by punishing offenders more severely. On the other hand, many social workers and social scientists would initiate mammoth programs designed to bring about the Great Society, thus removing the social causes of crime.

Both of these approaches overlook the organizational dimension of police departments as a factor determining the effectiveness of law enforcement efforts to eliminate organized crime. One approach adheres to a beehive perspective of police departments: every department in every city has the same form of organization, and the only way to increase the sting and the honey is to add more bees. Advocates of the other approach are concerned with the dangers of a police state and the use of police departments as tools by unscrupulous politicians.

Police departments must be put in a new, unbiased perspective if progress is to be made either in understanding or in controlling organized crime. It is especially important to realize that departments differ in their operations and that they are capable of dramatically altering the extent to which they are effective in the fight against crime. Concern with the internal organization of departments and with the relationship between departments and the organizational environments in which they operate is crucial in obtaining this new perspective.

From Robert Edward Mitchell, "Organization as a Key to Police Effectiveness." Reprinted by special permission from the *Journal of Crime and Delinquency* volume 4, number 4, October 1968.

One cannot examine police effectiveness independently of criminals, city governments, courts, and others with whom the police have an occupational concern. In America the significance of the police derives to a considerable extent from the magnitude of crime. About two million major crimes a year are reported, and the value of stolen property is estimated at $600 million. It seems reasonable to predict that the crime problem will become even more serious in the future. It is said, for example, that crime is increasing five times faster than the population.

The growth of lawlessness is not, however, a unique American phenonenon. In England and Wales, the number of "persons found guilty of indictable offenses" per 100,000 population increased from 502 in 1955 to 747 in 1960. In Sweden, "crimes known to the police," standardized for the size of population, have also shown an increase over the years.

Crime-reporting procedures vary so greatly from one country to the next that international comparisons of crime rates are not reliable. Nevertheless, current information—admittedly inadequate—suggests the dismal hypothesis that societies have a normal rate of crime. This rate, it seems is predicted by a nation's level of industrialization, so that we can look in the future to an ever increasing crime problem in all societies around the world.

If this prophecy is reasonably accurate, the police will play an increasingly important role in society. This role need not be one of strategic hamlets in which precinct stations serve as control centers in the war against a hostile, lawless countryside. Two sets of statistics, neither one of which is guaranteed to be accurate, suggest that the police are able, when properly organized, to influence the rate at which crime rates will increase or decrease.

Table 1.—Arrest Rate (Number of Arrests Per 100,000 Population) for Three Types of Organized Crime [a]

Type of Crime	1950	1960	Ten-Year Difference
Narcotic and Drug Law Violations	10.2	25.5	15.3
Prostitution and Commercialized Vice	41.4	24.3	−17.1
Gambling	138.7	113.0	−25.7

[a]Figures obtained from *Uniform Crime Reports for the United States*, 1950, 1960.

First, some types of crime are increasing more slowly than others, and a few rates are actually decreasing. Table 1 presents the arrest rates for three examples of organized crime, each of which is, when compared with most other types of crime, relatively easy to control by energetic and effective police action. In the ten-year period 1950–60, the arrest rate for violations of narcotic and drug laws more than doubled. In contrast, the arrest rate for prostitution and commercialized vice was almost halved, and arrests for gambling also decreased. These figures do not mean that police departments are becoming less concerned with organized crime or that the gap is widening between arrest rates and rates at which these crimes are actually committed in the population at large. Rather, in part, the lower rates probably reflect increased effectiveness in performance of police duties.

Second, crime rates vary sharply from city to city. These differences suggest either that police departments in some cities are more effective than others or that they differ widely in what they consider a crime. In any event, they suggest that departments differ greatly in performance and, inferentially, in their ability to control and eliminate crime. Table 2 presents differences in crime rates between cities of approximately the same size within the same state. The size factor is a crude statistical control for the complex of factors that tend to produce criminal activity, and the state factor is a crude statistical control for differences in legal definitions of crime. Overall, the difference in crime rates for paired cities is quite startling.

Police departments are differentiated in several other ways. In California, for example, the Oakland and San Francisco departments are considered by many to have a better relationship with minority groups than does Los Angeles. In dealing with civil liberties, some departments have been known to tolerate overzealous search and seizure procedures, practices which invite the federal courts to enter into the administration of criminal justice at the local level (see *Mapp v. Ohio,* 367 U.S. 643 [1961]). More generally, some departments—for example, Milwaukee and Los Angeles— have national reputations today for being "clean" departments, while others —for example, Chicago and Boston—suffer from poor reputations. These reputations refer to the amount of police corruption and inefficiency, which are themselves partly responsible for the crime problem.

In the last ten years a great number of examples of police-criminal collusion have come to the public's attention. A partial list of departments with known unsavory incidents would include Baltimore, Burlington (Vt.), Chicago, Denver, Detroit, Hudson County (N.J.), Los Angeles, Miami, Nashville, New York, New Orleans, Omaha, San Francisco, Tulsa, and Washington, D.C.—cities in every region of the country.

Some departments are, as Sutherland put it, "systematically lawless." "This does not mean," he noted, "that every policeman is lawless, but that as a system the police operate in a lawless manner." Police graft is a good example of systematic lawlessness.

Royal Commission studies in England, as well as many local, state, and national studies in America, have documented such lawlessness as

Table 2.—Crime Rate (Crimes Reported[a] Per 100,000 Population) for Selected Cities, 1956[b]

Cities	Population	Crime Rate
Illinois		
Peoria	113,000	2,290
Rockford	119,000	1,063
Ohio		
Cincinnati	522,000	1,320
Columbus	431,000	610
Massachusetts		
New Bedford	110,000	1,750
Cambridge	113,000	858
Michigan		
Flint	195,000	3,015
Grand Rapids	200,000	1,683
California		
Oakland	455,000	3,010
San Diego	468,000	1,790
Connecticut		
Hartford	186,000	1,525
Bridgeport	175,000	998
Oklahoma		
Oklahoma City	285,000	2,690
Tulsa	239,000	2,038

[a]These are "Part 1" crimes—criminal homicide, rape, robbery, aggravated assault, burglary, larceny, and auto theft.

[b]Vernon L. Hoy, "The Police Specialist in District Stations" (M.Sc. Pub. Adm. thesis, University of Southern California, School of Public Administration, June 1958), pp. 85-90.

proof of the existence of organized criminal groups. In such instances, the criminal world tends to control the overall performance of entire police departments. However, there is considerable evidence that departments are able to change for the better. In many cities the police, for some as yet unknown reason, have been able to drastically reduce incidents of organized crimes. Prostitution, gambling, and narcotics seem to be especially amenable to police control.

Police Operations

The few social scientists who have studied the police have focused almost exclusively upon the situation of the individual policeman. By doing so, they overlook the organizational dimension of crime control, a perspective that can be approached primarily through a comparative study of departments. A narrow concern with the individual policeman can also lead to erroneous findings of what are thought to be unique hazards. For example, one study claimed that feelings of inadequate public recognition and even outright community disrespect contributed to the policeman's proclivity to employ unwarranted force in the performance of his tasks.[1] Of course, other studies have found that although ministers and college professors also feel they are not given adequate community recognition, these feelings do not lead them to any noticeable misuse of their position to manipulate parishioners and students.[2] Furthermore, there is no evidence to date that differences in the use of force by individual policemen, or departmental differences in the use of force, are in any way related to differences in felt deprivation on the part of individual policemen. Although a study of the individual policeman is not without value, the limitations of this perspective deserve notice.

A concern with police systems also has its limitations, but it can lead to a better understanding of a department's effectiveness in its program against organized crime. Specifically, if we consider effectiveness not only as a significant and measurable concept but also as a characteristic of organizations rather than of individuals, a number of social science approaches to the study of organizations can be adopted to throw new light on police systems. For example, it is possible to study how departments which differ in internal organization, as well as in their relations to various community groups, also differ in their ability to control organized crime. Although such studies have not actually been conducted, some scattered

---

[1]William A. Westley, "Violence and the Police." *American Journal of Sociology,* July 1953, pp. 34-41.

[2]Robert Edward Mitchell, "When Ministers and Their Parishioners Have Different Class Positions," *Review of Religious Research,* Fall 1965, pp. 28-41.

evidence indicates the value of such an organizational or "systemic" approach to police operations.

Inside Police Departments

A fairly large though dull corpus of literature has been compiled on how to reduce costs and allocate resources within police departments. It includes a folklore on how to keep police systems healthy and effective, making unfounded assertions that relate salaries, vacations, promotions, and swing shifts to the morale of departments.

Such conjectures refer to an entire police department, but the major responsibility for the control of organized crime rests heavily on certain special groups within the department, especially vice squads, detective bureaus, and intelligence units. These typically are élite groups: their salary scales are higher, they recruit the more able men, their responsibilities are intellectually more demanding, and they are able to work in mufti. Yet in many cities these élite elements have not been notably successful against organized crime. In fact, since vice squads often desert to the enemy, a closer scrutiny of them may provide hints on how to organize police departments for a more effective offense against organized crime.

Vice squads are organized in a number of different ways. In some cities their functions are distributed throughout the force; in others, there is a strict division of labor, including constraints on what patrolmen and detectives can do in vice cases. In some instances the squad concerns itself with juvenile vice, while in others this is primarily the responsibility of special juvenile officers. Some vice squads have special narcotics and other details. Some rotate their members so that continually new, relatively unsullied men are charged with the often undesirable, tempting work. In some large departments the squad operates out of a central headquarters; in others the vice squad work is divided into multipurpose details, each of which operates out of a local precinct.

These variations have developed as means to control not only criminals but also police. However, despite local claims made for particular variations, no systematic information has ever been marshaled to prove that any one organizational pattern is more effective than another. Furthermore, it is unlikely that any such assessment of effectiveness can be made without first placing departments within the larger context of their operation.

A major key to effectiveness is found in the external challenges and obstacles to law enforcement, for these help define both the goals of police departments and the means available to them. How are departments affected by the general community, other legal agencies, political and civil authorities, and the criminal world itself?

The Community

Police in many communities have ample reason to complain about the public's failure to assist them in preventing avoidable crime. People are murdered and robbed because of their neighbors' apathy, and criminals are let free because witnesses to their crime refuse to "get involved." Such attitudes certainly make it harder for the police to perform their work effectively. They also suggest that fiction and myth surround the role assigned to police in American society. The police picture themselves as operating under conditions similar to those in England, while, in fact, the American public has a continental perspective of law enforcement. The distinction between these systems was recently drawn by a Royal Commission which referred to a fundamental contrast "between the Continental principle of placing responsibility for the maintenance of law and order upon the executive government and arming it with powers of direct enforcement, and the British principle that it is the right and duty of each citizen to preserve the peace and bring the malefactors to justice, with its corollary that the police are merely paid to act on the citizens's behalf."

> The contrast on this view is seen in small things and big things alike: the British police are unarmed, but most policemen on the Continent carry arms; and political and secret police appear to flourish on the Continent, for their role as agents of the state leaves them a prey to political extremists.[3]

A number of recent legal measures have been designed to swing the American population over from the Continental to the British pattern. For example, some Good Samaritan bills hold a citizen liable to legal prosecution for failing to comply with a policeman's request for assistance. If such legislation is successful, perhaps it will make deputies of us all and thereby place the public on a par with the police in a situation similar to that which legally exists in England, where, in the view of the common law, a policeman is only "a person paid to perform, as a matter of duty, acts which if he were so minded he might have done voluntarily."[4]

However, the history of guerrilla warfare teaches us that it is not easy to transform a hostile peasantry into informers and collaborators. After all, the police are not spearheading a revolutionary attack on society, and their work does not have a visible impact on the economic, political, and social welfare of the population. Therefore, the effect of this moralistic approach to the crime problem is questionable. Nevertheless, its possible benefits should not be neglected. Certainly, studies should be conducted on how these Good Samaritan laws affect the public's attitudes and the effectiveness of police departments.

[3]Royal Commission on the Police, *Final Report* (London: H.M.S.O., 1962).
[4]Ibid.

Other Legal and Quasi-Legal Systems

Local police departments operate within and are affected by a system of legal agencies. The federal government has treasury, narcotics, Internal Revenue, and postal police groups as well as the FBI; the state, the county, and the local community often have comparable groups, including quasi-official crime commissions, and, of course, district attorneys. In addition to these law enforcement agencies, there is also the court system, including judges, lawyers, bondsmen, and the like.

Courts have a singularly important impact on the operation and effectiveness of departments, for they are the major mechanisms serving to control the police. They help define the law by the evidence they admit, the proportion of defendants they convict and sentence, and the severity of the judgments they hand down—actions which reward and punish police behavior and thereby help the policeman define and enforce the law. The important implications of these processes for the police are seen perhaps most clearly in the English experience with a 1948 bill on juvenile first offenders, which resulted in a 60 per cent drop in the number of juveniles sent to prison. Investigations related to such First Offender bills revealed a wide diversity among the thousand or so magistrate courts in England. Some courts committed to prison as little as 8 per cent of the accused; others, as much as 40 per cent.[5] While these figures may reflect differences in police departments and public prosecutors, as well as in the courts, they also suggest that departments differ in their experiences with the courts and that police behavior that is rewarded in one community is punished in another.

My informal interviews with American lawyers indicate that these same problems occur here and are seriously aggravated by the political appointment of often unqualified men to the bench. An unprofessional court system amenable to political pressure results in practices which discourage and demoralize police departments: judges issue "quickie" writs releasing offenders "with connections," they throw cases out of court, and in some communities they publicly chastise the arresting police officers. The lawyers suggested that police officers soon learn it is useless to arrest certain criminals or to crack down on certain types of crime.

In many communities police departments can become effective only if the courts are first reformed. California's Special Crime Study Commission on Organized Crime forcefully made this same point in 1950.[6] The Commission also noted that "there are about 75 police, justices, and municipal courts or departments thereof in Los Angeles County with criminal

---

[5]Ibid.
[6]California Special Crime Study Commission on Organized Crime, *Third Progress Report*, 1950.

jurisdiction." For the most part, they are completely independent units with "almost as many interpretations of the criminal laws as there are judges." This proliferation of satellite cities within a single metropolitan area[7] increases the likelihood that organized criminal elements will be able to locate at least one safe haven from which to manage their affairs in the larger area. In such areas, it is not enough to reform one community; all of them need attention.

Therefore, the effectiveness of police departments seems to be affected by the operation of the courts—by the proportion of all police arrests that eventually result in conviction, the quality of sentencing, the court records on specific offenses, the types of evidence admitted, the record on writs of habeas corpus, practices regarding first offenders, and the like. Effectiveness may also be influenced by the typical operations of lawyers, bondsmen, parole officers, district attorneys, and others who are involved in the administration of criminal justice and therefore impinge on and affect the performance of police tasks.

Political Parties and Local Governments

Police departments, as well as the courts, have to be considered in the still wider perspective of the communities in which they operate and the people who appoint and pay them. Earlier journalistic critiques of the police were typically placed within this larger framework, and charges were made that political parties and city governments subverted the performance and effectiveness of police departments. In this connection Sutherland noted that "Formally, the police department is organized to operate for the welfare of society; informally, it is organized for the welfare of the politicians."[8] Since the politicians are assumed to have considerable influence on the courts and upon government administration, and since it is also often assumed that politicians are influenced by criminal elements in the community, it seems likely that the effectiveness of the police is related to the ethical standards and practices of politicians and public servants. This relationship was noted in 1894-95 by the Lexow Committee in New York City, where it was found that the same system of bribery used by criminals was also used by commission merchants, contractors, pushcart vendors, and bootblacks who wanted to use the public streets for private business. In other words, the police alone were not corrupt; corruption characterized the entire governmental system. There is no reason to suppose that this characterization

---

[7]Los Angeles County had forty-six separate law enforcement agencies in 1950, and Chicago had more than four hundred independent police forces within fifty miles of the center of the city.

[8]Edwin H. Sutherland, *Principles of Criminology,* 5th ed. (Philadelphia: J. B. Lippincott, 1955).

is not applicable today. A report by the California Crime Study Commission in 1949 indicated that "it is common practice of slot machine operators throughout the country to pay 10 per cent to 20 per cent of their gross profit for protection and graft. . . . $400,000,000 is being spent annually by the slot machine racketeers for bribery and corruption of public executive officers."[9]

> All criminals are more or less dependent upon their social contacts with more respectable members of society and this is particularly true of those engaged in commercial forms of crime. For them, friendship with political figures is absolutely essential. In no other way can the criminal groups and syndicates obtain that immunity from interference by law enforcement agencies which is just as essential to successful gang operations as the discipline imposed by acts of violence.[10]

The World of Organized Crime

Some cynics would debate whether criminals are more deplorable and antisocial than police departments and city halls. Certainly many observers would agree with William Foote Whyte's assertion that "the primary function of the police department is not the enforcement of the law but the regulation of illegal activities."[11] Numerous crime investigations as well as Whyte's study of Cornerville support this claim. Furthermore, they suggest that crime, like the police, can be viewed as a system. The police as a system or group seem to interact with crime as a system in the process of regulating it. Examples of how these mutually interpenetrating systems operate were noted recently by a grand jury in Kansas City, which accused the police of cooperating with criminal elements, giving them a monopoly over local crime in return for assistance in controlling disruptive criminal activities. In Denver, the absence of a strong criminal system seems to have contributed to the openly criminal activities of the police: police salaries were not supplemented by illegal gratuities, and the police excursion into criminal activities was not countered by entrenched organized criminal interests. In other cities, organized crime actually seems to regulate police activities, keeping them relatively honest.

It is probably useful to view police-criminal behavior from a sociological perspective of intergroup relations. The police and criminal systems represent conflict groups, each trying to regulate the behavior of the other. This process is mediated by a variety of middlemen—bondsmen, lawyers, marginal criminal elements, ex-policemen, judges, politicians, or, as the California crime commission stated in 1950, by some of the "more respect-

---

[9]California Special Crime Study Commission on Organized Crime, *Second Progress Report*, 1949.

[10]*Third Progress Report.*

[11]William Foote Whyte, *Street Corner Society* (Chicago: University of Chicago Press, 1955).

able members of society." The public becomes aware of this interaction through its most common manifestations: graft, corruption, and the payoff.

If this intergroup perspective is tenable, it follows that the way and the extent to which the two groups are organized will affect the course of their mutual relations. Put in another way, the organization of crime affects those groups charged with controlling it. This means that an understanding of the organization and operation of crime is necessary for a full understanding of the actual performance of police departments. An understanding of other organizations in the community is also necessary for an understanding of police departments.

However, the merging of this double perspective from which departments and their environments have been viewed raises a crucial question. If the effectiveness of police departments is so heavily influenced by the organization of the community, other legal and quasi-legal agencies, politicians, city administrations, and the criminal world itself, is it possible that departments can by their own independent efforts become more effective in their campaign against organized crime? Or, given this interorganizational system which we have pictured, is greater police effectiveness dependent on a balanced program of reform of all the relevant social actors in this social system? More specifically, what independent influence can an internal reorganization of a police department have upon the obstacles to effectiveness raised by the outside community? These questions have in the past been the concern primarily of policy-makers, as suggested in the earlier mentioned ideological conflict between groups which adhere to the beehive theory of police work and those who direct their primary attention to eliminating the causes of crime. On the other hand, it has been our argument that greater attention should be given to reforming police departments internally so that they can cope more effectively with the external obstacles created by groups in the larger community.

Ineffectiveness and Democracy

Much of the social science literature on crime and, especially, juvenile delinquency, refers to deviant subcultures. Cloward and Ohlin concern themselves specifically with how delinquent subcultures are created, sustained, and, possibly, transformed.[12] One might also expect that ineffective, corrupt police departments would have characteristically antisocial, deviant cultures. For example, the members of such departments might adhere to life philosophies which hold that man is inherently evil, that he is not to be trusted, that he must be held responsible for all his actions, that the wrongdoer is incapable of being reformed, and that physical force and

---

[12]Richard Cloward and Lloyd Ohlin, *Delinquency and Opportunity* (New York: Free Press, 1960).

coercion are the only worthwhile tools the policeman has—all views which may contribute to the control of crime but which at the same time contravene many honored American values. One might also expect the members of such departments to place little value on strict adherence to the law and to believe that deviation is normal and therefore not deviant, that there is no reason to expect the police to act any differently from the rest of the normally corrupt society, and that life is a gamble, requiring risks but also affording opportunities for personal profit—all views which encourage poor police performance.

However, it is important to distinguish corruption from ineffectiveness. Police departments with identical cultures can differ greatly from one another simply because of the different ways they are organized. Of course, some departments are so ill-adapted to their environments that pressures are created which lead almost inevitably to a socially undesirable culture completely at odds with the publicly stated goals of the police. But, if studies of industrial, medical, military, and other organizations have any relevance to police organizations, we would expect that the way a department is organized will affect the stresses which its members feel in their occupational roles and also the ways in which they react to these stresses. When the stresses are of a certain kind, and when they are distributed in a certain pattern within the department, ineffectiveness and possibly corruption will be the product.

It is dangerous to assume, as so many human relations experts do, that stress is necessarily undesirable and that organizations should be internally re-arranged in order to relieve any personal frustrations which employees experience in the course of fulfilling their job responsibilities. On the contrary, the viability of other features of American life may depend on the continued relative ineffectiveness of police departments and the perpetual frustration of policemen. Re-organization for complete effectiveness in the fight against crime might place the police in a position where they can easily violate many constitutionally guaranteed rights. This is a danger to which we must be alert, but it should not be allowed to delay overdue efforts to discover ways to increase the effectiveness of this significant sector of American governmental operations.

CHAPTER 10

Uncertainties in Police Work: The Relevance of Recruits' Backgrounds and Training

John H. McNamara

John H. McNamara is currently conducting research on poverty. The former Director of Research and Evaluation, Economic Opportunity Commission of Santa Clara County, California, Mr. McNamara has published papers on alcoholism, urban contact patterns, and scalogram analysis. This article is based on a thorough study of the New York City Police Department and the New York City Police Academy.

Recruit Training and Uncertainties Regarding Legality of Police Actions

The difficulties for any recruit training program in transmitting a working knowledge of both procedural and substantive laws are many and complex. Earlier it was pointed out that American federal, state, and local legislative laws combined with the judical decisions making up the common law system do not constitute a well constructed axiomatic system. That is, one cannot discern general principles consistent with one another that would allow a police officer to make decisions regarding the legality of his actions with any marked degree of confidence in the correctness of his decision.

The system of laws with which a police officer must operate is thus not one that can easily or succinctly be presented. Further, police departments, with some justification, feel strongly that errors made by police personnel regarding the legality of their actions are likely to have severe consequences for the individual officer as well as for the department as a whole. It is not surprising, therefore, to find the academic curriculum of the New York City Police Academy heavily loaded with detailed presentations of procedural and substantive laws from a variety of sources: New York

State Penal Law, New York State Code of Criminal Procedure, New York City Administrative and Health Codes, the Federal Constitution and its amendments, etc. Although some instructors tried to present the general history and political philosophy underlying this system of laws, both class presentation and the recruits' program of study largely consisted of stating or memorizing page after page of laws and the conditions associated with different laws.

One indicator of the extent to which recruits failed to derive any general sense of the legality of police actions was found in the responses of 250 recruits to the following item: "*According to my instructors* the following are the most important *principles of law* as far as patrolmen on patrol are concerned." (The item was followed by space for written descriptions of three separate principles.) We were unable to find a manageable number of categories that adequately summarized the range of responses and thus could not code the responses. The responses ranged from "patrol on the left (side of the street)" to "protection of life, limb, and property." The same item was given again to some of the same group after they had completed two years in field assignments; the results were the same.

Along with a lack of consensus among the recruits regarding basic principles of law, there developed an increased support for the belief that police lack the basic legal authority appropriate to their position. Responses of recruits tested at the beginning and end of their training to questionnaire items concerning such authority were found to move in the direction of belief that police have insufficient legal authority. The movement of beliefs further continued in the same direction during the first year of assignment to field work. A second group, tested after two years in the field, showed a general tendency to be slightly more convinced of the insufficiency of police authority than the group with one year in the field (Table 8). The largest proportionate increase in the belief that police have insufficient legal authority, however, took place between the beginning (T_1) and the end (T_2) of the recruit training.

There is also a large change in the recruits' attitudes regarding the sufficiency of police legal authority after they have had one year of field experience. This finding is consistent with our hypotheses that a "cultural discontinuity" existed between the police academy curriculum and the later requirements of the field assignments.[39] We had sufficient reason to believe that the curriculum would not include discussion of many of the informal practices that were widespread in the department, particularly those in violation of the *Rules and Procedures*. Police academy personnel were reluctant to discuss these practices because they feared their discussion

---

[39]See R. Benedict, "Continuities and Discontinuities in Cultural Conditioning," *Psychiatry*, Vol. 1 (1938), pp. 161-7.

Table 8.—Changes over Time in Recruits' Beliefs in the Sufficiency of Police Legal Authority (in percent)

Item	Time[a]	No Answer	Strongly Agree	Agree	Uncertain	Disagree	Strongly Disagree
A	T_1	1	5	19	29	35	11
	T_2	0	14	30	16	35	5
	T_3	1	24	39	17	13	6
	T_4	1	27	36	18	18	0
B	T_1	1	6	13	46	25	9
	T_2	0	12	33	30	21	5
	T_3	1	14	41	18	22	4
	T_4	1	17	43	19	17	3
C	T_1	1	10	29	36	21	3
	T_2	0	13	40	26	20	1
	T_3	1	27	43	21	7	1
	T_4	1	30	48	15	6	0
D	T_1	1	12	64	8	14	1
	T_2	1	5	57	8	24	5
	T_3	1	1	38	13	39	8
	T_4	1	1	34	17	31	16

Item A: "The present system of state and local laws has undermined the patrolman's authority to a dangerous extent."

Item B: "The courts have tended in recent years to discount the testimony of patrolmen where there are no other witnesses or there is no other proof regarding an alleged crime, offense, or violation."

Item C: "A number of pressure groups have been successful in getting legislation and court decisions that severely restrict the police actions that patrolmen can take."

Item D: "Generally speaking, patrolmen today have enough legal authority to get their jobs done efficiently."

[a]The symbols T_1, T_2, and T_3 refer to one group tested at the beginning of its recruit training (T_1), at the end of its recruit training (T_2), and after one year in field assignments (T_3). The N's are, respectively, 171, 164, and 137. The symbol T_4 refers to another group of eighty-three patrolmen with two years' experience in the field.

would be interpreted as a form of endorsement or legitimation of the patterned evasion of rules.

We believe one consequence of the failure of the academy personnel to discuss the informal practices would be that the patrolmen would later be required by social pressures from other officers in the field to follow the informal practices. In order to justify following these practices the recruits would eventually come to believe that there is insufficient authority granted the police officer by the courts and legislatures. One of Westley's findings concerning the use of unnecessary force by police officers on sex offenders is similar in that police believed that the force was justified because the courts were seen as failing to punish sex offenders adequately.[40]

It is interesting to note that the recruits do not change much in any consistent direction either during their training or during the first two years in the field with regard to the amount of legal discretion they believe is accorded to them by the supervisors and administration of the department. (See Table 9.) One reason why the recruits did not perceive the departmental hierarchy of authority to be as responsible for the insufficiency of police authority as the courts and legislatures may be that an officer's negative evaluation would hurt his career. Also many of the respondents may have remained unconvinced that the research was being conducted by an agency other than the department. A number of recruits expressed such a belief to the author and to one another. Although every effort was made to convince the respondents that their replies were to remain anonymous and that their responses would not affect their careers, some believed that they had been singled out by a unit at headquarters for investigation.

Along with the change toward a decreased belief in the sufficiency of police legal authority there was an accompanying increase in the authoritarianism of patrolmen as measured by the mean scores on the F-scale. The scores increased from a mean of 4.15 for a group of recruits tested just before they began training to a mean of 4.18 at the end of training to a mean of 4.31 at the end of the first year in the field. Another group of 83 patrolmen with two years' experience had a mean score of 4.46. Assuming the comparability of the above groups and a continued increase in the F-scale [authoritarian personality syndrome] scores with more experience, we can hypothesize that in time the discrepancy between the police officers' attitude and the courts' thinking regarding criminal law will increase, since the authoritarian orientation is probably negatively related to an emphasis on personal rights as against property rights. We cannot explore the implications of this change rigorously at this point, but it seems likely that it is related to the police's feeling that their authority has been subverted by forces outside the department.

---

[40]W. A. Westley, "Violence and the Police," *American Journal of Sociology* Vol. 59 (1953), pp. 34-41.

Table 9.—Changes in Recruits' Beliefs Concerning Discretion Allowed by Supervisors and Administration (in percent)

Item	Time[a]	No Answer	Strongly Agree	Agree	Uncertain	Disagree	Strongly Disagree
A	T_1	1	2	16	25	46	10
	T_2	1	1	20	14	57	7
	T_3	1	4	15	18	52	10
	T_4	1	6	23	11	52	7
B	T_1	1	3	6	39	46	5
	T_2	0	1	11	30	51	7
	T_3	1	1	22	22	50	4
	T_4	1	8	21	25	45	0
C	T_1	2	2	17	31	38	10
	T_2	0	2	15	27	51	5
	T_3	1	8	25	12	50	4
	T_4	1	7	23	15	47	7
D	T_1	1	6	32	44	15	2
	T_2	0	5	45	33	16	1
	T_3	1	5	52	20	18	4
	T_4	1	7	55	16	20	0

Item A: "The department does not seem to allow patrolmen enough discretion regarding the arrests they might make or summons they might serve."

Item B: "One of the major problems with law enforcement is that each patrolman is not given enough latitude by his supervisors to handle the police problems in his area of responsibility."

Item C: "Patrolmen often fail to take necessary police action due to a feeling that supervisors will disapprove of their actions."

Item D: "Police supervisors almost never instruct a patrolman to reverse his plans when he has planned to make an arrest or to issue a summons."

[a]See Table 8, footnote [a].

Table 10 indicates the officers' attitude toward the use of force in a somewhat ambiguous situation. The percentage of recruits endorsing the use of force increased between the beginning of their training (T_1) and the end of their stay in the police academy (T_2). We should note that the recruits reported informally that some differences existed among the instructors as to their orders regarding the conditions under which force should be used and the conditions determining the degree of force to be used. The major difference apparently existed between the "academic" instructors and the instructors in firearms and physical training. The latter group of instructors, primarily patrolmen, were more likely to endorse the more frequent use of force and the use of more serious force than the academic instructors, who generally were either sergeants or lieutenants. Thus some inconsistencies in the recruits' training were related to the hierarchical position of their instructors. The academic instructors adhered more closely to the expectations of the administration of the department.

Table 10.—Responses to: "If a Patrolman Thinks He May Have to Use Force in a Situation He Should Use It Right after His Entrance into the Situation in Order to Gain the Advantage of Surprise" (in percent)

Time[a]	No Answer	Strongly Agree	Agree	Uncertain	Disagree	Strongly Disagree
T_1	0	6	33	22	36	3
T_2	0	8	38	13	37	4
T_3	1	8	40	10	38	3
T_4	0	6	26	18	46	4

[a]See footnote Table 8, footnote [a].

We previously hypothesized that a major rationale underlying the use of force was the attempt to cope with disrespect shown to police. Westley found that disrespect for police was the most frequently mentioned justification by police for the use of force.[41] Piliavin and Briar similarly found that disrespect shown by juveniles to police often was grounds for taking juveniles into custody.[42] The patrolmen tested in the New York City Police Department do not strongly concur that disrespect shown to police provides a sufficient condition for the use of force. The responses to an item intended

---

[41]Ibid.

[42]I. Piliavin and S. Briar, "Police Encounters with Juveniles," *American Journal of Sociology*, 70 (1964): 206-14.

Table 11.—Responses to: "Most Officers Agree That Some Force Is Necessary and Justified When a Citizen Unjustly Insults and Curses a Police Officer." (in percent)

Year in Academy	Time when Tested	Strongly Agree	Agree	Uncertain	Disagree	Strongly Disagree	N
1961	End of training	5	33	28	28	6	(107)
	Two years in field	4	44	10	39	3	(83)
1962	Start of training	2	25	15	50	8	(171)
	End of training	3	23	18	49	7	(164)
	One year in field	1	34	16	45	4	(137)
1963	Third month of training	2	30	15	46	7	(296)
	Fourth month of training	4	31	19	43	3	(266)

to measure their perception of the degree of consensus among police officers concerning the use of force against abusive citizens (Table 11) indicate that the majority of patrolmen tested at different time periods during their first two years on the force do not agree that such consensus exist. The table does indicate, however, that their field experience somewhat influenced the patrolmens' perception, the change being that more officers agreed that the group supported the use of force in the case of disrespect shown to officers.

The faith in the use of force was also based upon considerations other than those we have just discussed. As indicated in Table 12, the majority of the patrolmen entered the department with the view that police need "more leeway and fewer restrictions on the use of force" in order to reduce the serious police problems of "tough neighborhoods." This view of the recruits was little changed at the end of their training but increased after one year of field work to the point where 74% endorsed this view.

Table 12.—Justifications for the Use of Force (in percent)

Item	Time[a]	No Answer	Strongly Agree	Agree	Uncertain	Disagree	Strongly Disagree
A	T_1	0	14	43	23	17	3
	T_2	1	16	42	17	23	1
	T_3	0	30	44	14	12	0
	T_4	0	39	39	13	8	0
B	T_1	0	3	18	31	44	4
	T_2	0	4	26	15	47	8
	T_3	1	7	39	12	36	4
	T_4	0	12	30	14	40	4

Item A: "If patrolmen working in the tough neighborhoods had more leeway and fewer restrictions on the use of force many of the serious police problems in those neighborhoods would be greatly reduced."
Item B: "A patrolman who frequently ignores challenges to fight from citizens will probably make it harder for other patrolmen to work his post or sector."

[a]See Table 8, footnote [a].

Another means by which force frequently is legitimated by police is the view that a patrolman's failure to accept "challenges to fight" will cause the more aggressive residents in an area to feel that they can "get away with anything" or feel they can "push the police around." The degree of agreement with this sentiment is indicated in the responses to item B in Table 12. As shown, the degree of agreement was slight at the outset of training (T_1); it increased during the training and then increased more during the first year of field experience (T_3), at the end of which the modal response was agreement with the item.

As we can see from the three tables concerning the officers' attitudes toward the use of force in situations that are legally marginal, by no means does a consensus exist among the more experienced patrolmen. The attitudes favorable to the use of force in such situations, however, are more likely to form following the academy training rather than during the training. It is apparent that the academy does not immunize the recruits against the sort of changes that academy personnel would find undesirable. The author's impression is that this is probably a consequence of the academy's failure to provide properly controlled counterarguments endorsing the opposite view from the desired one. In turn, this failure seems to be caused by a fear that discussion of beliefs or practices at variance with the position of the administration will be taken by all relevant parties as endorsement of these beliefs or practices. Whether or not this fear was justified, it seemed to have the opposite effect from that intended, in as much as the recruits later moved closer to positions seen as inappropriate by the administration of the department.[43]

Recruit Training and Uncertainties Regarding Police Prestige

As we indicated . . . the recruits' perception of the prestige accorded the role of the police officer by the general public was that the appointment to the force was seen as upwardly mobile. The element of prestige assigned to the role has special personal significance for each officer in that the role has what may be termed a "transcendental" character. That is, both while on duty or off, the nature of the officer's interaction with any other person is likely to be affected by his and by the other person's knowledge that he is a police officer. When recruits are told that it is a "twenty-four-hour-a-day job," they are unlikely to realize the full significance of the statement. Although they may know that they will be required to wear their revolvers at all times they are away from their homes, they are not likely to realize that, as happened to one recruit, their girl friend's father may not allow them to enter his house.

Nor are they likely to be aware of the number of times they will be told of the ineffective or corrupt action of other police officers by persons

---

[43]See P. F. Secord and C. W. Backman, *Social Psychology* (New York: McGraw-Hill Book Co., 1964), for a recent review of research on the consequences of presenting counterarguments for attitude change.

anxious to seek some psychological redress. They also may not realize that any purchase made by themselves or by their family members may be scrutinized by neighbors or by some investigating unit in the department as a sign that they have become corrupt and have decided to "be on the take" or to begin "shaking down" motorists, bar owners, or grocery store operators that violate the sabbath laws.

In the academy a good deal of effort was made to instill some "pride in the job." The recruits were told that the department was "over a hundred years old and proud of its tradition." Moreover, some handout material entitled *Recruit Issue Material,* which described the contemporary department as the "finest" informed the recruit that he must keep it "the finest." In order to do so the recruit "must be dedicated, disciplined, courageous, patient, and forebearing." Further, he "may not achieve the material rewards of other professions, but he has the greatest opportunities for spiritual satisfaction." (One wag, after reading the last quoted statement, indicated his disagreement by pointing out that the department does not have a particularly high rate of deaths in the line of duty.)

During recruit training the professionalization of police work was stressed as a realistic objective for all members of the force. Academy personnel also stressed the technology of police work and encouraged the recruits to take extra courses in police science. (Recruits received ten semester hours credit for the academy training toward a Bachelor's degree at New York City College Baruch School.)

During the training period in the academy recruits were also exposed to some work experiences both of a police nature and of a clerical and janitorial nature. The types of police work one group was exposed to were primarily traffic control, parade duty (in which officers stand alongside the parade route and maintain order among spectators), and patrol car duty with an experienced patrolmen for one eight-hour period. By far the most interesting experience for the recruits was the opportunity to observe closely the patrolmen in the patrol car. The clerical work was primarily filing of forms and work in the various offices of the academy. The other work was transporting police barriers (similar to a sawhorse) to various areas of the city and setting them up.

In general, the recruits thought that the clerical and janitorial work was somewhat inconsistent with their newly acquired status. Ninety-eight per cent of one group of 164 recruits at the end of their training indicated they felt they should have had more patrol car experience, whereas only 15% felt they should have been given more clerical work and only 7% felt they should have had more assignments involving the transportation of police barriers. Interestingly enough, only 12% felt they should have had more parade duty. Since the duty usually consists of standing in one spot and observing the spectators, they considered it boring. The reluctance of the academy personnel to have the recruits patrol with experienced patrolmen because of their fear that the recruits would be exposed to officially improper performance of duties was somewhat borne out by the experience of the above group of 164 recruits. When the recruits were asked to indicate whether the experiences they had in the field "coincided or conflicted with academy teaching," 4% indicated that their experience with traffic control conflicted, 6% indicated that parade duty conflicted, and 14% indicated that their assignment to a patrol car conflicted with what they had been taught at the academy. The last assignment, of course, was one in which the patrolmen were not so closely supervised and one in which a much broader range of types of police duties were likely to be encountered.

We indicated earlier that recruits at the beginning of their training are not likely to agree that the prestige attached to the position of patrolman has been increasing (Table 13). At the end of their training there was little change in their feeling, or much change after their first year in the field (T_3). The group of patrolmen with two years of field experience (T_4) had a slight tendency to disagree more with the statement in Table 13, than the other group but did not differ markedly. The four months of training did little to increase the officers' faith that their work was becoming more recognized by the public as having much prestige.

Table 13.—Changes in Responses to: "The Respect that Citizens Have for a Patrolman and His Position Has Been Steadily Increasing Over the Years (in percent)

Time[a]	No Answer	Strongly Agree	Agree	Uncertain	Disagree	Strongly Disagree
T_1	0	3	9	16	45	27
T_2	1	5	13	11	54	16
T_3	0	3	13	13	56	15
T_4	0	2	6	11	59	22

[a]See Table 8, footnote [a].

In this regard, two different groups of officers who had had some field experience were asked to "indicate how you think the general public feels the prestige of jobs you had before coming on to the force compares with police work." Their responses (Table 14) were compared with what they had indicated at the start of their training. . . . It seems that there was a shift toward reevaluation of their past jobs as having more prestige than indicated at the time they entered the department. Of course, the influence of the academy training cannot be inferred rigorously from this table, but it would appear that the patrolmen were again not immunized against the pressures of police work which serve to convince officers that their position does not have sufficient prestige assigned to it to facilitate their carrying out police duties. That police have somewhat high aspirations for the prestige level of police work is clear from the responses of the patrolmen with one or two years' field experience to the following: "Police work should be ranked alongside that of doctors or lawyers." Seventy-five per cent of the experienced men agreed with the statement and only 15% disagreed. Thus the problem of living with the discrepancy between the desired status and the perceived actual status of patrolman exists for the majority of officers. One manner in which the problem is resolved has been investigated by Niederhoffer in his study of the development of cynicism among police.[44]

Recruit Training and Uncertainties
Regarding Interpersonal Skills

The curriculum of the recruit training school in the academy has a number of class hours scheduled during which recruits were exposed to such topics as "the personal element in police work," "groups of people," "courtesy," "racial prejudice and common sense," "child development and psychology," and "the adolescent gang." These topics were covered primarily by lectures given by the academic instructors in formal class meetings. In addition, instructors often used examples drawn from their own experience with the public that dealt with interpersonal problems in the police officer's relations with the public. For the most part, any principles regarding interpersonal skills were presented either in the form of rather general prescriptions, for example, "be firm but courteous," or in the form of rules of thumb which individual instructors had evolved from their own experience in patrol work. Many of these latter prescriptions were quite ingenious, such as the recommendation that a patrolman when issuing a traffic ticket to a motorist find out whether the motorist is from the neighborhood. If the motorist was from the neighborhood, the patrolman was to indicate that he would not cite the motorist for any additional violation the officer noticed, since the motorist was from the area. If the motorist was not from the area, this fact also ostensibly served to keep the officer from issuing more than one citation. Presumably, motorists found either justification plausible because it was consonant with their desire to avoid additional citations.

The major difficulty in any attempt to transmit knowledge concerning interpersonal skills or in any attempt to improve these skills is that little exists in the way of such knowledge. This lack of knowledge is matched by

---

[44]See A. Niederhoffer, "A Study of Police Cynicism" (Ph.D. diss., Department of Sociology, New York University, 1963).

Table 14.—Prestige Seen as Assigned by the "General Public" to Jobs Police Officers Had Prior to Entering Police Work (Prestige of Past Jobs Relative to Police Work in percent)

Year in Academy	When Tested	Much Higher	Somewhat Higher	About the Same	Somewhat Lower	Much Lower	(N)[c]
1961	Start of training[a]	7	11	24	49	9	(105)
	Two years in field[b]	13	20	21	39	7	(83)
1962	Start of training[a]	2	10	27	45	16	(163)
	One year in field[b]	8	19	21	45	7	(164)

[a]See Table 6, footnote [a] for item and coding. (Some differences exist between the items given before training and after field experience.)

[b]This item is presented in the above paragraph. (The response categories in the table were presented to officers.)

[c]The "no answer" respondents are excluded from this table.

196

the inadequacy of most measures used to improve such skills. Although laboratory studies of social interaction may yield some knowledge about a limited number of variables and relationships, the utility of such knowledge is restricted, since it must be applied in noncontrolled settings. Furthermore, there are few clear-cut and reliable methods by which one can proceed from experimental findings to the application of these findings in everyday life.

For police, the range of situations in which they must interact with citizens is at least as broad as that for any other occupation. Recruits had few, if any, opportunities to test their interpersonal skills, to develop them or to integrate them with the skills and knowledge acquired during their stay in the academy. Their first opportunity to do so was in the field after they had left the academy. In the field, unfortunately, errors were frequently irreversible and lessons learned "the hard way" were quite costly to both the officers and citizens involved.

Since the task of developing and maintaining these skills is an extremely difficult one, many academy personnel involved in the selection and training of recruits tended to treat the matter as one of having common sense or not having it. They assumed that common sense is something you have or you do not, that is, an ability that cannot be developed or taught. Common sense was also a characteristic highly valued by the patrolmen tested both in the academy and in the field. The groups at the different time periods indicated in Table 11 never had more than 7% in agreement with the statement "Well developed skills of selfdefense are more useful than common sense to a patrolman." Similarly, only 10% or less of each of the same groups tested at different times agreed that "One of the least important problems for patrolmen is that of gaining the cooperation of the public." The recruits were aware, at a general level of discourse, that their task involves some interpersonal skills in order that it be accomplished. But their judgment of the difficulty of this task varies greatly at different stages in their early careers.

The responses to the items in Table 15 show that the recruits entered the department somewhat skeptical of the degree to which patrolmen received the needed cooperation from the public (item A). Thirty-two per cent agreed, at that point, that "Patrolmen almost never receive the cooperation from the public that is needed . . ." At the end of the training period (T_2) the per cent agreeing with the statement decreased to only 18%. At the latter point, we might consider that the academy training had prepared the recruits effectively, since it is useful for patrolmen to believe that at least some of the general public will assist police in their duties. As pointed out earlier, police can be greatly assisted in a variety of ways by the general public, but it is important for them to believe in at least the possibility they can and will receive this cooperation in order for them to seek it out. After the patrolmen had completed one year in the field, however, their responses moved closer to those they gave as beginning recruits, with the per cent in agreement about the lack of cooperation even higher (46%).

A similar trend can be observed in the remaining items in Table 15. The recruits became more convinced during their training that public cooperation and assistance are not extremely rare commodities, but then shifted during their first year's field experience toward a skepticism regarding the availability of such commodities. A second group of patrolmen with two years in the field either was similar in their responses to the group with one year in the field or was even more convinced that they could not rely on much help from the public. This trend seems to be opposite to that observed in medical students by Becker and Geer, in which the students became more cynical about humanitarian values during their training in medical schools but regained their former idealism after they completed their training.[45] As were the changes in medical students, the changes in the police recruits' attitudes can probably be seen as a function of the kinds of social support for them. Much of the support in the academy for the recruits' attitudes comes from the instructors, whereas in the field it is more likely to stem from other patrolmen and additionally from the recruits' experiences with citizens. Which of the two sources of support in the field contributed more to the change toward an increased lack of faith in public cooperation is not clear, but probably both were operative.

A related process of change occurred with regard to the belief that respect in tough neighborhoods for police is dependent on the extent to which police are willing to use force. (See Table 16.) At the end of their training (T_2), the recruits are more likely to disagree with the position that force serves as a solution to the problem of respect for the police than they were at the beginning of their training (T_1). However, following their first year in the field, they moved in the opposite direction to a point where twice as large a percentage of patrolmen (51%) agreed with the statement as the percentage (26%) at the end of the recruit training. The group of patrolmen with two years in the field tended slightly to be in even more agreement with the statement.

The implications of the changes shown in Tables 15 and 16 for the interpersonal tactic of *information gathering* would seem to be in the negative direction. That is, an increased reliance on the use of force and a lack of trust in the public's cooperation and assistance would create difficulties for patrolmen in acquiring the necessary information on which to base a decision concerning the handling of individuals or groups of citizens. If patrolmen believe they are not likely to receive help, they would presumably

---

[45]H. S. Becker and B. Geer, "The Fate of Idealism in Medical School," *American Sociological Review*, 23 (1958): 50-6.

Table 15.—Recruits' Estimates of Cooperation from Public
(in percent)

Item	Time[a]	No Answer	Strongly Agree	Agree	Uncertain	Disagree	Strongly Disagree
A	T_1	0	7	25	25	39	4
	T_2	1	2	16	18	62	1
	T_3	1	9	37	12	41	1
	T_4	0	10	40	14	34	2
B	T_1	1	3	36	34	26	1
	T_2	0	3	33	24	39	1
	T_3	0	6	46	17	30	2
	T_4	0	10	51	10	30	0
C	T_1	1	2	40	33	22	2
	T_2	1	3	62	19	15	0
	T_3	1	2	42	15	37	2
	T_4	0	2	40	18	39	1
D	T_1	1	1	34	34	26	4
	T_2	0	4	41	27	21	7
	T_3	0	2	42	21	29	6
	T_4	0	1	38	22	34	5

Item A: "Patrolmen almost never receive the cooperation from the public that is needed to handle police work properly."
Item B: "It is usually quite difficult to persuade people to give patrolmen the information they need."
Item C: "The public in general is usually quite helpful to a patrolman who can use the public's help."
Item D: "Most people will try in some way to help a patrolman who is being attacked on the street."

[a]Table 8, footnote [a].

be less likely to seek help in gathering information. Similarly, if they rely heavily on force, they may be able to gather information, but its reliability is that much more suspect than information received without the use of force.

Table 16.—Responses to: "Respect for the Police in a Tough Neighborhood Depends on the Willingness of Patrolmen to Use Force Frequently and Effectively" (in percent)

Time[a]	No Answer	Strongly Agree	Agree	Uncertain	Disagree	Strongly Disagree
T_1	0	6	26	31	34	3
T_2	0	5	21	19	49	5
T_3	1	7	44	14	28	5
T_4	0	13	42	20	24	1

[a]See Table 8, footnote [a].

The increases in the F-Scale scores ... [authoritarian personality syndrome] should also be negatively related to the ability of the patrolmen to do interpersonal testing, since one distinguishing characteristic of the authoritarian personality is the tendency to ignore or not perceive a wide range of differences among people. This would be particularly true in the case where the differences may be related to status or to such perceived attributes as respect for law and order. Patrolmen must interact with many persons from the lower socio-economic levels whose orientation toward the legal system is seen by the patrolmen as at variance with the proper level of respect due the law. These perceived disparities between their own and the citizens' status levels and orientations toward the legal system would create some difficulty for patrolmen who score high on the F-Scale with regard to their perception of the unique values or needs of such individual citizens. For such patrolmen, the salience of the above differences between themselves and citizens would probably obviate the necessity for information gathering prior to their making a decision about how to gain the citizen's compliance.

Even though new patrolmen may face some difficulties in taking the role of citizens with whom they will interact, they seem to be quite aware of the general necessity for their *clarification of expectations.* A group of 266 recruits at the end of their training were similar to 221 patrolmen with one or two years in the field in their distribution of responses to the following: "Generally, police make things much easier to handle if they immediately make clear to people why they were called to the scene." Only 10% of each group disagreed with the statement. The two groups similarly agreed that "A patrolman's authority is not weakened by his giving citizens a few alternative ways in which they can cooperate with the patrolman." (Only 8% in each group disagreed with the statement.)

A slight difference existed between the recruit and experienced groups with regard to the public's understanding of laws which patrolmen enforce. The experienced patrolmen, with one and two years in the field, were somewhat more likely to feel that the public understands the laws patrolmen enforce than were the recruits tested at the end of their training. This difference follows from the experienced patrolmen's increased familiarity with laws, if we assume that they project their own familiarity onto the general public and that recruits are more likely to be aware of the difference between a police officer's understanding and the public's understanding of legal matters because of their recent status as part of the public. (See Table 17.)

Table 17.—Patrolmen's View of Public Understanding of Laws (in percent)

Item	Group	No Answer	Strongly Agree	Agree	Uncertain	Disagree	Strongly Disagree
A	Recruits	0	6	50	18	25	1
	Experienced patrolmen	1	5	40	11	41	2
B	Recruits	1	4	48	19	27	3
	Experienced patrolmen	0	4	67	8	20	1

Item A: "Few people really understand the laws that police must enforce."
Item B: "Most citizens seem to have a pretty good working knowledge of their legal rights and obligations."

There are few differences between the experienced group and the group of recruits tested at the end of their training in regard to some hypothesized correlates of the interpersonal tactic of *exploiting or* utilizing the values of citizens. As seen in Table 18, the majority in each group indicated agreement with the prescription that police should not altercast citizens into a criminal role (item A). This attitude would obviate some of the many difficulties for police officers in handling violators that result from the officers' failure to create or reestablish the conditions in which a citizen's normal values are operative and can hence be utilized by the officers in gaining compliance.

Table 18.—Correlates of Exploiting or Utilizing Values: Facilitators (in percent)

Item	Group	No Answer	Strongly Agree	Agree	Uncertain	Disagree	Strongly Disagree
A	Recruits	0	5	62	17	16	0
	Experienced patrolmen	1	2	55	15	26	1
B	Recruits	0	1	12	31	55	1
	Experienced patrolmen	0	0	16	17	65	2

Item A: "A patrolman generally should not try to make a person who has violated some law feel like a criminal."
Item B: "Complainants or witnesses don't like to give all the necessary information to police chiefly because they resent police in general."

Both groups are also similar in their disagreement with the proposition that citizens' resentment of police causes them to withhold needed information (item B). The attitude that citizens resent police in general is probably one that causes individual officers to interact in a defensive manner with citizens. Such interaction would make it difficult for the officer to devise an approach which recognizes the values of citizens and utilizes them. Thus, in at least the respects measured by the items in Table 18, police are prepared to deal with the problem of utilizing the values of citizens.

In other respects the attitudes of the officers do not seem so well prepared for the task of utilizing the values of citizens. Again, the groups of experienced and recruit patrolmen were similar in their responses to the items in Table 19. There was a marked agreement with the statement that police expectations are "only natural" (item A). One of the more striking features of the police officer's role, however, is that not only are many of his own actions such that if he were not a policeman his actions would be met by a strong societal reaction, but also his requests for compliance from citizens often involve punitive consequences for the citizens, who generally do not see themselves as deserving of these consequences, particularly at the time the officer makes the request. A police officer's failure to recognize the extraordinary nature of his expectations would present certain problems for him in attempting to work with or through the values of citizens with whom he interacts.

Table 19.—Correlates of Exploiting or Utilizing Values: Inhibitors (in percent)

Item	Group	No Answer	Strongly Agree	Agree	Uncertain	Disagree	Strongly Disagree
A	Recruits	0	5	70	14	11	0
	Experienced patrolmen	0	3	80	11	6	0
B	Recruits	0	3	36	30	30	1
	Experienced patrolmen	0	2	33	20	42	3
C	Recruits	0	1	38	31	28	2
	Experienced patrolmen	0	2	38	28	31	1

Item A: "The things that patrolmen want citizens to do in accordance with the law are only natural."
Item B: "A patrolman should generally try to make offenders feel as though they were really law-abiding but had just made this one mistake."
Item C: "A patrolman can be pretty sure he will gain compliance from a person who appears to be somewhat frightened of the patrolman."

Similarly, a patrolman who fails to see the utility of manifestly treating an offender as law-abiding probably experiences some difficulty in attempting to utilize the values of an offender in gaining compliance. The responses to item B in Table 19 would seem to contradict the responses to item A in Table 18 in that the responses in Table 19 indicate a lack of agreement that officers should generally make the effort to induce this sense of being law-abiding. The two items differ, of course, regarding the degree to which officers should take steps to avoid giving citizens the impression the officers consider them to be criminals. Hence, item B in Table 19 may not be an adequate measure of beliefs concerning the utility of the tactic of attempting to "normalize" the situation of the citizen in order that his usual values be operative. Further, the tactic requires that the values of the citizen be congruent in some sense with the values implicit in the relevant law being enforced. As Miller points out, the values of members of the lower classes conflict in a number of dimensions with middle-class values and particularly in a way that would create problems for police officers.[46]

The final problem for officers in using the values of citizens stems from their failure to reject the notion that fear of an officer implies compliance on a citizen's part (item C in Table 19). Again, both groups showed a similar tendency to be slightly more in agreement with the statement that a citizen's frightened appearance implies his compliance. That fear is an unstable solution to the problem of gaining compliance has been shown in a number of research settings. Strict reliance on fear, although not necessarily implied by agreement with item C, should then create a rather unstable set of relations between police and public. Nevertheless, some police conceive of the police officer's role as requiring behavior aimed at inducing fear in citizens. The police objection to abolition of the death penalty rests to a great extent on this conception of the role. Similarly, it seems that the failure to develop a nonlethal alternative to the police revolver can be traced to the reluctance of police to give up what they perceive as an essential role component as well as a necessary deterrent. The legal basis on which the use of revolvers rests, however, is that of simply stopping someone from committing a serious crime or escaping from apprehension. Again, reliance on fear is a tactic that obviates the utilization of values because of the stress level induced in the citizen. The relationship between stress levels and rationality (taken here to refer to behavior consistent with the individual citizen's values) has clearly been shown to become negative with increases in stress beyond a critical point.[47]

The interpersonal skills characterized as involving both a decisive and impersonal *presentation of self* apparently are affected to some extent by the academy training program. As shown in Table 12, during training recruits increased their degree of agreement with the proposition (item B) that a patrolman's ignoring of challenges from citizens to fight creates a problem for other patrolmen in the area. The same group further increased its agreement with the statement during the first year of field experience. This attitude would not serve to assist patrolmen in maintaining the appearance of emotional distance that is particularly important in situations in which officers take punitive action. That is, by responding to challenges of this sort the officer is likely to appear to be acting on his own and not as a representative of the law. Hence, his requests for compliance may be rejected by a citizen on the grounds that no personal obligations exist between himself and the officer.

---

[46]W. B. Miller, "Lower Class Culture as a Generating Milieu of Gang Delinquency," *Journal of Social Issues,* 14 (1958).

[47]See C. E. Osgood, *An Alternative to War or Surrender,* (Urbana: Illini Books, 1962), for an excellent and succinct discussion of this relationship applied to military and political relations among hostile nations.

A similar change can be discerned in Table 11, in which the agreement slightly increased over time for three groups of patrolmen that "Most officers agree that some force is necessary and justified when a citizen unjustly insults and curses a police officer." Patrolmen apparently come to perceive more support from their fellow officers for actions which are not consistent with the need for police impersonality. As indicated earlier, the changes primarily take place during assignment to the field. There was little change during recruit training in regard to the recruits' perception of consensus regarding the use of force under such conditions. The later increases probably reflect, to some extent, the increasing identification of the patrolman with his role as well as an increasing familiarity with a wider range of types of officers and police behavior.

The patrolmen tested after some field experience indicate a marked awareness of the value of an impersonal demeanor when attempting to handle a noncriminal dispute. As shown in Table 20 there is an unusually high degree of agreement with item A regarding the value of not appearing to take sides in such disputes. It would appear that the power problems of coalition formation in the triad are well known to police, who are required to handle disputes between husband and wife, landlord and tenant, merchant and customer, etc.

The patrolmen show less consensus on the matter of maintaining an impersonal appearance through pointing to the courts as having "the final say" and hence indirectly pointing to their function as delimited or delineated and somewhat independent of their personal convictions regarding a "citizen's case," (item B). Although a majority in each group indicated disagreement that a patrolman loses some authority by such a tactic, the majorities are slim. Patrolmen in agreement with this item presumably are less likely to use the alternative, for example, in interaction with a motorist who disagrees with the patrolman that any traffic violation occurred, of indicating that the citizen can contest the officer's decision and that the officer considers it proper for the citizen to do so. This action need not be supported by a lecture on the virtues of the democratic state or the adversary system in American courts. Nor would the well-worn "tell it to the judge" seem appropriate. If appropriately used, the tactic can help prevent a citizen from thinking that the patrolman has a personal interest in "getting" the citizen.

The third item (item C) in Table 20 was constructed as a measure of the extent to which patrolmen feel that the appearance of emotional involvement on their part assists them in situations in which some punitive action has been presented as likely. The patrolmen in each group were fairly evenly split between agreement and disagreement that patrolmen "are helped considerably" by an appearance of anger in such situations. A significant number of patrolmen assumed that the credibility of the threat of force depended on their appearing angry. The difficulty with this assumption is that anger reduces the perceived impersonality of the officer and consequently places him in a position where he is likely to be seen as personally competing with a citizen. This perceived personal competition, in turn, implies a different set of rules governing the patrolman-citizen interaction. These rules allow for the exchange of punitive actions.

The appearance of anger has the further potential disadvantage of reducing the decisive appearance of the officer, inasmuch as emotion often implies an ambivalent state. Hence, the risks of using an angry appearance to support the credibility of a threat are great enough so that the tactic can be considered useful only under carefully defined conditions. Data are not available on the degree of agreement that the patrolmen might have given this item at the start or at the completion of their training. Personal observation of interaction between some academy personnel and the recruits, however, indicated that the recruits were not without police role models in which the association between an appearance of anger and punitive action occurred.

Table 20.—Correlates of Impersonal Presentation of Self
(in percent)

Item	Time[a]	No Answer	Strongly Agree	Agree	Uncertain	Disagree	Strongly Disagree
A	T_3	0	26	69	0	4	0
	T_4	0	20	71	1	7	0
B	T_3	0	0	28	19	52	2
	T_4	0	0	37	8	54	1
C	T_3	0	2	39	12	47	1
	T_4	0	0	44	17	36	3

Item A: "A patrolman should invariably avoid appearing to take any side in a dispute where no crime has been committed."
Item B: "Patrolmen generally will appear less authoritative if they tell a citizen that a court has the final say about the citizen's case."
Item C: "When patrolmen indicate they will use the force necessary to gain compliance from a citizen, they are helped considerably if the citizen thinks they are getting angry."

[a]See Table 8. footnote [a].

Recruit Training and Uncertainties
From Organizational Sources

As indicated in the section concerned with background characteristics of police officers, recruits were exposed to some of the *semimilitary aspects of police work* in the selection process. Prior to their appointment they had undergone a character investigation, in which the sincerity of their motives or the truth of information they had given may have been openly questioned by an investigator. It is in the selection process that the potential recruit also learns that "all doubts are to be resolved in favor of the department"; that is, unless the appropriate police personnel are completely satisfied, the applicant is to be disapproved as a candidate for the position of patrolman.

Once the candidate enters the department, he is immediately presented with information that supports the ascendancy of the organization over the individual. On the first page of the first lesson plan used by academy instructors, the introduction to the hour lecture, "Note Taking and Study," ends with the following: "What you don't learn, or principles which you fail to accept may result in improper performance of police duty and possibly may also lead to your appearance as a defendant in a department trial."

The second hour of academic lectures reviewed a number of rules of the police academy and of the department in general. The introduction to the hour ends with the following: "Your compliance with these rules will go a long way in helping your first steps toward a successful career in this department." In the second hour the recruit is referred to the handout material entitled *Recruit Issue Material.* This material covers a number of areas in the training program and also contains nine pages of 117 rules and regulations of the Police Academy Recruit Training School. The rules and regulations vary greatly with regard to their specificity, from using a specific entrance to the building to one rather comprehensive rule: "Conduct, disorder or neglect prejudicial to good order, efficiency or discipline, whether or not specifically mentioned in the Rules and Procedures, including cowardice or making a false statement is prohibited."

The recruit, on or off duty, is further explicitly enjoined from drinking "intoxicants at any time to an extent making him unfit for duty," from entering "at any time, any premises licensed for 'on-premises consumption of alcoholic beverages except when necessary in the performance of police duty'," and while on the street in uniform, from eating, smoking, chewing gum or tobacco, reading newspapers or other material, running, loitering, using vile or indecent language, and "expectorating." While at home ("the official residence") the recruit is expected not to be absent "between midnight and 6:00 A.M. except when necessary in the performance of police duty or while expeditiously traveling to or from an assigned duty, or with permission of the Commanding Officer, Police Academy."

The Introduction to the *Recruit Issue Material* ends with a paragraph containing the following.

> ... Of necessity, our discipline is severe and our program is rigorous. You will be confronted with many regulations. You may not understand the purpose of each rule or requirement, but each is designed with a purpose and tested by time.... There is no easy way.... The man who cooperates, works with the Academy, will find his training period most rewarding. The shirkers will be eliminated.

The comprehensive nature of his commitment to the police force and the potentially punitive consequences of his failure to fulfill any aspect of that commitment are thus made clear early in his training to the incoming recruit. He may find, for example, that his failure to report immediately a sickness that keeps him from attending classes in the morning results in a police patrol car calling on his home in the afternoon. He may also find that the character investigation continues on during his stay in the academy and that his sexual behavior as a bachelor has become a matter of departmental concern.

For the most part, recruits do not appear to evaluate negatively the rather close supervision and rather large number of rules and regulations in the academy. As might be predicted on the basis of their past work experiences and on the basis of their F-scale scores, they tend not to find the atmosphere repressive or overly restrictive. As was indicated earlier in Table 7, one group of 171 recruits in their first week of training perceived supervision throughout the department as close and, further, did not evaluate this as problematic. The recruits' perception of supervision throughout the department as close or strict probably assists them in their adjustment to the semimilitary conditions of the academy.

One other factor that may account for the recruits' positive evaluation of the dominant supervisory style is the belief that supervisors are obligated not only to observe patrolmen closely but also to give patrolmen whatever assistance they can. The responses in Table 21 are indicative of the extent to which patrolmen see their supervisors as obligated to exchange assistance for the patrolmen's positive evaluation of close supervision and the patrolmen's complaint behavior implied by this evaluation. The recruits also did not disagree that the assistance is forthcoming from supervisors, as indicated by their responses to item C in Table 21. After some experience in the field, however, the patrolmen were less likely to agree that their supervisors "are extremely helpful toward patrolmen." By far the larger number still agreed (T_3 and T_4) with the statement, but a trend away from endorsement of this item can be discerned.

As shown in Table 21 the patrolmen changed little with respect to their agreement that supervisors carry heavy obligations to patrolmen (items A and B). We can hypothesize that an imbalance between the perceived obligations of supervisors to patrolmen and the perceived extent to which supervisors fulfill these obligations exists for the experienced patrolmen. The manner in which this imbalance is resolved cannot be rigorously

Table 21.—Patrolmen's View of Their Supervisors' Obligations (in percent)

Item	Time [a]	No Answer	Strongly Agree	Agree	Uncertain	Disagree	Strongly Disagree
A	T_1	0	23	60	16	1	0
	T_2	0	24	62	11	2	1
	T_3	1	26	63	5	4	1
	T_4	0	25	63	6	6	0
B	T_1	0	17	56	22	4	1
	T_2	0	17	65	11	6	1
	T_3	0	17	63	16	4	0
	T_4	0	18	63	11	7	1
C	T_1	0	12	54	31	3	0
	T_2	1	8	56	29	5	1
	T_3	2	6	47	23	18	4
	T_4	0	4	40	35	19	2

Item A: "A patrolman is officially entitled to all the help he needs from his supervisors."
Item B: "Supervisors are expected to give help without any reservations to patrolmen who need help with police problems."
Item C: "Supervisors in the police department are extremely helpful toward patrolmen."

[a]See Table 8, footnote [a].

identified, but it seems to consist, in part, of a restructuring of the patrolmen's view of supervisors. The restructuring often takes the form of viewing supervisors as somehow personally lacking in courage or as failing to be hierarchically independent of higher ranking supervisors. This latter view probably underlies the small degree of disagreement (17%) on part of the experienced patrolmen with a statement that "Police supervisors usually go along with each other when one wants to take disciplinary action against a patrolman."

The changes in the general views of patrolmen regarding the disciplinary or punitive practices and policies of the department are somewhat more marked than their view of the closeness of supervision. The patrolmen, as recruits, tended to see the discipline to which they were exposed in the academy as fair, impartially administered, effective, and necessary for the organization. In a combined group of 271 recruits tested at the end of their training, 49 (18%) had received one or more "delinquencies" during their stay at the academy. The delinquencies were officially recorded violations of academy and department rules and regulations. Recruits were given a hearing or trial with academy personnel presiding, and if found guilty were usually given extra work assignments as punishment. The separate responses of the two combined groups are listed in Table 22 and show the extent to which the recruits endorsed the general policy of discipline.

Their endorsement of the general policy is not quite matched, however, by their endorsement of the administration of delinquencies nor by their belief in the effectiveness of the delinquencies. Although more than three-fourths of the recruits agree that the rules and regulations are worthwhile (item D) and that delinquencies are necessary for organizational order (item E), only one-half or less agreed that the delinquencies were fair, deserved, and effective (items A, B, and C respectively.) It is the author's impression that the discrepancy between the level of agreement with the general policy and the level of agreement concerning the propriety of implementing the policy of discipline was associated with a process of "personalizing" the disciplinary system similar to the process previously mentioned. That is, as the recruits progressed through their training they became more likely to account for the delinquencies given to recruits by pointing to personal characteristics of the police superior officer who charged a recruit with a violation of rules and regulations. Some instructors, for example, came to be known as "petty" and others as "hairy" (punitive). Still, the majority of the recruits did not come to see the administration of discipline in these personalized terms during their training.

During the training period the recruits apparently also changed their view of the extent to which punitive techniques are utilized by supervisors in the field. A slight trend can be discerned in Table 23 toward a view of supervision as less punitive than the view expressed at the beginning of the recruit training. At the end of the training period, the percentage of recruits in disagreement with the statement that police supervisors use punishment as their main method of ensuring effective performance (item A) rose to 53% from an initial 35% at the outset of training. Similarly, more recruits disagreed at the end of their training that patrolmen frequently are found guilty of rule violations and severely punished (item B) than at the begin-

Table 22.—Recruits' Perception of Academy Disciplinary System (in percent)

Item	Group	No Answer	Strongly Agree	Agree	Uncertain	Disagree	Strongly Disagree	(N)
A	1960	16	9	41	22	5	7	(107)
B	1961	4	10	35	26	20	6	(164)
C	1961	4	3	43	34	15	4	(164)
D	1961	2	9	68	12	8	1	(164)
E	1961	2	12	64	7	13	2	(164)

Item A: "Do you agree that the delinquencies and complaints given to your company were fair?"

Item B: "Do you agree that only the recruits who most deserved delinquencies were the ones who received them?"

Item C: "Do you agree that the delinquencies had the effect the instructors wanted on those who received them?"

Item D: "Do you agree that the rules and regulations which serve as a basis for delinquencies are worthwhile?"

Item E: "Do you agree that delinquencies are necessary in order to keep recruits' behavior in line with the rules and regulations?"

ning of their training. After one year in the field, however, (T_3), the group returned to a view closer to their view at the beginning of training. A second group of patrolmen (T_4) with two years in the field tended to perceive their supervisors as even more punitive.

Table 23.—Perception of Field Supervisors' Punitive Tactics (in percent)

Item	Time [a]	No Answer	Strongly Agree	Agree	Uncertain	Disagree	Strongly Disagree
A	T_1	1	8	30	25	29	6
	T_2	1	5	25	16	46	7
	T_3	0	10	29	14	44	3
	T_4	0	12	42	11	31	4
B	T_1	0	7	13	26	43	11
	T_2	0	3	15	18	53	12
	T_3	1	9	21	18	41	10
	T_4	1	11	27	18	35	8

Item A: "The main method used by supervisors to keep their men working properly is that of punishment for ineffective performance."
Item B: "Patrolmen frequently are found guilty of violating departmental rules and procedures and are consequently penalized severely."

[a]See Table 8, footnote [a].

The 221 patrolmen with field experience whose responses are listed in Table 23 actually received a reported total of eight complaints (officially recorded violations of rules), four of which were given to the group of 83 patrolmen with two years in the field. No individual patrolman in either experienced group received more than one complaint. On the other hand, there are twenty-two reported instances in which patrolmen in these two groups were given departmental recognition (medals officially given for acts of heroism and bravery as well as for "good collars," that is, worthwhile arrests of persons who have committed serious crimes where the arrest may have required some ingenuity on the part of the patrolman).

Additionally, six patrolman in the two groups reported they had received civilian complaints. These were primarily complaints from citizens alleging police brutality and abusiveness. None of the complaints were reported as leading to a verdict of guilty by the Civilian Complaint Review Board, a hearing board made up of civilian and uniformed personnel in the department. It is interesting to note that the experienced patrolmen generally considered the departmental handling of the civilian complaints less fair than the handling of complaints issued by police supervisors. In Table 24 we can see the relative degree to which the handling of civilian complaints (item A) and the administration of departmental complaints (item B) met the standards of fairness held by patrolmen. The handling of civilian complaints was seen as fair by only 14% in each group, whereas departmental complaints were seen as fair by a slightly larger percentage. The responses of the two groups are almost identical regarding departmental complaints, but the more experienced group held somewhat stronger negative attitudes than did the less experienced group concerning civilian complaints. In general, both groups justified their stand by indicating that the investigation by the department of civilian complaints was either biased in favor of the civilian's position or inadequate.

In contrast, both groups were more favorably inclined toward the fairness of the system of departmental awards (item C). The less experienced group, however, seems to have witheld judgment more so than the group with two years in the field, since 50% of the former group indicated they did not know how to rank the system. This would appear to follow from the nature of their field experience relative to that of the group with two years. The less experienced men were less likely to find themselves in situations in which they would be required to show bravery or heroism, as they were less likely to patrol in cars. Foot patrolman were less likely to be summoned in an emergency because of the ease and rapidity of establishing communications with the patrolmen in radio cars. Therefore, they were less often considered for an award.

The patrolmens' evaluations of more specific aspects of the disciplinary system in the field may help to clarify their feelings. The experienced patrolmen were asked to evaluate the practice of having outside supervisors or "shoe-flies" observe the men. These supervisors were police captains not assigned to a specific precinct who were perceived by patrolmen primarily as punitive agents. The practice seemed potentially quite useful in that it relieved the supervisors of a given unit somewhat from having to take punitive action against patrolmen with whom they worked. It was felt that in this way the supervisors and patrolmen in a given unit would function more effectively as a team.

As indicated by their responses to items A and B in Table 25, the patrolmen show little sympathy with this solution. Only 7% of each group agreed that the system of outside supervision serves effectively as such a solution. Among the reasons indicated earlier for their dislike of such a system was the feeling on the part of patrolmen that these outside supervisors were rated on the basis of the number of complaints they issued to patrolmen (something akin to the "quota system" citizens see as operative

Table 24.—Perceived Fairness of Departmental Handling of "Complaints" and Departmental Awards (in percent)

Item	Group[a]	No Answer	Very Fair	Somewhat Fair	Don't Know	Somewhat Unfair	Very Unfair
A	1961	2	8	6	21	38	25
	1962	0	6	8	36	25	24
B	1961	0	5	18	33	31	13
	1962	0	7	17	31	27	18
C	1961	1	8	39	30	15	6
	1962	1	11	25	50	12	1

Item A: "In general, how do you feel about the fairness of the department's handling of civilian complaints?"

Item B: "In general, how do you feel about the fairness of disciplinary action in the department?"

Item C: "In general, how do you feel about the fairness of departmental recognition?"

[a]The groups are identified by year of graduation from the academy. The 1961 group had two years in the field (N = 84) and the 1962 group had one year in the field (N = 137).

in the issuance of traffic tickets). A related reason for the objections by patrolmen to the system of outside supervision was their belief that complaints given by these supervisors were based on isolated instances of violations of departmental rules rather than on a patrolman's total performance. The responses to item B in Table 25, in which only 5% of each group disagreed with this sentiment, indicate the extent to which patrolmen shared this view of the outside supervisors' administration of discipline.

Table 25.—Evaluation by Experienced Patrolmen of Discipline in the Field (in percent)

Item	Group[a]	No Answer	Strongly Agree	Agree	Uncertain	Disagree	Strongly Disagree
A	1961	1	0	7	11	35	46
	1962	0	0	7	11	35	47
B	1961	0	35	45	15	1	4
	1962	0	29	47	18	5	0
C	1961	0	6	32	25	30	7
	1962	0	6	34	29	26	5
D	1961	0	27	35	26	10	2
	1962	0	12	38	29	19	2
E	1961	0	11	21	7	54	7
	1962	0	7	21	7	54	11

Item A: "The system of outside supervision (shoo-flies) seems to be a good solution to the problem of discipline."
Item B: "Outside supervisors rarely take into consideration the past record of a patrolman."
Item C: "More often than not, a patrolman becomes too cautious after getting a complaint."
Item D: "Disciplining a patrolman usually has the effect of making him a less active cop."
Item E: "Most patrolmen spend the major part of their tours watching for supervisors."

[a]See Table 24, footnote [a].

The patrolmen further saw the general system of departmental discipline as dysfunctional in the sense that being given a complaint often leads to a withdrawal on the part of a patrolman from his duties (items C and D). In each group a slightly larger percentage of patrolmen agree than disagree with the belief that patrolmen become "too cautious" after receiving a complaint, and in both groups there is marked agreement that disciplining a patrolman usually results in his becoming a "less active cop." This shared feeling regarding the dysfunctional results of punishment is somewhat substantiated elsewhere, where it has been shown to be a common consequence in laboratory studies involving the use of punishment.[48] The nature of the patrolman's role is such that if he is not appropriately motivated, his actions may become quite ineffective because he must of necessity often handle threatening and distasteful situations often without assistance from either supervisors or other patrolmen.

One further point may be made about the disciplinary system. It appeared to the author that the system often engendered more concern on the part of patrolmen with what their supervisors were up to than concern with the problems of the citizenry. A strongly worded item (item E) was presented to the patrolmen and produced a disagreement on the part of approximately two-thirds of the respondents. Twenty-nine per cent of the group showed some agreement that "*most* patrolmen spend the *major* part of their tours watching for supervisors." In view of the strong wording of the item, this percentage of agreement is somewhat high. Whether or not the patrolmen were accurately reporting the practices of most patrolmen, their perception of the disciplinary system and its effects on the patrolman rather clearly indicates an unfavorable view. We might interpret this attitude as a function of a perceived discrepancy between the patrolmen's "investment" (in terms of experience in the field) and a form of supervision seen as inappropriate or as appropriate only for "rookies."[49] The phenomenon of police inactivity thus is not only a fear of punishment but also a result of a perceived failure of the department to honor its end of the exchange. At the same time, supervisors probably impute a more voluntaristic set of motives to more experienced patrolmen who violate rules and regulations, since experience implies an increased awareness or knowledge of these rules. This voluntaristic view of behavior, by the same token, is probably used by patrolmen in viewing their supervisors. Given the likelihood of behavior being viewed as voluntaristic, we can expect that much of the interaction between supervisors and patrolmen will conform to the characteristics of a "punishment-centered bureaucracy."[50]

---

[48]See E. R. Hilgard, *Theories of Learning* (New York: Appleton-Century, Crofts, 1956), esp. pp. 112-3.

[49]See C. C. Homans, *Social Behavior* (New York: Harcourt, Brace and World, 1961), esp. pp. 75-8 and Chap. 12, "Justice," for a discussion of the manner in which a person's investments in an interaction or organization influences the manner in which he perceives his "costs" of interaction or membership in an organization.

[50]See A. W. Gouldner, *loc. cit.,* and also G. Nettler, *loc. cit.,* regarding the relationship between punitiveness and a voluntaristic view of deviance.

As pointed out previously, the recruits felt that both the rules of the academy and the rules and regulations of the department contained in the departmental handbook, *Rules and Procedures,* are necessary and proper. In Table 22, recruits at the end of their training indicated their support of the rules and regulations as a basis for punitive action against recruits. Similarly, they believed that conformity to the rules and regulations required the system of delinquencies.

In response to an item asking the same sample of recruits to rank their study materials with regard to "how useful they will be in the field," the *Rules and Procedures* was ranked the most useful over lecture notes, the penal code, the code of criminal procedures, and other publications having to do with traffic law and the administrative and health codes. The question of the particular utility of the handbook is interesting, since there was a high level of *disagreement* (69%) with the statement that "patrolmen who rely entirely on the *Rules and Procedures* of the department are probably excellent police officers." Another group of 107 recruits earlier tested at the end of their training responded similarly to the following: "If a patrolman relied entirely on the *Rules and Procedures* of the department to do his work, he probably would be: a terrible police officer (36%); an average police officer (19%); a good police officer (33%); an excellent police officer (12%)."

The importance of the *Rules and Procedures* to the patrolmen apparently then did not stem from their belief that conformity to its provisions ensured adequate or outstanding performance—more likely from its punishment—legitimating function, as delineated by Gouldner.[51] Although there are no data directly bearing on this point, the recruits were probably quite concerned with knowing the rules and regulations, since 90% of the 1962 graduates agreed that "any violation of the rules and regulations of the department can be the basis for disciplinary action against patrolmen." Knowledge of the rules and regulations, if the above interpretation is accurate, would then protect a patrolman in two ways. He would be more likely to avoid violating a rule (when the violation was detectible, at least), and he would also be better prepared to defend himself against what he might perceive as the arbitrary use of authority by a supervisor. Nevertheless, the patrolmen did not see many situations in which they could or should refuse to obey an order from a superior. Only 10% of the same group agreed that "there are quite a few situations in which patrolmen are not officially required to obey orders from superior officers." Similarly, only 10% disagreed that "generally, it is a wise policy for a patrolman to do almost anything a superior officer orders."

After the recruits have had some field experience they appear still to remember the phrase in the introduction to the *Rules and Procedures,* since approximately three-quarters of each experienced group agreed that any

[51]A. W. Gouldner, *Patterns of Industrial Bureaucracy* (Glencoe, Ill.: The Free Press, 1954), pp. 168-72.

violation of rules may provide a supervisor with a basis for some punitive action (item A in Table 26). In this connection increasing experience had inclined the patrolmen with two years in the field to agree less that the *Rules and Procedures* is meant as a "guide" for patrolmen (item B). Sixty-seven per cent of the patrolmen with only one year in the field (the 1962 group)

Table 26.—Rules and Procedures as Seen by Experienced Patrolmen (in percent)

Item	Group[a]	No Answer	Strongly Agree	Agree	Uncertain	Disagree	Strongly Disagree
A	1961	1	23	54	9	12	1
	1962	2	21	55	4	7	1
B	1961	0	8	43	13	25	11
	1962	0	8	59	7	21	5
C	1961	0	21	60	7	12	0
	1962	0	22	58	9	10	1
D	1961	0	10	45	8	35	2
	1962	1	4	36	15	42	2
E	1961	0	2	53	14	29	2
	1962	0	3	64	15	16	2

Item A: "Any violation of the rules and regulations of the department can be the basis for disciplinary action against patrolmen."
Item B: "The *Rules and Procedures* is meant to be a guide for patrol-men and not something to be followed to the letter."
Item C: "It is impossible to always follow the *Rules and Procedures* to the letter and still do an efficient job in police work."
Item D: "A patrolman, for his own good, should never deviate from the provisions contained in the *Rules and Procedures*."
Item E: "Most supervisors are careful to fit the *Rules and Procedures* to the situation rather than insisting the *Rules and Procedures* have to be followed regardless of the situation."

[a]See Table 24, footnote [a].

agreed with the item, whereas 51% of the men with two years showed agreement. Both groups, however, show the same rather high level of agreement that efficient police work would be impossible if an officer were to follow the *Rules and Procedures* to the letter (item C).

It is interesting to note, in view of the agreement that efficient police work cannot be accomplished by adhering to the letter of the *Rules and Procedures,* that the majority (55%) of the men with two years in the field agree that a patrolman, "for his own good," should adhere closely to the *Rules and Procedures* (item D). A smaller percentage (40%) of the men with one year in the field agreed with this item. A smaller percentage (18%) of this last group also showed disagreement with the statement that supervisors do, in fact, use the *Rules and Procedures* as something more akin to a guide (item E). Thirty-one per cent of the more experienced group indicated disagreement with this item.

Thus, adherence to the *Rules and Procedures* is probably a function of the extent to which patrolmen believe this adherence serves to protect their careers as well as a function of their perception that the supervisors are rule-bound. Since this adherence conflicts with the patrolmen's feelings about what is effective police work, we might expect that the patrolmen who experience this conflict will find few intrinsic satisfactions in their work.

The responses to items intended to measure the officers' perception of the intrinsic satisfactions of a *career* in police work are presented in Table 27 and indicate the extent to which the experienced patrolmen perceive their work as intrinsically satisfying. Both groups of patrolmen are split almost equally with regard to whether the intrinsic satisfactions balance off the dissatisfactions associated with police work (item A). There is more agreement within both groups that a recruit's expectations that the work will be intrinsically satisfying are unrealistic (item B) and even more agreement that the economic benefits of the work are necessary to keep patrolmen "on the job" (item C).

Another indication of the extent to which the patrolmen are satisfied with the work is the anticipated length of time they expect to remain in the department. Two groups of respondents were asked in 1961 and 1962 at the outset of their training how long they expected to stay on the force. They were asked the same question again in 1963 after one group completed two years and the other one year in the field. Their responses in Table 28 show a tendency for both groups to foreshorten their anticipated stay in the department after completing their training and some experience in the field.

Similarly, the level of aspiration of the patrolmen both with regard to promotion to higher ranks and with regard to assignment to the detective division or to other desired assignments (the "details") changed. The patrolmen in the 1961 group in Table 28 appreciably changed their reported expectations regarding where they would be assigned after ten years on the job. Twenty-five per cent of the group at the beginning of their training indicated they expected to be in the patrol force or in the safety (traffic) division, but after two years in the field 56% of the group indicated they expected to be in one of these assignments when they have completed ten

Table 27.—Perceived Intrinsic Satisfactions in Police Work
(in percent)

Item	Group[a]	No Answer	Strongly Agree	Agree	Uncertain	Disagree	Strongly Disagree
A	1961	1	2	47	6	34	10
	1962	0	4	40	16	35	5
B	1961	0	12	41	18	29	0
	1962	0	7	48	20	24	1
C	1961	0	20	53	9	17	1
	1962	0	18	44	17	20	1

Item A: "All in all, there are enough satisfactions just in performing police duties to make up for the headaches of the job."
Item B: "A recruit who thinks he is going to get much personal satisfaction just from performing police duties is due for a rude awakening."
Item C: "It would be difficult to keep most patrolmen on the job if it weren't for the salary and other benefits connected with the job."

[a]See Table 24, footnote [a].

years on the job. Those expecting to still be a patrolman after ten years on the job increased from 3% at the outset of their training to 20% after two years in the field. Finally, although 62% of the group with two years in the field indicated they were studying for the next examination for promotion

Table 28.—Responses of Patrolmen to: "Approximately how many
years do you expect to stay on the force?" (in percent)

Group[a]	When Tested	Less than 20	20 to 25	25 to 30	30 to 35	35 or More
1961	1961	8	67	16	4	5
	1963	14	73	8	4	1
1962	1962	9	65	19	5	2
	1963	8	79	9	2	2

[a]See Table 24, footnote [a].

to sergeant, only 20% reported they were studying more than eight hours a week, on the average, for the next test.

It is not the case that the patrolmen failed to see the advantages of rank. On the contrary, they tend to see the relative advantages as marked for superior officers in the department. The experienced patrolmen indicated a high level of agreement that privileges are quite different for superior officers. In Table 29 the two groups of patrolmen with experience agreed pretty much that patrolmen have few privileges relative to their supervisors (item A). They show even more agreement with the frequently heard statement that "It's a bosses' job."

Table 29.—Patrolmen's View of Their Privileges Relative to Those of Police Superior Officers (in percent)

Item	Group[a]	No Answer	Strongly Agree	Agree	Uncertain	Disagree	Strongly Disagree
A	1961	0	20	36	17	27	0
	1962	2	13	41	15	29	0
B	1961	0	33	42	14	11	0
	1962	1	25	44	9	13	0

Item A: "Patrolmen have almost no privileges compared with what their supervisors have."
Item B: "It's a bosses' job."

[a]See Table 24, footnote [a].

The patrolmen apparently changed their view of the extent to which patrolmen could rely on a "rabbi" or "hook" (a patron) to help them get the transfers or assignments they wanted (Table 30). In only 8% of the 1962 group at the end of their training agreed that patrolmen often got jobs they wanted as a personal favor, but after one year in the field 33% agreed (item A). The 1961 graduates after two years in the field were even more in agreement; 54% of this latter group agreed with item A.

The distribution of responses to an evaluative statement regarding this practice changed little for both the 1961 and 1962 graduates between their graduation and the time they were tested after some field experience. The modal response—to a statement that this practice is in the interests of the department as a whole—was that of "uncertain" for both groups at both points in time. From an individual patrolman's personal point of view the practice was both desirable and potentially undesirable, since he was not

Table 30.—Attitudes Toward the "Rabbi" System (in percent)

Item	Group[a]	When Tested	No Answer	Strongly Agree	Agree	Uncertain	Disagree	Strongly Disagree
A	1962	End of training[b]	1	1	7	28	47	16
		One year in field	2	12	21	29	29	7
	1961	Two years in field	0	16	38	18	22	6
B	1962	End of training	0	1	19	45	27	8
		One year in field	2	2	22	44	25	5
	1961	End of training	3	7	28	40	14	8
		Two years in field	0	10	24	42	22	2

Item A: "Transfers or assignments are quite often made as a personal favor to a patrolman."
Item B: "Transfers or assignments made in this way usually work out all right for the department as a whole."

[a]See Table 24, footnote [a].
[b]The N's at the end of training for the 1961 and 1962 academy graduates were, respectively, 108 and 164.

likely to be the only patrolman with a "rabbi." Thus, although the "rabbi" system may have given some sense of confidence about one's future in the department when an individual faced problems with the formal organization, the system did not guarantee that any one individual patrolman could better his lot relative to other patrolmen. Of course, sponsors varied in the degree they were "hung heavy," (that is, influential or powerful in the organization), and those with an influential sponsor could anticipate some ease in getting the sort of duty they desired.

This informal solution to the problem of getting a desired assignment is of course not the only solution to an individual patrolman's career problems in the organization. The high degree of perceived cohesiveness among patrolmen at the beginning of their training does not seem to be appreciably affected by their field experiences. As shown in Table 31, patrolmen tested at a number of different points in the early phase of their careers tend to be in strong agreement that the patrolmen constitute a "brotherhood" (item A) and that assistance from other patrolmen is not a rare commodity (items B and C). They further concur with one another in disagreeing that a significant number of patrolmen will avoid helping other patrolmen (item D). This cohesiveness is not only related to difficulties associated with handling citizens or police problems but also extends to the difficulties associated with a patrolman's relations with other officers, particularly with his supervisors.

The experienced patrolmen tested after one and two years in the field were more likely than not to agree that they should try on their own to participate informally in the education of police recruits. In Table 32 the majority of the experienced patrolmen in both groups endorsed statements to the effect that experienced patrolmen should familiarize recruits on field training exercises with practices and conditions at variance with academy training (items A and B).

The experienced men also concurred strongly with one another that experienced patrolmen do, in fact, contribute more to the job socialization of new patrolmen than do their supervisors (item C and D). The informal organization is probably maintained in this manner. Moreover, the experienced patrolmen are likely to feel that their sharing of knowledge is required behavior. Probably the individual novice patrolman quite often welcomes their help. He may often find himself embroiled in a number of difficulties both with other patrolmen and with supervisors, since the academy training generally avoids discussion of many common practices which, to a greater or lesser degree, violate the rules of the department. Many experienced patrolmen and supervisors thought the academy had an "unrealistic" or "impractical" orientation. In attempting to present the "ideals" of police work, academy personnel were considered by many older officers to be overlooking critical aspects of police work. It was thus a common feeling among older officers that academy personnel must have never actually worked in the field units. For such officers in the field units this view of instructors served to explain the fact that the typical recruit was unaware of what experienced officers considered as important practices in the field.

Table 31.—Perceived Cohesiveness among Patrolmen (in percent)

Item	Group[a]	No Answer	Strongly Agree	Agree	Uncertain	Disagree	Strongly Disagree
A	T_1	0	29	43	14	13	1
	T_2	1	25	47	11	14	2
	T_3	0	20	49	11	17	3
	T_4	0	17	52	6	20	5
B	T_1	1	42	40	8	8	1
	T_2	0	57	31	4	8	6
	T_3	1	61	26	4	7	1
	T_4	1	47	34	5	12	1
C	T_1	1	54	42	2	1	0
	T_2	5	58	34	2	1	0
	T_3	0	69	28	1	0	2
	T_4	0	64	33	2	0	1
D	T_1	0	4	20	26	39	11
	T_2	0	2	20	17	43	18
	T_3	0	3	19	11	46	21
	T_4	0	2	28	16	42	12

Item A: "The police department is really a large brotherhood in which each patrolman does his best to help all other patrolmen."
Item B: "A patrolman can always count on getting assistance from other patrolmen whenever he needs it."
Item C: "Patrolmen will quite automatically join in to help other patrolmen when it is apparent that help is needed."
Item D: "There is a significant number of patrolmen who will try to get out of doing anything to help other patrolmen."

[a]See Table 8, footnote [a].

The samples of patrolmen who received their academy training in 1961 and 1962 were not so negative in their evaluation of the training they received in the academy. Their responses (in 1963) to two items are some-what but not markedly unfavorable relative to the attitudes of "old-timers" (Table 33). Although the patrolmen in both groups are more likely to agree than disagree that the training would provide a more useful basis for the work (item A), approximately two-thirds of them disagreed that the training is more dysfunctional than functional (item B). Nevertheless, their overall response would not be encouraging to academy personnel.

Perhaps even less encouraging are the responses to the set of items in Table 34. It has been stressed throughout this report that the problems of uncertainty for police create a large variety of difficulties for them. Although social scientists are familiar with police misconduct in regard to their use of force and other more visible areas of job performance, for the most part there has been almost no discussion of police inactivity. The responses in Table 34 bear on this problem rather directly and support the earlier thesis that inactivity becomes an informal prescription for patrolmen

Table 32.—Perceived Role of Experienced Patrolmen Vis-á-Vis Police Recruits (in percent)

Item	Group[a]	No Answer	Strongly Agree	Agree	Uncertain	Disagree	Strongly Disagree
A	1961	0	4	47	13	33	3
	1962	0	8	48	16	24	4
B	1961	0	2	51	18	28	1
	1962	0	4	52	15	27	2
C	1961	0	26	61	8	5	0
	1962	0	21	67	7	4	1
D	1961	0	17	72	5	5	1
	1962	1	18	66	7	7	1

Item A: "When experienced patrolmen have the chance they should let recruits who are on field training exercises know about the things the academy instructors won't talk about."

Item B: "Experienced patrolmen should let recruits in field training exercises know just how actual police work differs from the ideals taught at the academy."

Item C: "A new patrolman learns more from the older patrolmen than from his supervisors."

Item D: "The more experienced patrolmen generally do more to help a newer patrolman adjust to the job than do his supervisors."

[a]See Table 24, footnote [a].

in the context of the uncertainties they face. The patrolmen are in some agreement that patrolmen should not "go looking for situations requiring police attention" (item A). Furthermore, the more experienced patrolmen (the 1961 group) strongly supported the statement that active patrolmen are those who "usually get into trouble with their supervisors" (item B). It would appear that the less experienced group had not yet attained the level of disenchantment of the more experienced group, which had a majority in agreement with this statement. Whether the 1962 graduates were moving in the same direction of the 1961 group is not clear, but almost one-quarter of the later graduates indicated they were uncertain concerning these particular costs to them of being an "active-cop."

Table 33.—Evaluation of Academy Training by Recent Graduates (in percent)

Item	Group[a]	No Answer	Strongly Agree	Agree	Uncertain	Disagree	Strongly Disagree
A	1961	0	6	39	25	29	1
	1962	0	10	35	23	32	0
B	1961	0	0	22	19	52	7
	1962	0	1	16	17	62	4

Item A: "The academy should change its training program a great deal in order to make it more useful for newer patrolmen."
Item B: "There is some truth to the statement that a new patrolman may be hurt more than helped by the training he gets in the academy."

[a]See Table 24, footnote [a].

Table 34.—Patrolmen's Evaluation of Level of Job Activity (in percent)

Item	Group[a]	No Answer	Strongly Agree	Agree	Uncertain	Disagree	Strongly Disagree
A	1961	0	5	60	13	22	0
	1962	0	5	54	17	22	2
B	1961	0	4	51	15	28	2
	1962	0	6	29	24	39	0

Item A: "A patrolman will usually get along better on the job if he doesn't go looking for situations requiring police attention but handles them as the situations arise."
Item B: "Patrolmen who are always out looking for situations requiring police attention are the ones who usually get into trouble with their supervisors."

[a]See Table 24, footnote [a].

Summary

We have presented some aspects of the training of police recruits and their first field experiences as these bear on the uncertainties experienced by police officers. Particular attention has been given to problems of adjustment to the role experienced by new patrolmen in the New York City Police Department.

The difficulties in organizing knowledge about the legal basis of police authority and in transmitting it to recruits are many. These difficulties are partly a function of the complexities of law and partly a function of a departmental concern that police officers be prepared to defend themselves from criticism through knowledge of the letter of the law rather than its spirit. Although not mentioned in our discussion, these difficulties may account in part for some officers' view of the law as fixed and immutable. Such a view of the law can create difficulties because it predisposes police to seek out quasi-legal or illegal solutions to their perceived problems.

In attempting to develop an *esprit de corps,* the academy seems not to have been successful in immunizing patrolmen against experiencing a strong feeling that their work is one that rates quite low in prestige in the eyes of their public. At the same time, the emphasis on police professionalization in recruit training probably increases the patrolmen's perception of the discrepancy between the socio-economic status that officers should have and the status they actually have.

We have seen that the academy's attempt to prepare recruits for the problems associated with face-to-face interaction with the public was problematic with respect to the appropriateness of content, for example, the admonitions to "be firm but courteous" and to "use your common sense," and with respect to the pedagogical methods used to transmit this knowledge, that is, the classroom lecture. Further, the reluctance of the academy to develop a comprehensive series of field training exercises was particularly problematic in regard to the development of interpersonal skills of the recruits.

This same reluctance to expose recruits to the field conditions associated with patrol presented problems for their adjustment to uncertainties stemming from the department, particularly the policies and beliefs about patrolman-supervisor interaction. Although it is difficult to conceive of a training program that would prepare recruits effectively for immersion in the belief system about supervision and use of punitive tactics by supervisors and the administration, the academy experiences of the recruits were likely to create a receptivity to the belief that supervisors often took punitive actions. Another problem was that of the recruits' receptivity to beliefs questioning the appropriateness of the administration of negative sanctions and to a belief in the damaging effects of such sanctions on the careers of patrolmen.

We consider that the training received by the recruits did not immunize them against other central attitudes that underlie ineffective performance. A case in point is the development, following the end of recruit training, of increased support for the use of force in situations where the legal basis is unclear. The development of attitudes supporting inactivity or apathy toward police problems encountered in the field, as related to the fear of punishment, was also discussed and presented as having severe consequences in view of the fact that the job performance of patrolmen is not supervised at the time a problem occurs and the fact that the nature of the work is often distasteful and threatening.

Perhaps our most significant inference from the analysis of the data on the New York Police Department is that a training program for police recruits faces two major dilemmas in preparing recruits for their later duties in the field. The first involves the question of whether to emphasize training strategies aimed at the development of self-directed and autonomous personnel or to emphasize strategies aimed at developing personnel over whom the organization can easily exercise control. It appears that the second strategy is the one most often emphasized.

The second dilemma is that involving the inconsistencies between what the academy considers ideal practices in police work and what the majority of men in the field consider to be the customary and perhaps more practical procedures in the field. The training program appeared to emphasize the former approach.

The costs to the department, as a whole, of choosing these alternatives have been described. Whether the costs might have been greater if the opposite strategies were chosen is not clear. Further, it is not even clear, that the dilemmas are as they appear to be; the conflict between control and autonomy and the conflict between ideal and actual may be more apparent than real. For example, the longer period of training undergone by professionals increases the control by the profession of the individual professional through the process of socialization rather than through direct control. In this manner social control and self-control become synonymous.

Similarly, a better strategy to resolve the perceived conflict between ideal and actual practices might be to conceive of the conflict as a problem of adapting innovations in police work to the context of traditional practices in the field. That is, rather than conceive of ideal police work as being irreconcilable with many aspects of actual police work, training personnel perhaps should make every effort to introduce what they consider ideal practice into the training in such a way that it does not call for a major scrapping of what the men in the field units consider to be "tried and true." In this way, the ideal practices would be less likely to call forth a defensive reaction from personnel who see their own position or their advantages as threatened by innovations. The net effect of such a strategy should then be less subversion of academy training by experienced men in the field.

Under most circumstances one can expect that a change of any sort will have a number of costs for an organization. For police departments, which will always be strongly affected by social change in the larger society, an orientation that accepts change and its costs as a condition of organizational existence is far more functional than either the "reformer" or the conservative orientations that call for total change or none at all. The costs of the battle between reformers and the entrenched interests in police departments are not few. The conflict has often caused both factions to expend enormous amounts of time and energy conducting the battle on terrain not worth winning. The consequence for the "rookie" in police work is that he must choose between one faction or the other and his choice of one precludes conforming to the expectations of the other. From his point of view, withdrawal from the conflict may be the only possible solution to a conflict that he may see as irrelevant to the major objectives of law enforcement.

CHAPTER 11

The Oral Board

John Guidici

John Guidici is Instructor in Police Science at Merritt Junior College. He retired from the Oakland Police Department in 1969 after more than twenty years of public service.

Progressive police officials are attempting to solve their recruitment problems realistically. Their task is difficult because there is no real unanimity of opinion among the administrators as to the personal qualities essential to the adequate performance of police duty. The various qualities most often identified as necessary are, at best, opinions developed without the benefit of scientific measurement. There has been little basic research undertaken in the field of police personnel selection. Hence, as important as the police function is to the maintenance of society the procedures employed in the recruitment and selection of law enforcement personnel are still, in large measure, left to uncertain techniques.

The first standards adopted related to physical attributes and the successful completion of a medical examination. As the nature of police service has become more complex attention has been given to the need to consider other qualities of the candidate. Police administrators have become aware of the fact that some assessment must be made of each candidate's mental development, emotional maturity and stability, personal morality and occupational interest. There is considerable evidence to support the thesis that these less tangible qualities are perhaps more significant than the physical attributes. Standards of performance within the service are subject to continuous upgrading. With the advance of performance standards and the extension of specialization attention has been re-directed toward the up-grading of recruitment and selection processes.

From John Guidici, "The Oral Board," in Richard H. Blum, ed., *Police Selection,* 1964. Reprinted through the courtesy of Charles C. Thomas, Publisher, Springfield, Illinois.

The basic obstacle to more effective hiring of police personnel is the present limitation of testing devices and procedures used to screen candidates. Certain qualifications can be measured without difficulty, for example, "height" and "weight." However, other qualities such as "enthusiasm," "judgment," "adaptability," etc., present a real challenge. In addition to measurement testing devices must satisfy the requirements of "validity" and "reliability." The police administrator wants to select candidates who as policemen will exercise competent judgment in the many stressful situations that are common to police work. The problem has been to find a testing device that will prove discrete and will measure adequately the existence and extent of the desired quality. Some police officials question the value of some of the more sophisticated tests being used as psychological measurements. They tend to favor the personal interview approach and base the selection on personal reaction to the candidate. They admit the technique is not "scientific" yet the results are more direct and have been reasonably acceptable.* This expression of trust in the interview process gives support to the use of an "oral board" in personnel selection.

Many police and personnel administrators consider the oral interview particularly suitable to the selection of law enforcement officers. There are a number of reasons for this belief. Historically, the employment interview is undoubtedly the oldest selection device known to man. It is not difficult to imagine interrogation of job seekers by employers long before there are any formalized evaluations of applicants and their capacities. In a number of personnel selection systems the practice of questioning applicants and observing them in an interview situation is the most important phase of the screening process. In many other systems the oral interview is considered a valuable addition to a series of more formal testing devices.

Before considering the oral interview in detail and its relation to other screening devices it is important to review the objectives of an employment examination. An examination conducted to select police recruits should accomplish three basic goals:

1. The examination should test the qualifications of each candidate with respect to predetermined standards that have been established,

2. The examination should provide some measure of the potential capacity for growth and effectiveness in the service for each successful candidate, and

3. The examination should provide a means of ranking the various candidates as to their qualifications.

Obviously there are many candidates who, by every available standard or requirement, as imprecise as the standard may be, will possess acceptable qualities justifying their hire. The question remains, "Will they perform well

---

*This argument is only valid in a small department.

during their long career as law enforcement officers?" It is not enough that applicants possess the requisite physical, mental, emotional and moral capacities for the job. The good candidate must also be motivated by a desire to perform adequately that will extend over his career even when confronted with frustrations that tend to overshadow job satisfactions.

Whereas the first two goals mentioned above related to the candidate and the job the third goal is a mechanical factor that is introduced solely to provide an orderly means of presenting candidates to the department administrator for appointment. This consideration arises due to the competitive aspect of the examination process within the philosophic framework of American civil service. It is reasonable to assume that some difference in potential will exist between the several candidates in a group. Ranking the successful candidates on the basis of test scores is a crude attempt to indicate relative capacities. Under the many limitations of personnel testing the ranking device is a more adequate measure of present capacity than it is of future potential for police service. The reduction of test scores to one numerical value for the purpose of ranking candidates tends to reduce the significance of the individual test measurements. Attempts have been made to counter this defect by weighting various test measurements in order of importance in job performance.

Intelligent personnel administrators are well aware of the problems associated with the assessment of men in relation to specific jobs. The direction of our efforts and the course of action we must pursue is clear. This fact is well documented in the several chapters of this book as well as in many of the references identified in the bibliography.

All authorities are in agreement that the examination and associated procedures used in the selection of men for law enforcement should be:

1. Valid,
2. Reliable,
3. Politically and socially acceptable,
4. Free from arbitrary manipulation,
5. Relatively simple to administer,
6. Inexpensive to conduct and evaluate, and
7. Possessed of a host of other "practical" virtues.

This is not to say that the field of law enforcement is totally lacking in requirements, standards, or testing devices which will measure applicants with reference to those standards. Many of these requirements and standards have been determined subjectively yet experience indicates that they have considerable demonstrated merit. For example, there is the general awareness that physical condition is an important factor in police performance. Most police executives and the public generally are of the belief that physical standards must be high. Thus, more attention is now given to the relationship of weight to height, superior motor coordination, freedom from potentially disabling defects and similar physical qualities. Devices to test these qualities are readily available everywhere. For another example consider the matter of police intelligence. We find broad acceptance of the proposition that law enforcement officers should be of above average intelligence if they are to function adequately. True the question of "how much" above is still being debated professionally but instruments are available which will tell us how intelligent a given applicant may be. However, a definite sense of uncertainty is felt when we move onward into the less well developed areas of personality and its testing.

It is certain that most police administrators will agree that a suitable police officer candidate will be characterized by such qualities as alertness, enthusiasm, loyalty; that he will possess a high degree of initiative, resourcefulness, self confidence and that he will have some understanding of what he will be undertaking in order to avoid future discouragement and disappointment. Almost universally, observers of the field of personnel management agree that no completely valid written tests have been found to measure the quality and quantity of each of these characteristics present in a given applicant. Of course research in these matters continues briskly. There has been some notable work done in isolating such personality characteristics as aggressiveness, dominance and recessiveness. The implications of this and similar research are still not clearly understood by police officials although this material might be useful in police personnel selection.

It is because of the "uncertain" elements in the above described testing methods that persons hiring police officers have turned to the oral interview. There is a substantial feeling that "experienced men" will be able to distinguish between those applicants who may or may not have the qualities which will make them successful policemen. The feeling persists that we are dealing with a situation in which the criteria for successful police performance are not clearly defined and where testing methods are not perfect.

Some justification for this point of view may be found in the fact that many men of good qualities have been selected for employment without formal testing procedures. Frequently these men have been hired solely on the basis of an oral interview. Yet serious doubts exist about the values of the interviewing technique. Ordway and O'Brien[1] comment;

> "The oral process has been open to criticism because of the nature of the personality factors, if any, utilized; the kind of evidence, if any, adduced; and the subjectivity of the standards, if any, employed in rating."

And Stahl[2] notes in his text:

> "The oral test has long served as a basic selection tool in private employment but has been more slowly accepted in the public field. This conservatism arises out of three considerations: (1) the difficulty of developing valid and reliable oral tests; (2) the difficulty of securing a reviewable record on an oral test, and (3) public suspicion of the oral as a channel for the exertion of political influence through the destruction of anonymity."

This observation by Stahl opens two topics for discussion. The first is the distinction between "private" and "public" employment. The second topic concerns the safeguards that seem necessary and which create such concern in the personnel selection practices for public employment. In differentiating between private and public employment we recognize that all employment involves a contractual relationship between an employer and a worker. If the employer is engaged in private enterprise a worker involved with him would be in private employment. If the employer is a governmental or "public" agency then the worker might be said to be in public employment. In either case employment occurs when there is work to be done and when, generally, the employer is satisfied that an applicant can do the required tasks. In neither case does an applicant have any inherent "right" to a position except as provided by law, rule or contract. The fact that public employment is supported by public funds does not alter this premise in any way.

Despite the fact that applicants for employment have no special "rights" to a position in either public or private employment there are some real differences in the respective situations. Essentially in private employment the relationship between the employer and the applicants are private ones without a competitive aspect. However, applicants in the public service are competing against others and they are entitled to assurance that their competitive position is safeguarded. In public employment, as found in the formalized civic service or merit systems at least, there are more limitations and restrictions in the selection of personnel than are found in private employment. Many of these restrictions are imposed for the purpose of maintaining equality of opportunity for the respective candidates.

Because of the criticisms noted by Stahl and other competent observers there are many who would prohibit, eliminate or restrict the use of the oral interview in the personnel selection process in law enforcement. But the use of the oral interview as an integral part of the selection procedure in the police service has produced some significant successes, imperfect though the system may be. It is the personal observation of many police officials that obvious misfits who have survived the "objective" portions of entrance examinations have, on numberless occasions, been detected and "washed out" by oral interviews. It is true there are, at present, grave limitations on the oral interview procedure. Substantial differences of opinions exist among professionals about given candidates following a series of interviews. A specially chosen oral interview board of competent police officers did approve applicants who, in the opinions of others, seem to have serious defects of psychological or psychiatric natures.

Despite the limitations of the interview techniques it has some advantages which are unique. For example there is an aspect of law enforcement which is, in a word, physical. No amount of data, no matter how precise, can convey to an employer the sense of "presence" which characterizes the applicant. In the interview this quality is identifiable rather easily. Further, the interview provides a real opportunity to tie together the separate tests and examinations which, taken together, constitute the employment process. Correctly used the interview is a device for clarifying or verifying the unanswered questions and inferences which arise in the other phases of the testing activity. This can be done in no other way. Our choice therefore does not appear to be whether or not the oral interview shall be used as a part of the selection process in the law enforcement but rather, how can it be improved so as to be a more effective instrument in the employment of potentially competent and effective peace officers.

The Oral Interview Board

In personnel management the term "oral interview" is used in a number of differing contexts. It may be used to informally screen applicants for positions exempt from civil service or a merit system or for special assignment within a class or grade. It is also used in a variety of ways in the examination of candidates for promotion from grade to grade. For the purpose of the discussion here the term "oral interview" describes the situation in which the applicant formally faces an interviewer or interviewers or when he participates as a member of a group of applicants under observation. The purpose of the interview is to provide an opportunity for the applicant to present his case and to enable the interviewer to observe and question him.

In private employment, the most common practice is to have most, if not all, applicants for technical, clerical and similar positions interviewed by a single "interviewer." In the larger companies, and in many progressive smaller ones, this interviewer is a professional personnel management employee who has special skills in this exacting work. More often than not this technician is a college graduate in psychology or personnel management. He brings to the interview situation the particular knowledge and skills which, it is hoped, will produce the best possible results.

In public employment, the situation is usually quite different. In order to eliminate or minimize the criticisms mentioned earlier every effort is directed toward making the oral interview process as "fair" as possible. The one significant development designed to make the interview more acceptable in public personnel practice is to have the applicant observed and heard by a number of interviewers. The several interviewers generally sit together and as a group constitute what is commonly known as an "Oral Board" or an "Oral Interview Board." The candidate is then presented to the group and the formal interviewing follows. It is with this form of the "oral interview" that this chapter is concerned.

It should be recognized at the outset that the meeting of an oral board to interview applicant for positions in law enforcement is but one part of a competent oral interview procedure. The interviewers on a board have key roles in the success of the system. However there is another key figure known as the "examiner" or "personnel technician." In the paragraphs that follow the term "examiner" will appear frequently and his relationship to the oral interview system and to the interviewers must be clearly understood.

Basically there are two essential parts of a competent oral interview procedure in law enforcement. The two parts are (1) a program, and (2) the interviewers. The examiner has the great responsibility of providing the program. It is his task to assure that this program is adequately prepared, competently implemented and meaningfully interpreted. Usually but not always the examiner is or should be a professional personnel man. Regardless, the responsibilities must be met if the oral interview system is to be a success.

The second part of the oral interview process is the interviewer. It is the responsibility of law enforcement officers assigned to this duty to so conduct themselves in the interview situation that the greatest possible benefit will accrue to the police service. This requires a high degree of competent and close attention. It is clear that there must be a close working relationship between examiners and interviewers if the oral interview procedure is going to improve as a personnel selection technique. It is the unanimous opinion of the civil service personnel and the law enforcement officers who worked with Dr. Blum in his studies that such a relationship could and would lead to exciting new concepts of the oral interview in law enforcement.

A successful oral board interview is the direct result of program planning. Whatever failures and lack of effectiveness we find in the oral board procedure can be traced to gross underplanning. It appears quite frequently that the person responsible for the oral interviewing of police candidates is not aware of the needs of the service. He makes no demands upon the interviewers except that they be available on the desired date. The only test for a reporting form is that it be capable of reproduction without difficulty. This kind of preparation may be relatively inexpensive but, in its application, it is not effective.

The first step in planning a program for an oral board is to identify the objectives of the interviewing procedure and commit them to writing. This will focus the attention of everyone concerned upon the basic purposes of the procedure. The goals of the test must be described in such a way that all the interviewing is directed toward the accomplishment of the desired ends. The orientation of oral interviews towards specific goals will enable us to make intelligent evaluations of the results. Not only will we see the results of a given board operation but, in addition, we will be able to determine if the long range benefits of this procedure are being achieved.

A good statement of objectives will define and limit the scope of the oral testing. It will directly affect the manner and length of time candidates are questioned and will assist in a more reliable evaluation of their responses. A clear understanding of the purpose of an oral interview will assist in the design of reports to be used in recording results. It will surely be of great assistance to the interviewers by clarifying the role they play on the board. In many ways then, statements of purpose will aid in the production, implementation and evaluations of the oral interviews so that they become more valuable instruments in police personnel selection.

After establishing his objectives the examiner must identify the specific traits which he wishes the testing to cover. Authorities almost unanimously agree that the oral interview technique should not be used to test personal qualities and attributes which can be examined in some other, more objective fashion. It is at this point that an examiner will find himself on unfamiliar ground. He will find little authoritative documentation about the personal qualities needed for successful performance in law enforcement. For example the question of how "aggressive" or how "authoritarian" a policeman must or must not be has never been resolved. Indeed all we know is there must be an enormous amount of research work done in police personnel management before this kind of question can be answered.

Despite the uncertainty about the specific traits to be sought out by the oral board there is a feeling among police executives that appropriate traits can be identified in oral interviews. In Blum's[3] study the members of an oral board commented upon the characteristics they noted in the applicants they passed or failed. In describing these characteristics the board identified successful candidates with such things as:

> "Good appearance, able to speak up, forceful, able to fit into discipline, capable of being trained, sincere, flexible, uses good English, energetic, mature, sustained interest in personal advancement, genuine interest in becoming a peace officer, stability, wholesome, conscientious, good past experience in police work, good educational background, well adjusted."

Similarly a wide range of negative characteristics were noted in the candidates who were failed by the board. Admittedly these are opinions but they are considered opinions. The officers who gave them are police commanders with considerable training and many years of experience. The opinions were based upon lengthy and perceptive interviewing of the applicants. It is reasonable therefore, to assume these opinions have considerable merit. Obviously before we can positively identify a potentially successful candidate there will have to be more precise definitions of the required traits. Perhaps this will come from similar studies and other experimentation.

The examiner's next step should be to identify the topics of discussion which should be explored in the interview. The chosen areas, if properly explored by the interviewers, should cause the candidate to give responses which can be interpreted in terms of his character, his life experience, and his chances for success in police work. To some examiners this may seem to be needless preparation and to some interviewers, excessive regimentation. Nevertheless a planned effort to elicit significant responses from the candidates will be more productive than any unplanned activity. The more common areas of interviewing include education, previous work experience, military experience, civic and social activities and similar topics. This is not to say that interviewers should have no latitude for exploring avenues which open during discussions. Quite to the contrary, experienced interviewers should operate flexibly in their questioning. The course suggested here is a device for keeping the questioning within fruitful areas, keeping in mind the limited available time for each interview.

The next consideration in the program planning is how to record and report the evaluations of the interviewers. Unlike other portions of the entrance examination procedure the end product of the oral interview is not produced by the candidate. This report rather is the personal analysis of an observer about a candidate based upon what that candidate said and did in the observer's presence. The construction of any kind of a formalized report presents great difficulty to an examiner because of the amount of material which can be covered in even a short interview.

The usual report of an interview includes a listing of the personality traits or other factors which the examiner wants to know about the applicants. Opposite each factor there is usually a scale of values. These values give the interviewer a convenient way to report his opinions about the subject. At the present state of development of the oral interview procedure in police work, the traits listed will range widely. Such simple ones as "Appearance" will be frequently found together with such ones as "Ability to organize work." Even in the case of the first trait the interviewer can comment only on the basis of one meeting with the candidate. An intelligent comment about the second is almost impossible since such a characteristic is difficult to evaluate correctly even when the subject is under observation for long periods of time. As further research mentioned above is undertaken more positive assertion can be made about the traits which the interviewers should seek in an applicant. On the basis of the discussion in Blum's[3,6] studies, it appears that such positive characteristics as appearance, forcefulness, sincerity, flexibility, language usage and habits, wholesomeness, stability, and others did impress the oral board members. Conversely, board members were impressed by such negative traits as selfishness, introversion, untruthfulness, passiveness, hesitancy, egotism and more of like character. Obviously not all traits can be described in any one report and there is question that any should be listed. Until that time when a more stable and generalized listing can be provided, each examiner must identify those qualities which he and his police chief feel to be most important for their department's use.

Perhaps even more troublesome is the problem of "scoring" the results of the interview. As pointed out above there is usually a scale of values opposite each listed trait or characteristic. The scales range from simple "pass-fail" or "suitable-not suitable" to systems in which final grades are given in terms of hundredths of one per cent. An attempt has been made to avoid the "grading" aspect by the use of descriptive phrases associated with the trait under consideration. These phrases presumably give the interviewer a convenient way to identify the response of the subject.

It must be borne in mind that the human personality is so complex that it is not possible to produce any "pure," "positive" results or score from an interview. It is difficult to isolate a single trait and describe it much less to give it numeric value. It is significant that in other professions results of similar interviews are consistently reported in narrative form rather than in numbers. This is so because many physical, mental and emotional states cannot be described except by descriptive words and phrases. In such cases a continuing series of observations are recorded until the practitioner arrives at a conclusion. At this point the professional may give an opinion and this is recorded for what it is—an opinion, no more, no less. Yet for a variety of reasons it seems necessary in public employment that the observations of the interviewers be reduced to some numerical value no matter how inappropriate this action may be. Principally this is done to satisfy the need to "rank" groups of applicants. Ranking by examination is considered the "fair" way to ensure equality of opportunity in public employment. Since this is most often done by the assigning of "grades" it follows that this must be done in oral interviews in order that the grading of the respective parts of an entrance examination will be compatible. Because of this obligation and because of the limitations described there has been produced a wide variety of forms, reports, charts, listings and other instruments designed to record the opinions of the interviewer. To date no one form has demonstrated remarkable superiority over another.

The discussion of scoring raises the point of standards. It is exceedingly important that the examiner establish firm standards against which the given factor is to be graded. It is commonly observed that, in the absence of specific instructions and frequently even when instructions are quite precise, individual interviewers will judge a response of a subject quite differently. Thus a response to a question concerning intra-unit loyalty is subject to several interpretations each dependent upon the inclinations of the respective interviewers. In many of these cases the difference is attributable to the several standards existing among the interviewers. Generally the greater the homogeneity of the interviewing group the more likely that the standards used will be similar. In the final analysis however, it is the responsibility of the examiner to define the terms and set the criteria against which the candidates are to be judged.

In addition to designating the standards for the various factors in the interview the examiner must establish a pass-fail point. The examiner must also determine whether or not non-acceptability in one factor constitutes grounds for complete rejection of the applicant. The determination of a pass-fail point is never simple and requires the complex balancing of multiple criteria. In some cases the point is more easily identified. For example any untruthfulness during an interview would certainly constitute grounds for rejection. But at what point, for example, does withdrawn or taciturn behavior render a man unfit for service in a particular department? It is apparent that as the examiner prepares his oral interview program there must be many consultations with the affected law enforcement agency.

The discussion of "non-acceptability" raises several questions which indicate a need for more research in the matter of grading interviews. In a system based upon or identified with a numerical scoring system it is possible for an applicant to be rated below passing in one factor but still have an acceptable "average" score. It seems more logical and valid that non-acceptability in any one factor ought to be cause for complete rejection of the candidate. It would appear then that the scoring of individual factors is unnecessary except as a guide to the individual interviewer. In those systems where the oral interview "scores" are used to rank applicants it is usually the average or composite score which is used to compute the final entrance examination results. Perhaps in the final analysis we are wasting time attempting to isolate and score a variety of traits. Research may eventually indicate that the best that can be said of a candidate is that he is, in the opinion of a given interviewer, "Eminently Qualified," "Well Qualified," "Qualified" or "Not Qualified." There is perhaps a case for this point of view at present. Most personnel technicians are in agreement that it is impossible to grade human attributes even grossly but we do so to conform to an existing system. Perhaps we should be looking forward to changing the basis on which "fairness" is established in public employment.

Finally the examiner must make certain that all the interviewers understand the importance of using approximately the same numerical values in scoring candidates. It is possible for one oral board member to materially affect the ranking of candidates by using abnormally high or low scores or by using a range of scores substantially different than his fellow board members. This becomes a part of the preparation of the interviewing program and is essential to the maintenance of uniformity.

We come now to the other essential element in the oral interview process. It is very important that qualified interviewers be assigned to service on oral boards. It will be of little avail to carefully prepare a good interviewing program only to have it undone by incompetent interviewing. It is difficult to understand why so much inexpert employment interviewing is accepted in law enforcement hiring practice in view of the great respect held for competent interrogation and interviewing in our other police activities.

No doubt part of the difficulty is based upon a lack of understanding on the part of executives who are responsible for the assignment of police personnel to oral interview boards. All too frequently such assignments are made on the basis of "availability" of officers at a given time without much regard for their interviewing competence. It is all too frequently presumed that because an assigned officer is a policeman he is, therefore, a competent interviewer. What has not been clearly understood is that employment interviewing is an activity calling for particular skills of the highest order. In a American Management Association study Mandell[4] states:

> "The (employment) interviewer has one of the most complex of all jobs. He needs some knowledge of psychology; he should have a thorough and up-to-date knowledge of job requirements in general and those of his organization in particular; and he must be able to relate these factors to the problem at hand and so project the behavior of the applicant. And he must base his difficult task upon the inadequate information obtained in an artificial situation: the interview."

Samuel Ordway[5] also recognized the problem when he observed:

> "The effectiveness of the oral test depends in great part on the skill of the examiners (interviewers). Thus, the examiner should possess considerable aptitude for his work before he is selected to serve as a member of an examining board. Skill in the procedure of the interview, however, may be acquired and perfected through training."

It is suggested here that responsible police departments and other agencies in the field of police personnel management jointly establish minimum standards for qualification as an interviewer or as a member of a police oral board. Perhaps one of the requirements would be some minimal educational preparation in psychology and employment interviewing. Another interesting approach might be the establishment of an appropriate "apprenticeship." Thus an officer desiring to qualify as an interviewer or oral board member would be required to sit through a number of interviewing sessions solely as a student observer. He would not participate in the interviewing. He could question board members or discuss problems with them between interviews or following the close of the session. After such orientation, perhaps the student interviewer could sit on a number of boards as a "junior" member until he has demonstrated that he was properly qualified. Only then would he be considered a full fledged board member or oral interviewer. An apprenticeship such as this would substantially upgrade the performance of oral interview boards in the police service. In view of the important relationship between oral board performance and the selection of recruits in law enforcement this would be an important step forward in police personnel management.

When the examiner comes to the point of creating an oral board to interview candidates for police service he is faced with the problem of selecting board members. Two questions arise. First, should the composition of the board be limited to police officers or should it include laymen? Second, should the board be limited to members of the police agency for which the candidates are being chosen or should it include persons from other jurisdictions. Both questions avoid the basic problem.

One of the criticisms of the oral board noted earlier is that it is subject to manipulation. The examiner must therefore create an interview situation which is as objective and unbiased as possible. A close examination of this situation reveals that the solution is not where the interviewers come from but rather the degree of their competence. Thus if a police department has capable interviewers on its staff it may be more effective to use their services. Presumably they would be most competent to evaluate applicants in terms of the needs of the service. If, on the other hand, police interviewers with the necessary skills are not readily available it may be necessary to use laymen. A competent layman would be a better board member than an incompetent or possibly even just an inexperienced police officer. It can be said then that the composition of an oral interview board must logically depend on where competent interviewers can be found, within or without the law enforcement agency.

The next step following the selection of board members is the "briefing" session for the interviewing group. At this point the examiner and interviewers meet for the purpose of clarifying the "ground rules" about the forthcoming interviewing session or sessions. The briefing is held primarily to ensure that the several interviewers have a common understanding about the purpose, scope and limitations of the oral interview procedure in which they are to participate. Here too is an opportunity to clarify any misunderstandings or to resolve any questions about the content and value systems which are a part of the program. This is the time when scoring is discussed and a semblance of uniformity is reached.

Ideally, the meeting between the examiner and the interviewers should take place well in advance of the oral board session itself. In practice, it is most often done in the few minutes between the arrival of the last interviewer at the scene of the interview and the appearance of the first applicant to be interviewed. This perfunctory orientation of interviewers to the examiner's program cannot provide the kind of understanding needed to ensure a successful oral examination. Even when the program material has previously been studied by the interviewers an hour is probably the minimum time to prepare. In some cases the preparation may take even longer. Nevertheless, only this studied approach to the interviewing sessions can produce the maximum benefits which can be obtained from oral interviewing.

No attempt is made in this chapter to describe the actual interview procedure. There is ample literature describing the most appropriate physical settings for the conducting of oral boards and an extensive literature on the techniques of interviewing. . . . There are however a number of points which merit our attention in the actual conducting of interviews involving applicants for positions in police work.

The members of the oral board described in Blum's studies[3, 6] are unanimously agreed that the most valuable asset to the interviewing process were the "background investigations" which were made on each applicant who was scheduled to appear before the board. Significant leads for depth interviewing were found in other documents such as the application and test results. But more and better information upon which to base questions was found in the investigation reports. The statements of neighbors, employers, teachers, tradesmen and others provided clues to behavior of the applicants which were not to be found otherwise. The conclusion of the board members is that such investigation should be made on all applicants to be interviewed by an oral board even though such investigations are expensive and oftentimes difficult to make.

Another point concerns one aspect of the physical appearance of candidates as they faced a board. Just as interviewers become accustomed to the interview situation so too may interviewees! An oral interview is apt to be an unnerving experience for a candidate who has never been before a board. On the other hand a candidate who has appeared before several boards may display a coolness and emotional control as a result of his experience. Board members must weigh "symptoms" of distress carefully having due regard for the applicants age, background and employment experience.

Finally there is great caution which must be used in phrasing questions directed to the applicants. The use of "loaded," "leading" or "stress" questions should be avoided. Questions which by their nature elicit incorrect or invalid answers from the candidates thus giving the interviewer an opportunity to place them in a defensive position serve no useful purpose. Questions which have no acceptable answers or those which are beyond the applicants knowledge or experience are also unsuitable. And questions which call for a candidate's statement of what he "would do" under certain circumstances are not acceptable. Generally questioning of candidates should be directed toward the determination of facts. The interview is a place to enlarge upon information which is presently available about the applicant, to clarify doubtful information and to seek out new information. The board must concern itself with facts not suppositions.

At the conclusion of each oral interview session there is an opportunity to engage in some interesting and productive study of the oral interview process. This can be done by a "debriefing" or critique. It seems certain that if each oral interview session were examined critically and in depth immediately upon its completion much could be gained. Among the facets of the procedure which could be examined are: the success or failure of the session to meet the objectives, whether or not the traits sought were identified; how suitable the value systems were and how well the scoring met the needs of the program, and finally what strengths and weaknesses were disclosed in the interviewing techniques. When time is taken objectively to assess individual oral board sessions then such sessions will improve in quality.

These then are the basic ingredients for a successful oral board procedure. (1) The program material should be set down formally in writing to the greatest extent possible. It is particularly important that program materials be readily available for the oral board members. The examiner should be able to provide each board member with a written program consisting of not less than: (a) a statement of objectives of the proposed interviewing procedure; (b) an exact identification of the attitudes, traits, knowledge, skill and other characteristics which the examiner wants considered and evaluated; (c) a definition of the terms used; (d) the criteria, standard or values which will be applied in the consideration and evaluation of the qualities, and finally (e) a description of the scoring system to be used in reporting the evaluations of the interviewer. This basic material should be distributed to the board members several days before the scheduled interviews for their study.

(2) The successful oral board procedure is a product of the interviewers. It requires a high degree of knowledge and skill in order effectively to implement the interview procedure. It is important therefore that we seek a substantial measure of competence in the members of oral boards who propose to evaluate the candidates for service in law enforcement.

The place of the oral interview generally and the oral interview board specifically in the selection of police officer candidates is assured. Experience has clearly shown that the oral interview is an important and meaningful device in screening men. It may be, in fact, the best instrument we now possess to do our selection job. Present literature concludes that no "objective" testing process or device existing today will demonstrate the presence of certain desirable qualities in police candidates. We are confident that the value of interviewing will be more extensively developed as time goes by.

It is hoped that the foregoing discussion will have focused the attention of the reader upon the immediate necessity for further research and documentation in the use of the oral interview in law enforcement personnel selection. It will be through the orderly process of study that this useful technique will be made more valid and of greater reliability.

Footnotes

1. Ordway, S. H., Jr., and O'Brien, J. C., *An Approach to More Objective Oral Tests.* Pamphlet No. 2, Society for Personnel Administration, Washington D.C., 1939.

2. Stahl, O. G., *Public Personnel Administration.* New York, Harper Brothers (4th ed.) 1956.

3. Blum, R. H., Goggin, W., and Whitmore, E. J., "A study in deputy sheriff selection procedures," *Police,* 6, no. 2 (1961):59-63. (See also the full mimeographed report of this study.)

4. Mandell, M. M., *The Employment Interview.* American Management Association, Research Study No. 47.

5. Committee on Oral Tests in Public Personnel Selection, Samuel H. Ordway, Jr. Chairman, "Oral Tests in Public Personnel Selection; A Report Submitted to the Civil Service Assembly." Civil Service Assembly of the United States and Canada, Chicago, 1943.

6. Blum, R. H., *et al,* A further study of deputy sheriff selection procedures. *Police,* 6, no. 4 (1962):77-79. (See also the full mimeographed report of this study.)

Part II   Selected Correlated References

Blum, R. H., W. L. Goggin, and E. Whitmore. "A Study of Deputy Sheriff Selection Procedures." *Police.* (November-December 1961). Good comprehensive research on selection procedures: oral boards, psychological tests, etc.

Bristow, A. P., and E. C. Gabard. *Decision-Making in Police Administration.* Springfield, Ill: Charles C. Thomas, 1961. An administrative overview of policy decisions in law enforcement.

Gammage, A. Z. *Your Future in Law Enforcement.* New York: Richard Rosen Press, 1961. Up-to-date description of job opportunities in law enforcement and related training.

Gammage, A. Z. *Police Training in the United States.* Springfield, Ill.: Charles C. Thomas, 1963. This book affords the prospective police officer the opportunity to survey the field of law-enforcement training and employment available in police work.

Germann, A. C. *Police Executive Development.* Springfield, Ill.: Charles C. Thomas, 1962. A good overview of managerial staff development in the police organization.

Institute for Training in Municipal Administration. *Municipal Police Administration.* The International City Managers' Association, Chicago, 1961. Covers aspects of police administration and lines of communication as well as other areas of administrative control.

Institute on Police Management for Supervisory and Administrative Personnel. *Police Management for Supervisory and Administrative Personnel.* Springfield, Ill.: Charles C. Thomas, 1963. A discussion of the title subject within an administrative framework.

Larsen, G. *An Introduction to Police Personnel Management.* Chicago: Northwestern University Traffic Institute, 1959. A good presentation of administrative problems relating to personnel matters.

Leonard, V. A. *Police Organization and Management.* New York: Foundation Press, 1964. Thoroughly covers the organizational and administrative aspects of police agencies.

Pomeroy, W. "The Administrative Setting." in R. H. Blum ed., *Police Selection.* Springfield, Ill.: Charles C. Thomas, 1964. A discussion of organizational matters peculiar to department administration.

Smith, B. *Police Systems in the United States.* New York: Harper & Row, 1949. Police organizations throughout the United States are analyzed and discussed.

The Challenge of Crime in a Free Society. A report by the President's Commission on Law Enforcement and Administration of Justice. Washington, D.C.: U.S. Government Printing Office, 1967.

United States Government Organization Manual. General Services Administration. Washington, D.C.: U.S. Government Printing Office, 1967. Describes federal government agencies and their particular responsibilities.

Wilson, O. W. *Police Administration.* New York: McGraw-Hill Book Co., 1963. A classic discussion of administrative function in law enforcement.

Wilson, O. W. *Police Planning.* Springfield, Ill.: Charles C. Thomas, 1952. A classic in the area of organization, communication, and principles of police planning.

Part III

The Elements, Process, and Techniques of Criminal Investigation

Part Three of this volume takes into account the technical aspects of law enforcement, in particular the areas of criminal investigation and interrogation. It points out that the ultimate goal of criminal investigation is to introduce legally obtained evidence into a court of law so that the guilty party may be convicted. In order to present useful evidence, the basic techniques of investigation must be mastered.

These tasks are frequently depicted as being glamorous, but are, instead, time-consuming and tedious. They require that the investigator be familiar with the current technical advances in the field of investigation. The use of sophisticated communication systems, improved laboratory techniques, and the implementation of electronic data processing are examples of such advancements. Thus, it is necessary that the investigator be involved in a process of continuing education.

Through these readings, the student will become acquainted with facets of the investigative process such as identification, surveillance, interrogation, collection of evidence, detention, and arrest.

Not to be overlooked, however, is the need to protect the rights of the individual who is accused. The famous *Miranda* decision, which serves to protect those rights, is cited frequently throughout this volume.

CHAPTER 12

The Investigative Process

James W. Osterburg

James W. Osterburg is Professor at the University of Illinois (Chicago Circle Campus), Department of Criminal Justice, Chicago, Illinois. He has served as Visiting Professor at the School of Criminology, University of California at Berkeley and as faculty member of the Department of Police Administration, Indiana University, Bloomington. This paper was presented in the spring of 1967 at a symposium on Law Enforcement Science held at the Illinois Institute of Technology.

The simplest view of criminal investigation is offered by suggesting that when answers to the questions—who, what, when, where, how, and why—are obtained the investigation is well launched, if not completed. A more sophisticated concept recognizes similarities between criminal investigation and the study of history. Both involve an inquiry into events of the past, a time differential being one of the greatest differences between them. An even more general concept views all methods of inquiry as having some elements in common; however, each discipline develops special investigative procedures which are particularly suited to it.

There are only a few textbooks that are barely suitable for use in an introductory college course on criminal investigation. Indeed the literature of the field in general is quite scant; almost all of the books written in recent times are included in the references.[1]

From James W. Osterburg, "The Investigative Process." Reprinted by special permission of the *Journal of Criminal Law, Criminology and Police Science* (Northwestern University School of Law), copyright © 1968, March issue, volume 59, number 1.

[1]C. E. O'Hara, *Fundamentals of Criminal Investigation* (Thomas, 1956).

W. Dienstein, *Technics for the Crime Investigator* (Thomas, 1952).

H. Soderman and J. J. O'Connell, *Modern Criminal Investigation,* 5th ed., rev. by C. E. O'Hara (Funks & Wagnalls, 1962).

M. J. Fitzgerald, *Handbook of Criminal Investigation* (Greenberg, 1951).

H. Gross and R. L. Jackson, *Criminal Investigation,* 5th ed. (Sweet and Maxwell, Ltd., 1962).

Table 1.—History and Criminal Investigation as Methods of Study of Past Events

Sources of information common to both; available ancillary disciplines

Source of Information		Ancillary Disciplines Available to Assist In the Study of a Past Event	
History	Criminal Investigation	History	Criminal Investigation
Physical Evidence			
1. Fossils	1. Impressions (Tool, Tire, Shoe)	1. Paleontology	1. Criminalistics
2. Bones	2. Narcotics	2. Geology	2. Chemistry
3. Material Remains of Man	3. Paint	3. Zoology	3. Physics
	4. Bullets	4. Physical Anthropology	4. Immunology
	5. Blood	5. Archaeology	5. Botany
	6. Flora		
Records and Documents			
1. Memoirs	1. Fraudulent Checks	1. Art History	1. Criminalistics
2. Letters	2. Threatening Notes	2. Linguistics	2. Questioned Document Expertise
3. Official Documents	3. Kidnap Letters	3. Information Theory-Storage and Retrieval	3. Photography
4. Manuscripts	4. Miscellaneous Documents		
5. Books			
6. Paintings			
People			
1. Folklore Tales	1. Victim	1. Cultural Anthropology	1. Techniques rather than disciplines are available. Questioning Surveillance Informants
2. Cultural Survivals	2. Eyewitnesses	2. Ethnology	
	3. Suspects		
	4. Others related to victim, suspects, and crime scene		

Investigation as a Process for
the Study of the Past

The general sources of information open to investigators concerned with a past event are: physical evidence, records and documents, and people. The disparity between the developed disciplines available to the historian as contrasted with the criminal investigator is significant. It suggests the need for a considerable increase in the support of much more academic study of criminal investigative methodology. Table 1 is perhaps the simplest means to illustrate the difference.

The contrast in sophistication of the theoretical and methodological aids available to the historian with those at the disposal of the detective suggests that considerable effort is needed to raise criminal investigation from the level of a crude craft to that of a professional discipline. The reasons why this has not occurred sooner are legion, but the most important is that practitioners themselves have never demanded that the necessary resources be made available. An ostensibly ever-rising crime rate, the United States Supreme Court, and a Presidential Crime Commission have brought this problem into perspective. The First National Symposium on Law Enforcement Science and Technology held in March 1967 at the Illinois Institute of Technology in Chicago was a partial response to the now recognized need for a general improvement in law enforcement practice.

Before proceeding with a description of the various aspects of criminal investigation some mention must be made of constitutional restrictions which, in the United States, are imposed on the process. These limitations restrict the use of certain procedures and hence make the process operate at less than peak efficiency. In a democracy, this is a price that must be paid because other values—such as man's inherent dignity—are given higher priority. Mention will be made later in this paper on the effects of certain decisions on the particular phase of the process under consideration. This will be done to indicate the effects of legal requirements especially on the application of science to the criminal investigative process.

Physical Evidence

There are two distinct aspects to physical evidence: crime scene search, and the examination of the evidence in a crime laboratory. The literature of Criminalistics[2] is much more advanced than the general literature of criminal investigation.

---

[2]P. L. Kirk, *Crime Investigation* (Interscience, 1953).

L. C. Nickolls, *The Scientific Investigation of Crime* (Butterworth, 1956).

C. E. O'Hara and J. W. Osterburg, *An Introduction to Criminalistics* (Macmillan, 1949).

A. Svensson and O. Wendel, *Techniques of Crime Scene Investigation,* 2nd. rev. Amer. ed., Ed. J. D. Nicol (Elsevier, 1965).

Crime Scene Search

The crime scene search is the starting point of most investigations. This search is usually the responsibility of the detective assigned to the case; however, large departments may have supplementary specialists available. The search involves (a) the recognition, collection, and preservation of physical evidence; (b) the determination of the modus operandi of the criminal.

Modus operandi files are maintained by many police departments to record the unusual facts or peculiarities associated with the commission of a crime. For example, the detective notes that a criminal has entered a building in some uncommon manner. If several such burglaries are investigated they may be grouped together through recognition of the "M.O." Thus, various clues from associated crimes might be pooled to identify the criminal or to provide information for planning surveillance strategy and tactics in order to apprehend him during some future attempt at a similar crime. While this aspect of crime scene search must be mentioned, it has produced a somewhat limited return under present operating conditions.

Role of the Crime Laboratory

The examination of the crime scene for physical evidence is usually one of the first steps in the investigative process. To be successful the detective must have an understanding of the crime laboratory and its limitations; he must be taught to recognize not only common types of crime scene evidence but also that which is not obvious; he must, in addition, be very familiar with the requirements of the scientist, as well as those of the lawyer, in the collection and preservation of clue materials.

Physical evidence—blood, paint chips, tool impressions, bullets, fingerprints, heroin, alcoholic beverages, and so on—is examined in a crime laboratory. This discussion of the role of the laboratory is given from the viewpoint of the field detective and not from that of the laboratory expert. The last two examples of physical evidence—heroin and alcoholic beverages —are typical of substances submitted for analysis. A few confirmatory tests are often all that are required to establish the nature of the substance. Classical "wet" chemistry or instrumental analyses suffice to answer promptly the general form of inquiry, viz., "This white powder is alleged to contain heroin. It is requested that the powder be analyzed." In most cases the allegation is correct, and analysis is quite simple. The other

R. F. Turner, *Forensic Science and Laboratory Technics* (Thomas, 1949).

J. Glaister, *Medical Jurisprudence and Toxicology,* 9th ed. (Williams & Wilkins, 1950).

T. A. Gonzoles, M. Vance, M. Helpern, and C. J. Umberger, *Legal Medicine, Pathology and Toxicology,* 2nd ed. (Appleton-Century-Crofts, 1954).

R. B. H. Gradwohl, *Legal Medicine* (Mosby, 1954).

extreme is the problem of identification of a general unknown. Fortunately, this later problem does not arise too often and may never be solved if the quantity of evidence is limited in amount.

One of the basic tasks of the crime laboratory is the identification of substances. Quite frequently this is contraband, or materials otherwise regulated by law. A chemist's testimony is required to establish that a necessary "element" (as ethyl alcohol or heroin) is present in order to comply with the definition of the particular crime. When all of the elements of the crime are established, the commission of a crime has been established. The laboratory has shown only that a crime has been committed but not that a particular person has committed it. Personal observations of a police officer or an eyewitness provide the evidence necessary to identify the perpetrator.

When the crime laboratory, through the examination of physical evidence, establishes a connection between the crime scene or victim and the criminal it has achieved another of its major purposes. The term *associative evidence* is applied to those physical traces which, through laboratory examination and evaluation, are shown to be in one-to-one correspondence.

The development of associative evidence is accomplished most often by a comparison of crime scene evidence with test evidence related to the criminal. Thus, a crime bullet is shown to have been fired by a suspect's gun by comparison with a bullet deliberately fired through the suspected gun. Similarly a crime scene impression is related to a tool, tire, or shoe by making a comparison exemplar with the suspected implement.

The formidable obstacle to obtaining comparison standards imposed by the Mapp and the Miranda decisions will only be alluded to here as a problem. This is worthy in itself of a dialogue between scientists, civil libertarians, and lawyers. Indeed, the fundamental division between the needs of science for known standards and the limitations unwittingly placed upon their collection must be reconciled if science is to make any great contribution to the administration of justice.

Some mention must be made of the fact that a laboratory finding can be most useful during interrogation. One of the necessary conditions in obtaining a confession is the realization by the suspect that evidence is available against him. Clue materials which may be examined in his presence are particularly valuable, especially if the result is visible—as the development of a fingerprint, a color change in a chemical test, or a photograph showing any associative evidence developed in the case.

Another exceedingly important role the laboratory plays in the investigative process is the exoneration of the innocent through the examination and evaluation of physical evidence. The measure of personal and institutional satisfaction is unbounded when a possible miscarriage of justice is prevented.

Records as a Source of Information

The use of records in law enforcement is treated largely from the administrative point of view in the scant literature of the field with almost no consideration given to their use as an investigative aid. What has been written is largely useless for the obvious application of computer technology to this problem. Some creative, exploratory thinking in this area has been undertaken by the staff of the New York State Intelligence and Information System.

To be of greatest value to the investigative process, records must be thought of as stored information which is there to be retrieved by the imaginative investigator. Thus, whether files are maintained expressly for criminal investigative purposes or exist as a necessary concomitant to good business practice, stored information may serve in the following ways:

To follow-up or provide new leads.

To identify the perpetrator.

To trace and locate a suspect or criminal.

To recover stolen or lost property.

Follow-up or Provide New Leads

The laundry and dry cleaner mark file and the fraudulent check file, if properly maintained, are examples of law enforcement information useful for follow-up purposes. The state automobile license plate file is an example of a governmental file maintained for one purpose but nevertheless useful for follow-up; however, this file could be more useful for police purposes if, for example, the color of the car was required to be provided on the registration form. This is an example of how some files presently operated in various other agencies of government could be made more useful for law enforcement and at almost no cost.

The many directories compiled by the telephone companies, both for public and intracompany usage, are especially helpful for follow-up purposes.

The pawn broker file is a good example to illustrate how new leads are provided. In addition to a handwriting specimen, i.e., a signature on the pawn slip, a personal description of the person who pledged a stolen article may sometimes be obtained. At times the behavior of the individual seeking to pawn an item is so suspicious, or the item is recognized as probably stolen, that the shop owner surreptitiously telephones the local police, meanwhile detaining the customer on some pretext. The city directory, although a private publication and therefore not available for every city, is a source of additional information on the residential and business community. Quite often this directory is used in connection with partial information obtained verbally from some other person who was contacted during the investigation.

Identify the Perpetrator

The criminal photograph file (or the rogues' gallery as it is sometimes called) and the modus operandi file are probably as successful as any files maintained for identification purposes. The two files are often in the same quarters and supplement each other. The latent fingerprint file enjoys very limited success in the identification of criminals on the basis of fingerprints alone. When computer technology addresses itself to the problem of fingerprint identity instead of fingerprint classification, a breakthrough of major importance may occur. The problem is formidable and may require that the storage of single fingerprints in a computer be accomplished first.

Trace and Locate a Suspect or Criminal

When the identity of a criminal is known but he (or a suspect) is absent from his usual places of abode, work, and recreation, the investigator is faced with a problem of tracing and locating that person. The basis of this effort is the knowledge that people are gregarious and that they tend to flee to places familiar to them. Thus, the police in those areas can be alerted to be on the lookout; the transfer of any school records of a child may be used to trace the parent; relatives or friends may be placed under surveillance— these are some measures that may be taken to trace and locate a person after flight. Since in general most people require some continuity in their business pursuits (and in the use of public utilities), business records are often quite useful for tracing purposes. In especially important cases, wanted circulars and posters may be distributed.

Although this is a discussion of the use of records in tracing missing persons, mention was made of surveillance and the use of posters. This illustrates some of the difficulties in describing investigation as a process. It would certainly be misleading merely to describe the use of records for this purpose. The mere mention of each technique at the appropriate place later in the discussion might result in some lack of appreciation that several approaches to the solution of the problem are in the process simultaneously. There are many other places in this treatment of investigative procedure where similar comments would be in order; however, having made the point once, we shall pass over it in the future for the sake of economy if not to avoid tedium.

Recover Stolen or Lost Property

The major problem in accomplishing this objective is to make certain that the complainant's description of the property coincides with its description when it comes under police cognizance either directly or through a pawn shop. Through carefully structured forms this problem is readily solved. Computers are also obviously useful. Their large memory and the considered selection of property discriminants makes possible the operation of a system over a much wider area than was heretofore possible. Thus traveling a hundred miles or crossing a state line to pawn a stolen article will not preclude the possibility of detection if the law enforcement computer systems are interfaced.

Data Surveillance

It is perhaps as appropriate at this point as anywhere in the paper to comment on some concern already being shown over the intrusion of privacy by computers. Westin has made a most succinct statement of both sides in this issue.[3]

> ... if society were to follow the technological and social-engineering possibilities, it is entirely possible that basic information about each major aspect of the individual's life will be collected in various functional master memory systems. His complete educational record from preschool nursery to postgraduate courses could be in the educational master file, including the results of all intelligence, aptitude, and personality tests taken during his lifetime. The individual's complete employment record would form another master computer dossier containing every job held, the rate of pay, efficiency ratings, employer evaluations, personality tests, recommendations, outside interests, family relation to work, and more, all available on instant printout when the individual is being considered for new employment. The master credit file could contain all the information needed to do a thorough financial analysis of the individual, including such items as his income, fixed expenditures, pattern of past discretionary spending, savings, investment, and predicted expenses based on personal and family history, and predicted promotion levels. Other central dossiers might deal with health, civic activity, and criminal records. Every person could have a personal identification number, and computer scanning of a cardholder's fingerprint or voiceprint would serve to control assumption of another's identity number. These computer transaction systems and central record files of the future could bring enormous benefits to mankind—in the form of planning, efficiency, and social control. Unless the issue of privacy is in the forefront of the planning and administration of such future computer systems, however, the possibilities of data surveillance over the individual in 1984 could be chilling ...
>
> A few thoughtful spokesmen, including some within the computer community, have begun to raise questions about safeguarding privacy and liberty in the age of the electronic dossier. But, so far, these voices have been a small cautionary note in the larger rousing chorus of computer designers

---

[3]A. F. Westin, *Science, Privacy, and Freedom: Issues and Proposals for the 1970's.* "Part I —The Current Impact of Surveillance on Privacy," *Columbia Law Rev.,* 66, 1003 (1966), at p. 1013-1014.

and users who are pressing for integrated, freely circulating information systems. Serious as the problem of physical surveillance devices is in the 1960's and promises to be in the 1970's, it may be dwarfed completely by the surveillance of individual and group life that unlimited use of electronic data systems could bring to American life in the next decade.

While this may seem a departure from a description of the investigative process, it is necessary for many suggestions will undoubtedly be made at this conference concerning the use of computers to improve investigative efficiency. It is wise to recognize that there are values other than effectiveness that must be considered. Political scientists, lawyers, and civil libertarians must be brought into the dialogue promptly.

People as a Source of Information

The victim of a crime or an eyewitness to it are obvious sources of information; less obvious but nonetheless valuable at times are informants[4] and relatives or associates of suspects. Of course considerable effort is involved in obtaining information from informants. They need to be cultivated constantly if any dividends are to result. Surveillance of a suspect or his associates is another source of information; however surveillance of any degree of sophistication requires a commitment of resources in men and vehicles that only the larger and better equipped departments can afford.

Questioning

A distinction is made between interviewing and interrogation. While both have much in common, the essential difference is perhaps best suggested by the words: antipathy, uncooperativeness, hostility. Thus victims and eyewitnesses are interviewed; suspects and criminals are interrogated. The Miranda decision rendered by the United States Supreme Court has established a set of guidelines governing the questioning of persons under detention when the aim is obtaining incriminating information. Predictions concerning the impact of these rules range from "disaster" by the police to "forced innovative improvement" in the entire investigative process by civil libertarians.

Information from people ranges from confessions, through clues of value for follow-up purposes, to details of no value to the investigator. In the post-Miranda era confessions are likely to be fewer in number and more skill and specialization will be required to obtain them. It remains to be seen whether or not follow-up clues are affected by Miranda through application of the "fruit of the poisonous tree doctrine." For example, can a weapon

---

[4]M. Harney and J. C. Cross, *The Informer in Law Enforcement* (Thomas, 1960).

mentioned in an illegal confession be used as evidence in its own right if the source through which it was located was the confession? Presumably the Court will rule on this in the future. Of course follow-up clues provided through interviewing are unaffected by Miranda.

Investigative behavior involving a follow-up clue may result in:

Checking or hunting through a record file.

Talking with other people.

Searching for physical evidence.

Additional follow-up continues until all leads are exhausted and no more are forthcoming or the perpetrator's identity has been established. The "mix" of physical evidence, records, and questioning that spells success obviously differs from case to case.

Personal Descriptions

The victim or eyewitness to a crime is often able to describe the criminal. The problem of transferring this information to other law enforcement personnel or to the public at large has been attempted in three ways: portrait parle or a printed verbal description of the physical characteristics and clothing of the criminal, use of a police artist to capture the likeness, and use of a mechanical device to combine a limited choice of salient features—forehead, hairline, eyebrows, eyes, nose, mouth, chin, ears, and so on.

The police artist makes possible an almost infinite variety of feature nuances to capture the Gestalt image; mechanical recording is more limited in reproducing the likeness but more rapid transmission of image data is possible. The use of electronic data processing to retrieve images of possible suspects from a file is an obvious application of computer technology to investigation. A significant expenditure of funds to build such a file, the need for more research and development, and the training of users of the file to acquire the proper input information are some of the obstacles to current widespread use of this technique.

Surveillance

Surveillance, referred to earlier in this paper, may be described as the unobtrusive observation of a person, place, or thing. A "person" is usually a suspect or a relative or friend of a suspect; however, any individual is a potential subject of a surveillance if there are reasonable grounds to believe that discreet observance of his activity might provide significant information.

Examples of "places" include liquor stores, supermarkets, banks, drug stores, or other places where transactions are largely in cash, or where contraband such as narcotics is available. Residences and places of business hardly need mention. Indeed *any* place may become sufficiently interesting to place it under surveillance.

"Things" which are worth watching secretly include: automobiles, the ransom dropped at a designated spot, and the fruits or instruments of a crime which were hidden immediately after its commission. In the latter situation, their discovery is made through other investigative procedure without the knowledge of the perpetrator.

Surveillance has a dual function in police work. One facet serves the investigative role; the other fulfills the preventive function. The objectives of surveillance, expressed concisely, are:

To locate a suspect.

To obtain detailed information concerning the nature and scope of a suspect's activities.

To prevent the commission of a crime.

There is a temptation to discuss surveillance as though it is an independent investigative technique. It is, of course, seldom so. For example, information acquired through legitimate wiretapping or interviewing often supplements and confirms facts developed through surveillance. Investigative techniques complement each other. The successful detective is the one who knows how to season his efforts with the proper amount of each.

Activities of a Suspect

An investigator needs details of the nature and scope of a suspect's activities for the following reasons:

To obtain evidence necessary to establish probable cause for a search warrant or arrest.

To identify the associates of a suspect and to infer from their observed behavior, as a group, any criminal intentions or plans they may have.

To obtain information for the interrogation of a suspect.

Behavior of Suspect and Associates

There may come a point in an investigation where it seems unlikely that a sufficient amount of evidence will be produced to establish guilt of a suspect beyond a reasonable doubt; however, by using his judgment and perhaps information from other sources, the investigator may have substantial grounds for believing the person is engaged in criminal activity. Under these circumstances the suspect may be placed under surveillance. If an efficient, professional criminal is involved, considerable manpower and equipment are required. While with some luck there may be a quick, satisfactory outcome, it is more likely that weeks or even months will be required before results are achieved.

Information for Interrogation

Horowitz[5] has analyzed the conditions necessary to obtain a confession. Of these there are two which may be assisted by information obtained through surveillance. The necessary, but by themselves insufficient, conditions referred to require the suspect to believe that:

Evidence against him is available;

Forces inimical to his interest are being employed with maximum effort.

The detailed, personal facts that a thorough surveillance puts at the disposal of an investigator can be devastating if used adroitly during an interrogation. Revealing, at an auspicious moment, some inconsequential detail about a person's behavior can lead him to believe his life is an open book to the police. After a few such clever uses of information, and if the other necessary conditions outlined by Horowitz have been met, an admission or confession may result. For an innocent person, of course, the internal pressure of guilt knowledge is not coupled with the other requisites for confession, and so none is likely to be obtained. Confirmation of the confession by checking details admitted to by the subject must be followed through diligently.

The decision to invest significant surveillance resources and the stage in the process where such a decision is made are dependent upon many factors: other priority needs, availability of a surveillance team, and other investigative developments as the case progresses. The economist's concept of "tradeoff" is applicable in arriving at a decision whether to continue the surveillance or not.

Technology has produced sophisticated electronic equipment that is useful for surveillance purposes. If such devices are not to be outlawed completely it behooves the law enforcement fraternity to pay heed to the clear message transmitted in the Westin paper.[6] Certainly some safeguards are necessary. A colloquy with those concerned with the invasion of privacy would be profitable. Until this discord is solved it will be hazardous to build the investigative process on the assumption that this source of information will be legally available for long in the future. The problem should be met head on rather than by covert usage and an "ostrich head-in-the-sand" approach.

[5]M. Horowitz, "Psychology of Confession," *J. Crim. Law, Criminal., and Pol. Sci.,* 47, 197 (1956).

[6]Westin, *Science, Privacy, and Freedom.*

Motives

Crimes may be divided into two classes from the standpoint of motive. Crimes such as robbery, rape, and burglary have "universal" motives which are of little value in furthering the investigation. Other crimes may have "particularized motives", for example, homicide, arson, and assault. In these crimes, when the motive is discovered, the relationship between victim and criminal may be deduced. The high clearance rate for homicide is based, at least in part, on this logic. Experience is helpful in ferreting out the particular motive for a crime. In some crimes a determination of who has benefited from its commission is suggestive as to motive; in others it is through adroit interviewing that the motive may be learned.

Criminal Investigation—Art or Science

It is convenient to view investigation as part of a continuum with the left-hand limit representing the "art" aspects and the right-hand limit the "science" aspects of the process. Also some people are better endowed naturally with the attributes of a "good" detective.[7]

Intelligence

Curiosity and imagination

Keen observation and retentive memory

Knowledge of life and people

Technical "know-how"

Perseverance

Freedom from bias and prejudice

Honesty and courage

Sensitivity, discretion, and tact

Physical fitness and neat appearance

Report writing ability.

Others less gifted may nevertheless become acceptable investigators if the elements of investigation are reduced to procedures and principles that are teachable. The rapidity and efficiency of this accomplishment will determine our future ability to educate and train investigators.

At the present time we are at an undefined point somewhere along the continuum and, hopefully, we are moving toward the science end of the spectrum. However, criminal investigation is not yet a process that can be

[7]As developed in class discussion with police officers and regular academic students.

characterized in steps or by precepts which, when followed, will unerringly lead to a solution of a crime. It can be perhaps better compared to cooking —the ingredients are the same for all chefs; but what they do to and with them, how they add and blend the items, how much heat (or energy) they apply—these are the factors which make the difference between a routine and an exceptional outcome, success or failure.

CHAPTER 13

The Crime Scene

William Dienstein

William Dienstein is Associate Professor of Criminology at Fresno State College, Fresno, California and a noted lecturer in the fields of criminology and police science. In addition to writing numerous articles for professional journals, he is the author of: *How to Write a Narrative Investigative Report* and *Are You Guilty?: An Introduction to the Administration of Criminal Justice in the United States.*

The clues that lead to the solution of an offense lie in the scene of the crime. Therefore, the investigator must be aware of what constitutes evidence, what are the clues, where they may be found, and how they may be protected, collected, and preserved.

When the investigator is sent to the scene of a crime, what must he know, what must he do, in order to insure that the solution of the case will not be bungled by improper initial procedure?

Evidence

In general, evidence is anything that may be presented in determining the truth about a fact in question. Evidence is that which supplies the means of arriving at the truth. Evidence may be any matter of fact from which another matter of fact may be inferred. So far as the investigator is concerned, everything at the scene of a crime that can be used in ascertaining what in fact occurred constitutes evidence.

Evidence is obtained through one or more of the five senses: seeing, hearing, feeling, smelling, or tasting. It is this evidence, unearthed by the investigator through the use of these senses during the course of his investi-

From Dienstein, William, *Technics For The Crime Investigator,* 4th ed., 1962. Reprinted through the courtesy of Charles C. Thomas, Publisher, Springfield, Illinois.

gation, that enables him to reconstruct the happening, to identify the person or persons involved, and to destroy the alibis of suspects.

From the crime scene, evidence is gathered to establish the fact of the offense and the identity of the perpetrator. To prove the commission of an offense, the steps which make up the offense must be established. An analogy may be made to the climbing of a ladder. Let us say that each rung is a step toward the criminal act itself. The criminal act is the top rung of the ladder. If a person starts to climb the ladder, the criminal act is not consummated until each rung is mounted and the top rung is reached. In the commission of a crime, all the steps which constitute the crime must be taken. These steps are considered the elements of the crime. Should any step be missing, the total act falls short of the criminal act.

The investigator must establish each step of the crime in order to prove the offense, and in order to establish each step, he must be aware of the elements in each offense. The elements of a crime are the aggregate of those factors necessary to constitute the particular offense. Two elements most common to all offenses are the act and the intent. The elements are indicated in the statutory definition of the particular offense.

For example, the elements of the crime of murder are that the victim named or described is dead; that the death of the victim resulted from an act or an omission of the accused; that the accused had a premeditated design to kill, or intended to kill or to inflict great bodily harm, or was engaged in an act inherently dangerous to others, such as an act which shows wanton disregard of human life. Unless all three of the above elements are established through investigation, the crime of murder is not proved, although some other offense may be proved.

The investigator must bear in mind the elements of the offense committed. The scene must be inspected to reveal proof for the establishment of each of the elements. The notes of the investigator are the basis for a full and complete account of all that was done, observed, and learned during the search. The facts discovered by the investigator, which tend to establish the elements of the offense, constitute a part of the evidence of the case. Each of these elements must be proved before the accused can be convicted of the offense charged.

Cases may be won or lost depending on the manner in which evidence has been collected, handled, preserved, and identified. No evidence will be of any value unless it meets the requisites of proper treatment. The investigator cannot know at the outset of a case which of the articles and traces he discovers will be used in legal proceedings. Consequently, he must handle all such findings in a manner that will permit their introduction in court as evidence if required.

Physical evidence found at the scene of an offense may permit the investigator to reconstruct the manner in which the act was committed.

Such evidence may also indentify the perpetrator. He may have left a personal article which can be traced to him because of description or marking; he may have left his fingerprints upon the scene; he may have left a shoe print; he may have left his trademark of operation.

There are two types of evidence found at a crime scene: fixed or immovable evidence and movable evidence. The principal types of fixed evidence which will be encountered by the investigator include latent fingerprints, shoe prints, tire prints, tool marks, writings or markings on fixed objects, instruments of sabotage, and such objects as cannot be removed from the scene because of bulk, weight, or other factors.

Movable evidence is a finding which can be easily and readily removed from the scene and stored until needed for further use during the investigation. This type of evidence is less difficult to handle since no reproduction is required to establish it. Movable evidence is often classified as to the examination to which it may be subjected. The type of examination accorded it determines the specific kind of handling.

In addition to proper handling, preservation, and identification of evidence, it is necessary that the "chain of custody" be maintained. The chain of custody refers to the possession of the evidence. From the moment the investigator discovers a bit of evidence until it is presented in court, the continuous possession of that evidence must be established. The evidence must be accounted for by receipt when transfer of possession is made. Time, date, and place must be noted as well as to whom it was given, by whom, and for what purpose. Each person who has had in his possession a bit of evidence must testify that it did not leave his possession during his period of custody, that it was either under his immediate care or placed in a locked compartment to which he alone had access, and that the evidence was in no way altered or contaminated.

As an example of the conditions which may break the chain of custody, the instance of a kerosene container is cited. At the scene of a fire, a container for kerosene was found. The container was finally traced to a suspect, and it was established that the container belonged to the suspect. During the suspect's trial, it was established that the fire marshal had kept the can in the back of his car, and that the car had been left unattended and unlocked for periods of varying lengths as he went about his business. The kerosene container was not admitted as evidence, and the case was lost.

If the possession of the evidence is unaccountable for a moment, the evidence is rendered inadmissible. For it to be accepted in court, it must be shown that the article presented is in the same condition, except where analysis may have required the use of a portion of it, as when found. If possession cannot be established, it is assumed that the article has been altered or could have been altered.

A general rule to be followed by every investigator is: *Nothing at a crime scene is too insignificant for proper treatment.* Cases are never lost because too much evidence has been gathered and preserved. Cases are often lost because the investigator decided that a certain article or trace was unimportant and failed to collect and preserve it. A lazy investigator finds crime scene searches for evidence a bore. Such a person is a detriment to any agency and should be given an immediate opportunity to seek employment more consistent with his temperament.

Protection and Search

Evidence is always present at the scene of the commission of any offense. Whether or not evidence is found is another matter. That it is not found, does not prove its absence. Failure to find evidence upon a crime scene may be due among other things to faulty crime scene protection, careless search, inadequate search, limited facilities, poor investigation, poor technique, or ignorance.

The investigator is seldom the first to arrive at the scene of a crime. Usually the first peace officer to arrive is the uniformed officer. He is the person who is responsible for the initial protection of the crime scene. How well he does his job may determine the outcome of an investigation.

The perpetrator of a criminal act must leave traces of his actions. These traces are a part of the crime scene. They can be easily destroyed, intentionally or unintentionally, by permitting persons to wander about the scene before it has been photographed, sketched, and searched. The importance of preserving the crime scene in its original condition cannot be overemphasized. The untampered crime scene can reveal the story of what occurred there. If the crime scene has been tampered with in any way, erroneous conclusions may be reached and the crime may never be solved.

Upon arrival at the scene of an offense, the first step of the uniformed officer is to establish protection about the perimeter of the scene in order that no personnel other than the investigator in charge or those that he permits to do so may enter.

"Has anyone been allowed to enter the scene?" will be the first question the investigator will ask when he arrives at a crime scene. The investigator will strengthen the protection of the scene by the use of uniformed officers and barricades where necessary. *One person must be in charge of the crime scene.* He will direct the protection and search.

The investigator will note the time of the arrival of the first officer at the scene, who was present, what was said, and whether or not everything is exactly as it was when the officer arrived. From here on the senior or assigned investigator becomes the search commander who is responsible for search discipline.

The names and addresses of all persons found on or adjacent to the scene are obtained. They are questioned primarily as to their exact location at the time of the commission of the offense. No effort is made at interrogation at this time. They are then removed from the scene and separated. Other officers may be assigned to take a statement from each one. Witnesses should not be permitted to talk to each other until they have been questioned carefully and complete statements taken.

The first action of the search commander, after making certain that witnesses have been detained and are being kept apart, is to assure himself that the area has been protected. Protection is not only against curious bystanders but against curious officials. All too often the investigator is confronted with a horde of curious officials in and out of uniform who, if permitted to inspect the crime scene, would unintentionally destroy any traces present.

The next step involves a preliminary survey of the scene and is accomplished simultaneously with the establishment of crime scene protection. The investigator gets an over-all picture of the area in which the offense occurred. This is done with composure and without haste. It is an orientation for the investigator and enables him to get the whole picture.

The investigator will start "cold." That is, he will have no preconceived notions of what happened, how it happened, and who might have done it. What he finds and where he finds it will be the facts upon which he does his thinking. Starting an investigation with a preconceived notion will lead an investigator into gross errors by causing him to look for those things which establish his preconceived idea and to overlook the things which disprove it. This is usually an unconscious working of the mind of the investigator, and he would be the first to deny that he is trying to prove his idea. Conclusions must arise from the findings; findings cannot arise from conclusions.

During the initial overview and the later observation and search of the scene, *nothing is touched, picked up, or moved until it has been photographed, located on a sketch, and minutely described as to location, condition, and any other pertinent observation.*

Upon completion of the preliminary survey and the removal of witnesses, the examination of the scene begins. Photography plays a very important part in this stage of the investigation. The search commander will have the scene reproduced photographically in order to have an accurate and permanent record available. He will make certain that the entire area is photographed.

The investigator cannot belittle the fact that the actual solution of the offense is in the scene of the crime. It is from the search of the crime scene and adjacent areas that the means of the approach to the scene by the perpetrator is established and the means of escape from the scene is discovered. Therefore, proper protection of the scene includes these adjacent areas. Proper protection makes it possible for a "true" photograph to be made of the immediate vicinity of the crime scene. Only a true picture can be presented in court as evidence. If it can be shown that some object in the scene has been tampered with before the picture was taken or that persons or objects are in the photographed scene which were not there originally, then the picture cannot be used as evidence. The importance of keeping the crime scene intact until photographs have been taken cannot be overestimated.

If the body of a victim is on the scene, the investigator will assure himself that the body has been photographed from all angles. The photographer will remain until the search is completed in case close-ups are needed of traces and conditions which the search commander wants recorded.

At the same time the area protection and photography are accomplished, the investigator is conducting a preliminary survey and determining his plan of action. He will direct a sketch to be made of the area in addition to the photographs. The sketching is begun as soon as possible. The drawing may be freehand, but accuracy must be maintained. The sketch should be oriented by compass directions. All objects indicated on the sketch must be located accurately by measurements. The search commander will indicate what is to be included and what is to be excluded from the sketch. The location of the camera from which each picture is taken can be recorded on the sketch. The advantage of a sketch over a photograph is that the sketch will include only certain essential items, whereas the photograph will reproduce everything within its range and field.

Upon completion of the initial photography, areas and objects are designated for search and inspection. Whether more than one investigator will make the detailed search will depend upon the commander. The searcher will suggest to the commander what objects will be dusted for latent prints and what objects will be removed as evidence. The search must be thorough and accurate. Nothing is taken for granted. Everything that may be of possible significance is recorded. No reliance is placed on memory.

The search commander will be the person who will mark all evidence for purposes of identification. If discovered by another searcher, the commander will direct that the evidence and its location in the scene be reproduced by sketch and/or photograph. The reason for having only one person actually handle all the evidence discovered upon the scene should be obvious: the chain of custody is reduced. The searcher who discovers the evidence remains a witness to the handling and marking.

Teamwork is essential to a crime scene search. The presence of technicians, investigators, and uniformed officers can give rise to conflict. Each has a specific job to do. Each specific job is a part of the larger job of the search. The search commander must direct all activity and reduce conflict to a minimum. Each technician and investigator will make notes of his own findings. In addition, the search commander will maintain a set of master notes which will include the findings of all his assistants. Nothing on the scene should be moved without clearance from the search commander.

The search of a crime scene is not limited to the search for objects. There is search for traces of objects—indications as to where an object may have been. To carry out an effective search is one of the most difficult tasks an investigator can be called upon to undertake.

In addition to the mechanics of a search, all personnel in the area must be alert to what goes on about them. During the course of his presence at the scene, the investigator may overhear the unguarded remarks of witnesses or others having a knowledge of the situation. Some slip of the tongue may furnish the clue which will be instrumental in the solution of the case.

All search personnel will be guarded in their talk to prevent the disclosure of information to unauthorized persons. Very often, henchmen of the perpetrator of an offense will "hang around" a crime scene while a search is in progress to learn how much the police discover. They will report their findings to the perpetrator. It is good practice to be alert for those who seem to display an unwarranted interest in the goings-on, and also for those who seem to be too nonchalant in their behavior, but manage to be as close as permitted.

Clues on the Crime Scene

Protection of the crime scene is essential to preserve fingerprints, footprints, tire markings, tool marks, spent bullets, stains, and the various traces left in the accomplishment of the crime.

It is probable that persons who were on the scene of the crime, prior, during, or immediately after its commission, have left their *fingerprints* on some object. Such fingerprints may be developed and photographed if they are not smeared or obliterated by prowlers. These fingerprints definitely establish the presence of certain persons at the crime scene.

It is necessary to protect the environs of a crime scene to preserve *footprints* for photographing and the making of plaster casts. Footprints have been valuable evidence in a chain of incriminating facts. Although shoes vary but little in shape of the sole and heel, each will carry the manufacturer's trademark and particular design. After a few days wear, certain individual characteristics and peculiarities will appear on the surface of the sole and heel, making identification possible. Prints from *rubber heels* can be left on nearly all types of smooth floor covering and on the ground itself. If the shoe surface has come in contact with some removable material such as blood, grease, or dust, the imprint may be made with this material.

These surface prints are photographed with a scale by the side. Comparison prints from the shoes of a suspect may be obtained by inking the soles and heels with an ink roller and having the suspect walk over white paper. Footprints should be photographed before an attempt is made to reproduce them by plaster casts. The risk of destroying the print is ever present when making a cast.

It is also possible to identify traces of *socks.* These traces may be visible or latent, and are dealt with in much the same manner as fingerprints. Identification is based on the comparison of the structure of the fabric.

The surroundings of a crime scene may contain traces of a vehicle used in the perpetration of the crime. *Tire marks* may be found. These may aid the investigator in his case. They are first photographed and then reproduced by making a plaster cast. If the imprint is made on a sensitive surface which may not bear the weight of the plaster, the surface is prepared by spraying with shellac. Care is taken that the spray is not directed at the impression. It may destroy the imprint. Spray against a piece of board or card and allow the spray to fall upon the surface. Ordinary plaster of Paris is used in making the cast. Never pour the plaster directly on the imprint. Break the pouring with a spatula or stick and allow the plaster to flow into the imprint rather than onto it from a height.

Crime scenes are protected so that *traces of tools* used in the commission of the offense are not obliterated. Any tools, jimmies, hatchets, axes, hammers, cutters, pliers, knives, can openers will leave markings on any material softer than the tool itself. It is possible with the aid of the microscope to examine the surface on which the tool trace appears and to identify the tool making the trace with the same degree of accuracy that a bullet is identified with the weapon from which it is fired. Tool traces are photographed, casts made of the impression, or the trace is cut out and preserved as evidence.

Spent *bullets* may be found upon the crime scene if unauthorized persons are kept off until after the search has been completed. It is easy to kick a bullet some distance. Stepping on it may remove or add marks to the surface, making identification impossible. Spent bullets may reveal the caliber and type of gun used and upon comparison will definitely establish the weapon from which fired. Bullets are first examined for adhering particles which are examined microscopically. Therefore, they should not be fingered or picked up by any person other than the investigator.

Whether or not a blow or a bullet struck a window pane from within or without may be of special significance. A *glass fracture* created by a bullet will show small flakes blown away on the side opposite the entrance of the bullet. It is more difficult to determine from which side a blunt object has smashed a window.

When a blow strikes a glass surface, the glass gives with the blow because of its elasticity. When the limit of elasticity is reached, the glass breaks along radial lines starting from the point of impact or force. These radial lines (lines spreading out from a center as rays of light) originate on the side opposite from the side of impact because this side is subjected to stretching and, therefore, breaks first. The front surface is pushed in by the force. The back surface bends and bursts. While these radial fractures are taking place, glass triangles are formed between the radial lines and the point of break. The glass triangles will also bend away from the direction of the applied force. The bending stretches the glass to its limits of elasticity, and the glass breaks in concentric circles, as the ripples form in a pond, on the side to which the force is applied. An examination of the edges of the glass fragments will make it possible to determine from which side the blow was struck. Consequently, it is important that the glass fragments and the glass remaining in a window or elsewhere be protected from tampering or handling so that it may be properly collected and preserved for expert examination.

Various *stains* may be found on the crime scene. Bloodstains are most common and can reveal much information. They are easily smeared and removed by footsteps, however, and for this reason it is important that unauthorized personnel let stains alone. One famous murder case was complicated by the fact that one of the police officers present was so tidy he tried to wipe up bloodstains in a bathroom. Had the stains been protected for examination and photography as to their shape, size, and position, valuable evidence could have been revealed.

Traces of cloth may be found on a crime scene. These are the negative prints of the cloth. If the fabric has a characteristic pattern or has been repaired, it may be of importance. These traces are photographed under oblique light. If possible, casts are made. Comparisons are made with the suspect fabric.

Traces of dust open vast possibilities. A garment left on the scene of an offense may reveal from dust traces the areas which the wearer of the garment frequents. Dust is peculiar to certain factories, plants, and areas. Because of this, search for a suspect can be directed to places where the particular kind of dust exists.

It will become evident with experience that almost anything may constitute a clue in a criminal investigation. *Everything must be recorded; nothing must be overlooked as too insignificant or unimportant to record.*

Photographs and Sketches

Crime scene photographs and sketches are of three general types: the locality, the immediate grounds, and the details of the scene. The reproduction of the locality gives a picture of the scene of the crime and its surroundings including such items as neighboring buildings, streets, sidewalks, and the like. Locality reproductions may be especially valuable in certain types of cases.

The reproduction of the grounds describes the scene of the crime with its nearest immediate surroundings: the house with garden, the room with other rooms on the same floor, etc.

The reproduction of the details describes the scene only—for example, the room in which the offense was committed and the details of that room. One type of sketch is known as a cross-projection in which the floor, walls, and ceiling are drawn on the same surface.

The sketch and photographs may become important evidence. In order for these to be admissible into evidence, it must be proved that they are accurate reproductions and show the scene as it was when the first official arrived. It is not sufficient to sketch and photograph the immediate scene upon which the offense was perpetrated. Surrounding and adjacent areas may be important and should be recorded, including roadways, buildings, paths, and the like.

It must be pointed out, even though it may appear obvious, that photographic coverage of a crime scene may require the taking of a dozen or more pictures. The danger of taking too many pictures is much less than of taking too few.

It is essential that each photograph be completely and accurately identified as to:

1. Subject of photograph.
2. Where taken.
3. Time of day.
4. Date.
5. Light source.
6. Distance from lens to subject.
7. Kind of camera.
8. Type of lens.
9. Aperture (stop opening).
10. Type of film.
11. Shutter speed.
12. Height of lens from the ground.
13. Name of person taking photograph.
14. Name of witness to the taking of photograph.
15. Name of person developing and printing photograph with date and time.

If a camera is not available, then a sketch is essential. Photographs and sketches may be used to supplement each other. Each serves a particular purpose. The photograph is not selective. It shows everything in front of the lens. The sketch permits the selection of those objects thought to be more important or which it is desired to emphasize or point up. Another use of the sketch as a complement to the photograph is that upon it may be indicated the position of the camera from which pictures of the scene were taken.

Some of the general rules for sketching a crime scene are:

1. Decide what is to be sketched.

2. Determine compass directions and draw them on the sketch.

3. Control all measurements. Do not rely on others to give them to you.

4. Use a measuring instrument of wood, steel, or plastic. Do not estimate distances by footsteps or other inaccurate means.

5. Represent distance between objects accurately.

6. Locate objects exactly.

7. Include only the essentials in the drawing. Do not overcrowd the sketch. The advantage of a sketch over a photograph is that irrelevant and non-essential things can be excluded.

8. Make any corrections of the sketch while on the scene. Do not wait until later.

9. Draw to scale. Indicate the scale on the sketch.

10. Include in notes on the sketch the date, time, and weather conditions (even if indoors), degree of light, witnesses, and name of person making sketch.

Sketching may be somewhat simplified by using graph or cross section paper. It must be remembered that the scale, title, date, time, location, weather conditions, compass directions, and name of the person making the drawing are a part of the sketch. Sketching is not something that can be done in an offhand manner. It is a job which requires practice, and is best done by one trained to draw.

The photograph and/or sketch of the crime scene serve to outline the evidential facts and circumstances to a judge and jury. The appearance of the crime scene is thereby recorded in such a manner that witnesses, prosecutors, attorneys, judges, and juries can get a clear picture of it. Crime scenes are not permanent. By the time a case is brought to trial, the scene may have been so altered as to make a reconstruction impossible. The photographs and sketches are the only evidence remaining of the scene. The history of criminal investigation shows many cases which have been lost because an accurate description of the scene of the crime was not preserved.

A good sketch or photograph provides for an adequate description of the scene.

As an example of the value of photographs of the locality of the crime scene, the following case is cited: An assault and rape had occurred in an uninhabited area within a rapidly growing community. The scene of the act was photographed. The photographer then placed his camera on the scene and took pictures in all directions away from the scene so that a complete circle was made. During the course of the trial some six months later, the defense introduced the point that the subject of the attacked was in reality a willing participant, and had she not been, she would have screamed and help would have been immediate. Since the time of the offense, the area had been subdivided and built up to such an extent that there was no resemblance between the scene at the time of the offense and at the time of the trial. The court and jury wanted to see the scene as it had been at the time of the offense. Verbal descriptions would have been meaningless. The pictures of the scene were introduced into evidence. The pictures showed no buildings of any sort within a mile of the scene. The accused was convicted. It was learned later that the pictures had balanced the scales against the accused. The story of the defense had taken such hold on the jury that they were ready to accept the fact of willingness on the part of the victim and her charge against the accused as vindictiveness until they saw the crime scene and the surrounding area.

As already indicated, crime scene protection permits accurate reproduction of the scene by sketching and photography. A photograph is an excellent supplement to a sketch for the reason that it records everything within the range of the camera. Small details may escape initial observation. It may be valuable to be able to re-study the crime scene. A question may arise concerning some detail of the scene after the scene has been altered. A photograph is always a ready reference.

The value of photographs is emphasized by the following: A body with a bullet hole in the head is found lying on a bed. A pistol is clasped in the victim's hand. The usual examination is made, and seeing no trace of violence, the investigator concludes he is dealing with a suicide. As it is difficult to obtain a photographer at the moment or the investigator has something else to do, he doesn't bother with a photograph or sketch. The body is removed, buried, and the case report is written as closed. Later, doubts arise. The deceased is believed to be the victim of a murder. It is no longer possible to examine carefully the hand which held the pistol to determine if the fingers are in a natural or unnatural position. It is no longer possible to determine whether or not traces of violence were present in the room. A series of good photographs would be of inestimable value as a basis for the decision in determining whether the case should be reopened.

A series of good photographs is a permanent reconstruction of the crime scene and is always available. A photograph is an excellent court exhibit. Also, a photograph may show things not recognizable to the eyes. A photograph was made of the body of a woman found seated on a park bench. It was assumed that she died a natural death since there were no marks of violence. The photograph revealed the seat outline of someone who had set next to her. The morning dew made this visible to the eye of the camera, but not to the human eye.

The photograph and sketch are artificial memories. They enable a complete recall of the scene at a later period, even months or years later. They are exact reproductions of the scene and constitute evidence of the scene. Long after the scene is destroyed, the photograph and sketch can be used to bring it back to reality. They permit the re-examination of the scene after any hope of reconstruction at the actual scene would be impossible. The photograph permits detailed and prolonged study of the crime scene by the investigator.

Handling and Preservation of Evidence

Scene: A house in a residential area. Within the house,
a body on the floor of a room.

The photography of the general area has been accomplished. Photographs are taken as the investigator progresses into the house. At the doorway to the room in which the body lies, the investigator pauses, carefully looking at the floor before he steps into the room. He notices a spent bullet near this entrance. A photograph is taken showing the location of the bullet in relation to a fixed object in the room so that it can be spotted later on the overall photograph of the room. The investigator picks up the bullet and marks it on the base or nose (ogive) for identification. His mark will be one unique to him but will not be an "X." In his notebook he will make an entry of the finding, showing the mark used and naming witnesses to the finding. A sharp pointed instrument may be used to mark the bullet. The bullet is placed in cotton in a pill box large enough to hold it. The box is sealed with a piece of cellulose tape and marked as to contents. The witnesses' initials are added to the markings as well as the name of the deceased.

The portions of the bullet which must be protected from damage are the sides on which there are engravings caused by passage of the bullet through the bore of the weapon from which it was fired. These engravings or striations are the "fingerprints" or personal signature of the weapon from which the bullet was fired, and are the basis for later identification by comparison with a test bullet fired from the suspect weapon.

A small pool of blood receives the attention of the investigator. A photograph is taken showing the location of the blood to some fixed object in the room. A close-up may be taken. The investigator collects a sample of this blood by soaking sterile filter paper in it. The blood-soaked filter paper is then placed in a sterile jar or test tube. The tube is labeled for complete identification including the unique mark or initials of the investigator. The container is sealed. The notes of the investigator will contain information as to where found, witnesses, method of collecting, handling, and preservation.

The next object noted is a revolver. It is photographed in position. The investigator picks it up by forefinger and thumb on the edges of the trigger guard. The weapon may be unloaded at the scene if fingerprint technicians are present to dust the weapon for prints. If not, the weapon will be placed in a container, tied to the bottom, and taken to the firearms technician. The portions to be protected are the smooth surfaces of the outside of the weapon which may contain fingerprints. If the weapon is to be unloaded, care is taken not to smudge any possible prints on it, and the investigator should not leave his own prints on the weapon, unless it is established that the outer surface of the gun contains no fingerprints.

It should be noted that the unfired rounds ejected from the cylinder may contain fingerprints on the shell or cartridge case. This should be protected. Each cartridge or shell is placed in an envelope, preferably a cellophane envelope, and sealed. An identification tag is attached to the container and proper entry is made in the investigator's notebook.

The shells of the fired rounds are marked on the side near the mouth or on the inside of the open end with the identifying mark of the finder and then placed in a cellophane envelope which is also properly marked and sealed. The shell can be identified by markings of the firing pin, breech face, and if a pistol by the additional markings of the ejector and extractor. These markings must be protected.

The body is next observed. It is photographed from several angles to determine its location in relation to a fixed object or objects and its position. A vertical photograph is valuable. It may be necessary to take the picture from a table or ladder. Then the body and garments are examined carefully. Visible markings are photographed and noted.

Strands of hair are observed to be clutched in the right hand. A close-up photograph is taken. The hand is opened and the hair is removed by the use of rubber tipped tweezers and placed in a test tube stoppered with a cork covered with pure animal lard. The container is marked and notations are made in the notebook. The reason for the use of the lard is that hair secretes aromas and fluids from the body which will evaporate. Lard will retain the effluvia and is subject to analysis.

A bullet hole is observed in the clothing. A close-up photograph is taken. The importance of this evidence is that if the weapon was fired close to the garment, the powder pattern of the unburned and partially burned powder expelled from the muzzle of the weapon is likely to be present. This pattern is important to the investigator and may determine the distance from which the weapon was fired. If blood is still oozing, place some clean material under the outer garment to prevent the blood from washing away any powder grains and destroying the pattern. The garment is allowed to dry, if wet, by natural means, then folded carefully with the outer surface outward and placed in a cellophane bag or wrapping. Do not use newspaper or anything other than clean wrapping paper if cellophane paper is not available. Do not hasten drying by artifical means.

Scrapings are taken from the fingernails of the victim and placed in small, clean containers. It is better to place scrapings from under each fingernail in separate containers, mark each container for identification, and seal. Proper entries will be made in the notebook.

Dust and dirt from the garments of the victim or suspect are subject to scientific analysis, and may provide evidence as to where he may have been or with what he may have had contact.

Stained areas are noted on the floor. These are photographed. The stains are removed by scraping with a sterile knife blade, or if necessary by removing a piece of the surface on which found. The material is placed in a container, sealed, and marked for identification. If an area appears to have been washed, cracks in the floor where pieces join will contain particles of the dried fluid sufficient for identification. This may be scraped out by using a sterile penknife or gouged out or a portion of the flooring removed.

If the stain is on a non-porous material such as cement, marble, or tile and cannot be scraped or removed, a portion of the stain may be dissolved out by placing a piece of filter paper previously soaked in distilled water over the stain. If there is no distilled water available, whatever water is used to wet the filter paper must be taken as a control sample for the laboratory technician. After a time it will be noted that the filter paper will become discolored if the stain begins to dissolve. The paper is picked up, placed in a sterile tube, sealed, and marked.

Areas where latent fingerprints may be present are photographed. The areas are then dusted. If fingerprints develop, they are photographed. If a latent print is found on an immovable object, then the print may be lifted, by the use of commercial rubber tape made for the purpose or by using cellulose tape, and placed on contrasting colored paper. Photographs and tape or paper are marked as previously described.

Further examination of the scene discloses a forced entry into the room. Photographs of the marks left by the tools used to gain entry are made. If possible, the area containing the marks is removed. If not, a mold of the markings is made by the use of moulage, plasticine, modeling clay, paraffin, or dental wax.

A note or some sort of documentary evidence is found. It is photographed where found, picked up with tweezers, placed unfolded in a cellophane container, sealed, and labeled.

In the driveway tire impressions are discovered. These are photographed, first with a long-shot to orient the marking to the scene, and then vertical close-ups are taken showing at least twelve inches of the track, with and without a rule. In addition, where possible, a plaster of Paris cast is made of the tire marking.

Blood-stained soil is removed after being photographed for position and placed in clean containers. Control samples of soil from adjacent areas are essential. The control samples are handled in the same way as the blood-stained soil. Containers are marked for identification.

Where toxicological examination of organs of the body may be required as in suspected poison cases and the facilities of a laboratory are not nearby, it becomes the duty of the investigator to see that proper precautions are taken during the autopsy so that samples may be sent to a laboratory.

Each organ or part thereof removed by the autopsy surgeon is placed in a separate, all glass container. No preservatives are used. Each container is sealed and labeled. The autopsy surgeon as well as the investigator will initial the label. The containers may be packed with dry ice or ice in sawdust, building insulation, damp paper, or damp excelsior. Care should be taken that the contents will not freeze, but will be kept cool to cold.

Throughout the handling, identification, and preservation of evidence, the chain of custody must be maintained. If articles are to be transported by common carrier to an examiner, establishment of custody is shown by registry or insurance and signed receipts of acceptance of the article.

In gathering evidence, the investigator will note all items in a notebook, mark all movable items with his special identification, date, time, place where found, witnesses if any, and seal in containers, also so marked. Fixed evidence is reproduced. The reproduction is identified by the same type of information as is used in marking movable evidence. Nothing at a crime scene is too insignificant to be dismissed. Nothing is touched or moved until it has been photographed or sketched with pertinent observations attached. The possession of evidence must be clearly established at all times, from the time it is first collected until it is presented in court.

Articles of evidence are the essence of the case. Their collection, handling, and preservation require the utmost care.

CHAPTER 14

Surveillance

Col. Maurice J. Fitzgerald, CMP, U. S. Army

Col. Maurice J. Fitzgerald is one of the foremost authorities on criminal investigation methodology. His expertise developed through training and practical experience with the New York Police Department and the United States Army.

A close watch over any place, building, or person is a surveillance. It is usually reserved for use in important cases as all surveillance work requires the use of additional personnel. In some cases many assistants are required, and almost any surveillance requires that the investigator be assisted by at least one or two other investigators.

In police terminology a static or fixed surveillance is known as a "plant," and the close observation of any individual or motor vehicle, in movement from place to place, is known as "tailing."

A "plant" may be established to initiate a "tail" on some suspect. And when a suspect is tailed to his home or place of business a plant may be established to ascertain persons that visit him.

While close observation of a person's mail, telegrams, or telephone conversations are a close surveillance to a certain extent, this term is not used in connection with a mail or telegram "cover," the tapping of a telephone, or the use of other listening devices. However, such techniques are useful in supplementing a surveillance, whether it is a plant or a tail.

Hard and fast rules cannot be set forth for procedure to be used in establishing a close watch over any place or person. The investigator himself must determine the exact technique to be used, must determine to what extent the surveillance will be maintained, and he also must determine when the surveillance has served its purpose.

Purpose

The purpose of a surveillance may be any one or more of the following:

(1) To secure information.

(2) To effect the arrest of a criminal or the apprehension of a suspect or material witness.

(3) To discover a crime.

(4) To prevent a crime.

In the majority of cases it is information that the investigator is seeking, but plants to discover crime are required in cases such as those involving rackets, and are a necessity in some instances to prevent robberies of storekeepers.

In some cases a great deal of information may be sought, in others perhaps only minor details to clarify one phase of the investigation may be all that is required. The attempt to discover a crime or a series of crimes may require the tailing of several members of a large safe mob for a week or two, or it may only be necessary to cover a premises on one night.

Plants to prevent robberies are usually the result of an investigation into several robberies. The investigator fails to secure any real information except that they are all the work of one man or one mob and that certain types of stores are the favorite victims, or that the robberies are confined to a certain neighborhood. In such cases plants are established not only to prevent crime but also to close out the investigation by the apprehension of the criminal or criminals.

Plants

A plant may be established upon the home or apartment of a person, to cover a certain place of business, or may even extend to a neighborhood —an area of several blocks in some instances.

The purpose of the plant and the physical set-up of the premises to be covered determine the number of assistants that an investigator will require to maintain it.

If the purpose of a plant is to serve as a starting point for tailing a suspect and his associates, then additional personnel are required. If the premises concerned has several entrances, it will require what might be termed two or three separate, but related, plants at the one premises. Such coverage requires not only the personnel necessary for full coverage of all entrances, but relief personnel and at least one additional man for communication between the investigators assigned to the various entrances.

When the purpose of a plant is such that only temporary coverage is necessary, then an outside plant is usually sufficient. If a lengthy plant may be required, then provision should be made for acquiring a suitable room, office, store, or apartment. While an investigator can maintain an outdoor plant for quite some time by changing his points of observation, his methods of concealment, and his assistants, it is highly desirable to secure an inside location if the plant is going to be over an extended period of time.

Naturally, the first requirement of any plant is observation. On inside plants telescopes, binoculars and telephoto lenses on cameras are all aids to observation. Such aids permit establishment of an inside plant at some distance from the premises to be observed.

An outdoor plant can be a simple or an elaborate one. The investigator can station himself in a nearby doorway or parked automobile or he may resort to various subterfuges ranging from sitting in an apparently disabled automobile, bus, or taxi-cab to digging a hole in the street. One investigator secured the cooperation of a nearby home owner, and his assistants spent two days replanting the shrubbery on the front lawn, obtaining fine observation as they worked.

Another officer secured the cooperation of a local bus company and spent a full day—in a bus driver's uniform—sitting in an apparently disabled bus right in front of the suspect's home.

If appropriate space for an indoor plant is available, it should be rented under an assumed identity or a fictitious firm name. However, it is usually necessary to secure the cooperation of a landlord or tenant of the appropriate premises. It is not desirable to reveal all the facts of the investigation to secure such cooperation. The investigator should identify himself, then make a broad statement as to the purpose for which he needs the premises.

Care must be exercised in approaching landlords and tenants in such instances. Prior to the approach a check should be made as to their reliability and trustworthiness. Remember that the success of the plant depends on their ability to keep silent about the presence of the investigator and his assistants.

Sometimes an ordinary plant cannot be established. Then it may be necessary for the investigator to plant himself or one of his assistants as an employee at the premises concerned. Again, cooperation of the employer —if not connected with the suspect or the investigation—can be sought, but it is advisable to exhaust every means of securing such employment through normal channels before seeking such cooperation.

When a plant is established to prevent crime and apprehend the criminals as they attempt to commit it, the same rule of observation applicable to all plants should serve as a guide in picking out a suitable place of concealment. However, another point the investigator must keep in mind is his field of fire in the event the criminal tries to shoot his way out of the trap.

Such plants are mainly for stick-up men—armed men, men willing to shoot to make good their escape. In previous years the rear of the store to be covered was always selected as the ideal place of concealment. This sometimes resulted in an exchange of fire—with no hits—and the escape of the criminal or criminals. The truly ideal location is between the criminal and his avenue of escape.

Personally, I favor an outdoor location if it will give good visibility of the premises under observation. If two men are assigned to such a plant they should be together. Do not split up a team in such cases as they are more effective both in observation and in apprehending the criminal when working together. And never place one man or team in a position where their field of fire may include the post of another man or team.

I recall one case in a large eastern city. One team was placed in the rear of the store, another in a parked automobile opposite the store. When the shooting started both teams fired at the bandits in the store, one from the rear and one from outside. Fortunately none of the officers were wounded—either by bandit fire or the fire of the other team.

Tailing

Before endeavoring to tail any person the investigator must know in his own mind and must thoroughly instruct his assistants as to whether a "close" or a "loose" tail is desired. In a close tail it is important that contact be maintained; discovery by the suspect that he is being followed is a secondary consideration. A loose tail is the exact opposite—under no circumstances must the tail be revealed to the suspect.

A "one-man" tail is a difficult one, in all cases it must be a close one or the person being followed will be lost. It is readily noted by anyone just turning a corner, stopping, then watching for the investigator to come around the corner. Unless a loose tail is sufficient coverage a one-man tail is almost useless. However, when observation has disclosed a regular routine on the part of the suspect, then it is sufficient. The investigator can then readily relocate the suspect in the event he does lose contact.

A variation of the one-man tail is to have several investigators rotate on the assignment, either by days or by the time of the day. Perhaps one man would work Mondays, another the following day, etc., or one would take the mornings and the others the evening and the night time. This is the "relay" technique and prevents the suspect from readily identifying the investigator or his assistants and thereby becoming aware of the tail.

A two to four man squad can operate much better than a single investigator. They can use either the "leap-frog" or the "group" technique.

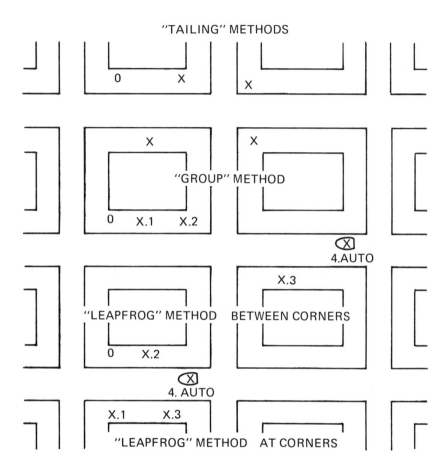

Note.—0 = suspect, X = investigator.
#1 is in a position to observe suspect and then fall back to #3 position; #2 is moving up, and #3 is closing on the #2 position.

When "leap-frogging" only one of the squad maintains contact with the suspect. It is a close tail, with the other members of the squad keeping contact with those immediately ahead of them. At stated intervals of five to six minutes, or upon signal, the man immediately behind the one keeping contact will move up and take his place, the one that had been in contact will stop, look in a show window or wait at a traffic light, then take his place behind the last man of the group. This procedure is continued in rotation as long as the tail is maintained.

Such method is particularly desirable when it is believed the subject may use a motor vehicle. The last man of the team drives an automobile and at a pre-arranged signal (removel of hat, changing a paper from one hand to the other, etc.) passed through the squad, the car moves up. The members of the squad jump in the car if time permits; otherwise the driver continues the tail.

When several men are assigned to a "group" tail, each man maintains contact with the subject. One may be abreast of him on the opposite side of the street, another behind him, and others in similar positions. In order to prevent discovery such positions can be exchanged between members of the group, but they do not leap-frog—each tries to maintain contact. This is a really close tail and is necessary only when discovery is preferable to losing the subject.

In any tail job the investigator in contact with the suspect may be forced to use public transportation such as trains, buses, trolleys, etc., and this presents a problem in concealment. If the suspect boards a train of several cars, the investigator should place himself in a car other than the one in which the suspect is located, but in such a position that he can observe the suspect.

Buses and trolleys present a difficult problem. Care must be exercised that the investigator is not spotted by the suspect. Sit in *front* of the suspect if possible (he can usually be observed by glancing in the window opposite his seat). If the conveyance is crowded with no seats available, I believe in standing as close to the suspect as possible. If he is suspicious, it may throw him off.

If the bus or trolley has two doors, however, it is advisable to place yourself close to one of them, the one furthest from the suspect. When he leaves by one door, the investigator can leave by the other one. On leaving such a conveyance the investigator must stall for time until the suspect moves off. A pause to light a cigarette, look at street signs, consult a notebook or piece of paper are all devices to gain time. However, when an alert suspect is being loosely tailed, it may be necessary to start walking. In such cases the investigator must risk losing contact. He must walk to the nearest corner as rapidly as possible, then seek some vantage point to regain contact.

No matter how many men are assigned to a tail job, this problem of not losing contact when the suspect boards a train, bus, or trolley is always present. It is for this reason that many investigators never work with less than one co-worker, and he operates an automobile. If the suspect boards a trolley or bus, it is much safer to maintain contact by following such trolley or bus in an auto. Unless a close tail is imperative—perhaps the suspect may make contact with someone on the bus or trolley—this is a better procedure than having an investigator board the same conveyance.

Do's and Don't's of Surveillance

Do dress for the neighborhood. A man wearing a suit may stand out in a slum area, and a man dressed in overalls will certainly attract attention in hotels or large office buildings, unless he pretends to be an employee.

Do watch for a "check" tail. The suspect may have someone following him just to see if he is being watched (wives of suspects excel at this).

Do use care at corners, either afoot or when in an automobile. They are the favorite spots for a check as to whether a tail exists.

Do relax. Just because the suspect may have looked your way once or twice doesn't mean he is fully aware of the fact that you are following him. Most inexperienced investigators are too sensitive on this point.

Do prepare for a confrontation—discovery by a suspect and questioning by him—and make appropriate plans for an immediate arrest or a general denial.

Do arrange for some central means of communication between personnel assigned to a tail, and between such personnel and their office or headquarters.

Do prepare plans for use when contact is lost.

Do talk to other people—loungers or passers-by—ask directions, pass the time of day, etc. If possible nod to some of them, say "hello." Many persons, such as mailmen, small merchants, and taxi-drivers, respond to these acts. Remember that if a suspect is suspicious, such apparent familiarity with persons in the neighborhood may allay his fears.

Don't use disguises. Be natural—it's your best disguise.

Don't act in a furtive manner, "slink," walk on the inside of sidewalks, hide in doorways, etc.

Don't keep your eyes fastened on the suspect's back. Look around naturally.

Don't do anything that will unnecessarily attract attention to you or your co-workers.

CHAPTER 15

The Law and Practice of Field Interrogation

Wayland D. Pilcher

Wayland D. Pilcher received his LL.B. from the University of
Texas Law School. In 1966 Mr. Pilcher became the first Police
Legal Advisor in Corpus Christi and one of the first to hold that
position in police administration in the United States.

A workable, qualitative definition of the term "field interrogation" is almost impossible to devise. We will have to be content, then, with a descriptive definition. For the purposes of this article, a field interrogation is any situation in which a police officer asks questions, pertaining to a crime or a suspected crime, of a citizen prior to the time when the citizen is taken, by force or consent, to a police station for further processing. The terms "field stop" and "field contact" are to be considered as synonymous with the term "field interrogation."

It would seem, at first glance, that the term "field interrogation" should be susceptible of a fairly accurate definition. But first glances can be deceptive. There are several revealing and important reasons why any definition of the term "field interrogation" must be, at least in some degree, arbitrary.

The necessity to be arbitrary in the definition of the term "field interrogation" arises primarily because there are so few clear-cut cases where the practice of field interrogation has been examined, analyzed, or defined.[1] At the root of this definitional problem is the wide disparity between the criminal law, as developed by appellate courts, and police practice. To the police officer, an arrest and a field interrogation are entirely distinct concepts.[2] Each has its own purpose, and the techniques used in the streets are

---

From Wayland D. Pilcher, "The Law and Practice of Field Interrogation." Reprinted by special permission of the *Journal of Law, Criminology and Police Science* (Northwestern University School of Law), copyright © 1967, December issue, volume 58, number 4.
[1]31 *Brklyn. L. Rev.* 175 (1964).
[2]Bristow, *Field Interrogation* 5–6 (2d ed. 1964).

quite different. Generally, from the policeman's standpoint, he "arrests" a person when he takes this person to the police station to be charged with a specific crime. On the other hand, he is engaged in the practice of "field interrogation" when he "checks out" a person to determine who he is, what he has been doing, and attempts to obtain an explanation of his actions. Our appellate courts apparently have not made this distinction until very recently. Instead, the courts, when they have faced the real issues at all, have talked in terms of "arrest."

Once the term "arrest" is used by an appellate court it is immediately handicapped. In the first place, the traditional concept of arrest is encrusted with the barnacles of an ancient time which has long since passed. Our present concept of arrest was fairly accurately described by Matthew Hale before 1676.[3] In feudal England, law enforcement, or at least the bringing of an accused person before a magistrate, was the responsibility of the people in the community and the citizens were organized in groups of hundreds in order to apprehend the perpetrator of a crime. In theory, when a crime was perpetrated and the person suspected of committing the crime was attempting to evade capture, the general populace was supposed to evoke a "hue and cry" to pursue the criminal in much the same manner that the posse operates in a western movie.

Such a system of apprehending criminals apparently worked satisfactorily in a static, rural society where each person in the community was intimately acquainted with every other person. The system described above eventually evolved into the Justice of the Peace system wherein the Justice of the Peace was not only a magistrate but also had the responsibility of preserving the peace within his jurisdiction and was the chief law enforcement officer. But the Justice of the Peace system proved inadequate in the face of urbanization and a marked increase in criminal activity.[4]

As cities began to develop, a system of night watchmen was evolved. The actual authority of the night watchman is somewhat vague, but apparently his only function was to take into custody persons who were suspicious or who were committing a crime and hold such persons until dawn, when they could be handed over to the regular law enforcement apparatus.[5] At the same time there developed in England a system of rewards and pardons to encourage citizens to apprehend criminals and bring them before a judicial officer for the criminal process to commence. The first organized police force in the Anglo-American heritage was not established until 1829 when the London metropolitan police force was created by act of Parliament over vigorous opposition. Thus, as one writer states:

---

[3]"Detention, Arrest and Salt Lake City Police Practice," 9 *Utah L. Rev.* 593 (1965).

[4]*Ibid.*

[5]Kuh, "Reflections On New York's 'Stop and Frisk' Law And Its Claimed Unconstitutionality," 56 *J. Crim. L., C. & P.S.* 32 (1964).

... the law of arrest was developed in the context of a citizen enforcement system where arrests were often motivated by greed for "blood money," private vendetta, or hope of pardon for the arresting person's own crime.[6]

The development of arrest law was probably also influenced by the post arrest predicament of the arrested person in early England. Persons charged with serious offenses were rarely admitted to bail and conditions in the jails of the time were horrible. Jails were run as a private business and fees were charged for the most elementary "privileges." Those persons arrested who did not have the means to purchase better accommodations were huddled together, often in irons, in dark, filthy, rooms and in close proximity to depravity and disease. Under such conditions, an arrest could be, and often was, equivalent to a death sentence.[7]

The concept of the individual citizen as a law enforcer is not merely of interest to medieval scholars; it is very much alive in some parts of the United States today. For example, the State of Texas completely revised its Code of Criminal Procedure in 1965, and this "modern" code provided the individual citizen with exactly the same authority to make arrests without warrant as the authority granted to the peace officer, with one exception.[8]

It is part of our judicial heritage that courts do not determine abstract questions of law. Therefore, field interrogation situations which are decided by courts usually are cast in the context of a situation where the field interrogation has in fact played a part in an arrest, a subsequent charge, and a trial. Furthermore, the discussion of field interrogation practices then arises under a motion to suppress, an objection to the introduction of evidence, or a discussion of the existence or nonexistence of probable cause to make the arrest.[9] Unfortunately, at least at the trial court level, the prosecutor is usually faced with meeting the defense attorney on these grounds and attempting to convince the court that: (a) probable cause for an arrest did exist, or (b) the evidence in issue was obtained prior to the time that an arrest occurred. The crucial questions in field interrogation suffer from being presented in this light.

In the first place, in most field contacts, probable cause, in a classic sense, does not exist. The traditional elements of probable cause are (1) that the peace officer knows a specific crime has been committed and (2) that

---

[6]"Salt Lake City Police Practice," *Utah L. Rev.,* at 595.

[7]*Ibid.*

[8]*Tex. Ann. Code of Crim. Proc.* Ch. 14 (1965). This exception provided that peace officers could only make arrests for felonies which did not occur in their presence if (a) the peace officer were informed by a credible person that an individual committed a felony, (b) that the person so accused was attempting to escape, and (c) that there is no time to procure a warrant. *See* Art. 14.04.

[9]LaFave, "Detention For Investigation By The Police: An Analysis Of Current Practice," 1962 *Wash. U. L. Q.* 360.

the peace officer has probable cause to believe that a specific individual has committed the specific crime.[10] If these elements are present, then the officer would more than likely simply arrest the individual, charge him, and there would be no field interrogation problem. As a result, the line is usually drawn on the rather artful definition of what is an arrest; the defense attorney naturally insists that the arrest occurred at the very instant the person was stopped and the prosecution insists with equal vigor that the arrest occurred at some nonspecific time after the individual was approached by the peace officer. With very few exceptions the courts tend to fall into this definitional trap. Therefore, we have numerous courts which hold that the slightest interference with a person's freedom of movement is an "arrest,"[11] and a large number of other decisions which define an arrest as "the taking into custody a person so that he may answer for a crime."[12] Thus, the critical issues involved in the practice of field interrogation are obscured by the semantic battle over the definition of "arrest."

Neither of these definitions reaches the essential issues which are involved in the field interrogation. Each of these definitions tends to beg the question, and a court's decision automatically follows from its choice of definition. To say that a peace officer must have probable cause to make an arrest at the very first instant where a citizen's full freedom of locomotion is impeded in any way can lead to some fantastic results. For example: let us assume that an officer is informed that a person has just been killed in a particular room in a particular building. The officer rushes in and finds it full of people. Most people would be willing to concede, at this point, that the officer has probable cause to believe that a crime has been committed; however, he has absolutely no idea that any specific person in this room has committed the crime. It would follow then that the officer must stand there totally helpless while the people in the room with the dead body silently file out, leaving eventually no one left but one confused and frustrated police officer and one dead body.

On the other hand, the definition of arrest as the taking of a person into custody to answer for a crime can lead to some equally fantastic results. This latter definition, if applied logically, would authorize an officer to take people into custody and theoretically detain them for an unknown length of time. There would be no arrest unless the officer's purpose in taking the individual was to charge him with a crime. The odious "dragnet" fits very comfortably in this latter definition.[13] In addition, this latter definition of arrest makes the determination of whether or not an arrest has occurred

---

[10]6 C.J.S. "Arrest," §6G(2) 587.

[11]Barrett, "Police Practices And The Law—From Arrest To Release Or Charge," 50 *Cal. L. Rev.* 32 (1962).

[12]Perkins, "The Law of Arrest," 25 *Iowa L. Rev.* 201 (1940).

[13]100 *U. Pa. L. Rev.* 1186 (1952).

resolve around the subjective intent of a police officer. It is submitted that the officer's subjective intent is not a particularly desirable point at which to determine such a crucial question of an arrest, even when it is mitigated by the general rule that the officer's intent can be determined from extraneous evidence and is not dependent solely upon his word as to what was his intent.

It is the author's suggestion that the very critical question involving individual liberties and protection of society against crime are not served by leaning on artificial and obscure definitions.

Another reason for the lack of legislative and judicial attention to the question of field interrogation is the simple fact that such attention was irrelevant in the many jurisdictions which did not have an exclusionary rule, and where a person who was unlawfully detained or arrested had no remedy other than a theoretical cause of action against the arresting officer for false arrest or false imprisonment. However, recent decisions by the Supreme Court of the United States, especially in the cases of *Mapp v. Ohio*,[14] *Miranda v. Arizona*,[15] and *Wong Sun v. United States*[16] have made the initial contact between the police officer and the citizen not only relevant, but in many situations critical.

Prior to any further discussions relating to field interrogation it is necessary that we examine the Constitution of the United States with relation to the right of an individual to be free from arrest. After all, if the Constitution requires that no individual can be detained in any manner unless the officer has classic probable cause to make an arrest without a warrant, then any future discussion of balancing of public interest with individual rights is irrelevant. The Fourth Amendment to the United States Constitution reads as follows:

> The right of the people to be secure in their persons, houses, papers and effects, against unreasonable searches and seizures, shall not be violated, and no warrants shall issue, but upon probable cause, supported by oath or affirmation, and particularly describing the place to be searched, and the persons or things to be seized.

It seems clear that the framers of this particular amendment did not have in mind arrest and searches as we think of them today. Historically, the framers of the Constitution placed the Fourth Amendment in the Bill of Rights to prohibit general warrants and writs of assistance.[17] The writs of assistance were widely used and abused in the thirteen colonies. They

[14]367 U.S. 643 (1961).

[15]384 U.S. 436 (1966).

[16]371 U.S. 471 (1963).

[17]Leagre, "The Fourth Amendment And The Law Of Arrest," 54 *J. Crim. L.,* C. & P.S. 393, 396-397 (1963).

were writs which authorized the officers to search anywhere at anytime for contraband. Furthermore, these writs were for an indefinite period of time, usually for the life of the sovereign who was then reigning.[18] At one point in the drafting of the Fourth Amendment it only contained the latter portion, which spoke specifically of warrants. The insertion of the first part of the amendment against "unreasonable searches and seizures" probably was not intended to impose additional standards, but to serve merely as a preface to the prohibition of general warrants.[19] However, there seems little doubt that the Supreme Court has, and probably correctly so, given life and meaning to the first portion of the Fourth Amendment by interpreting the amendment to carry an overriding requirement of "reasonableness" to the entire field.[20]

In the process of imposing this penumbra of reasonableness to searches and seizures the Court has also emasculated the rather simplistic argument that the Constitution prohibits only unreasonable searches and seizures; that a reasonable search is constitutional. This type of argument is invalid, or more accurately a simple truism, because it overlooks the fact that "unreasonable" as applied to searches and seizures is a word of art and has, over the decades, obtained a specific legal meaning over and above the meaning as applied in general usage.

It should be noted at this point that the Fourth Amendment does not use the word "arrest" at all. Instead it uses the word "seizure" which is, in effect, much broader than the word "arrest." Few people would argue that no person could ever be "seized" in the sense of being detained unless "probable cause" existed. We have many examples of this outside of the criminal field. A quarantine to protect the community from contagious disease,[21] the picking up of a lost child on the streets, the detention of a person who is entering the United States from a foreign country or the restraint of a person who is attempting to commit suicide are all examples of detentions which are "reasonable" but which do not involve an arrest.[22]

One may well wonder how the whole concept of "probable cause" arose to apply to situations where an officer stops a person on the street for the purpose of investigating a crime. Apparently, the rationale runs something like this: (1) the Fourth Amendment states that no warrant shall issue but upon probable cause particularly describing the person to be seized; (2) this applies to warrants of arrest as well as search warrants; and (3) obviously the standard required to arrest a person without a warrant must be at least as high as the standard required to arrest a person with a warrant.

---

[18] *Ibid.* at 397.
[19] *Ibid.* at 397-398.
[20] *Ibid.* at 399.
[21] Waite, "The Law Of Arrest," 24 *Tex. L. Rev.* 279 (1946).
[22] Leagre, "The Fourth Amendment" at 406-407.

Thus we have reached the rather ironic situation in which a constitutional provision which was originally designed to prohibit governmental authorities from ransacking houses and personal effects anytime they wanted to has now been interpreted, by some persons at least, to also prohibit police officers from stopping an individual who, at 2:00 in the morning, breaks and runs at the first sight of a patrol car.

Arrest Versus Detention

At this point we will deepen our inquiry and ask some of the more fundamental questions which arise when a police officer stops a citizen on the street. Basically, the issues boil down to the following questions: Is there any significant difference between a detention and an arrest? If there are valid distinctions, are there sufficient policy reasons to recognize and authorize the police to draw their own distinctions between detention and arrest?

First, let us ask ourselves just what happens to a person who is placed under "arrest," regardless of exactly how the word is defined or exactly when the arrest occurs. Let us assume that a person is walking down a street in a city and a peace officer, with more than adequate probable cause, approaches and places him under arrest. The individual is very probably searched on the spot, and then taken to a police station where he is booked on some charge. He may be interrogated at this point if he waives his right to counsel, as required by *Miranda v. Arizona,* and even if he is not interrogated, he is placed in jail unless he makes bond. He is given the opportunity to have a preliminary hearing to determine whether or not there is "probable cause" to hold him pending indictment or other procedure to bring him to trial. If such probable cause exists, he either remains in jail, or out on bond, until he is tried by a judge or a jury. At this point he is found guilty or innocent of the crime as charged and he is either released or retaken into custody. Let us further assume that this particular individual is not guilty of the crime with which he is charged and he is released after a not guilty finding by the trier of fact.

On the other hand, let us take a situation where a person is "detained." In this circumstance he is stopped on the street, usually asked to identify himself and give some explanation of what he has been doing and his movements in the neighborhood. He may even be required to stand by while the officer investigating or detaining him checks with the police station to see if he is wanted. There might possibly even be a further detention while witnesses to a crime attempt to identify him. If the individual is under suspicion of committing a major crime and he has an alibi he might even be taken to the police station and held there until his alibi can be checked. Under many circumstances he will probably be searched to a greater or lesser extent. We will assume once again that the individual is innocent of the crime, if any, of which he is suspected and that he is released from his detention.

It cannot be too strongly emphasized at this point that we are not discussing the detention of a person that a police officer picks up at random. In all cases relating to field interrogation or detention we are assuming that the police officer has certain facts which draw his attention to the individual being detained or interrogated in the field, but these facts fall short of classic probable cause to make an arrest. The author knows of no responsible authority who advocates authorizing police officers to pick a citizen at random off the street, detain him, interrogate him or confine him in any way unless there were some circumstances which set this particular individual apart from the general public.

In order to make this latter point especially clear, perhaps it would be best to outline the type of situation which the author is speaking about when he uses the word detention. A good example occurred while the author was serving as Police Legal Advisor to the Police Department of the City of Corpus Christi, Texas and was one in which he specifically suggested that the officers detain a person without making an arrest. The circumstances of the detention were as follows: At 1:00 A.M., an individual knocked on the door of a citizen and asked if this particular citizen could spare a bandage. The person who knocked on the door was bleeding rather profusely from a cut of unknown origin on his hand. The homeowner, who was a city official, called the police and reported the incident while his wife obtained a bandage for the injured person. When a patrol car approached the house, two persons, not counting the injured party, were sitting out in front in an automobile. As soon as the patrol car came into view, the two individuals, both young males, drove off at a high rate of speed. They got approximately three-fourths of a block when they were stopped by another patrol car coming from the other direction. The type of clothing worn by these three young men and the type of car they were driving rather clearly indicated that they did not live in the neighborhood in which they were found. When questioned separately, the individuals gave at least two names to the police officers and came up with three conflicting stories as to what they were doing at this particular place and at this particular time of night. None of the persons would give any information as to how the injured individual cut his hand. All three of the persons were held on the street for approximately 30 minutes while the police officers checked with headquarters to determine whether or not any crime, such as burglary, had occurred that night to the knowledge of the police department in which a person suffered a cut on the hand. While this check was being conducted, another patrol car examined two nearby schools which were the source of frequent cases of burglary or vandalism. Neither the check by the patrol car nor the check through headquarters indicated that these particular people had been involved in any specific crime. The young men were permitted to leave after they had identified themselves finally to the satisfaction of the patrolmen and after the injured party had been given first aid. It should be noted that all three of these individuals were distinctly held against their will, although no force was necessary, and it should be further noted that the officers at the scene had no "probable cause" to make an arrest for a specific crime.

This type of detention apparently meets the approval of a rather significant majority of commentators. A relatively recent article states:

> The stop, contrasted with an arrest, is relatively short, less conspicuous, and less humiliating to the person stopped and offers much less chance for police coercion. Moreover the attempts to apply a single standard of probable cause to all interferences is likely to lead to a standard either so diluted that the individual is not adequately protected or so strict that much apparently reasonable police investigation is unlawful.[23]

Professor Wayne R. La Fave has asked a number of extremely pertinent questions relating to field interrogations. He asks whether it makes any difference that the field interrogation typically results in a much shorter period of detention than an actual arrest. Does it make any difference that the suspect will not have an arrest record, or that the suspect will not consider himself under arrest? He also inquires whether or not the person subjected to field interrogation has suffered as much damage to his reputation as an actual arrest. He apparently concludes that there is a good deal of difference between a detention and an arrest and he observes, "A conversation with a policeman on the street corner is not likely to be mistaken by the public as an arrest as is the actual taking of the suspect to the station for further questioning."[24]

Another writer has observed that "The London Police, who have been proclaimed as models for American police agencies, have been stopping several hundred thousand people a year and asking to see the contents of bags they are carrying or inquiring as to the possession of other property which might have been stolen."[25]

Still another author goes to the extreme of postulating the proposition that a policeman's authority to conduct a field interrogation is in reality an exercise of the detained individual's affirmative right to be given an opportunity to be heard before he is arrested.[26] Presumably this "right" is based

---

[23]Recent Statute, 78 *Harv. L. Rev.* 473, 474-75 (1964).

[24]LaFave, "Detention for Investigation" at 364.

[25]Ronayne, "The Right To Investigate and New York's 'Stop And Frisk' Law," 33 *Fordham L. Rev.* 211, 214 (1964).

[26]Perkins, "Law Of Arrest" at 261.

on some sort of free speech rationale rather than on the more familiar right to remain silent as contained in the Fifth Amendment.[27]

Even among the writers who belittle the distinction between arrest and detention there is usually a concession that there is a difference in (a) the limitation on the length of a detention, (b) the lack of an arrest record, and (c) the fact that the detained person can truthfully answer "no" if asked if he has even been arrested. This latter element is becoming more and more important in our society today when individuals must fill out all types of forms, many of which ask questions relating to the person's "police record." However, the suggestion that there is a valid distinction between an arrest and a detention in fact, if not in law, does not mean to imply that an interrogation, no matter how short, by a police officer on the street is totally innocuous. When a person is stopped on the street and asked questions by a police officer there is undoubtedly a good deal of pressure on this individual to respond to the police officer's questions. After all, what are a person's alternatives when he is faced with the situation where he is the subject of a field interrogation? In practice, he has only five alternatives: (1) he can confess to a crime, (2) he can offer his identification and give plausible reasons for being present and give an explanation of his recent movements, (3) he can attempt to flee, (4) he can tell a lie, or (5) he can refuse to answer any questions at all. To a thoughtful person a confession or flight are obviously out of the question. This conduct will only tend to confirm the police officer's original suspicion, whatever that may have been, which caused the officer to single the person out in the first place. This, in effect, leaves a person only three alternatives: cooperate, refuse to answer any question, or lie.

Regardless of the legal effect of a refusal to answer, the practical effect of such a refusal will be to confirm an officer's suspicion. A lie is dangerous because it can be used as a factor in probable cause to make an arrest if it is detected and will, at least, heighten the officer's suspicion. Thus, as a practical matter, a person detained has no satisfactory alternative but to identify himself and attempt to convince the police officer that he is an upstanding citizen with nothing to fear from the law.

By way of summary then, what are the distinctions between a detention and an arrest? First, the detention or custody is limited. It is true that in some rare instances field interrogation or field detention will go beyond the few minutes which it normally takes. However, even at its most extreme, a field detention is likely not to take anywhere near the time that a formal arrest will consume. We must bear in mind that a traditional arrest usually

---

[27]For additional authorities which generally support some type of field detention, see 37 *Mich. L. Rev.* 311 (1938); "The Law Of Arrest: Constitutionality Of Detention and Frisk Acts," 59 *Nw. U.L. Rev.* 641 (1964); 28 *Va. L. Rev.* 315 (1942); 14 *Syracuse L. Rev.* 505.

carries with it a processing period during which the individual under arrest is fingerprinted, has his picture taken and is usually interrogated unless he refuses to answer any questions. Of course, almost every state requires that the individual be released on bond or taken "immediately" before a magistrate. But the bond procedure can consume 30 to 45 minutes, counting the time that the person under arrest gets in touch with a bondsman and has all of the papers signed.

Secondly, a person who is subjected to a field detention and a field interrogation does not have on his record, which will be with him for the rest of his life, the fact that he has been charged with a crime. In most states a person who is arrested, no matter how capriciously, is still saddled with that vague and indefinable thing which scares employers away—a "police record." The individual has this albatross hanging around his neck regardless of the outcome of his trial—even though he may be totally exonerated and even collect damages from the peace officer who illegally arrested him. It is true that some police departments maintain informal or "nonofficial" records of field interrogations which they feel will be significant in the future. But this is an entirely different process than the maintenance of an official arrest record.

Thirdly, since a detained person has virtually no idea that he has in fact been "arrested," in spite of some courts' definitions, he can truthfully answer "no" to the inevitable question, "Have you ever been arrested or convicted of any crime other than a traffic offense?"

Finally, we must consider the detained person's reputation. It is almost inconceivable that a person who has been the subject of a field interrogation does any significant damage to his reputation when his friends and neighbors see him talking to a police officer on the street corner. Any damage to reputation under such circumstances is certainly far less than the damage which might occur if these same friends and neighbors saw the individual being taken off, handcuffed, in the back seat of a police car. This difference in damage to reputation is particularly important if the crime under investigation is one involving extreme emotional reactions from the neighborhood, such as child-molesting, homosexual activity, or the like.

The fact that the actual distinction between an arrest and a detention is a real distinction is a far cry from saying that the distinction is significant enough to treat the arrest differently from the field interrogation in terms of public policy. One of the most vigorous foes of field interrogation and detention is Professor Caleb Foote.[28] Although he laces his works with a great deal of emotionalism, he nevertheless makes some points which can hardly be ignored. He challenges, to begin with, the necessity for any type

---

[28]See Foote, "The Fourth Amendment: Obstacle Or Necessity In The Law Of Arrest?" in *Police Power and Individual Freedom* (Sowle ed. 1962).

of general detention statute or practice which is separate from the traditional law of arrest. And, as might be suspected, he insists that arrest is "an actual restraint of the person to be arrested,"[29] which occurs at the moment an individual is no longer a free agent to do as he pleases.

Professor Foote insists that we do not have enough information to determine the necessity of field interrogation. He states: "Factual assumptions made about police arrest practices today necessarily rest upon political philosophy or armchair speculation seasoned with scattered and unreliable statistics, isolated studies, personal experiences or undocumented police claims." He is, of course, correct that criminal law, especially as it involves the work of the police officer on the street, has suffered and is still suffering from a gross lack of concrete, reliable data. But the social sciences cannot remain static because our methods of information-gathering do not fit in the admirable and convincing matrix which the physical sciences have managed to develop.

Professor Foote argues that the need for field interrogation and detention would disappear if we have more and better trained police officers. He states:

> The chief disadvantages of these alternatives are that they cost money and require the exercise of political and administrative statesmanship whereas enacting new arrest laws offers the illusion of doing something about crime without financial or political complications and has a natural appeal to political expediency. I suspect that in police work, as elsewhere, one generally gets no more than he pays for, and that legislation of police power is a wholly inadequate substitute for responsible police fiscal and personnel policy.
>
> The importance of seeking alternatives within the present legal framework is emphasized when one examines the impact of police arrest practices upon our constitutional respect for privacy. The right to be let alone—to be able to sit in one's own house or drive one's own car or walk the streets without unwarranted police instrusion—is surely one of the most important factors to be weighed in achieving a balance between individual liberty and public necessity. Ironically, it is this factor about which we know the least. Although we are often inadequate, we collect at least some data on the number of crimes reported, the number of crimes cleared by arrest and the mortality between charge and conviction. We also have figures purporting to state the number of persons arrested but usually this only reflects cases where the police have booked, fingerprinted and charged the suspect. We cannot even guess at the true arrest rate because we have no data on the number of people whose liberty is restrained but who after investigation are released without charge. Under these circumstances to try to make an intelligent evaluation of how the right of privacy fares under present conditions and how proposed changes in the law would affect it is very much like trying to

---

[29] *Ibid.* at 30.

compute batting averages when one knows only the number of hits for each player but has no data on the number of times at bat.[30]

Professor Foote sidesteps the problems of the hypothetical emergency situation, such as the right of the police to temporarily detain a person found near a fresh corpse, by stating: "Whatever the law may be in such situations, the reasonableness of the police action is conditioned by an immediate crisis and would have no general application."[31] Then he refers to Mr. Justice Jackson's dissenting opinion in the case of *Brinegar v. United States,*[32] where the Justice appears to approve of a situation in which police officers might throw a roadblock around a neighborhood and search every outgoing car when this is "the only way to save a threatened life and detect a vicious crime," whereas he would disapprove of "a roadblock and universal search to salvage a few bottles of bourbon and catch a bootlegger." The fact that Professor Foote himself draws a distinction between emergency situations and everyday police problems seems to be flatly contradictory to his position that the Constitution permits only one single standard of probable cause. Once it is admitted that a police officer may take certain steps in an "emergency" situation, but that the officer may not take the same steps in a "non-emergency" situation, it is obvious that the authority of the police officer to arrest or detain a person depends on the type, degree, or even existence of an emergency. Therefore, the whole scope of the inquiry ceases to be whether or not the officer has the authority to detain a person, but rather the essential question is—under what type of "emergency" circumstances may an officer detain a person?

One engaged in library research in the field of police detention is struck by the fact that there is almost no dialogue between the persons who want to strictly limit the policeman's authority to detain a person and those advocates of broadening the officer's authority to make a detention. There are numerous articles, of course, but they are in effect monologues which are, this author suspects, largely directed at people who have already become convinced. In other words, the scholarly debaters are simply not speaking the same language at all.[33]

Those authors who tend to advocate broadening a policeman's authority to detain a person usually stress the "practicalities" of on-the-spot police work. They can point to numerous situations where reasonableness and common sense would dictate that a police officer make a detention, but where the circumstances are such that the officer would normally be beyond his authority in making such a detention. These advocates usually fail to

---

[30] *Ibid.* at 33.
[31] *Ibid.* at 35.
[32] 338 U.S. 160 (1949).
[33] Compare 12 *Okla. L. Rev.* 154 (1959) with 12 *Okla. L. Rev.* 160 (1959).

come to grips with the legal and constitutional issues which are involved in any exercise of authority by a police officer in the field other than to say, perhaps, "well, the Constitution of the United States only prohibits unreasonable searches and seizures and therby permits searches and seizures which are reasonable."

On the other hand, those individuals who advocate strictly limiting a police officer's power tend to avoid concrete discussions of hypothetical, or even real, situations where a police officer could be expected to act "reasonably" and use good common sense. These advocates prefer instead to discuss the legalistic issues involved and to become enmeshed in esoteric discussions of "arrest" and "probable cause."

What is too often overlooked is that no constitutional right, privilege or guarantee is absolute. The whole idea of law, as a decisional process, is an attempt to apply certain principles to everyday life to the extent that they are meaningful and pliable. The task of building Utopias is left to the philosopher. The task of the working lawyer is to develop certain principles and practices which will guarantee the maximum of public order and crime prevention and at the same time permit the maximum of constitutional freedoms to the individual citizen.

Specific Issues

So far, the problem of field detention and interrogation have been discussed in somewhat general terms. It would be useful, now, to examine some of the more narrow and specific issues which will arise in a field interrogation or detention situation.

Use of Force

One of the issues which courts and legislatures have been particularly reluctant to face is the question of what force, if any, a police officer should be authorized to use in a detention less than an arrest. Neither the Uniform Arrest Act nor the "Stop and Frisk" law of New York mention the question of force. Very few courts have been faced with this question, since experience seems to show that only an infinitesimal group of people attempt to resist a mere street stop. Furthermore, it is this author's very firm suspicion, based on two years' on-the-street work and observation with police departments, that in those rare instances where the police must use force in what would ordinarily be a field detention situation, the officer has a tendency to take the position that he approached the resisting individual initially for the purpose of making an arrest, usually for some vagrancy type offense.

However, the fact that the use of force in a field detention situation is seldom clearly placed in issue during the course of trial does not mean that the question of force is not an important one to which we should address our attention. About the only legislative enactments, in the criminal law area, which specifically deal with force are the merchant detention statutes designed to combat shoplifting. In addition, the provision of the American Law Institute's Code of Pre-Arraignment Procedure, which has not been enacted by any state, also clearly faces the issue of force in a field interrogation or detention context. Both the ALI code and the typical merchant detention statute state that the person who is detaining or stopping an individual may use all reasonable force short of deadly force.

It is quite understandable why legislatures and courts are loathe to face the issue of force. A field detention, virtually by definition, is the stopping of a person when there is no probable cause to believe the person who is the subject of the stop has committed a crime. It seems rather extreme, therefore, to authorize a police officer to forcefully wrestle with an individual and perhaps handcuff him for the purpose of asking that individual his name and address and what he has been doing.

Some writers evade the issue of force by stating that all the police officer is doing is walking up and asking a person a question in much the same way a private individual would do. Therefore, the implication is that the police officer is doing no more than any other individual could do, thus the question of force, if not irrelevant, tends to fade away. In other words, if A, a private citizen, stops B on street and asks of him directions to the bus station, it is quite possible that B would simply continue on his way without answering at all. A would probably classify B as an extremely rude person; however, we simply do not consider the question of how much force A may be permitted to use against B in order to obtain an answer to his question because force, in such a context, is simply unthinkable. Therefore, to equate a police officer with the private citizen in a field detention situation is to lose touch with reality.

The author has observed more than 400 field stops in two different states and he has never seen a situation where force has been necessary. It is almost inconceivable that the type of questions which were asked during these field stops, and some of the questions were rather searching, would have been tolerated by the detained person unless they were being asked by a police officer. The only conclusion which can be drawn from these observations is that the presence of a police officer, no matter how pleasant his demeanor, implies the potential use of force—force at least to effectuate the stop if not to compel the answers.

Another method of evading the question of force in a detention situation is to take the position that any force used was, in fact, for some purpose other than detaining an individual. An excellent example of this technique is found in the case of *High v. State*.[34] In this case the police officers were

---

[34]217 S.W. 2d 774 (Tenn. 1949).

informed by a passing motorist that a disturbance was taking place at a certain location. The officers rushed to the location and saw a car driving away with one person in it. They stopped the car and found that the driver was intoxicated. There was apparently no evidence, such as erratic driving, to indicate that the driver was intoxicated prior to the time he was stopped by the officers. The Supreme Court of Tennessee upheld the conviction for driving while intoxicated. It held that the stopping of the automobile was not a technical arrest and that the officers simply stopped the car for the purpose of quelling the disturbance of which they had been informed and found that the driver was intoxicated. The court rather unimaginatively overlooked the fact that there was no disturbance to quell at the time the officers stopped the car and, as a matter of fact, no disturbance ever took place in the presence of the officers other, perhaps, than the disturbance which may have occurred during the course of taking the driver into custody for the offense of driving while intoxicated.

The only case to face the issue of force squarely is *Cannon v. State.*[35] In this case the defendant followed a woman to her house and accused her of speeding while she had been driving an automobile. The defendant was obviously drunk. Two officers arrived and took the defendant, against his will, to the police station for an intoxication test. He apparently failed the test and was charged with driving while intoxicated. It was the theory of the state that he was not placed under arrest until after he had failed his test for intoxication and that the intervening detention was authorized by Delaware's version of the Uniform Arrest Act. The defendant contended that the detention statute did not authorize the use of force and contemplated only voluntary detention. The Delaware Supreme Court, without much discussion, rejected such a contention out of hand. The court held that such a construction of Delaware's detention statute would make the statute meaningless.

It is obvious that the Delaware Supreme Court in the *Cannon* case articulated the proper rule of law. It is admittedly offensive to contemplate force being used against a private citizen when the private citizen is not being placed under arrest based on probable cause. The necessity of force will occur in extremely rare instances in the field detention context. But even so we should face the fact that a field detention authorization must carry with it the right of the officer to use force in making a detention. If such authorization is not present then we have not given the officer the tool which he needs to gain the maximum benefit from a field detention and interrogation authority. Indeed, a detention statute without the right to use force may lead to a situation where the general public, which has relatively little to fear with or from a field detention statute, will be subjected to being

---

[35]168 A. 2d 108 (Del. 1961).

stopped and questioned, but the small corps of criminals at whom the detention statute is primarily aimed, will have no reason to fear it since they know they will not be required to pay any attention to the officer when he approaches them. This would lead to the further result that the general public would be limited in their freedom and there would be no corresponding gain to society as a whole.

Privilege Against Self-Incrimination

Another issue involved in a field detention and interrogation is the question of the detainee's right not to answer the questions on the basis that the answers might incriminate him. There seems to be absolutely no question that a person who is subjected to a field interrogation cannot be required to answer questions of an incriminatory nature. Any other interpretation of a statutory or common law right of field detention would be squarely contrary to the Fifth Amendment's protection aginst self-incrimination. However, there does seem to be some question as to the effect of a person's refusal to answer the police officer's question. This question is usually framed in the context of whether or not the refusal to answer questions can be taken into consideration as one of the factors or elements in determining probable cause to make an arrest for a specific offense.

It has been held that flight from an officer to avoid answering questions can be a factor in determining probable cause.[36] By the same token, contradictory stories given in rapid succession, and obvious lies can also be taken into consideration in determining probable cause.[37] Chief Justice Traynor of the California Supreme Court stated, as dictum, in the case of *People v. Simon*[38] that "there is, of course, nothing unreasonable in an officer's questioning persons outdoors at night [citing authorities] and it is possible that in some circumstances even a refusal to answer would, in the light of other evidence, justify an arrest." There are, of course, other authorities that do not agree; they state that an exercise of a person's privilege against self-incrimination cannot be used as a factor in determining probable cause.

The only provision of the ALI's Model Code of Pre-Arraignment Procedure which was specifically rejected was the provision which would permit a failure to comply with an obligation imposed by the code to be used in determining probable cause for an arrest. It was the intention of the drafters, as shown by the commentary accompanying the draft, to permit the refusal to answer authorized questions by police officers to be used as a factor in determining probable cause.

---

[36]See Scurlock, "Arrest In Missouri," 29 *U. Kan. City L. Rev.* 117, 125 (1961).
[37]*State v. Hedman,* 130 N.W. 2d 628 (Minn. 1964).
[38]290 P. 2d 531 (Cal. 1955).

States which have adopted the Uniform Arrest Act provide that any person, questioned by an officer, who fails to identify himself or explain his actions to the satisfaction of the officer may be detained further for a period of detention not to exceed two hours. The statutory wording seems to indicate quite clearly that a refusal to answer the officer's questions, even on the basis of a privilege of self-incrimination, could result in the individual being taken to the police station and held there until he does answer the officer's questions or until two hours expire. However, research does not reveal any case with that specific holding. In fact, no cases from the states which have adopted the Uniform Arrest Act have been found which even discuss the effect of a failure to answer the officer's questions.

There is authority for the proposition, of course, that while the Constitution does not require a person to incriminate himself, the Constitution does not state that the exercise of the privilege cannot be used for any other purpose.[39] Recent decisions of the Supreme Court seem to indicate that the purposes for which an invocation of the privilege against self-incrimination are used have been severely limited, although the court has not overruled the above stated principle in its entirety.[40] Nevertheless, the court has been especially alert and sensitive to any situation in which the use of the privilege against self-incrimination could be interpreted as an admission of guilt.[41] It would seem, therefore, that the use of the privilege against self-incrimination in a context where a detained person refuses to answer any of the officer's questions would fall in the "admission of guilt" category and be held to be constitutionally protected; in other words, a refusal to answer questions during field interrogation cannot be used as a factor in determining subsequent probable cause to make an arrest.

Thus far we have been discussing a situation in which a detained person refuses to answer any of the police officer's questions, except perhaps for name and address. A different conclusion might be reached if a detained person answered most of the officer's questions but refused to answer certain questions relating to a specific subject. Under such circumstances, if the officer considered refusal to answer a portion of his questions in his determination of probable cause to make an arrest, his determination might be upheld. True, he would be implying that the detainee was admitting guilt by his refusal to answer certain questions and would therefore be subject to the previously outlined constitutional objections. On the other hand, such conduct on the part of the detained individual might come closer to the "contradictory or evasive answer" category which has been recognized as a factor in probable cause.

---

[39]See *Konigsberg* v. *State Bar of California*, 353 U.S. 232 (1957); *Orloff* v. *Willoughby*, 345 U.S. 83 (1953) and *Kimm* v. *Rosenberg*, 363 U.S. 405 (1960).

[40]*Garrity* v. *New Jersey*, 385 U.S. 493 (1967); *Spevack* v. *Klein*, 385 U.S. 511 (1967).

[41]*Siochower* v. *Board* 350 U.S. 551 (1956).

The field research did not disclose a single instance where a detained person absolutely refused to answer any of the police officer's questions. On those rather rare instances when answers were refused, the subject matter usually did not involve probability of a crime, but rather third persons whom the detainee preferred not to name. Most instances of refusal occurred when the officer asked the detainee where he had been and he replied that he had been to see his girlfriend. When the officer would inquire as to her name and address, presumably for the purpose of verification, the detained individual would refuse to answer, perhaps out of chivalry or perhaps out of wisdom.

It is the author's opinion that an officer who has so little probable cause to make an arrest that the refusal of a person to answer his questions will swing the decision one way or the other, in all likelihood has a pretty weak arrest to begin with. A reviewing court would probably find "insufficient probable cause" without a detailed and careful examination of the constitutional issues involved. It is also the author's conclusion, based upon field research, that a person who answers questions with extreme reluctance almost invariably attracts the full attention of the questioning officer to the extent that the officer starts attempting to find probable cause to make an arrest. Even when probable cause is not found, the person who answered the questions evasively or with extreme reluctance can almost certainly be assured that he will be under some type of surveillance. The time and duration of this surveillance will, of course, depend on numerous circumstances. Therefore, even if a refusal to answer the officer's questions does not constitute probable cause for an immediate arrest, such refusal to answer is seldom to the detainee's advantage.

Length of Detention

The length of a field detention is an issue of particularly vital importance. Various statutory enactments permit a detention for any period of time ranging from twenty minutes, in the case of the ALI Code of Pre-Arraignment Procedure, to two hours in the case of the Uniform Arrest Act. Other statutes, such as New York's "Stop and Frisk" Act, and the common law right to field detention, do not contain any specific time period for the detention. Presumably cases falling in the latter category could result in a detention for a "reasonable" period of time.

In discussing the length of detention, the conflicting balance of values is rather obvious. On one hand, it is quite obvious that a field detention is especially capable of police abuse. In addition, those persons who advocate a field detention of some type stress the fact that the invasion of a person's right to free mobility is so slight as to justify the use of field detention as a law enforcement tool. On the other hand, if the length of detention is made so short as to dilute the effectiveness of such a detention as a law enforcement aid, then very little has been gained by authorizing such detention.

One argument against having any specific period of detention named at all is that any time limit set by a statutory enactment will be considered by the officer as the usual length of time which he can detain a person and, therefore, there will be a tendency for officers to detain persons for the maximum period of time even when the use of this maximum period of time is not necessary. This conduct on the part of the police officer would, in the author's opinion, be especially true in those cases where the officer, by virtue of his experience and "street wisdom," feels intuitively that the individual he is detaining has committed some crime, but the officer just can't quite "pin anything on him." On the other hand, the phrase "for a reasonable period of time" can be interpreted many ways under certain circumstances. This might result in a field detention statute being used as an excuse for a general investigative custody for a number of hours. Such a use would, of course, be contrary to the general purpose of field interrogation statutes which are primarily designed to authorize the police officer to obtain the name, address and explanation of actions from the individual who has been stopped. Naturally there will be some cases where the officer, using reasonableness and common sense, will desire to detain a person for a more protracted length of time pending a further investigation. However, the field research done by the author, coupled with his field experience, indicate that the need for an extended detention is an extremely rare event. This field research and subsequent experience, which will be described in some detail hereafter, indicate that the vast majority of field detentions consume less than six minutes. Indeed, the only field detention observed by the author which exceeded thirty minutes occurred in the City of Chicago when the police department's highly touted computer broke down and, as a result, an individual was detained for almost an hour until the clerical staff at headquarters could determine whether or not the detained person was wanted for an offense. He was.

Any detention statute should have a maximum length of detention expressed therein and that length of detention should be approximately thirty minutes. Such a period of time would be sufficient to cover the overwhelming majority of situations in which a field detention would be desirable. In addition, the existence of a thirty-minute time limit would clearly indicate to the officer that the statute is designed to permit only the most minor of detentions and is not to be used as an excuse to take a person into custody while an investigation is in process. A thirty-minute time period would also tend to cancel out those situations where the individual police officer, for one reason or another, decided to hold a detained person for the full time alloted by the statute. Even where this abuse does occur, a detention for a half-hour is a relatively minor invasion of a person's general right to free locomotion.

Exclusionary Rule

The vexing question always arises regarding what remedy would be available if a person has been detained beyond the thirty-minute maximum time period advocated in this article. For example, though no exclusionary rule governing violations of the ALI twenty minute limitation has yet been drafted, conceivably the drafters could take the position that *all* evidence obtained during the stop—that taken before the expiration of twenty minutes as well as that taken thereafter—should be excluded because the stop, considered as a whole, was illegal. This would be, to say the least, a most unfortunate and, indeed, unfair rule. We would then have a situation where the search of a person, which almost always occurs very early in the stop, would result in the discovery of legally admissible evidence, but if the detained person gave a prolonged explanation regarding his conduct or his possession of the contraband, then this evidence, which was originally valid and admissible, would, at the 21st minute of detention, suddenly become inadmissible. Such a "now you see it, now you don't" rule of exclusion is unnecessary, impractical, and logically inconsistent. An exclusionary rule which covered only those items discovered as a result of a search *after* the maximum period of detention had elapsed might be acceptable, but evidence obtained as the result of the search during the permissible time period should be admissible, regardless of subsequent circumstances. If the officer exceeds the period of detention, such violations of the statute can more effectively be dealt with by use of other disciplinary techniques which will be subsequently discussed.

Scope of Questions

Another issue involved in a field interrogation situation relates to the types of questions which may be asked a detained person. This issue has been created primarily as a result of the Supreme Court's decisions in the *Escobedo*[42] and *Miranda* cases.

The *Miranda* case will be discussed at some length hereafter to determine if it applies to a field interrogation situation at all. However, assuming that the *Miranda* case could apply to a field interrogation, the issue remains as to whether or not *Miranda* would apply to every field interrogation.

It seems valid to classify field interrogation into three broad categories. The first is where a police officer has some reason to believe that the detained party has committed a crime. Perhaps the belief is not of such a nature as to constitute probable cause, but at least the officer has, prior to

---

[42]378 U.S. 478 (1964).

the stop, a very specific situation or set of circumstances about which he desires to question the detained person. In the second, it is believed that the person to be detained has done something, or his presence is so out of character with the neighborhood, that the officer desires a *general explanation* regarding the individual's *movements.* Finally, we have the circumstance wherein a detained person may be a *witness* to a crime or have information relating to a specific crime which the peace officer feels would be valuable. Of course, these three general categories of detentions are very broad and each category is capable of being broken down into an almost infinite variety of sub-categories.

There seems to be little doubt that no *Miranda* warning would be required in the third class of field interrogation involving a witness. This is the type of interrogation in which there is no thought, at least initially, that the detained person has committed a crime or is guilty of any other unlawful conduct. Indeed, the *Miranda* case itself excludes this type of questioning from the requirement of a warning.[43] The second category of field interrogation would, at first glance, also seem to be outside the scope of the *Miranda* decision. After all, there is no probable cause for an arrest, and there is in fact no "custody" or arrest as those terms have been used and interpreted by a majority of the cases. Furthermore, the officer is usually not concentrating his questions upon a specific crime or circumstance but rather is asking the individual for nothing more than his name, address and explanation of his presence and actions.

We must remember, however, that the field stop, if properly used, is not a "random sampling" of persons in the community. Under court decisions which validate the common law field interrogation and the stop and frisk statutes, an officer is authorized to make a stop only when an individual's conduct raises a certain degree of suspicion in the officer's mind that the person stopped has committed, is committing, or is about to commit a crime. Therefore, a person subjected to a field stop is being investigated as a suspect for a crime even though the exact nature of the crime may be unknown to the officer at the time of the stop. True, the detained individual is not the "focus of suspicion" that he would be if the officer had extraneous evidence to the fact that the detained person had committed a specific crime, but this does not remove the fact that the detained person is suspected of doing something illegal. Nevertheless, the author believes that the *Escobedo* and *Miranda* cases would not apply to this second category of field detention. *Escobedo* and the four cases decided in *Miranda* all involved circumstances where individuals were very clearly under arrest and had been in fact taken to places of detention. The interrogators in those cases employed techniques which were designed to obtain confessions from the individual

---

[43]384 U.S. 436 at 477-78.

involved to be used in evidence against him in a specific case which was under investigation. The field interrogation, on the other hand, is not designed so much to obtain a confession of a specific crime as it is to determine or obtain information relating to the detained person's conduct. As long as the interrogation officer confines himself to such questions as "what are you doing out here at this time of the morning?", there is little likelihood that he would be required to give the *Miranda* warning at this first approach to the individual to be detained.

The first category of field stop, that of questioning a person with relation to his guilt concerning a specific crime or series of crimes, is an entirely different matter. Here we have a situation where the "focus of suspicion" is relatively firm and it would appear that if *Miranda* applies to questioning away from the stationhouse at all, it would apply in this type of circumstance. Hence, the officer would be required to give the *Miranda* warning if he wanted to use the individual's statements as evidence against the individual in a criminal case. In addition, we can predict with a relatively high degree of accuracy that the Supreme Court is going to be rather sensitive to investigative techniques which can be reasonably construed as designed to evade the *Miranda* decision. Approaching a person whom a police officer believes has committed a specific crime and interrogating him with relation to that specific crime on a street corner under the disguise of a field stop might very easily be interpreted as such an evasion.

In summation, no warnings are necessary under the *Miranda* decision to persons who have been subjected to a field stop except in those cases where the interrogation relates to a specific crime which an officer has probable cause to believe, or at least suspects, that the detained person has committed.

Records of the Stop

Another issue involved in field stops is whether the police ought to record the detention. This issue probably has an emotional content which far exceeds its true importance. The New York "Stop and Frisk" Act, as well as the Uniform Arrest Act, are quite specific in stating that field detentions should not be recorded as arrests in any official police record. On the other hand, the ALI Model Code of Pre-Arraignment Procedure requires each field stop to be recorded and sets forth in some detail the information to be kept. The importance of record keeping insofar as the general public is concerned is perhaps exemplified by a public controversy which broke out in the City of Chicago in the winter of 1965–66. That police department's policy is to conduct field stops even though Illinois has no enabling legislation and the Illinois courts have not clearly sustained a peace officer's common law authority to make field detentions. In spite of the fundamental issues which surround field interrogations, the opponents of such a departmental policy opposed most vigorously the Chicago police department's practice of making notations of field stops and then retaining them for a thirty-day period. If newspaper support is any indication of general public approval, it would appear that the people of Chicago approve the practice of field stops even in spite of their alleged "illegality"[44]; nevertheless, even the newspapers which generally supported the policy of a field interrogation expressed discomfort over the record-keeping practice.[45]

Those states which prohibit the keeping of records of field stops do so, presumably, in an attempt to make the consequences of such a stop as innocuous as possible. In fact, as indicated earlier, the lack of a detained person's "police record" as the result of the stop is one of the primary points which distinguishes a field interrogation from an arrest. A good deal of public sentiment can be aroused by charging that police departments are compiling dossiers on individuals to be used for some vague, future and unknown (but presumably sinister) purpose.

Police officials, on the other hand, support the idea of keeping records which are to be maintained for a limited period of time on a number of grounds. First, such records provide leads if it should be later determined that a crime was committed in a certain neighborhood. The theory is that the investigating officers would check the field stop records to find out which suspiciously acting persons were in the general area of the crime at the time it was committed. Police officers, especially administrators and supervisors, can also use the field interrogation records as a method of supervision and internal control of the patrolmen under their command. In short, they can have some indication of which patrolmen are aggressively checking their beats and which ones are dragging their feet.

Most importantly, records of field stops are invaluable to police supervisors when a citizen complains that he was rudely approached or otherwise mistreated during the course of a field interrogation. In a large metropolitan police department it would be next to impossible to determine which officers were involved in the complaint unless there was a record of the incident.[46] We can only presume that this latter use of records is what the drafters of the ALI Code had in mind when they required that rather extensive records be maintained. This presumption is reinforced when we notice that there is, among other information to be recorded, information of witnesses present during the field stops and whether or not the detained person objected to the stop. It is also worthy of note that the ALI drafters went to rather elaborate precautions to limit potential abuse of the field stop, yet did

---

[44]*Chicago Sun-Times,* January 19, 1966, at 31.

[45]*Ibid.*

[46]"The Law Of Arrest: Constitutionality Of Detention And Frisk Acts," 59 *Nw. U.L. Rev.* 641, 654 (1964).

not see fit to require that the records kept of the field stop be destroyed after a limited period of time. Under the ALI provisions these records could be maintained indefinitely. The only conclusion which can be drawn from this circumstance is that the ALI drafters did not consider maintenance of records to be a significant source of unwarranted exercise of police powers.

It is the author's opinion that field stops should not be recorded as arrests and should not be considered as "a police record." By "police record" we mean that an authorized person in a police position who was checking on a specific individual would not be routinely informed of any field stops. Beyond this limitation, the keeping or nonkeeping of records is largely a false issue. It would appear that if the lack of records would make a policy of field interrogation more palatable to a particular community, records should not be kept, not for a law enforcement or legal reason, but from the standpoint of public acceptance and police department public relations.

The Search

Of the various issues which may arise in the course of a field interrogation, probably the most critical and controversial issue is that of a search of the detained person. This is a vital issue because a person arrested after a field stop is frequently arrested for the possession of contraband which is discovered as a result of a search. In addition, it is one of the most difficult issues to grapple with. The overwhelming majority of authorities seem to approve of the idea of permitting police officers to make field stops and conduct inquiries. However, there is a much more substantial difference in opinion when the inquiry includes a search.

One line of reasoning holds fast to the idea that absolutely no search of a person is constitutionally permissible unless that search is conducted under the authority of a search warrant or as an incident to a lawful arrest.[47] It naturally follows, according to this rationale, that if a field stop is not an arrest, then there can be no search of a person until such time as an arrest has occurred. The dissent in the case of the *People v. Rivera*[48] took this position. Justice Fuld predicated his dissent on the basis that a search without consent and without a warrant is constitutional only if it is an incident to a lawful arrest. He brushed aside any suggestions that a frisk is distinguished from a search by pointing out that neither the Fourth Amendment nor the law of torts distinguishes between a cursory search and an elaborate one. He then stated: "This is nothing but exercise in semantics;

---

[47]See Collings, "Toward Workable Rules of Search and Seizure—An *Amicus Curiae* Brief," 50 *Cal. L. Rev.* 421 (1962).

[48]201 N.E. 2d 32, 35 (N.Y. 1964) (dissenting opinion).

a search by any other name is still a search."[49] It is, perhaps, interesting to note that the judge dissented only on the question of the right of an officer to search as an incident to a field stop. The highest court in New York was unanimous in agreeing that officers had a common-law authority to stop and question an individual.

Another writer also doubts that a search of any nature is permissible. He appears to base this conclusion on the fact that arrests without warrants are well known and have been traditionally used whereas searches without warrants have been more strictly proscribed. He states that a very important distinction exists between arrests and searches, and adds: "Whereas the basic postulate is that a search without warrant is *per se* unreasonable and is to be tolerated only in certain circumstances . . . arrest without warrant is hardly treated as exceptional."[50] And a recently published, comprehensive analysis of street stops also expresses doubt that gradations of search are constitutionally permissible.[51]

In general, a majority of the authorities approving a street stop at all would authorize a cursory search, "a frisk," for the self-protection of the police officer. While such a modified search does not fit neatly into a traditional view of search and seizure law, it does conform more closely to the realities of the street. As one author states, "Hale, Hawkins and Blackstone never saw a 4 inch automatic pistol, but to officers who have, it does not seem unreasonable to search a person being questioned who may be armed."[52] A 1964 article points out that 26% of the police officers killed in the four previous years were making an arrest or transporting prisoners. Another 18 were killed investigating reports of suspicious persons, and 63 were killed interrupting robberies or burglaries, even though the officer did not know, in all cases, that he was in fact interrupting a crime in progress.[53]

There appears to be virtually no suggestion from any responsible source that a police officer be authorized to make a general evidentiary search incident to a field interrogation. The Uniform Arrest Act, New York's "Stop and Frisk" Act, and the ALI Proposed Code of Pre-Arraignment Procedure all strictly tie the authority of an officer to make a search of any kind incident to a field stop to the officer's need for protection. This same limitation is also contained in the case law of those states, notably California, which recognize a police officer's right to stop and question an individual as a part of that state's common law. Thus far, the author has not been able to find any state which recognizes a statutory or common-law

---

[49]201 N.E. 2d at 35.
[50]Scurlock, "Arrest in Missouri" at 118.
[51]Recent Statute, 78 *Harv. L. Rev.* 473, 476-477 (1964). See also *Johnson* v. *United States,* 333 U.S. 10 (1948) and *Trupiano* v. *United States,* 334 U.S. 699 (1948).
[52]Comment, 39 *Cal. L. Rev.* 96, 109 (1951).
[53]Ronayne, "Right to Investigate" at 237.

right to stop and question persons, but prohibits the police officer from conducting any type of search of him.

There is a distinct tendency, however, for the courts to scrutinize a search with considerably more care than they review the probable cause to investigate a stopped person's activity. An excellent example of this is the case of *People v. Rodriguez.*[54] In this case a motion to suppress evidence of policy slips was granted. The policy slips were uncovered while a police officer was frisking an individual for weapons. The court reasoned that a cursory search, or patting down of the outside clothing to determine whether or not a person was carrying a weapon would not have revealed policy slips, hence the court held that this type of search must, by the very nature of the evidence uncovered, have been beyond the frisk which was contemplated under the New York statute and was an unlawful search.

Another such case is *People v. Simon.*[55] In this case a police officer saw the defendant and another person walking in a warehouse district late at night. The officer stopped and searched the defendant and, in the course of said search, found a quantity of marijuana. Defendant was charged with illegal possession of that drug. The California Supreme Court set the information aside and released the defendant. Chief Justice Traynor pointed out that under California law a search may be before or after an arrest but probable cause must exist prior to the search or it is invalid. In this case, the officer simply stopped the defendant and thoroughly searched him before he asked defendant to identify himself or explain his conduct. The Court pointed out that there is nothing unreasonable in an officer's questioning of a person who is outdoors late at night. However, in this case the type of search indicated that the officer was engaged in a general search for evidence without probable cause, which is, of course, unlawful. A later California case, also written by Chief Justice Traynor, does clearly recognize the right of an officer to request a suspect to "submit to a superficial search for concealed weapons."[56]

In summation, the majority of the authorities which have faced the issue of the search seem to take the position that even though the constitutional language relating to searches has no exceptions, courts, in the light of experience, have engrafted certain exceptions such as a search incident to an arrest or a search by consent.[57] These authorities tend to engage in a balancing of social values and reach the conclusion that, ". . . as long as the frisk is strictly limited, this invasion seems outweighed by the necessity to protect the questioning policeman."[58]

---

[54]262 N.Y.S. 2d 859 (Cty. Ct. 1965).
[55]290 P. 2d 531 (Cal. 1955).
[56]*People* v. *Mickelson,* 380 P. 2d 658 (Cal. 1963).
[57]Leagre, "The Fourth Amendment" at 339.
[58]Recent Statute, 78 *Harv. L. Rev.* 473, 476-77 (1964).

This general rationale is also well summarized in the commentary to the stop and frisk provision of the ALI Model Code of Pre-Arraignment Procedure:

> . . . an officer, if he reasonably believes his safety so requires, may search a person stopped pursuant to this section. He may search only to the extent necessary to discover any dangerous weapon which may on that occasion be used against him. The search envisioned here should not usually be more intensive than "an external feeling of the clothing" that is, the traditional "frisk." The subsection also authorizes a search of the immediate surroundings of the person for the same purpose and under the same limitations. By immediate surroundings, the draft intends to designate any place (for example, a lady's handbag) where a weapon may be concealed, and which during the interview remains in easy reach of the person.
>
> The Reporters included this authority to search with some reluctance. Many people would find being subjected even to the limited search authorized by this subsection offensive and humiliating. Nevertheless, the important purpose which this section as a whole is intended to serve would be frustrated if no search were authorized. Police officers will not, and should not, be asked to risk an encounter with a person who may be armed unless they can protect themselves by "frisking" the person at the outset. Where the authority to stop has been recognized, the search for dangerous weapons has also generally been recognized as a necessary concomitant to it.
>
> The draft seeks to minimize as far as possible the recourse to such searches by limiting their scope to the specific need which is their justification. The very extensive search which may accompany an arrest is clearly not within the terms of this provision.[59]

Thus far, we have discussed a number of authorities which take the position (a) that no search at all is permissible under any circumstances which constitute less than probable cause to make an arrest, and (b) that some type of limited search, for the protection of the officer involved, is permissible. A third alternative has been suggested. It would authorize police officers to conduct a limited search for deadly weapons and would go further by not permitting into evidence any item recovered by the search except weapons. Presumably the reasoning behind such a suggestion is that the authority of a police officer to frisk an individual for deadly weapons would not be abused by being used as an excuse to conduct a general search of the detained person for other types of contraband. In other words, it would remove any motive for the officer to conduct a thorough search for items other than weapons since the other items could not be used in obtaining a conviction.

At first blush such a proposal sounds rather attractive. It would allow the officer to protect himself and greatly reduce the temptation to abuse the

---

[59]*Model Code of Pre-Arraignment Procedure, Tentative Draft No. 1* (March 1, 1966), 101.

authority to frisk. However, such a proposal, like most simplistic solutions to extremely complex problems, can lead to some illogical situations. In general, if this proposal were followed we may encounter a situation of a police officer making a perfectly proper frisk and uncovering what could very well be evidence of a major crime, but immunity would be accorded the stopped person because the seized evidence was not an instrumentality dangerous to the officer. Indeed, we could easily reach the point where a police officer would not stop persons whom the officer suspects are guilty of possessing narcotics, burglary tools, stolen property or other contraband out of fear that he might accidently find some of this contraband on the person during the frisk and thereby taint its validity. This possibility is not merely a product of the author's imagination. In fact, one case now pending before the Supreme Court involving New York's "Stop and Frisk" Act is just such an example.

The question naturally arises: If there is so little judicial or scholarly opposition to the authority of a police officer to stop an individual and ask an explanation of his movements, why do we then find a rather significant opposition to the right of a law enforcement officer to conduct a frisk as an incident to the street stop? It is this author's opinion that some of the concern relating to a frisk is based on the very real potential for abuse in a field situation.

To begin with, most openminded students of the problems related to field interrogation can easily see the distinction between a field stop and arrest. There is a relatively clear distinction between a four or five minute conversation with a policeman on a street corner, as in the case of a field stop, and, on the other hand, an arrest in which the individual is taken to a police station, charged with a crime, fingerprinted, "mugged," and in general caught up in the entire criminal law process. However, the distinction between a frisk and a more thorough search is an even finer distinction than that between a field stop and an arrest. It is quite easy to define a frisk as the patting down of the outer clothing for the purpose of determining by touch the existence of a concealed weapon. However, in actual field practice, a police officer will frequently face situations in which a simple "frisk," to be effective for self-protection, may turn into a reasonably thorough search—even assuming the good faith of the police officer. For example, cold weather, when people are wearing numerous garments and heavy clothing, creates something of a problem. Even the educated fingers of a veteran police officer have difficulty in checking for knives and small weapons beneath extremely bulky clothing. Requiring an individual to unbutton his topcoat and perhaps a jacket underneath the topcoat, then checking the various layers of clothing for a reasonably available weapon can have all the appearances of a rather thorough search. Such a search is certainly necessary to protect the officer in some instances, but it also goes considerably beyond the mere patting down of the outer clothing as discussed by the courts. Hatbands, boot tops, and collar linings are favorite places for concealment of certain types of sharp bladed weapons, yet it is extremely difficult to check these parts of a person's clothing by simply running a hand over them, and this is especially true if the weapon is made of flexible material such as leather or plastic, or a safety razor.

The most common confiscated weapon which the author has seen in two years' field experience with police departments is a small Spanish or Italian automatic pistol, which sells for $8-$15 and which fits in an adult male's hand without being seen. Such weapons, while lacking in accuracy and precision, are extremely effective at point-blank range. Yet this is the type of weapon which an officer is supposed to protect himself against by patting down the outer clothing.

In addition to the sophistication and increasing availability of commercial weapons, the officer in the street must contend with an occasional ingenious homemade weapon. The author has seen a homemade "zip gun" capable of firing a single .22 or .25 caliber bullet which was designed and constructed to be concealed in a common cigarette lighter. From outward appearances, this weapon would have a very low threshold of reliability and accuracy but it did work when tested. Therefore, in the hands of a certain type of person, the very act of casually lighting a cigarette could spell death or serious injury to a police officer.

Another troublesome problem in defining the limits of a frisk is the question of items being carried by the detained individual. There is a very real threat to officers making street stops under certain circumstances when the detained individual is carrying open boxes, grocery sacks or even handbags. This is an especially relevant problem in view of the fact that the carrying of some such items very late at night and in certain portions of a city would be the very type of circumstance which would attract a police officer's attention to the individual in the first place.

The purpose of the preceding discussion is not to develop any definite line between a frisk and a search. Rather, the purpose is to demonstrate that a peace officer, in order to protect himself, is going to have to engage in some type of search which will exceed the casual patting down of the outer clothing. In balancing the degree of intrusion of the freedom of personal movement over and against the effectiveness of a law enforcement technique, we must not delude ourselves into believing that the degree of intrusion, insofar as the frisk is concerned, can be effectively limited to a fleeting three or four second patting down of outer clothing.

There is still an additional reason why the frisk of the person causes more concern than the original stopping of the individual. The statutory and common-law authority of a police officer to stop an individual on the street is based on "reasonable suspicion" that the individual stopped has commited, is about to commit, or is going to commit a crime. While it is conceded that the term "reasonable suspicion" has not been the subject of extensive case law, nevertheless a reading of the few cases which have interpreted and analyzed this and similar terms indicates that the appellate courts have some general concept of what these terms mean and the circumstances to which they apply. In general these terms mean that a person must be engaged in some type of conduct or be in some circumstances which remove him from the general class of ordinary citizens in the same area at the same time and, further, that these circumstances must suggest to a reasonably prudent officer that the individual is engaged, or is about to engage, in some illegal act. While such a criterion is necessarily vague, it would appear that it is no more vague or incapable of review than the classic concept of "probable cause to arrest."

It should be noticed, however, that the statutory authority for an officer to make a frisk as an incident to a street stop is dependent on the officer's "reasonable belief that he is in danger." Yet research has not revealed a single case in which the officer's "belief that he is in danger" was ever subjected to appellate review. This presumably means that the authority of an officer to frisk an individual, which can be a much more serious intrusion of the individual's liberty than the original stop, is going to be based on the criterion of whether or not the officer has a right to stop the individual. It is understandable that a judge would be somewhat hesitant to review the officer's judgment as to whether or not he was in danger. After all, it is the police officer's life which is at stake and a judge would be naturally hesitant to review this highly personal decision. But if the authority of an officer to make a frisk is to be constitutionally upheld and properly applied and opposition to the frisk abated somewhat, the courts are going to have to grapple with the question of standards which justify a frisk.

The concept of "reasonable belief of danger" is going to have to be determined and developed by case law in conformance with our common law tradition. But it appears that the very first question which must be decided prior to the development of case law is whether or not the courts are going to require objective criteria to take into account generally surrounding circumstances which do not necessarily apply to a specific individual being stopped. In other words, does an officer have to testify to certain movements or conduct on the part of the specific individual stopped in order to justify a belief in danger, or will the court take into consideration the general character of the neighborhood, the time of day, the availability of assistance to the officer, the general type of crime which the detained person is suspected of committing and other circumstances of a like nature? The author believes that general circumstances such as those mentioned must be taken into account in determining "reasonable belief of danger." Any attempt to require some suspicious movement—such as the reaching for a glove compartment or a hip pocket on the part of the individual detained —would not comport with the reality of the streets.

At this point, we should realistically face the fact that we are actually not talking about the protection of citizens from the intrusion of a frisk but are discussing admissibility of evidence. There is not the slightest doubt that an officer who believes that he may be in danger, based on any conceivable criteria, is going to conduct a frisk. If the officer feels his life is at stake he will protect himself first and the question of admissibility of evidence will have extremely low priority. However, the judicial development of some case law, at least to the extent of crystalizing the concept of "reasonable belief of danger," will reassure those individuals who may have reservations about granting a police officer the authority to conduct a frisk. At least it will indicate that the criteria to conduct the frisk will be subject to judicial review and not left to the whim of each individual police officer.

There is one final reason why some persons might have reservations about authorizing a frisk as opposed to authorizing a field stop. This involves the question of the detained person's reputation or embarrassment. It is relatively easy for a well-trained police officer to conduct a short field stop involving a short period of questioning of an individual and make such a practice inconspicuous to the other persons in the vicinity. However, a frisk is more difficult to conceal from other citizens, especially when it also includes checking of shopping bags or the more heavy-handed frisk necessary for heavy or bulky clothing. Associated with the question of reputation is the attitude of the person who has been stopped. The field research for this article, as well as the author's experience in the field, has been that individuals who are merely questioned almost never raise objections to being stopped, especially if the interrogating officer's demeanor is one of politeness and efficiency. Almost every objection of any degree observed has been in a situation where the detained person was subjected to a frisk. Indeed, this author's personal experiences while residing in the City of Chicago bear out the field observation. He was subjected to a field stop by Chicago police officers on two occasions. During both incidents it was quite understandable that his conduct, when viewed by a police officer from a distance of a block or so away, could be considered suspicious. Under both circumstances, a short explanation of that conduct satisfied the officers that the seemingly suspicious conduct was, in fact, reasonable and innocuous. The author departed from both field stops with a generally favorable impression of the officers concerned, especially their politeness and alertness. However, if the field stop had resulted in a frisk of either the person or an automobile, the author strongly suspects his own feelings would have been less favorable and some degree of resentment would have been present.

A corollary to the question of reputation is the fact that a frisk is much more subject to abuse by police officers than a field stop. Assuming that a police officer desires to harass a particular individual and this harassment took the form of stopping the individual at every conceivable opportunity, it would no doubt be annoying and somewhat damaging to the individual's standing and reputation in his community. However, if the harassment took the form of a thorough frisk, it could become extremely oppressive, especially if the officer managed to conduct the frisk in open view and in relatively crowded public places. This type of harassment by conducting frequent personal searches is not a figment of some civil libertarian's overactive imagination. It exists today, in varying degrees, to the extent that a slang expression has been developed to cover the situation. Harassment by frequent personal stops and searches is known in one big city as "jacking-up" an individual. This practice of "jacking-up" a citizen is usually accomplished by means of unlawful detentions and searches. Any statutory or common-law scheme to add new tools to the arsenal of law enforcement officers must be especially constructed to assure that it does not, at the same time, legalize a presently existing abuse.

Miranda and the Field Interrogation

One of the more pressing constitutional problems involved in the area of field interrogation is the question of what effect, if any, the recent decision of the Supreme Court in *Miranda* has on field stops. There is an assumption, which is probably valid, that the requirement that a person be warned of his right to silence, that any statement he makes may be used against him, that he is entitled to an attorney either of his own selection or appointed for him if he cannot afford one, would hamper the use of the field stop as a technique to uncover crime. Certainly, an exercise of the full *Miranda* ritual would have a tendency to alarm a citizen whose suspicious conduct resulted from completely and innocuous motives. It is the judgment of the author that *Miranda* does not apply to the typical field interrogation. However, this case has such importance and potentially far-reaching effect on the process of criminal investigation that it will be discussed separately and in some detail, apart from other constitutional issues.

To begin with, all four of the cases which were decided by the Supreme Court in the *Miranda* opinion involved persons who had been arrested and taken to the police station and interrogated for the purpose of obtaining a confession.[60] In each of the cases, a confession was obtained after lengthy detention and interrogation at the station house. Before examining the language of the court, it is of interest to note that Mr. Chief Justice Warren, who wrote the majority opinion, does not use the word "arrest" in the opinion. He therefore avoids the semantic and definitional difficulty which has been the stumbling block of many other courts and which was

---

[60]384 U.S. at 440.

discussed at the very outset of this article. Instead of using the word "arrest" the majority almost always uses the word "custody." Therefore, for our purposes, it behooves us to examine some of the language of the majority opinion to determine whether or not an interference with a person's freedom to move about the streets for the purpose of inquiring of the individual his name, address, and explanation of actions is the type of "custody" to which *Miranda* is addressed.

In the very first paragraph of the majority's opinion, we find the statement ". . . we deal with the admissibility of statements obtained from an individual who is subjected to custodial police interrogation . . ."[61] The Court then points out that in each of the cases before it law enforcement officials took the defendant into custody and interrogated him at the police station. By way of introduction to the rationale of the majority's opinion, Mr. Chief Justice Warren stated:

> Our holding will be spelled out with some specificity in the pages which follow but briefly stated it is this: the prosecution may not use statements, whether exculpatory or inculpatory, stemming from custodial interrogation of the defendant unless it demonstrates the use of procedural safeguards effective to secure the privilege against self-incrimination. *By custodial interrogation, we mean questioning initiated by law enforcement officers after a person has been taken into custody or otherwise deprived of his freedom of action in any significant way.*[62]

It is submitted that the word "custody" means that an individual has been taken physically from the street or other place and confined. This interpretation of the word "custody" is reinforced by additional quotations which will follow. But the Court also indicated that the *Miranda* rule would have to be followed in any other situation which deprived a person of his freedom of action "in any significant way." At this point in the opinion it is not clear what the Court means by being deprived of freedom of action in any significant way. This statement implies that *Miranda* is applicable to situations in which the suspect is not actually confined in a police station or jail, but, by the same token, it also implies that there can be a deprivation of freedom of action in an insignificant way, to which *Miranda* would not apply. As the opinion progresses we find the following:

> The Constitutional issue we decide in each of these cases is the admissibility of statements obtained from a defendant questioned while in custody and deprived of his freedom of action. In each, the defendant was questioned by police officers, detectives, by a prosecuting attorney *in a room in which he was cut off from the outside world.*[63]

---

[61]384 U.S. at 439.
[62]384 U.S. at 444 (emphasis added.)
[63]384 U.S. at 445 (emphasis added).

The Court then observed that all four cases were similar in that "They all thus share salient features—*incommunicado interrogation of individuals in a police dominated atmosphere,* resulting in self-incriminating statements without full warnings of constitutional rights."[64] The Court added that "An understanding of the nature and setting of this in-custody interrogation is essential to our decisions today."[65]

At this point the Court goes into a discussion of reports of physical abuse of prisoners in order to obtain confessions, primarily the Wickersham report of 1931 and three Law Review articles dated 1930, 1932 and 1936. The Court then points out that "Interrogations still take place in privacy," and that "Privacy results in secrecy and this in turn results in a gap in our knowledge as to what in fact goes on in the interrogation room."[66] The Court next discusses at some length two well known and widely used manuals of police interrogation wherein the authors discuss psychological techniques of gaining the confidence of the suspect and obtaining a confession thereby. The Court then states: "Even without employing brutality, the 'third degree' or the specific strategems described above, the very fact of custodial interrogation exacts a heavy toll on individual liberty and trades on the weakness of the individuals."[67] The majority also observed: "It is obvious that such an *interrogation environment* is created for no purpose other than to subject the individual to the will of his examiner. This atmosphere carries its own badge of intimidation. To be sure, this is not physical intimidation, but it is equally destructive to human dignity. *The current practice of incommunicado interrogation* is at odds with one or our nation's most cherished principles—that the individual may not be impelled to incriminate himself."[68] The Court at a later point states: "We have concluded that without proper safeguards the process of in-custody interrogation of persons suspected or accused of a crime contains inherently compelling pressures which work to undermine the individual's will to resist and to compel him to speak where he would not otherwise do so freely."[69]

As the opinion progresses, its application to field interrogation based on reasonable suspicion becomes less certain. We find a statement to the effect that, "the principles announced today deal with the protection which must be given to the privilege against self-incrimination when the individual is first subjected to police interrogation while in custody at the station or

---

[64]*Ibid.* (emphasis added).
[65]*Ibid.*
[66]384 U.S. at 448.
[67]384 U.S. at 455-56.
[68]384 U.S. at 457-58.
[69]384 U.S. at 467.

otherwise deprived of his freedom of *action in any way.*"[70] The preceding quotation very clearly supports the earlier implication that the word "custody" means confinement at a police station but instead of talking in terms of deprivation of freedom of action in any *significant* way which the court discussed early in the opinion, we now find the opinion turning to the deprivation of freedom of action in *any* way. Of course, if this preceding statement is interpreted to be the holding of the court in *Miranda,* certainly the field stop is a deprivation of freedom of action "in any way." If this apparent contradiction in the opinion were not enough, in the very next paragraph we find the court saying that "investigation [of a crime] may include inquiry of persons not under restraint." And then the court said:

> General on-the-scene questioning as to facts surrounding a crime or other general questioning of citizens in the fact-finding process is not affected by our holding. It is an act of responsible citizenship for individuals to give whatever information they may have to aid in law enforcement. In such situations the compelling atmosphere inherent in the process of in-custody interrogation is not necessarily present.[71]

The preceding quotation could easily be interpreted as applying to witnesses only and not to a person who is suspected of committing a crime. However, such an interpretation is weakened because the Court attaches a footnote at the end of the foregoing quotation. This footnote cites with approval the police practice of visiting ". . . the house or place of business of a *suspect* and there questioning him, probably in the presence of a relative or friend."[72]

It is submitted that this latter quotation rather effectively destroys the idea that the general non-custodial investigation of crime referred to in the *Miranda* quotation applies only to witnesses. Based on the preceding quotations, it is the author's conclusion that *Miranda* was striking at what the Court considered the inherently coercive circumstances and atmosphere of a place of confinement and does not apply to general inquiries made in public places and in public view which do not have the attributes of a jail or station house. *Miranda,* therefore, does not apply to the typical field interrogation.

There are situations, of course, which could develop in the field which would bring about an atmosphere and circumstances similar to a station house questioning and in which *Miranda* would apply. For example, a person is stopped and a general field interrogation, or the evidence obtained

---

[70]The quotation in the text came from an advance sheet, 16 L.Ed.2d 725, No. 7 July 6, 1966. However, the official report inserts the word "significant" between the words "any" and "way," 384 U.S. at 477.

[71]384 U.S. at 477-78.

[72]384 U.S. at 478, n. 46.

as a result of a frisk, indicates that the detained person has been guilty of a major crime. If he is placed in a police car and interrogated at significant length by police officers with relation to the individual's guilt of the crime, the circumstances would not be significantly different from the inherently coercive in-custody interrogation which was generally condemned by *Miranda*. Then too, a police station is not the only place where a person can be taken into physical custody and "cut off from the rest of the world." If a police officer stops an individual in a store on suspicion of shoplifting, and takes him to some isolated room in the back of the store and proceeds to interrogate him for the purpose of obtaining a confession, there can be relatively little doubt that *Miranda* would apply. Examples such as the two which have just been mentioned would be exceedingly rare, however, and to apply *Miranda* would have little effect on the general practice of field interrogation. In summation, the entire thrust of the rationale of *Miranda v. Arizona* is such that it does not apply to field interrogations so long as the stop is for a relatively short period of time, is conducted in public, or in a non-police dominated atmosphere, and the questioning, at least initially, is confined to the general conduct of the individual and is not an interrogation relating to the individual's involvement in a specific crime for the purpose of obtaining a confession.

Field Research

In order to obtain factual data for this article, the author made arrangements with the Chicago Police Department to ride with various units of that department's Patrol Division in November and December of 1965, and in April and May of 1966.

Method

The information set forth hereafter in this article resulted from observation in Task Force Areas 6, 1, and 4 and in Patrol Districts 11, 2, 20, and 16. The author would report to the relevant area or district headquarters at 6:00 P.M. after a supervisory officer had been notified that an observer would be present. The author would then be assigned to one unit for the night's observation. The officers involved were given an explanation of the purpose of the observer's presence and were requested to conduct themselves as though they were on a routine patrol mission. (The possible effect on the police officers' conduct due to the presence of the observer is discussed hereafter.) The author would accompany the officers during the entire eight-hour shift, making notes on certain stops which were made. The data contained herein includes only those contacts in the field which were not primarily concerned with the apprehending of a particular person for the commission of a specific criminal act. The type of police activity under investigation in this report is the stopping of individuals who were allegedly engaged in "suspicious" activity and operates under the various labels such as "field challenge," "field interrogation," "stop and frisk," and "stop and quiz."

Explanation of Data

The phrase "total persons contacted" represents the number of persons the officer spoke to in an official capacity. For example, if an automobile with three occupants was stopped and only the driver was asked to identify himself, one person was counted as "contacted." If all occupants were questioned or asked to identify themselves, three persons were counted as "contacted."

The phrase "vehicles stopped" is self-explanatory; it also includes a few instances (less than ten) when persons were questioned after being observed in a parked car.

The phrase "frisk of a person or car" means, in relation to a person, the running of the officer's hands over the outside of a person's clothing as a check for concealed weapons. If during the course of a frisk the officer felt an object which, in his opinion, could have been a weapon, the incident is counted as a frisk, even though the officer went into the person's clothing after feeling the object. The frisk of a car is defined as a superficial shining of a flashlight inside the automobile to observe items which would be in plain view; it also includes the shining of lights under the seats and other potential hiding places which are accessible without rearranging any items in the car.

The phrase "search of a person or car" is defined, in relation to an individual, as the examining of the inside of a person's pockets or minutely examining a piece of clothing; for example, taking a person's hat off and turning the sweatband inside out. Basically, any physical investigation which extended beyond the feeling of a subject's outer clothing is counted as a search. The looking inside of packages or sacks is not counted as a search unless the officer shifted the contents of the parcel around or lifted some items of the parcel in order to examine all of the contents of the package. Any such rearranging of the contents of a parcel is counted as a search. A search of an automobile is defined as any conduct which goes beyond a superficial checking of the interior of an automobile. The opening of glove compartments, trunks, or boxes inside a car are examples of searches. Any time the officer felt it necessary to rearrange any of the contents of an automobile it was counted as a search.

The phrase "approval" represents the number of persons who affirmatively congratulated the officers for being alert or expressed their appreciation of the officer's presence.

The phrase "Protest 1" represents the number of persons who did not verbally protest at being stopped, but who displayed objective signs of annoyance or inconvenience.

The phrase "Protest 2" represents the number of persons who were visibly upset at being questioned and expressed such disapproval verbally.

Using the definitions contained above, the data obtained is as follows:

Total persons contacted, 297;	Search of person or car, 142;
Vehicles stopped, 129;	Approval, 4;
Persons arrested, 11;[73]	Protest 1, 8; and
Frisk of person or cars, 187;	Protest 2, 7;[74]

Validity of Data

The most difficult problem in this type of field survey is the interpersonal relationship between the police officer and the observer. As stated earlier, each unit was requested to carry out its function as though the observer was not present. The author is under no delusion that the request was complied with entirely. However, even though the observer is an "outsider" there are some techniques which can be used to minimize the possible distortive effect of the observer's presence: (A) The author always rode the entire shift with a single unit. After a few hours in the close confines of a patrol car, the officers would begin to become more accustomed to the observer's presence and this would, in turn, tend to make the observations more valid. (B) The normal practice would be to ride with a different unit each night until the observer found a team which seemed to be comfortable with him and the observer with them; then the observer would ride with that unit for the balance of the time he was in the particular area or district. (C) The observer attempted to show by his actions that he knew how to conduct himself in a field contact situation; the author's previous experience with another police department in another state tended to relieve the officers' natural apprehension that the observer might do something foolish in a potentially delicate situation. (D) In all of the author's relationships with the officers, he operated on the theory that establishing a good rapport was his job, thus taking the burden off the officer to keep the observer "entertained."

Although we must assume that the presence of a non-policeman had an effect on the conduct of the officers, it does not automatically follow that the officer's altered conduct will always reflect favorably on the police department or the field contact practice. For example, one night the author accompanied two officers who were so polite to the public that they actually gave the appearance of being obsequious. It is interesting to note that almost

---

[73]Persons arrested: rape, 1; unlawful carrying of weapon, 5; attempted auto theft, 2; gambling, 1; theft, 1 and driving while license revoked, 1.

[74]This figure includes one protest, in an overwhelmingly Negro area, which was primarily directed to the fact that a white person (the author) was in the area; the two officers accompanying the author were both Negroes.

half of the "Protest 2" incidents occurred in that one tour of duty. Of course, it is possible that this was just a coincidence or a "bad night." On the other hand, it is psychologically valid to state that a grovelling police officer will get a large share of complaints because he does not command the respect of the people with whom he is dealing. In addition, the number of "searches" was considerably higher than the author anticipated. Perhaps this resulted from the officers' attempt to impress the observer with the very thorough job which they were doing.

There is another reason for believing that the observer's presence did not seriously distort the collected data. With the single exception pointed out above, the officers with whom the observer rode conducted themselves in fundamentally the same manner. If the presence of an observer was radically altering police conduct, it follows that more than three dozen policemen would have to react to an observer's presence in a uniform manner and would have to keep up the "act" for more than 300 hours. The author finds such a suggestion somewhat difficult to accept.

General Observations

The average length of time a citizen was detained by a field stop was between two and three minutes. One person was detained about 20 minutes until the victim of an armed robbery arrived and made a negative identification. One driver was detained for more than 45 minutes while a name check was being made. This delay occurred on a Friday night while there was a computer malfunction; the person was arrested when it was reported that his driver's license had been revoked. Other than these two instances a detention did not last over five or six minutes and, of course, the overwhelming majority were much less than that.

The author was impressed at the length to which most officers went in order to keep from drawing attention to the fact that a person was being questioned. The officers would stand quite close to the detained individual in order to speak in low tones. Very few of the frisks or searches of a person were conducted in the traditional "hands-on-the-wall" manner. The normal technique used, even for a search, was for an officer to stand directly in front of the detained individual and conduct his frisk from this position. The only movement which the detained person was required to make was to hold his arms out from his sides a few inches in order that the officer could feel under the armpits and the chest pockets. This technique of frisking is not in accordance with good police practice and is, in fact, dangerous to the officer since it places him in a vulnerable position in the event that the frisked person decides to attack the officer.[75] Nevertheless, this kind of frisking technique was almost invariably used since it can be done in a very inconspicuous manner by an experienced officer.

---

[75]Vallow, *Police Arrest and Search*, 45-55 (1962).

The normal technique of a frisk or search of the person is to require the individual to place his hands on a vehicle or wall and to extend his feet out from the object which is supporting his hands. The only times this frisk was observed during the course of the author's observation was in certain situations where more than two persons were being frisked or where the detained person gave some distinctly objective sign that he had a weapon. Examples of this latter category occurred when an individual would reach under the seat of his car or would put his hand in his pocket when the officers identified themselves as policemen and would be hesitant in removing his hand when ordered to do so.

A number of the officers explained to the observer that the attempts to make the stop as inconspicuous as possible were done to keep from drawing a crowd which could potentially create a problem for the officer on the street. While such a motive may not be based on the highest principles of civil liberties, it does minimize the embarrassment factor.

The fact that a field stop, especially accompanied by a frisk or search, is humiliating to some degree is recognized by a general policy followed by the officers in the field in Chicago. Males are almost never subjected to field stops when accompanied by females. The theory behind such a policy is that a man, either alone or accompanied by other men, will not normally object to being stopped and frisked. However, the same man, in the same circumstances, accompanied by a wife or girl friend, will feel that his masculine role as a protector is challenged by such a field stop and thus he may offer objection or resistance. This writer observed three instances of field stops involving females, but in only one instance was a female involved to the extent that she was listed under a category of "total persons contacted."

Most of the persons contacted were involved in some type of "suspicious activity" which was discernible to the observer. Of course, the term "suspicious activity" is, to a large extent, a subjective evaluation. And, we must remember, that the observer was not a trained police officer nor familiar with the neighborhoods in which he rode. Of the 297 persons contacted, 243 of them were engaged in some type of conduct which the author would classify as "suspicious." Most of the suspicious activity involved attempts, in varying degrees, to evade police officers as soon as the individuals recognized a police car, or involved persons who might be fairly classed as loitering or lurking in back alleys, dark doorways or similar locations late at night.

The author did notice that the number of field stops is a factor in the supervisory control of patrolmen in the Task Force. This is quite readily understandable, especially for a unit such as the Task Force which is given a considerable independence and which does not answer routine calls. This is not meant to imply that a "quota" system exists, in the strict sense of the word. Nevertheless, in each Task Force area headquarters a monthly list is posted in a prominent place on the bulletin board which indicates, among other things, the number of field stops which each Task Force officer has made. In addition, there does appear to be pressure on the patrolmen to "show some activity." In areas of a high crime rate and dense population, this system, insofar as the observer could determine, causes little problems. However, in some relatively quiet districts this real or imagined pressure could lead to a number of field contacts in which there is no suspicion of any kind. This author also observed, that in the relatively quiet residential areas, an officer would patrol for five or six hours without making any field stops and then, as his tour of duty came to a close, would stop two or three people within the course of an hour whose only suspicious activity appeared to be their presence in the neighborhood. Such conduct can only be classified as an abuse of the field stop technique. It is strongly suggested that any police department using the field stop practice should make it scrupulously clear to the officers involved that stops should be made only in reasonably suspicious circumstances and that there is not going to be the slightest hint of a "quota" system by which the officers' efficiency or competence is to be judged.

The data set forth is not intended to be a definitive study, based on scientific methods, of the field interrogation practice of the Chicago Police Department. Rather, the data is descriptive and to some degree subjective even though a conscious effort was made to obtain a balanced view of the field interrogation method by selecting districts and areas of varying crime rates and ethnic groups. The statistics contained above indicate that 3.6% of the persons stopped were eventually arrested, all as a result of information or physical evidence obtained by virtue of the detention. Statistics from the Task Force rate of arrest of "field challenges" indicate that out of more than 250,000 field contacts the arrest rate was approximately 3.2%. This close relationship between the author's sample data and the total statistics indicate that his experience and observation offer a statistically valid insight into one police department's experience and practice—especially if we use the figures contained herein as a general guide and do not attempt to use them as highly precise tools.

The collection of this data naturally gives rise to the question of whether or not the advantages of a systematic field interrogation program outweigh its disadvantages. In the final analysis, such a question is based on a person's concept of values rather than on some mathematical formula. Nevertheless, we can make some generalizations.

The value of a field interrogation program exceeds the 3.6% of the arrests made because it keeps persons with a criminal inclination on the defensive. Any police department that follows a practice of centering its attention only on responses to crimes already committed places itself in a position, not of preventing crime, but of reacting to criminal activity. Such a practice gives the criminal the initiative in that he is almost totally free to determine the time, place, and circumstance under which he will commit a crime.[76] But a well planned and a well conceived program of field interrogation leaves the criminal without all of the options. An aggressive and controlled program of patrol to determine who is on the streets, what the explanation for their presence is (assuming the individual is engaged in some unusual activity), will throw an indeterminable variable into any preconceived plan to commit a crime. In addition, such a practice of field interrogation is designed to give the general public, including the vast majority of law-abiding citizens, the feeling of police "presence." This will in turn, hopefully, help to instill in the general public a confidence in the alertness and efficiency of the police department.

As indicated previously, there was very little abuse observed in the course of the original stop. The data indicates that, on the average, the patrol units which were under observation stopped about one person an hour. Considering the general nature of criminal activity in the city of Chicago, this number of stops per hour is not excessive.

The foregoing data and observations indicate, however, that the field interrogation practice does have some disadvantages. The data indicates that approximately 5% of the individuals contacted show visible signs of anger or resentment at the intrusion. It can be assumed that an unknown number of additional people were more successful in hiding their feelings about their detention. Nevertheless, it is the author's impression, based on observing the demeanor and manner of speech of persons detained during the course of the field survey, that an overwhelming majority of the individuals stopped cooperated willingly with the police officer, if not out of a sense of civic duty at least with the attitude that this temporary delay be ended as quickly as possible. The observer also noted that all but one of the protests occurred in predominantly Negro districts of Chicago. It is likely, therefore, that field interrogation practice, in all probability, adds to the general deterioration in the relationship between policemen and minority groups.

Already noted, the extent of the search in many instances was surprising. Over one-third of the field detentions resulted in searches which far exceeded even that which proponents of "stop and frisk" advocate. Certainly the searches, except in two or three instances, went far beyond the type of search which would be necessary to protect a police officer. Slightly more than one-half of these extensive searches were made in high crime rate, Negro areas which had been the scene of large scale rioting the year before (1964). Most of the officers in these districts were quite candid in explaining that they were aware the search was unlawful and that no

---

[76]See Bristow, "Field Interrogation."

conviction could be supported on the basis of evidence obtained by the search. However, they further explained that the purpose of these extensive searches was to confiscate firearms in the event of future riots and that a conviction for unlawful carrying of a firearm was largely irrelevant. Such conduct also widens the gap between police officers and the Negro minority, especially in the vicinity of Chicago's Eleventh District. On the other hand, the officers' prediction of future riots in the summer of 1966 did prove accurate and the author feels certain that the same officers who had to face the rioters felt quite justified in previously removing a number of firearms from the area of the riots.

In general, the "field challenge" practice of Chicago's police department has advantages which outweigh the disadvantages. It is submitted, however, that the number of extensive searches is not only unlawful, but unnecessary, and that such a practice of extensive searching be discontinued or at least not be permitted to hide under the cloak of legitimate field interrogation practice. If the Chicago police department decides to conduct clearly unlawful general searches in areas of potential rioting, then the department should, as a matter of policy, do so openly and explicitly. In this way the courts and the municipal officials responsible for such a policy can clearly and cleanly be judged by the responsible citizenry. To conduct general searches under the guise of field interrogation does not make the searches any more lawful, and such a practice endangers, through abuse, the legitimate use of the tool of field interrogation.

It is interesting to note that out of the approximately 300 persons subjected to a field stop, not one single individual indicated in any way that he would not answer the police officer's question. The author heard a number of highly unskillful lies, but observed no one who chose to resort to silence.

Conclusion

It appears that the primary opposition to authorizing temporary police detentions is the fact that such authority is capable of abuse by police officers. This fear has some validity and cannot be brushed aside easily. But an effective law enforcement tool should not be completely negated because it is subject to potential abuse.

In dealing with the problem of abuse of authority, it is suggested that attention be directed toward the potential abuse rather than the authority itself. Thus far the technique of the courts in handling abuse of police authority has been through the exclusionary rule which prohibits the introduction of illegally seized evidence—a technique that, in the main, has been ineffective. It is ineffective because it does not actually prevent the abuse itself but only strikes at a consequence of the abuse. For instance, if police officers kick in the door of a person's home in the middle of the night and ransack it without probable cause, and if, in fact, the officers find no incriminating evidence, there can be no doubt that a very gross abuse of police authority has occurred—and yet there is no evidence to exclude. By the same token, even if some contraband is found, when the prosecuting attorney learns of the method by which the evidence was obtained, there is little likelihood that a charge will be placed against the home owner for possession of contraband. Once again the courts' exclusionary technique becomes a futility.

Traditional civil suits against police officers are largely ineffective because of the difficulty of satisfying a judgment in a substantial amount against a relatively impecunious policeman.

As regards remedial action by disciplinary measures directed at the offending officer, this seems quite unrealistic to contemplate when consideration is given to the fact that the officer in our hypothetical case actually obtained highly incriminating evidence even though his conduct was illegal. This places the police administrator in the awkward position, as far as the general public and his subordinates are concerned, of disciplining a policeman who caught a criminal. In addition, a competent defense attorney would almost certainly get a good deal of mileage at the trial of the case against the possessor of the contraband out of the fact that the evidence against him was obtained in a manner so grossly abusive as to result in a policeman's discharge or suspension.

The author's recommendation is that the governmental agency by whom the offending officer is employed should be made civilly liable for abuses in field detention *arising out of malice, bad faith, or gross negligence.* It is suggested that a field detention statute carry with it this creation of civil liability against the agency employing the police officer.

In order to make civil liability meaningful, it is further suggested that a certain sum of money be assumed as damages in case of such abuse— perhaps a sum in the neighborhood of $500.00, plus reasonable attorney's fees. A provision should also be included which would permit the plaintiff to collect a higher amount upon proof of actual damage. This concept of a minimum is necessary, however, because in the ordinary situation an individual subjected to police misconduct either has not suffered any actual damage or else the damages which he has suffered are so speculative as to be extremely difficult to prove. This recommendation is made with the full knowledge that, initially, at least, this statutory liability would result in a rash of ill-founded and even fraudulent lawsuits.

The author is confident that a governmental agency, faced with the prospect of a budget-wrecking series of lawsuits, would very quickly and very vigorously establish and enforce criteria and standards for field interrogations, and would also resort to a wide range of administrative sanctions to insure that the criteria are followed. If this result occurred, the courts would be impelled to accept the principle that civil rights and liberties can be adequately protected by police administration without court interference.

It must be emphasized that the civil liability suggested herein is only for abuses which are the result of malice, bad faith, or gross negligence. The fact that a police officer simply made an error in judgment, would not be the basis for liability. In other words, is is contemplated that no action would lie if unwarranted motives were absent, as when the officer had legitimate "reasonable suspicion" as a basis for the original stop.

Field detention interrogation is both a constitutional and a necessary tool in the fight against crime. It must, however, be used with discretion, and for the legitimate purposes for which it was intended. The police officer in the street must take seriously the admonition of the great French statesman, Talleyrand, when he said, "above all, not too much zeal."

Part III   Selected Correlated References

Fricke, Charles W., and LeRoy M. Kolbreck. *Criminal Investigation.* Los Angeles: Legal Book Corp., 1962. Good introductory textbook for police-science students. Does not go into great detail and depth.

Inbau, Fred E., and John E. Reid. *Criminal Interrogation and Confessions.* Baltimore: The Williams and Wilkins Co., 1962. One of the most widely recognized references and authorities on the subject of interrogation.

Jones, Leland V. *Scientific Investigation and Physical Evidence.* Springfield, Ill.: Charles C. Thomas, Pub., 1959. An introduction to proper methods of investigation, and the collection, care, and preservation of evidence.

Kirk, Paul L. *Crime Investigation.* New York: John Wiley and Sons, 1953. A detailed reference and guide for the criminalistics student, laboratory technician, and criminal investigator.

Kirk, Paul L., and Lowell W. Bradford, *The Crime Laboratory.* Springfield, Ill.: Charles C. Thomas, Pub., 1965. A good discussion in considerable depth of the organization and operation of the crime laboratory.

O'Hara, Charles E., and James W. Osterburg. *An Introduction to Criminalistics.* New York: The Macmillan Co., 1949. A most useful, concise, and easy to understand reference for every student in criminal investigation. Explains and details easy-to-follow procedures.

O'Hara, Charles E. *Fundamentals of Criminal Investigation.* Springfield, Ill.: Charles C. Thomas, Pub., 1966. The student, police instructor, and criminal investigator will find this presentation to be most valuable as a basic guide to criminal investigation. Well illustrated.

Soderman, Harry, and John J. O'Connell. *Modern Criminal Investigation.* New York: Funk and Wagnalls, 1962. This well-written text discusses basic, advanced, and technical elements of criminal investigation. Widely accepted and adopted by the law-enforcement profession as a basic reference. Used as a basic textbook in law-enforcement education and training programs throughout the world. Well researched, documented, and illustrated. Should be in every police, law, and student library.

Turner, William W. *Criminalistics.* San Francisco: Aqueduct Books, 1965. An excellent reference for the many facets involved in criminalistics. Well researched and written. Especially helpful to police officers and lawyers.

Weston, P., and K. Wells. *Criminal Investigation: Basic Perspectives.* Englewood Cliffs, N.J.: Prentice-Hall, Inc., 1971. Essentials of Law Enforcement Series, 1971. A concise treatment of the basic essentials and principles of criminal investigation. This paperback is written in nontechnical language thus making it less difficult for the student not sophisticated in the techniques of criminal investigation.

Part IV

Traffic Control and Criminal Law: Analysis, Methods and Procedures

The initial portion of this section discusses the goals, the dilemmas, and the challenge of police patrol. Along with the aforementioned areas, the authors focus on current procedures and innovations in police patrol, showing how the functions performed by the patrolmen are essential to police work. *The theme of police patrol is that the most important person in the police organization is the patrol officer.*

Much of the work performed by patrol officers in traffic control is centered around the theme of prevention. The authors point out that it is through this effort, by issuing warning notices, citations, and conducting traffic enforcement education, that violations and accidents are prevented. The many different types of patrol are described. They include *foot patrol,* which is probably the oldest and most common type of uniformed police patrol known and is employed extensively throughout the world; *horse*

335

patrol, next to foot patrol, the oldest type police patrol utilized; *bicycle patrol,* utilized quite frequently prior to the introduction of the automobile to the police patrol service; *automobile patrol,* recognized as standard police patrol service; *patrol with scooters and motorcycles; police canine patrol,* initially utilized as an aid to police officers in Europe; *marine patrol,* routinely used by cities with close proximity to bodies of water, and other specialized types of patrol.

In providing personal safety and property security to citizens within the community, peace officers are not necessarily concerned with "legal technicalities." However, out of pure necessity, peace officers are generally expected to understand criminal and civil law. The authors of Chapters 18 and 19 paint a vivid picture of the working basis for the policeman's conception of criminal law. Chapter 19 then looks at police-citizen confrontations and the pros and cons of "search and seizure" protection guaranteed by the Fourth Amendment.

CHAPTER 16

Methods of Patrol

G. Douglas Gourley and Allen P. Bristow

G. Douglas Gourley is Director of the Department of Police Science and Administration at Los Angeles State College, Los Angeles. He has authored or co-authored: *Public Relations and the Police, Effective Municipal Organization, Effective Police Organization and Management, A Bibliography of Criminal Procedure,* and *A Bibliography of Police Public Relations.*

Allen P. Bristow is Professor in the Department of Police Science and Administration at Los Angeles College, Los Angeles. In addition to writing numerous articles for professional journals, Professor Bristow has authored or co-authored: *Decision-Making in Police Administration, Effective Police Manpower Utilization, Introduction to Modern Police Firearms, Police Disaster Operations, and Police Supervision Readings.*

The methods by which the police patrol their district are as varied as the population and terrain they must protect. This chapter discusses those methods and systems in common use, as well as several which may become more popular in the future.

Foot Patrol

The oldest form of police patrol is naturally the foot beat. Dating long before 1829 and the first Metropolitan Police organized by Sir Robert Peel, the foot beat is still very much on the police scene. The majority of large American cities employ foot-beat men in varying degrees, especially in the highly concentrated population or high crime incident areas. Only a few of

From Douglas G. Gourley and Allen P. Bristow, *Patrol Administration,* 1961. Reprinted through the courtesy of Charles C. Thomas, Publisher, Springfield, Illinois.

the smaller communities use foot-beat men. With large areas to cover and the trend being towards shopping centers which de-emphasize the downtown business area, foot patrol is becoming increasingly impractical.

One of the strongest arguments for the foot beat is that the officer gets to know persons in his district. This can also have its disadvantages when care is not taken to prevent favoritism, loitering, mooching, and gossiping. One of the main problems in connection with a foot beat is the matter of communication. If a solitary officer becomes involved in real trouble, he must go to a call box or a telephone which is not always convenient or possible. Only in a few communities are patrolmen equipped with transistor radios. Occasionally, the press or a special interest group sets up a wail to "put the patrolman back on the beat so the women will be safe from the rapists that lurk in the shadows." Many police authorities resent such pressure tactics and have stated that the foot beat is obsolete, and that the cost of foot patrol is prohibitive. Except for crowded downtown areas or where there is a high concentration of people or crime, it would seem that methods of patrol other than foot patrol will be found most efficient.

Automobile Patrol

Under most circumstances automobile patrol will be found most effective. The automobile allows the officer to be mobile, and reduces his reliance on the station. Within the vehicles can be kept the riotgun, flares, fire and rescue equipment, spotlights, radio, and a stock of all necessary reports and maps. This equipment cannot be carried by the foot-beat man, and there are occasions when he needs such items. The patrol car provides protection against the elements and is almost always operational. A major feature is the car radio which keeps the officer in constant touch with his station.

The One-Man Patrol Car

Originally, police patrols were conducted by squads or larger groups of officers which, with the advent of the patrol car, were reduced to groups of four and then two. As communications improved, patrols become more independent of station control; and this permitted greater decentralization of man power. But as far as motorized patrol is concerned, for almost twenty years (1930 to 1950) the majority of patrol forces in this country continued to staff patrol cars with two officers.

During the last decade, as patrol data has become more available, there has occurred an almost universal trend toward the one-man car. Statistical studies from Wichita, Kansas City, San Diego, and other jurisdictions have shown that one-man patrol is far more effective than was the former two-man system. Companion studies have illustrated that the patrolman is as safe, if not more safe, when patroling alone. In the face of these results, those patrol administrators who are not already considering conversion to one-man patrol face requests by legislative and public groups to investigate its feasibility.

Generally speaking, the authors favor the *true* one-man car system but wish to caution patrol administrators to avoid selecting any program which falls short of the *true* one-man car system.

The True One-Man Car System

To establish what is referred to as the true one-man system, the patrol administrator must satisfy the following conditions.

Patrol Districts

Patrol districts must be re-evaluated and reorganized. Assuming the two-man car districts were correctly laid out, each one-man car district must contain only approximately one-half the area and activity that existed under the two-man car districts. In addition, careful consideration should be given to the arteries leading from one district to another to permit maximum access when assistance is needed. Patrol hazards requiring more frequent patrol inspection should be located on the boundary between districts.

A mistake frequently made in the conversion to a one-man car system is to reduce by half the number of officers and leave the patrol districts at nearly their original size. Pressure is often placed on the patrol administrator by economy minded public officials to simply remove one patrolman from each existing patrol car. While it is true that this could give the city a one-man car system, the results would be dangerous and not in the best interests of the community because inadequate police coverage would result.

Vehicle Equipment

Every effort should be made to alter patrol vehicles to the requirements of one-man operation. Protective screens and door locks for prisoner transportation are mandatory if prisoners are to be transported by one officer. The police shotgun, mounted in a visible position is important for psychological effect and availability. The combination automatic siren and public address system is strongly recommended. Communications equipment should be as efficient as possible, and here the steering post microphone with a foot operated "mike" button should receive consideration.

The automatic transmission is also quite important for a one-man car system. Other special equipment items such as portable desks, equipment racks, etc. made necessary by the peculiar nature of the area, should be considered.

Communications System

The heart of the one-man car system lies in effective communications. The three-way radio becomes a must and officers should be encouraged to use the car to car frequency to relay information and co-ordinate other activities.

Under normal conditions the dispatcher should be responsible for no more than fifteen cars. If the dispatcher is also required to operate a telephone complaint board, this maximum should be reduced drastically. The dispatcher must be kept informed at all times of the status and location of each car. When his work load does not permit this, another dispatcher must be added. Radio car activity boards should be developed to assist dispatchers in car control.

Total radio broadcast time should be evaluated and additional frequencies added where necessary. It becomes even more important in a one-man car operation that an emergency broadcast made by a patrolmen not be covered by other radio transmissions.

The selection and training of dispatchers also becomes important in the one-man car system. This key person must be able to understand every activity which occurs. It therefore becomes mandatory that the dispatcher be a patrolman, rotated back to radio-car assignment periodically. Only an experienced and responsible patrolman can evaluate situations and determine the proper dispatching of units. To employ a civilian or unexperienced officer at this task is dangerous.

Various dispatching techniques must be developed, standardized; and dispatchers must be trained. For instance, decisions must be made in advance as to the dispatching sequence under special conditions, on how many units to dispatch to given situations, and what follow-up system to use when units do not report conditions on a call within a prescribed time.

Training

Many techniques change when patrolmen work alone. It should not be assumed by the patrol administrator that these techniques will at once become apparent and will be adopted by the patrolmen. In-service training or "re-training" must be established, particularly in the areas of: (1) pull-over techniques, (2) prisoner search or security, (3) communications techniques, (4) major crime apprehensions, and (5) field interrogation techniques, to name only a few.

Philosophy

The one-man car operation will be successful only to the degree that the patrolmen accept and understand it. Great attention must be paid to gaining their acceptance and approval by carefully explaining: (1) why the system is being adopted, (2) what it will accomplish, (3) how it will work, and (4) what will be expected of them.

Probably the greatest resistance to the one-man car system is on the part of the patrolmen. They argue that it is not safe and frequently reject the statistical proof that is presented to them. Their arguments are developed primarily on an *emotional* basis. Actually, the strongest reason that they can objectively advance is the lonely aspect of one-man patrol.

Patrolmen should be made to understand that they *will not* be expected to take the chances they once did with a partner; that it is expected some situations will occur for which they must seek assistance.

The patrolmen must be made to realize that a call for assistance is not a sign of weakness but good police procedure. Some police officers consider it is a reflection on their competency or courage to request assistance even on routine drunk arrests. Under the one-man car system, most arrests should not be attempted until two officers are present. This is not always possible, of course, but highly desirable.

If patrolmen produce only 75% of the activity alone that they accomplished while with a partner, the *total* produced by both working separately will equal 150%.

Many methods of indoctrinating patrolmen exist. One method is to prepare a booklet which presents the case for one-man patrol as well as suggested techniques. . . .

When the authors speak, hereafter, of the one-man car system they refer to the *true* one-man car system which has been developed in line with the suggested criteria.

Special Conditions

Although the authors generally recommend the one-man car system, it must be stressed that this system is appropriate only for certain communities. To attempt such a patrol system in a rural area with inadequate cars to back up officers would be foolhardy. Several state and county police agencies have attempted conversion to one-man patrol with disappointing results, due largely to the great size of their patrol area.

The temperament of a community is another factor in determining the advisability of a one-man car system. If the area is anti-police, tough, and incidents of assaults on police are frequent, the one-man car would be dangerous. Some communities, which are generally appropriate for the one-man car but which have some tough districts, use a modified one-man system.

Such a system would place several two-man units in the tough patrol districts. Other agencies establish roving two-man cars which are assigned to all serious calls, along with the one-man car which has beat responsibility.

The patrol administrator should, therefore, examine carefully his community to determine if it will lend itself to the one-man car system. His decision should be based on these factors and not political pressure or the urge to conform with other localities. His decision should also consider his willingness to expend the funds and effort required to establish a *true* one-man car system.

Advantages

The one-man car system does not guarantee a crime-free community, but it does have a number of advantages over the two-man system. These advantages are not limited to operations but extend as well to the administration, public relations, and personnel aspects of the department.

Efficiency

Of primary interest to the patrol administrator is the increased efficiency to be gained from the one-man system. All studies on converted one-man systems show a gain in: (1) arrests, (2) citations, (3) field interrogations, and (4) other measurable work units. At the same time a marked reduction is noted in reported crimes which are subject to the repressive influence of patrol.

The increased repressive influence of the one-man system is reflected in the fact that the number of miles driven were almost doubled. In some of the cities, it was observed that total mileage increased more than twice the average under the two-man system. This might indicate that the patrolman alone tends to keep the car on the road more than when he rode with a partner.

A reduction in average arrival time to calls was also noted by most studies, probably due to the decrease in size of patrol areas. This reduction in arrival time probably is responsible in part for the increase in arrests, as well as an improvement in general public relations.

Statistically unmeasurable are the favorable public relations effects or repressive effects of the public observing many more patrol cars cruising through the community. It would appear logical that the public notices *patrol cars,* not the number of officers in them. One of the authors recently observed a major disturbance quelled by a one-man car system. When the arrests had been made and the officers began to leave, it was amazing to observe how few patrolmen were actually at the scene. The number of police vehicles at the scene presented a distinctive "show of force" to the crowd, which would not have been available under the two-man car system.

Discipline

Infractions and misconduct on the part of officers patrolling alone seem to be considerably less than under the two-man system. The reason for this has never been adequately established although it would appear that an increased ability for supervisors to place responsibility may be part of the answer. It is the opinion of some police administrators that when the officer is alone there is no "dare" aspect and no opportunity to impress a partner with misconduct. Others cite the fact that it is more difficult for an officer who is alone to become involved in disciplinary situations. They point out that officers cannot depend on a partner to listen for calls while they sleep, become involved with women, or enter a bar.

Another aspect of conduct which would seem to be improved by one-man patrol is simple courtesy. An officer working alone, it would seem, speaks more courteously to the public. The reason for this has not been determined, it may be because he lacks the moral support of the partner or does not need to impress the partner with his callousness.

Supervision

When officers work alone, it is much easier to evaluate their performance. Quite often a situation occurs, under the two-man system, where one partner becomes unproductive; and this condition is concealed by a more energetic partner who literally "carries" the defective officer. Under the one-man system, each patrolman may be compared with the others on performance and productivity.

A single officer may be held more closely responsible for conditions in his district than two patrolmen. When suspensions occur, only one man is off duty instead of two.

The matter of personality conflicts and changes of partners does not occur under the one-man system. In addition, rumors and griping are reduced, thus increasing morale. Under a well supervised one-man car system, the time in which officers can complain and trade grievances with each other is reduced to the time they spend in the locker room.

Alertness

One of the theories of one-man patrol is that, knowing he does not have the protection of a partner, the single patrolman will be more alert. Unfortunately, no objective method exists to measure or compare alertness. Accident rates compared between the two systems seem to bear out this theory, however.

The increase in the number of field interrogations indicated by cities which have converted to the one-man system indicates that another possible advantage exists. Perhaps patrolmen working alone tend to "play their hunches" more than when accompanied by a partner. When alone, no one, other than the patrolman knows about the "hunches" that did not develop arrests.

Disadvantages

In discussions on the merits of the two systems, the most usual objection raised to the one-man car system is the safety of the patrolman. The studies on comparative fatality and injury rates which have been made to date seem to indicate that there is no appreciable difference between the two systems. There do exist other disadvantages, however, which do not usually enter into such discussions.

Expense

The cost of obtaining twice the number of patrol cars is not the only expense incurred in transition to the one-man car system. All automotive costs will increase, gas, oil, tires, etc. In addition, not only required equipment must be purchased for the new cars, but the *extra* equipment necessary for the system must be purchased for *all* cars. Dispatching problems may also cause an increase in expense, both in equipment and personnel.

Secondary expenses probably will occur due to increased efficiency. An increase in prisoners, prosecutions, follow-up investigations, and reports will add to the budget.

Witnesses

Prosecutions may suffer due to lack of testimony. In many cases, only one patrolman will be able to testify to the elements of a crime, as he may be the only witness present other than a possible victim. In addition, when working alone, the patrolman has no witness for his acts in case of civil suit. The lack of a partner may also induce false complaints regarding the officer's conduct on the part of angry citizens.

Training

The traditional method of training patrolmen in the techniques of patrol is by "break-in" with an experienced officer. This naturally results in a two-man operation. If attrition is high on the patrol force, it would seem that some two-man cars would have to be maintained for training, even under the one-man system.

Back-Up

The theory of one-man patrol is greatly dependent on the availability of a neighboring unit, should assistance be needed. There exists, however, no iron clad method to insure that units will be available for assistance. Even if a dispatching technique were established to keep one unit clear for each unit committed on a call, there would be no assurance that units would not simultaneously go out of service on observations.

Conspicuous Patrol Cars

Of concern to the public from time to time is the method of distinctively marking patrol cars. The public, or influential segments thereof, have exerted great pressure to require patrol vehicles, particularly those involved in traffic functions, to be conspicuously painted. In some states this pressure has resulted in legislation which *requires* the police to so mark their patrol vehicles.

Public Opinion

Surveys indicate that the public is divided on the question. Those who favor marked cars present two general arguments. The first is that a citizen will be unable to recognize an unmarked patrol car, hence may be unable to summon assistance. The second concerns the fear that a motorist will never be sure who is stopping him, the police or a "red light bandit." The authors choose not to comment on these two improbable and remote arguments, except that such persons are probably more concerned with the theory that traffic enforcement should be "sportsmanlike."

Other segments of the public have no opinion on the subject or feel that any method the police use to reduce traffic accidents and prevent crime is acceptable.

If the patrol administrator is so fortunate as to be able to make the decision on a basis of merit, without public opinion or political pressure, the problem becomes a simple matter of evaluation of need and purpose.

Advantages

A conspicuously marked patrol car tends to further the preventive or repressive aspect of patrol. A car which stands out will be seen by more persons, while on patrol, than a plain car. When the objective is to suppress crime, particularly by one-man car patrol, distinctly marked cars are a necessity.

Disadvantages

When the emphasis is on apprehension, whether it be motorists or pedestrians, patrolmen are at a marked disadvantaged in conspicuous cars. It is particularly difficult to get close enough to apprehend such wary criminals as addicts or purse-snatchers when in a conspicuous car.

Compromise

Some agencies, particularly the California Highway Patrol, have compromised in such a way as to gain the advantages of both the marked and unmarked car. Only the side doors are painted white, and no warning devices are mounted on the roof or fenders. Red spotlights are mounted in normal position and kept turned down when not in use. From the front, this type of car appears to be a normal sedan; from a side or any quarter, it is a distinctly marked patrol car.

Another similar technique is to mount brackets on the sides of the patrol car. When conspicuous patrol is desired, white panels bearing police identification are mounted in a few seconds. This device is particularly valuable in communities where officers own their own patrol cars.

Police Boats

The majority of port cities have maritime police units that are responsible for dock areas. The United States Coast Guard assumes reponsibility for most of the police problems on the water. New York and San Francisco use patrol launches that have regular patrol beats. These boats are equipped with a variety of weapons and rescue equipment. Normally, a coastal police department can draw on the service of private boat owners or request the services of the Navy or Coast Guard. The airplane can usually handle any needed patrol over a water area; and, if seacraft are needed, they may be procured through the voluntary channels available.

The Use of the Bicycle in Patrol

The bicycle has been used by a majority of the European police departments for many years, and a number of Asian departments such as Hong Kong also use them. In the United States the bicycle is all but ignored as a piece of police equipment, except by private patrols.

The Lakeland, Florida, Police Department has utilized bicycles for several years with great success. Three bicycle patrolmen are assigned from 11:00 P.M. to 7:00 A.M. This city reports that such a patrol has greatly reduced night-time burglaries and thefts.

The prowler call is one of the most common patrol calls and yet seldom does a radio car crew see a prowler, much less arrest one. Being practically silent, the bicycle would be an ideal method of responding to a prowler call. This would be especially true in new residential tracts where a car can be heard and seen easily. Naturally, it would not be practical to have a police bicycle patrol in large metropolitan areas, but having one radio car in a district equipped with a bicycle might be feasible. The British and German airborne units during World War II had folding and collapsible bicycles. Such a unit could be easily kept in the back seat of a patrol car. Thus when a prowler call is dispatched, the bicycle equipped car would respond and stop within a block of the address. One officer could ride the bicycle to the location; the driver could then circle the area. In an area that has been plagued with prowlers, a regular bicycle patrol could be established. Equipped with a walkie-talkie, the officer could patrol while keeping in constant touch with patrol cars in the area.

With the application of a little imagination, the bicycle could well have a place on the American police scene.

Horse Patrol

With the advent of technology came the practical elimination of the horse in police patrol. Mounted police were used in all of the largest American cities; but with the development of the motorcycle and radio car, horse patrol has almost disappeared. The expense of keeping horses and training men to ride them was too great considering their limited uses.

The utilization of mounted police in crowd-control situations is the most valuable of their functions. The patrolman sits high above the crowd where he can observe agitators and, if necessary, use his night stick to advantage. Also, most persons, especially urbanites, have a fear of horses and the big police horse was normally respected. Yet the horse, being flesh and blood, has frailties. A sudden slash of a razor, a lighted cigar thrown at its head, or a jagged bottle twisted into his flanks can cause the animal to panic. In a riot a horse could easily be killed, throwing his rider into the midst of a hostile mob. It has been found that a motorcycle in the hands of a skilled rider can accomplish as much as a horse in crowd-control situations.

The horse for general patrol in a city area is very impractical. The sound of its hoofs against pavement disallows any chance of arrest during the commission of a crime. The Texas Rangers and the U.S. Border Patrol use horses to a limited extent in rugged areas. Even here, though, the aircraft, patrol car, and jeep have largely replaced the traditional western pony.

Horse-mounted police reserves, however, are popular in the Western United States. Perhaps the largest organization of this kind is the Los Angeles County Sheriff's Mounted Posse. These reserves receive extensive search and rescue training and perform valuable rescue work, especially in the mountain areas. There are occasions where the country is so rugged that only a horse can navigate the terrain. This type of rescue station is more peculiar to a sheriff's department than the average police department.

The Police Dog

A controversial subject currently under discussion in police circles is the use of dogs in patrol. The military have employed dogs with great success since the early stages of World War II, and Europeans have used dogs in police work for some time. In the United States dogs have been adopted by some departments and are being studied by many others. This subject is discussed in great detail . . . [elsewhere].

The Use of Aircraft in Patrol

The air age is rapidly changing our social concepts; and, in line with the times, law enforcement agencies are beginning to make greater use of aircraft in the patrol function. The United States Border Patrol pioneered in the use of aircraft to pinpoint situations and direct ground forces. The use of aircraft, particularly the helicopter, by rural law enforcement agencies in rescue work is almost common. Traffic enforcement by aircraft is now developing rapidly in rural areas and is being closely paralleled in metropolitan districts by the almost universal use of helicopters for traffic control.

The Washington State Highway Patrol uses light planes and helicopters along its highway network with great success. The Virginia State Police use planes for special events such as football games where there is extreme traffic congestion. The Sioux City Police Department has adapted their aircraft for pursuit of escaping vehicles. The airplane can cover an enormous area in far less time than it would take a fleet of patrol cars. Once the felon's vehicle is sighted, the Sioux City light-plane radios the exact location and begins directing the setting up of roadblocks. If the felon leaves the car and tries to flee on foot, then the plane makes a low level strafing run. This tree-top flying usually unnerves all but the most hardened criminal.

Police planes are usually equipped with radios and are in direct contact with ground units. If the aircraft is not equipped with a radio, the walkie-talkie tuned to the police frequency has been found to be satisfactory for short ranges. Many departments which use planes extensively have the roofs of their patrol cars painted with the number of the individual car so it can be spotted from the air. Los Angeles County Sheriff's Department cars have a gold star painted on a white background which is distinctly visible from the air.

Few departments actually own and operate their own planes. The majority depend on aerial volunteers. These volunteers are usually deputized by sheriff's departments which affords the pilots the authority of a peace officer. The California Highway Patrol now uses an airplane to patrol the desert area which is too desolate and large to patrol solely by car. This area has a heavy flow of traffic between Los Angeles and Las Vegas, and a light plane is invaluable in observing accidents on these desert highways. Many lives are saved as the injured do not have to wait for an ambulance until the chance observation of a patrol car or motorist.

CHAPTER 17

Aggressive Patrol

George W. O'Connor and Charles Vanderbosch

George W. O'Connor and Charles Vanderbosch of the Professional Standards Division, International Association Chiefs of Police are highly respected in the law enforcement field as researchers and authors. They have written and edited numerous articles, monographs, and training aids on police-community relations.

Law enforcement agencies have a specific task to perform for the communities they serve. First and foremost, crime must be controlled and prevented. When police fail in this primary duty, they then must perform a variety of duties designed to apprehend the offender and to recover stolen property.

Achieving Prevention

To successfully prevent criminal activity, the beat officer must be familiar with the conditions which create crimes.

In every crime there exists a combination of factors:

1. *The desire of the criminal to commit a crime.*
2. *The opportunity—or the belief in the existence of the opportunity —to commit the crime.*

Police action cannot deal effectively with the DESIRE of the offender. But it can and must deal directly with the criminal's *belief* that the opportunity for criminal activity is present.

To create the *belief* that the opportunity does NOT exist, the police take measures which place them most frequently in the locations of criminal

From George W. O'Connor and Charles Vanderbosch, *The Patrol Operation,* copyright 1971. Reprinted with the permission of the International Association of Chiefs of Police, Washington, D.C.

activity at the times when that activity is greatest. In other words, the criminal must be convinced that there is such continuous police coverage and in such strength that the risks involved are too great.

The criminal is a gambler. He measures his desire to commit a crime against the chances of being caught. When the chances of arrest are low—when patrol coverage is weak or lacking, for example—the crime will be committed and the criminal will escape. However, where aggressive patrol constantly impresses upon the criminal the idea that his activity will either be observed or will result immediately in his pursuit and capture, the risks are considered to be too great.

The effect that patrol will have upon criminal activity depends upon the type of crime involved. The individual who becomes so enraged that he commits a homicide will not be controlled to any great extent by motorized or foot patrol. The person desperate for narcotics will take far greater risks than the criminal whose "habit" has been satisfied.

Just as some crimes are not easily prevented or controlled by patrol, others are unquestionably reduced in the fact of aggressive patrol activity.

The person planning a burglary can be convinced that the opportunity to do so does not exist where he knows patrol officers are active and alert. As he studies police habits, he knows that the beat patrolled by the officer who frequently "checks the doors" of the business establishments is not a safe one in which to work. He knows that the frequent and irregular patrol pattern is such that he cannot rely upon any fixed amount of time in which to strike without running the risk of having the patrol car turn a corner and catch him in the act.

Basic Methods of Prevention

There are two basic methods for engaging in aggressive, preventive patrol:

1. Check frequently the physical security of business premises to prevent burglary and robbery.
2. Check frequently the citizen—to stop the suspicious person, to question his identity and his activities, to be constantly alert for persons within the beat who are up to no apparent good.

Crime prevention is the responsibility of more than just the police. The citizen himself must be reminded of his obligation to make his store secure through the installation of proper locks, lights and alarms. He must be reminded to lock his car, to notify police of his extended absences from home, to avoid hazardous locations during certain hours. In short, the citizen must be interested in his own protection. Frequently, this interest must be stimulated by the person most familiar with hazards of the beat officer.

Crimes against property—such as burglaries and larcenies from autos —can be reduced markedly by aggressive patrol tactics, in combination with a continuous appeal for citizen concern and cooperation.

The professional officer does more than ride about his beat waiting for calls for service from radio. He actively engages in preventive patrol. This primary activity goes far beyond looking. It involves frequent stops to check on both the doors and windows of buildings and the actions of suspicious persons.

The Professional Crime Fighter

There are a number of specific techniques that the professional develops in becoming a fully effective crime fighter. He goes beyond the confines of his automobile to challenge suspicious persons—persons whose glances and actions betray possible criminal intent; persons who appear not to belong on the beat.

Crime prevention cannot be accomplished from the front seat of an automobile—it can only be done on the street or in the bars or in the alleys when and where the criminal is most likely to strike.

He physically checks the security of business premises. This means more than shining a spotlight on doors and windows. He positively determines that they are not only closed but locked.

He continuously alerts citizens to take sensible precautions to avoid becoming victims of the criminal.

The beat officer who fails aggressively to seek and correct crime breeding conditions is an officer who fails to serve. The man who feels that patrol involves only responding to radio calls is a man who is performing only the secondary task to which he is assigned.

Early in his career, each officer must clearly understand that he will never fully accomplish total prevention—even when aggressive patrol makes the risks for the criminal considerably higher.

The awareness that total prevention is an unattainable goal does not deter the professional officer from fully devoting his energies to as much prevention as is humanly possible . . . and this amount of prevention is considerable.

It is clearly apparent that at least fifty percent of auto thefts could be prevented *if* people would lock their cars, would remove the keys, would place their ignition on lock instead of on off.

The officer fully intent upon providing the police service for which he was hired and trained can markedly reduce the purse snatchings, the muggings, the rapes and the thefts from autos on his beat. He will force the burglars to give up attacks on the businesses and homes on his beat and he will put prostitutes and gamblers virtually out of business *if* he will engage actively in continuous, aggressive patrol.

Responding to calls for service is of vital importance and every officer is prepared to do so without hesitation. The more difficult task which faces most men is that of keeping themselves busy between calls. It is this self-starting activity which is of primary importance in the overall fight against the rising crime rates. It is this constant movement and activity which has the greatest effect upon the criminal's belief that the opportunity to commit the crime is not present—or if it is present, it is an opportunity which is only a fleeting one which involves too great a risk of arrest.

Citizen Complaints

The professional patrolman—the man who recognizes the breadth and the depth of his responsibility for providing a *vital* public service—completes his tour of duty with mixed emotions.

He knows that his community is a better place in which to live for his having spent eight hours on the street. He also knows there is the possibility that he may be confronted at his next roll call with word that a citizen has complained against him.

Despite this harassment, this attempt to "get-back," the professional goes back on the street to provide another tour of service—knowing that the complainer and the ensuing investigation are all part of the job.

It is most unlikely that the professional policeman could complete a year without being the subject of a citizen complaint. The public is fully aware of the law enforcement profession's serious attentions towards alleged officer misconduct. A small portion of that citizenry knows they can intimidate by threatening to complain. The professional patrolman recognizes this. He knows that when he does his job he is going to make a number of people unhappy—those who receive summonses, those who go to jail and those who are warned against future or impending violations.

The real professional is a man who fully recognizes that as the controller of human conduct, as the regulator of human behavior, he himself must be above criticism. He must be warm and friendly to some—but not too warm. He must be cool and detached with others. He must never react to the verbal abuse, the threats, the insults. Reaction to these reduces him to the same low level of the insulter.

Being the enforcement agent for a community is a difficult task and the professional knows it. He knows that the only way to avoid giving the appearance of being slow, surly and corrupt is to continuously exhibit behavior which is efficient, polite and of unquestionable integrity.

The professional officer is like the competent umpire in a baseball game. The call is made on the basis of what is seen. That action results in both delight and anger. Call a "strike" and the batter is unhappy. The pitcher and the catcher are pleased. Call a "ball" and the reactions are reversed. Stop a traffic violator and he is unhappy. Fail to stop a violator and the other drivers being threatened or inconvenienced by his behavior are unhappy.

Aggressive patrol *cannot please* all of the people all of the time. It can and *must protect* most of the people all of the time.

Calling a pitch a "ball" when it bounces in front of the plate is easy. The difficult calls—the ones that just miss the corner of the plate—are not easy but they are necessary. The boos of the crowd do not stop the umpire from calling them as he sees them. Nor do unfounded citizens' complaints deter the professional patrolman from continuing to seek out the criminals and the violators.

The professional police officer accepts all types of information from all available sources. He follows leads, he interviews people and he evaluates the original information in terms of further developments—in terms of supporting information.

When the department receives a "tip" that Citizen Doe is "making book" in the corner barber shop, the investigation begins. When a citizen calls, reports a burglary in progress and hangs up without giving his name and address, the beat car is dispatched and the call is investigated. Every call is investigated and the report submitted.

How does the professional officer look upon the anonymous complaint, the chronic beef, the phoney allegation of misconduct? He accepts them for what they are worth—nothing but harassment.

He knows they are a part of the job. He knows that to pull away from the job, to lay back or to adopt an attitude of "stay clean by doing nothing" means defeat. He knows that the false complaint is designed to stop him from doing the aggressive patrol job that must be done to provide complete and adequate police protection.

The product of inaction is crime. The product of action is dedicated professional service and public safety.

The Supervisor's Role

The Supervisor of the aggressive patrolman has a more difficult task than the supervisor of the lethargic beat man.

The professional patrolman is going to seek out problems on his beat. He will go beyond the confines of his beat to assist and "cover in" for men on adjacent beats. He is going to stop traffic violators and he is going to take enforcement action. He will be out of his vehicle checking doors and suspicious persons frequently enough that he will not be immediately available for radio assignments. The complaints from the disgruntled, from the violators and from the suspicious will be made.

The supervisor stands in a difficult position. He must know his subordinate. He must be ready to take immediate positive action to determine the truth or falsity of the complaint. Above all, he must not presume guilt and then wait to be convinced of innocence. He will accept the information of the complaint. He will notify the accused officer and he will presume that the officer was justified in his acts—until the facts clearly show otherwise.

The supervisor is not asked to stand up and support or defend the officer whom he knows is wrong. The wrongdoer must stand by himself and must face the consequences of his own weaknesses. However, until that wrongdoing is substantiated by good, solid facts, the supervisor and the commander must be objective and must be fair to *all* parties.

The supervisor and the commander must respect both the feelings of the complainant who steps forward and personally registers a complaint and the feelings of the accused. They must not broadcast throughout the community the fact that a complaint has been received, but must wait until the investigation is complete and the facts are clearly shown and guilt or innocence is known.

CHAPTER 18

Police Attitudes Toward Criminal Law

Jerome H. Skolnick

Dr. Jerome H. Skolnick is Professor of Criminology at the University of California at Berkeley and Research Criminologist at the Center for Study of Law and Society, U.C., Berkeley. Professor Skolnick has authored or co-authored numerous works including: *Problems of the Family, Society and the Legal Order: A Reader in Sociology of Law, Social Problems: Crisis in American Institutions, Controlling Crime: The Social Organization of Criminal Justice, Family in Transition,* and *The Politics of Protest* (ed.).

A professor of law recently concluded that there are two prevalent models of the criminal process in the United States, the "due process model" and the "crime control model."[1] The due process model views the criminal process as conforming to the rule of law. It is a model stressing the possibilities of human error, especially the frailty of authority under pressure. Above all, it is a model emphasizing *legal* guilt over *factual* guilt. Thus, an accused is to be held guilty if, and only if, the factual determinations made against him have been presented in a procedurally regular fashion by lawfully constituted authorities acting within duly allocated competences.

For example, the convicting tribunal must have jurisdiction and venue, the power to deal with this kind of case in an appropriate locality and the case must have been brought within a limited time. Lest there be "double jeopardy," the accused must not have been previously convicted or acquitted of the same or a substantially similar offense. He must also fall into the category of persons who can be considered criminally responsible, thus excluding children and the insane. Such requirements for legal guilt,

From Jerome H. Skolnick, *Justice without Trial,* copyright 1966. Reprinted by permission of John Wiley & Sons, Inc., New York.
[1]Herbert L. Packer, "Two Models of the Criminal Process," *University of Pennsylvania Law Review,* 113 (November, 1964), 1-68.

and there are others running through the criminal law process, have nothing to do with whether the State can prove that the accused committed the act that is charged as the offense against him. If these procedural criteria are not met, the accused is *legally* innocent.

The crime control model, by contrast, emphasizes *factual* guilt. Its chief principle is efficiency through rational administration or "the system's capacity to apprehend, try, convict, and dispose of a high proportion of criminal offenders whose offenses become known."[2] This model stresses social control over individual justice. Its operative norms are those of a productive enterprise; its success is gauged by a high rate of apprehension and conviction in the context of mass administration of criminal law.

Previous chapters have discussed features of law enforcement drawing the policeman toward the crime-control model. The ability of known "criminals" to frustrate and harass law enforcement, the commitment of the police department to structures for apprehending criminals, and the perceived demands of political superiors for evidence of the policeman's ability and initiative, all combine, in the context of nontotalitarian norms about the initiative of workers, to bring policemen to interpret procedural requirements as frustrating the efficient administration of criminal justice.

This chapter further examines factors contributing to this process. It might be thought, for example, that instances of factual guilt not meeting legal criteria in dramatic crimes—homicide, rape—are what impels the policeman toward the crime control model. That is doubtless true, but I believe its force is overrated, even by policemen themselves in their own propaganda. From my observations, I would suggest that equally, if not more important, is the presence of procedural requirements in routine cases, especially those where the character of the defendant is clear. This chapter analyzes the legal processing of prostitution cases from this viewpoint and shows how the policeman's self-conception as a "craftsman" contributes to the seeming irrationality of procedural requirements based upon the rule of law.

Problems of Obtaining Evidence

The detective sees himself as a craftsman charged with carrying out assignments that, when stated generally, seem simple. In their complex particulars, however, these tasks may demand considerable skill. One such general task is finding facts; another is finding them in such a way as to allow them to be introduced as evidence; and finally, the facts must be strong enough to meet legal standards of proof and inference. That is, it is not enough that the policeman personally concludes, with complete confi-

---

[2] *Ibid.,* p. 10.

dence in his experienced judgment, that the defendant is guilty. He must also meet legal criteria to transform personal knowledge and feelings into a conviction.

The Westville district attorney's office, for example, requires eyewitness testimony to a solicitation before it will press the charges. If a prostitute has solicited a policeman or a special employee, the police have no problem in producing such evidence. Suppose, however, the police were to arrest a man and woman in a hotel room after following them because the man was white, the woman black, and the neighborhood colored. To achieve a conviction under these circumstances, the police must obtain a story from one of the parties incriminating the other. Take the following observed situation:

> After half an hour of "detecting," by listening in at closed doors of a cheap hotel, two vice control policemen decide the couple they are after is behind the door of room 14. They knock on the door; the girl answers. They identify themselves as policemen and immediately "split the pair" in order to determine whether the man's story and the woman's jibe. Among other things each says, the man claims he has known this girl for a while, the girl that she met him tonight. The policemen decide to take the pair to the squadroom for further interrogation. One policeman drives while the other sits between the pair and allows no talking in the patrol car.

At this juncture, the police see their task clearly. They must obtain a story from the man which incriminates the woman. The man, however, may actually be as guilty as the woman—guiltier if, as is often the case, he solicited her. The police justify their tactic on grounds of expediency; without testimony of the man they would be unable to secure a conviction against the woman. Recognizing that the women may not be deterred by the shame, inconvenience, and expense of arrest and conviction, since professional prostitutes regard arrest as a predictable part of a precarious career, while their customers might be, law enforcement officials interviewed nevertheless doubted that it would be more effective to have a policy of arresting men.[3] The case described below exemplifies the department's prostitution policy in practice:

> The man was a white serviceman, thirty-two years old, the woman a twenty-one-year-old Negro. When they were brought into the vice control squadroom, the woman was placed in a holding cell, a concrete windowless structure, approximately the size of a "walk-in" closet. The lights were not

---

[3]The rationale of the prosecutor bears a close resemblance to the "functional" explanation offered by Kingsley Davis. See his article, "Prostitution," in Robert K. Merton and Robert A. Nisbet (ed.), *Contemporary Social Problems* (New York: Harcourt, Brace and World, 1961); pp. 273-274.

turned on. The man was brought into an interrogation room, about the same size as a holding cell, but brightly lit and containing a small table and three chairs, one for the interviewee, one for the interrogator, and one for a witness (usually another policeman—in my role as participant-observer I continued to identify myself as a policeman by the simple expedient of not identifying myself otherwise).

The first thing the man was told was that he could walk out the door if only he would tell the truth—"All we want to know is when she set the price, how much, and for what. We know already because we were listening at the door, but we want to hear the truth from you." (Actually, we did not know; we could not hear very well through the door.) The man told a long rambling story which did not incriminate the woman, and he was placed in a holding cell while she was being interrogated. Like him, she denied solicitation had occurred, although she admitted that she had never seen the man before and that she was living with a "boy friend" in the room where she was found with the serviceman.

She was taken out of the interrogation room, and the man was brought back in. This time the man admitted that the woman had been sitting on his lap, had gotten up after he had unbottoned her blouse and said, "Let's get down to business."

In this second interview the man recalled that he had replied, "How much?"

When the interrogator asked the man what the woman's response had been, the serviceman said, "She didn't say anything."

The interrogator pointed out to the serviceman how improbable his story was, had him tell it again, told him to try and remember a little bit more, used flattery, sarcasm, threatening glances, pleaded for understanding, and finally, after about an hour of grilling, gave up. Obviously frustrated and annoyed, he called me outside and said, "See what we're up against. If we can't get this guy's cooperation we haven't got anything to book her on. We've got to let them both go, even though we're damned sure there was a solicitation here. But unless that guy says she set a price, our case won't stand up in court. But I'm going to tell the S.O.B. off before I let him go."

We returned to the interrogation room, handed the serviceman back his ID card, and the policeman "told the man off," which included advice to the effect that if didn't like what he was being told, the serviceman could see him on the street anytime and settle the matter. The serviceman was very deferential, claimed he had told all he could remember, only the truth, and thanked the policeman. My impression was that the serviceman was an old hand at this game and knew just which parts of the story to leave out, although it is also possible that the woman did not respond to his "How much?" thinking the serviceman was a special employee of the police department or a policeman.

It never occurred to the policeman to arrest the serviceman (who had admitted soliciting the woman), mostly because men as a rule are freed, but also because the Westville police have a standing arrangement to turn over all servicemen arrested on vice activities to the service police. They feel that if they were to prosecute a serviceman, he would be placed in "double jeopardy" since he would be subject to sanctions by the service as well as by the civil government. Besides, most policemen are former servicemen themselves, and are inclined to give a soldier or sailor a break whenever possible. What bothered the policeman about this serviceman was not that he "was out looking for a piece of tail"—policemen expect no less of servicemen—but that he had refused to incriminate the girl. "After all," the policeman explained to the serviceman, "we do cooperate with the service police and try to give you guys a break."

> When the man left, we opened the door to the holding cell and found the girl sobbing quietly. The officer told her how he was going to "give her a break" and let her go "this time" (when in fact he simply had insufficient evidence to convict). Then he told her that since he had done her a favor, he would like one in return. There followed a detailed explanation of a purchase of marihuana that he wanted her to make as a "special employee."

She agreed, under the circumstances, for what probably were a number of reasons. First, she was likely participating in various petty illegal activities. Thus, in the course of the interrogation it developed that she was living in Westville with a "boy friend" and at the same time was married to a serviceman stationed fifteen hundred miles away. Secondly, to a Negro girl from the South, the power of the police must appear awesome. She had already been locked up in a dark cell for more than an hour, and was not so secure in her position that she could refuse a policeman a favor. Finally, "to sweeten the deal" she was offered a small sum to act as a "special employee." To the girl, however, the most important consideration was probably the good will of the police, whom she might expect to encounter in the future.

To the policeman, such an evening's work is largely a frustrating failure, even though it is all part of his job and even though he has enlisted an informant. He has uncovered a solicitation, but because of the "technicalities" of criminal law is unable to "score," to obtain evidence sufficient to convict. Even if he is able to secure such evidence on the night of the arrest, however, it often happens that policemen are further frustrated by certain constitutional aspects of criminal procedure, such as the defendant's right to be freed on bail. In the administrative context of the processing of a criminal case, constitutional protections for the defendant come to be regarded primarily as administrative obstacles.

The Policeman's View of Criminal Justice

Although the policeman may have enough evidence to book a woman for solicitation or prostitution, unless she is held for a venereal disease check it is possible for the defendant to bail out immediately after being booked. The bail for a prostitution charge is always five hundred and twenty-five dollars (in Westville), no matter how many prior arrests and convictions the woman may have incurred. Bail bondsmen charge 10 per cent of the bail, which means that a prostitute must raise fifty-two and a half dollars to gain her immediate release. The defendant is given the right to have the sergeant at the jail make two phone calls to raise bail. Some prostitutes will have the sergeant call their pimp or a "steady trick." Others, who have been on the street for a long time, have an informal "credit" arrangement with a bail bondsman. Thus, it is rare for a well-organized, working prostitute to be unable to make bail, although a young, inexperienced girl without "connections" may remain in jail until her trial (or plea of guilty, after which she may be given probation). Under these circumstances, an experienced prostitute can be back on the street within several hours after arrest. If it is early enough in the evening, she may continue to ply her trade.[4]

The ease with which a prostitute is able to return to illegal activity is frustrating to the policeman. In his opinion, if the community wants to keep prostitutes off the streets, a system permitting them to return within a couple of hours after arrest is irrational. Thus, to the policeman, pretrial release is basically an irrational right given to the defendant by a state already tendering defendants an unreasonable measure of solicitude at every stage of the process.

Furthermore, and even more important, the policeman does not feel that he will have "his day in court." As one vice control man put it, "Our worst problem with whores is the plea of not guilty." When the suspect is booked, she is given a date in court, the date itself varying depending upon whether she makes bail or not. If she does not make bail and is booked before 2 A.M., she is placed on the same day's calendar (provided she has not been arrested on a Friday or Saturday night, in which event she will be placed on Monday morning's calendar). After 2 A.M. she is placed on the calendar for the following day. Appearing before the judge the following morning, she is charged, reminded of her rights to an attorney, and of the availability of the public defender for indigent defendants. (Usually there will be a deputy public defender present in the courtroom.) Sometimes the defendant will elect to plead guilty immediately, but most of the time she will request the services of a private attorney or of the public defender. In turn, the public defender will routinely request, and will be routinely granted, a day's continuance in order to interview his client.

The next day the public defender may plead his client guilty, or he may request a date for trial. On a misdemeanor, the defendant must be tried within thirty days, but the situation of the defendant who makes bail and

[4]Unless she has been held for a venereal disease check.

the one who does not is enormously different, since the defendant who cannot make bail must spend the time between being charged and the trial date in the county jail. This period of time, which may be less than thirty days, is known in the system as "dead time," since the judge need not take it into account in sentencing, although he may. Accordingly, it is generally in the interest of the defendant who cannot make bail to have guilt or innocence decided as quickly as possible in order to minimize "dead time." This period of pretrial detention may also serve as an incentive for a defendant to plead guilty when the chances for acquittal are regarded by her attorney as problematic.

When the policeman complains of the "problem . . . of the plea of not guilty" he is referring to the woman who makes bail, not to the defendant serving "dead time" in the county jail.[5] In contrast to the defendant who cannot make bail, it is generally in the interest of the bonded defendant to prolong the trial date. She has a sense of freedom which she does not wish to lose by undergoing the hazards of a trial and a possible finding of guilt.[6] In addition to a psychologically founded impetus to remove oneself from the adjudicatory process, there are legal and social reasons for so doing. In order to convict, the prosecution must present a witness who will testify that the woman solicited him. If the witness is a serviceman, he may be shipped out of the area in the meantime, thus destroying the prosecutor's case. Or he may die, or even change his mind about testifying. As one deputy district attorney put it, "A postponement may not hurt us, but it cannot do us any good. Our cases never get better as they get older."

Furthermore, if a woman is a professional prostitute, she may be rearrested one or several times while the initial case is pending. With several counts against her (and a crowded court calendar), there is some implicit pressure on the district attorney to settle for a plea of guilty on one of the counts, since the judge is unlikely to impose a heavier sentence for several counts than for only one. Thus, the pretrial period for the prostitute out on bail is one of "freedom" in a double sense: she not only maintains her normal citizenship rights but she also enjoys a degree of immunity from prosecution for illegal activities during this period. Finally, if the judge does

---

[5]On the importance of bail in the administration of criminal justice see Caleb Foote, "The Bail System and Equal Justice," *Federal Probation,* 19 (1955), 43; C. E. Ares, A. Rankin, and H. J. Sturz, "The Manhattan Bail Project: An Interim Report," *New York University Law Review,* 38 (1963) 67 ff; Patricia Wald, "Pretrial Detention and Ultimate Freedom: A Statistical Study—Foreword," *New York University Law Review,* 39 (1964) 631-640; and Anne Rankin, "The Effect of Pretrial Detention," *ibid.,* 641-655. For a bibliography and general discussion of bail reform see Daniel J. Freed and Patricia M. Wald, *Bail in the United States* (New York: The Vera Foundation, 1964).

[6]I have encountered only one defendant who *wanted* to go to prison, and this was a lower class Negro male who had spent eight years in state prison and wanted to go back to his "home." Indeed, he had committed a harmless petty theft to effect his return.

fine her, the woman will have had additional time to earn some money to pay off the fine and her attorney's fees.

The postponement of cases is consequently a source of irritation to the police, who feel that it interferes with the purpose and outcome of their duties. In addition, a postponement may involve some personal inconvenience for the vice control man. Whatever his stated shift may be, an officer always tries to complete a specific assignment. The work of a prostitution detail necessarily includes the handling of discontinuous and relatively short assignments, usually running a few hours. These assignments are, however, unpredictable enough to insure that actual hours may run into overtime. It is not uncommon for a vice control policeman to work into the early hours of morning and still be required to make a court appearance at 9 or 10 A.M. In addition, it may happen that a court appearance scheduled for 10 A.M. does not end until noon, and may drag on until afternoon. Since most vice control men work at 6 P.M. to 2 A.M. shift, it simply may not "pay" to return home at either end of a shift because of a court assignment, especially if the officer commutes. Consequently, a postponed case may result in notable inconvenience for the policeman.

The district attorney's office attempts to remedy this possibility by sending out subpoenas two weeks in advance of trial to police officers. Defense attorneys are called a day before a case is ready "to go" to guarantee that the defense attorney will not request a postponement at the last minute. Even with such precautions, however, it occasionally happens that policemen fail to be notified of postponements.

Moreover, police feel that judges are too lenient with defense attorneys who request postponements. The police perceive postponements as defense "tactics" (as indeed they are) and regard these as unfair and unethical. Furthermore, the police feel that judges, as a rule, give them less consideration than they give to defense attorneys. The policeman see attorneys as demanding and receiving a degree of "consideration" irrelevant to their role in the legal process. Thus, the police claim, a defense attorney may privately request and receive a postponement from a judge, with the implicit (if not explicit) understanding that the reason for the postponement is the client's inability to pay the attorney.

Although police charges may tend to be overstated, in fact there are built-in pressures upon the judge to cooperate with defense attorneys (aside from identification as fellow professionals), while the police have relatively little informal access to the judge and no direct means of interfering with his work. Their pressures usually must be filtered through the office of the district attorney, except in some instances where a judge is a former distinct attorney, friendly to police. By contrast, the defense attorney has more than conversational influence. He may refuse to "be reasonable" and insist upon his client's legal right to trial by jury within the thirty days trial deadline

Table 1.—Disposition of Persons Charged with Prostitution and
Related Sex Offenses by the Westville Prosecuting Attorney,
August 1962-February 1963[*]

Charge

Disposition	Solicitation or Prostitution (647b PC)	Pandering (266 PC)	Female Impersonation (3408 PC)	Total
Dismissed	21	1	4	26
Probation	2	–	–	2
Not guilty	4	–	–	4
Fine	29	–	1	30
Judgment suspended	18	–	2	20
Jail	12	1	6	19
Continued	14	–	–	14
Total	100	2	13	115

[*] This period of time happened, by chance, to be the period covered in the prosecuting attorney's "vice book" when the attempt was made to secure disposition data.
Thus, data for this period of time were used because of accessibility, which was
related to currency. It is doubtful that any systematic bias was thereby introduced.

period in cases which normally could be settled by the accused's plea of
guilty. If this were to happen with any frequency, the calendar could
become clogged, and the State would lose some cases simply because these
could not be adjudicated within the legally prescribed time period. Furthermore, if this were to happen, the judge who handles the jury trial calender
would be called to task by the presiding judge of the municipal court.[7] That
is, administratively speaking, the most important task of the judge is to keep
his calendar moving. In order to accomplish this, he must keep the prosecuting attorney and the defense attorney operating "within bounds." A
judge who permits either side to become excessively balky impedes the
achievement of this goal. A judge can exercise the full limit of his authority
with a specific defense attorney or two, perhaps one considered a "nut" by

[7] Each month a record is kept, and distributed to all municipal court judges, of the disposition
of jury trials for that month. At the bottom, in capital letters and distinctly set apart, is a
sentence which reads "CASES DISMISSED UNDER SEC. 1382 P.C.," the thirty-day trial provision
requirement. It should be, according to the administrative standards of the court, followed
by the word "NONE."

the community of defense attorneys. He cannot, however, lightly disregard the ordinary defense attorney's "reasonable" request that he be afforded an opportunity to be paid for his services. Neither can the district attorney, since the defense attorney can also interfere with the work of the district attorney. Thus, on the basis of the potential sanctions built into the structure of the judicial system, the judge unavoidably tends to inconvenience the policeman rather than the defense attorney.

Statistics reflect the analysis of the social structure. Only a small proportion of persons charged in Westville with solicitation or prostitution receive jail sentences. Of the eighty-six closed cases appearing in the files of the district attorney's office between August 1962 and February 1963 (an additional fourteen were being continued), only 14 per cent received jail sentences. Five per cent of those charged with solicitation or prostitution were found not guilty at trial; 24 per cent were dismissed outright by the judge; and 34 per cent received fines. These, however, are regarded by prostitutes, by defense attorneys, and by police as the equivalent of "license fees" for continuing prostitution activities.

The remaining 21 per cent were given sentences of from thirty to one hundred and eighty days in the county jail, with judgment suspended. The consequences of such a sentence are ambiguous. Technically, if a woman under a suspended sentence for prostitution is arrested once again during the period under which judgment has been suspended (usually a year or two), she may at the discretion of a judge be required to serve her earlier jail sentence plus any new one imposed. In practice, however, Westville judges take earlier suspended sentences into account only after conviction, and some judges will, after a period of a year or so, ignore the earlier suspended sentence and "merely" fine the prostitute for her most recent conviction. When this happens, both police and prosecuting attorney feel that justice has been thwarted.

"Pleading Out" Prostitution Cases

When the police do bring prostitution cases to court, they will typically put pressure upon the district attorney not to accept a plea of guilty in exchange for a fine. Since police have recurring relations with prostitutes, they have a considerable stake in influencing outcome. If interactions between police and prostitutes were minimal and nonrecurring, the policeman's authority would not be challenged by the possibility of a defendant escaping conviction. But policemen need prostitutes—as informers, for instance—and are also regularly called upon to control them. Consequently, an arrest which does not lead to conviction and a jail sentence undermines the policeman's ability to constitute an authoritative threat to the prostitute.

It may happen, however, that the district attorney has little choice in whether to accept a plea of guilty. In chambers, the bargaining is largely between judge and defense attorney over sentence. The district attorney can do little more than represent the police position to the judge in chambers. He obviously cannot refuse to accept a plea of guilty, because if the issue were to go to trial the defendant might be acquitted by a jury. Even if she were found guilty, the judge might still impose a fine rather than a jail sentence. In a prostitution case, consequently, the significant representation by counsel takes place in the judge's chambers before trial, and the outcome will tend to vary with the private moral conceptions of the judge.

This is not, however, to assert, as many attorneys would, that it is impossible to generalize about the outcome of such an interaction because it "all depends upon the personalities of the people involved." What an attorney means by such a statement is that the interaction is not entirely predictable, since its outcome depends on who the parties are and what their prior relations have been. This assertion is true, of course, but it still appears that the variations in "role" explain far more than variations in the "personality" of those occupying such roles. For example, during the study, a vigorous defense attorney became a judge. While he maintains privately the position that it is senseless to jail prostitutes, as a judge he does so if the woman has been convicted with some frequency, about twice in a year's time. Furthermore, he still talks privately like a defense attorney, but acts publicly like a judge. He feels that in his role as a judge he must adjudicate between parties, not simply uphold the defense attorney's point of view as presented in the context of a negotiation. Finally, he realizes that the defense attorney may not privately agree with the position he takes in a negotiation but also takes it in line with role obligations.

The following is a description of negotiations in another judge's chambers of five prostitution cases. It is typical in the sense that it expresses how the differing role obligations of judge, defense attorney, and district attorney shape the interaction and its income.

> Present were the judge, the defense attorney, the district attorney, and the writer. The vice control officers were not permitted to participate directly in the bargaining. While the group was being assembled, the district attorney whispered to me: "While I'm supposed to be abstractly responsible to the community for anything I do, actually I'm directly responsible to the officer who makes the arrest. He's the person that I have to explain any of my actions to."
>
> When everybody was seated, negotiations were opened by the defense attorney, one of the most experienced and respected in the county, and a Negro himself, who was defending five Negro women accused of prostitution.
>
> "Judge," he said, "These girls don't want any time so I know I'm going to have a lot of difficulty making a deal, but I want to say that I don't really

think that these girls are so responsible. I think the police created the whole thing. All the girls were trying to do was make a little Christmas money." Everybody smiled at this remark, including the defense attorney.

It is important to note that the defense attorney began bargaining with the judge, not with the district attorney. All concerned understood that what was being bargained over was sentence, not charge. Among some defense attorneys this ploy is known as "wiring the judge" before "copping out."

The defense attorney continued, "Do you think it will do any good to go through with these cases individually? I sort of want to know how you feel about them, Judge, because if you feel you are going to have to give them time, then it doesn't even pay to waste any of our time talking further."

It was clear that, faced with the prospect of five jury trials, and the criterion of efficiency, the judge was not going offhandedly to declare the impossibility of a fine, even though there was no timewaiver problem in these cases. Thus, the opening move by the defense attorney was a strong one.

The judge responded by explaining his attitude toward prostitutes. He said that a long and checkered history of prostitution showed that there wasn't much that could be done to help these girls. . . . "I would like somehow in some way to rehabilitate the girls, to change their life pattern, and if they are new at the game I am willing to give them a break. But if they have spent a great deal of time as prostitutes, I feel that the only thing I can honestly do as a judge is to give them punishment so as to deter them from committing the same kind of acts in the future."

The defense attorney replied, "Judge, privately I agree with you, but as an attorney I have to see what I can do for my clients."

The judge indicated that he understood the defense attorney's position and was not holding him to account personally, but that as a judge he also had to do his job. The judge suggested that they take the cases one at a time and see what they could do with them. The defense attorney was agreeable: "Why don't you look at Jane Darrow's record, Judge, and see what you would give her, without any comment from me."

The judge began to look at Jane's record and as he was doing so, the defense attorney, instead of holding back comments as he had promised, keep making side remarks which emphasized the general "social problem" nature of prostitution as against the individual culpability of his clients. "If only they'd tear down these shack-up hotels and put up some street lights there wouldn't be so much of a problem."

Actually, the defense attorney was expressing his conception of the kinds of broad "sociological" reasons which would impress a "liberal" white judge. The attorney was acting on behalf of his clients in saying these things, because what he said did not reflect accurately his own private moral conceptions. These are rather complex, because as a Negro attorney in

what, from where it sits, is at best a "liberal" white community, he sometimes expresses apparently contradictory moral sentiments. However, on
the subject of prostitution, he will privately express the idea that prostitutes
earn their living in the best way that they know how; that they provide a
service for which men are willing to pay; and that unless they create a public
health problem they should not be harassed by the community. Furthermore, that within the Negro community, with opportunities for earning a
living limited as they are, prostitution is often tolerated, if not accepted,
morally.

    Apparently Jane was the worst offender of the lot, with the worst
record, because the defense attorney said, "Judge, she's had the gamut, the
record, but I'll tell you, she just won't plead, knowing she's going to jail. In
fact," said the Defense attorney, "if I gave them Jane, they'd give up all the
others."

One couldn't quite tell who the "them" was, whether it was the
district attorney or the vice control squad, but it seemed to be the vice
control squad, and the defense attorney appeared cognizant of the pressures
from this source on the district attorney.

    The judge asked the defense attorney what his defense would be. He
replied, "Well Judge, you know the man that went into that house and they
caught coming in and out, he was simply—he was an old friend of the family.
He'd known this girl for years, and her mother and father were old family
friends, and he just went in there because he was a friend of the family. When
he came out these vice squad officers said to him, 'Do you know what kind
of a woman she is?' and he said, 'I don't care what kind of a woman she is,
she's an old friend of mine.' He'll testify to that, Judge."

    The defense attorney added that the arresting officer was Rogers. The
defense attorney contended that if Rogers took the stand he'd "wipe up the
courtroom with him" because Rogers, he said, made the worst impression
possible.

    The judge didn't commit himself on Jane Darrow, but went on to a
couple of the other cases and looked over the records of the girls. He commented along the way that he'd probably have to give some of them "time,"
although maybe some of them could get away without any "time," because
he felt that some of the cases contained an element of entrapment. The district
attorney agreed there probably was an element of entrapment in some of the
cases.

    The defense attorney said, however, he wasn't going to argue entrap-
ment, because when you argue entrapment you admit that the solicitation had
been made and this doesn't always turn out too well for your client in a jury
trial.

    The judge asked rhetorically—since he already knew the answer—"I
don't suppose most of them want probation?" The defense attorney agreed
with the judge, who responded by saying, "All these are old-timers, isn't that
right?"

The defense attorney said, "All but one, Diane Smith. She doesn't want probation, though, because she doesn't want any probation officer coming around to her house on this charge. She's got a daughter graduating from Cedarville High."

The defense attorney then repeated that these girls didn't want any time and presented to the judge the technique of moral rationalization used by the prostitute. He said that these girls felt that they weren't doing anything that was very wrong; that they weren't doing anything that was very different from what other women do, except that they slept with a number of men, instead of one; that they earned their money fair and square, in an exchange of sex for money; and that it was a private exchange that they felt wasn't wrong to make. He further argued that a sentence of time wasn't going to change the behavior of any of these girls.

The judge said in reply that none of these girls had ever gotten one hundred and eighty days and the defense attorneys shot back that one of them had and was still out on the streets. The judge looked at her record and agreed that one of them had.

The judge said that he felt that perhaps the time spend in jail might not in fact do these girls any good, but he wasn't going to agree beforehand not to give any of them any "time." The defense attorney said he felt that he could beat some of these cases, but that he would not like to have to.

The defense attorney brought up once again, as he had throughout the interview, the fact that these trials would be so time-consuming on everybody's part, and it would be a good idea to not have to go through the business of trial. He tried to show that he was sort of on the judge's side, that he did not really think too much of these girls. He placed himself in the position of a poor guy representing clients who are making large demands upon him, and there was nothing he could do but hold to a fast, hard bargain. It was the ancient "I'd like to, but my partner won't let me" bargaining routine—"My client is the one who insists that there be no time."

The judge said, "Well, I guess then we'd better have some jury trials. I just won't agree to tie my hands in advance as to sentencing." The defense attorney said, "Okay, I guess we'd better. We'll just have to write them up on the calendar." As he left, the defense attorney thanked the judge and the judge said, "What are you thanking me for? I haven't done anything for you." The defense attorney smiled and said, "Oh, that's all right, Judge, I understand your position in this."

We all left the judge's chambers and went out into the courtoom. The district attorney immediately went over to the members of the vice control squad who were present and told them that no deals had been made. They were very happy, almost jubilant. They said that they didn't want any deals to be made, that even if they had to lose some of the cases, they wanted to go through with court trials.

They left the courtroom and were interivewed in the corridor. Asked why they were so happy that no deals had been made, since it would require a lot of court time for them, one said,

> We don't care about that. We don't even mind working overtime and not getting paid for it. What we don't like is being dealt out in the judge's chambers." He continued, "We ride around all night and, when we make an arrest, we feel that the arrest ought to stick. If we set up a case, then we want to see it go through. When we write one up, we want to see it move. We don't want it dealt out. . . . We don't even care if we lose some of the cases. We want to indicate how many arrests we've made, and we want to show that we went to trial with them. Many of these cases are dismissed out of hand, and if they're dismissed, the judge that they are coming before now doesn't know why a girl had a case dismissed earlier. What often happens is that a girl will come before the judge and he'll try to give her a break so he will dismiss the case. But the next time she's arrested, she may not come before the same judge, and that judge will look at the dismissal and think that she was brought up on a wrong beef, when it's just that the other judge was feeling sorry for her.

Administrative Bias of the Craftsman

The hostility the policeman expresses toward the prostitute is not, however, unconditional. The policeman does not express the same antagonism toward the prostitute who does not "play the system for all it's worth," or the prostitute who is "cooperative with law enforcement." His objection to the prostitute is best understood in light of his stance toward principles of criminal procedure.

The policeman views criminal procedure with the *administrative bias of the craftsman,* a prejudice contradictory to due process of law. That is, the policeman tends to emphasize his own expertness and specialized abilities to make judgments about the measures to be applied to apprehend "criminals," as well as the ability to estimate accurately the guilt or innocence of suspects. He sees himself as a craftsman, at his best, a master of his trade. As such, he feels he ought to be free to employ the techniques of his trade, and that the *system* ought to provide regulations contributing to his freedom to improvise, rather than constricting it. There is in his attitude toward judges, for instance, a sentiment akin to that of Shaw's epigram, "Those who can, do; those who cannot, teach." Like other doers, he tends to be resentful of critics who measure his value by abstract principles rather than the "reality" of the world he knows and lives and sees.

To further understand the consequence of his craftsman's bias, it must be understood that the policeman draws a moral distinction between criminal law and criminal procedure. (I have never heard a policeman actually articulate, argue, and defend the distinction, but it is implicit in his general outlook.) The distinction is drawn somewhat as follows: The substantive law of crimes is intended to control the behavior of people who willfully injure persons or property, or who engage in behaviors eventually having such a consequence, as the use of narcotics. Criminal procedure, by contrast, is intended to control authorities, not criminals. As such, it does not fall into the same *moral* class of constraints as substantive criminal law. If a policeman were himself to use narcotics, or to steal, or to assault, *outside the line of duty,* much the same standards would be applied to him by other policemen as to the ordinary citizen. When, however, the issue concerns the policeman's freedom to carry out his *duties,* another *moral* realm is entered.

Statements are often made, typically by civil libertarians, to the effect that "policemen ought not to break the law in carrying it out." From sociological vantage, the important point is the different meaning of the word "law" as used by the policeman and by his critics. Unlike the policeman, civil libertarians do not in this context draw a moral distinction between the law of crimes and criminal procedure. This is not, for the moment, to suggest that civil libertarians are wrong in the demands they make upon police. No policy judgment need be implied here. Rather, it is important to make a conceptual distinction which will help to understand the policeman's attitude toward legal constraints.

In contrast to the criminal law presumption that a man is innocent until proven guilty, the policeman tends to maintain an administrative presumption of regularity, in effect, a presumption of guilt. When he makes an arrest and decides to book a suspect, the officer feels that the suspect has committed the crime as charged. He believes that as a specialist in crime, he has the *ability to distinguish between guilt and innocence.* If pressed, and in public, most police would not advocate that criminal trials are generally unnecessary. If one talks to policemen for a period of time in private, however, the impression is gained that the policeman feels that most trials are a waste of taxpayers' money since, as one law enforcement spokesman put it, "We do not charge innocent men." Indeed, the policeman sees himself as a merciful administrator of justice as well. Vice control men feel, for example, that any "breaks" a particular defendant deserves have already been meted out according to personal discretionary standards of police, appropriate in their operational environment.

The administrative presumption or regularity may well prevail among all persons in the system, defense lawyers, judges and juries, although in differing degree. Arthur Train states the regularity presumption nicely when he says:

> People as a rule don't go rushing around charging each other with
> being crooks unless they have some reason for it. Thus, at the very beginning

the law flies in the face of probabilities when it tells us that a man accused of crime must be presumed to be innocent. In point of fact, whatever presumption there is (and this varies with the circumstances) is all the other way, greater or less depending upon the particular attitude of mind and experience of the individual.[8]

Placed in the routine context of criminal law administration, the presumption of regularity is the most obvious and commonplace assumption that can be made. That is, it *is* reasonable to assume that trained people do their jobs properly. To understand the force of this assumption, one need only observe several *voir dire* examinations of jurors in criminal cases, and notice the stress placed by the defense attorney on communicating to the jury the right of the defendant as to a presumption of innocence, and the burden of proof of the prosecution to prove its case beyond a reasonable doubt. Prosecutors, at least in Westville, prefer to try cases before experienced jurors, and defense attorneys before a "greener" panel because each perceives that the greater the experience of a juror, the more likely he is to attribute a presumption of regularity ot law enforcement, rather than a presumption of innocence to the defendant.

Among criminal lawyers, this is the fundamental distinction between those who are regarded as "prosecution-minded" and those who are termed "defense-minded." The "prosecution-minded" lawyer envisions the adjudication of criminality as a "rational" administrative task, placing much confidence in "specialists" whose job it is to deal with criminals. The "defense-minded" lawyer, on the other hand, emphasizes the peril of interfering with the liberty of a human being. He sees the sanctions as being so high that it is dangerous not to presume the innocence of the defendant. Furthermore, he is troubled that the police will behave in an arbitrary fashion, with greater concern for their own stake in the outcome than for the society's interest in justice. The consequence (and a deep and inevitable source of tension under the circumstances) is that the policeman must feel his work is being "interfered with" well beyond what a "rational" system would demand.

Accordingly, the policeman feels that criminal procedure has been unfairly weighted against him. In the policeman's administrative eyes, any "balance of advantage" lies not with the State but with the defendant. The policeman finds it difficult to fathom and to justify a system which, on the one hand, requires that he be increasingly knowledgeable and competent in general areas as well as those relating specifically to police work, and, on the other, sometimes nullifies his best efforts by interposing seemingly irrational requirements and procedural delays.

---

[8]Arthur Train, *Courts and Criminals* (New York: Scribner's, 1921), p. 15.

The Quasi-Magisterial Role of the Prosecutor

One channel for tempering police resentment toward criminal law is the office of the prosecutor. By representing the law as an authoritative symbol, the prosecutor tends to curb police hostilities toward legal strictures. The prosecutor thus plays a quasi-magisterial role, somewhere between policeman and judge, a role he eases out of as the case progresses. In the early stages, the prosecutor acts more like the magistrate; in the later stages, he necessarily comes to represent law enforcement.

The initial contact of policeman with prosecutor occurs when the former brings a complaint to be charged. This encounter may be critical, because it is an important point for making decisions about the conception of the case—whether the complaint should be dismissed, whether the charge should be reduced to a lesser offense or to a misdemeanor. On most occasions, police do not attempt to influence the deputy district attorney one way or the other. During the study, forty-eight attempts were observed in which police tried to influence a municipal district attorney's decision.[9] In forty, the police argued for a heavier charge, and in eight, for a lighter one. The deputy accepted the policeman's argument in slightly more than one-quarter of the cases. The deputy, however, rarely made an outright refusal. Instead, he usually made one of two explanations: (1) that the defendant would not likely receive a more severe sentence as a result of a heavier charge; or (2) that if the officer were to obtain additional evidence, the deputy would charge as requested.

In most felony cases, if the defendant is "held to answer" to the superior court, his file containing his rap sheet, arrest report, preliminary hearing, and an assessment by the municipal deputy is sent to the "screening deputy" in the county prosecutor's office for the purpose of filing an "information."[10] The assessment by the municipal deputy is supposed to alert the "screening" deputy to particular problems or items of information. For instance, it may be noted that the prosecution witness "makes a lousy impression on the stand" or that, despite such a fact, the complaining witness does not want to drop charges.[11]

In deciding the charge or charges upon which to file an information, the "screening" deputy will again frequently talk to the policeman. It should be understood, in terms of the state hierarchy of the prosecutor's

---

[9]The figures were gathered in two municipal prosecutors' offices in the county studied. They should be interpreted with caution as they represent no sample of a known population. There was, however, a high degree of inter-interpreter reliability for the two offices observed.

[10]Usually, cases of general public concern are presented to a grand jury for "indictment." Functionally, however, the "information" and "indictment" are equivalents. See Fred M. Henderson and William L. Ritzi, "Grand Jury Proceedings," in *California Criminal Law Practice* (California Continuing Education of the Bar, 1964), pp. 251-273.

[11]In rape cases, such a request will usually be honored.

office, that deputies on the county level are of higher status than those at the municipal level (except for those holding positions of rank in the municipal level (except for those holding positions of rank in the municipal offices, especially Westville's). Thus, only after a deputy gains experience on the municipal level, will he be sent up to the county office (unless he has compensatory outside experience). In this respect, the municipal offices serve as "farm teams" for the county office.

As a result, the "screening deputy" in the county office will view more critically the work of the municipal deputy, and will also understand that the municipal deputy may be subject to some greater degree of police influence. The "screening deputy" may interview the policeman and the complainant himself, depending upon whether he has questions as to the charge, or perceives discrepancies between the charge and the evidence brought out at the preliminary hearing. (The screening deputy is empowered to change the charge, providing the offense in the information was encompassed within the same behavioral transaction as the original charge.)

Usually, changes are in the direction of charging the defendant *less* seriously than the deputy did down below. Not only is the municipal deputy subject to greater police pressure but he is also wary of undercharging, since the charge can always be reduced on the information. Overcharging is usually regarded as an "error" by the "screening deputy," but an understandable one. As one "screening deputy" who, like most county deputies, had formerly been in a municipal office said:

> If I were down there I'd probably do the same thing. If you don't have to try the case, then you can be a lot looser in what you charge, and a lot of the time these guys just get careless. But if they had to take this case into court and try it, they would be a lot more careful. I know that if I had to try a case that I was charging, I'd be a lot more careful.

Of course, the screening deputy's anticipation of courtroom exposure makes him less likely to accept the request of a policeman. While the municipal deputy might be willing to "take the heat" from the "screening deputy" for overcharging (to maintain friendly relations with the police) the "screening deputy" is less interested in these relations than in not losing, which is different from winning. If the case should come to trial "overcharged," the defendant may gain an acquittal, while with a lesser charge, he may be found guilty on the same facts. Deputies are called upon to educate policemen that agreement to a lesser charge does not represent capitulation, so much as reality: a considered judgment that the defendant would probably be convicted of the lesser offense, but not of the greater.

When an information is filed, the case passes on to the "calendar man," the representative of the district attorney in the courtroom on issues pertaining to date of trial. He must be prepared to say whether a case is likely to "go" or not, and therefore must keep in close touch with defense attorneys. He thus functions as the routine "plea bargainer" for the prosecutor. The calendar man's dealings with police are minimal, unless a "problem," such as the wish to protect the identity of an informant, is noted on the assessment sheet coming up from the municipal deputy.

If the case is not "settled" on the day the information is read, it is assigned to a trial deputy (although it may still be, and frequently is, pleaded out before trial). When the trial deputy enters the picture, the case is his to prepare for the courtroom. Frequently, such preparation requires further interviewing of witnesses, especially of police, who are as a practical matter easily available. By my observation, when the trial deputy questions the police, he is not at all reluctant to criticize the policeman's actions in the case. For instance, in one such interaction observed, the policeman was told that his failure to caution the defendant in a recorded statement might prejudice the jury unfavorably. According to several deputies questioned on this matter, it is indeed the policy of the office to "educate" policemen.

Furthermore, the police seem not to resent such "correction," and appear to enjoy their roles as "assistants" to the higher-ranking law enforcement personnel. Unlike the municipal district attorney, the county deputy is generally an experienced courtroom operative, and is more likely to be accepted by the police, who tend to weigh experience heavily. He is perceived in a fashion similar to that in which the captain of a team or a higher military officer would be viewed—possibly with some resentment, but with clear acknowledgement of his right (and duty) to correct errors. At the superior court level, the policeman and the district attorney become part of the same team. Thus, although the prosecutor plays a magisterial role in the sense of assessing with a critical eye the validity of complaints and the strength of a case, he ultimately represents law enforcement. In playing this role, however, he is not only interprets criminal law to the policeman, but also, in the process of interpretation, *legitimizes its authority* and tempers police resentment toward criminal law.

Conclusion

This chapter has described a portion of the working basis for the policeman's conception of criminal law. By examining the processing of prostitution cases, it has shown how the policeman develops the craftsman's administrative bias; he sees the world in probabilistic terms. When he sees a black girl and a white serviceman enter a hotel together, he assumes an act of prostitution is in the offing. To him, these are not constitutionally protected citizens, but predictable actors whose misbehavior he usually judges correctly. Sometimes, to be sure, he may be in error. The probabilities, however, are so strong, he feels, that his judgment is rarely going to be wrong.

Given that assumption, he finds it utterly unjustifiable to have imposed upon him a series of "obstacles" that (1) impede the exercise of his expert opinion, and (2) permit criminals to frustrate the stated aims of the community as expressed in substantive criminal law. For him, due process of law is, therefore, not merely a set of constitutional guarantees for the defendant, but also *a set of working conditions* which, under increasingly liberal opinions by the courts, are likewise becoming increasingly arduous. No comparable worker, he would assert, is given so little consideration. Thus, by presuming the defendant to be innocent as the first in a series of frustrating obstacles, the State requires the policeman to work in a milieu filled with extraneous and, to him, needless restrictions. If these were "rational" he might countenance them. In his world of fact, however, they appear highly irrational, since they do not conform to his experience. One cannot "presume" a defendant to be innocent when the character and actions of the defendant so strongly suggest guilt. The very notion of making a presumption so frequently contrary to fact violates his craftsman-like conception of self, and induces negative attitudes toward due process of law. The policeman, in short, is primarily interested in *factual* guilt. Indeed, the idea of *legal* guilt leaves him cold and hostile.

To a degree, these feelings are tempered through the quasi-magisterial role of the prosecutor. In the latter, the policeman finds a man who is both a sympathetic ally and an interpreter of constitutional legality. The prosecutor need not be successful in making the policeman approve of the strictures of due process of law, which he typically does not admire himself. By accepting their legitimacy, however, he demonstrates to the policeman that it is at once possible to disagree with the rules of the game as they are laid down, and at the same time to carry out the enforcement of substantive criminal law—if one learns skillfully how to interpret these rules into action.

CHAPTER 19

The Fourth Amendment and Police-Citizen Confrontations

Lawrence P. Tiffany

Lawrence P. Tiffany is Professor of Law at The University of Denver. He received his A.B. (1961) and his LL.B. (1963) degrees from Washington University, and his S.J.D. (1967) from the University of Wisconsin.

The question of the constitutionality of police field interrogation practices has generated great interest in the past several years. Although courts have litigated this question for decades,[1] a major discussion of the problem did not appear in legal literature until 1960.[2] In 1964 the New York legislature enacted a statute authorizing police to stop and frisk suspects who could not be arrested.[3] That statute attracted considerable attention to the problem. Since then, the frequency of litigation of field interrogation issues has increased, and over fifty publications now exist on the subject. The problem has been discussed extensively by the American Law Institute in connection with the initial draft of the *Model Code of Pre-Arraignment Procedure*[4] and in the American Bar Foundation's Survey of Administration of Criminal Justice in the United States.[5] The report of the President's

---

From Lawrence P. Tiffany, "The Fourth Amendment and Police-Citizen Confrontations." Reprinted by special permission of the *Journal of Criminal Law, Criminology and Police Science,* (Northwestern University School of Law), copyright © 1969, December issue, volume 60, number 4.

[1]California has the most extensive case law on field interrogation, and its development there is traceable to *Gisske* v. *Sanders,* 9 Cal. App. 13, 98 Pac. 43 (1908).

[2]Remington, "The Law Relating to 'on the Street' Detention, Questioning and Frisking of Suspected Persons and Police Arrest Privileges in General," 51 *J. Crim. L.C. & P.S.* 386 (1960).

[3]*N.Y. Code Crim. Proc.* §180-a (McKinney Supp. 1967).

[4]ALI *Model Code of Pre-Arraignment Procedure* §2.02 (Tent. Draft No. 1, 1966). The discussion of this section is reported in 43 ALI *Proceedings* 52-157 (1966).

[5]LaFave, *Arrest: The Decision to Take a Suspect into Custody* 289-97 (1965); Tiffany, McIntyre and Rotenberg, *Detection of Crime: Stopping and Questioning, Search and Seizure, Encouragement and Entrapment* 6-94 (1967) [hereinafter cited as *Detection*]. Descriptive material is also found in American Bar Foundation, *Law Enforcement in the Metropolis* 18-22 (1967).

Commission of Law Enforcement and Administration of Justice discussed the practice briefly and concluded that police authority to stop, question, and frisk suspicious persons who cannot be arrested should be made explicit.[6]

The Court gave an opinion on that question for the first time in 1968.[7] The caution with which they did so reflects the legal complexity of the problems associated with police on-the-street practices (particularly those motivated by a desire to prevent crime), the exceptionally divergent responses to those practices in case law and legal literature, and the recognition that police-citizen confrontations on the street are major contributing factors to increased racial tensions. The Task Force on Police concluded that:

> Misuse of field interrogations . . . is causing serious friction with minority groups in many localities. This is becoming particularly true as more police departments adopt "aggressive patrol" in which officers are encouraged routinely to stop and question persons on the street who are unknown to them, who are suspicious, or whose purpose for being abroad is not readily evident. The Michigan State survey found that both minority group leaders and persons sympathetic to minority groups throughout the country were almost unanimous in labelling field interrogation as a principal problem in police-community relations.[8]

The Chief Justice gave recognition to the importance of the question: "We would," he wrote, "be less than candid if we did not acknowledge that this question thrusts to the fore difficult and troublesome issues regarding a sensitive area of police activity—issues which have never before been squarely presented to this Court."[9]

---

[6] The President's Commission on Law Enforcement and Administration of Justice, *The Challenge of Crime in a Free Society* 95 (1967). See also The President's Commission on Law Enforcement and Administration of Justice, *Task Force Report: The Police* 183-86 (1967). Supporting documents treat the problems in more detail. *See* V Field Surveys, The Nat'l Center on Police and Community Relations at Michigan State University, *A National Survey of Police and Community Relations* 327-36 (1967); IV Field Surveys, Lohman & Misner, *The Police and the Community: The Dynamics of Their Relationship in a Changing Society* (Vols. 1 & 2, 1967); Black & Reiss, "Patterns of Behavior in Police and Citizen Transactions," in III Field Surveys, *2 Studies of Crime and Law Enforcement in Major Metropolitan Areas* (1967).

[7] *Terry* v. *Ohio*, 392 U.S. 1 (1968), and *Sibron* v. *New York*, 392 U.S. 40 (1968). *Sibron* is a consolidation of two cases, the other one being *Peters* v. *New York*. Certiorari was dismissed in a fourth case as improvidently granted. *Wainwright* v. *City of New Orleans*, 392 U.S. 598 (1968).

[8] The President's Commission on Law Enforcement and Administration of Justice, *Task Force Report: The Police* 184 (1967).

[9] *Terry* v. *Ohio*, 392 U.S. 1, 9-10 (1968). The issue was presented to the Court by the government in *Rios* v. *United States*, 364 U.S. 253, (1960). The government there had argued "that a police officer may stop any person for the purpose of inquiry on less information than

There are many difficult issues involved in the field interrogation controversy, and it would have been surprising had the Court tried to resolve a major part of them. But it is equally surprising how narrow the scope of the decisions was. *Terry,* the most important of the cases, holds only that when an officer is investigating a suspicious person the officer may frisk him for dangerous weapons if he has evidence that reasonably leads him to believe that the suspect is armed and dangerous. Such a search is not unreasonable under the fourth amendment despite the lack of probable cause to arrest if it is limited to patting down the exterior clothing of the suspect. The authority to frisk is superfluous when the officer arrests on probable cause and searches the suspect incident to that arrest.

The Court did not deal with the problem of detention prior to frisking, with interrogation, or with the constitutionality of the New York stop-and-frisk statute. These are issues which many observers believed were central to the litigation of these three cases. The Court also failed to say whether states may still choose to define suspicious conduct as a substantive offense to permit arrest and conviction under circumstances which, under *Terry,* would only permit a frisk.[10] They did not discuss the admissibility of evidence other than weapons turned up by a *Terry* frisk. The number of issues left undecided are sufficient to encourage litigation for years to come. The reasons why these opinions are so narrow in scope must obviously be speculative at this time, but the answer may be important to an accurate appraisal of these decisions.

The first explanation is the most obvious: The issues involved in police field interrogation practices are so difficult to resolve and so new to the Court that they could not reach acceptable agreement on any question beyond the need to frisk under *Terry* circumstances. A second explanation is also possible: The actual consensus may have been to avoid these issues, not because the Court could not reach sufficient agreement on them, but because the Court thought it would be unwise to adopt fixed rules on the first occasion of significant national awareness of the problems inherent in these practices. These explanations are not mutually exclusive, of course,

---

would constitute probable cause for arrest; and that any temporary detention that may be involved in the act of making inquiry does not constitute an arrest." Brief for United States, p. 24. *Rios* is discussed more fully in Tiffany, "Field Interrogation: Administrative, Judicial and Legislative Approaches," 43 *Denver L.J.* 389, 401-04 (1966).

[10]In addition to a statute which authorizes field interrogation, New York also has a statute which provides that a person is guilty of loitering when he:

Loiters, remains or wanders in or about a place without apparent reason and under circumstances which justify suspicion that he may be engaged or about to engage in crime, and, upon inquiry by a peace officer, refuses to identify himself or fails to give a reasonably credible account of his conduct and purposes.

N.Y. Penal Law §240.35(6) (McKinney Supp. 1967). The statute is discussed in Schwartz, "Stop and Frisk," 58 *J. Crim. L.C.* & P.S. 433, 459 (1967).

but the second explanation, which suggests a wait-and-see posture, carries with it important implications about the responsibility of police departments for field interrogation practices.

Police departments typically have eschewed public acknowledgment of any responsibility for policy formulation.[11] Even less often have they initiated and involved themselves in public evaluation of whatever policies might exist within their departments. Most departments have behaved this way with respect to field interrogation practices. Indeed, many deny they stop and question suspects who may not be arrested.

One consequence of the failure of the police to permit critical and public evaluation of their practices is that courts are forced to do so without the benefit of any significant agency or community participation in the decision-making process. Secondly, it should not be surprising if much of the public continues to be hostile toward police practices when there has been no opportunity for public participation in formulation of the policies underlying those practices.

It is true that the Court in *Terry* deliberately adopted a wait-and-see attitude toward field interrogation practices, then the obligation of local officials—particularly the police—is clear. For whatever reasons, departments now have the opportunity to begin the process of publicly developing fair and workable standards to guide their on-the-street practices and to develop adequate control mechanisms to insure compliance with them.

But development of evidentiary and procedural standards to which police ought to adhere in conducting field interrogations will be retarded to the extent that antecedent questions about the scope of field interrogation authority are left unresolved. The effort here is not to reexamine the full range of issues involved in these practices. It is, instead, to focus attention on two questions that are of fundamental importance in any attempt to resolve problems relating to field interrogation and to examine the adequacy of the Court's response to these questions. The first of these questions is whether police may properly use field interrogation to control the conduct of a person they believe is about to commit a crime. The second question is whether notions about consent ought to be given legal recognition in the field interrogation context. These questions are raised following a brief discussion of the three opinions.

A Summary of the Cases

Terry v. Ohio

A Cleveland detective observed Terry and co-defendant Chilton engaged in a behavior that suggested to him they were "casing" a downtown store for a daylight robbery. For ten or twelve minutes they engaged in repeated observations of the store and then returned to converse with one

---

[11]LaFave, *Arrest* at 510-14.

another on a streetcorner. During this time, a third man, Katz, briefly conversed with both of them on the corner. Terry and Chilton left the streetcorner and walked in the opposite direction from the store they had been observing. As they again met with Katz, the detective approached the three men and asked their names. He testified that he received a "mumbled" response. He turned Terry around, frisked him, and felt a hard object which he believed to be a gun in the breast pocket of his overcoat but was unable to remove it. He ordered all three men into a nearby store, removed Terry's overcoat, and retrieved a gun. He ordered all three men to raise their hands and face the wall. A frisk of Chilton also turned up a gun. Terry was convicted of carrying a concealed weapon after his pretrial motion to suppress the gun was denied by the trial court.

An Ohio Court of Appeals[12] held that the activites of the defendant were sufficiently suspicious to permit inquiry and that an officer may frisk for self-protection incident to such an inquiry. The Supreme Court of Ohio dismissed petitioner's appeal on the ground that no substantial constitutional question was involved,[13] and the United States Supreme Court granted certiorari.[14]

In an eight-to-one decision, the Court affirmed the conviction. Chief Justice Warren wrote the majority opinion, concurred in by Justices Brennan, Stewart, Fortas, and Marshall. Justices Harlan, Black, and White wrote separate concurring opinions. Justice Douglas dissented.

The defense argued that the Court should not legitimate any interference with a citizen in the absence of probable cause to arrest because to do so would lend unwanted support to other, more objectionable practices than those involved in this case. The Court acknowledged that such practices do occur but replied that "a rigid and unthinking application of the exclusionary rule, in futile protest against practices which it can never be used effectively to control, may exact a high toll in human injury and frustration of efforts to prevent crime."[15]

On the government's side, the argument was made that the practices involved in this case were insufficiently odious to call the fourth amendment into play because the actions of the officer did not constitute a "search" or an "arrest." But the Court avoided their previous arrest-or-nothing type of analysis and concluded that the practices were sufficiently odious to require justification even though they do not amount to "arrests."[16] They are subject to fourth amendment standards including the application of the exclusionary rule when such standards are violated.

---

[12]*State* v. *Terry*, 5 Ohio App. 2d 122, 214 N.E.2d 114 (Cuyahoga County 1966).
[13]*Terry* v. *Ohio*, 392 U.S. 1, 8 (1968).
[14]387 U.S. 929 (1967).
[15]*Terry* v. *Ohio*, 392 U.S. 1, 15 (1968).
[16]The arrest-or-nothing approach was used in *Rios* v. *United States*, 364 U.S. 253 (1960),

Those standards are not satisfied by good faith of the officer. The action must be based on "specific and articulable facts which, taken together with rational inferences from those facts, reasonably warrant that intrusion."[17] The interest in crime detection and prevention as well as the need to protect himself and others justified the frisk in this case. The majority held:

> Our evaluation of the proper balance that has to be struck in this type of case leads us to conclude that there must be a narrowly drawn authority to permit a reasonable search for weapons for the protection of the police officer, where he has reason to believe that he is dealing with an armed and dangerous individual, regardless of whether he has probable cause to arrest the individual for a crime.[18]

Sibron v. New York

Although *Sibron* and *Peters* were decided in the same opinion by the majority of the Court, they are clearly discussed as separate cases. Arresting Officer Martin, during eight hours of patrol, observed Sibron

> in conversation with six or eight persons whom he ... knew from past experience to be narcotics addicts. The officer testified that he did not overhear any of these conversations, and that he did not see anything pass between Sibron and any of the others. Late in the evening Sibron entered a restaurant. Patrolman Martin saw Sibron speak with three more known addicts inside the restaurant. Once again, nothing was overheard and nothing was seen to pass between Sibron and the addicts. Sibron sat down and ordered pie and coffee, and as he was eating Patrolman Martin approached him and told him to come outside. Once outside, the officer said to Sibron, "You know what I am after." According to the officer, Sibron "mumbled something and reached into his pocket." Simultaneously, Patrolman Martin thrust his hand into the same pocket, discovering several glassine envelopes, which, it turned out, contained heroin.[19]

Henry v. *United States,* 361 U.S. 98 (1959), and Brinegar v. *United States,* 338 U.S. 160 (1949). The statement in *Rios* is typical:

But the Government argues that the policemen approached the standing taxi only for the purpose of routine interrogation, and that they had no intent to detain the petitioner beyond the momentary requirements of such a mission. If the petitioner thereafter voluntarily revealed the package of narcotics to the officers' view, a lawful arrest could then have been supported by their reasonable cause to believe that a felony was being committed in their presence. The validity of the search thus turns upon the narrow question of when the arrest occurred, and the answer to that question depends upon an evaluation of the conflicting testimony of those who were there that night.

364 U.S. at 262 (footnote omitted).

[17] *Terry* v. *Ohio,* 392 U.S. 1, 21 (1968) (footnote omitted).

[18] *Ibid.* at 27.

[19] *Sibron* v. *New York,* 392 U.S. 40, 45 (1968).

With some ambivalence, the trial court concluded that the officer had probable cause to arrest Sibron and that the search was properly incident to that arrest. The court did not rely on the New York stop-and-frisk statute. The New York Court of Appeals affirmed without opinion,[20] but the dissent there indicated that the majority decision was based on the New York statute.[21] That statute was also urged as justification for the police conduct in the state's initial brief filed with the United States Supreme Court opposing jurisdiction.[22] After probable jurisdiction was noted by the Court, the New York County Attorney tendered a confession of error.[23]

Despite claims that the issue in Sibron's case was moot, and despite the confession of error, the Court decided the case on the merits. At the same time, the Court refused to decide the constitutionality of the New York statute.[24]

The Court, in five opinions, reversed Sibron's conviction. Chief Justice Warren again wrote the majority opinion, concurred in by Justices Brennan, White, Stewart, and Marshall. Justice Douglas, in a separate opinion, seemed to agree with the approach of the majority. Justice Harlan reiterated the analysis he advocated in *Terry*.[25] Justice Fortas would have given more weight to the confession of error, and Justice Black dissented on the ground that the police action was taken in reasonable self-defense.

The majority, as they had in *Terry*, defined the frisk as the intrusion that had to be justified because, they concluded, the record was unclear whether Sibron was under restraint before the search occurred. They held that the evidentiary requirement for a self-protective search was not present in this case, and that the search was not properly limited in scope because it extended beyond patting down the exterior of the suspect's clothing. Thus, *Sibron* was clearly an effort to indicate that the thrust of *Terry* was not to give the constitutional imprimatur to coercive intrusions based on evidence as slight as that present in this case.

Peters v. New York.

During the afternoon, an off-duty New York City patrolman, Lasky, heard noises at his sixth-floor apartment door. He received a telephone call and after he hung up, he looked into the hall through a peep-hole in his door

---

[20] *People* v. *Sibron*, 18 N.Y.2d 603, 219 N.E.2d 196, 272 N.Y.S.2d 374 (1966).

[21] *Ibid.* at 604, 219 N.E.2d at 197, 272 N.Y.S.2d at 376.

[22] *Sibron* v. *New York*, 392 U.S. 40, 47-48 (1968).

[23] *Ibid.* at 48.

[24] *Ibid.* at 61. The failure of the Court to deal with the New York stop-and-frisk statute undoubtedly came as a surprise to many observers. The position of the majority seems to have been that the statute is so vague that the Court could not tell exactly what is authorized and therefore could not determine its constitutionality. *Ibid.* at 60-61 n.20.

[25] See text accompanying footnotes 54-57.

and saw two men tiptoeing down the hall. He did not recognize them as residents of his apartment building. He telephoned the local Mount Vernon police, completed dressing, and returned to the door. The strangers were then tiptoeing toward the stairway although an elevator was available. As Lasky emerged into the hall armed and slammed his apartment door the suspects fled down the stairs. He apprehended one of them after a chase covering a flight and a half of stairs. The other man escaped. The officer asked the detained suspect what he was doing in the building. Peters claimed he was looking for a girlfriend but said he would not identify her because she was married. The officer took him down another half flight of stairs to the fourth floor and frisked him. He felt something hard in the suspect's pants pocket and testified it "could have been" a knife. He removed an unsealed opaque plastic envelope and found burglary tools in it. The suspect was convicted on his guilty plea for unlawful possession of burglary tools after the trial court denied his pretrial motion to suppress the evidence obtained by Officer Lasky.

Every member of the Court except Justice Harlan agreed that probable cause existed to arrest Peters for attempted burglary. The New York Court of Appeals had clearly felt the conduct of the officer could be justified only on the basis of the stop-and-frisk statute.[26] The notion that probable cause existed to arrest for any crime was not mentioned in their opinion. The majority of the Court adverted to this rationale of the New York Court of Appeals, but observed: "This may be the justification for the search under state law. We think, however, that for purposes of the Fourth Amendment the search was properly incident to a lawful arrest. By the time Officer Lasky caught up with Peters on the stairway between the fourth and fifth floors of the apartment building, he had probable cause to arrest him for attempted burglary."[27] As if *Terry* had never been decided, the Court found that Peters was arrested the moment he was restrained and that the search was incident to that lawful arrest. Despite their conclusion that Peters was properly arrested, the Court justified the subsequent search with the conclusion that "Officer Lasky did not engage in an unrestrained and thorough-going examination of Peters and his personal effects. He seized him to cut short his flight, and he searched him primarily for weapons. While patting down his outer clothing, Officer Lasky discovered an object in his pocket which might have been used as a weapon."[28] This language appears to be a justification for a *Terry*-type frisk rather than a statement of traditional authority to search incident to an arrest. Certainly, searches justified as "incidental" to arrest are not limited to searching for weapons, nor are they restricted to patting-down outer clothing.

---

[26] *People* v. *Peters,* 18 N.Y.2d 238, 219 N.E.2d 595, 273 N.Y.S.2d 217 (1966).

[27] *Sibron* v. *New York,* 392 U.S. 40, 66 (1968).

[28] *Ibid.* at 67.

These problems again prompted Justice Harlan to concur specially. He disagreed with the majority's conclusions that probable cause to arrest existed at the time Peters was restrained. He also objected to what appeared to be a reversion by the majority to the earlier arrest-or-nothing analysis of cases like *Rios* which the Court had expressly eschewed in *Terry.* Indeed, *Rios* and *Henry* are prominent in the majority opinion. Part of the disagreement also seems to be whether probable cause to arrest and the arrest must precede the search as the majority opinion implied, or whether it suffices if probable cause to arrest exists prior to the search, whether or not the arrest has actually occurred. Justice Harlan argued that "[t]here is *no* case in which a defendant may validly say, 'Although the officer had a right to arrest me at the moment when he seized me and searched my person, the search is invalid because he did not in fact arrest me until afterwards.' "[29]

Field Interrogation as a Control on Intending Criminals

Glanville Williams has argued that "[i]n a rational system of justice the police would be given every encouragement to intervene early where a suspect is clearly bent on crime. Yet in England, if the police come to the scene too early they may find that they can do nothing with the intending offender except admonish him."[30] The formal law situation has not been strikingly different in American jurisdictions. The important—and unanswered—question is this: Is it part of the function of the police to try to prevent crime by physically interrupting persons believed to be contemplating a crime? Remarkably little attention has been given to this question. Present field interrogation practices raise this issue.

Many police feel they need authority to engage in what they call "aggressive, preventive patrol" practices. Police departments are often assigned and accept responsibility for crime rates in a city, and they often gauge their effectiveness as police not so much by the percentage of crimes "cleared" but by whether or not they can reduce the incidence of crime. Procedural restrictions on police interferences with citizens, on the other hand, usually have been thought to limit police authority to those instances in which the police have evidence indicating a suspect probably has committed a crime.[31]

The tensions between these competing assumptions about the proper scope of police authority have been exposed predominately in the vagrancy

---

[29]*Ibid.* at 77 (concurring opinion). Similar views of the propriety of a search-then-arrest sequence is gaining judicial support. See *e.g., Holt* v. *Simpson,* 340 F.2d 853 (7th Cir. 1965). The problem is discussed in Barrett, "Personal Rights, Property Rights, and the Fourth Amendment," 1960 *Sup. Ct. Rev.* 46.

[30]Williams, "Police Control of Intending Criminals," 1955 *Crim. L. Rev.* 66.

[31]See Tiffany, "Field Interrogation: Administrative, Judicial and Legislative Approaches," 43 *Denver L.J.* 389, 395-98 (1966).

law controversy. The New York Court of Appeals, for example, declared unconstitutional the New York vagrancy statute partly because the authority to arrest under these types of laws was used by the police to avoid restrictions imposed by substantive and procedural codes.[32] A second practice which raises the issue is the unsystematic legislative responses to particular inchoate behavior such as both *Terry* and *Peters* involved. The suspect who was intending to commit armed robbery can be arrested because he will be found to be in the possession of a concealed weapon. So, too, in many states, the incipient burglar may be arrested if he brought along specialized tools, but not otherwise. Convictions for anything but vagrancy under these circumstances are not possible unless exceptional, fortuitous circumstances are also present. Preparation to commit a crime is not made criminal *per se* so that whether an intending criminal may be arrested for prosecution is essentially left to chance. This discrepancy between what police assume to be their role and the limitations imposed by rules embodying a contrary assumption is probably largely responsible for the long life accorded vagrancy laws and is reflected in the proliferation of possession-with-intent type of statutes.

Field interrogation raises the same question. Both case law and existing statutes authorizing field interrogation permit police to stop, question, and frisk when they have evidence indicating that the suspect is about to commit a crime. Indeed, the Model State Statute on "Stop and Frisk" which has been prepared and distributed by the Americans for Effective Law Enforcement provides: "Whenever any peace officer of this state encounters any person under circumstances which reasonably indicate that such person has committed, is committing, or is about to commit a criminal offense, he may detain such person." The position paper which accompanies the circulation of this proposal makes it clear that the field interrogation authority includes the power to engage in detention designed to prevent the commission of crime as well as to detect perpetrators:

> Even when the police are forced to release the suspect because of his refusal to answer questions or because no evidence of an attempted crime is found at the scene, the very act of temporary detention and questioning may deter, at least for that night, a potential criminal act of violence. That, in itself, would be a worthwhile result, since the duty of the police is not only to apprehend persons who have already committed criminal acts, but also to prevent crimes from occurring in the first place.[33]

Thus, these rules do encourage the police to intervene early, but the police may not arrest unless the frisk turns up something upon which to base a prosecution.

---

[32] *Fenster* v. *Leary,* 20 N.Y.2d 309, 229 N.E.2d 426, 282 N.Y.S.2d 739 (1967).

[33] The model act and the accompanying commentary can be obtained from Americans for Effective Law Enforcement, Inc., 33 North Dearborn Street, Chicago, Illinois 60602.

To the extent that field interrogation practices are conceived to range well beyond conviction-oriented processes and to include as well efforts to control intending criminals by non-conviction means, questions are raised whether these preventive practices can realistically be separated from other, less desirable practices and whether such preventive practices can be controlled.

Field interrogation is only one of the specific practices engaged in by police under the rubric "aggressive, preventive patrol." Many other practices are attributable to the same orientation to prevent crime from being committed in the first place. The following paragraphs are a description of one such practice, the so-called "battle of the corner."[34]

Both uniformed patrolmen and members of the Juvenile Aid Division, but primarily the former, engage in constant confrontation with Negro youths who congregate on streetcorners in the urban area. The youths insist on what is called corner-lounging, and the police insist on dispersing them. Recalcitrance is punished by arrest. The study concluded:

> Interviews with both juveniles and District policemen reveals something of the dynamics of the 'battle of the corner.' Both apparently see these encounters as challenges to their manhood. Neither party expresses a willingness to allow the corner to go to the other by default. In many respects, both parties view the encounters as a game, albeit a deadly serious game. Among some of the younger officers, one encounters a sense of dedication never to lose the battle of the corner. Part of the young policeman's lore is the fact that losing the battle is seen as one of the most serious 'defeats' a policeman can suffer. Older officers, of course, have often tired of these encounters and unconsciously avoid 'showdowns.' Many of them, however, also reveal an unwillingness to lose if a showdown is unavoidable.
>
> 'The drawing of the battle lines,' however, has apparently been as much the consequence of public pressure as it has been the product of the policeman's action. In numerous interviews, policemen justify their dispersal of corner-lounging groups on the basis of complaints from the public. Visitations to various neighborhoods in the city and to various District police confirms the fact that there are many public complaints about corner-lounging groups creating a disturbance or shouting insults or obscenities. Furthermore, many policemen use their selective experience to point to the fact that many groups assemble on the corner as a prelude to more serious misbehavior and delinquency.[35]

The relationship of this type of practice to field interrogation depends largely upon one's definition of field interrogation.[36] The practices often

---

[34] IV Field Surveys, Lohman & Misner, *The Police and the Community: The Dynamics of Their Relationship in a Changing Society,* vol. 2, at 156 (1967).

[35] *Ibid.*

[36] See *Detection, supra* note 5, ch. 1.

involve questioning, detention, and searching. Nevertheless, they are functionally different from those situations in which the police are trying to obtain information about the commission of crime. The point is not that the kind of field interrogation involved in *Terry* is indistinguishable from these preventive practices; it is rather that police have not made sufficient efforts to maintain the distinction in practice.[37] Related prevention practices often shade imperceptibly into police assumption of control of movement in public places, at least in high crime areas at night.[38] Such practices are often what the police take "crime prevention" to mean.

One of the ironies of empirical research into the field-interrogation question is that the most difficult problem of such research is to isolate conceptually those instances in which the police stop and question a person whose conduct has raised a fair question as to his involvement in criminal activity from all the other things that patrol officers do, including indiscriminately conducted stop-and-search programs designed to confiscate guns, and harassment of teenagers in minority areas.[39] There are probably few observers who would completely deny the utility and necessity of stopping and questioning suspects when probable cause to arrest does not exist—if, that is, temporary on-the-street detention power would be carefully limited in actual day-to-day police practices. Just as obviously, present street practices in many cities are unjustified and harmful.

Thus, one of the dominant themes running through the controversy over the legitimacy of field interrogation relates primarily to the anticipated (and present) abuse of the power to interfere with persons who may not be arrested. Aggressive tactics are common. They are often largely motivated by poorly articulated efforts to somehow prevent crimes and are encouraged in many instances by police efforts to remain "in charge" of the streets. The importance of *Terry* in this context is whether Court authorization for the police to "deal with" possibly intending criminals in ways not involving efforts to prosecute will be interpreted by the police as lending support to such tactics.

Chief Justice Warren adverted at some length to the inadequacy of the exclusionary rule as a control on police-citizen encounters which are not motivated by a desire on the part of the police to secure evidence usable in a criminal prosecution. For the majority in *Terry,* he observed: "Regardless of how effective the rule may be where obtaining convictions is an important objective of the police, it is powerless to deter invasions of constitutionally guaranteed rights where the police either have no interest in prosecuting or are willing to forego successful prosecution in the interest of serving some

---

[37]See text accompanying footnote 11.
[38]See *Detection, supra* note 5, ch. 1.
[39]*Ibid.*

other goal."[40] Yet the Court concluded, in response to defense arguments, that the existence of a "protean variety" of street encounters ought not to result in "a rigid and unthinking application of the exclusionary rule, in futile protest against practices which it can never be used effectively to control. . . ."[41] Further, the Court said, "our approval of legitimate and restrained investigative conduct undertaken on the basis of ample factual justification should in no way discourage the employment of other remedies than the exclusionary rule to curtail abuses for which that sanction may prove inappropriate."[42]

It is important, however, to determine exactly what the Court means by "legitimate and restrained investigative conduct." There is language in these cases which indicates that at least several members of the Court are willing to recognize police authority to interfere with persons despite the indication that the "suspect" cannot be convicted of any offense. The majority in *Terry* said a legitimate state interest is "effective crime prevention and detection."[43] Justice White, speaking about the frisk in that case, said: "Perhaps the frisk itself, where proper, will have beneficial results whether questions are asked or not. If weapons are found, an arrest will follow. If none are found, *the frisk may nevertheless serve preventive ends because of its unmistakable message that suspicion has been aroused.*"[44] Even Justice Douglas, dissenting, argued that searches and seizures must be predicated on probable cause, but that fourth amendment standards are satisfied if the officer has probable cause to believe that "a crime was *about* to be committed."[45]

Justice Harlan concluded in his concurring opinion that the officer's conduct in *Sibron* fell below *Terry* standards and observed: "There must be something at least in the activities of the person being observed or in his surroundings that affirmatively suggests particular criminal activity, completed, current, *or intended.*"[46]

Justice Harlan agreed that *Peters* should be affirmed, but on the basis of the right to stop and question, not on the majority's view that probable cause to arrest existed. He observed that probable cause has been taken to mean: "Evidence that would warrant a prudent and reasonable man . . . in believing that a particular person has committed or is committing a crime."[47] The omission of reference to future conduct of the suspect was

---

[40]*Terry* v. *Ohio,* 392 U.S. 1, 14 (1968) (footnote omitted).
[41]*Ibid.* at 15.
[42]*Ibid.*
[43]*Ibid.* at 22
[44]*Ibid* at 34-35 (concurring opinion) (emphasis added).
[45]*Ibid.* at 35 (dissenting opinion) (emphasis added).
[46]*Sibron* v. *New York,* 392 U.S. 40, 73 (1968) (concurring opinion) (emphasis added).
[47]*Ibid.* at 75 (footnote omitted).

deliberate: "unlike probable cause to arrest, reasonable grounds to stop do not depend on any degree of likelihood that a crime *has* been committed. *An officer may forcibly intrude upon an incipient crime even where he could not make an arrest for the simple reason that there is nothing to arrest anyone for.* Hence although Officer Lasky had small reason to believe that a crime had been committed, his right to stop Peters can be justified if he had *a reasonable suspicion that he was about to attempt burglary.*"[48] Justice Douglas, concurring in the affirmance of Peters' conviction, took this position: "I would hold that at the time Lasky seized petitioner, he had probable cause to believe that petitioner was on some kind of burglary or housebreaking mission."[49]

One implication of this language is that preventive—or at least anticipatory—searches and seizures are not necessarily incompatible with the fourth amendment. But *Terry* does little to resolve the uncertainty. Indeed, the ambiguous fourth amendment status of police coercive intrusions which are not designed to secure convictions is significantly perpetuated by these cases. Certainly, the question is important enough to require more critical evaluation than the Court has thus far given it. It is not clear that a majority of the Court would be willing to unambiguously hold that there are instances in which the police may coercively intrude upon a person they believe may be contemplating the commission of a crime. It is clear, however, that the exclusionary rule will have little or no impact as a control device on this species of anticipatory detention because of the underlying assumption of that rule that overly aggressive police tactics are designed to secure convictions. But the Court gives considerable support to those "preventive" practices despite recognition that such practices may be beyond the control of the judiciary.

The Role of Consent in Field Interrogation Practices

Another important question in field interrogation practices is left unresolved by the *Terry* doctrine and follows both from the fact that the Court did not address the question of limitations upon the purposes of legitimate field interrogations and from the fact that the Court declined to deal with the question of detention prior to the frisk of the suspects. Because the police were obviously dealing with suspects in all three cases, the Court addressed only the question of police-suspect confrontations. Thus, the question whether judicial application of notions about consent might vary significantly when the person confronted is believed to be a witness, in contrast to the instance in which he is believed to a perpetrator, was not

---

[48]*Ibid* at 78 (emphasis added).
[49]*Ibid.* at 69 (concurring opinion).

clarified.[50]   But even when it is clear that the police are dealing with a suspect, the Court seems willing to give considerable latitude to consent doctrines.

The Court in *Terry* refused to treat the initial confrontation as involving restraint.

> We thus decide nothing today concerning the constitutional propriety of an investigative 'seizure' upon less than probable cause for purposes of 'detention' and/or interrogation. Obviously, not all personal intercourse between policemen and citizens involves 'seizures' of persons. Only when the officer, by means of physical force or show of authority, has in some way restrained the liberty of a citizen may we conclude that a 'seizure' has occurred. We cannot tell with any certainty upon this record whether any such 'seizure' took place here prior to Officer McFadden's initiation of physical contact for purposes of searching Terry for weapons and we thus may assume that up to that point no intrusion upon constitutionally protected rights had occurred.[51]

The Court took a parallel position in *Sibron:* "We are not called upon to decide in this case whether there was a 'seizure' of Sibron inside the restaurant antecedent to the physical seizure which accompanied the search."[52] The Court concluded that the record would not permit a determination "whether Sibron accompanied Patrolman Martin outside in submission to a show of force or authority which left him no choice, or whether

---

[50]The pre-*Terry* draft of the ALI *Model Code of Pre-Arraignment Procedure* (Tent. Draft No. 1, 1966) does provide for authority to interrogate witnesses. Section 2.02(1) provides:

Stopping of Persons Having Knowledge of Crime. A law enforcement officer lawfully present in any place may, if he has reasonable cause to believe that a felony or misdemeanor has been committed and that any person has knowledge which may be of material aid to the investigation thereof, order such person to remain in or near such place in the officer's presence for a period of not more than twenty minutes.

Police authority in this section which covers both suspects and witnesses is more restricted than when only a suspect is involved. Section 2.02(2), which covers only suspects, has a lower evidentiary standard:

Stopping of Persons in Suspicious Circumstances. A law enforcement officer lawfully present in any place may, if a person is observed in circumstances which suggest that he has committed or is about to commit a felony or misdemeanor, and such action is reasonably necessary to enable the officer to determine the lawfulness of that person's conduct, order that person to remain in or near such place in the officer's presence for a period of not more than twenty minutes.

However, the difference in standards may be illusory, because in any high crime area, the police always have reasonable cause to believe that a crime has been committed unless the section is interpreted to be more limited in terms of location or immediacy than the language requires.

[51]*Terry* v. *Ohio,* 392 U.S. 1, 19 n. 16 (1968).

[52]*Sibron* v. *New York,* 392 U.S. 40, 63 (1968).

he went voluntarily in a spirit of apparent cooperation with the officer's investigation."[53] On the other hand, in *Terry,* the Court pointed out that "[i]t is quite plain that the Fourth Amendment governs 'seizures' of the person which do not eventuate in a trip to the station house and prosecution for crime—'arrests' in traditional terminology. It must be recognized that whenever a police officer accosts an individual and restrains his freedom to walk away, he has 'seized' that person."[54]

One result of the Court's refusal to treat the initial confrontation in these cases as involving detention was that the Court was called upon to determine only the propriety of the frisk and thus avoided a decision about the evidentiary basis of an initial investigatory detention not accompanied by a frisk. This, of course, obscures the question whether there are differences in the standards justifying the two actions.

The more important question left unanswered is: When, if ever, should a confrontation between a police officer and a suspect not be treated as involving restraint? The Court was careful to point out that the treatment of the initial confrontations in these two cases as being without restraint had no material impact on the disposition. At some point between confrontation and taking a suspect to the station restraint occurs, and the only guidance given on the question is that restraint will be found to be involved when there is a "show of force," a term left undefined by the Court. Whether a "confrontation" of a suspect *is* a "show of force," or whether that term should refer to something like display of weapons, is an important question to resolve.

The majority view that Terry and Sibron may have voluntarily cooperated in their undoing led Justice Harlan to feel "constrained to fill in a few gaps. . . ."[55] He differed from the approach of Chief Justice Warren in two major respects. First, "if the frisk is justified in order to protect the officer during an encounter with a citizen, the officer must have constitutional grounds to insist on an encounter, to make a *forcible* stop."[56] Second, "[w]here such a stop is reasonable, however, the right to frisk must be immediate and automatic if the reason for the stop is, as here, an articulable suspicion of a crime of violence."[57] He concluded that "Officer McFadden's right to interrupt Terry's freedom of movement and invade his privacy arose only because circumstances warranted forcing an encounter with Terry in an effort to prevent or investigate a crime. Once that forced encounter was justified, however, the officer's right to take suitable measures

---

[53] *Ibid.*
[54] *Terry* v. *Ohio,* 392 U.S. 1, 16 (1968).
[55] *Ibid.* at 31 (concurring opinion).
[56] *Ibid.* at 32.
[57] *Ibid.* at 33.

for his own safety followed automatically" when the original suspicion related to a crime of violence.[58]

In a large majority of encounters between police and citizens, or even between police and suspects, it is quite ambiguous whether the citizen is under restraint, if that term refers to whether or not he can walk away. One of the main problems with assuming, in the absence of clear evidence to the contrary, that suspects may voluntarily cooperate with the police during a field interrogation is that the right to be free from the annoyance of public inquiries by the police may belong only to those persons who are willing to risk resolution of the ambiguity inherent in those encounters. This is an especially undesirable judicial policy given the fact that refusal to "cooperate" with beat-patrol officers is often viewed by them both as an indication that the suspect is in fact guilty of something and as an attempt on the suspect's part to undermine the authority of the investigating officer.[59] Furthermore, the suspect has no way to decide whether the investigating officer has authority to stop him or not.

It may have been somewhat understandable that the judiciary would rely on notions of consent or cooperation to resolve fourth amendment problems in this context when they were required to choose between consent and arrest as the only justifications for evidence acquisition by police. But recognition of coercive investigative authority in the absence of probable cause to arrest ought to alleviate the pressure to resolve ambiguous confrontations by creation of a presumption of consent. In terms of an evidentiary antecedent, a request for cooperation need not be reasonable in the constitutional sense, and even the *Terry* evidence-of-guilt standard need not be met.

An additional problem with the consent doctrine in this context is that it is doubtful that courts could realistically and uniformly resolve factual matters which involve the subtle psychological interaction in police-suspect confrontations.[60] Difficulty of adjudication alone might be insufficient reason to deny the police needed authority to investigate crime. The question is whether the need to use consent doctrines still exists. It would be an unfortunate diversion from the significant fourth amendment issues involved in field interrogation to focus on whether the suspect voluntarily cooperated rather than focusing on the justification for the police conduct involved.

A dichotomic approach to that problem expressed in terms of "detention" versus "voluntary cooperation" is less than helpful. To observe that not all police-suspect confrontations are coercive is beside the point. If

---

[58] *Ibid.* at 34.

[59] *Detection, supra* note 5, at 57.

[60] See *e.g.,* Project, "Interrogations in New Haven: The Impact of *Miranda,*" 76 *Yale L.J.* 1519 (1967).

courts will be unable realistically to evaluate the assorted reasons suspects may appear to be cooperative with an investigating officer, the task is to select the policy that would be most responsive to the need to resolve the competing interests. The Court's recognition that any restraint of suspects by police brings that conduct within the fourth amendment's requirement of reasonableness will provide little protection as long as police can take legal advantage of the ambiguity inherent in most street confrontations.

Conclusion

Too often the assumption has been made that when the courts deal with something called "criminal procedure" they are concomitantly dealing with most of the significant problem areas of police conduct. The Court candidly recognized that this assumption is grossly inaccurate. In large part this litigation hiatus is due not so much to the ambit of the fourth amendment as it is to the scope of remedies used to control and limit police activities. The exclusionary rule, of course, is currently the most frequently invoked remedy. The formal limitations on that remedy are numerous, and the conditions under which it may be thought to be effective are quite limited. First, it cannot be effective unless illegally obtained evidence is needed by the state to convict the defendant, and this will not be the case when improper police conduct does not result in state acquisition of evidence or when the state has other evidence sufficient to convict. Second, many procedural obstacles exist to limit the frequency of invocation of the rule. If the appropriate motion is not made at the appropriate time, the issues may escape formal litigation. Given the predominance of the guilty plea system in all jurisdictions, it is likely that most questions of police illegality become only additional factors in the bargaining process. The defendant must also have satisfied "standing" requirements to move to suppress. Third, indirect uses may still be made of illegally obtained evidence, such as by introduction at trial of that evidence to impeach the defendant; and, the so-called "fruits" doctrine cannot prevent all indirect benefit to the police.

Finally—and this is the main problem—the exclusionary rule derives whatever efficacy it may have from the underlying assumption that when the police engage in illegal conduct it is for the purpose of securing a conviction. The fallacy in this assumption has been amply documented.[61] It should be hoped that the Court's explicit recognition of this limitation in *Terry* will contribute to increased attention to that "protean variety" of police-citizen confrontations which do not contemplate prosecution. Preoccupation with the propriety of methods of obtaining convictions has been the natural result of preoccupation with appellate cases. The point is not to belittle the significance of concern with the manner of obtaining convic-

---

[61]See *e.g.*, LaFave, *Arrest* at 289-97.

tions; obviously, research of the type now underway concerning the impact of *Miranda,*[62] as one example, is vital to any sensible rulemaking designed to control conviction-oriented aspects of police practices. The point is that conviction processes are not all that is important about police practices. Indeed there is some evidence that conviction processes are becoming relatively less important as the way in which our criminal justice systems manage rulebreaking.[63]

Development of meaningful controls over this aspect of police work will require more adequate identification and description of those practices and identification of the pressures or conditions contributing to their widespread existence. Most important is recognition that control over nonconviction processes cannot be relegated to the courts armed only with the exclusionary rule.

Whether police on-the-street intrusive practices are oriented toward conviction or not, the need for adequate standards and controls is difficult to overstate. One interpretation of *Terry* is that the Court for the moment has left the initial responsibility for this to the relevant administrative agencies. The problems are difficult, but it is important that they be resolved intelligently and as quickly as possible. In the absence of positive departmental responses which give some indication of police awareness of an obligation to accept the opportunity provided by *Terry* to behave like responsible administrative agencies, it is likely that future field interrogation cases decided by the Court will contain less doctrinal ambiguity and will be more restrictive on police.

The likelihood exists, of course, that *Terry* will not be viewed this way by police officials. Because of the vagueness of the language used on many of the important issues and because of the approval of the police conduct leading to Terry's conviction, *Terry* may be taken as broad approval of current police field interrogation practices. If that view of *Terry* is prevalent and has the effect of encouraging present aggressive police tactics on the street, the dominant impact of *Terry* may be to encourage more and more judicial intervention to curtail those practices.[64]

---

[62]An excellent comment on *Miranda* research may be found in ALI *Model Code of Pre-Arraignment Procedure,* Part II (Study Draft No. 1, 1968).

[63]Linton, "Administrative Stabilization of Conviction Rates," August 1968 (unpublished paper).

[64]"This attitude [of justifying failure to observe procedural restrictions imposed by courts] often prompts the imposition of even greater restrictions on police authority. Courts are undoubtedly influenced by their assumption as to how police will react to legal requirements. If there is confidence that they will stay well within defined limits, their powers may be stated broadly; but, if it is thought that they will regularly exceed the limits, the tendency is to impose severe and perhaps unrealistic limitations upon their authority."
LaFave, *Arrest* at 512 (footnotes omitted).

The major doctrinal implication of *Terry* was underscored by Justice Douglas in his dissent: He pointed out that "[w]e hold today that the police have greater authority to make a 'seizure' and conduct a 'search' than a judge has to authorize such action."[65] Presumably this is so because it is thought that judges are limited to the traditional warrant-issuance process, and that the prerequisite under that procedure will continue to be a higher evidentiary standard ("probable cause") than is required of police by *Terry* for field interrogation ("reasonableness"). Obviously the role of magistrates in enforcing the fourth amendment has never been as significant as the authority exercised by contemporary police,[66] and this is true despite the fact that the Court still romantically treats arrests without warrants as the "exceptional" case and extols the virtues of the warrant process.[67] But *Terry* represents the most important instance of doctrinal recognition of this reality. The response of police administrators to *Terry* may be one of the most important factors controlling the longevity of this doctrinal shift.

A few of the current problems that inhere in judicial efforts to control the police practice of field interrogation have already been identified. The exclusionary rule cannot control police activity which is not directed toward conviction, and judicial reliance on notions of consent removes field interrogation from the ambit of fourth amendment requirements because no "seizure" is found to have occurred. But there is still another dimension to the problem. Judicial efforts to control "the police" often seem to be based on an assumption that police departments are monolithic. As a result little distinction has been made between efforts to control the police hierarchy in the United States on the one hand and efforts to control the patrolman

---

[65] *Terry* v. *Ohio,* 392 U.S. 1, 36 (1968) (dissenting opinion).

[66] Barrett, "Criminal Justice: The Problem of Mass Production," in *The Courts, the Public, and the Law Explosion* 85, 117-18 (Jones ed. 1965). Professor La Fave has concluded:

> The assumption apparently is that greater protection for the individual is afforded by the warrant procedure, since an arrest will be made only if an impartial judicial officer, upon careful evaluation of the evidence presented to him, determines that adequate grounds for an arrest exist. But, at least in Kansas, Michigan, and Wisconsin, it is clear that the warrant process does not serve this function. Rather, the decision is made in the office of the prosecutor and the judge routinely signs the arrest warrant without any independent inquiry into the facts and circumstances of the individual case.

LaFave, *Arrest* at 502-03. See also *Detection, supra* note 5, ch. 8; Miller & Tiffany, "Prosecutor Dominance of the Warrant Decision: A Study of Current Practices," 1964 *Wash. U.L.Q.* 1, 17:

> "It is difficult to analyze comparatively the formal law and current administrative practices in the area of control over warrant issuance without concluding that an aura of unreality surrounds the problem. Nowhere does the declared law seem so at odds with the facts of the law in action. Yet the formal law statements—as well as expressed concern over the situation—seem, on the surface at least, to be aimed at shadows. The substance is not at all what the commentators seem to assume it is."

[67] *E.g., Warden* v. *Hayden,* 387 U.S. 294 (1967).

on the other. Efforts to control the hierarchy assumes that the high-level administrators have effective control over patrolmen. Efforts to control the patrolman assumes that he is more responsive to external judicial control than he is to the requirements of his sergeant. Both of these assumptions are of doubtful validity.

It is especially the doubt about how much control the police higher echelon has over the day-to-day decision-making of the officer on patrol that renders fatuous any predictions about the efficacy of adoption of field interrogation standards by many departments in the wake of *Terry.*[68] Still, the adoption of such administrative rules is a necessary step in the development of administrative or other mechanisms designed to bring police "aggressive, preventive patrol" practices under control. Thus, the ability of departments to acquire control of the behavior of their patrolmen on the street is also likely to be of significance for the survival of what is now taken to be rather broad authority to maintain police field interrogation practices.

---

[68]Several police departments have issued training bulletins on Stop-and-Frisk, among them being: Chicago, Denver, Gary, New York City, Pittsburgh, and San Jose, California. In each of these cases, the bulletins were written by the department's legal advisor.

Part IV   Selected Correlated References

Applegate, Rex. *Kill or Get Killed.* Harrisburg, Pa.: Stackpole Books, 1961. A good reference on self-protection and effective procedures for handling criminal suspects.

Baker, J. S. *Traffic Accident Investigator's Manual for Police.* 2nd ed. Evanston, Ill.: Traffic Institute of Northwestern University, 1957. A detailed and comprehensive handbook devoted to the study of accident investigations.

Bradford, L. W. "Drinking Driver Enforcement Problems." *Journal of Criminal Law, Criminology and Police Science.* Vol. 57, No. 4 (December 1966). Mr. Bradford writes about peace officers' attempts to enforce laws relating to driving while under the influence of alcoholic beverages. Enforcement of such laws are complicated, according to Mr. Bradford, by the differences between moderate drinkers and alcoholics.

Bristow, A. P., and J. B. Williams. *Criminal Procedure and the Administration of Justice.* rev. ed. Beverly Hills, Ca.: Glencoe Press, 1966. A concise and up-to-date work on the law, judicial, and post-judicial system of justice in the United States. An excellent reference.

Cahn, E., ed. "Criminal Guilt." *Social Meaning of Legal Concepts.* Vol. 2. New York: New York University Press, 1950. A clear statement regarding the isolated subject of legally defined guilt.

Chapman, Samuel, ed. *Police Patrol Readings.* Springfield, Ill.: Charles C. Thomas, Pub., 1964. This volume represents some of the best articles compiled by an author on police patrol. Also by the same author: "The Dog in Law Enforcement." *Police.* (June 1960); "Whether to Use Police Dogs." *Police.* (September-October 1961).

Fricke, Charles W., and A. L. Alarcon. *California Criminal Law.* 9th ed. Los Angeles: Legal Book Corp., 1965. An excellent reference on California law and its provisions; explanations in easy to understand language.

Hall, Livingston, and Yale Kamisor. *Modern Criminal Procedure.* 2nd ed. St. Paul, Minn.: West Publishing Co., 1966. An excellent reference of correct procedure, legal terms, definitions, and implications, applicable to all systems of justice in the United States.

LaFave, Wayne R. *Arrest.* Boston: Little, Brown and Co., 1965. An outstanding discussion on the subject of arrest and its varied ramifications throughout the United States. This reference is a must for every student and law-enforcement officer.

Payton, George T. *Patrol Procedures.* 2nd ed. Los Angeles: Legal Book Corp., 1966. This reference is the only one of its kind. A good presentation of proper patrol procedures. It has been widely acclaimed and adopted as a basic text in police-science courses dealing with police patrol.

Tappan, P. W. *Crime, Justice and Correction.* New York: McGraw-Hill Book Co., 1960. Chapters 10 through 13 orient enforcement of law in the legally defined judicial process.

Traffic Law Enforcement Series. 2nd ed. Evanston, Ill.: Traffic Institute of Northwestern University. A series of training manuals published for inclusion in a loose-leaf notebook. An excellent publication for practitioners and students enrolled in law-enforcement programs.

Whisenand, P. M., and J. L. Cline. *Patrol Operations.* Englewood Cliffs, N.J.: Prentice-Hall, Inc. Essentials of Law Enforcement Series, 1971. The authors cover patrol functions as a series of overlapping activities. They discuss each activity separately and review the standard performance technique involved.

Part V

Police Relations with the Community and with the Youthful Offender

In the concluding part of this volume, the subject of police image is discussed by men who have unique combinations of instructional and service experience. They point out that the establishment and maintenance of a favorable police image is a very effective encouragement to voluntary law observance and, therefore, a crime deterrent. Chapters 20 and 21 note examples of police activities that are geared to the attainment of public support. They stress in particular the judicious use of force, the long-range effect of police contact with juveniles, and the value of promoting leadership among more interested segments of the community.

The sad plight of the law enforcement officer, in regard to respect for law and order, is vividly portrayed by J. D. Lohman. He points out that many of the problems that confront law enforcement agencies in the urban areas are directly attributable to the "changing American scene." Wholesale and radical transformations are sharply modifying the conditions of contemporary community life and posing new problems for law enforcement agencies. One significant factor is that the cities are becoming the residence of lower-class Negro groups, while whites are moving to the suburbs. This widespread resettlement has coincided with problems of housing, income, etc.

If it is correct that law enforcement has reached a point where citizenry respect can no longer be taken for granted, then it might be said further that at least one police goal is in jeopardy—that of gaining support for police activities. Chapter 22 underscores the fact that police need all the support they can get in a democratic society.

The chapter entitled, "Juvenile Offenders: Special Problems" is taken from the editor's publication *Law Enforcement and the Youthful Offender: Juvenile Procedures,* where he examines those areas of delinquent activity that law enforcement agencies find extremely difficult to deal with. These special problems require considerable flexibility and, due to their uniqueness, a great deal of serious thought. Special handling is required when dealing with juvenile gangs, and the use of narcotics by juveniles. These are not routine law violations, and the author analyzes the causes of such violations. In addition, he reviews the role of the police in protecting the community, investigating the offense, and arriving at an intelligent disposition.

CHAPTER 20

Issues in Human Relations: Threats and Challenges

Nelson A. Watson

Nelson A. Watson, until his death in 1971, was Director of the Professional Standards Division, International Association of Chiefs of Police. Dr. Watson contributed many articles and books invaluable to the literature of the police science field.

"Cool it! Here comes the fuzz!"

Or — for those old enough to remember—

"Cheese it!—Da cops!"

Or — the mistake that many parents make when trying to discipline a young child—

"You behave yourself or the policeman will come and get you!"

In all of these statements and unfortunately in the opinion of a lot of otherwise intelligent people, the image of the police officer implies a threat.

Threats and challenges, which in some respects are alike, are two specific kinds of human relations. Both are important to police. In this paper we shall consider these issues in human relations with particular attention to their meaning in the police field.

The first thing we should do before getting to the specifics is to set the stage by mentioning a few things about human relations in general. Let us start by noting that human relations means all of the many types of interactions that occur between and among people. These interactions or relationships all have certain characteristics or dimensions by which we evaluate and react to them. In passing, it will serve our purpose to consider what some of these dimensions are.

Dimensions of Human Relations

First of all, there is obviously a *time* dimension. Any given relationship between two people can be brief or long lasting. A relationship such as father-son is a lifetime matter. Husband-wife is shorter as is employer-employee. Now, such role relationships are common to practically everyone —there are very few of us who are hermits or recluses. We all have many role relationships. A policeman-violator relationship is one you encounter in your daily work and it is ordinarily fairly brief.

The time dimension applies to all types of human relations—they begin, they change, or they end. Some are momentary and some are permanent.

Probably you have at some time almost bumped into someone coming toward you. You try to side step and he side steps in the same direction. Then both of you move the other way. Finally, you get the confusion resolved and with a chuckle or a muttered apology, you pass and move on. You may feel amused or annoyed, but this human relationship is a brief one.

Someone may ask a policeman for directions and, upon receiving an answer, go his way whereupon this momentary relationship ends. Two officers may be competing for a promotion to the same vacancy. A rivalry develops which may continue long after the vacancy is filled by the winner. Sex is a factor which permanently affects relationships. The fact that A is male and B female affects their relationship as long as they live.

There are other kinds of relationships in addition to the various roles we play which are important in our contacts with people and which are also affected by the time dimension. For instance, in the relationship between two people, one may be dominant and the other submissive. This arrangement may continue as long as the two are associated. On the other hand, some event may reverse the situation. In the police world, for example, Sergeant A may be dominated by Lieutenant B, but when Sergeant A is promoted to lieutenant, he may gradually come to dominate Lieutenant B.

Another such relationship is attraction-repulsion. No doubt you and many of your acquaintances are mutually attracted to each other. These are your friends and some of your relatives. There may be certain acquaintances toward whom you feel negatively—people you dislike for various reasons. Such feelings between you and other people can be very long lasting or very short. They can also reverse their direction.

Another dimension is the *importance* or salience of the relationship to the person. Some of your relationships with others are of great importance to you and some are not. Person A may value very highly the friendship of B. B may or may not hold a similar view regarding A. John may have deep-seated feelings of inferiority which make it important for him to try to dominate others. Such feelings are sometimes at the root of bragging and bullying. The more important the relationship is to the person, the more likely he is to exert effort to establish it or to keep it going, or if it is a negative relationship, to break it up.

Extensity or *pervasiveness* is another dimension. A particular relationship between A and B may pervade or extend to everything that goes on between them—love or hate, for example. Then again, disagreement or anger may characterize their relationship only in connection with certain specific issues such as money, sex, or drinking.

Still another dimension is the *pleasant-unpleasant* tone of the relationship. There are many words in our language to describe quality: like-dislike, love-hate, good-bad, and so on. This is a *negative-positive* dimension.

And, in addition to having a negative-positive direction, these feelings exist in some degree of intensity. Pleasure may vary from mild euphoria to intense ecstacy. Pain may run from little more than discomfort to excruciating agony. This is an *intensity* dimension.

We should also mention the *degree of clarity* of the relationship. Sometimes it is easy to interpret the feelings and the intentions of another person. He may be cheerful and friendly and his intentions are clearly harmless—maybe even helpful. Or his general demeanor may indicate that he is full of hate and anger and that his intentions are really dangerous. But there are times when it is not possible to determine clearly what the other person's feelings and intentions are. The situation is ambiguous and it is hard to know what to expect. In the police field this ambiguity is sometimes produced through deliberate attempts to deceive. A con man, for example, exudes a friendship that is only a front. He uses this false front to lure his "pigeon" into the trap. We could call this dimension "uncertainty" since it would result in some degree of uncertainty as to the proper response. Another source of ambiguity is the "poker face." A person may deliberately try to hide his feelings or he may simply be rather inexpressive.

It should be understood that these dimensions are not independent of each other. The easiest way to think of this is in terms of the time dimension. You cannot have negative or positive feelings about something that does not last for some amount of time. Similarly, any relationship experienced to some degree of intensity must be a feeling *about* something—it extends to or encompasses things. Also, it will be of some degree of importance. Say a person has a good relationship with his neighbor. They like each other. They cooperate in many things. They seek each other's company with reasonable frequency. They are mutually dependent in some ways. The relationship between them extends to many of their areas of interest such as gardening, house repairs, their children, etc. It is of importance to them. There is no ambiguity in it. It is pleasant and it lasts for a long time. Looking at it this way, it is plain to see that none of these dimensions can exist alone.

The Psychological Field of Human Relations

The dimensions we have been discussing, except for time, are psychological and not physical quantities and even time has psychological attributes. It must be clearly understood that the relationships we are discussing also are psychological. All human relations take place in a psychological field. They may or may not require the physical presence of the parties, for the relationships can exist even if the parties have not actually ever met in person. What is really required is psychological, not physical presence. If A is to have a relationship, any kind of relationship, with Patrolman X, Patrolman X must exist within the psychological field or environment of A. It is not necessary, however, for A to be part of the psychological field of Patrolman X. So far as X is concerned, A might not even exist.

Similarly, for Patrolman X to have a relationship with A, A must exist within the psychological field of Patrolman X. In this case, X may not exist for A.

If the relationship is mutual, on the other hand, each must exist within the psychological field of the other. To say that "each must exist" means that the relationship must have some degree of the various dimensions we discussed. It must continue over some period of time. It will have some degree of importance to each. It will be either negative or positive and of a certain level of intensity and clarity. It is through these dimensions that the nature of the relationship is interpreted and understood by the two parties.

Let us take some examples to illustrate these important points. First, consider the one-sided case in which A has a psychological relationship with Patrolman X but where the relationship is not shared by the officer. Say A is a dope pusher but Patrolman X, at this point, has no way of knowing it. A is wary of Patrolman X, but the officer does not even notice A. For him, A is only one of the many generalized others or anonymous people known to X to be present, but not seen as individuals. Schematically, it might be as shown in Figure 1.

The diagrams, vastly oversimplified, show that A is not even in the psychological field of Patrolman X, but Patrolman X does occupy a central position in the field of A. It may be that X is merely the specific officer who on this occasion has been singled out of A's generalized wariness of all police. In this case, A might have a fear of (high intensity) or anxiety about (low intensity) all policeman (negative direction) of which he is also aware (clarity) and which affects much of what he does (extensity) every day (time dimension). This relationship may be of great importance to him. On this occasion, it is Patrolman X who becomes the specific focus of A's general relationship with police as an institution. His personal relationship with X may well cease as soon as X is out of sight.

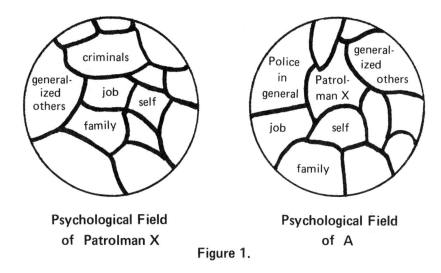

**Psychological Field
of Patrolman X**

**Psychological Field
of A**

Figure 1.

It is easy to see how the situation could be reversed. Patrolman X might regard A as a suspect who matches a description of a wanted man. A would then be within the psychological field of X. However, A might not be the wanted man and having no feelings of guilt, Patrolman X would perhaps not be an object of awareness within his psychological field.

Then, to complete the picture, observe that for the relationship to be mutual, both must be in the psychological field of the other. Unless this is so, there cannot be any interaction between them. If neither is within the psychological field of the other, there is no relationship at all.

Anyone can think up all kinds of reasons for each to be within the psychological field of the other, whether physically present or not. Human relations become very important when an officer stops a motorist for a traffic violation. Each is present and a psychological relationship exists. After the encounter comes to an end and each goes his independent way, the relationship continues for a time even though physically neither is in the presence of the other. There may be feelings of embarrassment, resentment, hostility and so on which persist for a long time. Moreover, if the motorist is a person who already had a psychological relationship with the officer, such as a high school classmate, for example, this incident will, without doubt, color the relationship in the future. What was a "beautiful friendship" may now be a strained coolness or even complete avoidance—a shift from positive to negative.

Police officers should understand that their official contacts with people are often matters of great concern. What is routine to the officer may be of overriding importance to the private citizen. The authority with which you are invested may be very threatening to him or her. Lets say you stop a women for a traffic violation and all that happens is that you issue a ticket or perhaps only a warning. To you it is a common occurrence, but to her it is a very disturbing event. As an everyday part of your job, it is certainly not going to make you angry or agitated to the point where you lost control of yourself. She, however, might be so alarmed or so excited that she begins to cry or maybe to tell you off in no uncertain terms.

Measured on the time dimension, you promptly dismiss the incident from your mind and go on to other business. The housewife does not. She may fuss and fume about it for hours. In fact, perhaps even months or years later when she meets a policeman at a social gathering, she belabors him with a detailed description of the incident—by now properly embellished and twisted to her own purposes. Or if it is fear that she experiences, she may be miserable in dread all afternoon wondering what her husband is going to say when he gets home. Time-wise, the relationship for her can be quite lasting.

In this incident also we have an illustration of the interplay of the dimensions. It is probably correct to say that if a relationship is experienced intensely, its effect will persist longer than that of one of low intensity. In the case just described, you had no intense feelings and you do not dwell on the matter very long. But the woman went through what was an intensely shocking experience in her relationship with you and it affects her for a much longer period of time. Likewise, what happened affects her behavior more extensively than it does yours. The incident does not change your outlook toward housewives in general, but it may have a significant effect on her attitude toward all policemen. This is the essence of a stereotype. No matter how well you behaved yourself or how courteous and considerate you were, she may have taken a dislike to you which she henceforth displaces onto other officers. You may be sure that some traces of the temporary relationship you had with this housewife and her traffic ticket will remain with her even when you are not present.

All of us have psychological relationships with others in which the psychological presence of the other is practically as important in governing our behavior as is the physical presence. Consider, for example, a wife, one's children, the boss, and so on. What a person does is modified to some extent by the realization that his behavior will be approved or disapproved by such people should they find out about it.

The Nature of Threats and Challenges

Threats and challenges are two important kinds of human relations with which policemen are often faced. Everyone will realize that threats and challenges can originate from circumstances not involving people. The weather can be threatening. A dog can be seen as a threat by a newspaper boy or a mailman. Mt. Everest can be seen as a challenge "because it is there." Par is a challenge to a golfer. Threats and challenges such as these, however, are not "issues in human relations" in the sense we are considering. Our discussion will concern only interpersonal relations in which threats or challenges play a part.

Every experienced officer will readily appreciate that some of the encounters he has with people are threatening either to him or to the other person. In some encounters, the officer is challenged by the other person. Likewise, the officer himself is sometimes seen as a challenge by certain other people. In either case, the situation can be unpleasant and difficult.

While threats and challenges are not the same, they do have some elements in common. A threat may not necessarily be a challenge, but a challenge usually is somewhat of a threat. Each may be accompanied by a feeling of anxiety or fear. Both would have some effect on one's motives and aspirations. Both would tend to modify a person's behavior. In this process, both would be perceived, integrated, and acted upon in different ways depending upon the person's personality complex. Sometimes a man who is threatened may react to the threat as a challenge almost as though he were saying, "Go ahead. I dare you!" If a man has a strong need to prove himself or to be dominant, he might rise to a threat or a challenge in a recklessly aggressive manner. One who has a strong need for self-preservation (security) or to be well liked may react to a challenge by trying to compromise, i.e. to avoid conflict and to resolve the matter by talking it over. Threats and challenges will be seen and acted upon by different personalities in different ways.

A threat is an internal phenomenon—*a state of mind*—in which a person believes that certain combinations of physical, social, and/or psychological factors are menacing to his well-being. He perceives in the situation the possibility of damage or harm to either his physical self (the body) or his psychological self (the ego). Robbery and extortion are crimes in which the psychological base is a threat. The same is the case with forcible rape.

A challenge is a dare and it is like a threat in that if it is not successfully thwarted something of a harmful nature will happen. Baiting of the police by demonstrators or potential rioters is a challenge.

A threat is a temporizing expression of aggressive intent. A challenge is a call to action in which the intent is to move toward more or less immediate resolution of some conflict. The person making either a threat or a challenge is attempting to gain superiority, mastery, or control of the behavior of the "victim." Threats and challenges may be explicit or they may be implied; they may be real or they may be imagined. Some threats are only bluffs.

How Threats and Challenges Work

It is important to understand that for a threat or a challenge to work they must be perceived as such by the intended "victim or receiver." A threat is not a threat unless a person sees it as such. If A threatens B, it will have no effect on B's behavior unless he knows about it and perceives the action as threatening. It is also true, of course, that B may think A is threatening him and act accordingly even though A has no such intention. The same is true of a challenge. At the same time, it is not necessary for B to be acquainted with A. Police are often notified by public figures and lesser known people of the receipt of threatening letters or telephone calls. Often the threatening party is unknown. Nevertheless, even in these cases, the threatened person's behavior may in fact be modified by the anonymous threat.

Another factor in the relationship which makes a big difference is the relative status or power position of the two parties. A threat is not likely to succeed unless one believes that the person making it has the power to do what he says he will do. If he is the boss, he may have sufficient economic power and authority to carry it through. If the threat comes from a parent to a child, the superiority of the threatener is usually recognized and accepted. However, if the child is a rebellious juvenile who is seriously challenging the parent's authority, the situation may be quite different. The power of a bully who threatens a smaller boy is raw physical force. The power of public opinion can be psychologically threatening to one who is tempted to do something off color such as accepting a bribe or engaging in an illicit sexual escapade.

Still another factor which makes quite a difference is the evaluation of the threat by the person threatened. If it is not perceived and evaluated as being important, it is unlikely to have much effect. The threatened action must seem sufficiently harmful. The person must believe he is going to be hurt. When a little girl says to her brother, "Stop that or I'll tell mommie on you," the little boy may not be alarmed at all because he knows nothing much will happen even if she does. Contrast that with a kidnapping in which the life of the victim is endangered. Here the threat is extreme and the likelihood that it will succeed is much greater. For some people threats which could produce "loss of face" are very serious.

When we put together the potential power to carry out the threat and the potential damage of the threatened action, we find interesting relationships. Low power–low damage would not produce much behavior modification. Low power–high damage and high power–low damage might produce some. High power–high damage would be the most effective.

There are many factors that have a bearing on how the threatened action will be valued by the threatened person. Among these are economic

	Low Power	**High Power**
Low Damage	Threat is ignored or produces only mild and passing reaction.	Threat produces moderate to strong anxiety and reaction.
High Damage	Threat produces mild to moderate anxiety and reaction.	Threat produces strong anxiety and strong defensive reaction.

Figure 2.

Scheme showing how most people would react to different combinations of threatening conditions. A person who is high-strung or very jittery may react strongly even to low-power, low-damage threats.

and social status and personality structure. An introvert might be terror-stricken by the prospect of making a speech, whereas it may be welcomed by an extrovert. The possibility of arrest is not the same to a skid-row bum as it is to a Superintendent of Schools. It seems evident that some people risk criminal behavior because they believe the threat of arrest and imprisonment to be low.

Guilt is a psychological factor of importance in any extortion case. "Protection" type extortion cases are based on the threat of economic catastrophy and no guilt is involved, as a rule. Other extortion, however, may be based on threats to disclose misconduct—theft, embezzlement, sexual misbehavior or deviation, and the like. This is, in part, the basis for denying security clearance to homosexuals, for example. If the threatened party is actually guilty, his reaction to the threat will probably be very different from that of one who is innocent.

Personality structure is an important factor in determining reaction to threats and challenges. One who has an inflated opinion of himself and who is use to having his own way is more likely to react aggressively than is a "milk toast" type of person. A worrywart who is timid or chronically anxious is likely to find threats and challenges disturbing or even devastating whereas a more normal person might shrug them off. One whose personality tends toward paranoia even "sees" threats when they do not exist. This may be because he is chronically anxious or fearful without any good reason. It is not logical to be afraid without having something to be afraid of, so a person like this sees various people or groups as threatening. This serves to justify his fears.

The psychological effects of threats and challenges and behavioral reactions to them are of considerable importance to the police. Policemen are often challenged and they are often threatened. Moreover, they themselves issue both challenges and threats. It would be wise, therefore, for an officer to know about these important types of human relations.

Threats and Challenges in Police Work

In many everyday situations on the street, a policeman finds himself threatened or challenged. How many times has an officer encountered a traffic offender who, as a "friend" of the chief or the mayor, threatens to have him transferred or fired? How many times has an officer found himself facing a man with a gun? Not infrequently a suspect makes threatening moves and remarks when being arrested. In riots, police are under high-power, high-damage threats of being injured or being killed. Police generally regard the attitudes and behavior of the Black Panthers and certain other organizations of black youths as threatening. Some of the behavior of campus protesters is challenging to the police and some of it is threatening. The deliberate provocation and insults of the New Left on the campuses are seen by some as challenges.

For the purposes of improving our understanding of human relations, it may be useful to describe various levels or kinds of threats:

1. *Verbal Emotional Release.* Some people become upset under pressure. Their emotions produce internal tensions which reach a level they cannot contain. Sooner or later they begin blowing off steam. They may become verbally abusive and threatening. They have little possibility of actually doing what they are threatening to do and no real intention of trying it. Many a police officer has encountered people like this. It is often apparent that the chatter is just so much "hot air." The officer calmly proceeds to write the ticket or to hold the prisoner for the paddy wagon without getting involved in a verbal free for all. He knows the best procedure is simply to let the person talk, in the meantime maintaining his composure—*and* his control of the situation.

2. *Real Threats.* Some people are not "badmouthing" just to relieve the tensions; they mean it and eventually they will try to follow through with their threats. It is not always possible to tell. Of course, if a man says, "OK cop! You asked for it," and pulls a gun, his intentions should be taken at face value. Your reaction should be immediate and decisive. This is not the time to wait to find out whether he really means it.

3. *Threats Intended as Offensive Weapons.* Some threats are made in a calculated manner, the intention being to provoke the officer into a response. In a sense, these threats are challenges. There really is no intention to follow through if the officer does not "take the bait." The challenge is issued in the form of a threat hoping to goad the officer into some injudicious or unprofessional conduct which can then be used as a basis for charges of abuse or brutality. Strict adherence to professional standards is the best defense against this type.

4. *Latent Symbolic Threats.* The three types of threats just described occur on a face-to-face basis during interpersonal contacts. This fourth type, which is really as important as the others, does not necessarily involve face-to-face matters. This type is based upon certain kinds of beliefs. A person may come to believe, either as a result of personal experience or because of things he has been told, that certain objects, situations, or people are potentially dangerous. We call these threats *latent* because, like attitudes, they are always there waiting just below the conscious level ready to spring into action when the symbol with which they are associated is perceived. We call them *symbolic* because the thing which activates them is possibly only a representative of a general class of things—in other words, a symbol.

To clarify these points let us take an example. Suppose a hoodlum has been arrested on several occasions for robbery, assault, and carrying a concealed weapon. He has been convicted of robbery and has served time. Under the Stop and Frisk Law he has been questioned a number of times resulting in an arrest and conviction for carrying a concealed weapon. To him, anyone wearing a uniform and a badge is a latent symbolic threat. His awareness of the police as a threat is activated when he is planning a "hit" and everytime he sees an officer or a patrol car. Both the uniform and the patrol car are symbols in which the essence of the threat is concentrated.

This is a human relations mechanism to which we must be alert in our own work. As human beings, police officers are as much subject to this psychological process as anyone else. If we are not informed and knowledgeable about such things, we may well be misled by latent symbolic threats. For example, one could make the mistake of regarding all college students who wear beards, sandals and "odd" clothing as anti-police. Experience with some such people during campus disorders may lead to the false conclusion that they are all that way and the trappings become symbols for behavior. The same is true of young Negro males, all of whom may come to be regarded as potentially dangerous and criminals.

Another example of current interest involves the latent symbolic threat represented by police officers in the minds of some people. Suppose some officer does mistreat a person—perhaps a juvenile. Say he abuses the boy verbally or maybe physically punishes him. For this boy, any officer—even you, an officer just trying to do your job within the rules—becomes a latent symbolic threat. In fact, this attitude may well be passed on by the boy to others thus making it difficult for all concerned.

5. *Situational Threats.* The least obvious or the most subtle threats we face, I call situational. They operate unilaterally on an intrapersonal basis. They are implicit in many of the situations and circumstances commonly encountered in our daily lives. They often operate without our realizing it. The subtlety in these threats results from the fact that, while they influence our behavior much like any other threat, we do not think of them as threats. Moreover, they are deeply personal and do not affect everyone the same way. What any individual does about them depends heavily upon his social conditioning, his sense of values, his aspirations, and many other personal characteristics. These situational threats are steeped in tradition and culture and very important in governing our conduct.

We need not go into these things exhaustively so let us remove the mystery by giving a few examples.

> *Example #1:* You are a policeman. It is generally accepted than an officer is supposed to be thoroughly masculine. Now, without really realizing it, you are careful to act in speech and deed the way you think a man should act. You dare not run the risk (expose yourself to the threat) of being called weak, timid, or (Heaven forbid!) a fag. This leads some officers to act *unnecessarily* tough.
>
> *Example #2:* The general feeling among the patrolmen you work with is that the decisions of the Supreme Court over the last few years are entirely too liberal, that they give suspects and violators too much advantage, and that they severely restrict the police. Not infrequently officers are heard to say that there seems to be some Communist influence at work. You have taken a course in Constitutional Law at the local college and you believe the decisions and guidelines for police should have been in effect long ago. Further, you feel that the decisions resulted from bad police practice in the first place. Also, some of the officers, especially some of the old timers, have been rather open in making fun of you for "wasting" your time going to college. The result of this general atmosphere is that you tend to keep your opinions to yourself. With feelings running as high as they are, you realize that the others might ostracize you if you try to "buck the tide."
>
> *Example #3:* Your field lieutenant is very opinionated and a stickler for detail. He insists that things be done his way or "by the book." You are hoping for promotion to sergeant and your lieutenant is the one who has the

task of preparing your performance rating. A situation arises in which you must take action. In your opinion, it seems clear that the best procedure both for the department and for the person involved, due to unusual circumstances in this specific case, is to make an exception to the "book." However, if you do, you might incur the wrath of the lieutenant causing him to give you a lower rating. The threat to your ambition to be promoted is very real.

Threats to police officers are more often implied than overt. The policeman is regarded by most people as a powerful person and an open threat is deemed to be rather risky. Most people would, therefore, avoid coming right out with it and instead would threaten by implication. Looking at it from the officers' point of view, this puts him in the position of *assuming* the making of a threat. Since officers are assaulted or perhaps verbally abused rather often, many are led to assume that a person is threatening when really he is not. When a person shows an attitude of hostility, he may or may not be dangerous. The same may be said for attitudes of fear, anger, or unusual excitement. In other words, these attitudes do not always produce dangerous behavior. It must be admitted, however, that they do often enough to warrant caution and preparedness.

Much the same might be said about challenges. A new, young officer assigned to patrol on foot in a slum area may meet an implied challenge from the "dudes hanging on the corner." These youths are going to test the officer. One way or another, he has to meet the challenge or he will not be able to continue patrolling there. This does not necessarily mean that he must resort to physical combat, though that may be what the "dudes" have in mind. Finding a way to handle the challenge without physical violence is preferable.

Juveniles often contrive strategies designed to challenge the police. It is part of their gamemanship which we sometimes refer to as deviltry. Unfortunately, much of it is a lot more serious than the old Halloween trick of upsetting garbage cans. Policemen can well do without such challenges as a high-speed chase after a youth in a stolen car. The challenges issued by juveniles are often especially irritating to policemen because of their insolence and lack of decency and respect. The fact that we understand them to be part of the process of growing up, establishing independence, and testing of authority does little to make them acceptable.

In one case, a man observed an incident in which an officer was arresting a juvenile. The boy called the officer some nasty names, told him to get his hands off him, that he was a teenager, and that the officer could not do anything to him. The officer had to physically restrain the boy so he would not run away. All the while the youth was using abusive, vile, and insulting language. The man who observed this, realizing that the officer could not punish the boy, asked if the officer wanted him to "take care of him for you!" The officer replied, "No, I'll handle it. If you hit him, I'd have to arrest you for assault. He's only trying to get me to 'blow my cool,' but it won't work. The officer handled this challenge well. He was not goaded into injudicious action and, needless to say, the boy did not get away.

A point of great significance relative to challenges was recently brought to the author's attention. One of the leaders of a nationally publicized protest said that part of the campaign strategy was to get the police to overreact by baiting them. The hope was that the police would become violent; that they would panic and do things which would cause non-involved people to condemn them thus generating sympathy for the protesters. The leaders were disappointed when they were unable to goad the police into unprofessional conduct and they felt that the campaign was not as effective as it would have been if the police had behaved badly.

The process of communication is seriously curtailed because of people's reaction to latent symbolic threats and situational threats. An important factor in both types is that these threats often involve the perception of other people as "different" and therefore unfriendly—maybe even dangerous. Many people have a tendency to suspect and dislike people who are unlike themselves. People who are "different" may be perceived as the embodiment of latent symbolic and situational threats. This would produce a negative position on the pleasant-unpleasant dimension.

One of the several elements of the culture of youth has been called the "conspiracy of secrecy." Youths sense the embodiment of latent symbolic and situational threats in their elders (and vice versa, by the way). This makes them wary and interferes with effective communication. When either party to a contact has reservations, doubts, and suspicions which cause him to hold back, the effectiveness of the interaction is reduced.

Police often complain that Negroes are uncooperative in criminal cases in that they withhold information which might lead to a solution of the case. This is the conspiracy of secrecy in another setting. The circumstances are familiar to policemen everywhere. A detective looking for a suspect questions people in the neighborhood, all of whom claim they never heard of the man even though the officer knows the suspect has lived there for years. The detective is convinced they are not telling the truth and are, in fact, protecting the suspect. It must be admitted that this can be a result of antipathies between the police and some people. Clearly, to the extent that this feeling exists, the resulting "conspiracy of secrecy" works to the disadvantage of society.

The same mechanism is at the bottom of demands for police review boards. Charges have been made that police themselves engage in a protective "conspiracy of silence." The idea is that no policeman is going to tell the whole truth about a case in which a fellow officer is accused of harassment, abuse, or brutality toward a complainant. The natural follow-up to this belief is that any investigation conducted of police by police will turn out to be a whitewash. The so-called conspiracy of silence and the conspiracy of secrecy run head on into each other. As a result, some people believe it would be futile to complain about police abuse and feel they must take the matter into their own hands outside the law.

The reduction of the threat potential in these latent symbolic and situational types would undoubtedly relieve the tensions associated with them. A more productive level of communication would result and the entire atmosphere would be improved.

The Professional Approach

What happens in many cases in which an officer is challenged is that the challenger is trying to get the officer to step out of his professional role. It is as though he were saying, "Look, Buster! You wouldn't be such a big shot if you didn't have that gun and badge." As the wielder of public power and authority, the officer is the dispenser of public discipline. In this capacity, he is required by law to exercise his authority according to rules. The rules do now allow the officer to vent his personal spleen on anyone. They do not provide for the administration of punishment by the police. Vindictiveness or harassment on the part of an officer are as much against the rules as are criminal actions.

A policeman is not an ordinary person. He is a professional and, as such, his conduct must conform to the rules. It is offensive to have people call us "pigs," but we cannot permit ourselves to retaliate in violation of the rules because to do so threatens destruction of the system we are sworn to defend. Moreover, to abandon the professional prescriptions for conduct is to walk into a trap and trapping you is the objective of the challenger.

The widely held concept of the police role produces an overemphasis on the policeman-violator relationship. Seldom is a policeman thought of as a helper even though a large part of his time is spent in rendering various kinds of service. The common concept of the role of a fireman, on the contrary, emphasizes the helper notion. It is unrealistic to expect that anytime soon we are going to be able to persuade people that the policeman is a helping person despite the fact that each time a violator is brought to justice the public good is promoted.

Adopting the professional role as a model for conduct and conforming to it in the face of provocation, frustration, and temptation is not only correct and commendable, it is also a source of great strength for an officer. It tilts the balance of power in the officer's favor. Officers who are consistently professional in conduct and bearing are in an advantageous position. They are clearly demonstrating their superiority and, as a result, people afford them the respect and admiration their professional behavior has earned. When an officer weakens and abandons his professional posture, the conduct which results may assume several forms, all of which are seen by the public as deserving of condemnation. Depending upon the circumstances, this nonprofessional conduct may be anything from vulgar language and petty abuse through unwarranted physical punishment and harassment of questionable legality up to outright criminality. Those who seriously challenge police by baiting and provocation want the officer to shed his professional armament and succumb to anger or panic. They want to reduce him to their level. The best way to handle such people is to adhere steadfastly to the professional code.

Needless to say, an officer should not make threats which he cannot or does not intend to carry through if necessary. To do so weakens his position when his "hand is called" and leaves a residue of animosity which will plague him and other officers in the future.

Group Reactions and Police-Community Relations

One of the most important aspects of human relations involving threats and challenges, especially the former, concerns the expectations held by the parties to the encounter. There are many references in police literature to the effect that Negro slum or ghetto residents, Puerto Ricans, Mexican-American, and other minority persons expect to be treated rudely or abusively by police. For their part, many police officers expect to meet with hostility and resistance or even violence from these same people. These very expectations come to be regarded as threats and inevitably they produce behavioral reactions. The behavioral reactions are then taken by the other group as evidence of existence of the threat and we have a "self-fulfilling prophesy." It is a vicious circle and if the tensions and hostility are to be reduced, we must find a way to break it.

The police in many places have taken constructive steps toward breaking this vicious circle. This is one of the objectives of police-community relations programs. Training programs in human relations for police have been offered. Efforts have been made to reach out to the people through Boys Clubs, Block Parent Plans, Crime Check or Crime Stop Programs, Juvenile Recreation Programs, Store-front Operations to bring police service closer to the locality, and similar activities.

Many times when these questions are discussed in police meetings and training schools, the officers say, in effect, "We're willing, but what about them? Whose telling them? There has to be some give on both sides; it can't be a one-way street." And, they are so right! There must be a change of attitude on "both sides." In fact, a large part of the problem lies in the widespread and unquestioned acceptance of the existence of "sides." The fact of the matter is that the vast majority of the people and the police should be allied in the fight on crime and the pursuit of justice and order.

The hard and practical fact which we must accept, unpalatable though it may be, is that it is the police who have to tell "them." In some cases, the police themselves go directly to the people. In others, the "telling" is done by community organizations with which the police work. Obviously, not everyone can be reached and despite our best efforts, there will always be a lot of residual hatred and hostility. But a well-conceived realistic approach to the human relations problems in police-citizen contacts must be an indispensable part of the daily activities of every police officer before real progress can be made.

Overcoming mistrust and hostility—so far as the *police* function in the community is concerned—is a *police* problem. Overcoming mistrust and hostility—so far as the broad social problems of our time are concerned —is a problem for all people toward which public and private effort must be directed. There is no question that some of the problems the police face result from the failures of society at large. And in this sense, it must be understood that there are no community problems which are not to some extent police problems because of the "fall out" resulting in crime and disorder. The police mission per se, however, must be carried on both at the policy level and by each individual officer in his daily performance of duty without aggravating the broad underlying social problems and without producing problems because of police failures.

Large numbers of people who now see the policeman as a threat must be convinced through good human relations practices by officers that they and the police are seeking the same goals and that, therefore, he is not a threat. The only ones for whom the police should be threatening are criminals and those who seriously abridge the rights of others. The relationship between the ordinary citizen of any race, creed, or political persuasion and the police should be characterized by mutual respect and good will. This becomes very important when making contacts with complainants, witnesses, and victims—yes, and even suspects. Too often the interviewing officer gives the other person the impression that he is the criminal, that he is not trusted, that he is the one who is "wrong." The person contacted is made to feel uncomfortable or even fearful. This is hardly the way to get cooperation. Now everyone knows that some complainants, some witnesses, some victims can't be trusted, but if you start off by giving that impression, you will have at least one strike against you from the beginning. Give the person the benefit of the doubt. There is plenty of time to take care of the other angle later if it turns out that way.

Probably all experienced officers have encountered people who think the world is against them. They see threatening people and things all around them. Such people are not necessarily psychotic. Some of them may have gotten off to a bad start from the time they were born. Perhaps the father was unknown and the mother did not want the child in the first place. As time went by, the child was taught from the attitudes of people around him that he was regarded as being in the way. He was neglected and abused. His personality developed in such a way that the effects of this treatment showed. He grew up showing a sour and suspicious disposition which discouraged people from contacts with him. Again, we have a vicious circle. People like this expect others to be hostile or cruel or at least indifferent. Since they expect to be hurt, they often reject others in advance in order to keep from being rejected by them. As a matter of fact, sometimes these people even reject themselves. From their earliest days, they have been led to believe they are not worth much and they hate themselves. For them, police may be especially significant. Police have been chosen as the representatives of all those hostile others who have been cruel or indifferent and who wish to keep them down. Therefore, in the police they see concentrated the threats of the hostile world.

There are many people who believe that their misfortunes and hardships are the results of prejudices and discrimination. For them, exploitation of the weak by the powerful is a fact of life. Their future seems bleak and hopeless. They believe that hostile forces unfairly threaten them from all sides. In the list of these forces as they see them is the power of those on top which has been delegated to the police to guarantee that the status quo is maintained. Obviously, this is not a condition that is peculiar to Negroes or other ethnic minorities; it is found in individuals of all types.

Persons who believe themselves disadvantaged because of prejudices and discrimination may react in a number of ways. In the first place, since they are constantly threatened with various hardships, they must find a source for the threats—someone or something on whom to blame their misfortunes. Normally this will be some person or group although occasionally one may be superstitious enough to blame it on the stars or some other supernatural force. When a person or group is blamed, it is some group close at hand. Throughout history, many groups have been so blamed: Jews, Catholics, Protestants (currently in Northern Ireland), Negroes, whites, and so on through a long list we need not present here. In a lot of cases, there is more than one source. In fact, if a person is sufficiently paranoid, he may think practically everybody is threatening him. In the second place, people who really are prejudiced and bigoted are likely also to be poorly educated, limited in their abilities, superstitious, and strongly authoritarian.

People who believe themselves unfairly disadvantaged may react by becoming aggressively militant. Some Negroes, for example, convinced that their troubles stem from white racism, agitate aggressively for change and may even riot. They may physically attack whites or if none are available, they may attack their property—"Burn, baby, burn." Of course, since the police, most of whom are white, are always there, they are natural targets for the militance. The militance may take other forms such as writings, speeches, marches, or picketing. Not all militance is undesirable. A strike by a labor union is a form of militance. It is entirely legitimate for people to be aggressively militant in order to advance themselves so long as they remain within the law. People who make threats are acting aggressively, and aggression is also a way to meet threats and challenges.

There is an opposite kind of reaction. Instead of attacking the source of threat or frustration, people may elect to move away from it. They may withdraw into a world of their own, give up, or perhaps deny that there is a problem and try to ignore it. In a broader sense, anyone who sees his problems as overwhelming and hopeless may withdraw and not try to fight back. The withdrawal can take a variety of forms. People who withdraw can take solace in all kinds of substitute adjustments. Among the havens often used are hobbies, religion, and even antisocial or abnormal activities such as crime, drug addiction, and neurotic or psychotic personality disorders.

It is interesting and disturbing to note that some people claim to see similar kinds of behavior on the part of some policemen. It has been said that the police are themselves a minority group and as such are subject to certain disadvantages and discriminations. Some police have been charged with what amounts to aggressive militance in their behavior toward certain groups such as campus demonstrators, hippies, and black people. Some claim the police, in giving expression to their militance, have been violent, that they have used unnecessary force, that they have been bigoted and intolerant, and that they have overstepped the bounds of their authority. Frequently this alleged behavior is attributed to the recruitment of the policeman chiefly from the lower classes where physical aggression is more often a reaction to frustration. Low pay, little education and inadequate training, low social status, and general resentment of police even among people who ought to know better are circumstances said to contribute to the problem.

The people who make these charges sometimes name the groups they think serve as scapegoats on whom the police may blame their troubles. The groups named include liberals, hippies, intellectuals, do-gooders, politicians, the Supreme Court, and civil rights activists, among others.

It should be obvious that among a group of 400,000 people—an estimate of the number of police officers in the nation—there will be all kinds of personalities. It would be expected that some policemen meet their problems aggressively just as people in other occupations do. It would also be expected that some would withdraw just as other people do. Have you ever heard of an officer who resolved the question of promotion by saying it would not do any good to take the examination because he did not carry any weight with the right people? This is a form of withdrawal—even if it is true. The important point is, that, as indicated earlier, the policeman's best approach to his problems is reliance on the professional code. While it may be all right for the average citizen to follow his personal inclinations, it is not for a policeman. An officer is a public official and public officials do not have the right to inject their personalities into their public duties.

Minimizing the Effects of the Threatening Police Image

Every officer should be aware that he is symbolically threatening to many people. His uniform and accouterments are badges of authority. He is regarded as a disciplinarian, a wielder of power, someone to be feared. His very presence constitutes a threat to many people even when they are not doing anything deserving the officer's attention. It is a common experience for people to slow down on high-speed highways when they see a patrol car even though they are not exceeding the speed limit. Undoubtedly, a lot of people immediately make a behavioral inventory (Am I doing anything wrong?) and become wary when they see a policeman approaching. This wariness, uneasiness or apprehension is part of the aura of threat with which the police are surrounded. The officer is thus often seen as a person to be avoided.

The fact that many people see the officer as a threat has some undesirable consequences. The tendency to avoid him is one. Another is a lack of cooperation by some people because they are reluctant to contact the police. Still another is the belief by certain kinds of people that they and the police are enemies and this often produces a tendency to act aggressively against officers. It has been suggested that if we disarm the police they would not seem to be so threatening. We are not willing to go along with that suggestion. It would certainly be wonderful as an ideal, but in the harsh realities of today's urban jungles, peopled as they are by armed thugs and unbalanced madmen hidden among and often indistinguishable from the decent people, it would be foolhardy.

The fact that a policeman is regarded as a threatening person by a law violator is legitimate; he should be a threat to such people. That he should be regarded as a threat and a person to be avoided by law abiding citizens is not legitimate. Law abiding citizens and police should be pulling together in a common cause: the prevention of crime and the promotion of justice and order.

What can police officers do about problems growing out of human relations in which threats or challenges are significant issues? Should we take a fatalistic view to the effect that this is the way human nature is and there is nothing we can do to change it? We think not. We think there are some human relations techniques which policemen can cultivate with good effect. Observation and experience teaches us that there are many officers who have developed excellent human relations skills. They seem to be able to relate to people better than most. They seldom get into trouble. They have a knack of dealing effectively with almost everyone. Why? Is it in part because they are able to present themselves in a nonthreatening way? Is it because they have found ways of minimizing the threat with which their identity as a policeman endows them? Is it, in part, because they have learned how to handle threats and challenges hurled at them?

There are some techniques which officers ought to cultivate for strengthening their human relations skills. Learning how to be an effective person is essentially a matter of developing skill in relating to others. When you think about it, does it not seem logical that if a person believes you are going to give him a hard time, he will try to avoid you or, failing that, he will be unreceptive or perhaps hostile? Don't you find yourself tensing up when you think someone is going to make trouble for you? An unpleasant and difficult situation will surely result if by your approach you give a person reason for that belief. The unfortunate fact is that many times a difficult situation can and does develop in a police matter even though you have no intention of giving the other fellow a hard time because (1) he expects it, and (2) you do nothing to offset his expectation. As we have already explained, such strained relationships are inherent in widely held concepts of the police role. People expect the relationship to be an adversary one. This means we must take special measures to relieve the strains. If by your approach in a non-adversary contact, you can avoid appearing to be threatening, you will have overcome a major obstacle to an effective contact. Moreover, if you avoid downgrading the other fellow and avoid giving the impression that you regard him as a threat you will have removed some more obstacles.

Following are some guidelines to help improve your human relations skills:

1. Don't be trapped into unprofessional conduct by a threat or a challenge.

2. Make sure everything you do is calculated to enhance your reputation as a good officer—one who is firm, but fair and just.

3. When you are faced with a threat and you can't tell how serious it is, try to "buy time" in which to size up the situation by engaging the person in conversation. Make a comment or ask a question to divert his attention if possible.

4. Don't show hostility even if the other fellow does. Many times a quiet, calm and reasonable manner will cause his hostility to evaporate or at least to simmer down. And an important point is that the next time he will not be so hostile because he doesn't think you are.

5. Reduce your "threat" potential. Avoid a grim or expressionless countenance. Be an approachable human being. Too many officers habitually appear gruff and forbidding.

6. Cultivate a pleasant, friendly manner when making nonadversary contacts. Be ready with a smile, a pleasant word, a humorous comment when appropriate.

7. Let your general demeanor and especially your facial expression and tone of voice indicate that you respect the other person as a human being.

8. Let the other fellow know by your reception of him that you don't expect trouble from him and that you don't consider him a nuisance. (Maybe you do, but don't let it show.)

9. Show an interest in the other fellow's problem. Maybe you can't do anything about it, but often it is a great help just to be a good listener. Most people will respond in kind.

10. Go out of your way to contact people in the interest of improving police-community relations. Even though your department may have a unit which specializes in community relations, never forget that you are the real key to good police-community cooperation. No group of specialists can establish or build really effective police-community relations without you. More important, however, is the *fact* that effective police-community relations means more to you than to anyone else. This means that you more than anyone else should be actively working toward the establishment of or the improvement of police-community relations. The essence of good working relations between the people and the police is to be found in the way you handle yourself. You and your fellow officers on the street can do more to improve (and to destroy) police-community relations in one day than your specialized unit and your command staff can ever do.

11. There is an old show business maxim which runs, "Always leave 'em laughing." Let us paraphrase that and say "Always leave 'em feeling satisfied." There are people who react to an arrest or a traffic ticket by feeling that the officer was fair, and was just doing his job, and that they had it coming. They don't like it, but they have to admit the officer did his job properly. When you render a service or react to a request, show some interest and give some explanation. This will promote good feelings which if carried on consistently by the entire force will have a cumulative effect resulting in vastly improved human relations.

12. Try in every way you can to encourage people to work with the police for their own protection. Let the average citizen know that, far from being a threat, you are interested in being a help. Drive home the point that he is threatened by crime and disorder, not by the police.

In conclusion, it seems wise to caution readers to be realistic about the threats and challenges posed by others. Remember that some threats are real. Don't let your guard down while trying to be reasonable and decent. At the same time, do not assume that everyone is out to get you. Do conduct yourself according to the best of our professional standards and traditions. Keep calm and try to get threateners and challengers to see reason. Don't be goaded into name calling or violence. Names will not hurt you, but when it is unavoidable, don't hesitate to use legitimate force to protect yourself from physical harm.

CHAPTER 21

Current Decline in Respect for Law and Order

Joseph D. Lohman

Joseph D. Lohman, until his death in 1969, was Dean of the
School of Criminology, University of California at Berkeley. He was
a noted lecturer and writer, his latest publication being, "The Handling of Juveniles From Offense to Disposition," a research project
sponsored by the United States Department of Health, Education,
and Welfare.

It has become a virtual byword in these times to speak of the "declining respect for law and authority." In every quarter we seem agreed on the
note, sounded daily by all of the mass media, that the citizenry is not only
failing in honoring specific laws but also displays a mounting disregard for
the "rule of law" itself as an essential aspect of the democratic way of life.
But even as we echo a common concern, it is not so clear that we are all
agreed as to what we mean and to whom and to what we are referring.

It is true that national crime figures are approaching a point where
law and order might well begin to break down, just as it did in the notorious
communities of America's frontier west. Indeed, crime is currently outrac-
ing our capacity to deal with it, increasing four times as fast as our rapidly
growing population and doubling in the past 20 years with no improvement
in sight.

Crime Is Heaviest in Urban Areas

With the trend toward increased urbanization and the metropolitan
pattern of distribution, the conditions traditionally associated with a plurality of conduct norms, with deviant behavior and crime, have been accentuated. Throughout history the "great-city" has been the setting par

From: Joseph D. Lohman, "Current Decline in Respect for Law and Order," *Federal Probation,* vol. 31, no. 4, December 1967. Reprinted through the courtesy of *Federal Probation,*
Washington, D.C.

excellence for crime and the criminal. But it should be apparent that the increasing lawlessness is only a surface symptom of a more deep-seated and more pervasive malaise. Many of us seem determined to fail in our assumption, if not our understanding, that crime is the lengthened shadow of the community. While the community is changing drastically, we are still straightjacketed by its old shadow. We recognize statistical changes—over 4 million people added to the United States population since 1960 and more than 115 million now living in metropolitan areas. But we fail to see that the emergent metropolitan society is something more than new numbers and a new distribution of the population. There has been initiated a totally new set and complex of social relations. It is the newly emergent social groupings of the developing community whose strivings and aspirations have brought about a new condition of confrontation within the society. In the "great-city" impersonal relations and individual detachment are the prevailing condition. The individual works, plays, and worships at places remote from where he lives. Control by family, friends, and neighbors is atomized. The individual has become more than ever before, a face in the crowd—bored, lonely, part of the great market for vice and crime.

These enormous metropolitan concentrations—around Los Angeles, Chicago, Detroit, New York, and many other areas—consist of people newly settled and for the most part strangers to one another. Their's is a dormitory existence. They do not know their neighbors, let alone relate to them in any continuing or effective way. The anonymity, the strangeness, the impersonality of the great metropolitan communities have become a standard condition of life in these United States. There have been created an enormous mobility and fluidity of life and a sense of detachment, even irresponsibility, on the part of every individual to everyone else. It is this new way of life which magnifies the whole problem of law and order heretofore identified with the marginal world of the ghettos. In the boredom, the dullness, the chronic frustration of this new urban society, the individual counts for little. He is attended to even less and hence he becomes a ready customer for any exciting answer to his dull and uneventful existence.

Persons Respond Differently to Law

Not only the market and pattern for vice but, also a conception of self as one of the excluded—an outsider—is built upon just such massive and indiscriminate collections of individuals. Their interests and appetites, while cultivated by the conditions of life engendered by the "great-city," are outlawed by our legal system. Correspondingly, the police are confronted by widespread desires for gambling, sexual gratification, thrill giving or pacifying drugs, freedom from the effects of unbridled competition, and other sundry restraints. In view of the current chronic confrontations between the law and the practices which have been generated in great sections of the population of our cities it is instructive to recall an observation made, over 25 years ago, shortly after the repeal of the Prohibition amendment, by a leading American criminologist.

> American culture does not demand or approve obedience to all laws. . . . The slogan "obey the laws" is never meant to be taken without qualification. It is but a slight exaggeration to say that *most* conservative people believe that *other* people should obey *most* of the *most important laws most* of the time. . . . The implied injunction—"break no laws"—is not obeyed even by the most meticulously moral.[1]

In a textbook for new police recruits, and anticipating the rebuffs they will encounter, three leading police scholars with long experience in police affairs had this to say in confirmation of that commentary:

> Those who enter the service may expect to find that his very finest efforts for the community will often be misunderstood, resented and sometimes bitterly opposed by otherwise good citizens simply because they themselves are inconvenienced. And too there exist in almost every community, a certain number of citizens who resent authority in any form, delight in community disturbances and do all they can to obstruct the conduct of police business. Those who enter the service may expect to find, in many situations, exhaustive testing of their patience, stability and objectivity.[2]

In their different perspectives the police and the scholars of crime have painted up the failing respect for the law. The tensions which have been engendered between the law and the various elements of the community upon which it is enforced could make life intolerable in our urban society. A clue to the search for an answer to our dilemma may be indicated in A. V. Dicey's lectures on Law and Opinion in England during the 19th century. Dicey observed that:

> Individuals, indeed, and still more frequently classes do constantly support laws or institutions which they deem beneficial to themselves, but which certainly are in fact injurious to the rest of the world. But the explanation of this conduct will be found in nine cases out of ten to be that men come easily to believe that arrangements agreeable to themselves are beneficial to others; a man's interest gives a bias to his judgment far oftener than it corrupts his heart.[3]

---

[1]Donald R. Taft, *Criminology* (New York: The Macmillan Company, 1942), p. 234.

[2]A. C. Germann, F. D. Day, and R. J. Gallati, *An Introduction to Law Enforcement*, 1962.

[3]A. V. Dicey, "Law and Opinion in England," 1905, pp. 4-15.

Let me add to this insightful passage another sobering reflection on the American scene which Alexis De Tocqueville offered us in his search for the principles which were forging the American character. De Tocqueville identified individualism as a characteristic product of democracy. Its first effects he saw as weakening the sense of public responsibility, turning to selfishness and the default of citizenship unless the constitutional structure is designed to encourage association in free institutions, ". . . conducted by the men who reside there, (hence) the same persons are always in contact, and they are, in a manner, forced to be acquainted and to adapt themselves to one another."[4]   Dicey and De Tocqueville in large measure anticipated the bases of our current dilemma. Each in his own way has set forth the possible social and cultural sources of the current tendency toward a polarity of interest and resulting confrontation between the newly emergent interest groups, and the traditional and established authority.

Lack of respect for law very often is assumed to be evidence of a willful disregard for legitimate authority and evidence of personal defect and shortcoming. We have much to learn about the mysteries by which societies generate an abnormal response within their own circle. But this has become increasingly apparent. It is the social structure itself which contributes to such behavior. Indeed, it is the self-same social structure expressing its force and influence in an ambivalent manner which produces on one hand the conforming individual, the person respectful of the social codes, and on the other, the deviant and lawbreaker who are disrespectful of the law. It *may well be that what we observe as "disrespect for law" is a normal reaction of normal people to an abnormal condition.*

Many of the problems which are confronting us today have meanings and hence a significance which are quite different from what we have traditionally ascribed to them or to the situations they represent. For example, there is much said these days about the estrangement of the young and the old; we speak of young people's being "alienated" and estranged from the adult community. We refer to persons frequently as members of groups which do not identify with the general community, who live to themselves in some separate place according to their own standards. We see them at least in some measure at odds with the norms and values, with the law, and with established institutions of the society.

I should like to suggest that this estrangement, this alienation, of individuals can be regarded in a quite different way. It will profit us, for a moment, to examine the agencies, institutions, and organizations to which we uncritically subscribe, and to apply the notions, which we have applied to individuals, to the institutions themselves. I believe it might properly be suggested that even as we speak of persons as being estranged and alienated

---

[4]Alexis De Tocqueville, *Democracy in America,* Vol. II, 1840, p. 103.

from the conventions, the norms, the institutions of society, we may be confronted in the current day by a crisis of these same institutions. For it can be seen that the institutions are not necessarily as one with the changing social scene. They do not readily reflect in themselves the trends, and so there are, indeed, stresses in education. There are stresses in welfare. There are stresses in law enforcement. It is these crises and the dilemma of our traditional services which need to be made explicit.

One might appropriately refer to the traditional services as alienated and estranged from some people—indeed, many people—rather than always the reverse.

Traditional Structures Are Being Changed

Some very profound changes of revolutionary proportions are taking place in American society. These changes are responsible for structuring the relations of certain individuals to us even as our administrative organizations have structured our relations to them. It is important for us to see that problem as it is posed in context. The contemporary American revolution involves, among others, three factors that have challenged the traditional institutional structures: the explosive rate of population increase; the doctrine of civil rights, an ideological force which has no precedent in recent history; the impact of technology which is producing a shape of things for which we have not bargained and which is profoundly affecting great numbers of the population. These tremendous changes are more than facts in themselves—they are the condition for the creation of a new pattern of human relations in this country. We often find it difficult to perceive this new pattern, primarily because our relationships are traditionally structured and we are disposed to maintain the traditional structure.

Let us take a brief look at the influences which are transforming the community and creating a new and formidable pattern of subcultures. The subcultures present to us a pattern of adaptive behavior which we tend, for the most part, to treat as the behavior of unique individuals rather than as a manifestation of collective experience. The members of subcultures are a phenomenon of collectivity and they cannot be meaningfully addressed if their behavior is viewed as that of exceptional individuals. We cannot engage them effectively as individuals because they are under a collective influence to which they are correspondingly responsive, and which is in competition, even overt conflict, with the remote and formal influences of the school, the police, and other institutions of society. Such agencies and institutions, by their very structure and organization, exclude these individuals, hence, affirming their behavior on which we then proceed to pass judgment as evidence of individual shortcomings rather than as a manifestation of their informal social life.

Crime Is Adaptive Behavior

Crime can be considered as merely a highly dramatic expression of the whole problem of social deviance—a variation from true north, so to speak, from the central tendencies of society. Crime, though a nonconformist expression, is as much a reflection of the patterning of social life as are the conformist expressions of society. In truth, it must be seen, more frequently than we are disposed, as an instance of adaptive and conforming behavior, and recognized as such. Crime, like other behavior, is a reflection of the community. In this sense, it is important for us to recognize that the problems with increasing incidence, for example, juvenile delinquency and other mass expressions of youthful behavior, are a projection of deep-seated processes at work in the life of the community. Over one-half of the United States population will soon be under 25 years of age, and 60 percent of serious crime is committed by those 18 years old and under. Thus, youngsters who are marginal in society must be regarded not only in relation to the society as a whole but also in relation to the social patterns of their local communities. It is sometimes overgeneralized that youngsters who are marginal in school are, therefore, marginal in their communities. But the society which produces the conformist and conventional middle-class youngster also produces the nonconformist, the deviant or delinquent youngster who is not effectively engaged by the conventional institutions of society.

The nonconformists are not qualitatively different from other young people. They are not persons who are necessarily unable to adjust and who cannot have effective relations in any kind of social context. Too frequently we speak about the necessity for "socializing" young offenders, apparently assuming that they are sterile creatures lacking the capacity for living in a state of realistic accommodation with their fellows. The truth is that many whom we tend to regard as maladjusted are, as a matter of fact, frequently in a remarkable state of adjustment. Such people may, indeed, be extremely socialized, but their socialization may involve commitments to groups at variance with the norms and standards of other groups in the society. These young people are social beings and we must not fail to see them as such. If they are socialized with reference to exotic and questionable groups, we must see this as the reality, and focus on the terms and conditions of their socialization rather than treat them as persons unable to adjust. The point is that social problems are more frequently a conflict between groups rather than a conflict between individuals and a group. Conflict is resulting today from the emergence of significant pools of collective experience, taking on the proportions of subcultures, which are, almost by definition, in many respects in opposition to the wider culture.

Lives at Odds With Life in the Community

Negro-Americans, Mexican-Americans—indeed, youth in general—live in a world which is apart from the total social world of others. They participate in a lesser degree in the general life of the community, and thus there develops among them a definition of life, in some measure, at odds with the life of the community. Parenthetically, I might add that this is true of our senior citizens as well. American society today tends to be centrifugal in character; its elements are being forced apart, thus forming smaller groups, each with its own local pool of experience and culture. This is true of young people, of the poverty-stricken, and of members of racial minorities.

Prior to the midtwentieth century, the patterns of American society were centripetal; they were directed to one standard, one norm, one set of values. The European immigrants of the 19th and early 20th centuries searched for a way to participate in the society as a whole and to be one with it. They wanted to become acquainted with its customs, arts, skills, and technology. The concept of the "hyphenated" American on the whole de-emphasized ethnic origins and emphasized the melting pot process—the transition from what they had been to what they were all to become in the new society. The reverse of this tendency is markedly in evidence at the present time. The impact of changes in population, civil rights, and technology has had the effect of driving the society apart and forcing it to manifest itself in local pools of experience, i.e., subcultures, which are the mainsprings of the problem behavior we see on every side. More often than we have recognized, the attitudes, values, and perspectives of great numbers of the population stem from their allegiance to these subcultures, not from fundamental and intrinsic differences. We must continue to explore the mystery of the process which causes a society to manifest itself in so many different ways.

Our problem youth, whatever the nature of their problem, are not objects, independent of and unrelated to our treatment of them. The machinery for dealing with them is definitional. A youngster who is singled out for attention is regarded by the community as being somehow different. Consequently, he develops a different attitude toward himself, and others view him differently. Dealing with him may create a new set of social relationships, whereas not so dealing with him may mean, in fact, that he is not distinguished from others in the common, ongoing processes of society. It is certainly true that there are latent, and as yet unreported, effects which result from the way in which we address our problems. Our developing knowledge increasingly focuses on these secret effects which often overshadow the influences that already have been identified in particular relationships.

It is ironic that segregation in the United States today, after the passage of the antisegregation laws, is far more widespread than when segregation legally existed. One reason, of course, is that greater numbers of people are involved. The second and more important reason is that a subtle *de facto* system of discrimination has come into existence. The practice of subtle discrimination is pervasive, and it often serves as a more accurate measure of the attitudes of individuals than an expressed declaration to members of minority groups.

Let me state this in another way. At the present time, many people are inclined to question the propriety of the civil rights movement. Why, they ask, do Negroes feel it necessary to mount a civil rights program when they have already been emancipated from the traditional system? It is easy to reply that Negroes do this because they have tasted the fruits of freedom and want more, but this answer is not the whole of the matter. White Americans believe that nonwhite Americans have achieved their victory and established their positions as free, independent, and equal citizens. This simply is not so; it is untrue and a few examples will suffice to prove its falseness.

Consider the Negroes' position in the large cities of the North in terms of residence. More Negroes live under conditions of residential segregation today than 20 years ago. This is true of every northern city—Chicago, Detroit, San Francisco, New York, to name only a few. Negroes have moved into all the northern cities, but as they have moved in, the whites have moved out to the peripheral suburban areas. This has created a new pattern of social relations whose distinguishing feature is greater segregation of whites from Negroes and Negroes from whites than ever before in our history. A generation ago, in Chicago, 50 percent of the nonwhites lived in communities in the city in which half the population was white. Today there are almost a million Negroes in Chicago, and 85 percent of them live in communities in which more than 85 percent of the population is nonwhite. A whole generation is living under much more segregated conditions than their forebears. This is illustrative of conditions throughout the country, and it refutes the widespread idea that progress in residential desegregation has been made in which Negroes should take satisfaction.

Lack of Opportunity

With reference to the changing technology, automation has produced results very different from those generally assumed to be the case. It is a popular belief that Negroes have achieved new occupational opportunities and status. The truth is that Negro unemployment ranges from 12 to 20 percent in many communities; in some communities as many as 40 percent of the youthful nonwhites are unemployed. These figures are in sharp contrast to the national unemployment rate of 4 to 5 percent. In certain respects, since the end of World War II, the position of the Negroes with regard to employment has deteriorated rather than advanced. Negroes were employed during the war, often in upgraded positions, and they held jobs which they never had previously held. The end of the war and the subsequent development of automation (which has very special implications for blue collar workers) resulted in pushing Negroes out of jobs and into the ranks of the unemployed. The Negro, therefore, is deeply concerned about employment, but the suburban whites who see Negro pickets in front of grocery stores and factories do not understand the reason for the concern. Negroes picket because they know that things are not as good as they are declared to be, but whites do not understand this fact and their failure to understand it means that they will communicate a gross misconception to a whole generation.

People who are solicitous about the welfare of Negroes know that the black-skinned child who wants to be President does not have a very good chance, and most of us believe that it might be well for him to concentrate on a reasonable goal; we suggest to him that he should not aspire to middle-class activities since he will find it difficult, if not impossible, to enter into them. More frequently than we realize, our solicitousness adds fuel to the fire of his bitter recognition of what he sees as a discriminatory and segregated social system. The helping services remind him that he should not aspire to the impossible; to him it is the butt end of the stick. When we attempt to be friendly, kind, and encouraging he finds us guilty of patronizing, and in this way we may be an instrument of the social structure and organization in a quite different way than we realize.

Marginal Groups in an Affluent Society

It is, indeed, ironic that a society at the height of its affluence should find it necessary to mount a war on poverty. In our society of today there are large groups of people who are not necessary for the maintenance of the affluent society. We are no longer dependent on the sweat and toil of many people in order to assure productivity. Why do we now focus on the marginal groups if they are not needed economically in the affluent society? We must concentrate our attention on them because the condition of their marginality has produced deprivation, and deprivation is a phenomenon which generates problems. The human animal, of course, attempts to find answers to problems. The subcultures are, in short, the problem-solving answers to their situations of stress and trial. Correspondingly, the subculture, which many of us see only as the evidence of a set of negative attributes and only to be deplored, is to many individuals a solution to their life's problems. It is their means of making life tolerable under the conditions of their deprivation. I refer to something more than physical environment, something more than the slums that we see as an environmental problem for many of our youngsters. I refer to the way in which people live their answers to their problem, respond to the lack of jobs, answer to their condition of deprivation forced upon them by the enveloping social structure. Their answers are the positive, organizing principles of their lives and they bring their answers into the school, the playground, the factory, and the law. In short, they bring their answers into the wider society which, for the most part, in its present structuring of professions and services, is not prepared to recognize that the answers have positive values.

We tell them, "assume our habits, culture, and attitudes and accept us on our conditions." This leaves them without any resource for working in the situations which actually confront them. Failure is their experience, for we do not give them rewards that are contingent upon their own natural learnings and adjustments to the world of deprivation from which they come. Their material and psychological deprivation has generated problem-solving responses. The residual piling up of the problem-solving responses has produced the subcultures of the deprived groups. In this background lies the significance of the behavior of the Negro child who comes from a black ghetto. If he is combative or inattentive, it is almost a certainty that a significant cultural pattern is there. His defiant attitude has in his milieu a survival value and his hostility is a partial answer to the situation in which he finds himself.

We are experiencing an eclipse of the formal controls of society because of the prior claims these subcultures have upon these individuals. There is a natural antagonism between the children of the slums, the racial groups and the police, as well as the general community. Today the "real" controls are in the area of the local, the primary, the face-to-face experience of these groups which are at odds with the general society.

We may very well ask, "Why is it students have no sense of shame and guilt as young persons formerly exhibited?" It appears to many that they have become cold, callous, inhuman agents without the essential characteristics of the youth which they remember. But there is a sense of shame and guilt. Shame reinforces locally defined, nonconforming behavior. In the current cultural communities of America, a variety of subcultures has made shame and guilt problematical. They reflect the local subcultures to which the young people relate. Hence, it produces nonconformity rather than conformity to the established norms of the general society, and correspondingly, it emphasizes attitudes which have local value. The power of the subculture to effect this reversal of values and norms is not fully appreciated. We are still asking ourselves why it is that formal ordering and forbidding techniques are not able to produce conformity. If the policeman's lot in the past years has been, as Gilbert and Sullivan said, "An unhappy one," it is likely to be an even unhappier one in the future, unless there is an alteration in the development of these young people. We are continuing to subscribe to the notion that we can police the community without having it formally supported by the informal systems of control.

New Patterns of Population Concentration

The tremendous population flux and growth of recent years brought on, between 1950 and 1960, a new pattern of population concentration in the major cities of the United States. The 12 largest cities of the United States lost nearly 2 million white residents who were replaced by 2 million Negro residents in the short 10-year period. This transformation was accompanied by a disproportionate change in the youth population within those cities. Washington, D.C., has a nonwhite population of well over 65 percent, but the public schools enroll just over 90 percent nonwhite. Chicago reported this year that over 51 percent of the students in the public schools were from the subculture of the Negro world. Only a quarter of the total population of that city is Negro. The city of Philadelphia has a non-white school population of well over 50 percent, whereas 33 percent of the total population of that city is nonwhite. The public schools of our major cities are confronted with a population, one-third to one-half of which come out of a subculture with characteristics which challenge the capacity of our schools to engage them.

In 1951, one out of every 10 children in the 12 largest cities of the United States was identified as culturally disadvantaged by the public schools. Today, it is more than one in three who are referred to in these terms. They represent problems of background that make it impossible to move them along in the school system at the same pace as other more advantaged youngsters. Projecting the trends, it now appears the ratio may well be one in two in the major metropolitan centers by 1980.

The Need To Be Wanted

The problem of young people, generally, is not wholly different from that of minority group youth. Many young people relate to the adult community in such ways as to suffer low self-esteem, and hence see themselves as unimportant and insignificant. Therefore, they must compensate by developing attitudes, norms, and values which do give them a sense of worth and importance. And more frequently than is good for the society, this turns out to be a condition of defense, a condition of rebellion, rather than a condition of identity with the adult culture. So the deprived or disadvantaged young people of our time, in increasing numbers, can be seen as demonstrating a cultural self-image which reflects a contraculture, representing rebellion and opposition to the norms and standards of the wider community. On picket lines, or in gang groups in alleys and by ways of the slum, they can be seen as reacting to, and rejecting the larger community.

The changing social scene has made it difficult or impossible for the young to attain the chief hope of every self-sustaining individual, namely, the realization of personal work satisfaction, or the finding of one's self in one's life task or work. Paul Goodman has stated the issues succinctly when he writes, "It's hard to grow up when there isn't enough man's work." In normal conditions a large part of security comes from knowing that your contribution is useful and the rest from knowing that it is uniquely yours —that "they" need you. Earlier generations in the United States have been needed because the very life of the family—bread on the table or coal in the kitchen range—depended on their contributions. Even for the slum child, scavenging along the railroad tracks to get coal, it wasn't difficult, however irksome the task, to understand that this was a meaningful and important function that he was performing. He was wanted. What he was doing was needed and it was significant in this sense. Hence, chores, as we know them, were something more than these mere irksome invasions of childish freedom; they were meaningful additions to the family income. The family larder, indeed the security of the family itself, often depended on the contribution of its youthful members.

But in these times, in these United States, we no longer have, for the most part, the same needs of our children. For example, we no longer need them to support us in old age as was the case before the advent of the collective institutionalized social security system. Indeed, for economic reasons and more recently for technological reasons, the adult world finds little need for youth. For the most part, they are in the way; they are a burden. To a large extent youth has been transformed from an economic asset for the average parent into his greatest economic liability. The fact that the child has become an income tax deduction has by no means made up the difference. The prolongation of childhood and the child labor laws, quite apart from the impact of automation and technology, and the cost of bringing up and educating a child for as much as 15 to 20 years or more of his life without any return, means that the economic grounds for a mutual need of the generations have passed with the times. In short, the economic roles, the obligations and responsibilities, the rewards, even the power relations between the young and the old, are only shadows of the recent past. The powers and responsibilities of each are unclear and tenuous. Indeed, in some respects, the relationships have been completely reversed. A factor which threatens to take from youth its sense of importance and usefulness—its sense of being needed—is threatening vast numbers of the adult society as well, for the automated machine has made all too many able-bodied men in the prime of their lives face an uncertain future of chronic indigence and insecurity.

Youth, itself, feeling insecure because of its marginal position in a society that no longer depends upon it for economic survival, is tempted to use the power this reversal between the generations has conferred on it to be accuser and judge of its elders. Hence, we witness the ubiquitous pattern of rebelliousness in present-day youth. This rebelliousness is manifest, to be sure, in a plurality of ways by different kinds of deviant patterns, including on the one hand, crime and delinquency, on the other hand, radical and conservative political activism of every hue, and still again, a variety of Bohemian life-styles. The Free-Speech Movement at Berkeley included supporters of Goldwater, Johnson, as well as radicals of the extreme left. But, nevertheless, these patterns are inclusive of the broad reaches and more numerous conventional elements of the whole world of youth. We are becoming increasingly aware of the existence of a variety of subcultures which are a product of the problem-solving disposition of human groups when confronted by specific and recurrent life problems. These are, in turn, a reflection of both the broad encompassing and the narrow and specific changes in the social and economic situation confronting young people in general, and in particular, as members of differentiated cultural, economic, and racial groups.

While it is true that only a small percentage of young people participate overtly in acting out the spirit of rebellion, many more are vulnerable and the general spirit of rebellion may well extend to greater numbers. The result may be a profound modification of the traditional patterns of power and authority. This is already indicated by the increasing incidents of attacks upon the police and other symbols of power and authority by young people.

Our society has been developing a complex of subcultures which are driving us apart into local communities and groups, and in which the members are interacting among themselves and producing their own distinctive norms and values. These are the current subcultures of youth, of race, of suburbia, and of income (high and low). It is the reality of these subcultures which is so confounding to the established institutional structures and those who man them. It is not that there is a culture of crime. It is that there is such a plurality of subcultures that the problem of the individual's adjustment to commonly accepted norms is confounded and that deviance and opposition to law and authority are generated as a matter of course. Crime, delinquency, disrespect for law and the police are its logical accompaniment. We must develop means for modifying and preparing personnel to play quite new and meaningful roles. A paradox of the new metropolitan developments is that we are constantly moving toward self-defeating extremes in our desperate and uninformed effort to keep abreast of the changing community. The heartlands of our great metropolitan centers are becoming the provinces of the new minorities. These groups are a potential threat. They may express themselves in the traditional patterns of organized crime as well as the current disturbances. They have come out of a segregated, discriminatory experience in search of freedom and opportunity into a social environment which in many respects continues as restrictive as the older pattern. It is then not only crime which becomes the abortive fruit of the failure to understand this changing community.

The unwitting processes of the middle-class suburban drift and the transformation of vast areas of central cities into enormous racial slums have profound social and political implications. The traditional alliances between crime and politics have focused on the immigrant community and the slum. We may very well usher in a new era of unprecedented political conflict between the cities and their suburbs, with aggravating overtones of race tension and conflict as an additional feature to the existing patterns of organized crime. To ignore the social, economic, and cultural disabilities under which these populations labor, to try to contain their volcanic eruptions by the mere expedient of repressive and antiquated police measures, can only have the effect of force-feeding the fires which are smoldering in the core of our metropolitan communities.

Often We Fail To Know and To Understand

In short, many of the problems which confront us stem from the failure of the public to know and to understand the new dimensions and ramifications of community life. Traditional police measures will not repress and contain these populations. The fact is that our most professional police organizations have had no more success than others in containing such disturbances. No amount of focusing on police measures which accent repression in the traditional approach to the problem can have any prospect of success.

An effective law enforcement function must be familiar with and equal to its target. The ultimate answer is to see crime and violence, not just as problems in law enforcement, but as problems in education, family organization, employment opportunity, and housing. These are the structures which incubate deviance, and hence, crime, delinquency, and violence. They are the structures which breed disrespect for law and the police. It is a myth that man's behavior can be changed directly. It can be changed only by altering the conditions which underlie his behavior. We must, in this instance, treat the causes and not just the effects of crime and violence. In short, the demonstrations of the current day and the eruptions of a racial or youthful nature are evidence that we are at a critical juncture in the history of the United States and the development of its communities. That juncture is the emergence of a new kind of community—the metropolitan community which is not merely a bigger place, not merely a change in population or size or a change in geographic location. The distinguishing features of the new metropolitan concentration is that it represents a whole new set of human relations, and those human relations must be the condition of action of the law and the police. The new community cannot be policed in terms which were appropriate to the village communities or to the urban centers which preceded the new great and complex metropolitan centers.

The remedy of the failing respect for law is not a simple one, but the sober admonitions of Dicey and De Tocqueville point the way. In our democratic system, the power to make and implement the law lies with the majority of the community. It is to the majority that we must look in remedying the insensitivity and intransigence of the society in its relation to the groups who live marginal to the centers of power. The young, the poor, and the minority groups have frequently viewed the law as not of their making or to their interest; like unto the law of a foreign power and the police as an army of occupation. Those who are thrice defined in their exclusion and deprivation—the young, the poor, and those of minority status—have been sharpest in their protest, most militant in their behavior, and least respectful of the law. As Dicey observed, "Men come easily to believe that arrangements agreeable to themselves are beneficial to others."

In going our separate ways and abandoning so many to an excluded life of deprivation we are realizing the selfishness of individualism of which De Tocqueville forewarned the democracies. This individualism has its extreme expression in the polarities of youth and age, of black and white, of the affluent and the poor.

Our remedy for disrespect for law is not to be found in merely admonishing the populace and seeing all who oppose it as without reason. Our remedy will be found in a greater dialogue and a fuller participation in the counsels and decisions of the majority by those who have been and continue to be excluded from the making and implementation of the law. The remedy is in "just laws," democratically designed and sensitively enforced.

CHAPTER 22

Police Perception of Riot Activity

Thomas D. Kitch

Thomas D. Kitch is an attorney with the firm of Fleeson, Gooing, Coulson, and Kitch, Wichita, Kansas. Mr. Kitch attended the University of Chicago Law School where he received a J.D. (law) in 1969.

The information for this study is taken from questionnaires which were completed by 476 Chicago police officers on Saturday, May 17, 1968, in classrooms at the Northwestern University Law School. The questionnaire was prepared by the staff of the Chicago Riot Study Committee, which was formed at the request of Mayor Daley to "conduct a complete and detailed factual investigation into the events immediately preceeding, on, and subsequent to April 4, 1968, in Chicago"—the disorders which occurred after the assassination of Dr. Martin Luther King, Jr.[1]

From Thomas D. Kitch, "Police Perception of Riot Activity." Reprinted by special permission from the *Journal of Research in Crime and Delinquency,* Volume 7, Number 2, July, 1970.

[1]Chicago Riot Study Committee, "Report of the Chicago Riot Study, Committee to the Honorable Richard J. Daley" monograph: Chicago, Illinois: [n.p.], August 1, 1968, p. 5. This report will also be referred to as the Austin Committee Report, after Judge Richard B. Austin, chairman of the committee. The following questions were selected for analysis:

(1) Where were you on duty April 5? April 6? April 7? (a) South Side? West Side? Near North? These answers are tabulated in Table I.

(2) Can you identify the looters in terms of age, sex, residence, strangers, other qualities? These answers are not presented in tabulated form.

(3) From your observations of the crowd, what percentage were looters? These answers are tabulated in Table II.

(4) Based on your personal observations, what percentage of the looters were arrested?

(5) Do you believe there was a plan or conspiracy to cause the riot? These answers are tabulated in Table IV.

(6) Do you believe there was a plan or conspiracy to exploit the riot if it began? These answers are tabulated in Table V.

(7) What do you believe could or should be done to arrest all looters? These answers are not presented in tabulated form.

As described in the fourth chapter of the Austin Committee Report, the purpose of the police questionnaire was to obtain each officer's

> evaluation of conditions that confronted him during the riot, his response, by the use of force, to certain situations, and his suggestions for the prevention of riots.[2]

The Austin Committee staff administered the questionnaire at two separate sessions on May 17, 1968—one in the morning and one in the afternoon—each lasting about three hours. Subjects were provided by the Chicago Police Department and the committee staff had no control over the selection of those officers who attended the sessions, although it was suggested that the officers be selected from districts which had been at the center of the April disorders. The high degree of compliance with this request is indicated by Table I, which shows that only 13 respondents reported no riot duty from April 5 through April 7.[3] It appears that the police department simply posted signup sheets in the districts which had been involved in the riot. All officers participating in the mass interview were paid in full by the department. Since the volunteers were collected in the space of two days, the committee staff is convinced that little or no "screening" of the interviewees took place (see Table I).

All participants remained anonymous, although one observer estimated that nearly 20 percent of the subjects were Black and that very few officers above the rank of sergeant were present. The questionnaire was 30 pages long and over 14,000 pages of testimony were collected at the conclusion of the interview.

---

(8) Would the use of tear gas, Mace, or dogs have brought the riots under quicker control? Are there any other devices you would suggest to be used to bring a riot under control? These answers are not presented in tabulated form.

(9) Would the greater use of deadly force have brought the riots under quicker control? These answers are tabulated in Table VI.

(10) Do you feel the department policy on deadly forces as outlined in Order 67-14 hinders or obstructs you in controlling riots? These answers are tabulated in Table VII.

(11) Do you believe that a specially trained reserve auxiliary police force to assist the police during a riot would be an effective unit for riot control? These answers are tabulated in Table VIII.

(12) What, in your opinion, brought the looting, arson, and violence to an end in the area in which you were on duty? These answers are not presented in tabulated form.

(13) What suggestions do you have to prevent future riots? These answers are not presented in tabulated form.

[2] Chicago Riot Study Committee, "Chicago Riot Study" p. 38.

[3] Note that this number of respondents actually constitutes about three percent of the 476 officers who answered the question. The discussion of the riot is generally limited to the events which occurred on Friday, before the arrival of the National Guard at 12:00 midnight—the period of time when most policemen were confronted with the most serious riot activity of the entire weekend.

Of the 463 officers who reported the location of their riot duty, several indicated they had been in more than one area. Thus, a total of 554 answers were given under the three areas, with the preponderance of WEST SIDE answers indicating that this area was the center of riot activity.

The emphasis of this brief study will be upon the police officer's perception of the conditions which confronted him during the riot. The average police officer is frustrated by what he determines to be a general lack of interest, knowledge, or concern on the part of the public. After the April disorders, one policeman expressed a deep sense of isolation:

> I, as a police officer who has seen things trying to be done, can only say that if the news media and television would upgrade their shows to show it like it is, and not of an isolated incident of mistake by one officer out of ten thousand. We, too, are human and have families, and have our debts and problems. If the resources were to show that we are in classes of society as other people are, they might think of police officers as nice people; instead of making a lot of money or shooting everything that walks or beating everybody up. Get the people on our side and maybe this insane disrespect will subside.[4]

Table I.—Where the Respondents Were on Duty (April 5-7)

	Number	Percent
South Side	107	19
West Side	350	62
Near North Side	97	17
Does not apply (desk personnel or not assigned to riot duty)	13	2
Total	567	100

Many officers think that the majority of people support them in their attempt to bring law and order to the ghetto. This attitude is the obverse of the one expressed by those policemen who think they are "isolated" from the community in which they work: "Rule with an iron hand . . . Forget about public opinion. I think the majority of the public wants this." These two opinions probably represent the initial responses of most police officers

---

[4]All quotations are transcribed verbatim.

to criticism of their performance during the riot in Chicago after Dr. King's death. Unfortunately, it is doubtful that either respondent has had meaningful contact with law-abiding members of the Black community.[5]

The most ominous aspect of police perception of the civil disorders is racism:

> I noticed some people wanted only to destroy and destroy and destroy, whether it be a white merchant or a Negro merchant. This is the real danger, "no-purpose destruction." And yet, it does show me something about the Negro people, something I haven't seen before, or didn't want to believe, but something that is definitely there, in their personality, or psyches, or what have you.

Many police officers rejected such generalizations:

> Give the local persons more authority in their community and equal portions of opportunity in the city. This will stop those 75-80 percent of the looters who under normal conditions would not do this thing.

But the attitude of the police toward ghetto residents was much affected by the April disorders. Many officers wrote that the riot duty involved some of the most "difficult" and "hard" work of their careers. The basis for this determination is a combination of frustration with superior officers, and disgust with the rioters. Since the police were often told to "act with restraint" in the early part of the riot, many individual officers were forced to handle minor assignments, such as directing traffic and protecting firemen, until reinforcements arrived or the looters moved on to other areas. The corresponding sense of impotence was simply compounded by the news coverage:

> ... but I think the TV news camera made asses of us, in that police officers were photographed letting people carry items down the street.

A. General Conditions in the Riot Areas

During the first two days of the April disorders, policemen frequently patrolled troublesome areas in four-man squad cars. These squad cars were

---

[5]One example of this lack of contact is the feeling that "pressure" on the police department comes from outside the ghetto community:

G. O. 67-14 [a Chicago Police Department order limiting the use of deadly force] and the training bulletins, and newspaper editorials, and the pressure from the extreme element in political and religious circles indicated that society does not want you to maintain order or protect property if you must deny a man his constitutional right to due process of law by using deadly force even when the law provides for it.

often given vague or contradictory directions and many officers later reported difficulty in communicating by radio with the district stations.[6]

> Better communication between command and live personnel is needed, officers received assignments which had to be abandoned when arriving on the scene. An approach of arrest and securing a certain intersection or riot area could be an improvement over the ill effect of moving to a new location, and passing looters on the way.

Whenever the police left their cars, they were frequently confronted with residents who were openly hostile ("as it stands, the individual officer has his hands full protecting himself from objects thrown at him by the crowds that gather, and cannot concentrate on capturing looters") and often engaged in activities which were clearly illegal.

> Let's put it this way, when you have three policemen alone and you can't get to help, and you have about 100 people coming at you, what are you to do —let them beat you to death?[7]

In the midst of this turmoil, these small groups of policemen were faced with a serious dilemma—they could have attempted to arrest those violating the law or they could have attempted to restore order by remaining in the area to intimidate or:

> Where policemen on foot walked through an area without making many arrests—breaking crowds and attempting to shag looters from stores—only about 20-30 percent of the crowd would loot. In other areas, where cars with police were passing through, it was 65 percent or more.

Whenever an arrest was made, it was necessary for at least one of the officers to leave the area with the arrestee and lose valuable time booking him at the district station.

> In a situation such as 5 April, all looters could never be arrested. When 500 people converge on a store, four or five men in a car cannot possibly take into custody that amount of people.

Over one-fourth of the respondents indicated that inadequate transportation from the place of arrest to detention centers was the primary difficulty encountered by arresting officers.[8] As one patrolman pointed out:

---

[6]See Austin Committee recommendation No. 7, "Chicago Riot Study" p. 42.

[7]The respondent recommended the use of tear gas in such situations.

[8]This was the most common complaint in response to question 7 in note 1, "Chicago Riot Study".

Each arrest ties up a certain number of police—and the number of looters is so large, once an incident begins, that arrest of five percent of looters would be a good job.

The Austin Committee concluded that participation in the riot activity was limited to a:

small fraction of the city's total population, to a small fraction of the city's Black population, and to a small minority of the residents of the immediately affected areas.[9]

Police perception of the riot participants leads to a somewhat different conclusion. There was general agreement that residents, and not "outside agitators," were completely responsible for the riot in Chicago.[10] One officer referred to the period between the death of Dr. King (7:00 p.m. Thursday) and the initiation of mass arrests on the west side of Chicago (5:00 p.m. Friday) as a time when the residents were subjected to a continual harangue "against Whitey" by black militants living in the ghettos:

I feel the extremist element in the community has on numerous occasions, attempted to arouse the people into disorder after an incident involving the police. But they failed because they could not spread the word fast enough, here they had 12 to 16 hours.

As a result, those police who patrolled the riot areas on Friday afternoon were frequently outnumbered by the looters:

Many people saw that we were unable to do anything, and then began to loot themselves. A police officer is not going into a crowd of 50 or 100 people alone if he is afraid to use the force necessary to stop looting and also to protect his own life.

Several officers reported that the looters were "cocky" and that they taunted the police.

Most of these people knew that police would not shoot, but if deadly force was used the word gets around. Some of them would pass by you, and say sarcastically, "We know you can't shoot, why do you carry the gun"—"The police won't shoot, so we gonna loot."

Most residents simply ignored the police in the early stages of the riot. For reasons that are discussed below, the police did not use deadly force, police

---

[9]Chicago Riot Study Committee, "Chicago Riot Study," p. 79.

[10]The most common response to question two, was that the looters were residents of the affected areas. Only ten respondents thought that the looters were primarily strangers.

dogs, or tear gas on the first day of the riot. As one respondent pointed out, the decision to "shot the first looter" was never made:

> But those police that are first on the scene, for some reason, maybe lack of responsive leadership, do not take decisive action.

In fact, the most striking aspect of the entire Chicago riot may have been the limited amount of armed violence—neither the ghetto residents nor the police, with one serious exception, seemed eager to escalate the conflict from crimes against property to violence against the person.

One significant restraint upon police activity may simply have been the large number of ghetto residents involved in the looting of stores. As a result, one officer concluded:

> This kind of situation is best handled by the military—and although it may be well handled by regular police personnel in sufficient number—it could never be done by an auxiliary police force.

Since most police in the riot areas on Friday afternoon knew that the Illinois National Guard was preparing to patrol the streets,[11] many of the small groups of officers probably decided that they could do no more than "hold" certain areas until the Guard troops arrived.

Police perception of the degree of participation by ghetto residents is indicated by Tables II and III. The even distribution of answers in Table II can be attributed to the wide range of riot activity to which the respondents were exposed. However, the estimates in Table II make the results in Table III much more dramatic—even when a small percentage of the crowd was looting, an even smaller percentage was arrested. If a total of 1,000 people were arrested for property offenses during the riot,[12] nearly 50 percent of the respondents were convinced that this number of arrests was no greater than 5 percent of the actual number of looters—that at least 20,000 people took part in the looting. Certainly, 20,000 people do not represent a "small minority of the residents of the immediately affected areas." If only half of this number were looting early Friday evening, which was the most intense period of riot activity, they still would have outnumbered the 6,000 policemen which had been mobilized by this time.

---

[11]At about 2:00 p.m. on Friday, Mayor Daley called Acting Governor Shapiro to inform him that the National Guard would be needed. Chicago Riot Study Committee Report, "Chicago Riot Study" p. 12.

[12]Approximately 500 people were arrested on the charge of burglary. Many persons found carrying merchandise were charged with disorderly conduct. See "Criminal Justice in Extremis: Administration of Justice During the April 1968 Chicago Disorder," 36 University of Chicago Law Review 494. (Spring 1969). Thus, it is probable that more than 1,000 looters were actually arrested.

Several officers were disturbed by the broad participation of ghetto residents in the looting. Some respondents thought that the power of arrest, even if backed by adequate transportation for arrestees, was inappropriate:

To arrest all would be impossible unless you would want to arrest whole families together.

I observed three-year-old looters and 83-year-old looters in either case, would and should not be dealt with as criminals.

This may sound all wrong, but you first must understand that they have no fear of being arrested or locked up. When you understand that they do not have the same fear as you and I, you will finally be meeting the problem. Their values of right and wrong are quite different.

Table II.—Percentage of Crowd Engaged in Looting

	Number	Percent
0-20%	93	20
20-40%	64	14
40-60%	44	10
60-80%	90	20
80-100%	107	23
Don't know	62	13
Total	460	100

Table III.—Percentage of the Looters Arrested

	Number	Percent
1% or less	95	20
1%-5%	118	25
5%-20%	95	20
20%-30%	26	6
30%-50%	25	6
50%-90%	12	3
90%-100%	3	1
Don't know	86	19
Total	460	100%

It is now clear that the worst property damage occurred during the first twenty-four hours of the riot and that the great percentage of this damage was located in an area six blocks to the north (along Madison) and eight blocks to the south (along Roosevelt Road) to the Eisenhower Expressway from four to six miles directly west of the Loop. By 3:00 p.m. on Friday, April 5, the looting in this area of Chicago was so widespread that police were unable to take effective action against the offenders.[13] At the conclusion of its study of the Chicago Police Department, the Chicago Riot Study Committee suggested that "significant errors in command judgement" may have been made "in stationing more police manpower in the Loop than was necessary during the day of April 5 while less was put into the west side."[14] This criticism reveals an unrealistic assessment of the dilemma facing the police department. In short, the police department had great difficulty identifying the center of the disturbances which afflicted many parts of the city simultaneously on Friday, April 5. Due to the widespread nature of these disruptions, which tended to focus upon ghetto high schools (some of which are ten to fifteen miles apart) early Friday morning, and the demonstrations and property damage which accompanied them,[14a] department supervisors did not realize that the west side would become the focus for more serious riot activity until the middle of Friday afternoon. As a result, task force personnel were withdrawn to the Loop area at noon (when most of the ghetto high schools were dismissed) to await assignment. Tensions were heightened considerably when students from one west side high school actually marched into the downtown area and began harassing pedestrians and breaking windows.[15] Finally, it should be noted that the Loop may have served as an effective staging area for the distribution of police to the three areas in the city where significant riot activity was reported early Friday afternoon—the south side, the west side and the near north side, all of which could be reached in about the same amount of time from the southern edge of the Loop.

The looting activity on Friday afternoon (and throughout the weekend) tended to concentrate on clothing, appliance, general merchandise,

---

[13]The Austin Committee concluded that "many of those who were instrumental in the development of the riots and in the vandalism, looting and arson during the day of April 5 probably escaped arrest while those who joined later in illegal conduct were more often among those who were arrested." "Chicago Riot Study," p. 43.

[14]*Ibid.,* p. 43.

[14a]The most comprehensive section of the Austin Committee Report is the chapter describing the disruption of high schools in the ghetto communities.

[15]These students were quickly dispersed after only a few arrests were made. They came from Crane High School, about four miles directly west of the Loop and encountered "extensive" police protection when they arrived at the Civic Center.

liquor, and grocery stores, and pawn shops operated by whites.[16] The Chicago Riot Study Committee found "considerable evidence" to support the conclusion that "vandalism and looting were motivated in part by a desire to retaliate against sharp business practices of white merchants." Once a store had been emptied of its contents, it would be set on fire or, in some cases, consumed by fires set in other parts of the block. There was no evidence that a single Black-owned business was burned intentionally.[17]

One policeman witnessed the futile attempt of a clothing store owner on the west to bargain with looters:

> He told the people that they could take anything they wanted, but he asked that they not burn the store. They emptied the store and then they burned it.

Several officers stated that much of the initial breaking and entering was accomplished by young men between the ages of 15 and 20, who were subsequently joined in the stores by young and old alike. One policeman noted that deadly force might have been used to curtail the initial breaking and entering if

> all facts and circumstances were accurately put before the people by press and radio, i.e., policemen shot a 15-year-old youth going through store window. In actuality, the police shot a "M/N 6'1" 175 lbs, breaking into a store burglary."[18]

One witness observed that there was a "carnival" atmosphere in the air and that some looters demonstrated prodigious strength, such as one young man who was seen carrying a washing machine single-handedly from an appliance store on West Madison.

The extent of organization among the looters is difficult to determine. Several policemen reported seeing adults direct juveniles into stores to obtain loot, supposedly on the theory that any children arrested by the police would be excused because of their age.[18a] In any case, the looters often broke into stores in an organized fashion and at least one officer was amazed by the results:

---

[16]Austin Committee Report "Chicago Riot Study," p. 10.x.

[17]*Ibid.,* pp. 14; 74-5.

[18]The fact that the boy was attempting to commit a forcible felony would authorize the use of deadly force—if he were attempting to escape and this was the only manner in which he could be apprehended. See discussion in part F of this study.

[18a]This same theory has been applied to gangs: "I was told that the older gang members gave the younger boys orders to loot because the law would excuse them—it did."

Some west side merchants had steel doors put on the front and rear of their stores to keep out looters; the gates were still torn down and fires were started on the roofs of the buildings.

Witnesses generally agreed that it "was all youth on the afternoon of April 5th, but the majority were adults that night." Just as the youths who had sparked the demonstration from school to school became exhausted, the older members of the ghetto community began returning home from work, only to find their neighborhoods in chaos and the opportunity for loot very near.[19]

While the stores were the primary objects for arsonists, many Blacks who lived above the stores were made homeless by the fires. Adequate warning to the residents was either given or obvious from the situation, since no occupants were killed as a result of these fires. The first fire alarm was sounded about 4:00 p.m. on Friday afternoon. Generally, the fires moved westward along both sides of Madison, away from the downtown area. As the residents fled, they made little or no attempt to retrieve furniture or other items of personal property from their apartments. The Austin Committee reported that

> Blacks who lost their own homes in fires were not uniformly bitter. Some apparently felt that their homes were already so substandard that little was lost.[20]

Fire department officials testified that a somewhat stronger wind would have brought the entire west side into danger, as well as large segments of the near north and south sides of Chicago. Total insured losses arising from these fires, the great majority of which were set on the west side, were estimated at $14,000,000 with actual losses running much higher.[21] By 5:00 p.m., fires on the west side were burning as far as a mile apart and the water department was ordered to increase the water pressure. At 5:10 p.m., the fire commissioner ordered all firemen to report to the nearest fire house. By this time, traffic conditions seriously impeded the flow of replacements and the transportation of equipment to the area of the fires. The Mutual Aid Plan was put into effect at 5:20 p.m., with suburban fire departments sending men and equipment to outlying Chicago fire stations, so that more men and equipment could be released to fight fires in the ghetto areas. Major fires were either set or continued to spread until 11:00 p.m. Friday night, at which time there were more than 2,000 firemen and 100

---

[19]These residents also encountered heavy traffic when they attempted to return home. Both National Guard and police personnel had difficulty reaching their assigned areas due to heavy traffic Friday afternoon.

[20]Austin Committee Report, "Chicago Riot Study," p. 73.

[21]*Ibid.*, p. 20.

pieces of equipment on the west side alone. It was not until 4:00 a.m. that the fire commissioner declared the situation to be under control.[21] Throughout this period, firemen were frequently hampered by residents who threw rocks and bottles or turned on hydrants to reduce water pressure.[22]

In the area surrounding the Cabrini-Green housing complex on the near north side of Chicago, looting and burning occurred on a much smaller scale than on the west side, but both were still primarily directed toward white-owned and white-operated stores. The south side remained relatively calm, although some windows were broken during the evening along 63rd Street. Most of this activity was concentrated in the vicinity of Halstead and 63rd, about four-and-one-half miles southwest of the Loop. Once again, this vandalism was directed primarily toward white merchants.[23]

The simultaneous outbreak of violence and looting in many parts of the city on Friday frightened many policemen. It appears that a majority of the respondents were willing to attribute the riot to the death of Dr. King, although there was some disagreement as to the existence of a plan before the assassination:

> There were, I believe, such plans, but they weren't needed because of King's death.

> I believed there was a plan but they did not wait after King was killed. No, King's assasination was the excuse. But there was no conspiracy. But as it got started, more people got in the snow ball.

Few policemen offered concrete details to back up their allegations,[24] but several found a "conspiracy" in the following events and/or observations:

> It was planned on the part of West Side High School students.

> Yes, they were in groups.

> Yes, by the high school students at John Marshall. It was obvious when they were released from school, and approximately 1,500 of them started marching

---

[22]The fire commissioner later determined that interference with firemen was less serious than had been reported at the time. *Ibid.,* p.54. The Austin Committee determined that some sniping at firemen did take place; once while firemen were fighting a fire at 2850 West Madison on Friday night; once Friday evening in the vicinity of the fire house at 1044 North Orleans; once Friday afternoon when firemen were prevented from reaching a fire in a grocery store at 876 North Orleans (the building was completely destroyed before they could reach it); twice near the Cabrini-Green housing complex (1:00 a.m. Saturday morning and again Saturday afternoon). Austin Committee Report, *Ibid.,* p. 53.

[23]By Saturday night, the south side had become the focus of riot activity. Army troops patrolled this area on Sunday morning. The near north side also experienced more serious looting on Saturday than on Friday afternoon or evening.

[24]Specific allegations were made against the Garfield Organization, a Negro group which operated on the West Side of Chicago.

west on Madison. I believe that there was a plan for riot for 1967 but I don't believe that at the time of the riot it had blossomed to the point in which its leaders had wanted. They were not fully prepared for riot when Dr. King was assassinated.

Yes, because it was too spontaneous to be a random thing.

Yes, on the near north side, stores were held up, the money taken, and then the crowd was told: "We got what we wanted, you can take the rest."

As is indicated by Table IV, these answers were opposed by 225 officers who generally agreed with the following statements:

. . . if there was a master plan, the planners must have been idiots.

No. There may be a small plan by some people that say if a riot comes, I am going to get this place, but no organization.

No, because it started too quickly and all over not just in our city—it might have become involved after the riot started.

Table IV.—Whether There Was a Plan or Conspiracy to Cause the Riot

	Number	Percent
No	225	48
Yes	210	45
Don't know	31	7
Total	466	100

With reference to any planning which might have gone on Thursday night, the Austin Committee stated:

[A] few small groups . . . particularly on the west side were discussing the wisdom and means of a violent response to Dr. King's assassination. So far as the committee has been able to determine, these groups were small in number, small in membership, and were informal and ad hoc.[25]

Many respondents shifted their answers in Table V. The most common explanation for the existence of a conspiracy after the riot began was simply

---

[25]Austin Committee Report, "Chicago Riot Study," p. 5.

a restatement of the Austin Committee conclusion that white merchants had been the primary target for looters and arsonists:

> I don't believe it was planned as a whole, but once it got started, there was some planning in regard to what they would loot and burn.

Table V.—Whether There Was a Plan or Conspiracy to Exploit a Riot Once It Began

	Number	Percent
No	75	16
Yes	373	79
Don't know	19	5
Total	467	100

Other officers emphasized the high degree of organization among the looters:

> There appeared to be pre-practice when the proper time arrived, each person, even young children, knew their job.

> There were waves of persons—first, second, and third, to replace each other if wounded or arrested.

> ... the way it was handled, you would think the looters and rioters were working at their profession.

> ... But I will say it was well-organized. As if they had a ready plan in case of a disorder—that could be put into effect for instance, the arsons were started so as to pull police away from certain areas and then those areas would be looted.[26]

Some respondents found a conspiracy in the "motive" or "intent" of the rioters:

> Yes, by certain militant groups: *Black*—for better living conditions; *White*— merely to exploit the uneducated Negro in his own environment, by urging him to destroy "whitey" in his neighborhood.

> ... all the [weak ones] needed was an incident. A white police shooting or beating a Negro could have started it.

---

[26]This conception of arson activity was in the distinct minority, with most officers contending that the stores were not burned until they were looted.

Of course, why start one unless you have a higher motive. The amount of destruction that would prevail still would not be a complete result of the people's despair. Mainly, it is a way to draw attention. Attention to what—their plight. Granted, it isn't nice, but do the means justify the end? In the end, with small success, to get people to pay tribute (monetarily and sociologically) they become bolder, more confident, and try to extract more. However, there is a limit, and though they are still far from it, it will come. A stop that is.

Certain people are always moving for violence and in a tension situation, after the assassination, people (sheep) listened to them.

... leaders told rioters it was their duty to rectify injustices by violent methods. This allowed the people to "rationalize" their motives.

There are always groups of lawless-minded persons who are predetermined to take advantage of *any* situation which may arise.

These people have nothing, they don't work or want to work, and to get anything, rioting and looting are the only way.

The news media did not escape involvement in the "conspiracy":

CBS (WBBM—TV) and the *Chicago Sun-Times* are to be held accountable for much violence by rendering false and untrue coverage of the events of this national disgrace. In fact, the *Sun-Times,* in an effort to perpetuate the riots, eulogized the nine looters and arsonists who were shot during this period.[27]

... The first thing any person arrested during a riot will do is go to the paper of other agencies and tell how they were cruelly treated, beaten, kicked and the like, and the news media always plays this up and puts the police officers in a bad light.

Finally, several respondents produced evidence of a "plot":

Yes, because so few arsonists were arrested! Of course, the element of surprise was theirs initially, however, overall, few were arrested. Besides, evidence supporting this is shown through open and frank statements made by Rap Brown, Stokely Carmichael, and other Black militants. More evidence is available through undercover work producing knowledge of the Harlem area R.A.M. movement. This is enough to go on.

If I may quote a national magazine, it is the plot of the Communist party to exploit the Negro people into doing all their dirty work and destroying this great democracy that we live in.

The Garfield Organization, the Woodlawn Organization, and many others are Chicago chapters of R.A.M. ... Their sniper teams were not up to strength

---

[27]Four deaths which occurred during the riot were the source of much controversy. See discussion in part G of this report.

yet, at that time, thanks to the raid of the Negro National Rife Association. (See the book of R.A.M.).

Shortly after the riots, or toward the close of them, a number of adults were arrested and charged with arson, and conspiracy to commit arson. I certainly believe these were prime movers motivating a number of actions (looting, fires, etc.) by the rioters . . .

. . . I also believe there are groups in this country who hope to cause internal disorder by using the people in this country to commit some. I believe, after observing many incidents in past disorders of people coming into this city from out of state to nurture disharmony and rioting, and such a plan of conspiracy does exist.

The Communists wish to exploit the riot throughout the world, to destroy the image of the United States so that if there is a revolution, all the countries will think the white people got what they deserved.

As a final indication of police perception of the riot, it should be noted that over one-fourth of the respondents (140) indicated that the riot ended only when the participants ran out of buildings to loot and burn, while over 50 officers said violence ended because the rioters were worn out (29) or the residents had to return to work on Monday (12) or the looters simply got what they wanted (10).[28] These observations apparently refer to various periods of time on Friday, Saturday, and Sunday—when different areas of the city were actually occupied by the national guard (west side) and the army (south side).[28a] In short, there was a tendency to discount the importance of the National Guard: "We have sufficiently trained men to handle any situation, we did not need the National Guard; it was over when they appeared." In discussing the tension generated among policemen by the riot, it is important to realize that many of them strongly disagreed with the policy of containing the rioters until the arrival of professional military help:

I believe that the police department could handle it by themselves, and if they did, it may bring more respect to us from the people because if they know that the guard is the only deterant, we are at a loss to stop anything until they arrive.

. . . because it would become worse after people realize that they were only a reserve and are only available for the emergency.

---

[28]This analysis was made from answers to question 12, Austin Committee Report, "Chicago Riot Study".

[28a]The National Guard did not begin patrolling streets on the west side until 12 midnight on Friday; U.S. Army troops began patrolling streets on the south side on Sunday morning.

B. The Response of the Police Department

One police officer noted the lack of direction felt by many police in the field on the first day of the riot:

> Policemen are no more effective in this type of situation without good leadership than are soldiers in a combat area told to do the best you can.

Criticism of superior officers was frequent:[29]

> More supervisors on the street at trouble spots directing their men. These men are supposed to be leaders and should be out there alongside their men.

And sometimes extended to the police department itself:

> There was no department policy for the first two days; after that, it was not needed.

By 4:00 p.m. on Friday, the police department had mobilized almost 6,000 police officers—about half the entire police force. Those officers on the eight-hour shift which would usually end at 4:00 p.m. had their duty extended four hours and all members of the force began operating on twelve hour intervals. All off-duty days were cancelled and many uniformed personnel were shifted to uniformed street duty. Since this order was not given until after the beginning of the 8:00 a.m. to 4:00 p.m. shift, there was no significant increase in police manpower to deal with the disturbances in the early afternoon.[30] By the time the police entered the west side in sufficient numbers to permit the institution of mass arrest procedures (about 5:00 p.m.), a large number of stores had already been looted and burned. Between 4:00 p.m. and mid-evening, when the police force was operating at 140 percent of its normal size, the great majority of arrests for riot-related activity on April 5th were made.[31]

At 7:45 on Thursday night, all days off for members of the Field Services Bureau were canceled. This bureau contains 7,500 sworn members, making it much larger than the other two subdivisions of the police department (these are the Staff Services Bureau and the Inspectional Services Bureau). Commencing with the first watch (12 midnight to 8:00 a.m.), extra assignments were made to the second, third, tenth, eleventh, and twenty-first districts, which correspond to those areas of the ghetto with a history

---

[29]In response to question seven, Austin Committee Report, "Chicago Riot Study", 28 policemen advocated an improvement in command personnel.

[30]Austin Committee Report, "Chicago Riot Study," p. 13.

[31]*Ibid.*, p. 43. One-hundred-and-thirty-nine arrests were made between 6:00 p.m. and 9:00 p.m. on Friday evening.

of disturbances. Special three- and four-man prowl cars began patrolling those parts of the ghetto where people were likely to congregate.

Each police district has two or three "tactical force" teams which consist of one sergeant and ten patrolmen who have received extra training in riot control techniques.[32] In addition, the police department maintains a task force (of about 500 men) which is normally used to break trends in crime, often in response to complaints that a particular area of the city is getting insufficient protection against a particular type of crime, such as burglary, rape, or prostitution. Members of the task force receive 13 hours of special training in riot control each year. A particular district will appeal to the task force for additional aid only after its own tactical force teams have been unable to quell a disturbance.

C. The Mobilization Plan

In 1960, early in the superintendency of Orlando W. Wilson, an "Immediate Emergency Plan" was developed to deal with potential disturbances in the city. Under this plan, certain "mobile forces" were designated in each district, so that one district would exhaust its riot-oriented personnel before calling upon an adjacent district for help. After serious racial disturbances in the summer of 1965, a new "Mobilization Plan" was implemented. It was felt that emergency personnel should be drawn from districts far beyond the district of incidence, so that adjacent districts would be at full strength in case there was any "spill over" from the primary district.

By 9:20 p.m. on Thursday evening, more than 300 officers of the task force had been assigned to patrol in the ghetto areas. At about the same time, ten "incident control" teams were formed for the purpose of bringing immediate and specialized attention to situations which threatened to become serious disturbances. While designed to deter riots with an extensive show of force, these teams were also expected to avoid provocation of the residents in ghetto areas with a premature show of force or any other police action. The police department also contacted the Illinois National Guard on Thursday evening but it was determined that no call should go out until it became evident that the city police could not contain disturbances in the ghetto. Since the city was unusually quiet on Thursday night, the call for the guard was delayed until almost 18 hours after the police department itself was alerted to the possibility of trouble—until 2:00 p.m. on Friday afternoon, when the disruption of the high schools spread into the streets of Chicago.[33]

Since the outbursts in the ghetto schools were nearly simultaneous on Friday morning, much of the crowd control work at this time was handled

[32] *Ibid.*, pp. 43-4.
[33] *Ibid.*, p. 12.

by members of the task force and the tactical force teams from those districts where the schools were located. These efforts were successful in most cases but police personnel were distributed very widely over the city until noon, when most of the ghetto high schools were finally closed. As we have seen, many officers were then sent to the fringe of the Loop area. It is difficult to determine whether the reassignment of these men to the west side later in the afternoon was accomplished in accordance with any identifiable mobilization plan. The Austin Committee simply reports that 300 task force members and 53 tactical teams (623 men) were operating in the affected districts by Friday evening. As will become evident in the discussion below, the assignment of extra men to the west side on Friday afternoon may have been haphazard, with little or no real control being exercised over the small groups of officers which were shuttled into the riot area. As one respondent complained,

> . . . One reason being you can't find a lieutenant or above when the going gets hot is because they're all planning the action to be taken ten blocks away or at police headquarters.

Although this assessment was disputed,

> During the first and second day we had only our sergeants and lieutenants on the street and they did a good job with the small amount of district manpower available . . .

it is now clear that the police on the west side were organized in small units, frequently no larger than the number held by the patrol car (from four to six men) used to transport them to the scene.

D. Police Action in the Affected Areas

On April 5th and 6th, the police were confronted with several unusual circumstances. Several respondents complained that they arrived in riot areas after serious trouble had already developed, either because there was insufficient transportation ("We were starting to work at 3:00 p.m. and the riot began and we had no transportation available to go the scene until about 40 minutes later") or because their commanders did not know where the center of activity was. Many shopkeepers did not remain in the ghetto areas, so that police were deprived of the encouragement and aid which these individuals might have provided.

> Merchants should stay in their shops and be prepared to prosecute and assist police.
> Merchants should be easier to contact for police purposes (to sign complaints and claim property).

> If businessmen remained at their businesses and insisted on their help in
> assisting in helping control a situation that got out of hand. I mean by being
> there would have helped a lot.

Even when the merchants remained in the area, their activities, such as the
sale of merchandise at cost and without receipts (thereby leading police to
think the goods were stolen) often created more confusion than their presence cured. A good example of this confusion is the story told by one officer
about a clothing store owner on the west side:

> While loading several trailers with clothing, he told the crowd to please let
> him get the trailers loaded, and when the trailers left, he said they could have
> what was left in the store. We stopped and arrested numerous people who
> were carrying clothing down Pulaski and Madison. Several minutes later the
> police radio informed us that these people who were coming from Pulaski and
> Washington were not looters, but that the clothes were *given to them.* This
> was one of the most demoralizing acts to the policemen assigned to this area
> that I have ever witnessed.

Upon reporting for duty on April 5th, all police personnel were
apparently told to take aggressive action against all offenders.[34] By the
following morning, these instructions had been restated in terms of a directive, which was broadcast every hour: "Supervisors will insure that their
personnel take aggressive action against all law breakers."[35] This directive
may reflect criticism of officers by patrolmen:

> Friday, more arrests would have been made but some of our *esteemed* bosses
> had issued orders not to arrest persons observed carrying objects or groceries
> in order not to provoke another incident.
>
> We should have supervisors ready to back up his men on arresting—not back
> down in face of a crowd for apparent fear of being castigated for "discriminat-
> ing."
>
> More *direct* orders to arrest promptly in all instances where possible would
> enhance the number of arrests.[36]

Nevertheless, it is clear that police faced unfriendly crowds when they
entered areas where looting was reported on Friday afternoon. As a result,
it was very difficult to detect those "law breakers" which deserved "aggressive action." No crowds would divulge the identity of an arsonist, rock
thrower, or looter.

---

[34]Austin Committee Report, "Chicago Riot Study," p. 38.

[35]*Ibid.,* p. 38.

[36]Responses to question seven, *Ibid.*

> What was needed was a show of force by the police department in strength
> and numbers, with a definite plan, not just sketchy orders, or none at all.

Since those officers who were "first on the scene" feared that any threat or
use of deadly force would simply incense the residents further, there was
a definite lull in police activity between the time that the center of the riot
activity on West Madison was discovered and the time when the Mobilization Plan (or some form thereof) produced enough manpower to permit the
use of mass arrest procedures.

In the second phase of the disturbance, employers began to release
their employees from work early in all areas of the city and traffic congestion
became a major problem—both in the sense that access to the riot area for
police and fire personnel was severely hampered and in the sense that
valuable manpower was diverted to seal off the riot area and prevent the
entry of unsuspecting white motorists, who had been subject to attack by
roving bands of high school students earlier in the day. When the police
escorted the remaining whites out of the ghetto areas, the contrast between
the resident looters (who knew which stores were white-owned) and the
police (many of whom were unfamiliar with the areas in which they were
working) increased. Since the police did not know which stores would be
hit next, the looters and arsonists gained valuable flexibility in terms of
tactics. As a result, their selection of stores proved remarkably effective—
on the basis of a "victim survey" conducted by the Austin Committee, it
was determined that nearly all arson was directed toward white-owned and
white-operated businesses.[37]

Since police on the west side were outnumbered by looters on Friday
afternoon, their refusal to rely on the use of the threat of deadly force made
it very difficult for them to capture those offenders they wished to arrest.
Those observed looting or throwing rocks would simply disappear into
crowds or buildings near the stores. In its section on the Chicago Police,
the Austin Committee recommends that the police concentrate on "symbolic arrests" during the early stages of any disorder.[37a] In order to be
effective, such arrests would have to remove known instigators or leaders
from the scene of the disturbance. Even in the early stages of the looting
on Friday afternoon, police officers were not generally familiar with the
residents (mostly students) who were responsible for the disturbances. As
the day progressed, policemen were brought in from other districts and
recognition of leaders or organizers became even less likely. As one officer

---

[37] *Ibid.*, p. 75.

[37a] "Symbolic arrests" are defined as: . . . arrests of persons in clear violation of law who are
in leadership positions and who are arrested under circumstances which may have a sobering or subduing effect on numbers of other persons in the same area. *Ibid.*, p. 47.

observed, the arrestees "lived in the area of the looting but they were strangers to us as arresting officers." Furthermore, just as in the first few hours of the afternoon there had been no discernible focus to the unrest in the city as a whole, so there was no single identifiable crowd or group on the west side to which supervisory officers could direct their men in the late afternoon and early evening. One respondent noted that "people were everywhere they were not in one place advancing in one direction." Finally, the number of troublemakers was simply not small enough to permit police to make "symbolic" arrests with the expectation that cooler heads would prevail as a result.

Before police began arresting residents on a massive scale, many individual officers simply fell back to direct traffic or provide protection for firemen.

> On the first day, we were told not to bother with the looters but to protect the firemen. We were not near any stores that still had merchandise. But we could see the looters carrying things about a half block away.

An inconsistent arrest policy confused many policemen:

> Lack of arrests stems from the lack of leadership and the inconsistency of our command. In the first days of the riot, most command personnel were asking us to hold back and not to act, for fear that overt action would be detrimental to the department. On the subsequent days (when most stores had already been burnt out), orders came down to the effect that we should become aggressive and now make more arrests—what does one do? The department should just give out orders that anyone caught looting, regardless of age, must be arrested. Have crews take names of arresting officers—and they make out arrest slips.

One respondent thought the field commanders should be given more power:

> The trouble is that the field supervisors of the department at the rank of sergeant through captain have too little authority. Exempt ranks can only order certain measures.

Some officers simply thought it was a matter of courage:

> We need Bosses with more balls to order the arrest of looters.
>
> ... untie the policeman's hands. There are certain police officers the people respect and fear. My partner and I are among the few.

These men are suggesting that it did not take much effort or courage for a supervisor to order that nothing be done. Their intense dislike of this procedure indicates the amount of tension which undefined and general inactivity can cause policemen.[38]   Furthermore, several respondents indicated that they had lost faith in the arrest procedure itself:

> Arresting them doesn't seem to help because they don't care and will do the same thing when the next riot starts.

> I, personally, no longer have any desire to arrest the looters. It's been my experience that they beat me out of court back onto the street. I believe one good crack on the head does more good. If you give them a headache, they go home and usually stay there.

One officer thought it was important to take the initiative when dealing with disorderly crowds:

> Greater use of billy club[s] by police on person[s] rioting would make contact personal, and fear of one's own safety would be noted by [the] rioter and his actions would then be of self-defense and not law violation.

Another respondent wanted more freedom to deal effectively with offenders:

> I believe if police were let loose to do their job a little head knocking would go further than shooting them. People have no fear of the policemen because they know what he can and cannot do, they also know without to[o] much trouble, and civil liberties groups or even government group[s] will do their best to get a policeman fired.

Other officers refused to make the maximum number of arrests because there was no transportation to district stations available or because they could not identify the looters in the first place:

> Naturally, as many looters as possible should be arrested, but only if you are sure they are looters. Many people were carrying items from burning homes and stores for safety and it was impossible to distinguish them from some of the looters.

One patrolman hestitated to arrest all offenders because

> I didn't want to spend the next two months in court, so I didn't make as many as I could. I think that an officer . . . should be assigned a court key and all his cases would be held a certain day.

---

[38]In a recent study of the Chicago Police Department, (unpublished monogram) the Center for Industrial Research at the University of Chicago attempted to determine the characteristics (motivation, intellect, and behavior) which can be associated with those officers who perform well in the field. In analyzing the working environment of policemen in the patrol division, the study noted that police in this division must generally

... endure long periods of monotony in routine patrol, yet react quickly (almost instantaneously) and effectively to problem situations observed on the street or to orders issued by the radio dispatcher . . .

During the early stages of the riot, this inactivity became more frustrating than usual because they were observing "problem situations" on the street.

E. Mass Arrest

When the police department's Mobilization Plan began to produce reinforcements (around 5:00 p.m.), the inactivity of most officers on the west side ceased. In contrast to their behavior a few hours earlier, the police began to use the power of arrest with very little discretion:

> There may also have been a tendency on the part of the police to make arrests later on April 5 . . . in a less discriminating way than is desirable so that a number of persons who were on the streets on legitimate business, including efforts to discipline . . . children, were incarcerated along with actual violators of the law.[39]

This criticism by the Austin Committee seems to be reflected by the arrest statistics. Between noon and 3:00 p.m. on April 5, only 33 arrests were made for riot-related activity. For the next three-hour period, this number jumped from 33 to 63; and from 6:00 p.m. to 9:00 p.m. it increased to a total of 139 for the three-hour period. This was the greatest number of arrests made in any three-hour period during the entire disorder. In effect, the police department used the power of arrest to regain control of the streets on the west side of Chicago. Once the National Guard troops arrived (between 11:00 p.m. and 12:00 midnight), the police were able to maintain order by concentrating their arrest power in areas where new trouble broke out and leaving the guard troops to protect areas which had already been hit by the rioters.

Traditional training in crowd control proved ineffective. Until recently, all policemen initially received 14 weeks of general instruction in the Police Academy.[40] Each trainee would receive 17 hours of crowd-control techniques. Further instruction is provided in the form of weekly training bulletins, one or two of which might pertain to crowd control in the course of a year. A few respondents indicated that no training could have prepared them for riot duty:

> There is not any training available which is better than actual duty during riots.

> The police department is well-qualified and had gained knowledge thr[ough] experience and will become more efficient in the future in regards to riots.

Police were unable to disperse looters with the use of riot control formations, which are described in training bulletins as a "last resort" crowd-control technique. Since looting had entered the West Madison area in force, keeping the crowds off the streets was no longer a viable solution

---

[39]Austin Committee Report, "Chicago Riot Study," p. 43.
[40]As announced in a news release dated January 6, 1969, and entitled "Chicago Police Launch New Seven-Month Long Training Program Today," the police academy has expanded the old 14-week program by 17 more weeks of training.

to the problem—the residents simply entered one of many available stores (through the broken windows) or alleys whenever the police attempted to use a "wedge" (for breaking up crowds) or a "diagonal" (for moving crowds away from buildings and into an open area) or a "skirmish line" (a holding action to block entrance to a street or other area). One training bulletin explained the purpose of these maneuvers:

> Physical handling of a rioter is not the best recourse so it usually should be the last. Punishment is a function of the courts.

> An avenue of escape should always be left open. The primary purpose of a riot formation is to disperse the unruly mob, not to take them into custody. (TB, Vol. VIII, No. 15)

Since the primary purpose of police presence was the protection of property, it was necessary for them to combine crowd control with a clearing action that would rout the looters from the stores. One method employed by the police was to seal looters inside a store by blocking all the entrances, but this task was made difficult by the large number of broken windows in most stores. Furthermore, there was no easy way to rout the looters from the stores—tear gas was not usually available for this purpose and the police lost valuable time removing the arrestees one at a time.[41] Furthermore, many policemen were hesitant to enter alleys behind or beside these stores.[42]

Under these circumstances, the police department was faced with a mass arrest situation—both as a method of controlling the large number of policemen in the area and as a last resort in regaining control of the streets. One training bulletin warned against a "random" arrest procedure:

> Mass arrests made by many police in helter-skelter manner will serve absolutely no purpose as far as maintaining law and order is concerned. However, arrests made in an orderly and well-planned manner indicate a trained force prepared for such emergencies and will help convey to the demonstrators and to the rest of the city that they are dealing with a superior force. (TB, Vol. VII, No. 38)

Nevertheless, there was a great deal of confusion in the arrest, transporting, and booking of prisoners. One district simply had the desk sergeant sign all complaints; this accelerated the arrest procedure, but jeopardized convictions. As a result, the arrest procedure actually involved a great deal of chance—people were arrested if there were squadrolls available to transport

---

[41]See discussion of riot weaponry in part, Austin Committee Report, "Chicago Riot Study".

[42]Several firemen complained that police would not enter alleys, even when the firemen were forced to fight fires from them and even though arsonists often entered buildings from the side. *Ibid.*, 1, p. 55.

them to district stations, and squadrolls were available according to the speed with which district stations were able to process arrestees.[42a]

The arrest procedure became more deliberate when the National Guard was assigned to patrol certain areas, thereby freeing the police to pursue looters and arsonists elsewhere. However, it appears that no major fires were set in the west side area after 11:00 p.m. which was at least 30 minutes before the Guard troops actually entered this part of the city.[43] This would indicate that the massive number of arrests between 6:00 p.m. and 9:00 p.m. played a significant part in the reduction of violence on the west side. In short, the arbitrary use of the arrest power may have had a greater impact on the residents than an "orderly and well-planned" arrest procedure. And just as the people may have begun to resent the random nature of the arrests, both the National Guard and a new shift of police arrived. By this time, both residents and police were exhausted; a final indication of the success of the department procedure was the restraint exercised by both the residents and the police at this time (12:00 midnight) —instead of escalating into armed conflict, the disturbances on the west side quickly subsided. Of course, the slight amount of violence between the police and the residents may simply indicate that police-community relations were in relatively good shape—that the residents were more interested in loot than in taking revenge against police department personnel for some prior action in the community.[44] An equally plausible explanation is the involvement of both the police and the residents in a time-consuming arrest procedure—individual officers worried about finding transportation for prisoners; friends and relatives were concerned about the welfare of the arrestees; looters decided to hide their loot.[45]

It is generally assumed that police operate under a strict chain of command during civil disorders, so that the exercise of discretion by the individual officer is of minimal importance.[46] Under the Chicago Police

---

[42a]One respondent noted that "police wagons must not be held waiting with prisoners for long periods."

[43]*Ibid.,* p. 51.

[44]Almost all members of the force were aware that aggressive acts on their part might intensify the riot, as in the case of the "blind pig" raid in Detroit, the traffic arrest in Newark or the "pregnant woman" arrest in Los Angeles. But the April riot cannot be traced to any particular police action. Instead, the hostility of the residents was toward the white race in general and white-owned stores in particular.

[45]The distribution of duties between the Guard and the police also caused some difficulty; several officers arrested on the basis of information provided by Guardsman who either did not give his name at the time or later failed to appear to testify at the trial of the defendant.

[46]The disorders to which the police routinely respond are not large-scale. Riots and civil commotions are, in any given city, rare occurrences, and when they happen, the police act *en masse,* under civil leadership.

J. Q. Wilson, "What makes a better policeman?" *The Atlantic,* March, 1969, p. 130.

Department's Mobilization Plan, there is a great emphasis on the speed with which reinforcements can be gotten to a particular police district. However, there seems to have been little planning for the problem of sustaining the organization of such emergency personnel over long periods of time—for more than two or three hours. As more police cars entered a particular area, radio communication became more difficult. As a result, police units from outlying districts usually had to rely upon their own sergeants and lieutenants for direction. The tactics used by these semi-independent units were, in turn, controlled by General Order 67-14.[47]

F. Deadly Force and Riot Weaponry

Late Friday afternoon, mounting frustration with the looters and arsonists caused many policemen to consider the use of deadly force. In drafting their questionnaire for policemen, the primary concern of the Chicago Riot Study Committee was:

> whether the police, by more aggressive action in the use of deadly force, could have prevented much of the destruction and looting and could have apprehended more offenders.[48]

Although only three questions (two of which are analyzed here) and a series of hypotheticals were presented in connection with this issue, the committee staff apparently analyzed the responses with sufficient care to conclude:

> The police officers' response indicated, with some exceptions, a sound understanding of their role as law enforcement officers in the use of deadly force under the laws of the State of Illinois as implemented by General Order 67-14. The confused circumstances of civil disorder make it especially difficult for police to follow carefully and accurately General Order 67-14. That the police were able, with a few deplorable exceptions, to do so deserves the highest commendation and approval of all Chicagoans.[49]

The use of deadly force by a Chicago policeman is strictly controlled by General Order 67-14, which was issued by former Superintendent O. W. Wilson on May 16, 1967. Each member of the force received a copy of the order and was directed to request clarification of any part which he did not understand. The order was not designed for use during a civil disorder:

---

[47]General order 67-14 (an order which was issued by the Superintendent of Police in Chicago in 1967, copies of which are carried by all policemen in their patrol manuals).

[48]Austin Committee Report, "Chicago Riot Study", p. 38.

[49]It should be noted that this observation is not addressed to the question of the possible efficacy of more deadly force and that the Chicago Riot Study Committee never did address this issue directly.

This order, along with many other ambiguous orders tend to confuse, and ultimately make the use of deadly force unuseable during a riot.

An order for riot situations alone should be made.

No person will tell you when 67-14 is in force—the difference between burglary and looting.

Table VI.—Would the Greater Use of Deadly Force Have Brought the Riots under Quicker Control?

	Number	Percent
Yes (ranging from "definitely" to "probably")	248	53
No	127	27
Unknown	40	9
Under certain circumstances	38	8
If used at the beginning	10	2
Total	469	100

Table VII.—Do You Feel the Department Policy on Deadly Force as Outlined in Order 67-14 Hinders or Obstructs You in Controlling Riots?

	Number	Percent
Yes	196	41
No	189	40
Unknown	40	8
Order is irrelevant (it does not apply to riots and can never replace the individual judgement of the officer, who will ultimately be responsible for his action anyway)	21	4
Good theory (but the city and the Chicago Police Department do not follow it)	10	2
Sometimes (7); it works both ways (3); it is the law (4); use any force necessary (3); it made me stop and think (1)	18	4
Total	474	100

General Order 67-14

I. Purpose: This order establishes guidelines in accordance with the law and department policy for the use of force likely to cause death or great bodily harm.

II. The Law:

    A. Force likely to cause death or great bodily harm includes:

        1. The firing of a firearm in the direction of a person even though no intent to kill or inflict great bodily harm exists, or

        2. The firing of a firearm at a vehicle in which a person is riding.

    B. A peace officer may use force likely to cause death or great bodily harm in making an arrest or preventing the escape of a person in custody only when:

        1. he reasonably believes that such force is necessary to prevent death or great bodily harm to himself or another person;

        2. the subject has committed or attempted a forcible felony *and* the officer reasonably believes that such force is necessary in order to effect the arrest or prevent the escape;

        3. the subject is attempting to escape by use of a deadly weapon *and* the officer reasonably believes that such force is necessary in order to effect the arrest or prevent the escape; or

        4. the subject indicates that he will endanger human life or inflict great bodily harm unless he is taken into custody without delay *and* the officer reasonably believes that such force is necessary to effect the arrest or prevent the escape.

    C. Chapter 38, Section 2-8 of the Illinois Revised Statutes provides: Forcible felony means treason, murder, voluntary manslaughter, rape, robbery, burglary, arson, kidnapping, aggravated battery, and any other felony which involves the use of threat of physical force or violence against the individual.

III. A. Force likely to cause death or great bodily harm will not be used in instances where there is likelihood of serious injury being inflicted upon persons other than the person against whom the officer is authorized by law to use such force.

    B. The use of firearms will not be resorted to in instances where the consequences of such use would be likely to outweigh the police purpose served by such use. However, the immediate safeguarding of the life of the officer or a third party shall outweigh all other considerations.

    C. The following practices are specifically forbidden:

        1. Firing into crowds

        2. Firing over the heads of a crowd except on specific order of a member above the rank of captain.

        3. Firing at a fleeing car except one in which a person who has attempted or committed a forcible felony is riding.

        4. Firing warning shots in the case of individuals where the use of deadly force is not permitted, warning shots will not be fired when they are

likely to injure persons other than those against whom deadly force is authorized.

5. Firing into buildings or through doors when the person fired at is not clearly visible.

G.O. 67-14 defines deadly force ("the firing of a firearm in the direction of a person even though no intent to kill or inflict great bodily harm exists") and restates the Illinois law (Chapter 38, Section 7-5) before explaining the "Department Policy." As one officer observed, "the stated law of Illinois lays out the terms for using deadly force—how can a city lay out any other policy than state law? The statement of law which is most nearly applicable to riot situations is contained in part II.B.2 of the order.

> A peace officer may use force likely to cause death or great bodily harm . . . only when:
> 2. the subject has committed or attempted a forcible felony *and* the officer reasonably believes that such force is necessary to effect the arrest or prevent the escape . . .

Forcible felony is defined in Chapter 38, Section 2-8 of the Illinois Revised Statutes to include burglary and robbery, but to exclude looting. Thus, a forcible felony is usually thought to involve the threat of violence to a person or actual breaking and entering where property is concerned. Several policemen found the distinction between looting and forcible felonies tenuous:

> . . . Looting was formerly a felony, but in the 1967 session of the legislature it was made a misdemeanor. This was fought by many groups but Black and liberal elements forced its passage.

> Looting and burglary should be synonomous.

> As most officers were not clear as to whether the police department or the city would say the acts were acts of burglary (a forcible felony) or they would go with laws pertaining to "Looting Statutes (Misdemeanors)," which nobody understands or knows why such a law was put in Illinois law books.

> Do away with looting as a law because this is burglary and the jail sentence should be issued as such. Here again, we appear to live by two sets of laws. On the west side they call it looting, a misdemeanor by the state's attorney's rules, but north of say Fullerton Avenue, it's burglary, forcible felony which could very well result in the death of the offender.

> 67-14 is a ridiculous farce—the law is the law and should be enforced as it is written. The police department should be criticized for its lack of enforcement of existing law. The mayor and police chief should be impeached for not doing their duty—by protecting the city from these arsonists and looters.

Several respondents thought that their supervisors went beyond the law in advising them against the use of deadly force:[50]

It is ideal if the department went by what it says.

Arson and burglary are both felonies and should be treated as such. The police department should be required to enforce the law as it is written.

No. Let's face it. If the order had been followed and the law there would have been at least a hundred people killed or wounded. But if the same thing happened tomorrow, you still couldn't shoot 100 people (all ages and sexes) that you caught looting a department store.

These respondents are reacting to the expression of "Department Policy" in Section III— of G. O. 67-14.[51] Under III.A., a policeman is prohibited from using deadly force

in instances where there is a likelihood of serious injury being inflicted upon persons other than the person against whom the officer is authorized by law to use such force.

This part of the order clearly prohibits an officer from firing into a crowd of looters and onlookers, even if he is sure that one of them has committed a forcible felony.

Firing over heads, yes, too many kids lootin for fun or excitement—*I will not shoot kids.*

During such mass confusion, innocent people would get killed.

One respondent thought the police should act swiftly in civil disorders:

The communications media tends to report the injury and also death of some of the persons in the riot as innocent victims of unjust, unlawful acts by the police. There are far too many "Monday Morning Quarterbacks" who criticize the actions of a man who had a few seconds to act.

Department policy is stated in more general terms in Section III.B. of the order:

The use of firearms will not be resorted to in instances where the consequences of such use would be likely to outweigh the police purpose served by such use.

---

[50]Some respondents questioned the department policy in light of their experience with police duty after a tornado had struck the south side of Chicago in 1967: "If looters can be shot in other areas for natural disaster certainly we can carry on when the disaster is man made."

[51]The following disagreement is indicative of the general police attitude toward the order: "Any steadfast rule under *Combat* conditions is a hindrance." "It can be used to advantage by an officer using good sound judgment. Each case is unique."

Several respondents thought that the riot lasted a relatively short time, and that the rioters were not particularly hostile toward police:

> Crowd did not seem vicious. Policy [using deadly force] might have lost the controlling.

> No, I believe the lack of deadly force was a major cause of the quick termination of the riots. In some areas, the use of deadly force probably would have generally ended in "war" and unnecessary bloodshed—it is believed the early withholding of firearms resulted in an early end of disturbances.

> ... But it [deadly force] may also have turned the rioters from property violence to violence against police officers.

> I believe that lack of deadly force was a major cause of the quick termination of the riots. Also, the fact that the weapons to be used were already in the hands of the policemen but they weren't used, helped to keep a "shooting match" from starting. Police potential firepower vastly outnumbered the rioters and it was used with discretion.

> No ... In a riot, you already have a tense situation, the use of deadly force would prolong or enlarge the riot area ... This could make a three (3) day riot as of this past April last maybe three (3) weeks or more.

Regardless of these particular attitudes, Table VI indicates that 63 percent of the respondents (including the two percent who qualified their answer with the condition that deadly force be used immediately and the eight percent who added other conditions) thought there was insufficient use of deadly force during the April riots.

Most officers who recommended the use of deadly force realized the risk of retaliation ("hope and pray that the residents do not arm themselves to the teeth") and several (two percent) qualified their endorsement with the suggestion that deadly force be used early in the riot:

> Deadly force at the very beginning would have stopped riot. But when first offender is shot, you need a great show of force. And let all persons [know] that all looters and arsonists will be shot.

> Before the looting and burning began, yes!!! The decision has to come immediately. Once the incident reaches certain proportions, it's too late.

Those officers who did recommend the use of deadly force or some special riot-fighting device (e.g., Mace, tear gas, dogs, shot guns, carbines) generally believed that the crowds were primarily composed of two groups—the "hard core" criminal element, and the "onlookers," who might or might not participate in the looting, depending on the manner in which the police handled the initial offenders. Thus, one respondent thought that deadly force "at the beginning would bring down the amount of looters and make it easy to arrest the few brave ones."

After the use of deadly force, the rioters would have known it was going to be cleared up fast, and they would have become involved with their own personal well-being, thus bringing into play divisiveness, breaking any unified or semi-unified efforts to continue the riot. Most certainly it would—who wants to go down first?—is the thought of the average rioter.

Nothing will keep a person in his house and out of a riot area faster than the thought that he might be arrested, hurt, or even killed.

Yes, most of these people knew that police would not shoot, but if deadly force was used—the word gets around.

Deadly force would have brought the riot under control quicker at the cost of more deaths.

Other policemen approved the use of deadly force only in cases of self-defense or "if it took the ringleaders who seldom are the active looters." While eight percent of the respondents in Table VI qualified their endorsement of deadly force, it should be noted that these men still basically agreed that more deadly force should have been used during the April disorders.

Several officers attempted to distinguish between the threat of the use of deadly force and the actual use of deadly force:

But I think that a threat of deadly force as the mayor did (too late) would have.

Not the greater use, but the knowledge on the part of the crowds, that the police could and would use deadly force if necessary.

The threat of deadly force would. As an example, there were white watch service patrolmen with shotguns at some stores. Their presence prevented looting and burning.

Other respondents refused to engage in speculation about the relationship between threats and deterrence; some of these men chose to view the entire issue of deadly force in terms of the continuing relationship between the police department and the community:

Probably valuable [deadly force] in the immediate sense, but would cause more damage in the long run as far as personal feelings and trust in the Chicago Police Department. But the outcome of this method may in itself outweigh the supposed good of stopping the riot. In other words, a more serious gap would have developed between the police department and the citizen.

Few respondents had any doubts about the "supposed good of stopping the riot." For most, it was simply a question of "respect"—both for them and for the law:

> Too many people laughed in faces of police—they (rioters) knew police had no orders to shoot . . .

> The use of deadly force would have showed them that we were not going to put up with civil disobedience and break down of law and order.

> Show them who the law is before they show us who runs the city.

> The people causing these riots think it is a big joke. They have to be shown we have a police department that is not chicken.

The third part of the department policy statement in G. O. 67-14 contains practices which are strictly forbidden, such as the "firing over the heads of crowds except on specific order of a member above the rank of captain." With the exception of one incident near Austin High School on Friday morning, when the commander of the Austin District fired two shots over the heads of students, there is no record of any such action having been taken during the riot. As has been noted, most rioters simply sought to avoid contact with the police; it is certain that no captain wished to risk the possibility of becoming directly responsible for escalating the riot in his area —the only time such firing would have been definitely permissible would have been a situation in which the rioters threatened the police directly. One policeman thought the order was a hindrance because "you can never find a command rank personnel during a riot."

> Mostly, it is our exempt leaders—they don't want to tell us to use force because they have to answer to the politicians.

Furthermore, district autonomy and authority began to disappear when additional police moved into the West Madison area under the Mobilization Plan (see section G below). It is entirely possible that many police officers were not sure who was under whose command in the field; this made the decision to fire over a crowd's head all the more difficult—police at the other end of the block might have been operating under an entirely different procedure.

A few respondents refrained from the use of deadly force because they feared reprisal on the basis of political necessity:

> But if you, as an individual, did use it and killed someone, I believe there would be results toward the policemen such as was necessary to pacify the colored.

> I feel the police officer today is scared to use deadly force, because it seems that the city will not back him up and that the only reason he can use it is to protect himself . . .

Many policemen who objected to General Order 67-14 in Table VII were really objecting to the investigation by the police department which was sure to follow:

I was afraid to use my gun because my decision at that second would be investigated for years, by someone who wasn't even there, causing me to spend end-less hours writing reports.

When you're behind a desk, wearing white shirts, you can't say what deadly force to use. When you live, work, and walk among people you know will create a riot, then the feeling is different.

. . . it's the attitude of superiors, who are waiting for you to make a mistake, which is very possible in the heat of such incidents.

. . . I think there is a great necessity to stop these riots as soon as possible, and sometimes some innocent people may be injured. If this does happen, the policeman is in the middle.

I think the city and police courts department should back their police officers.

One officer saw his own actions in terms of the popular will:

. . . However, the city must be prepared to stand behind an honest effort, which turns out to be bad judgement. A blanket lid on all force, puts everyone down, giving all the edge to the rioters. I believe the good citizens of Chicago deserve the edge. If a mistake is made, let it be in their favor.

Several officers simply said they would take the responsibility for the decision to use deadly force:

The man who pulls the trigger still has to justify his actions and with hostile witnesses, might not shoot even though he knew he would be within the law to do so.

I think a policeman will use common sense to tell him when and when not to shoot. Different situations require different means.

I use my own discretion and no department order or mayor's statement will ever be my reason to use deadly force or not to use it—That's something I must live with the rest of my life . . . *I'll* be the one to go to prison if I goof up.

. . . The entire order merely states you will make the decision, be accountable for your actions, etc. This is as it should be, but no man can tell another what is the proper action to take unless he is standing right alongside of the situation.

A few respondents thought the order was a positive aid during the disturbances:

I think it is a good order, or you would wind up with an OK Corral situation in the street.

Not really—it is a good order. I thought the officers used generally commendable restraint and that this policy paid off in our area.

Instead of emphasizing the value of riot experience or the ineptitude of superior officers who lose contact with conditions in the streets, several officers recommended an improvement in the deployment of weapons available to the department:

> The size of the police units are not as important as the strength of their weapons and ability and permission to use them.

Many police officers were openly impressed by the array of weapons displayed by the National Guard and Army personnel. For example, all members of the National Guard were equipped with gas and gas masks and several officers had the power to order immediate use of the weapon. But, as several policemen bitterly observed:

> Tear gas would have helped us because if you're trying to get 200 people off a corner that is about the only way possible. The use of tear gas in breaking up large crowds would have been useful but we were unable to get the gas when we needed it.

> What is needed is some direction from the Top Brass who were not present although every general order states that a deputy chief or over only could give the orders to stop looting, etc. by using tear gas, dogs, etc.

The most popular weapon recommended by the respondents was the police dog:[52]

> Dogs! Dogs! Dogs! and more Dogs! They fear dogs more than guns or gas. They respect the animal more than the police.

> Unrestricted use of dogs on large mobs would prevent persons from getting the upper hand. These people are more afraid of dogs than a man with a .38 or a .45.

Several policemen allocated weapons according to the particular problem faced by the department in a certain area:

> Use gas for stores with looters in them (then make arrests); but dogs are best for crowd control. Tear gas might have helped in massive crowd gatherings to disperse them. Also Mace would be a personal boost to the police in non-deadly situations. Dogs should be used only in special situations, as the welfare of the dog must also be considered.

> . . . gas and dogs, when used, would discourage the bystander from staying in the area allowing police to deal only with the hard core of the mob—fewer

---

[52]In response to question eight, Austin Committee Report, "Chicago Riot Study" note 1, 110 respondents singled out police dogs and 90 specifically recommended the wider use of tear gas.

men can control and clear an area with gas. Barbed wire barricades to seal off clear area.

Many of the officers who recommended the use of dogs, tear gas, or high-pressure water hoses were aware that such weapons were made objectionable to the public as a result of their use in the South:

> ... Prior to the Birmingham riots, these dogs or the use of the dogs was the greatest asset our department had.[53]

> No, the use of dogs and gas would only aggravate the situation—deadly force is necessary to put fear into the offender.

> I don't agree with the thinking that using dogs is inhuman and cruel when you are dealing with a situation as serious as you have during a riot. No one likes to use force, but this is not a game being played, "the other side" is not playing the game with any set of rules or sportsmanship.

> Dogs! Dogs! Dogs! Dogs! and more Dogs! I hope I made my point. "Bull Conners" ruined one of the best crowd control methods the Chicago Police Department ever had by missing the canine.

G. Deterioration of District Authority

One serious problem with the Mobilization Plan is the maintenance of authority over the activites of all policemen who are moved into a particular district. This problem is most poignantly demonstrated by the deaths of four ghetto residents on the evening of April 5th. All four died within the space of three-and-one-half hours and within an area of two square blocks on Madison Street, about eight miles west of the Loop. Members of the police department were apparently aware of these deaths. As one respondent noted, "Manpower and some *unauthorized* killing of looters ended the riot." The Austin Committee investigated the incident:

> Two were shot from the street at 7:30 and 7:35 p.m., by rifle fire aimed into two stores at 4135 and 4113 West Madison Street, crowded with looters. Two were shot in an alley parallel to and between West Madison and West Monroe streets. None was resisting arrest according to the Committee's reasonably detailed and reliable information. Allegedly two police cars containing two to four white policemen in each car who were armed with rifles were in the two block area at this time and were seen shooting on the level into stores and shooting on the level in the alley in question.[54]

Such use of deadly force was in direct contradiction of section III.C.(5) of General Order 67-14, which prohibits "firing into buildings or through

---

[53]*Ibid.* p. 42: The canine units should be used with great discretion and regard for their irritating as well as their pacifying effect on various Chicago neighborhoods.

[54]*Ibid.* p. 37.

doors when the person fired at is not clearly visible." Furthermore, it other districts. It was also more difficult for these officers to check out alibis or explanations for a particular person's presence in a given area (e.g., employees who were caught in stores where they worked). With reference to the riot arrestees, one officer concluded: "They lived in the area of the looting but they were strangers to us as arresting officers." When police began to take the arrestees directly to the central headquarters at 11th and State in the early evening of April 5th, "screening" ceased to exist altogether.[57]

Those officers who were embarrassed or disturbed by the need for the National Guard and by their own inability to "head off" riots before they begin by arresting the leaders and getting to trouble spots quickly—recommended the use of counter-insurgency tactics by the department:

It appears that reinforcements from outlying districts often cruised through riot areas in their own police cars, without ever placing themselves under the command of a particular officer on the scene. If this is the case, many important decisions about the use of force and the power of arrest were probably made by the small groups of men in each of these cars. In short, the degree of centralized control over the activities of police in the riot areas is not at all clear.

The implementation of the police department's Mobilization Plan created other difficulties. Many merchants alleged that the police who came from other districts were much less assiduous in their attempts to control the looting.[56] As we have seen, lack of familiarity with the area probably caused most emergency personnel to proceed with caution, especially when it became necessary for them to pursue offenders into alleys or stores. The influx of new personnel also contributed to a general inability to "screen" arrestees at the station house; those who were known to be responsibile members of the community could not be recognized as such by police from seemed clear that the two men in the alley were not engaged in any forcible felony.

The most important element in the tragedy is the fact that the commander of the Fillmore Police District, in which the shootings took place, asserts that neither of the police cars involved was under his authority.[55]

---

[55] *Ibid.* p. 37.

[56] *Ibid.,* p. 74.

[57] The decision to bypass the district stations was probably based on the following factors: (1) There was concern that some of the station houses, such as the Fillmore District Station (which suffered the loss of all electric power and was the subject of some sniper fire on Friday evening), might not be far enough removed from the riot area to deter attempts by the rioters to free those being held; (2) There was a great deal of delay in the booking procedures at the district stations; (3) it was known that magistrates would be available at 11th and State to set bond.

I would use colored officers living in project areas to set off tear gas devices when needed from their strategic spots.

Keep a constant vigil in the ghettos so as to know when organizers are around.

Adequate communication with . . . the leaders to assist in every way possible to stop any conspiracy . . . school and playground authorities, church precinct captains and cooperative citizens.

Stop confusing legitimate civil rights with subversive groups. Stop sticking our head in the sand and refusing to see the vast strides the Communists are making in bringing about general sabotage.

All persons used in riot control should be aware of the area . . . be familiar with various groups in the area that should be kept under close surveillance.

However, it is doubtful that such attempts would be successful; one officer explained how he attempted to uncover evidence *before* the April riots:

My partner and I were told months ago that a riot would take place. I got a list of all the gangs in my district. Time after time, I've interrogated the younger ones (under 14 years old). I prepared myself for that day. But I did not know, until Dr. King's death. . . .

H. Auxiliary Police

The policemen of Chicago are steadfastly opposed to the creation of a special auxiliary force for use during riots. A full 70 percent of the respondents rejected the plan, proposed by Sheriff Woods and others, to give riot training to volunteers. The explanations accompanying the responses in Table VIII revealed a stubborn pride in the existing structure of the department and the responsibility of being a policeman:

(No) There are already enough morons playing police part time. Mainly the (sheriff bailiffs). *God Help Us!*

No, because this would exist too many problems dealing with command and communications. When we asked for help from the Guardsmen, they went the other way. You can have the Guard and the phony commanders.

. . . As Woods proposed, his posse would drill once a week for a few hours. I would not place a weapon in this person's hand because he would not be capable of handling this type of situation.

No. Unless a person is well trained in crowd control, and is capable of handling himself, he can start a riot, rather than prevent it.

... unless you deal with these people every day, you don't have enough knowledge of them to be entrusted with their lives.

Other respondents thought that more manpower simply was not the answer:

No. If we are not allowed to use force, neither will they. Let the policeman on the street do his job and we won't need a reserve nor the National Guard.

The Chicago Police Department could handle any trouble before and can handle any trouble in the future if we were backed by our bosses. They are all afraid of getting fired if they go too far.

Several respondents thought that the police department simply was not large enough to handle serious civil disorders:

Table VIII.—Would a Specially Trained Reserve Auxiliary Police Force Be of Assistance to the Police in the Control of Riots?

		Number	Percent
No	(the members of such a force would be poorly trained, unreliable and inexperienced)	178	38
No	(these answers were either unexplained or contained the basic assertion that the Chicago Police Department could handle any trouble if certain restrictions were removed)	129	28
Yes	(conditioned upon proper training)	52	11
Yes	(otherwise unexplained answer or accompanied by the observation that any increase in force would help)	46	10
Yes	(only if the reserve forces were given clerical duties or were used to drive trucks, guard detention centers, direct traffic)	22	5
No	(because the mobilization of the reserve would still be too slow)	21	4
	19	4	
	Total	467	100

Total Against = 328 or 70 percent
Total in Favor = 120 or 26 percent

Have an effective force ready to move into any area within two hours of an outbreak will contain it. But more manpower must be employed to be able to have this size force. We are not equipped at this time to handle all the areas that are potential riot areas.

Chicago needs at least 25,000–30,000 policemen, well equipped with sniper scope guns and mounted 50 calibre, 75 calibre M. guns and bazookas.

Many police officers were particularly critical of the type of person who was likely to volunteer for riot duty:

This would attract too many fanatics and racists. Crazy people.

No. The screening and training would be difficult. I think it would be easy for some intellectual subversive to filter through the screen . . . anyone who volunteers to fight in riots is a little goofy.

Reserves would comprise "police freaks," those not fit for actual police services and those wanting a "little action."

The regular police would have no confidence in them.

Why not subsidize the Rangers, [a youth gang] as they would have a greater understanding, and empathy for the situation? I do not think they would back you up in a tight spot.

No! They would have an "I don't give a damn, I won't be here next week" attitude.

No, because you would get those persons who wanted to be police, but something was wrong and they couldn't make it. Bad people.

No. I've seen auxiliary police forces in other cities and it seems they attract men who have tried to get on the regular force and failed. When they do get a uniform and badge they become drunk with power and cause more confusion and trouble than the rioters themselves.

Several policemen opposed the creation of an auxiliary police force on the ground that it would be illegitimate:

The auxiliary force may aid in all out rebellion of minority citizens who would believe that they were being put down by other than lawful means.

An auxiliary police force would do no good in assisting the police as it would give people the impression that other citizens were taking sides with the police and perhaps add more fuel to the fire which had already started.

Others thought the question of "respect" was no longer relevant:

Since the people who were in these past riots have little or no respect for a police officer, I doubt that they would pay any attention to an auxiliary officer.

In the context of the question dealing with auxiliary police, many respondents emphasized the importance of personal knowledge of the ghetto communities for the first time:

> No. Because training is not the only thing a policeman must have in riots. He must also be involved in the everyday relationships with the people, so that he may better understand their problems. And knowing the issues involved can sometimes very easily disperse a group by saying a few words. He must be involved not just during riots, but prior to [them] to be effective.

> . . . an auxiliary police force coming out on the street once in a great while may not know how to cope with certain problems. Some persons you are able to talk to, others are so brainwashed on racism, nothing or no one can handle them. I should say talk to them.

> . . . all persons used in riot control should be aware of . . . the various groups in the area that should be kept under close surveillance.

> No, the people used, no matter how well trained, would not have street experience. This takes years to learn.

> . . . One experience[d] policeman would be better than 20 of the [auxiliary policemen]. Take one rookie and let him work around some old timer, and a lot of knowledge will rub off. Where will their knowledge come from?

One respondent thought the establishment of an auxiliary police force "would cause additional sympathetic citizens—families of Aux Police." A few officers thought auxiliary police from the "target community" (the ghetto) would receive greater respect from the residents, although many wondered whether the auxiliary police force could ever be mobilized quickly enough to deal effectively with disturbances.

I. Attitudes Toward the Department and Ghetto Residents—the Prevention of Future Riots

Nearly one-fifth of the respondents (88) thought that nothing could be done to prevent future riots.[58] Thirty-three percent of the respondents (150) advocated the use of strong police action—vigorous enforcement of all laws with a strong show of force at the outset of any disturbance, relying on better supervision and mass arrest tactics, as well as swift trials and harsh punishment. A smaller number of police officers (44) indicated their concern with the improvement of community relations by the police department.

> Keep patrolmen on the same beats so that they become better acquainted with the residents of the beat. In closer association with the residents, a policeman

---

[58]These answers are selected from responses to question 13, Austin Committee Report, "Chicago Riot Study."

can be alerted to any kind of problem that could develop into a civil disorder. Working every day amongst these residents will establish him as part of the community and the large number of good people will confide in him. I think the Eighth District should be fully integrated, in fact, all districts should be integrated regardless of where the man lives because if you work in a district, you learn the people and the average police will gain respect of the people in the district and he will be allowed to move in that particular area faster than anyone else.

Train us (policemen) to do a better job in helping the citizen. The area of patrol is best controlled by the people who live in that area. Because things that happen in that area concern them and their family. When you work in one area and live in another, you seem to have a lack of concern.

If you don't deal with these people every day, you have a tendency to be overzealous in your work and know that undercover of a riot, some people would use this as an excuse to hurt more than help the situation.

A large number of respondents thought that riots would not end until ghetto conditions were eliminated. However, there was much disagreement about the significance of the riot in terms of the characteristics which could be attributed to ghetto dwellers in general in:

The Black people have had enough of be quiet and you'll get your freedom. In their minds they thought they were right in what they were doing.

These people understand only strength and lack of same denotes cowardice!

. . . make people work on the west side instead of drawing welfare. All they have to do now is loaf on the corner and drink. If they know they will get hurt because of their stealing and burning, they won't do it . . .

Most adults in the area call working men fools. And the teens are being taught the same.

As long as there are injustices against a group of people, if that group is pressed into a confined area, you will sooner or later get an explosion.

Society today differs from that of yesterday in that people used to do wrong and after they did wrong, they felt sorry. But today people don't care if they do wrong. Morality as a whole has changed—you can see this in young children.

Put these scum in jail and the others will not be in such a hurry to start something.

Treat all men like men—old people leave young people alone.

A lot of trouble is brewed by the big high-rise buildings which cause the police a lot of problems. Stop building big high-rises in slum areas.

There was considerable discussion about the role of the Black policeman:

> There is a need for more police and more Negro supervision in the police department in the Negro community.

> Put more Black policemen in Black communities. Most Negro police did nothing—they seemed to sympathize with the looters.

> . . . let Negro policemen arrest all known militants and wrongdoers. This will relieve the tensions.

> . . . Hire more Negro policemen because they are now and always will be the only force to prevent the spreading of a riot; and if Chicago will view the facts without the Negro policemen they already have, Chicago would have burned much worse than it did.

One officer thought the white policeman was the main problem.

> The Negro should be treated as any white man is treated. Weed out the prejudiced policeman from the Negro area and put him with his own people. Give the Negro better police protection from the white policeman. Don't treat or regard every Negro as a criminal. Stop harassing them on the street, just because he drives a big car or dresses neatly.

Complaints about the court system ("Impeach Judge Wendt!") were common and many policemen spoke of the lack of support for them in the Black community itself—evidenced most dramatically by the April riot. Their main objection, in terms of community support, was directed toward the "softhearted," "fuzzy minded" liberal—the isolated social worker, clergyman or organizer:

> To prevent riots or any other type of disturbance as they are called, you need backing without this, everything which you do is considered wrong. People have to stand behind their police department . . . Everytime a policeman uses force he thinks is necessary, you have persons and groups, clergy, jumping down him. This man is then thrown to the dogs. You then have people running about doing what they please. The laws should be strict.

This attitude is in direct contrast to the doubts experienced by a few policemen:

> There is not enough time or paper to explain it here. But we must examine ourselves. We must start to understand the problems of others and our own problems.

> Read a book and study Mexican, Indian, and Negro history, after that, take a look at the present, then and only then can you count on having a future.

Conclusion

Individual officers did not hesitate to express disagreement with department policy (or lack thereof) in regard to measures taken to quell the disturbances following the death of Dr. King. To the extent that such criticism is the result of frustration and confusion on the part of particular patrolmen, the Mobilization Plan is itself in need of adjustment with respect to coordination of four-man police cars, emergency radio communications and command authority in the field. In this sense, the Mobilization Plan is "successful" only when the individual policeman is not given time to worry about the significance of the behavior of the rioters—either in terms of disrespect for him personally, or in terms of his obligation to enforce the law.

The police observations which form the basis for this report were made nearly six weeks after the disturbances occurred. The residual degree of hostility expressed toward both the police department and the inhabitants of the riot-torn communities will no doubt reinforce the dilemma created when these same policemen, without prior experience or confidence in a particular community, are sent there to engage in the ticklish job of defusing a potentially serious disturbance. The complaining officers are now less capable of entering the black communities with a positive attitude toward the problems encountered by the inhabitants and will be less likely to develop an understanding of the tensions which produce disturbances. A strictly military approach to riot control, wherein the normal and discretionary law enforcement decisions of individual policemen are suspended, may therefore, be preferable when viewed in terms of the ongoing relationship between the community and the police.

The difficulty encountered by the Chicago police command in locating the center of the disturbances has been documented here. But even if the Mobilization Plan is implemented with a high degree of internal discipline and tactical precision in the future, success will continue to be doubtful because the plan's emphasis on mobility is simply an extension of a general reliance on vehicle "beat" patrol by the Chicago Police Department. During normal times, the department relies almost exclusively on private complaints to trigger deployment of police officers. As a result, police contact with law-abiding members of the Black community is severely limited. Ironically, the primary liability of this policy is revealed during civil disorders, when police are unable to identify responsible Black citizens or locate those stores which are likely to be looted due to poor community relations.

Perhaps the most compelling aspect of the police department's dilemma is its own failure to adopt a procedure which permits individual policemen to consciously discuss and acknowledge different attitudes, both among themselves and in the communities where they work. Few officers commented on their lack of contact with responsible members of the Black community, and it is doubtful that the extensive division of opinion among them about such matters as deadly force (Tables VI-VII), the existence of a conspiracy (Table IV), or the best way to prevent future riots is known to the respondents themselves. The hesitancy of the department to acknowledge the disagreement among its own personnel is probably due to the desire to maintain discipline and to control the behavior of individual officers with a rigorous system of reporting, record keeping, and exact knowledge of existing law. As a result, the division of opinion among policemen about issues covered in this study may simply be symptomatic of an inevitable unrest and frustration, which periodically find release in the violation of department regulations or through a loss of patience with individuals in the Black communities of Chicago.

Answers given by the policemen who volunteered to participate in the study of the riot in Chicago in April of 1968 show that at least 20,000 individuals probably participated actively in the looting. It is exceedingly difficult to state the duties of a policeman under such circusmtances and it is equally absurd to expect the policemen themselves to understand or accept the limitations of their own involvement in such chaos without extensive guidance from command personnel. As long as the latter were unable to handle the disturbances with crowd control techniques and were unequipped to initiate mass arrest procedures, the police in the field were simply told not to risk escalation of the conflict. In the early stages of the disturbance, many field commanders either did not realize the extent of the riot or else were afraid to admit to their own men that they were helpless —probably as a result of the fear that some of their personnel might engage in distasteful vigilante action. Such fear constitutes a serious lack of faith in the individual officer's capacity to understand the significance of the extensive unrest in the ghetto neighborhoods or to accept certain limitations on his own ability to restore order. At the height of the riot activity, the police department's reliance on discipline of its members to achieve control simply broke down, as many policemen were understandably shocked by the failure of their commanders to follow existing laws and regulations to the letter. It is this harm to their morale which did occur; it was the riot itself which directly challenged rigid assertion of department discipline as the most beneficial form of organization during the daily operation of the department.

If the Chicago police were encouraged to discuss the significance of the King riot in terms of the extent of their responsibility to the Black communities as well as to the maintenance of order in the city as a whole, the existing disagreement among the police themselves might be the basis for a greater awareness and acceptance of those cultural differences which have heretofore been the basis for frequent misunderstandings. More confidence in the police by their own commanders could induce more responsible and constructive police behavior, a change which would reduce the number of formal reporting procedures now used to instill discipline and maintain control. Both the community and the police might then overcome their tendency to view the police department as a monolithic, unresponsive institution. Under present conditions, the policeman's distrust of both his department and the Black community has only increased as a result of the riot which occurred in April, 1968.

CHAPTER 23

Juvenile Offenders: Special Problems

Edward Eldefonso

Edward Eldefonso is a Supervisor with the Santa Clara County Juvenile Probation Department, San Jose, California, and teaches police science courses at De Anza College. Mr. Eldefonso has authored or co-authored such words as *Law Enforcement and the Youthful Offender: Juvenile Procedures; Principles of Law Enforcement; Human Relations: Law Enforcement in a Changing Community; Police-Community Relations; Police and the Criminal Law;* and *An Introduction to Corrections: A Component of the Criminal Justice System* and is currently collaborating on *An Introduction to the Criminal Justice Process* and *The Criminal Justice Process: Human Approach.*

Although law enforcement agencies are accustomed to handling antisocial behavior pertaining to law violators, there are special problems which require considerably more flexibility and, due to their uniqueness, a great deal of cogitation. These are not the type of problems the police can handle in a more or less unvarying customary manner. Procedures for handling juvenile gangs, use of narcotics and alcoholic beverages by juveniles and the perplexing problem of sex offenses cannot be considered routine. Therefore, the prospective police officer should have some understanding of such problems.

Juvenile Gangs

The word gang has a long history in the United States, and some of that history sheds light on contemporary use of the term and on present social attitudes toward designated groups of adolescents throughout the country. In early English usage, *gang* was often employed as a synonym for

From Edward Eldefonso, *Law Enforcement and the Youthful Offender,* revised edition, 1973. Reprinted by permission of John Wiley & Sons, Inc., New York.

"a going," "a walking," or "a journey." In this sense, it traces its origin to the Scandinavian languages. As early as 1340, there was an Anglo-Saxon derivation which had a common meaning of "a number of things used together or forming a complete set." The above meanings were shortly combined so that gang came to stand for a crew of a ship or companies of mariners.

Although the word gang is usually associated with antisocial behavior or rebelling against authority, the gang in itself is not inherently vicious. Group activity is a necessary part of a growing child's life. The gang becomes dangerous if the street life from which it springs offers opportunities for delinquency, and if the leader of a gang is a bad influence. To the youngster who is in danger of becoming a delinquent, gang life often becomes particularly attractive. With others of his own age who may be as neglected as he is, he may get recognition and acceptance by adopting the ways of the gang. In such a manner, the goal he seeks—satisfaction—is obtained.

The influence of the gang, whether negative or positive, is particularly effective because it often completely answers the boy's needs. His desire for companionship and adventure is satisfied. He gets the feeling of belonging and of loyalty to the group. If the gang is delinquently orientated, the tougher he is the more recognition he gets. Furthermore, he may also find the discipline he needs. Gangs develop their own codes and rules of behavior, and demand that their members rigidly abide by them. Because a gang's control over boys' conduct often becomes stronger than that of their families or of the larger social group, attitudes and behavior patterns may result in delinquent activities.[1]

The etymology of the word "gang" provides a starting point from which to examine contemporary social views about juvenile gangs. The social views are constructed from an amalgam of fact, myth, and stereotype and, like all other such views, they tend to elicit and to preserve the process that they seek to describe. It is one of the noteworthy insights of social science that the isolation and labeling of forms of behavior tend to solidify, and sometimes increase, such behavior. Labeling provides a definitional framework in its recognition of a phenomenon, adding a further dimension to its previous characteristics. It is one thing to drink intoxicating beverages, but it is often quite another to violate the law by such behavior. It is one thing to hang around with a group of boys, but another thing to be a member of a gang; and the particular self and social definition imparted to the behavior may sometimes greatly affect the behavior itself.[2]

---

[1]J. E. Winters, *Crime and Kids* (Springfield, Illinois: Charles C. Thomas, 1959), p. 96.
[2]G. Geis, *Juvenile Gangs,* President's Committee on Juvenile Delinquency and Youth Crime (Washington, D.C.: Government Printing Office, June, 1965), p. 2.

Many attempts to indicate policies and lines of action that appear to offer the greatest hope for effective intervention with gangs whose activities have been defined as antisocial, or whose members appear to be caught up in a self-defeating way of life, have been extremely difficult. For one thing, generalizations derived from work with groups in particular areas are not necessarily applicable to other geographical areas. Gangs in Los Angeles, for instance, are notably more mobile, more automobile orientated, than gangs in New York or Chicago; therefore, programs directed toward a particular gang must take these factors into consideration.

Attempts to assess and to summarize even a fractional part of the literature, and to elicit training guidelines, must almost of necessity be tentative. As a first step, before looking at the issues involved directly with intervention work with gangs, an attempt will be made to review popular studies dealing with gangs so that the practitioner can familiarize himself with the present state of the field and place his own work into clear perspective.[3]

Gang Studies

A popular presentation of a delinquent gang as perceived by a layman was written by Harrison Salisbury, Pulitzer Prize winner, in a book, *The Shook-Up Generation,* after observing for a period of three months some of the juvenile gangs in New York. Salisbury pointed out that gangs often are "pitiful, tragic, dangerous," and that youth within them find it hard, if not impossible, to break away once a member.[4]

According to Salisbury, gangs are products of social deterioration and are mainly found in slum areas in the community. Lack of basic security in families, neighborhoods, and community life are experienced by the adolescent in these settings. The gang offers a dubious substitute for security which does not exist in the present and for which there is not promise in the future.

Salisbury indicated that there are means for working out the problems which have created delinquent gangs. He feels that the universal education principle is unrealistic in that youths learn at different rates and this creates great difficulty for the slow learner. Different children have different capacities and different chronological ages for maturation.

He also feels that social disorganization, which has occurred in many housing projects in the "slum" areas, may be improved by making the income requirements more flexible. This would help prevent mobility which is created by having families move when they reach a certain income bracket. Active social work would help to reduce conflict in the housing

---

[3] *Ibid.,* p. 3.
[4] H. E. Salisbury, *The Shook-Up Generation* (New York: Harper & Row, 1958), p. 42.

area and create more stability. Social programs would improve the house-keeping and family life habits of housing tenants and make such developments better places in which to live.

Schools, Salisbury insists, are in most instances the only place for security and refuge for the lower-class youth who is buffeted by poverty, family inadequacy, lack of formal and informal neighborhood organization.

Walter Miller, in his paper, "Lower-Class Culture as a Generating Milieu of Gang Delinquency,"[5] dealt with one type of delinquency that consisted of law-violating acts committed by members of adolescent street-corner groups in lower-class communities, and attributed this behavior to lower-class values. Miller attempted to show that the dominant component of motivation underlying these acts consisted in a direct attempt by the adolescent to adhere to forms of behavior, and to achieve standards of values as they are defined within the lower-class community itself. It is a long-established, distinctively patterned tradition with an integrity of its own rather than a so-called "delinquent subculture" which has arisen through conflict with the middle-class culture.

Miller presented six of the major concerns of lower-class culture, listed in degrees of explicit attention:

Trouble is of great concern in the lower-class population in that it results in the unwelcome or complicating involvement with official authorities or agencies of middle-class society. Substantial segments of the lower class, however, feel that "getting into trouble" is not in itself overtly defined as prestige, but as a means to an end.[6]

Toughness is demonstrated by physical prowess in which the lower-class individual exhibits strength and endurance and athletic skill. Masculinity is symbolized by a distinctive complex of acts and avoidance. Tattooing, absence of sentimentality, and non-concern with "art" and "literature" are indications of one's masculinity in the lower class.[7]

Smartness is the capacity of one to outsmart, outfox, outwit, dupe, or "con" another individual through maximum use of mental ability and a minimum use of physical effort. Examples of the individual in the lower class who utilizes this means for "success" are the professional gambler, the "con" artist, and the promoter.[8]

Excitement is an important characteristic feature of lower-class life which is expressed by the "night on the town" involving a pattern of activities in which alcohol, music, and sexual adventure are components.

---

[5]W. B. Miller, "Lower-Class Culture as a Generating Milieu of Gang Delinquency," *Journal of Social Issue*, Vol. XIV (Ann Arbor, Michigan: University of Michigan), p. 5.

[6]*Ibid.*, p. 8.

[7]*Ibid.*, p. 9.

[8]*Ibid.*, p. 11.

Fate is a characteristic in which lower-class individuals believe their lives are subject to a set of forces over which they have relatively little control. A distinction is made between two stages: being "lucky" or "in luck," and being "unlucky" or "jinxed."[9]

Autonomy, according to Miller, is a phenomenon in which the tough, rebellious independence often assumed by the lower-class person frequently conceals a powerful dependency craving. The adolescent street-corner group represents the adolescent variant of the lower-class social group. In many cases, it is the most stable and solidary primary group he has ever belonged to and provides a dependency on the peers faced with similar problems of adjustment.

Belonging is an important content of the lower-class group. One achieves "belonging" primarily by demonstrating knowledge of, and a determination to adhere to, the system of standards and valued qualities defined by the group. One maintains membership by acting in conformity with valued aspects of toughness, smartness, autonomy, etc.[10]

In conclusion, Miller states that the commission of crimes by members of adolescent street-corner groups is motivated primarily by the attempt to achieve ends, status, or conditions which are valued, and avoid those that are disvalued by the lower class.

Albert K. Cohen, in describing the development of a delinquent subculture in *Delinquent Boys,* calls attention to the crucial condition for the emergence of a new cultural form, as the existence in effective interaction with one another, of a number of individuals with similar problems of adjustment. These may be the entire membership of a group or only certain members similarly circumscribed within the group.[11] The adjustment problems of the working-class boy, according to Cohen, stem from the fact that he is unable to live in accordance with the middle-class standard of the dominant culture because of a disadvantageous social position.[12]

The working-class boy's problem is one of "status-frustration," the basis for which is created by early exposure to lower-class socialization. For example, middle-class value is to aspire to an occupational position of economic advantage and social prestige.

The working boy's aspirations are not necessarily considered a step toward economic mobility. Eventual "advancement" and "promotion" are not so important in the working class. "Planning" and "foresight" are often outside the range of values. The "pinch" of the present is far more demanding than the promise of the future. "Payoff" is considered an immediate

---

[9] *Ibid.,* p. 11.
[10] *Ibid.,* p. 14.
[11] A. K. Cohen, *Delinquent Boys,* (Glencoe, Illinois: The Free Press, 1955), p. 59.
[12] *Ibid.,* p. 135.

need, not eventual upgrading. The "ethic of responsibility" for the down-and-out in the family is imperative to the extent that one branch of the family will spend all it has for another in need, and the "law of reciprocity" holds, in that the same is expected in return in times of stress.

One is honest with particular persons, not honest in general. Persons in this socioeconomic group feel more at home in their own families and in their immediate neighborhood, and are ill-at-ease in secondary social contacts. Emotions appear to be released more spontaneously and there is free expression of aggression with no hesitancy to right. Little attempt is made to cultivate polish, sophistication, fluency, appearance, and personality, which are considered so necessary in the middle-class world.[13]

In contrast, the middle-class culture values ambition as a virtue and lack of it a serious defect. Responsibility is individual, and reliance and resourcefulness are considered essentials. Skills have to be developed so that there may be tangible achievements through outstanding performances, either in the scholastic, athletic, or the artistic areas. Forethought, conscious planning, and budgeting of time are considered of high value. Manners, courtesy, charm, and other skills in relationships are the basis for "selling of self" to others. Aggression is controlled, and violence and physical combat are frowned upon. Recreation has to be such that it is considered "wholesome," "constructive," and "not a waste of time." Property must be respected. To achieve status and success, Cohen states these are the ground rules of the prevailing culture in the United States.[14]

This socialization to lower-class values handicaps the working-class boy from achievement in the middle-class status system. Nevertheless, he must compete where achievement is judged by middle-class standards of behavior and performance.

The lower-class boy, relates Cohen, *finds the delinquent subculture a solution to his problems. It gives him a chance to belong, to amount to something, to develop his masculinity, to fight middle-class society.*

This solution for the "status-frustration" problem may not appear to be acceptable behavior, but it may appeal more than the already institutionalized solutions. When youngsters find it impossible to achieve status according to middle-class standards, they turn to development of "characteristics they do not possess and the kinds of conduct of which they are capable."[15]

Mob or gang action sets up its own "positive morality," a value structure to justify its conduct with a rapid transition into behavior accord-

---

[13] *Ibid.,* pp. 94-97.
[14] *Ibid.,* pp. 89-91.
[15] *Ibid.,* p. 65.

ing to the new "group standards" with emergence of a distinctive subculture.[16] These new values which emerge, according to Cohen, are opposed
to the larger cultural structure. The mechanism of "reaction formation"
takes place in which the delinquent seeks to obtain unequivocal status by
repudiating, once and for all, the norms of the middle-class culture.[17]

There is strong hostility and contempt for those who are not members
of the delinquent subculture. Anti-social behavior is indulged in simply
because it is considered disreputable by the dominant class. In order to gain
status in the delinquent gang, a member must constantly exhibit his defiance
of middle-class norms.

The corner-boy way of life "temporizes" with middle-class morality;
the full-fledged delinquent subculture does not. The boy who breaks clean
with middle-class morality has no inhibitions against aggressive and hostile
behavior toward the sources of his frustration. The corner boy who has not
embraced delinquent subculture and still compromises with middle-class
norms inhibits his hostility and aggression against the middle class. On the
other hand, delinquent subculture legitimatizes aggression.[18]

Cohen contends that the delinquent subculture is non-utilitarian, ma-
licious, and negativistic. By non-utilitarian, he means that the boys really
do not want the things they steal. They steal for the glory, for the "hell-
of-it," for the status. By malice, he means "an enjoyment in the discomfort
of others, a delight in the defiance of taboos." By negativistic, he means that
the delinquent subculture negates the values of the middle-class culture.
Other characteristics are short-run hedonism, by which he means that the
gang has very little interest in long-range goals, planned activity, practice
to develop skill and group autonomy, in which the gang has an intolerance
of restraints, except from the informal pressures within the group itself.
Relations with other groups tend to be indifferent, hostile, or rebellious.[19]

According to Cohen, the delinquent subculture is a solution to the
problems of status and success for the male rather than the female. Female
delinquency is usually involved with establishing a satisfactory relationship
with the opposite sex.

Intervention with Gangs

As previously indicated, some difficulty arises from attempts to generate ideas about gangs and work with gangs when the groups themselves
differ, often in radical and dramatic fashion, from one geographical locale
to another. Experimentation regarding different approaches to the understanding and the control of gang behavior has been carried on in various

[16] *Ibid.*, p. 66.
[17] *Ibid.*, p. 132.
[18] *Ibid.*, p. 23.
[19] *Ibid.*, pp. 25-28.

cities, and it would appear profitable to attempt to delineate some of these efforts against the background of their geographical setting. To do so, gang projects in New York City will be considered and, where appropriate, projects from other cities will be channeled into the presentation.

Most of the work with gangs in New York City today falls to the Youth Board. The efforts of the Board have been primarily directed toward the control of fighting or bopping gangs, a concentration that may indicate the more aggressive nature of gang behavior in New York, or may reflect the city's huge size and limited resources, necessitating a focus on those groups considered to be the most socially hazardous.

The New York City Youth Board was organized in 1947, and its earliest efforts to combat fighting gangs were carried on by means of subsidies to existing social agencies which were designed to encourage expansion of their on-going programs. This tactic proved ineffective, however, primarily because the established agencies were unable to set up the special kinds of undertakings necessary to cope with a problem which had not traditionally been defined as part of their assignment. The lesson concerning the tendency toward inflexibility in some social agencies, their inability to respond readily to new ideas and approaches, is one that must be kept in mind in all novel and imaginative programs. Procedures and paths must be discovered to deal with such institutional inertia—and often this is quite possible—or calculated steps must be taken to bypass such obstacles as expeditiously as possible.[20]

The Youth Board terminated its relationships with private agencies in 1950 and initiated a program of its own. Such programs involved assigning special "detached" workers into territories controlled by gangs, with instructions to the workers to establish a liaison with gang members and to exploit this liaison for the purpose of rechanneling gang activities into acceptable paths. The Youth Board assigned 11 workers to two high-delinquency areas in Brooklyn in 1950. The program proliferated rapidly and a decade later there were some 85 detached workers dealing with more than 100 gangs located throughout the city.[21]

According to the Youth Board, the prime goal of work with antisocial teenage gangs is the building of a bridge between the members of these groups and the community from which they have cut themselves off. From a handbook published by the Youth Board entitled *Reaching the Fighting Gang,* and enumerated in a publication by Hans W. Mattick and Nathan S. Caplan describing the rationale for the Chicago Youth Development Program, the philosophical aims of the Youth Board action program can be summarized as:[22]

---

[20]Geis, *Juvenile Gangs,* pp. 42-43.

[21]*Ibid.,* p. 43.

[22]*Ibid.,* p. 43.

1. To reduce the absolute amount of illegal and antisocial behavior attributable to the target population in the experimental area.

2. To change the behavior of individuals and groups in the contacted part of the target population, where necessary, from the more seriously antisocial to the less seriously, and from the less seriously antisocial to the conventional, within the class and the cultural norms of the local population.

3. To help individuals and groups in the contacted part of the target population meet their emotional needs for association, friendship, and status by providing conventionally organized and supervised activities for them, with a view to increasing their capacity for participation and autonomy.

4. To increase the objective opportunities for youth in the external environment, in the field of education, employment, and cultural experiences.

5. To help youth prepare themselves for conventional adult roles by providing guidance in the fields of education, work, family life, and citizenship through direct intervention in their life processes, especially in times of crises.

6. To relate the target population to local adults and institutions in positive ways so that communication channels between youth and adults may be developed through which a shared, conventional system of values may be transmitted.

7. To develop in parents and local adults a concern for local problems affecting youth welfare, and to organize them with a view to having them assume responsibility for the solution of local problems.

8. To create a positive change in attitude in both youth and adults, about the possibility of local self-help efforts to improve the local community, through active and cooperative intervention in community processes, and thus to create a more positive attitude toward the local community itself.[23]

There is a certain similarity between the Chicago goals and a more general operating statement preferred in New York by the Youth Board:[24]

Street club members can be reached and will respond to sympathy, acceptance, affection, and understanding when approached by adults who possess these characteristics and reach out to them on their own level.

The positive relationship that is developed between an adult worker and a street club can serve as a catalytic agent for modifying antisocial attitudes and behavior. This relationship can also be used to help the individual member meet his needs in more positive ways.

[23] *Ibid.*, p. 44.
[24] *Ibid.*, pp. 44-45.

According to the Youth Board in New York, there is no single simple formula for establishing initial liaison with gangs, but the most successful approach seems to stem from the suggestion that the particular circumstances be allowed to dictate the opening appeal of the worker to the boys. According to the Youth Board, there are various ways of establishing contact. Among these are hanging around, direct introduction, agency referral, referral by a service group, self-referral, and, during an emergency, self-introduction. These initial and beginning relationships are usually developed through marginal participation in group activities and conversation. One develops relationships through offering and providing services, by sharing personal information, by meeting the members' suspicions and tests, and dealing with them understandingly. If the worker can accept the group, their games, new foods, new dress habits or fads, he is moving toward acceptable contact with the group and its members.[25]

Having learned through experience, the Youth Board advises workers to select for initial contact those individuals who seem either to be more amenable, the most important, or the most available. There need be no concern if initial contact is not made with the leader, but instead with individuals more toward the outer fringes of the gang structure. Such persons will, if all goes well, represent channels of access to the upper echelons of the gang hierarchy. There will, of course, be continuous testing of the worker, attempts to determine the sincerity and the particular limits of his tolerance for the group and its behavior, and to establish with some precision the ground rules under which the worker is operating. It is obviously crucial that the worker himself know more or less exactly and establish clearly what these boundaries and principles are so that he can function properly and effectively.[26]

During the many years the Youth Board has been in operation there have been some conclusions and speculation regarding gang activities in areas falling under its jurisdiction. It is noted that two particular long-run trends merit notice. The first relates to the apparent change in the nature of youth gangs in New York, and perhaps elsewhere, particularly in relation to the emphasis on aggression and the movement toward the use of narcotic drugs. The second relates to the change in the role of girl auxiliaries to boys' gangs.

Nationwide surveys by leading authorities suggest that gang fighting is on the decline throughout the United States. There were said to be more than 500 fighting gangs in 29 high-hazard areas in New York City less than five years ago. Today, the number is put at about 130, with these showing quite varying characteristics. The Assassins of Manhattan's Park West area may be taken as a typical example of the transition. In 1959, the Assassins

---

[25] *Ibid.,* pp. 46-47.
[26] *Ibid.,* p. 47.

were involved in the worst outbreak of teen-age warfare New York had experienced in years. Because of the outbreak, many of their leaders were taken into custody by the police. The police crackdown is said to have contributed to the alleviation of aggression among the Assassins, and the growing number of gangs in more remote areas brought neighboring gangs, formerly intense rivals, into more relaxed relationships in the face of a defined common enemy.[27]

The Assassins changed their name to Socializers, and gradually shifted to more mild-mannered pursuits, keeping in line with their new look as a "cool" group:

> We're cool because everyone wants to grow up without worrying about it. The guys want to be like grown up. When I was jailed for carrying a zip gun, that was time wasted, man. You can't bring back that lost time. You can waste yourself, man.

Today, investigation reveals that all the boys who replaced the former Assassins in the area, as they outgrew gang membership, smoke marijuana. It is estimated that about 20 per cent use heroin more or less regularly. Use of drugs may, of course, represent even less desirable performance than the former pattern of fighting, which may at least have drained off hatreds and energies which, without outlet now, are turned to escapist stratagems through narcotics. If this is the case, it would be an indication of some of the complex social issues involved in *intervention programs* and the necessity to ascertain that they are directed to deal with basic underlying problems rather than only with manifest issues.

Drug addiction, among other things, usually results in the isolation of the addict from members of the gang partly because of his presumed unreliability in fulfilling group demands, and partly because of his vulnerability to arrest and to police pressures. Entry by a gang worker is a complicated problem because of the all-absorbing life of an addict.[28]

The second major change in New York gangs concerns the altered role of girl gangs. Girls affiliated with gangs, either formally or informally, represent a resource for good or bad that probably has not yet been adequately tapped. For one thing, it is believed that marriage, as much as anything else, tends to draw many boys from gang activity, partly from a sense of increased maturity, and partly because the girl offers feminine objections to the expenditure of time and money and to the dangers which may be involved in some gang associations. Girls in this sense become socializing forces. Walter Miller, has also pointed out in *Lower-Class Culture as a Generating Milieu of Gang Delinquency* that some gang members

---

[27] *Ibid.,* p. 48.
[28] *Ibid.,* p. 48.

use marriage as an excuse (and one which is oddly acceptable) for diminished participation in gang activities:

> One recently-married corner boy stated, "Sure, I'd like to go out drinking, but the old lady would kill me! She'd drag me out by my ear if I went into a bar!" She was not, of course, strong enough to do this, but the legitimacy of the "old lady's demand" was recognized by the group.

At the same time, younger girls in New York are said to be more often of late forming gangs of their own, and these gangs have become increasingly handmaidens of male lawbreaking. It is estimated by the Youth Board that some 8,000 New York boys are in gangs and, that the number of girl gang members is now 3,000. There is as yet very little work done by the Youth Board among the girls.[29]

Nearly all the girl gangs constitute units of boy gangs and use a variant of the same name. If the boys call themselves the Dead Beats, for example, the girls may name themselves the Dead Beats Debs, or Debutantes, or the Dead Beatrices. The girls' roles include those of weapon carriers and weapon concealing, sexual intimacy with the boys, prostitution to obtain money for narcotics for themselves and for their boy friends, and courier and errand-girl chores. Status in girl gangs generally accrues in terms of the rank of the girl's boy friend in his own gang; the higher his standing, the better her position will be. In this respect, the girls are said to be particularly resistive to efforts to work with them because of their special need for gang-derived security. They are also reported to be more responsible for fighting than was true in an earlier period. Sometimes they falsely claim that they were mistreated or approached by members of rival gangs in order to stir up trouble and create excitement about themselves.[30]

Increased aggressiveness of the behavior of girls associated with gangs in New York thus represents one among many new patterns emerging in that city. Some will find their way elsewhere, others have already begun in different areas, and some will remain peculiarly restricted to the city of their origin. Together, they may be blended into a general portrait of gang activity and, as previously indicated, they must be examined with great care in establishing proper procedures for intervention with gangs wherever such work is undertaken.

Experiences from cities other than New York shed additional light and perspective upon work with gangs. In Los Angeles, gang intervention programs are under the auspices of the Group Guidance Section of the Los Angeles County Probation Department, representing an administrative arrangement different from that usually found elsewhere. There has always

---

[29] *Ibid.*, pp. 50-51.
[30] *Ibid.*, p. 51.

been a lack of agreement among researchers as to the basic aspects of juvenile gang dynamics, and the fact that what is known about them is based on information collected in other geographical areas prompted the decision of the Los Angeles County Probation Department Research Office to go directly to the gang boys themselves for information about juvenile gangs. The Los Angeles Probation Department assumed that the best method of gaining a better understanding of the etiology and dynamics of the local gangs was to interview in depth several juvenile gang leaders. Such an approach resulted in an excellent publication[31] which will serve as a guide for the following discussion on gang activities in Los Angeles.

Joining the Gang

The Los Angeles Probation Department Research Office ascertained that although there was great variety in the reasons for gang involvement, there were also common elements. Among the diverse reasons were: (1) some boys followed in the footsteps of their brothers; (2) some reactivated dormant gangs; (3) some joined because their friends belonged; (4) some joined as a group from another club or gang; and (5) in one occasion, it was ascertained that one boy helped originate the group.[32]

The common elements included: the proximity of the mothers' residences, the existing personal ties among the members, and the almost accidental character of their involvement. In most cases, it appeared that the boys just "drifted" into gang membership.

One boy described how he met members of the Twenties every morning on the street corner, and finally, started to "hang around" with them. Later, he was "hanging around" when the Twenties became involved in a fight with the Businessmen, and was thereafter considered to be a member. His membership was fully established when he was an accomplice in a robbery of bus transfers worth $1.50. Here is how the boy described it:[33]

> At first, I cut it loose; I wasn't in any gang, but I used to just associate with them, you know. And so we got into this little fight with this Businessmen, and, you know, I helped; so I might as well consider myself as one of them. And then, we robbed that bus and went to jail and came out. Ever since then, we was big enough, you know.

Another boy described how he "hung around" with the Caballeros and the Midnight Choppers, two of the gangs attending his high school. However, neither of these groups interested him enough to seek formal membership; instead, he attempted to start his own "social club" which

---

[31] R. E. Rice and R. B. Christensen, *The Juvenile Gang: Its Structure, Function and Treatment,* Los Angeles County Probation Department Research Office, Report No. 24, 1965.
[32] *Ibid.,* p. 9.
[33] *Ibid.,* pp. 9-10.

lasted six months and then collapsed due to internal friction. This club was probably a "spontaneous gang" as some of its members were described as taking "some stuff" and were "kind of messed up." After the club broke up, most of the members joined an established gang, the Road Dancers.[34]

Two youngsters who followed in the footsteps of their older brothers gave some hints as to how gangs become traditional. Their descriptions of initial gang involvement are almost identical; here is one:[35]

> The Rebel Rousers, oh, well, came from our older brothers. They started it, and, when we got old enough, we took it over. I'd say I was about seven years old. I don't know when they first got together but I know when they first called themselves the Rebel Rousers, and my brother was one and I was one. When the club first started, I never run around as much as my brothers did, but I was a member. Most everybody was close together in age, you know. My brother's only three years older than I am. Since I was 13, I was involved in the fights.

The above quotation reveals one of the ways in which gangs are transmitted from year to year, a procedure which can, and often does, continue for generations.

Interviews with an older gang member who had reactivated a dormant gang revealed that the young inheritors of that traditional gang displayed a great deal of hostility toward "retired" members and attempted to pass themselves off as "tougher" than the older boys. The older member stated:[36]

> I know quite a few of the fellows in the present gang, but no real connection. They just considered us one of the older fellows. They don't consider anybody one of the greats, they try to tell us older fellows that the present club members are as great as anybody that has ever been in the club; but we don't believe them. Especially one of the younger groups, it's called the Midgets. They keep telling us they are the greatest. They try to say they fight more. Although I can remember when there were just younger fellows, we used to have more or less interclub squabbles, or just free-for-alls, us against them, we'd be in different groups, and I can't see where they're growing any tougher as the years have aged them.

Such competitive toughness is basically attributed to a great deal of tradition within their respective club.

The research completed by the Los Angeles Probation Department further reveals that the boys described above are from the southwest part of Los Angeles, an area of few and more recent gangs. Therefore, it has been

---

[34] *Ibid.,* p. 10.
[35] *Ibid.,* p. 11.
[36] *Ibid.,* p. 13.

only in the past several years that the traditional gang has become a factor in this part of the county; in previous years many spontaneous groups were formed, but they were easily dispersed or would lose momentum and disintegrate by themselves.[37]

In East Los Angeles, according to the Los Angeles Probation Department, the conditions are quite dissimilar and most gangs in this area have been in existence for two or more generations. The density is greater and each gang tends to incorporate a smaller geographical area. Until recently, the groups in this area, along with those in San Fernando Valley, have been the most violent in the county. It was gang activity in East Los Angeles that induced the Board of Supervisors to establish the Delinquency Prevention Unit within the Los Angeles County Probation Department in 1943.

The compact nature of the East Los Angeles gangs, along with the vase network of organized youth, has resulted in the situation which markedly affects the manner in which a boy is inducted into the gang. There is often a pattern of amalgamation of smaller gangs into one or more large groups, and often this territorial expansion leads to the destruction of their rival gangs. These amalgamations and expansions have something of the qualities of international treaties and invasions.[38]

It should be pointed out that there is a propensity for the youths to move from one gang to another. Such movement may be repeated several times during their adolescence. One of the interviewees from the East Los Angeles area describes his membership experience with several gangs as follows:[39]

> I must have been about 15 when I joined a big gang, or 14. But before that, I used to be from the Mariaches, it was small time. . . . I learned about 'em, let's see now, I moved in, you know, I didn't know they existed before. But as soon as I started hanging around with the guys, my neighbor especially, we're the ones that used to be pretty close, and there's this other club we used to belong to, from there we met some guys from the Mariaches and we got in. I was 13 when I went in there. This first one, I didn't last very long 'cause, as I said, it was small time, and we started seeing some bigger ones, so you get interested; I guess I lasted in the Mariaches about six, seven months in there. And when I initiated to get out ('Initiated out' usually requires a ritualistic beating by the gang members), I wanted to get out . . . and, well, this other guy, me and my neighbor friend, we used to be pretty tight, and he, well, he's the one that introduced us to the Lomitas. I was in there three years. But, before we was the Lomitas, we used to be the Chatos, from Fortieth Street, see, in our group, the Chatos transferred to the Lomitas and our 40 guys were Lomitas.

---

[37] *Ibid.*, p. 14.
[38] *Ibid.*, p. 14.
[39] *Ibid.*, p. 15.

Before the minor mentioned above had reached the age of 15 he had belonged to four separate gangs or groups, and at no time after age 12 was he without a group of organized peers. The minor eventually chose a gang with a reputation for long-standing violence and trouble in the community. After leaving the Lomitas, he joined two sponsored gangs and played an active role in each.

Another youngster who was raised in the vicinity where gangs flourished in the east part of Los Angeles refused to be inducted into a gang for several years. This youngster was subsequently harassed by the gang's membership. At the age of 16, this youngster started a club consisting of 30 boys, called the Diamontes, which met at Laguna Park for recreational and social activities. However, the pressure increased on him to join the Little Valley Gang which he had previously refused. Subsequently, his own club was often attacked by the Little Valley Gang. Unable to defend themselves, the Diamontes solicited the aid of two gangs operating in the same territory, and with whom they were friendly. These gangs, the Varrio Nuevo and the Headhunters, were feuding with the Little Valley Gang at the time, so they took up the defense of the Diamontes. Eventually, this led to the merging of the Diamontes with the Varrio Nuevo. According to R. E. Rice and S. Addams, who made a definitive study of this gang in "The Correctional Cost of Service and Unservice Gangs," this "harassed youngster" eventually became one of its leaders and, during the next three years the Varrio Nuevo became one of the most notorious in the East Los Angeles area.

The Los Angeles Probation Department researchers obtained five pages of transcript narration regarding the description of the complex story of this particular gang leader's gradual involvement in a gang. The gang leader summed it up as follows:[40]

> Well, the guys from Varrio Nuevo started moving into the park. And the guys from the Little Valley started moving toward the valley. They started pushing 'em back. This was in the summer of '58, and that's when I got into the gang. All of the guys from the park went down to the Estrada Courts, and the guys from the Varrio Nuevo, they said that if the Headhunters didn't break up and join the Varrio Nuevo, well, they would have to, you know, march. At that time, march meant get beat up or somethin'. And, at that time, the Headhunters had 150 guys, but they were all young, you know, and the guys from the Varrio Nuevo, they were more, you know, these guys have been fightin' for years, since early '40's. And they're younger boys, well, right now, the youngest guy's from Varrio Nuevo, they're 23. And they said we're goin' to need younger guys and you got to either break up or come in with us or don't come around—move out someplace else, you know, because they said that the Little Valley, we've got 'em on the go now and we want to keep 'em

---

[40] *Ibid.*, p. 17.

that way. We've already took over the park but we ain't got that many guys, you know. So we got together, the guys from the park, we had 30 guys, and the guys from the Headhunters, they had quite a few guys. So we went down to the court and decided whether we're going to get into the Varrio Nuevo or not. We got to the point, we said okay.

In Los Angeles County, Juvenile Probation Department researchers ascertained that there were two factors in joining a gang. One is the "drifting-in" quality of involvement. This, according to the experts in the gang research field, is considered quite unusual in that it has long been recognized by workers in the field that induction into a structured gang was usually a formal ritualistic event in the lives of its members. This position was subscribed to by such experts as William F. Whyte, author of *Streetcorner Society: the Social Structure of an Italian Slum;* Frederic M. Thrasher, author of *The Gang;* and Robert Summers, author of an article entitled, "Juvenile Gang Activity in Los Angeles County." There was nothing in the interviews conducted by Los Angeles researchers which supported the belief of formal ritualistic initiation.

The other factor is well known to street workers, and deals with the apparently high motivation that gang members have to join a group that is outside the mainstream of the dominant adolescent culture.[41]

There are many functions of gangs, most notably the social functions, defensive functions, and fighting. It appeared that the social functions were quite important in filling a large void in the lives of its members. Such functions were disorganized and the social activities were summed up by the Rebel Rousers:[42]

> When the club first got started, we didn't have no specific activities, you know, like every day we'd go over to the park and lay down and talk and drink all day. Not many 12-year-old boys go around drinking wine; but 'cause everybody else did it, I did it too. Maybe on weekends, everybody goin' to a swimmin' pool or somethin'. We usually stayed at one another's house, and stayed together most of the time, play cards, something like that. Everybody just stay at home during the day time, and come out at night. We'd go down to the park and talk. At night, them that was goin' to school they'd come down to the park.

It can be assumed that these types of social and delinquent activities were closely correlated. Considering the activities of gang members, it is not difficult to understand how violence follows the drinking of alcoholic beverages. On numerous occasions, the interviewees mentioned use of intoxicating beverages and the subsequent violent behavior of the indulgent members.

---

[41]*Ibid.,* p. 19.
[42]*Ibid.,* p. 21.

It is difficult to separate the social and defensive purpose of the gang due to the fact that social activities usually resulted in members defending themselves from aggressive acts. According to the researchers, the accounts of interviews made it quite difficult to determine whether fighting associated with dances and party crashing was more important than the social events themselves. The boys, however, mentioned each as a separate and mutually exclusive function of the gang. A Midnight Chopper told of the defensive aspect of the gang in these words:[43]

> There was really no major purpose for the gang. I think it was just all —everybody gettin' tired of bein' pushed around by other fellows, you know. They were willing to fight for their rights, but they just didn't have enough strength to.

Gang membership, according to certain members, might enhance the possibilities of a member being attacked by another juvenile. The concept that a boy's chances of being attacked are increased, rather than decreased, through gang membership is expressed more colorfully by the non-gang member. His comments were:[44]

> They know that when they don't get in it (the gang), they know that they're safe. If they do git in it, they know they ain't safe. They know that man gonna' always be on their tail. There's always gonna' be someone lookin' for 'em from another gang, no matter what gang they're in. A lotta guys say they gonna' join for protection, shoot, let 'em go in. Some of 'em do join gangs just for protection, but that's some protection.

Although the above might imply otherwise, the defensive aspect of the group, however, cannot be overlooked. The very fact that all the gang leaders described defense as one of the main purposes of the gang makes the concept itself important.

Fighting seemed to permeate all activities. This function, although unmentioned as either a direct or indirect purpose of the gang, had been amplified in activities such as party crashing, expansion of territory, defensive activities, and revenge. It is apparent, however, that the violence was not always planned. Over the past years, experience in working with gangs in Los Angeles County reveals that in most instances violence is an unplanned and situational occurrence.

Here is how a Rebel Rouser told of the feelings he had when fighting:[45]

---

[43] *Ibid.*, p. 24.
[44] *Ibid.*, p. 24.
[45] *Ibid.*, p. 28.

The feeling you get in a fight—you could call it excitement. You felt proud 'cause you fightin' for your name, you know. Protect your name, protect your part of town. You know, you be proud to stand up and fight for your name.

This quotation and others not included clearly indicate that violence is apparently one of the primary functions of gangs, and not a secondary one. At the same time, the lack of affect shown by these youths while describing some of their most violent activities may reflect a desire to repress memories of this behavior.

The city of Chicago has had a considerably longer and more intensive experience with gang work programs than Los Angeles. It was there that the Area Project, known sometimes as the Back-of-the-Yards Program, was first undertaken by Clifford Shaw in 1929.[46] This effort was designed to involve local residents as deeply as possible in the resolution of problems in their own neighborhoods.

The basic rationale of the Area Project was that the program regards as indispensable to the success of welfare activity, in general, and delinquency prevention, in particular, the participation of those who form a significant part of the social world of the recipients of help. This is seen not as a prescription of a panacea, but as a condition for progress in finding a solution. The program has remained experimental in the sense that it has continued to explore the question: What kind of participation is necessary on the part of which kinds of persons in terms of social role in the local society? But it has rested firmly and consistently on the conviction that no solution of a basic and lasting character is possible in the absence of such participation.

The Chicago Area Project stresses programs for recreation for children of the neighborhood and campaigns for community improvement. The project is also concerned about delinquency prevention and the neighborhood groups assist other agencies with their work, visit boys' community training schools, and provide support for parolees and persons similarly requiring assistance. Twenty-five years after its inception, the impact of the ground-breaking Chicago Area Project must remain somewhat speculative because of the difficulty of careful evaluation of such an endeavor.

It is extremely difficult to reach concrete conclusions as to when the intervention programs are at a point which would guaranty success. Such difficulty is attributed to the diversity of programs directed toward gangs, the complex nature of their ingredients, and the punitive nature of research findings. However, a number of general observations can be safely put forward.

---

[46]C. Shaw., *Delinquency Areas* (Chicago: Chicago University Press, 1929).

Boys, according to studies, will respond more readily to persons who are not severely detrimental; that is, individuals who do not criticize or condemn the habits and general deportment of the gang member. Standards and values adhered to by the intervention worker are not easily transmitted to persons with whom he works. Training, combined with experience and built upon original qualifications, represents the most desirable amalgam for effective gang work.

There are, generally, two types of programs: formal and informal. Formal programs tend to emphasize enhancement of skills, participation and success in relationships with various institutional segments of society, such as the world of employment or that of education, as well as family adaptations. Informal arrangements are usually directed toward creating greater ease and comfort in living, with the underlying belief that such items serve to create, besides law-abiding behavior, additional success in adjustment to the institutional structures.[47]

Agencies directing intervention programs will undoubtedly establish general operational guidelines. In all probability, their emphasis will be upon the particular strengths of the staff, the needs of the gang members, and the services and resources available in different geographical areas. Information presented here regarding such programs has endeavored to indicate major themes and patterns in various undertakings so as to provide some indication of what is being done and what might be potentially useful elsewhere, as well as to point out the wide range of approaches possible and the fact that it is not necessary to remain inexorably tied to a procedure which has proven to be a failure.

Police Role

As this chapter has attempted to point out, neither punitive methods nor adult-sponsored recreational programs are adequate in coping with street gangs. Revenge or simple punishment will not deter antisocial activities. Such methods only increase tensions and make behavior more hostile and aggressive. The main difficulties facing athletic-recreational and leisure-time programs is that the youngsters who need them the most are usually not participants in adult-sponsored activities of this kind. Such activities usually attract youngsters who have not displayed delinquent tendencies. Furthermore, many agencies that are attempting to organize programs with the delinquent youngster are not equipped to integrate into their total programs those autonomous street gangs which have already developed patterns of aggressive behavior. If the punitive approach is unsound, and if the provision of recreation through agencies tends to be ineffective, what other methods could be utilized and where do the police fit in?

---

[47]Geis, *Juvenile Gangs,* p. 58.

Law enforcement agencies throughout the United States recommend that an area project approach be adopted. The reason for such a recommendation is quite practical. Under the coordinating council program, each area of the community would have a committee composed of a cross-section of persons living in that particular neighborhood, including representatives of social agencies, schools, labor unions, churches, police, fraternal, and business organizations. One good example of this approach are the area programs being set up by the Economic Opportunity Commission (a federally subsidized agency) throughout the United States. Such an intervention group would have the objective of developing local resources to meet the needs of street gangs in that particular area. It should stimulate community action toward removing those factors in various neighborhoods which are inimical to the full development of a secure democratic way of life for all residents in the neighborhood.

The area in which the police can be quite helpful would be the identification of potential antisocial gangs and the transmitting of such information to trained workers sent into the streets to work with these gangs. The police should endeavor to obtain information concerning members, background information, prior criminal history, if any, and extensive information on gang leaders. This approach obviously calls for tact on the part of the investigating officer. These groups generally resent those in authority, and it must be impressed upon each group and its leaders that the objective of the officers is not to take the course of punitive action but to assist the area committee in supplying information concerning the gangs, their members, purposes, and desires.[48]

The area committee, with all information obtainable, would then direct the workers to try to direct the clubs along socially constructive lines. If the members of the gang respond positively to accepting understanding adults, the relationships with such adults would serve as a powerful force for personal and social adjustment.[49]

It is unfortunate that in many areas the lack of trained workers may make it necessary for someone else to attempt to perform this task. The police, then, have no alternative but to enter this field. Certainly, under most conditions, the police should not become directly involved in intervention work. However, if there is no other agency available, then someone must take the initiative if effective action against undesirable gang conditions is to be instituted. The approach utilized by the police would be that used by trained intervention workers. The police should relinquish this particular role as soon as some other agency can assume this task.

The following are suggestions offered by Inspector John E. Winters,

---

[48]Winters, *Crime and Kids*, p. 98.
[49]*Ibid.*, p. 99.

commanding officer, Youth Aide Division, Metropolitan Police Department, Washington, D.C., to police officers assigned to gang investigations:[50]

1. The investigating officer should not approach a gang with predetermined ideas and suggestions. Because the officer may be in a position to suggest rooms for club meetings, halls for dances, or locations for athletic activities, knowledge of the neighborhood and its resources is a must. Such referrals should only be done, however, if the group expresses a desire for such facilities.

2. The officer must become acquainted with members individually. The individual needs of the youngsters must be determined in order to make intelligent referrals to vocational, case-work, or psychiatric services, and seek assistance of the court if necessary.

3. The most important "tool" of an officer investigating gang activities is his ability to relate to gang members. The officer should have the type of personality which would enable him to converse and develop rapport with young people. He should be democratic, and able to accept the difference between his standards and those of the group without imposing his thinking or ideology upon them. Club members should not be protected from their responsibilities for, or the consequences of, their antisocial acts.

4. Understanding of procedures of various social services available in the community is an important part of an officer delegated to gang investigations.

5. The police should work in close cooperation with the area committee, if there is one; consult with specialists in case work, group work, and psychiatry.

6. The ultimate objective would be a self-governing federation of the various clubs in each area. This is important because through federation, the clubs' own leadership can be unified and steered toward constructive goals. In short, the police should function to gain the acceptance and confidence of these clubs and then use all the means at their disposal to work toward their objectives. These objectives, according to Inspector Winters, should be:
   a. The opportunity for the club to enjoy the normal adolescent group life that the street club potentially offers its members.
   b. The gradual development on the part of the club members of the feeling that they are needed and important members of the community and that they have a real part to play in the job of making their neighborhood a happier, more comfortable, more secure place in which to live.

---

[50] *Ibid.*, p. 99.

c. The opportunity for club members to develop a close relationship with accepting and understanding police officers, and to create in the minds of these young people that the police want to help, not prosecute.

The above recommendations offered by Inspector Winters are made on the premise that when there are other agencies available, the police should not enter the treatment field. Although there is no reason for law enforcement officers not to strike up friendly relationships with these groups, apprise interested citizens of the needs of groups, and provide whatever assistance is possible to those who are in the treatment field, it should be pointed out that treatment should be delegated to those who are trained to assume this role.

According to Inspector Winters, it must be borne in mind that:[51]

Though this approach has been successful in some communities, there are those hardbitten, sophisticated, and antisocial groups of young adults and teen-agers who would not respond to any approach. They are believed to consist of only a small percentage of the total. The only action that can be taken against these groups is constant surveillance, arrest, and prosecution for unlawful acts. In any determination of police action in a given situation, the welfare of the community must take precedence over the individual. For this reason, all investigations into group situations, whether designed to provide help for the group or to develop sufficiently for prosecution, should be made a matter of record.

Inspector Winters further states:[52]

A file should be maintained in the office of the juvenile unit. This file should identify groups by name and location. Cards on individual members should contain information relating to that individual such as any prior record of criminal activity or reports received on misbehavior, truancy, etc., the results of consultations with parents (a good technique that has produced constructive results), the school attended, etc. It has been established that the mere recording of pertinent information concerning a gang member has a deterring effect on the member with relation to antisocial activity. This file should not be a public record and should not be used as a basis for punitive action except where absolutely necessary. Its main purpose would be to furnish information to the community's coordinating council and, through that council, to the various area committees.

The fact remains that the police department's first approach to a gang situation should be that of a helping agency; i.e., assisting other agencies and

---

[51]*Ibid.,* p. 101.
[52]*Ibid.,* p. 101.

groups to redirect the gang's activities into constructive channels. However, it is the responsibility of the law enforcement agency to utilize aggressive and consistent action if intervention programs fail and the interest of the community are being threatened.

Adolescent Drug Addiction

During the last decade, there has been a continuous increase in the number of adolescents in our society, particularly in the large metropolitan areas, who have become involved in the use of narcotics. This has produced much controversy and discussion in this country, perhaps the most emotionally alarming one has been the nature of its relationship to criminality. This relationship has become the focus of even greater attention in these post war years, as the use of narcotics has spread in almost epidemic proportions among some sectors of our adolescent and young adult population, and as these youthful addicts, in ever-increasing numbers, have become involved in altercations with law enforcement agencies for violations of the narcotic drug laws and for other criminal offenses.

What is the nature of the adolescent who becomes involved in the use of drugs? Although the drug addict is not an individual who has remained aloof from crime, he is rarely many of the sensational things portrayed in the public mind. Those who have worked with the adolescent drug addict recognize him as an emotionally sick individual whose difficulties relate back to a life history of social and emotional maladjustment.

Extent of the Problem: Youthful World of Drugs[53]

Many thousands of Americans are addicted or habituated to alcohol, narcotics and other kinds of drugs. In New York City alone, there are an estimated 25,000 addicts. It has been calculated that New York City's addicts must raise from $500,000 to $700,000 per day to support their habit. To do so, many turn to such crimes as robbery, shoplifting, burglary, forgery, and prostitution. Although less severe, the picture is comparable in Chicago, Los Angeles, Detroit, and other major cities. Most qualified observers agree that the total consumption of drugs is increasing. Their estimates vary. Charles Hollander, Director of drug studies for the U.S. National Student Association in Washington, D.C., states: "Drug use has become so frequent among college students that it has regulated sexual activity to second place in popularity." Hollander further states that marihuana is a prime favorite, and independent research conducted during the 1967–68 Fall semester indicates an increased trend toward it. As an exam-

---

[53]E. Eldefonso, *Youth Problems and Law Enforcement* (Englewood Cliffs, New Jersey: Prentice-Hall, Inc., 1971.)

ple, Hollander cites reports that 20 percent of students at the University of Wisconsin at Milwaukee had admitted drug use; that one-third of nearly 10,000 students polled at the University of California at Los Angeles admitted smoking marihuana; and that 25 percent of 150 students in Essex County, New Jersey, had used marihuana or amphetamines—pep pills. *Newsweek's* February 1970 issue writes about the problem:

> The drug revolution, barely begun on college campuses a few years ago, has already swept the Nation's high schools, the use of drugs, particularly marihuana, is now an accepted fact of life from anywhere from 30 to 50 percent of all U.S. secondary-school students. "I'd compare buying dope today," says Eric Nelson, one of the brightest seniors at Newton (Mass.) High School, "with buying the school newspaper."
>
> Last month, surveys by both high school students and administrators pointed up just how widespread drug use really is. At Greenwich (Conn.) High School, the student newspaper took a sample of homeroom classes and reported that 46 percent of all seniors had smoked marihuana, 10 percent had tried LSD, and three percent had used heroin. "We do it," said a Greenwich senior who has already been accepted at the University of Connecticut, "because it's here, because we like it, and because it's one way to tell the grown-up world to go to hell." In Gross Pointe Park, Mich., a wealthy suburb of Detroit, school officials surveyed 2,650 students from the fifth through twelfth grades, and ended up with similar findings. About half the seniors had used drugs at least once; frequent users often start in the eighth and ninth grades, and most students obtain drugs from friends without spending money and usually get them in their own or friends' homes.

Although marijuana remains the favorite student drug (cost $20.00 an ounce—increase of $8 from last year and containing approximately 25 to 30 joints, or cigarettes), students also utilize mescaline (a form of peyote), speed (usually Methedrine), and LSD. Stimulants and depressants—"ups" and "downs" are also popular in high schools. The stimulants—amphetamines (diet pills, Dexedrine and Benezedrine) induce great bursts of energy and, quite frequently, are usually ingested before strenuous activities, such as sporting events or examinations. However, when the aforementioned drugs wear off, the user often has a difficult time. Therefore, a depressant is utilized—barbiturates. The "downs" include Seconal and Tuinals, both of which produce euphoria—an abnormal state of well-being and contentment not warranted by an individual's actual circumstances. Because "ups" and "downs" are only ten to fifteen cents each, the average student does not encounter any difficulty in acquiring money for his supply.

Heroin, which causes powerful addiction, long considered the affliction of the criminal, the derelict, the debauched, is increasingly attacking America's children. A New York City health official states that the medical profession has not accorded enough attention to devising ways to prevent

Table 1.—Percent of Young People Experimenting with Marijuana

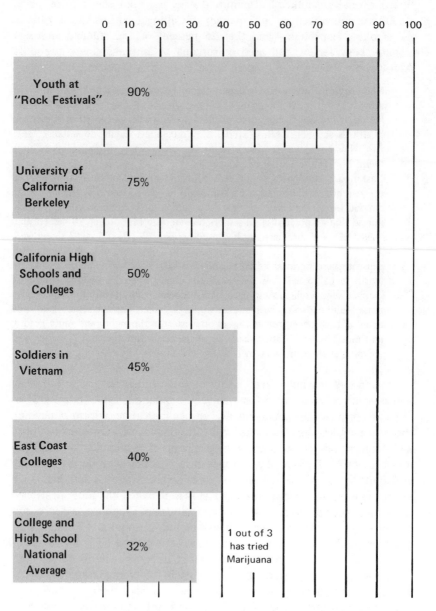

Sources: Gallup Poll: Estimates by Army medical officers, National Institute for Mental Health, and various individual college polls.

Reproduced by permission of Ambassador College.

unnatural deaths, including those from drug addiction, alcoholism and suicide. Dr. Michael M. Baden, New York's Deputy Chief Medical Examiner, states that heroin use is now the leading cause of deaths among teenagers in New York City, where drug addiction has become a major public health problem apart from extensive criminal aspects. Amplifying on drug addiction in New York, Dr. Baden reports that hepatitis, tetanus, endocarditis, bacterial infection of the heart, homocide, and suicide, are in high incidence in the heroin-user population. And, Dr. Baden further states, whereas deaths among teenagers constituted only four percent of the total in 1918, the situation has drastically changed. The total is now 25 percent, with the sharpest rises since 1967.

> Part of the dread in the danger of the problem is that it spreads all too invisibly. No one knows how many heroin addicts of any age there are in the U.S. But in New York City alone, where most experts think half the heroin users in the U.S. live, 224 teen-agers died from overdoses of heroin related infections last year, about a quarter of the city's 900 deaths from heroin use. So far this year, over 40 teen-agers have died because of heroin. There may be as many as 25,000 young addicts in New York City, and one expert fears the number may mushroom fantastically to 100,000 this summer. Cautious federal officials believe that heroin addiction below age 25 jumped 40 percent from 1968 to 1969. However imprecise the figure is, there is no doubt in the magnitude of the change, or the certitude that something frightening is sweeping into the corridors of U.S. schools and onto the pavements of America's playgrounds. It has not yet cropped up everywhere, but many experts believe that disaster looms large.[54]

The problem is by no means limited to the schools, of course; but, as previously stated, a large number of these abusers are of high-school age. Some are even younger. They will live short, empty lives with neither hope nor meaning. They no longer have a choice.

Most of the serious drug problems exist in the heart of the major cities where there are too many people, too little money, and too little to do. But drug abusers can be found everywhere from the worst slum area to the wealthiest suburb.

The common factor is the attempt to escape from either physical or emotional problems. Young people are particularly vulnerable. Usually, they are introduced to drugs by friends, not by "pushers." And it is quite different to refuse a favor or a dare from a friend. It is also harder still to resist a group, where you are the only hold out. It is a well-known fact that gangs and even otherwise amiable social groups are often the most responsible for the introduction of illegal drugs.

---

[54] *Time,* March 16, 1970, p. 16.

The figures mentioned are alarming, but they do not begin to reflect the real cost of the abuse of narcotics and certain other drugs. Thousands of drug abusers live for years in the shadows of society—only half alive, only half free. Data from the Federal Bureau of Narcotics indicate that the number of arrests for nonviolent property crimes was proportionately higher among addicts. In contrast, however, the number of arrests of addicts for violent offenses against a person, such as rape and aggravated assault, was only a fraction of the proportion constituted by such arrests among the population at large.[55]

In view of the above information, Harold Finestone states:[56]

> To adolescent groups who simultaneously evaluate highly adults who were engaged in a wide variety of criminal activity and adults who were addicted; and these valuations were reflected in both criminal activity and experimentation with narcotics. Thus, both the criminality and experimentation with narcotics stemmed, at least in part, from influences to which the youngsters were exposed, as represented by adult models within the local community. Both criminality and narcotics use came to be prestigeful forms of activity. In this sense, it is irrelevant to ask whether the delinquency preceded the addiction or vice versa. Many of those who became addicted and were forced to engage in crime to support the high cost of their addiction would probably have gone to engage in crime as adolescents regardless of whether or not they had become addicted. . . .
>
> The impression gained from interviewing adolescent addicts was that these addicts were petty thieves and petty 'operators' who, status-wise, were at the bottom of the criminal population or underworld. It is difficult to see how they could be otherwise. The typical young junkie spent so much of his time in a harried quest for narcotics, dodging the police, and in lockups, that he was hardly in a position to plan major crimes.

The extent of the problem is much more serious than previously indicated (Table 1.) Most statistics pointing out the use of narcotics derived from *only those reported* to the Federal Bureau of Narcotics from local law enforcement agencies. Furthermore, the data reported to the Bureau represents only those adolescent drug addicts who have been classified as bona fide addicts. On many occasions, youngsters who have abused the use of drugs and are in the process of experimenting have not come to the attention of the law enforcement agencies, or, when detected, are not viewed as "legitimate addicts." Therefore, the magnitude of the problem is much more extensive than the statistics compiled by the Federal, or for that matter, State Bureau of Narcotics indicates.

---

[55]H. Finestone, "Narcotics: Narcotics and Criminality," *Law and Contemporary Problems*, School of Law, Duke University, Vol. XXII, No. 1 (Winter, 1957), pp. 74.

[56]*Ibid.*, pp. 75-77.

Why Drugs?

To cope intelligently with drug problems, one needs to know more about what kind of appeals drugs offer. There are a number of reasons, but basically it is the individual who, because of an inadequate personality, fails to identify with mature adult goals. Because of his inability to formulate some type of identification with mature adult goals, such a person finds it necessary in making an adjustment in two areas: Since he is concerned with two adjustive objectives (1) creating a pleasure-seeking structured environment for himself in which he can pursue effortless pleasurable activities; and (2) eliminating the intrusive demands and responsibilities as associated with adult personality status. Such a person afflicted with a crippling personality turns to drugs because it is suited for realizing the above-mentioned hedonistic objectives.[57]

> After he takes his first few shots, the addict literally exclaims, "Boy, this is what I have been looking for all my life. What could be easier?" By merely injecting a needle under his skin, he satisfies his quest for immediate and effortless pleasure. Apart from the voluptuous thrill of the "kick," he reports increased self-confidence and feelings of self-esteem, decreased anxiety, and grandiose (of wealth, power, and omnipotence). Primary needs such as hunger and sex urges fade into the background, and, although not directly gratified, are rendered so uninsistent as to be incapable of generating anxiety or frustration when their satisfaction is threatened or denied. Fear of pain is also set aside as the threshold for pain perception is raised and as its anxiety-producing implications are minimized. In fact, because of the drug's specific inhibition of the self-critical faculty, the environment in general assumes a more benevolent and less threatening aspect.[58]

In viewing the available literature on drug abuse, it is noted that there are many other explanations and different ideas concerning the etiology of drug usage. Various disciplines (psychology, physiology, sociology, etc.) have contributed to literature on drug abuse. It is noted that many kinds of drug users are delineated, and the causes leading to use are thought to be multiple and frequently interrelated. However, the main theme of all the disciplines appears to concentrate on the user's personality. David P. Ausubel, a noted author and expert on drug abuse, concludes that:

> Differential susceptibility to drug addiction is primarily a reflection of the relative adjustive value which narcotics possess for different individuals. At any given moment, a person exposed to narcotics will only become an addict

---

[57]D. P. Ausubel, *Drug Addiction: Physiological, Psychological, and Sociological Aspects*, (New York: Random House, 1958), p. 95.

[58]*Ibid.*, pp. 44-45.

if the drug is able to do something significant for him psychologically, that is, to satisfy certain of his currently important needs.[59]

There are many other explanations as to the "why" of drug abuse. But, perhaps, the most definitive analysis of drug abuse among adolescents is Isador Chein's *The Road to H.* Isador Chein agrees with Ausubel's hypothesis that drug susceptibility is associated with the *adjustive* value of using drugs and paints a vivid picture when he concludes that:

> The evidence indicates that all addicts suffer from deep-rooted major personality disorders. Although psychiatric diagnoses are apt to vary, a particular set of symptoms seems to be common to most juvenile addicts. They are not able to enter into prolonged, close, friendly relations with either peers or adults; they have difficulties in assuming a masculine role; they are frequently overcome by a sense of futility, expectations of failure, and general depression; they are easily frustrated and made anxious, and they find frustration and anxiety intolerable.[60]

Furthermore, this is an era of rapid, revolutionary change that leaves adults, as well as youths, bewildered and uneasy as to what tomorrow may bring. There are crucial struggles over civil rights and social injustice. The war in Viet Nam is unpopular with many citizens, young and old. The cities show obvious decay; pollution of air, water, and land is increasing. Off stage is a menace of obliterating nuclear war.

Rapid social changes widens the "generation gap," states Dr. Kenneth Keniston, Yale psychologist, and the here-and-now becomes more important to the young who "can no longer commit themselves unquestionably to the life styles, attitudes, and skills of their parents. To do so is to condemn one's self to obsolescence in the modern world."

Many youths live under tremendous pressure to excel in school, and to some "school work seems contrived, a form of marking time, and hence irrelevant," states Dr. Dana L. Farnsworth, Director of University Health Services at Harvard.

Never in history have so many of the Nation's youth been so accustomed to affluence, with no worry about starvation, unemployment, or depression. Parents who have survived the great depression of the 1930's and work hard to get ahead and give their children a better break, find this view difficult to take.

Furthermore, they find many youths protesting that the society they are growing up in is materialistic, commercialized, impersonal, automatic, full of social injustice, making little allowance for the individual and his inner-feelings.

---

[59]D. P. Ausubel, "Causes and Types of Drug Addiction," *Key Issues,* Vol. 1, (Nov. 1961), p. 12.
[60]I. Chein, et. al., *The Road to H* (New York: Basic Books, Inc., 1964), p. 14.

Psychiatrists who have worked with many teen-agers and young adults, have concluded that the youngsters identify with a new notion that you can want experiences which are purely esthetic, purely on their own merits, even if they do not lead anywhere.

Portrait of an Adolescent Drug Addict

Identification of any drug addict, adolescent or adult, is vague because we usually do not recognize a drug addict until addiction is well established with the attendant personality and social habit regression. The recognition of an addict is, if not impossible, extremely difficult. The clue to the understanding of the adolescent drug addict, therefore, is dependent upon examining both his psychological and social development to see if it is possible to determine what commonalities of background have served to create his current difficulties. Generally, the teen-age drug addict comes from a rather deprived social environment that lacks the necessary resources which might endow him with greater potential for survival. Because of the basic lack of support from his environment in general and his family in particular, the adolescent addict is geared for failure rather than success, and in truth, as we have traced his life pattern, it can be readily seen that he has known failure rather intimately. His initial failure was in relationship to his family toward whom he looked for love and support but, instead, found rejection or lack of understanding. This failure later developed into social failure as he internalized profound feelings of insecurity and worthlessness. Therefore, the youth becomes a rather withdrawn, somewhat isolated individual who seems more of an inactive observer of life than a direct participant in it. He is unable and unwilling to extend himself in the everyday world because the spector of failure is always before him.[61]

This is clearly seen in the educational background of the adolescent drug user, where, despite the fact that his intelligence parallels that of the average population, he soon drops out of school after having completed poor work at a level significantly below his actual capabilities. It is rare to meet an adolescent user who has gone beyond the third or fourth year of high school.

Early in the period of an addict's experience with narcotics, the effect of the drug is dissipated in a few hours and no deviation from his normal routine occurs. The user may seem somewhat subdued, under no particular pressure, perhaps inclined to talk more than usual, and have a somewhat pleased feeling about his surroundings. Close scrutiny of his eyes reveals the tell-tale pinpoint pupils. When high, he is lethargic, sleepy, perhaps stuporous, dreamy, and with no particular interests but that of going to sleep. He

---

[61]L. Gold, "Toward an Understanding of Adolescent Drug Addiction," *Federal Probation,* Vol. XXII, No. 3 (September, 1958), p. 43.

may also be preoccupied with various fantasties of grandiose omnipotent type. Nausea, vomiting and intense scratching may be temporary side effects. If the individual continues with only occasional joy pops (as occasional injections are called), those probably will be the limit of the observable signs. Needle marks may be found if the individual were examined physically, but there are many users in the adolescent field who don't inject, but snort or sniff the drug, and among these there are no tell-tale physical marks. The locations of works, that is, the eye dropper, the needle, the bent spoon, or little cones that are utilized for inhalation of the drug, would be presumptive evidence.[62]

The adolescent drug user tends to be materialistic since, in a sense, he has ceased to believe that his emotional needs can be met in a positive manner. It is of interest to note that he is an individual who is ordinarily unable to retain whatever material possesions he has because they are needed to maintain a drug supply.

The drug user approaches life with a profound sense of inadequacy and helplessness which overwhelms him and causes him to flee from realities of everyday living. He seeks the comfortable vacuum that the drug offers him. The drug has value for the adolescent addict not solely because it can provide pleasurable sensations, but because it becomes a buffer between the user and the society which he fears.

Since he is an escapist, he is unable to relate to other people in a meaningful, constructive, realistic fashion. He can only take from others in a dependent and passive manner and is unable to give anything in return in either a physical or emotional sense. His basically dependent orientation tends to breed suspicion and resentment to the degree that it blocks the development of positive relationships with another person.[63]

The teen-age drug addict usually is involved in a conflictive relationship with parental figures. He feels that the parent does not understand him, and also anticipates that the parent will act in a manner that will be detrimental to his personal interests.

Many times, the parents of the drug addict are also inadequate people. They are unable to really live up to the criteria expected in a parent-child relationship. This quality of weakness that exists in a parental relationship is not solely a fact that occurs during a period of addiction, but it permeates the entire living situation. Because of his relatively unstable, immature personality structure, the teen-age drug addict perceives his environmental situation out of perspective. As a result, the individual experiences great difficulty where only moderate difficulty should exist.

---

[62]The New York Academy of Medicine, *Conference on Drug Addiction Among Adolescents,* (New York: The Blakiston Company, 1953), pp. 8-9.
[63]Gold, "Understanding of Adolescent Drug Addiction," p. 43.

Because he perceives the adult world as an unstable place, he prefers to seek out the security of an infantile type of relationship. So the infantile behavior may be not only the result of cultural deprivation, but also actually serve as a protection from dealing with the more complex situations and responsibilities that can be expected of one who aspires to be accepted as an adult.

In brief, according to *Conferences on Drug Addiction Among Adolescents,* held by The New York Academy of Medicine, the following are the three phases which a young addict will complete: (a) the early phase, when very little can be observed, in which perhaps the "works" (drug paraphernalia) is the only clue; (b) the later stage, in which the personality changes, the social group changes, and the appearance of needle marks (if the person is injecting himself) are the signs which will be detected; (c) later, the phase of physical dependency, in which the obstinance syndrome is the diagnostic clue.[64]

Personality is an important factor in the development of abuse. Some individuals seem particularly prone to psychic dependence: a desire for drugs that is entirely independent of physical symptoms or needs. It is not the direct effect of the drug—sedation or stimulation—which influences the development of psychic dependence, but rather the interpretation of this effect as euphoria or "feeling good" and the use of the drug to escape from reality. These people often succumb to alcohol. In fact, abuse of alcohol is often the first step on the road to the abuse of drugs.

The development of abuse is rooted in the repeated use of drugs as a way of solving life's problems. Eventually, the tendency to solve or hide from problems through the use of drugs interferes with normal personality functioning.

Chronic abuse of drugs is generally considered a symptom of mental or emotional illness. This illness does not fall into any one category such as schizophrenia or depression. (However, most drug abusers suffer from personality disorders.) Nor are all drug abusers alike from an emotional standpoint. Perhaps the only common characteristic is that drug abusers use drugs to a point where they can no longer manage without such support.

There is a significant difference between two classes of drug abusers: the adult abuser and the juvenile or "teen-age" abuser. The adult abuser of drugs commonly has a history of social maladjustment. The pressures and demands of society are too much for him to bear. Typically, he has a background of family difficulties, disciplinary problems, and trouble with the police. At some point, he finds that there are artificial ways to escape reality, anxiety, and his feelings of inadequacy in coping with life's problems. In escaping, he may turn to alcohol or drugs and draw a chemical

[64]The New York Academy of Medicine, *Conference on Drug Addiction,* p. 43.

curtain between himself and reality. Association with other drug abusers is an important factor in developing a dependency on drugs.

The juvenile or "teen-ager" presents a more complex picture. Going through adolescence is, under the best of circumstances, a difficult and complex process. Some authorities feel that boredom and lack of definite goals contribute to juvenile troubles. One salient feature of adolescence is the need that all juveniles have to be accepted and "to belong." For many, a juvenile gang fills this need. By conforming to the gang's code of behavior, the youngster gains recognition in his group. Often the degree of recognition is in direct proportion to the juvenile's willingness to defy legal, social, and parental authority. Juvenile drug abuse frequently stems from this "gang psychology." It usually begins in a gang or party setting. One member of the group starts, and the rest go along for fear of appearing "chicken."

One aspect of drug abuse is the fact that many abusers will use any substance that gives them a "thrill." "Airplane" glue, lighter fluid, gasoline, nutmeg, and ether have all been used. Because of their easy availability, many of these substances are often used by children and teen-agers.

Varieties and Types of Drugs Abused

Wise police officers will try to lead from the strength of knowledge in discussing drugs with teen-agers. Only that way are they likely to be effective; only that way can they speak intelligently.

Knowledge in this case must be based on the facts about the drugs themselves—what they are like and what they do to people.

The following is a rundown[65] on the principal drugs being used or abused by teen-agers and young adults.

Stimulants

Amphetamines, first produced in the 1920's for medical use, are stimulants to the central nervous system and are best known for their ability to combat fatigue and sleepiness. They are also sometimes used to curb appetite in medically supervised weight reduction programs. The most commonly used stimulants are amphetamine (Benzedrine), dextroamphetamine (Dexedrine), and methamphetamine (Methedrine).

Slang terms for these drugs by some people who misuse them include "pep pills," "bennies," and "speed."

Examples

Benzedrine (Bennies), Methedrine (Crystal), Dexedrine (Dexies, Xmas Trees), and Cocaine (Coke, Snow).

---

[65]Excellent resources in this area are: G. McLean and H. Bowen's Pamphlet on "Facts You Need to Know About Drug Abuse," (Palo Alto, Calif.: Darr Publishing Co., 1970), and the same authors' book *High on the Campus* (Wheaton, Illinois: Tyndale House, 1970).

Abuse

Because the body develops a tolerance to amphetamines, abusers increase their dosages gradually, a factor which exaggerates the normal effects of these drugs and results in:

Euphoria	Restlessness
Alertness	Enlarged pupils
Reduction of awareness of fatigue	Sleeplessness
Excitability	Heavy perspiration
Tremor of the hands	Loss of appetite
Talkativeness	Weight loss

Stimulant drugs increase the heart rate, raise the blood pressure, cause palpitations (throbbing heart and rapid breathing), dilate the pupils, and cause dry mouth, sweating, headache, diarrhea, and paleness. They also depress the appetite.

Are these Stimulants Addicting?

Benzedrine, Dexedrine and other stimulant drugs do not produce physical dependence as do the "hard" drugs (drugs made from opium, i.e., morphine, paregoric, codeine, etc.) or narcotics. The body does not become physically dependent on their continued use. It does, however, develop a tolerance to these drugs, with larger and larger doses required to feel the effects.

There is another kind of dependence medical authorities note in connection with the abuse of stimulants. They call it "psychological" dependence, or a practice that can become a habit for mental or emotional reasons, with the person "getting used to" and turning to the drug for its effects.

Depressants

The *barbiturates* are a large family of drugs derived from barbituric acid, which was developed in Germany in the 19th Century. Since then, innumerable barbiturates have been synthesized and prepared for medical use under trade names such as Seconal, Phenobarbital, and Nembutal. These drugs are available in liquids, tablets, capsules, and various other forms.

Identification of Barbiturates

Barbiturates are known to drug abusers as barbs, candy, goof-balls, sleeping pills, or peanuts. Specific types are often named after their color or shape. For example, solid yellow capsules are known to abusers as yellows, yellow jackets, or nimbies. Red capsules are called reds, pinks, red birds, red devils, seggy, and seccy. Red and blue capsules are known as rainbows, red and blues, or double trouble. Solid blue capsules are known by abusers as blues, blue birds, blue devils, or blue heavens.

Examples

Seconal (Red Devils), Nembutal (Yellow Jackets), and Phenobarbital (Phennies).

Abuse

Continued and excessive dosages of barbiturates result in:

Euphoria	Loss of balance and falling
Impaired judgment	Quick temper
Reaction time is retarded	A quarrelsome disposition
Slurring speech	Coma (with danger of pneumonia and death)
Staggering	Sleep induction

Authorities consider the barbiturates highly dangerous when taken without medical advice and prescription. Because these drugs are commonly prescribed by doctors, many people mistakenly consider them safe to use freely and as they choose. They are not. Overdose can cause death.

Barbiturates distort how people see things and slow down their reactions and responses. They are an important cause of automobile accidents, especially when taken together with alcohol. Barbiturates tend to heighten the effects of alcohol.

Users may react to the drug more strongly at one time than at another. They may become confused about how many pills they have taken, and die of an accidental overdose. Barbiturates are a leading cause of accidental poison deaths in the United States.

Because they are easily obtained, and produce sleep readily, barbiturates are also one of the main methods people choose to commit suicide.

These drugs are physically addicting. The body needs increasingly higher doses to feel their effects. Some experts consider barbiturate addiction more difficult to cure than a narcotic dependency. If the drug is withdrawn abruptly, the user suffers withdrawal sickness with cramps, nausea, delirium and convulsions, and in some cases, sudden death. Therefore, withdrawal should take place in a hospital over a period of several weeks on gradually reduced dosages. It takes several months for the body to return to normal.

Glue-Sniffing

Plastic glues vary in chemical composition, depending on the specific formula used by the manufacturer, but all of these cements contain highly volatile organic solvents—substances considered in industry to be safe when inhaled in very low vapor concentration, but known to be dangerously toxic when inhaled in high concentration. Solvene is a prime constituent of most glues and of plastic cements.

The effects of glue sniffing are comparable, except in degree, to the effect of a general anesthetic upon the body. The glue sniffer experiences a tingling sensation in his head—a lightness and an exhilaration known to him as a "jag." If he continues to inhale the glue, he will experience a state similar to alcoholic intoxication.

Identification of Dangerous Glue

Quick-drying plastic cement, frequently called airplane glue, as well as certain solvents such as benzene, carbon tetrachloride, and ethyl alcohol, can be very harmful when breathed.

Abuse.   Inhalation of such toxic fluids commonly results in:

Euphoria	Slurred speech
Intoxication	Staggering
Dizziness	Irritability
Possible loss of consciousness	Rash, foolish, and even dangerous actions

The "glue-sniffer" commonly:

Has inflamed eyes	Loses appetite and weight
Has irritated nose and lung tissue	Feels constantly sick

LSD-25 D-Lysergic Acid Diethylamide Tartrate (A Hallucinogenic Drug)

Identification of LSD-25

LSD-25 is an odorless, tasteless, and colorless chemical which, when taken in even the smallest quantities, is likely to cause the mind to react in strange, unpredictable and uncontrollable ways.

People who use LSD say that it has a number of psychological effects. The first effects, they indicate, are likely to be sudden changes in their physical senses. Walls may appear to move, colors seem stronger and more brilliant. Users are likely to "see" unusual patterns unfolding before them. Flat objects seem to stand out in three dimensions. Taste, smell, hearing, and touch seem more acute. One sensory impression may be translated or merged into another; for example, music may appear as a color, and colors may seem to have a taste.

One of the most confusing yet common reactions among users is the feeling of two strong and opposite emotions at the same time—they can feel both happy and sad at once, or depressed and elated, or relaxed and tense. Arms and legs may feel both heavy and light.

Users also report a sensation of losing the normal feeling of boundaries between body and space. This sometimes gives them the notion they can fly or float with ease.

Effects can be different at different times in the same individual. Researchers have found, even in carefully controlled studies, that responses to the drug cannot be predicted. For this reason, users refer to "good trips" or "bad trips" to describe their experience.

As to the *physical* effects, an average dose of LSD, amounting to a speck, has an effect that lasts for about 8 to 10 hours. Users take it in a sugar cube, a cracker, a cookie, or can lick it off a stamp or other object impregnated with the drug. It increases the pulse and heart rate, causes a rise in blood pressure and temperature, dilated eye pupils, shaking of the hands and feet, cold sweaty palms, a flushed face or paleness, shivering, chills with goose pimples.

Is LSD Dangerous?

Recent reports from hospitals in areas where LSD is used without close medical supervision warn of definite dangers. These include: (1) *Panic.* The user may grow frightened because he cannot stop the drug's action, and he may fear he is losing his mind. (2) *Paranoia.* He may become increasingly suspicious, feeling that someone is trying to harm him or control his thinking. This feeling generally lasts 72 hours after the drug has worn off. (3) *Recurrence.* Days, weeks, or even months after the individual has stopped using LSD, the things he saw and felt while on the drug may recur and make him fear he is going insane. (4) *Accidental Death.* Because the LSD user may feel that he can fly or float, he may try to leap out of a high window or from other heights and fall to his death. Such accidents have been reported. Or he may drive or walk in front of a moving car because he thinks he cannot be harmed.

Marijuana

Marijuana is a drug found in the flowering tops and leaves of the Indian hemp plant, cannabis sativa. The plant grows in mild climates in countries around the world, especially in Mexico, Africa, India, and the Middle East. It also grows in the United States, where the drug is known as pot, tea, grass, weed, Mary Jane, and by other names.

For use as a drug, the leaves and flowers of the plant are dried and crushed or chopped into small pieces. This green product is usually rolled and smoked in short cigarettes or in pipes, or it can be taken in food. The cigarettes are commonly known as reefers, joints and sticks. The smoke from marijuana is easily recognized due to its sweet odor.

The strength of the drug differs from place to place, depending on where and how it is grown, how it is prepared for use, and how it is stored.

The marijuana available in the United States is much weaker than the kind grown in Asia, Africa, or the Near East.

When smoked, marijuana quickly enters the bloodstream and acts on the brain and nervous system. It affects the user's mood and thinking. Its pathway into the brain is not yet understood. Some scientists report that the drug accumulates in the liver. Because it may cause hallucinations when taken in very large doses, it is classed as a mild "hallucinogen." Just how the drug works in the body and how it produces its effects have not yet been discovered by medical science.

The long-term physical effects of taking marijuana are not yet known. The kind of research needed to learn the results of chronic use has not yet been done.

The more obvious physical reactions include rapid heart beat, lowering of body temperature, and sometimes reddening of the eyes. The drug also changes blood sugar levels, stimulates the appetite, and dehydrates the body. Users may get talkative, loud, unsteady, or drowsy, and find it hard to coordinate their movements.

The drug's effects on the emotions and senses vary widely, depending on the amount and strength of the marijuana used. The social setting in which it is taken and what the user expects also influence his reaction to the drug.

Usually, when it is smoked, marijuana's effect is felt quickly, in about 15 minutes. Its effects can last from two to four hours. The range of effects can vary from depression to a feeling of excitement. Some users, however, experience no change of mood at all. The sense of time and distance of many users frequently becomes distorted. A minute may seem like an hour. Something near may seem far away.

Dependence

Marijuana users may develop a psychological dependence. Because so many users of narcotics report previous use of marijuana, concern should be given not only to the habit-forming use of marijuana, but also to the serious possibility that it will serve as a stepping stone to more serious drug addiction.

Narcotics

The term "narcotic" refers, generally, to opium and pain-killing drugs made from opium, such as heroin, morphine, paregoric, and codeine. These and other opiates are obtained from the juice of the poppy fruit. Several synthetic drugs, such as Demerol and Dolophine, are also classed as narcotics. Opiates are widely used in medicine as pain killers. Cocaine, made from coca leaves, and marijuana are classified legally but not chemically as narcotic drugs.

Since heroin appears to be the narcotic used by most addicts today, these questions and answers deal mainly with heroin.

What is Narcotic Addiction?

When the abuser of a narcotic gets "hooked"—meaning addicted—his body requires repeated and larger doses of the drug. Once the habit starts, larger and larger doses are required to get the same effects. This happens because the body develops a "tolerance" for the drug.

One of the signs of heroin addiction is withdrawal sickness. When the addict stops using the drug, he may sweat, shake, get chills, diarrhea, nausea, and suffer sharp abdominal and leg cramps. Modern treatments help the addict through withdrawal stages. Science now has new evidence that the body's physical addiction may last much longer than previously believed.

There is another kind of drug dependence connected with the use of narcotics. This is known as psychological dependence. That is, taking the drug also becomes a habit for emotional reasons. For example, the addict comes to depend on the drug as a way to escape facing life.

Narcotic use can become even more of an escape than expected because large or unexpectedly pure doses can, and not uncommonly do, result in death.

What is the Effect of the Drug?

Typically, the first emotional reaction to heroin is reduction of tension, easing of fears and relief from worry. Feeling "high" may be followed by a period of inactivity bordering on stupor.

Heroin, which is usually mixed into a liquid solution and injected into a vein, appears to dull the edges of reality. Addicts have reported that heroin "makes my troubles roll off my mind," and "it makes me feel more sure of myself."

The drug depresses certain areas of the brain and may reduce hunger, thirst, and the sex drive. Because addicts do not usually feel hungry, their hospital care may include treatment for malnutrition. The drug may also reduce feelings of pain.

Withdrawal symptoms appear in the addicted person about 18 hours after the drug has been discontinued.

In general, effects of the drug are influenced by many factors. These include the user's personality, size and frequency of dose, and how the drug is taken.

Does Addiction Lead to Crime?

Some studies suggest that many of the known narcotic addicts had some trouble with the law before they became addicted. Once addicted, they may become even more involved with crime because it costs so much to support the heroin habit. For example, an addict may have to spend up to $75 to $100 to buy his day's supply of heroin.

Most authorities agree that the addict's involvement with crime is not a direct effect of the drug itself, but turning to crime is usually the only way he has of getting that much money. His crimes are nearly always thefts or other crimes against property, and not often crimes of passion or violence.

Drug Abuse

All the drugs commonly abused are either completely outlawed, as are heroin and marijuana, or they can be obtained only from the underworld peddler or from thieves or diversion of legitimate supplies from physicians, hospitals, or pharmacies. So the drug abuse problem immediately has legal aspects, and law enforcement becomes extremely important.

Crimes of violence are often committed by persons under delusions from stimulant drugs; the delusion that they are being watched or followed is common with stimulant users. Sex parties and violent assaults are rarely committed while under the influence of opiates or barbiturates because these depressants quiet the users and lessen sex drives. However, the use of depressant drugs can lead to violent assaults, holdups, and even murder when approaching withdrawal symptoms lead to desperation and the addict will take any risk to get drugs or the money to buy them.

Part of society's duty is that of passing necessary laws and upholding law-enforcement activities. Problems of enforcement are complicated in metropolitan areas and cities where there is a large import-export maritime business. New York and California's problems in controlling drug abuse are complicated by the smuggling of heroin and marijuana via ships, planes, and land travel, and by the lack of laws to control the importing of barbiturates and other dangerous drugs.

The problem of narcotics will continue and, without doubt, expand as long as there is ineffective control at the source of production. Therefore, law enforcement must seek ways and means of international control. Efforts to increase law-enforcement personnel at points of entry in order to insure closer inspection is probably the first step toward controlling the traffic. Stronger feeling or measures would deter some of the narcotic traffic, thereby lowering the profits inherent in this illegal trade.

Measures to control narcotic traffic depend on the degree of cooperation between nations. There is at the present time little effective control over production of raw materials. This is an area where immediate attention will have to be focused.

International control is only one aspect of the problems confronting law enforcement. As previously stated, as far as the adolescents are concerned, experimentation with the use of drugs is quite prevalent in the school setting. Therefore, the control of narcotic traffic nationally is of paramount importance to law enforcement agencies. Without "customers" narcotic traffic will dissipate. Social institutions can play an important part in the tremendous struggle to prevent narcotic use. Schools are in a position to be able to detect experimentation on the part of youngsters who will utilize such drugs for a "thrill."[66]

Investigative Techniques[67]

Common Methods of Hiding or Disguising Drugs

The search for drugs is one of the most difficult problems faced by an officer. Drugs may be in solid, powder, or liquid form. In its pure state, the "bulk" of a drug may be very small.

One popular way to carry illegally obtained drugs is to keep them in an old prescription bottle. The officer should be suspicious of any bottle with a worn or dirty label.

Illegally obtained drugs are often hidden in the bottom of a cigarette pack. The cigarettes are cut off and the pack appears normal. Drugs may also be found in fountain pens, cigarette lighters, toothpaste tubes, flashlights, and lipstick tubes which have had their contents removed. Tablets and capsules may be folded into letters, handkerchiefs, personal papers, books and newspapers, or secreted in the linings of clothing. Occasionally, drugs may be dissolved into innocent-appearing liquids.

Determining the Illegal Possession, Use, and Source of Drugs

There are many ways that a drug abuser comes into contact with the police. The officer may find drugs—or evidence of their use—during a routine check or in the course of an arrest for a totally unconnected offense. He may actually see a person taking drugs, find evidence of unusual behavior, or he may encounter a suicide attempt involving drugs.

In each of these cases, the officer seeks several items of information to build a successful case or save a life. He must be able to answer these questions:

Does the suspect have drugs in his possession?

What are the drugs and where did they come from?

Is the possession legal?

Has he taken doses of the drugs?

---

[66]J. P. Kenney, and D. G. Pursuit, *Police Work with Juveniles,* 2nd ed. (Springfield, Illinois: Charles C. Thomas, 1959), p. 175.
[67]Landis and Fletcher, pp. 13-15.

There are literally thousands of drugs on the market. Some require a physician's prescription, but many do not.

Prescription drugs can, generally speaking, be purchased only from pharmacists, but non-prescription items are often bought from supermarkets, variety stores, grocery stores, and newsstands. (Some doctors, particularly those in isolated areas, dispense drugs to their patients, rather than write prescriptions.)

The officer's best approach to questioning relies on the principle that a suspect is innocent until proven guilty. Such an attitude is essential in producing evidence that will be admissible in court, and, incidentally, often results in digging out the greatest amount of helpful evidence.

As the questioning proceeds, the officer should remember that many of the subject's answers can be verified later.

Questioning often follows this pattern:

Are you sick now? Have you been ill?

Who is your doctor? Did you receive a prescription?

Is this medicine yours? Does it belong to someone else?

Do you know what it is?

Where was the prescription filled?

When did you last take the medicine?

How long have you been taking the medicine?

What is the medicine being taken for?

Are you under the care of a doctor? Do you take the medicine according to his orders?

By using this questioning pattern, the officer has given the subject a logical alibi and, apparently, believes his story that he is ill. Hopefully, the subject will volunteer that the medicine is his and that he is taking it. The officer is, moreover, protected in case the subject is actually ill and is taking a legally prescribed medicine.

The officer should now attempt to verify the answers to his questions.

1. Doctor's Name. This should appear on the prescription label, and can be verified by telephoning the doctor.

2. Name of Pharmacy. This can be verified by calling the pharmacist.

3. Prescription Date. The pharmacist's records will help there.

4. How Medicine is Taken. Check number of tablets or capsules left in bottle against the number the pharmacist says he dispensed.

5.   Is the Medicine the Same as that Prescribed? Check with pharmacist. (Pharmacists give all prescriptions an individual number. This appears on the container which is given to the patient. The pharmacist will need this number to refer back to the original prescription.)

With this procedure, the officer has either confirmed or invalidated the subject's story. Remember that both physicians and pharmacists are generally most helpful and cooperative in such investigations.

Part V   Selected Correlated References

Banton, M. *The Policeman in the Community.* New York: Basic Books, 1964. An excellent discussion of law enforcement's role in community structure.

Barndt, J. *Why Black Power.* New York: Friendship Press, 1968. An excellent treatise of value to law enforcement through identifying and isolating the positive value of political and economic power for minorities.

Barrett, E. L. "Personal Rights, Property Rights and the Fourth Amendment." *1960 Supreme Court Review.* Chicago: University of Chicago Press, 1960. A fine discussion of the title subject with emphasis on the individual in constitutional government.

Coffey, A., E. Eldefonso, and W. Hartinger. *Human Relations: Law Enforcement in a Changing Community.* Englewood Cliffs, N.J.: Prentice-Hall, Inc., 1971. The entire volume discusses, at an introductory level, the scope of police-community relations. See also, by the same authors: *Police-Community Relations.* (paperback) New Jersey: Prentice-Hall, Inc., 1971.

Cohen, Albert K. *Delinquent Boys: The Culture of the Gang.* Glencoe, Ill.: The Free Press, 1955. The author discusses the adolescent boys of the lower-class and their gang activities. Cohen indicates that the lower-class boys form delinquent gangs as a reaction against the middle-class world. An excellent overview of lower-class gangs.

Davies, D. "Police, Law and the Individual." *Annals of the American Academy of Political and Social Science* Vol. 291 (1954) p. 145. Another well-done consideration of overall police relationship to community affairs.

Eldefonso, Edward. *Youth Problems and Law Enforcement.* (paperback) Englewood Cliffs, N.J.: Prentice-Hall, Inc., 1972. A concise overview of procedures utilized by contemporary law enforcement agencies in dealing with the youthful offender.

Grier, W. *Black Rage.* New York: Basic Books, 1967; along with E. Cleaver. *Soul on Ice.* New York: McGraw-Hill, 1968; J. Cohen. *Burn, Baby, Burn.* E. P. Dutton Press, 1967; R. Conet. *Rivers of Blood.* New York: Bantam Books, 1964. Each volume contributes new dimension to the magnitude of social unrest.

Harlan, L. *Separate and Unequal.* Univ. of No. Carolina Press, 1968; along with J. Conant. *Slums and Suburbs.* New York: McGraw-Hill Book Co., 1961. Both provide an excellent perception of the depth of cultural impingement on minority groups in institutions.

Harrington, M. *The Other America: Poverty in the United States.* Baltimore, Md.: Penguin Books, 1963. An extensive and "hard hitting" coverage of the title subject.

Heaps, W. A. *Riots, U.S.A., 1765–1965.* New York: The Seabury Press, 1966. This book covers the history of some of the riots and civil disorders of the 200 years of this nation.

Marx, J. *Officer, Tell Your Story: A Guide to Police Public Relations.* Springfield, Ill.: Charles C. Thomas, Pub., 1969. In reviewing the need for public support of police goals, this book deals with the attitudes and procedures of police agencies in the context of community relations programming.

Momboisse, R. *Community Relations and Riot Prevention.* Springfield, Ill.: Charles C. Thomas, Pub., 1969. The theme of this text is: *The only effective way to control a riot is to prevent it,* and this theme is reviewed in the context of community relations programming.

Momboisse, R. *Riots, Revolts and Insurrections.* Springfield, Ill.: Charles C. Thomas, Pub., 1969. In related context to the preceding annotated reference by the same author, this text examines the subject of the title in terms of standards and guidelines for police organizations.

Report of the National Advisory Commission on Civil Disorders. Washington, D.C.: U.S. Government Printing Office, 1968. The chairman of the committee responsible for this study was Otto Kerner, therefore, this study is often referred to as the Kerner Report. It provides an extensive study of several of the more recent riots in the United States as well as an intensive investigation of the conditions within the ghetto. Particularly, attention is directed towards the conditions in the ghetto as they are related to civil disorders.

Report of the National Commission on the Causes and Prevention of Violence: *Rights in Conflict.* Washington, D.C.: U.S. Government Printing Office, 1969. The investigation of the civil disorders and the police reaction surrounding the Democratic National Convention of 1968.

Skolnick, J. ed. *The Politics of Protest.* A Task Force Report — National Commission on the Causes and Prevention of Violence. A Clarion Book. New York: Simon and Schuster, 1969. A recent publication with a collection of contributions dealing with the facets of protest and politics.